Transferring Language Learning and Teaching From Face-to-Face to Online Settings

Christina Nicole Giannikas
Cyprus University of Technology, Cyprus

IGI Global
PUBLISHER of TIMELY KNOWLEDGE

A volume in the Advances in Mobile and Distance Learning (AMDL) Book Series

Published in the United States of America by
IGI Global
Information Science Reference (an imprint of IGI Global)
701 E. Chocolate Avenue
Hershey PA, USA 17033
Tel: 717-533-8845
Fax: 717-533-8661
E-mail: cust@igi-global.com
Web site: http://www.igi-global.com

Library of Congress Cataloging-in-Publication Data

Names: Giannikas, Christina Nicole, editor.
Title: Transferring language learning and teaching from face-to-face to online settings / Christina Giannikas, editor.
Description: Hershey, PA : Information Science Reference, [2021] | Includes bibliographical references and index. | Summary: "This edited volume offers a platform for exploring how the field of language teaching is adapting to changes that have derived from the pandemic, with a strong focus on the challenges faced and ways to move forward"-- Provided by publisher.
Identifiers: LCCN 2021040465 (print) | LCCN 2021040466 (ebook) | ISBN 9781799887171 (Hardcover) | ISBN 9781799887188 (Paperback) | ISBN 9781799887195 (eBook)
Subjects: LCSH: Language and languages--Computer-assisted instruction. | English language--Study and teaching--Computer-assisted instruction for foreign speakers. | Second language acquisition--Computer-assisted instruction.
Classification: LCC PE1128.3 .T73 2021 (print) | LCC PE1128.3 (ebook) | DDC 428.0078/5--dc23/eng/20211021
LC record available at https://lccn.loc.gov/2021040465
LC ebook record available at https://lccn.loc.gov/2021040466

This book is published in the IGI Global book series Advances in Mobile and Distance Learning (AMDL) (ISSN: 2327-1892; eISSN: 2327-1906)

British Cataloguing in Publication Data
A Cataloguing in Publication record for this book is available from the British Library.

All work contributed to this book is new, previously-unpublished material. The views expressed in this book are those of the authors, but not necessarily of the publisher.

For electronic access to this publication, please contact: eresources@igi-global.com.

Advances in Mobile and Distance Learning (AMDL) Book Series

Patricia Ordóñez de Pablos
Universidad de Oviedo, Spain

ISSN:2327-1892
EISSN:2327-1906

Mission

Private and public institutions have made great strides in the fields of mobile and distance learning in recent years, providing greater learning opportunities outside of a traditional classroom setting. While the online learning revolution has allowed for greater learning opportunities, it has also presented numerous challenges for students and educators alike. As research advances, online educational settings can continue to develop and advance the technologies available for learners of all ages.

The **Advances in Mobile and Distance Learning** (AMDL) Book Series publishes research encompassing a variety of topics related to all facets of mobile and distance learning. This series aims to be an essential resource for the timeliest research to help advance the development of new educational technologies and pedagogy for use in online classrooms.

Coverage

- Online Collaborative Learning
- Snack Learning
- Cloud Computing in Schools
- Administration and Organization
- Student-Student Interaction
- Distance Learning
- Accreditation
- Online Class Management
- Student Achievement and Satisfaction
- Virtual Universities

IGI Global is currently accepting manuscripts for publication within this series. To submit a proposal for a volume in this series, please contact our Acquisition Editors at Acquisitions@igi-global.com or visit: http://www.igi-global.com/publish/.

The Advances in Mobile and Distance Learning (AMDL) Book Series (ISSN 2327-1892) is published by IGI Global, 701 E. Chocolate Avenue, Hershey, PA 17033-1240, USA, www.igi-global.com. This series is composed of titles available for purchase individually; each title is edited to be contextually exclusive from any other title within the series. For pricing and ordering information please visit http://www.igi-global.com/book-series/advances-mobile-distance-learning/37162. Postmaster: Send all address changes to above address.

Titles in this Series

For a list of additional titles in this series, please visit: http://www.igi-global.com/book-series/advances-mobile-distance-learning/37162

Handbook of Research on Managing and Designing Online Courses in Synchronous and Asynchronous Environments
Gürhan Durak (Balıkesir University, Turkey) and Serkan Çankaya (İzmir Democracy University, Turkey)
Information Science Reference • © 2022 • 731pp • H/C (ISBN: 9781799887010) • US $245.00

Handbook of Research on Effective Online Language Teaching in a Disruptive Environment
Jean W. LeLoup (United States Air Force Academy, USA) and Pete Swanson (United States Air Force Academy, USA)
Information Science Reference • © 2022 • 490pp • H/C (ISBN: 9781799877202) • US $245.00

Designing Effective Distance and Blended Learning Environments in K-12
Thomas F. Driscoll III (Bristol Warren Regional School District, USA)
Information Science Reference • © 2022 • 389pp • H/C (ISBN: 9781799868293) • US $195.00

Educational Recovery for PK-12 Education During and After a Pandemic
Penelope D. Keough (National University, USA)
Information Science Reference • © 2021 • 283pp • H/C (ISBN: 9781799869528) • US $195.00

Handbook of Research on Transforming Teachers' Online Pedagogical Reasoning for Engaging K-12 Students in Virtual Learning
Margaret L. Niess (Oregon State University, USA) and Henry Gillow-Wiles (Oregon State University, USA)
Information Science Reference • © 2021 • 664pp • H/C (ISBN: 9781799872221) • US $425.00

The Black Experience and Navigating Higher Education Through a Virtual World
Kimetta R. Hairston (Bowie State University, USA) Wendy M. Edmonds (Bowie State University, USA) and Shanetia P. Clark (Salisbury University, USA)
Information Science Reference • © 2021 • 282pp • H/C (ISBN: 9781799875376) • US $195.00

Curriculum Development and Online Instruction for the 21st Century
Tamara Phillips Fudge (Purdue University Global, USA) and Susan Shepherd Ferebee (Purdue University Global, USA)
Information Science Reference • © 2021 • 400pp • H/C (ISBN: 9781799876533) • US $195.00

IGI Global
PUBLISHER of TIMELY KNOWLEDGE

701 East Chocolate Avenue, Hershey, PA 17033, USA
Tel: 717-533-8845 x100 • Fax: 717-533-8661
E-Mail: cust@igi-global.com • www.igi-global.com

Editorial Advisory Board

Table of Contents

Detailed Table of Contents

Preface

The abrupt global outbreak of the pandemic in late 2019-early 2020 led to Emergency Remote Teaching (ERT) in all fields of education across the globe. An abrupt shift to online learning and teaching, and the rapid planning and implementation of online instruction raised issues and questions among practitioners and researchers. As stated by UNESCO Director-General Audrey Azoulay: "We are entering uncharted territory and working with countries to find hi-tech, low-tech and no-tech solutions to assure the continuity of learning" (https://en.unesco.org/news/one-five-learners-kept-out-school-unesco-mobilizes-education-ministers-face-covid-19-crisis). In the blink of an eye educational authorities worldwide called for school closures to limit the spread of the pandemic, a situation which prompted UNESCO to urge countries to ensure flexible learning in formal and informal settings (Huang et al., 2020).

The abrupt shift to online learning and teaching shocked the majority of the language education community who had to become familiar with online tools, resources, and adjust teaching approaches overnight (Giannikas, 2020). According to the literature, the lack of sophisticated technology, experience, and training in developing online learning platforms is a massive challenge educators and academic institutions have faced worldwide (Mohammed et al., 2020). Furthermore, the International Telecommunication Union (2019) has stated that although 93% of the world's population resides within covered Internet zones, approximately 53% uses the Internet which is considered an obstacle when struggling to continue the educational process (Union I.T., 2019). Language teaching programs needed to respond to the need for distance education, with teachers working to transfer their material onto online platforms and/or learning management systems (LMS), even though their materials are not designed with distance learning in mind. Even in the midst of recovery, COVID-19 has led to language teaching programs extending their teaching online and trying to adjust the material to deliver high-quality practice. The education emergency caused by the pandemic has revealed that the world needs an education system that favors flexibility and resilience to equip educators to face unpredictable emergencies that may arise.

Transferring Language Learning and Teaching From Face-to-Face to Online Settings examines the phenomenon of emergency language education further and provides an avenue for language teachers and researchers to share their experience, thoughts, and suggestions about transferring their material and teaching approaches from face-to-face (f2f) to an online setting. The newly commissioned chapters of the book link the theoretical understanding and practical experience of ERT, and aspires to be a ground-breaking resource, bringing together the fields of language teaching, teacher training and professional development in a balanced relationship when faced with global challenges and crises. The edited volume can be of interest to a wide readership, such as scholars and researchers, undergraduate and postgraduate students, professional educational organisations, practitioners, teacher educators, policymakers, and administrators. Given its vibrant scope and nature, the volume addresses various needs and is an important primary source in Applied Linguistics courses as it accommodates diverse topics and it balances research and practice. Furthermore, this collection can also become a point of reference in pre- and in-service training of schoolteachers in general and language education as it offers a platform for exploring how the field of language teaching is adapting to changes that have derived from the pandemic, with a strong focus on the challenges faced and ways to move forward. covering topics such as digital pedagogy, Asynchronous Language Teaching, Synchronous Language Teaching, Virtual Communities and teacher education.

THE IMPORTANCE OF EACH CHAPTER

Each chapter of this edited volume displays a significant contribution to the field of language education in times of emergency. The authors have shed light on various aspects of ERT in many academic areas. Specifically, in the first chapter, "Online Teaching Satisfaction and Technostress at Japanese Universities During Emergency Remote Teaching," Matthew Apple and Daniel Mills discuss the situation in Japan. According to the authors, courses that were already prepared for face-to-face delivery from the start of the spring term suddenly needed to be delivered online via emergency remote teaching due to the pandemic. In order to understand the challenges that university faculty faced and to find ways to improve upon the situation if this becomes the "new normal," it is imperative to understand faculty satisfaction with online teaching and how these perceptions affect motivation and lifestyle. University faculty teaching English-language courses were recruited from several universities in Japan and asked to complete an online survey which consisted of demographics, questions related to online teacher satisfaction, teacher motivation, teacher lifestyle, and open-ended questions. Results indicated mixed feelings toward online education, negative evaluations of the lack of Japanese universities' preparedness for online long-distance learning, and concerns about the social and physical health of students and instructors.

The second chapter, "Pecha Kucha Presentations: Digital Adaptation and Online Communication in ESP Higher Education," by Soraya García-Sánchez, describes a comparative research analyses and reflections regarding the teaching and learning approaches designed to foster communicative English language skills under the modality of online education with real-time interaction and multimodal communicative mediation. Because of the global pandemic COVID-19, the higher educational community of three different subjects on English for Specific Purposes (ESP) modified their programs to full online education with different digital tools and interactive methods. A survey was used to analyze students' preferences regarding this abrupt change. Consequently, the delivery of communicative skills through mediated multimodal communication or interaction in English were explored with students' online speaking presentations, which followed the Pecha Kucha model. It is suggested that the multimodal Pecha Kucha speeches allowed participants to produce, receive, interact, and mediate their interpersonal communication with interactive comments, expressed synchronously via MS Teams or posted asynchronously on the forum via written or audio messages.

Chapter 3, with the title "Emergency Remote Teaching in Tertiary Education: Issues Raised, Solutions Given, and Lessons Learned," elaborates on the experience of a language practitioner and 22 students and discusses how they managed to cope with this unprecedented situation. The issues raised, the solutions given, and the lessons learned at the end of this endeavor are documented and shared throughout the chapter. Quantitative data were collected by a questionnaire addressed to the students at the end of this period. Qualitative data were collected by the practitioner's descriptive/reflective notes and by a semi-constructed interview of students. The results revealed that students' attitudes became more positive towards online learning at the end of their online experience. The practitioner's adaptability, continuous self-training, and positive attitude towards change were proved to be determining factors linked to students' positive attitudes in the end of the course.

The fourth chapter by Tamara Kavytska and Viktoriia Drobotun with the title "Online Teaching Writing to University Students: Negative Stereotypes Ruined" examines emergency online writing instruction aimed at enhancing integrated cause-and-effect writing in tertiary education. Specifically, the research compares two models of digital support in terms of their impact on the quality of cause-and-effect academic essays. The instruction relied on the integrated approach to writing instruction and the theory of online collaborative learning. The study was organized as experimental training with third-year university students (n=42) as participants who formed 2 experimental and 2 control groups. Results show a generally positive impact of both digitally supported instruction models on the overall quality of cause-and-effect writing. However, different aspects of the indicated writing appeared unevenly affected by digital support of the online course. With the training efficacy of both digital support models confirmed, the general conclusion drawn from the research lies in the idea that only a targeted selection of online technologies can produce a significant enhancement of the skills under training.

Chapter 5 with the title "University Students Going Online During the COVID-19 Pandemic: Experiences From a Blended Delivery Course Model in Greece" by Kia Karavas and Trisevgeni Liontou looks into making course content consistent, relevant, and meaningful to students. The authors discuss the transformation of a compulsory course of the Department of English Language and Literature of their university into a blended course with elements of a remote flipped classroom. This chapter aims to present the decisions taken for the adjustment of the course and to present university students' evaluation of this course focusing their opinions of the revised course structure and challenges they faced while completing the course. The results revealed that although the student response to fully online distance learning was not overwhelmingly positive, their response towards the flipped classroom model was. This points to the great potential the flipped classroom model can have for introducing pedagogies that combine distance learning with face-to-face teaching.

In Chapter 6, with the title "The Potential of a Telecollaborative Translation Course: Virtual Exchange During the Pandemic and Beyond," Raphaelle Beecroft and Petra Bauer look at the difficult global circumstances which pose a challenge for face-to-face exchange in higher education level language pedagogy, creating the need for innovative digital alternatives which can be integrated into internationalisation strategies. This chapter presents such an endeavour merging translation and telecollaboration which fosters an interplay of intercultural and functional communicative competence. Combining approaches from Translation Studies and Foreign Language Pedagogy, it is proposed that telecollaboration creates a plurilingual and pluricultural space within which participants from varying linguacultural backgrounds may collaborate on a common product – a translation. The translation process itself requires intercultural exchange in which participants engage in an immediate manner through online interaction. Preliminary results from a study focussing on a telecollaborative translation course implemented with Durham University German students and prospective English teachers from Karlsruhe University of Education, Germany are presented.

In Chapter 7, with the title "Teacher Online ELT Experiences in a Rural Primary School in China During the COVID-19 Pandemic," authors Di Liang and Xingtan Cao present their study which adopts narrative inquiry to report five English teachers' online teaching experiences in a rural primary school in China during the COVID-19 pandemic. From a sociocultural theoretical perspective, this study shows how the participating teachers navigated the transition in instructional mode and developed familiarity with online teaching over time. Using thematic analysis, the findings of this study reveal that the teachers showed anxiety toward online teaching, they formed a virtual community of practice, they incorporated lived experiences into online teaching, and that they called for professional development centered on online teaching and spoke to the changing needs for English teaching in the post-COVID era. Implications are provided regarding how the teachers could transfer face-to-face ELT to an online setting and how they could be better supported professionally by their school and colleagues.

In Chapter 8, "Teacher Practices Towards Providing Interaction During Online Education in K-8 Settings," authors Gizem Kara, Melis Dilek, and Aysegul Liman Kaban discuss what kind of practices teachers implement to offer interaction opportunities in online education in terms of learner-learner interaction, learner-instructor interaction, and learner-content interaction. The study included 55 English teachers who had online lessons during the pandemic. To collect data, a survey was distributed to English teachers who are teaching at K-8 levels and the results of the survey are analyzed quantitatively. The study has found that learner-learner interaction strategies are less implemented by the teachers in comparison to learner-content and learner-instructor interaction practices.

In Chapter 9, with the title "Influence of Positive Student-Teacher Interaction on the Meaning-Making Process in Virtual Learning: A Study in the Primary English Class," authors Agustin Reyes-Torres and Ana García-Perera present their study that focuses on the crucial role that teachers play to engage and to guide students to become meaning makers. To this end, the authors make use of the Pedagogy of Multiliteracies in the English Primary class to establish a positive students-teacher relationship as a determining factor to enhance the learning process. Qualitative research was conducted so as to explore to what extent these factors influence the meaning-making process. The findings are presented and elaborated upon in this paper. The researchers worked with three different groups of students in a public school in Valencia (Spain) before and during the lockdown enforced by COVID-19. The analysis of the data obtained reveals that academic achievement and students' engagement are influenced by the quality of the student-teacher relationship and the teacher's role as a mediator of knowledge.

In Chapter 10, "Digital Literacy in Language Education: The COVID-19 Era of Cyprus," authors Christina Giannikas, Dina Tsagari, and Trisevgeni Liontou discuss the abrupt shift to online learning and teaching, which shocked the majority of the language education community and prompted teachers to become familiar with online tools, resources, and adjust their teaching approaches overnight. Beyond the state of alarm, it is now evident that a nexus between innovation and ICT exists. The pandemic has highlighted the critical role of technology in language education. As part of a larger study, this book chapter focuses on language education in Cyprus and examines the issues facing language teachers' digital literacy and competence through the lens of complex and unpredictable adaptive systems. The data displayed and discussed in the chapter contradicts teachers' confidence of their digital literacy and competence of delivering language lessons online and what was applied in practice, and concludes by making specific recommendations at policy making, pedagogical and research level.

In Chapter 11, with the title "Accommodating New Challenges: EFL Student Teacher and Teacher Trainer Attitudes Towards Transferring Teacher-Training Online," Georgios Neocleous describes his research focusing on learning in times of COVID-19, the effectiveness of transferring language teaching from face-to-face to online settings in teacher education programs still remains under-explored. The purpose of this chapter is to delve deeper into student teachers and their instructors' attitudes to explore how the field of language teaching adapted to changes that have derived from the pandemic. The overarching research question the study attempted to address was: 1) What are the pre-service teacher attitudes and their instructors toward digital learning of EFL teacher-training amidst the global pandemic? The findings offer insights into how to adequately prepare and design online teaching and activities for teacher training programs in the future.

In Chapter 12, "Engendering WTC in Online Learning Spaces: Peer Connectivity Is More Important Than We May Think," Amelia Yarwood and Phillip Bennett look at how language learning environments have had to swiftly transition from traditional face-to-face learning to remote learning contexts since the start of the pandemic. This chapter interrogates factors related to students' Willingness To Communicate (WTC) in online-mediated discussions in a Japanese University classroom. Using a Self-Determination Theory framework to conduct a thematic analysis of data collected from focus group discussions, and the written reflections of English L2 learners (N=19), three main factors were found to contribute to a lack of WTC. Two of the three are unique to online learning: disruptive environmental factors and a thwarting of relatedness between classmates. The third factor, a perceived lack of communicative ability, although not unique to online learning, was amplified by the online environment. In order to address these factors which, contribute to a lack of WTC, a number of teaching interventions aimed at fostering communicative online classrooms are introduced.

Chapter 13, with the title "Exploring the Shaping of English Language Teacher Practices While Working With Refugees and Asylum Seekers During the COVID-19 Pandemic," by Gary Motteram, Susan Dawson, Richard Fay, Andres Mora, and Francesco Leoni, describes a project which began during the first wave of the COVID-19 pandemic in the UK. The project supported a group of UK-based ESOL (English for Speakers of Other Languages) teachers and volunteers as the pandemic forced them to move from face-to-face to online teaching with refugees and asylum seekers. Using an ecological perspective, the authors explore the different possibilities for action that the teachers and volunteers perceive in the ever-changing pandemic environment and consider how language teacher practices and the achievement of organisational aims have been shaped, and in turn are shaping, the online teaching. The chapter concludes by considering how the practices developed for the online teaching might now shape teaching as it returns, to a large extent, face-to-face.

In Chapter 14, "Language Teachers' Health: Emotions and Wellbeing in the COVID-19 Pandemic," Cristina Pardo-Ballester looks at an under-investigated setting of higher education and language teachers' psychological consequences, namely emotions and well-being. It is subsumed here under the broader field of "health" on four counts: before the Covid-19 pandemic, the onset, during the pandemic, and a future without a pandemic. There have been several studies on the beginning of the pandemic with a focus on the transition to emergency online teaching, but there is a scarcity of published data about prior experience with distance education before the pandemic. Moreover, most studies recently published about language teaching and the pandemic reported results with data collected during spring and summer 2020. This chapter documents language teachers' emotions and well-being from prior teaching experience, the onset of the emergency online transition in spring 2020 due to the Covid-19 pandemic through the end of spring 2021.

In Chapter 15, with the title "Building a K-12 Educator Community of Learners During Emergency Remote Learning," Melanie Wong presents how the ways that Kindergarten to Grade 12 (K-12) educators' support towards their English Language Learners (ELLs) have changed due to the pandemic. These circumstances have brought on unprecedented challenges as educators attempt to make learning relevant and learn a new digital terrain. The lingering question is how can teacher leaders support colleagues to teach during global crises and post-pandemic times. This auto-ethnography explores experiences of a K-12 teacher leader. Using a Multiliteracies and Learning by Design, the knowledge processes employed are explored. Using digital technologies, such as Microsoft Skype, educators were able to collaborate as a community of learners to exchange teaching ideas and best ELL practices at daily K-12 teacher drop-in sessions.

Finally, the volume closes with Chapter 16, "Understanding Teacher Burnout Coping Strategies During a Global Pandemic." Caleb Powers discusses the impromptu conversion to distance learning forced administrators to consider alternatives to providing quality education which often neglected to consider the toll asked of the teachers. Subsequently, these conditions contributed to an unprecedented surge in teacher burnout. This chapter explores the strategies of 165 U.S. world language teachers for coping with teacher burnout during the pandemic: 76.7% of respondents indicated an increase in burnout after the pandemic started. The most alarming trends in the data are the reduction of access to certain coping strategies, the degradation of effective strategies into ineffective ones, and the severe reduction of the time and energy available to engage in these strategies. These data indicate that teacher burnout should be a priority concern to prevent any further damage to our education systems.

THE IMPACT OF THIS BOOK

Covid-19 continues to dominate education, and although in the midst of recovery schools have re-opened in some contexts, there are still a large number of teachers who are working online. Due to the abrupt changes and need for adjustments to a new normal, it seems appropriate to look for effective responses to the language teaching challenges posed by the pandemic. This is why research has become vital, since the likelihood that the collective knowledge of the education community can reveal the reality of the learning environment and enhance remote teaching. This volume reflects teaching practices, learning strategies and research in a growing language learning community, where the unprecedented circumstances of the COVID-19 pandemic has prompted scholars in the field to develop new traditions and shed light on the way the education crisis was handled. The chapters reveal many strengths in their arguments, for example research methodologies and strategies, topics that are of interest to practitioners and researchers, the significance of effective teaching practices and equitable learning in the field, and the mental and emotional wellness of practitioners and students. The aspiration of the volume is to provide its readership with thought-provoking and inspiring chapters that will encourage further development in the field in these uncertain times.

REFERENCES

Giannikas Christina, N. (2020). Prioritizing when Education is in Crisis: The language teacher. *Humanising Language Teaching.*, *22*(3), 1755–9715.

Huang, C., Wang, Y., Li, X., Ren, L., Zhao, J., Hu, Y., Zhang, L., Fan, G., Xu, J., Gu, X., Cheng, Z., Yu, T., Xia, J., Wei, Y., Wu, W., Xie, X., Yin, W., Li, H., Liu, M., ... Cao, B. (2020). Clinical features of patients infected with 2019 novel coronavirus in Wuhan, China. *Lancet*, *395*(10223), 497–506. doi:10.1016/S0140-6736(20)30183-5 PMID:31986264

Mohmmed, A. O., Khidhir, B. A., Nazeer, A., & Vijayan, V. J. (2020). Emergency remote teaching during Coronavirus pandemic: The current trend and future directive at Middle East College Oman. *Innovative Infrastructure Solutions*, *5*(3), 72. doi:10.100741062-020-00326-7

Union, I.T. (2019). *Measuring digital development Facts and figures 2019*. International Telecommunication Union.

Acknowledgment

The editor would like to acknowledge the help of all the people involved in this project. First, my sincere gratitude goes to the authors who contributed their time and expertise to this book. Second, the editor wishes to acknowledge the valuable contributions of the reviewers regarding the improvement of quality, coherence, and content presentation of chapters. Many of the authors also served as referees; I highly appreciate their double task.

Christina Nicole Giannikas
Cyprus University of Technology, Cyprus

Chapter 1
Online Teaching Satisfaction and Technostress at Japanese Universities During Emergency Remote Teaching

Matthew T. Apple
https://orcid.org/0000-0002-7541-1352
Ritsumeikan University, Japan

Daniel J. Mills
Ritsumeikan University, Japan

ABSTRACT

As the COVID-19 pandemic hit Japan in early 2020, courses that were already prepared for face-to-face delivery from the start of the spring term in April suddenly needed to be delivered online via emergency remote teaching. In order to understand the challenges that university faculty faced and to find ways to improve upon the situation if this becomes the "new normal," it is imperative to understand faculty satisfaction with online teaching and how these perceptions affect motivation and lifestyle. University faculty teaching English-language courses were recruited from several universities in Japan and asked to complete an online survey which consisted of demographics, questions related to online teacher satisfaction, teacher motivation, teacher lifestyle, and open-ended questions. Results indicated mixed feelings toward online education, negative evaluations of the lack of Japanese universities' preparedness for online long-distance learning, and concerns about the social and physical health of students and instructors.

INTRODUCTION

In April 2020, the start of the academic year in Japan, the coronavirus suddenly disrupted the lives of university faculty. With very little warning, courses already prepared for face-to-face (F2F) delivery needed to be delivered online via emergency remote teaching (ERT). While ERT was not unique to Japan,

DOI: 10.4018/978-1-7998-8717-1.ch001

the general lack of long-distance learning programs and low level of technology usage in the Japanese educational system (Aoki, 2010; Funamori, 2017; Latchem et al., 2008) led to a large digital gap among instructors. Although some teachers were already adept at using technology for education, many were forced not only to learn how to use these tools but also how to apply them effectively in English as a Foreign Language (EFL) courses. The situation was exacerbated by the often conflicting and confusing messages sent to teachers by university administrators, who were scrambling to set guidelines for the new online classes yet had little or no knowledge of online teacher training, online course design and management, and online teaching pedagogy.

In order to understand the challenges that university faculty in Japan faced in the spring term of 2020 and find ways to improve upon the situation if this becomes the "new normal," it is imperative to understand faculty satisfaction with online teaching (Bolliger et al., 2014) and how these perceptions affect teacher motivation and lifestyle. To this end, the researchers conducted a sequential explanatory mixed-methods research project (Creswell, 2003) at the conclusion of the spring 2020 semester in August. Instructors teaching English-language courses at universities across Japan were invited via posts in online language teaching and research groups to complete an online survey, which consisted of demographic variables, Likert scale variables about online teacher satisfaction, technostress, teacher lifestyle, and online teaching motivation, and open response questions. After completing the survey, study participants were given the opportunity to participate in the second stage of the study, a semi-structured interview conducted via Zoom at the end of the academic year in March 2021 (Apple & Mills, 2021). This chapter presents the quantitative results of the initial survey, which represents the first stage of the mixed methods project.

BACKGROUND

Online Learning and Emergency Remote Teaching

Distance learning is an important part of the equitable delivery of education around the world (Lembani et al., 2020; Ridge & Waghid, 2001; Saykili, 2018). In the past, correspondence courses were delivered through the mail and later, as technology developed, via telephone, television, and video and audio recordings. Online learning differs from these earlier versions of technology-enhanced distance education in that it uses the internet as the main form of communication between instructors and students (Ko & Rossen, 2010). Online learning provides both instructors and students with the flexibility to teach and learn from anywhere and anytime. In addition to convenience, the vastness of the internet offers an endless supply of learning materials, authentic content, and even interactions with other learners and experts all over the world.

This medium of course delivery has been flourishing in the U.S., even before the COVID-19 pandemic forced most institutions online. According to 2019 data from the U.S. Department of Education, 35.3% of all students enrolled in degree-granting postsecondary institutions were participating in at least one online learning course (De Brey et al., 2021). However, the adoption of online learning in other countries has not been as robust. In a 2019 survey of European Union members, only 8% of respondents aged 16 to 74 reported taking an online course in the past three months. The highest percentage of online course participation came from Nordic countries such as Finland (21%) and Sweden (18%; Eurostat, 2020). This lack of online learning experience is especially true in Japan, where the country's Ministry of Education, Culture, Sports, Science and Technology (MEXT) does not commonly approve online courses for credit (Hata, 2020).

ERT is different from online learning in that it is an unplanned and temporary change in the method of course delivery brought on by a crisis situation (Hodges et al., 2020). Online learning still carries the reputation of being less effective than face-to-face (F2F) classes, but academic research does not support this assertion (Gierdowski et al., 2020; Hodges et al., 2020). Therefore, comparisons between online learning and ERT, where online classes are hastily prepared without proper training and support, can have long-lasting negative effects on how people view online learning. In a recent study of student technology usage of over 18,000 undergraduate students in six countries and 31 U.S. states, a large majority of respondents reported that they preferred either completely (37%) or mostly (32%) F2F learning environments (Gierdowski et al., 2020). As the authors of this study warned, such findings could demonstrate a preference for F2F learning environments based mostly on one negative experience rather than real evidence.

While the implementation of ERT was not ideal for both instructors and students, the situation has brought attention to the role that online learning will play at all levels of education in the future and highlighted how unprepared many institutions were in shifting to this form of course delivery in a crisis. This was particularly evident in Japan, a country often associated with high technology, where cultural factors, as well as a propensity towards traditional instructional methods, prevented the timely adoption of Information and Communications Technology (ICT) and online education (Hata, 2020). Over the years, Japan has introduced several top-down approaches in an attempt to incorporate technology into the curriculum, including The Vision for ICT Education in Japan, e-Japan Strategy, and the Smart Japan ICT Strategy (Nuncio, 2020). However, none of these approaches have created lasting change in terms of educational reform. The COVID-19 crisis and difficulties implementing ERT have given us the opportunity to study the affordances and challenges associated with online learning both in and out of a crisis. Such findings may play a key role in informing future practice.

Online Teaching Satisfaction

Online teaching satisfaction has been shown to be influenced by a number of factors. A factor analytic study of online teaching satisfaction of over 300 faculty members teaching online at universities in the U.S. state of Ohio found three factors to be important in measuring satisfaction in this environment: instructor–student interaction, the role of technology, and institutional support (Blundell et al., 2020). Bolliger and Wasilik (2009) also identified three factors in their research, which they labeled as instructor-related, student-related, and institution-related. However, a further refinement of their study expanded the initial faculty satisfaction instrument to include five factors: *instructor-to-student interaction*, *affordances*, *institutional support*, *student-to-student interaction*, and *course design, development, and teaching* (Bolliger et al., 2014). Furthermore, they found that faculty satisfaction was linked to overall course quality. This finding might be especially important in the case of ERT, in which neither faculty nor students were prepared for the switch online or had agreed to this method of course delivery.

As researchers and teachers around the world emerge from their first year of ERT, several studies are being published to share their initial experiences. Howe and Heitner's (2020) comparative study of 251 instructors found that teaching services and support were determiners of online teaching satisfaction during the COVID-19 pandemic. Another study that took place in a Saudi Arabian university also showed that the length of institutional support for online classes positively correlated with faculty satisfaction levels

(Alsuelmi, 2021). In contrast to these studies, a survey of 203 faculty members in Mainland China, Hong Kong, and Macau discovered that perceptions of the effectiveness of online courses was the only factor to significantly affect faculty satisfaction (Lei & So, 2021). The researchers believed this response was because all faculty respondents were teachers in the field of hospitality and tourism, which is a practical rather than theoretical field. However, as the results differed from studies in other environments, cultural factors may have played a role in the results. As additional studies examining faculty satisfaction with ERT are published, the unique determinants of satisfaction in this situation will be identified. However, a common theme of studies before and after the COVID-19 pandemic is the importance of institutional support as a determining factor of faculty satisfaction.

Institutional Support

Perhaps the most important aspect of distance education is the degree to which institutions support instructors (Milheim, 2001). For online education and ERT to work effectively, institutional support will comprise several aspects of the learning environment, including access to technology (hardware and software), adequate training and preparation, clear institutional policies and guidelines, technical support and troubleshooting assistance, and fair compensation and rewards.

There is an overall awareness among long-distance educators that online education requires a great deal of time on task to adequately prepare materials for learners and to assess student work adequately and fairly (much more so than F2F classes; Bower, 2001; Simonson et al., 2000). The lack of technical training, in particular, is a concern among educators, and many studies have identified a lack of ability to use technology and receive support to be major worries of faculty (e.g., Betts, 1998; O'Quinn & Corry, 2002). However, when institutional support is readily available and effectively delivered, online education, even during an emergency situation, can provide a number of affordances to both teachers and students.

Affordances

Affordances in online teaching and learning refers to the perceived benefits the practice provides in contrast to the traditional F2F classroom. However, it is important to understand that affordances do not necessarily equate to pedogeological usefulness. Affordances can be potential (the disposition of the environment to realize events under specific conditions) or actualized (i.e., real events; Heft, 2007). Both types of affordances can be perceived by observers, but affordances do not cause behavior or action; they merely provide a choice for the behavior (Kono, 2009, p. 361).

Flexibility and convenience are the two affordances identified the most in relation to online learning and teaching (Bolliger et al., 2014). Access and the utilization of a variety of resources are other important factors. Bolliger et al. (2014) observed, "Through effective use of the functionality of various learning tools, online instructors can provide pedagogically effective learning environments where the instruction is highly interactive, supportive, communicative, and social" (p. 185). Online learning allows for the blending of online and offline, in-class and out-of-class, and formal and informal learning. Informal and formal learning can be mutually beneficial (Benson, 2011; Cotterall & Reinders, 2001; Reinders & Benson, 2017), and computer-assisted language learning (CALL) can help develop student motivation, autonomy, and self-efficacy (Honarzad & Rassaei, 2019).

However, there are differences between online teaching and ERT. Watermeyer, Crick, Knight, and Goodall (2021) found that the majority of responses regarding ERT were negative. However, some of the faculty they surveyed believed that the ERT was an opportunity for "pedogeological reinvention" (p. 637) and would even make their job easier. Bolliger et al. (2014) warned that, while responses to the survey regarding the affordances of online learning were highly positive and asserted that such affordances would be "realized or utilized by instructors" (p. 192), many of the benefits of online learning technology cannot be fully realized without support and training. In summary, whether ERT can become the catalyst for actualizing the many affordances of online teaching is yet to be seen.

Teacher Motivation

Motivation is defined in general terms as a person's desire to make decisions and take action (Dörnyei & Ushioda, 2021). For teachers, motivation is multidimensional and developmental as they move through training and their careers (Prabjandee, 2020). A number of factors have been shown to influence motivation in the teaching profession. Using five factors based on Self-Determination Theory (Ryan & Deci, 2002, 2017), a study of teacher motivation among Spanish secondary school teachers ($N = 584$) found that work dedication was most strongly linked to intrinsic motivation and external regulation (Abós et al., 2018). However, in a study of pre-service EFL teachers in Patagonia and Argentina, Banegas and Busleiman (2014) found that teaching degree, autonomy, and individual activities were key to sustaining motivation for teaching online.

Teacher motivation has an effect on teacher engagement with students and their beliefs about educational approaches and goals. Given the importance of the teacher in guiding students through the learning process, understanding these affective factors in teachers is crucial. When instructors in higher education feel more autonomous and have a growth mindset, a belief that knowledge and abilities can be fostered and improved with effort (Dweck, 2008), they tend to use more motivational teaching approaches, such as providing encouragement, fostering enjoyment, and offering choices. Conversely, instructors who are more demanding and have a fixed mindset, the belief that some people are "born with" certain abilities that cannot be easily changed, tend to domineer students, use shame to coerce them, or even abandon them (Vermote et al., 2020). Likewise, students who perceive that teachers give them clear expectations and support their own learning autonomy tend to have better learning outcomes and exhibit fewer behavioral problems (Vansteenkiste et al., 2012).

Unfortunately, ERT has had a disruptive effect on teacher motivation in many learning contexts. A qualitative study of 10 teachers in Portugal and Brazil found that the sudden move to emergency remote teaching had a negative impact on motivation (Oliveira et al., 2021). Similar results were shown in a quantitative study of 202 professors at three universities in Poland, in which the researchers concluded that the COVID-19 pandemic had a negative effect on motivating job potential (Kulikowski et al., 2021). However, the timing of data collection may reveal different results. A study in Spain found that teacher motivation to use digital technology and improve their skills increased as they gained confidence in teaching online during the COVID-19 pandemic (Beardsley et al., 2021). As additional studies are published regarding teachers' experiences with ERT, a more complete picture will emerge regarding how the pandemic affected teacher motivation as well as what coping strategies and interventions were effectively used in educational systems worldwide.

Technostress

Technology has become ubiquitous in both our personal and professional lives. In higher education, universities all over the world seem to be on a constant crusade to integrate more and more technology into the curriculum in order to remain relevant and effective (Alghamdi & Holland, 2020; Habibi et al., 2020). While university faculty can see the benefits of instructional technology, the constant need to learn the latest applications as well as pressure to always remain connected and available can result in stress, which affects job performance (Li & Wang, 2020) and satisfaction (Lee & Lim, 2020; Maxwell, 2021).

A survey-based research study conducted at three private universities in the U.S. state of Texas revealed that faculty reported only low to moderate levels of technology fatigue, but the researchers suspected that participants were underreporting their stress levels (Halupa & Bolliger, 2020). One possible explanation of this is that faculty perceptions of technostress were reduced through the use of coping mechanisms prevalent among the participants such as "taking breaks and creating technology free zones or times" (p. 23).

While the previous study found no significant difference due to gender or age, researchers studying technostress in India among faculty observed different results. In a study surveying approximately 400 faculty members in the Indian state of Madhya Pradesh (Shivastava, 2020), only moderate levels of technostress were reported by the participants, but both males and older faculty members experienced more technology-related stress than their female and younger peers. These results contrasted with a recent study of German teachers adapting to technology integration during the COVID-19 pandemic, when it was discovered that female teachers experienced more stress and longer working hours (Klapproth et al., 2020). Thus, several factors can contribute to the reduction of technostress among faculty members, including administrative support and adequate resources for training (Halupa & Bolliger, 2020; Klapproth et al., 2020). Technology self-efficacy also plays a role because faculty can feel that they are less proficient than their students, who they perceive to be digital natives (Prensky, 2001).

Teacher Lifestyle

Due to the COVID-19 pandemic, people in many industries have had to adapt to remote work (Kniffin et al., 2021). This phenomenon has brought about several changes in lifestyle as workers struggle to adapt to new technologies and the blurring of work and personal life (Wang et al., 2021). With this adversity comes the benefits of more time, freedom, and the elimination of lengthy commutes and obligatory F2F meetings (Ozimek, 2020). However, according to a 2020 study of 570 full and part-time faculty, conducted by Course Hero, stress levels are at all-time highs among university educators. The resulting stress of switching from F2F to ERT has resulted in 40% of participants leaving academia. The ability to adapt to ERT was influenced by an educator's prior experience with online teaching (Roy & Covelli, 2021).

Bidwell, Grether, and Pedersen (2021) surveyed 114 faculty members at a U.S. state university concerning their perceptions of ERT. They found that balancing work and family life was a major concern. Considering the societal expectations placed on females regarding family obligations and the negative outcome this has on academic career advancement, it is likely that the switch to ERT had a disproportionate effect on women (Nash & Churchill, 2020; Staniscuaski et al., 2021).

Research Questions

Based on a careful reading of existing literature, our own experiences using technology in L2 education, and our knowledge of the EFL situation in Japan, we formulated three research questions to guide our study:

RQ1: What factors influence online teaching satisfaction for EFL university teachers in Japan?
RQ2: To what degree has technostress affected teaching motivation?
RQ3: What factors have led to changes in teacher lifestyle?

METHODOLOGY

This study represents the first stage of a larger project that employed a sequential exploratory mixed methods approach (Creswell, 2003). The second stage of the mixed methods project consists of in-depth follow-up interviews with several self-selected study participants, which were conducted after the Japanese 2020 academic year ended in March 2021 (Apple & Mills, 2021). Results of the first stage will be discussed in this chapter, based on data collected in August 2020 via an online survey comprising demographic variables, Likert category data *agree–disagree* items covering six psychological variables related to online education, and open response questions regarding the use of technology and reflections and reactions.

Study Participants

A total of 87 university instructors of English participated in the quantitative survey study. Thirty were tenured, full-time professors, 32 were on temporary full-time contracts, and 25 were part-time instructors. Eighteen of the tenured instructors and 13 of the full-time contract instructors also worked part-time at one or more additional universities. Seven of the part-time instructors worked at three different universities, and five were teaching at four different universities. An average of nine 90- or 100-minute courses were taught per week by study participants, with a range of three to 18 separate courses per week. The average age was 49, with the youngest at 28 and the oldest at 69. The average amount of teaching experience was just over 13 years; the most experienced had taught English for 42 years, but two participants had just started their teaching careers during the ERT situation. Most (n = 66) had master's degrees; 18 had doctoral degrees, 37 listed Teaching English to Speakers of Other Languages (TESL/TESOL) certificates in addition to terminal degrees, and three had bachelor's degrees. There were 48 male and 36 female participants (three did not indicate a gender). Of the 87 participants, 68 were English L1 speakers, and 12 were Japanese L1 speakers. Six were L1 speakers of other languages (three European and three Southeast Asian). One participant asked, "Why is this relevant?" and did not answer.

Questionnaire Instrument

The English–Japanese bilingual survey instrument in this study used demographic items, Likert-type category scales, and open-ended responses in an embedded design for data collection (Creswell, 2003). The quantitative items comprised six psychological factors (k = 30) related to online teaching. A six-point Likert scale was used, ranging from 1 (strongly disagree) to 6 (strongly agree) with no neutral point.

Online Teaching Satisfaction was operationalized as the three separate, related variables *Instructor-Student Online Interaction* (α = .86), *Affordances* (α = .85), and *Institutional Support* (α = .91), based on the factors and items used by Bolliger et al. (2014). One item in Instructor-Student Online Interaction was originally negatively worded but was changed to be positively worded to match the other items. One item from Affordances ("Online teaching allows me to reach a more diverse student population") was deleted as irrelevant in the Japanese EFL context. One item from Institutional Support ("My institution(s) provided fair compensation or incentives for teaching online") was also deleted, as Japanese universities do not normally have any online courses or programs, there was no choice but to teach online during the spring 2020 term coronavirus crisis, and EFL teachers did not receive any additional monetary compensation. Two factors from the original Online Teaching Satisfaction questionnaire were not used (Student-to-Student Interaction and Course Design/Development/Teaching), as they were irrelevant to the ERT situation.

Technostress (α = .85) items were taken from a subscale of the Technology Fatigue questionnaire (Halupa & Bolliger, 2020). One item ("I like using technology for teaching") was changed from positive to negative wording to match the other items. As the term "technology" could include audiovisual materials in a F2F setting, the word "online" was added to all items, to emphasize the online nature of the technology being used.

Teacher Lifestyle (α = .72) items were based on the American Federation of Teachers 2017 Educator Quality of Work Life Survey. As the original items were phrased in the form of a question, they were reworded into statement form for the Likert scale used in this study. One new item was added ("I am physically active"), as this was felt important given the nature of the ERT situation.

Online Teaching Motivation (α = .78) items were based on the factor Teaching Motivation in Abós et al. (2018). One item ("Learning how to improve my teaching methods is a waste of my time") was changed from negative to positive wording. The word "online" was added to each item to match the purpose of the present study and, indeed, all study participants had no choice but to teach entirely online at the time.

Open-ended response questions were designed to elicit details about each teacher's online situation, to give more depth in interpreting the Likert item results, and in particular to address Research Question 3 regarding teacher lifestyle. Questions asked about the availability of a course management system (CMS) or learning management system (LMS) at the university or universities where they taught; additional online tools, websites, software, and hardware used or desired; any online technology usage training provided by the university; changes in lifestyle due to suddenly needing to teach entirely online; and general feelings and thoughts about online and ERT teaching.

All questions were originally written in English, translated into Japanese by one of the researchers, and back-translated by an L1 speaker of Japanese to confirm accuracy. The survey was made available as a combined bilingual online survey via SurveyMonkey (http://www.surveymonkey.com), and links to the survey were posted on language teaching and research groups on various social media sites run by Japanese university EFL groups. All participation was voluntary, and no monetary compensation was offered.

Analysis Procedures

The data from the Likert category questions were first analyzed by the Rasch Rating Scale Model (Andrich, 1978; Rasch, 1960) to determine item fit to their intended constructs, obtain item–person maps for each construct to test for ceiling and floor effects, and to confirm construct validity using

Rasch principal components analysis of the residuals (PCAR). Rasch item and person reliability and separation measures were obtained, and traditional Cronbach's alpha estimates were also conducted for comparison. Traditional descriptive statistics were also calculated to confirm normal distribution (see Table 6 in the Appendix). A preliminary analysis indicated that four items (one each in Affordances, Technostress, Teacher Lifestyle, and Online Teaching Motivation) misfit their intended constructs. A bivariate correlation of disattentuated person measures of each construct with the misfitting item and without the misfitting item showed minimally improved Rasch item and person reliability. The Rasch PCAR indicated support for the construct validity of all six factors. Thus, all items were retained for further analysis. After combining items to compute a composite mean index score for each factor, correlational and multiple regression analyses were conducted to answer the first two research questions.

The open response questions were analyzed in two ways. First, all written responses were copied into an Excel sheet for open matrix analysis (Brown, 2001), and mentions of similar words for questions regarding CMS/LMS, software, websites, and digital devices used in online teaching were counted. Second, a coding analysis scheme was created for the two questions regarding changes in lifestyle and feelings about online teaching in general during the transcription of responses, in order to reduce the huge amount of data generated through the questionnaire into a smaller number of patterns that could be more easily interpreted (Brown, 2009, p. 211). After the initial coding analysis was completed, responses were clustered into larger categories, and another round of coding analysis was conducted. This resulted in a categorization of responses to lifestyle changes as *generally positive* or *generally negative* and to feelings about online teaching as *beneficial* or *not beneficial*.

RESULTS

In general, teachers slightly agreed with all six quantitative variables in the survey (Table 1). The composite index scores for Technostress (M = 17.52/30.00) and Teacher Lifestyle (M = 23.37/36.00) both showed agreement with the variables; however, the relatively high standard deviation (SD = 5.92 and SD = 5.84, respectively) also indicated differences among the respondents. Likewise, the composite index mean score for Institutional Support was barely above the statistical threshold for "agree" (M = 15.67/30.00), and the high standard deviation (SD = 6.59) indicated a wide range of experiences among teachers in the study. Given that the Institutional Support factor is only one aspect of the three factors comprising Online Teaching Satisfaction (OTS), we felt it prudent to consider each OTS factor both separately and combined when answering our research questions.

Table 1. Composite index scores for each factor relating to online teaching satisfaction

Factor	*k*	*M*	*SD*
Instructor–Student Online Interaction	5	19.45	4.82
Affordances	4	16.98	4.40
Institutional Support	5	15.67	6.59
Technostress	5	17.52	5.92
Teacher Lifestyle	6	23.37	5.84
Online Teaching Motivation	5	23.43	4.41

Note. N = 87.

In the open-ended response questions, the most commonly used LMS was Manaba (an English–Japanese bilingual LMS created by Asahi.com; used by 31 participants), followed by Google Classroom (26), Moodle (20), and Microsoft Teams (6). Seven universities had their own proprietary LMS. Two teachers used Blackboard, and two more used Webex. In most cases, the LMS available was not required; data elicited from study participants revealed that only 28 universities required the use of LMS or specific online teaching tools, demonstrating a lack of centralized or managed online learning technology. Many teachers listed other software and online tools as "LMS," which may have been due to unfamiliarity with the term. The most commonly used software among all teachers was Zoom (67), followed by YouTube (43), Flipgrid (31), and Quizlet (8). In total, teachers reported the usage of nearly 50 different programs or online websites for language learning. They relied largely on laptop computers (57), with fewer using a desktop computer (31). Several teachers reported using their smartphones (22) and tablet devices (14). There were virtually no differences among the tenured, full-time contract, or part-time teachers in the type of devices or software relied upon for ERT. Some (30) reported using multiple devices, particularly Apple computer technology, and several commented that they had to buy a new microphone, camera, or new computer in order to use videoconferencing software.

To answer our research questions, we relied mostly on the results of the quantitative data analysis (particularly for research questions one and two), with additional depth provided by results from the open response questions. Research Question 3 was primarily answered by examining responses to the open response questions regarding teacher lifestyle and feelings about online teaching.

Research Question 1: Results and Discussion

Research Question 1 asked which factors in the study influenced the online teaching satisfaction of EFL teachers in Japan during the spring 2020 term, in which they were obliged to teach all classes online. As the original study concerning teacher's satisfaction with online learning combined the variables of Instructor-Student Online Interaction, Affordances, and Institutional Support (Bolliger et al., 2014), those three variables were combined into a new variable called Online Teaching Satisfaction, and a correlational analysis was conducted with the other three psychological variables as well as the demographic variables *Teaching Position*, *Age*, and *Years of Experience* to answer Research Question 1 (Table 2). For the correlational analysis, Teaching Position was operationalized as 1 for full-time tenured, 2 for full-time contract, and 3 for part-time.

Technostress (r = -.34), Teacher Lifestyle (r = .49), and Online Teaching Motivation (r = .43) were all significantly and moderately correlated ($p < .01$) with Online Teaching Satisfaction. These results were not surprising, as previous research has demonstrated similar relationships between these factors. While not specific to technostress, research has shown that stress can have a negative impact on job performance (Li & Wang, 2020) and satisfaction (Lee & Lim, 2020; Maxwell, 2021). Furthermore, studies carried out during the pandemic have indicated that an unprecedented number of educators are leaving the field and that the switch to ERT during the pandemic has had a negative impact on motivation (Kulikowski et al., 2021; Oliveira et al., 2021). These results demonstrate the need for faculty and administrators to mitigate the negative impacts of ERT but providing suitable institutional support, training, resources, and work flexibility.

Surprisingly, years of experience only had a weak correlation with Online Teaching Satisfaction (r = .21) and Teacher Lifestyle (r = .23), at the $p < .05$ level. While years of experience did correlate negatively with teaching position, showing that older study participants were more likely to be part-time teachers, a follow-up ANOVA using Teaching Position as the independent variable showed no differences among the psychological variables. All teachers, regardless of age, position, or years of teaching experience, were essentially equally affected by the sudden move to online ERT. The lack of correlation between the factors of age, position, and years of teaching experience with online teaching satisfaction was unexpected. The researchers' assumption was that experience as well as a higher position in the university, which usually comes with fewer teaching hours and more financial resources, would positively correlate with higher satisfaction. The lack of this relationship may be explained by an overall dearth of experience with online teaching in Japan that essentially put everyone on uneven footing. These results demonstrate a need for continual digital transformation in Japanese education in order to equip all educators with the knowledge and technology necessary to meet the requirements of students in the 21st century.

Table 2. Correlational analysis of factors related to online teaching satisfaction

Factor	TPOS	Age	YExp	OTS	TECH	TLIF	OTM
Teaching Position	—						
Age	-.14	—					
Years of Experience	-.36**	.78**	—				
Online Teaching Satisfaction	-.02	.18	.21*	—			
Technostress	-.04	.05	-.08	-.34**	—		
Teacher Lifestyle	-.06	.15	.23*	.49**	-.73**	—	
Online Teaching Motivation	.04	-.03	.14	.43**	.50**	.48**	—

Note. TPOS = Teaching Position; YExp = Years of Experience; OTS = Online Teaching Satisfaction; TECH = Technostress; TLIF = Teacher Lifestyle; OTM = Online Teaching Motivation
$^*p < .05$, $^{**}p < .01$

To give more depth to the correlational analysis results, we turn to answers to the open response question regarding feelings toward online teaching. Most participants felt that the ERT situation might eventually lead both students and teachers to a better understanding of how language learning and teaching might make good use of online or "hybrid" (i.e., alternating F2F and CALL) learning methods (50). A representative quote from one teacher raises the possibility of using online teaching for personal and professional development:

I feel more effective now, better able to differentiate instruction for students who need it, better able to listen and respond to my students' needs, and I feel like I'm growing in my skill as a teacher more rapidly than I have in years. (Participant 21, tenured)

However, while several felt that online learning might lead to improved teaching methods and class management (21), and even that ERT may encourage students to become more independent (9), quite a few negative comments indicated pessimism about these same concerns. Thirteen comments were directed at the negative impact on social interaction among both students and teachers and students and students. A negative comment from one teacher also raised the fact that incoming Japanese university students have generally weak computer skills, as their secondary school education does not require computer use:

A big disadvantage is the lack of direct exposure to students who may need help during a lesson. That lack of presence also makes presentation of lessons feel unnatural since I can't see their faces or interact. Another disadvantage is the students' poor computer literacy combined with the fact that I can't interact smoothly with them to help overcome those problems. (Participant 63, tenured)

Finally, teachers were concerned with the lack of preparedness on the part of institutions. Many (20) complained that either no training was provided or that the training provided was only in Japanese and consisted of little more than a software handbook sent via email as a PDF file. A few commented that several students had WIFI issues that prevented them from effectively joining online live class meetings, while others complained that the administration gave no direct help but that tenured colleagues did. One wrote:

I think that teaching online is beneficial for students and teachers, IF we all, teachers and students, get an appropriate training and orientation from the institution. (Participant 54, part-time)

Teacher comments exemplify the reliance in Japanese universities on a decentralized program structure and course management run by individual professors rather than by administrators. English language programs were run essentially by a tenured faculty member, either alone or in conjunction with other tenured faculty members, almost on a one-to-one basis with little or no directives from a central university authority.

Research Question 2: Results and Discussion

As a preliminary step prior to multiple regression analysis to answer Research Question 2 regarding technostress and online teaching motivation, a follow-up correlational analysis was conducted using the separate factors Instructor-Student Online Interaction, Affordances, and Institutional Support (Table 3).

Table 3. Correlational analysis of all psychological factors in the study

Factor	ISOI	AFF	ISP	TECH	TLIF	OTM
Instructor-Student Online Interaction	—					
Affordances	.56**	—				
Institutional Support	.37**	.32**	—			
Technostress	-.42**	-.48**	-.01	—		
Teacher Lifestyle	.54**	.59**	.26*	-.75**	—	
Online Teaching Motivation	.38**	.55**	.05	-.47**	.49**	—

Note. ISOI = Instructor–Student Online Interaction; AFF = Affordances; ISP = Institutional Support; TECH = Technostress; TLIF = Teacher Lifestyle; OTM = Online Teaching Motivation

$*p < .05$, $**p < .01$

Technostress had significant correlations with four of the other five variables. However, it had barely any correlation with Institutional Support (r = -.01). Instead, Institutional Support was related to Instructor-

Student Online Interaction ($r = .37$) and Affordances ($r = .32$) at the $p < .01$ level and related to Teacher Lifestyle ($r = .26$) at $p < .05$. While this seems to corroborate the open responses regarding the general lack of institutional support at Japanese universities, these findings contradict research conducted in the U.S. that showed institutional support and adequate resources for training as significant determinants of Technostress (Halupa & Bolliger, 2020; Klapproth et al., 2020). Technostress did have a significant negative impact on Online Teaching Motivation ($r = -.47$). However, the factors Teacher Lifestyle ($r = .49$) and Affordances ($r = .55$) had stronger correlations with Online Teaching Motivation.

To partially answer Research Question 2, a standard multiple regression analysis was conducted with Technostress, Affordances, Teacher Lifestyle, and Instructor–Student Online Interaction as independent variables and Online Teaching Motivation as the dependent outcome variable. As Institutional Support had virtually no correlation with Online Teaching Motivation, it was excluded from the analysis. Preliminary diagnostics determined that four cases exceeded the recommended Mahalanobis distances of plus or minus 3.3 standard residuals. Cook's distance for all four was below the 1.0 value criteria for removing outliers (Tabachnick & Fidell, 2001, p. 69), and the cases were retained for further analysis. All statistical assumptions were met for multicollinearity and homoscedasticity. One case was removed in a pair-wise deletion for missing data, making $N = 86$ for the regression.

The multiple regression model was significant, [$F(4, 86) = 11.78$, $p < .0005$], with the adjusted R-square indicating that the four independent variables explained 33% of the variance in Online Teaching Motivation. Results showed that Affordances was the only variable making a significant contribution to predicting Online Teaching Motivation (Table 4). The influence of Affordances, as well as the surprising lack of influence by the variable Institutional Support, can be made clear with reference to an open-response comment:

I had access to everything I needed, but I realize that comes from a place of privilege as a tenured faculty member with a budget. It was distressing to see no allocation made for our part-timers. It's my opinion that funds should have been diverted toward equipment for PTT [part-time teaching] faculty, and more should have been done to support their needs. (Participant 21, tenured)

Table 4. Standard regression with online teaching motivation as the dependent variable

Factor	*B*	*SEM*	**β**	*t*	*p*
Instructor–Student Online Interaction	.030	.102	.033	.292	.771
Affordances	.373	.117	.373	3.183	.002
Technostress	-.150	.099	-.202	-1.520	.132
Teacher Lifestyle	.078	.112	.104	.698	.487

The standardized coefficient ($\beta = .37$) indicated that an increase of 1 standard deviation on the Affordances variable would increase Online Teaching Motivation scores by 1.6 (4.40 times .37). However, given that all teachers and all students during the spring 2020 term were forced to do all learning in an online environment, the variable Affordances, while statistically significant, may have less real value for determining English teachers' motivation while teaching online. A follow-up hierarchical regression was conducted in order to control for the influence of Affordances. Without affordances in the model, both Technostress and Teacher Lifestyle were significant (Table 5). The *R*-square change between the model with Affordances and the model without Affordances indicated that the three variables combined explained an additional 6% of the variance in Online Teaching Motivation. The lack of influence of Instructor-Student Online Interaction shows that despite the stress levels teachers were largely satisfied with their ability to remain in contact with students online. Whereas technostress experienced from the sudden move to ERT negatively affected teacher motivation, the change in lifestyle due to having to teach entirely online positively affected teacher motivation. Possible reasons for this seeming discrepancy will be discussed in the next section.

Table 5. Hierarchical regression model results controlling for affordances

Factor	*B*	*t*	*p*
Teacher Lifestyle	.257	2.354	.021
Technostress	-.271	-2.715	.008
Instructor-Student Online Interaction	.107	.979	.106

Research Question 3: Results and Discussion

Research Question 3, regarding factors related to Teacher Lifestyle, can be answered partly by the previous correlational analysis and partly by examining open responses. By far the strongest correlation in the quantitative data analysis was between Technostress and Teacher Lifestyle ($r = -.73$). This seems hardly surprising, given the sudden switch to ERT in April 2020 along with an emergency declaration by the Japanese government that led to partial lockdowns throughout the country, with most if not all university campuses completely closed to students, faculty, and staff for several weeks. For such a change to take place at the beginning of an academic term, without any plans in place should the need for ERT arise, it is nearly a given that job stress caused by technology usage would be first and foremost in teachers' minds. What became evident from the open responses was that universities in Japan by and large did not have adequate English teaching policies or programs in place prior to the switch to ERT and even during most of the lockdown across the country. Indeed, teachers commented on the levels of stress caused by this sudden shift by specifically mentioning the accompanying lack of institutional infrastructure support:

I feel that teachers risk being burnt out, but nobody at school really thinks about those things. Sigh. (Participant 58, tenured)

...when it [online teaching] is the sole option, it is stressful, especially as this is an entirely new approach to teaching for many of us. This has undoubtedly raised stress levels among both teachers and students. (Participant 23, tenured and part-time)

Regarding changes in teachers' lifestyles due to having to teach online, teacher responses were somewhat mixed, which partially explains the positive influence of Teacher Lifestyle on Online Teaching Motivation. Most of the positive comments about lifestyle changes (15) related to the lack of need for commuting to work, which allowed teachers more time to create materials and give adequate feedback to students. There were additional positive comments (5) about the fact that online teaching gave them more time for family and private life, which the teachers clearly appreciated. However, these positive comments were far outweighed by the number of negative comments about the enormous amount of time needed to prepare materials for online delivery and grading (22):

...watching hundreds of little videos and hundreds of uploaded homeworks, instead of glancing around at open books during class, and monitoring pairwork during class time. I was working 60~70 hours a week in semester 1. (Participant 16, tenured)

Everything takes so much longer! (Participant 42, part-time)

Just as many negative comments focused on the lack of physical activity resulting from telecommuting, leading to health concerns (22):

Too much screen time and not enough physical movement. I got sick with dizziness for a little over one week. (Participant 6, full-time contract and part-time)

Sitting for long periods in front of the computer caused some minor repetitive stress injuries. (Participant 27, full-time contract)

I felt like I was working 24 hours every day. (Participant 47, tenured and part-time)

I only had three days off during the semester! (Participant 11, full-time contract and part-time)

Further comments about the difficulties of separating work from home, particularly finding a workspace (8), worries over psychological issues such as isolation (8), and maintaining social relations with colleagues (7), show that, while study participants recognized some positive benefits of online teaching, they were largely unhappy and worried about their situations. The impact of the pandemic has had a profound effect on the way in which individuals and organizations function. While some of these changes were positive, the crisis has also served to highlight inequalities in our society and to force us to deal with them. The responses of our participants showed that for Japanese universities to implement effective online education in the future, either because of a crisis or to expand access to courses beyond the classroom, disparities between tenured and non-tenured faculty members need to be addressed and adequate support and training must be provided.

Practical Implications for Japanese University English Programs and Teachers

The most obvious practical implications of the findings in this study are the need for Japanese universities to establish transparent policies and to provide adequate support for distance learning using ICT in English programs. The general lack of ICT infrastructure for English education at many tertiary level institutions in Japan may come as a surprise to English educators and researchers outside the country, particularly given the common image of Japan as a technologically-advanced country. However, the dearth of documentation about distance learning programs in Japan in general indicates a lack of such programs prior to the pandemic. Thus, the lack of organized, well-planned institutional support for English teachers came as little surprise to us as experienced teachers in Japan.

Additionally, there is a lack of language support for teachers who do not speak fluent Japanese. A common complaint among non-Japanese speaker study participants was that institutionally-held meetings and workshops were in Japanese only, with English language technical support relegated to a PDF software manual. As neither of the authors of this chapter are in a position to influence educational policy at our university (let alone at other universities), we strongly suggest that non-Japanese teachers of English show initiative and actively seek ways to improve their ICT knowledge and online pedagogy (as well as to improve their Japanese language skills!). Working and studying about various software and websites together with other English teachers is also highly recommended, as is joining an online teaching support group. The best such example is Online Teaching Japan, a Facebook Group that started in March 2020 and now has nearly 3000 members from over 80 countries around the world (Online Teaching Japan, 27 Oct 2021). The national organizations Japan Association for Language Teaching (JALT) and English Teachers in Japan (ETJ) also hold regular online events about ICT-based instruction that are often free for all interested participants.

A final implication is for tenured university English instructors in Japan, who may be few and far between but are in a much better position to act as a go-between, particularly for part-time instructors who may be struggling with the needs at multiple places of employ. In fact, Japanese universities represented by the instructors in the study in many cases did ask tenured English instructors to pass along information regarding English program policy changes, in English, that was originally in Japanese and machine translated or translated by a tenured Japanese professor. However, asking teachers to read a software manual is simply not as effective as providing hands-on learning experiences prior to the start of a given academic term. As Japanese university ICT department workers generally speak little to no English and thus are not capable of holding English-language workshops for English-speaker instructors, the only Japanese university workers capable of holding such workshops are the tenured English instructors. Given that nearly half of Japanese university instructors are part-time and nearly a quarter are on non-renewable, five-year-limited contracts (Katayama & Masutani, 2018), English teachers must frequently move from university to university in order to continue their teaching careers. Unless Japanese universities move toward the implementation of institutionally-run workshops, tenured teachers are the only ones in a position to help incoming part-time and contract English teachers understand the online LMS and software being used at their respective institutions. This added responsibility may further increase technostress; hence planning and preparing for the next sudden ERT is crucial to avoid a repeat of the 2020 experience.

FUTURE RESEARCH DIRECTIONS

The COVID-19 pandemic that began in early 2020 is still with us and is likely to remain for the foreseeable future. Even with the quick implementation of various vaccines in some countries, certain countries were able to inoculate many of their citizens, while others have been unable to secure enough vaccines to do the same. Japan as a whole resisted implementing an effective vaccine system until early 2021, with the very first stage rolling out at approximately the same time period (February–March) that we conducted the second stage of our mixed-methods study, the first stage of which was presented in this chapter. A few universities set up English-language websites with information about online teaching policy changes starting in early 2021, and others formed working groups to establish procedures for switching between F2F, fully online, or hyflex courses (i.e., simultaneously teaching some students F2F and some students online in the same class meeting, a type of CALL instruction which in Japan is usually inaccurately termed "hybrid"). Our future research regarding the state of online English teaching and university teachers in Japan is ongoing and is likely to evolve along with our present situation (Apple & Mills, 2021).

As we continue to analyze the qualitative data provided us in interviews with self-selected study participants from the first stage of the study, we have come to realize that the educational and societal situation in Japan as it copes with the virus may necessitate ongoing research to continue to learn more about how institutional administrators, teachers, and students in Japan react to what is likely to continue to be a complicated mixture of F2F, blended, and online course delivery.

CONCLUSION

In the original questionnaire study by Bolliger et al. (2014) about online teaching satisfaction, it was assumed that the structure and software for online courses were provided via an online LMS through the host institution. In the sample population in our Japan-based study, nearly half of the study participants were obliged to create their own LMS because their host institution had no unified online or long-distance learning system in place. Indeed, the general lack of long-distance learning infrastructure at Japanese universities meant that when the ERT situation suddenly occurred, EFL teachers were forced to rely on a more or less hodge-podge variety of websites and social media software using their own knowledge of technology and their own devices with little to no support from their institutions. Rather than getting support from program administrators, they had to rely on the goodwill of teaching colleagues, particularly those who were fortunate enough to be in tenured teaching positions.

In terms of online teaching, teachers in our study were eager to point out that ERT is not online teaching. However, they remained concerned that their institutions in Japan showed no apparent change from the beginning to the end of the ERT situation. As teachers prepared for a partial or complete return to F2F classes at the end of August 2020, they were hopeful that things would change but remained skeptical and pessimistic:

It's a means to an end, ERT is a short-term solution. If it's to become a longer-term approach, training and increased infrastructure is needed for us and for students. (Participant 84, full-time contract)

ACKNOWLEDGMENT

We gratefully acknowledge the assistance of the administrators and members of the many English teaching associated groups on Facebook groups and, in particular, Online Teaching Japan, Kyoto JALT, Osaka JALT, Nara JALT, and West Tokyo JALT, who graciously allowed us to post our request for study participants and reposted our request throughout the internet.

This research received no specific grant from any funding agency in the public, commercial, or not-for-profit sectors.

REFERENCES

Abós, Á., Sevil, J., Martín-Albo, J., Aibar, A., & García-González, L. (2018). Validation evidence of the Motivation for Teaching Scale in secondary education. *The Spanish Journal of Psychology, 21*(9), 1–12. doi:10.1017jp.2018.11 PMID:29633687

Alghamdi, J., & Holland, C. (2020). A comparative analysis of policies, strategies and programmes for information and communication technology integration in education in the Kingdom of Saudi Arabia and the republic of Ireland. *Education and Information Technologies, 25*(6), 4721–4745. doi:10.100710639-020-10169-5

Alsuelmi, A. (2021). *Perceptions of faculty members on the value of distance education at two different types of institutions of higher education in The Kingdom of Saudi Arabia* [Doctoral dissertation, Kansas State University]. K-State Electronic Theses, Dissertations, and Reports.

American Federation of Teachers. (2017). *Educator quality of work life survey*. https://www.aft.org/sites/default/files/2017_eqwl_survey_web.pdf

Andrich, D. (1978). Scaling attitude items constructed and scored in the Likert tradition. *Educational and Psychological Measurement, 38*(3), 665–680. doi:10.1177/001316447803800308

Aoki, K. (2010). The use of ICT and e-learning in higher education in Japan. *World Academy of Science, Engineering and Technology, 42*, 854–858.

Apple, M. T., & Mills, D. (2021). *"Like a hamster on a spinning wheel": University instructor reactions to a year of teaching online* [Manuscript in preparation].

Banegas, D. J., & Manzur Busleimán, G. I. (2014). Motivating factors in online language teacher education in southern Argentina. *Computers & Education, 76*, 131–142. doi:10.1016/j.compedu.2014.03.014

Beardsley, M., Albó, L., Aragón, P., & Hernández-Leo, D. (2021). Emergency education effects on teacher abilities and motivation to use digital technologies. *British Journal of Educational Technology, 52*(4), 1455–1477. doi:10.1111/bjet.13101

Benson, P. (2011). Language learning and teaching beyond the classroom: An introduction to the field. In P. Benson & H. Reinders (Eds.), *Beyond the Language Classroom* (pp. 7–16). Palgrave Macmillan. doi:10.1057/9780230306790_2

Betts, K. S. (1998). An institutional overview: Factors influencing faculty participation in distance learning in postsecondary education in the United States: An institutional study. *Online Journal of Distance Learning Administration, 1*(3). https://www.westga.edu/~distance/betts13.html

Bidwell, L. M., Grether, S. T., & Pedersen, J. (2021). Disruption and difficulty: Student and faculty perceptions of the transition to online learning in the COVID-19 pandemic. In J. M. Ryan (Ed.), *COVID-19: Social consequences and cultural adaptations* (Vol. 2, pp. 31–46). Routledge.

Blundell, G. E., Castañeda, D. A., & Lee, J. (2020). A multi-institutional study of factors influencing faculty satisfaction with online teaching and learning. *Online Learning Journal, 24*(4), 229–253. doi:10.24059/olj.v24i4.2175

Bolliger, D. U., Inan, F. A., & Wasilik, O. (2014). Development and validation of the Online Instructor Satisfaction Measure (OISM). *Journal of Educational Technology & Society*, *17*(2), 183–195.

Bolliger, D. U., & Wasilik, O. (2009). Factors influencing faculty satisfaction with online teaching and learning in higher education. *Distance Education*, *30*(1), 103–116. doi:10.1080/01587910902845949

Bower, B. L. (2001). Distance education: Facing the faculty challenge. *Online Journal of Distance Learning Administration*, *4*(2), 1–6.

Brown, J. D. (2001). *Using surveys in language programs*. Cambridge University Press.

Brown, J. D. (2009). Open-response items in questionnaires. In J. Heigham & R. A. Croker (Eds.), *Qualitative research in applied linguistics: A practical introduction* (pp. 200–219). Palgrave MacMillan. doi:10.1057/9780230239517_10

Cotterall, S., & Reinders, H. (2001). Fortress or bridge? Learners' perceptions and practice in self access language learning. *Tesolanz*, *8*, 23–38.

Creswell, J. W. (2003). Research design: Qualitative, quantitative, and mixed method approaches. *Sage (Atlanta, Ga.)*.

De Brey, C., Snyder, T. D., Zhang, A., & Dillow, S. A. (2021). Digest of education statistics 2019 (NCES 2021-009). National Center for Education Statistics, Institute of Education Sciences, U.S. Department of Education.

Dörnyei, Z., & Ushioda, E. (2021). *Teaching and researching motivation* (3rd ed.). Routledge. doi:10.4324/9781351006743

Dweck, C. S. (2008). *Mindset: The new psychology of success*. Random House.

Eurostat. (2020, May 17). *People expanding their knowledge by learning online*. https://ec.europa.eu/eurostat/web/products-eurostat-news/-/edn-20200517-1

Funamori, M. (2017). The issues Japanese higher education face in the digital age: Are Japanese universities to blame for the slow progress towards an information-based society? *International Journal of Institutional Research and Management*, *1*(1), 37–51. doi:10.52731/ijirm.v1.i1.112

Gierdowski, D. C., Brooks, D. C., & Galanek, J. D. (2020). *EDUCAUSE 2020 student technology report: Supporting the whole student*. EDUCAUSE Research.

Habibi, A., Razak, R. A., Yusop, F. D., Mukminin, A., & Yaqin, L. N. (2020). Factors affecting ICT integration during teaching practices: A multiple case study of three Indonesian universities. *Qualitative Report*, *25*(5), 1127–1144. doi:10.46743/2160-3715/2020.4150

Halupa, C. P., & Bolliger, D. U. (2020). Technology fatigue of faculty in higher education. *Journal of Higher Education and Practice*, *11*(18), 16–26. doi:10.7176/JEP/11-18-02

Hata, A. (2020, April 22). Japan's students left behind as world embraces online classes: Red tape ensnares schools trying to adapt to new coronavirus restrictions. *Nikkei Asia*. https://asia.nikkei.com/Business/Education/Japan-s-students-left-behind-as-world-embraces-online-classes

Heft, H. (2007). Affordances and the body: An intentional analysis of Gibson's ecological approach to visual perception. *Journal for the Theory of Social Behaviour, 19*(1), 1–30. doi:10.1111/j.1468-5914.1989.tb00133.x

Hodges, C., Moore, S., Lockee, B., Trust, T., & Bond, A. (2020, March 27). The difference between Emergency Remote Teaching and Online Learning. *EDUCAUSE Review*. https://er.educause.edu/articles/2020/3/the-difference-between-emergency-remote-teaching-and-online-learning

Honarzad, R., & Rassaei, E. (2019). The role of EFL learners' autonomy, motivation and self-efficacy in using technology-based out-of-class language learning activities. *The JALT CALL Journal, 15*(3), 23–42. doi:10.29140/jaltcall.v15n3.170

Howe, D., & Heitner, K. L. (2020, October 1-2). *Faculty satisfaction teaching online in the time of COVID-19* [Paper presentation]. Walden University Research Conference 2020 (online). https://scholarworks.waldenu.edu/researchconference/2020/papers/9/

Katayama, K., & Masutani, F. (2018, May 20). Daigaku kyouin, hansuu ha hijoukin jyoukin mo yonbun no ichi ga "kigentsuki" [Half of university instructors are part-time and one-quarter of full-time instructors are on "fixed-term" contracts]. *Asahi Shimbun*. https://www.asahi.com/articles/ASL5M54SBL5MUTIL00Z.html

Klapproth, F., Federkeil, L., Heinschke, F., & Jungmann, T. (2020). Teachers' experiences of stress and their coping strategies during COVID-19 induced distance teaching. *Journal of Pedagogical Research, 4*(4), 444–452. doi:10.33902/JPR.2020062805

Kniffin, K. M., Narayanan, J., Anseel, F., Antonakis, J., Ashford, S. P., Bakker, A. B., Bamberger, P., Bapuji, H., Bhave, D. P., Choi, V. K., Creary, S. J., Demerouti, E., Flynn, F. J., Gefland, M. J., Greer, L. L., Johns, G., Kesebir, S., Klein, P. G., Lee, S. Y., ... Vugt, M. V. (2021). COVID-19 and the workplace: Implications, issues, and insights for future research and action. *The American Psychologist, 76*(1), 63–77. doi:10.1037/amp0000716 PMID:32772537

Ko, S., & Rossen, S. (2010). *Teaching online: A practical guide* (3rd ed.). Routledge. doi:10.4324/9780203855201

Kono, T. (2009). Social affordances and the possibility of ecological linguistics. *Integrative Psychological & Behavioral Science, 43*(4), 356–373. doi:10.100712124-009-9097-8 PMID:19609627

Kulikowski, K., Przytuła, S., & Sułkowski, Ł. (2021). The motivation of academics in remote teaching during the COVID-19 pandemic in Polish universities: Opening the debate on a new equilibrium in e-learning. *Sustainability, 13*(5), 2752. doi:10.3390u13052752

Latchem, C., Jung, I., Aoki, K., & Ozkul, A. E. (2008). The tortoise and the hare enigma in e-transformation in Japanese and Korean higher education. *British Journal of Educational Technology, 39*(4), 610–630. doi:10.1111/j.1467-8535.2007.00771.x

Lee, M., & Lim, K. Y. (2020). Do the technostress creators predict job satisfaction and teacher efficacy of primary school teachers in Korea? *Educational Technology International, 21*(1), 69–95.

Lei, S. I., & So, A. S. I. (2021). Online teaching and learning experiences during the COVID-19 pandemic: A comparison of teacher and student perceptions. *Journal of Hospitality & Tourism Education, 33*(3), 1–15. doi:10.1080/10963758.2021.1907196

Lembani, R., Gunter, A., Breines, M., & Dalu, M. T. B. (2020). The same course, different access: The digital divide between urban and rural distance education students in South Africa. *Journal of Geography in Higher Education, 44*(1), 70–84. doi:10.1080/03098265.2019.1694876

Li, L., & Wang, X. (2021). Technostress inhibitors and creators and their impacts on university teachers' work performance in higher education. *Cognition Technology and Work, 23*(2), 315–330. doi:10.100710111-020-00625-0

Maxwell, E. E. (2021). *Technostress factors as predictors of job Satisfaction among teachers in K–12 education* [Doctoral dissertation]. Grand Canyon University.

Milheim, W. (2001). Faculty and administrative strategies for the effective implementation of distance education. *British Journal of Educational Technology, 32*(5), 535–542. doi:10.1111/1467-8535.00223

Nash, M., & Churchill, B. (2020). Caring during COVID-19: A gendered analysis of Australian university responses to managing remote working and caring responsibilities. *Gender, Work and Organization, 27*(5), 833–846. doi:10.1111/gwao.12484 PMID:32837013

Nuncio, R. V. (2020). Benchmarking ICT for education in Japan: Best practices, trends, challenges and lessons learned for Philippine ICT-based education & development. *Asia–Pacific Social Science Review, 20*(2), 136–148.

O'Quinn, L., & Corry, M. (2002). Factors that deter faculty from participating in distance education. *Online Journal of Distance Learning Administration, 5*(4). https://www.westga.edu/~distance/ojdla/winter54/Quinn54.htm

Oliveira, G., Grenha Teixeira, J., Torres, A., & Morais, C. (2021). An exploratory study on the emergency remote education experience of higher education students and teachers during the COVID-19 pandemic. *British Journal of Educational Technology, 52*(4), 1357–1376. doi:10.1111/bjet.13112 PMID:34219758

Online Teaching Japan [David Juteau]. (2021, October 27). *OTJ has members from these countries...* Facebook. https://www.facebook.com/groups/603548090241536/posts/959027178026957

OzimekA. (2020). The future of remote work. https://papers.ssrn.com/sol3/papers.cfm?abstract_id = 3638597

Prabjandee, D. (2020). Multilayered motivation of becoming English teachers in Thailand: Beyond intrinsic, extrinsic, and altruistic reasons. *Teacher Learning and Professional Development, 5*(1), 49–61.

Prensky, M. (2001). Digital natives, digital immigrants. *On the Horizon, 9*(5), 1–6. doi:10.1108/10748120110424816

Rasch, G. (1960). *Probabilistic models for some intelligence and attainment tests*. University of Chicago.

Reinders, H., & Benson, P. (2017). Research agenda: Language learning beyond the classroom. *Language Teaching, 50*(4), 561–578. doi:10.1017/S0261444817000192

Ridge, E., & Waghid, Y. (2001). Equity and distance education. *Equity & Excellence in Education, 34*(3), 80–86. doi:10.1080/1066568010340310

Roy, S., & Covelli, B. (2021). COVID-19 induced transition from classroom to online mid semester: Case study on faculty and students' preferences and opinions. *Higher Learning Research Communications, 11*(0), 10–32. doi:10.18870/hlrc.v11i0.1197

Ryan, R. M., & Deci, E. L. (2002). Overview of self-determination theory: An organismic dialectical perspective. In E. L. Deci & R. M. Ryan (Eds.), *Handbook of self-determination research* (pp. 3–33). University of Rochester.

Ryan, R. M., & Deci, E. L. (2017). *Self-determination theory: Basic psychological needs in motivation, development, and wellness.* Guilford. doi:10.1521/978.14625/28806

Saykili, A. (2018). Distance education: Definitions, generations and key concepts and future directions. *International Journal of Contemporary Educational Research, 5*(1), 2–17.

Shivastava, A. (2020). Identifying and analyzing occupational stress factors among faculty of autonomous colleges n Madhya Pradesh. *Academic Leadership, 21*(04).

Simonson, M., Smaldino, S., Albright, M., & Zvacek, S. (2000). *Teaching and learning at a distance: Foundations of distance education.* Prentice Hall.

Staniscuaski, F., Kmetzsch, L., Soletti, R. C., Reichert, F., Zandonà, E., Ludwig, Z. M., Lima, E. F., Neumann, A., Schwartz, F. P., Mello-Carpes, P. B., Tamajusuku, A. S., Werneck, F. P., Ricachenevsky, F. K., Infanger, C., Seixas, A., Staats, C. C., & de Oliveira, L. (2021). Gender, race and parenthood impact academic productivity during the COVID-19 pandemic: From survey to action. *Frontiers in Psychology, 12*, 663252. Advance online publication. doi:10.3389/fpsyg.2021.663252 PMID:34054667

Tabachnick, B. G., & Fidell, L. S. (2001). *Using multivariate statistics* (4th ed.). Allyn & Bacon.

Vansteenkiste, M., Sierens, E., Goossens, L., Soenens, B., Dochy, F., Mouratidis, A., Aelterman, N., Haerens, L., & Beyers, W. (2012). Identifying configurations of perceived teacher autonomy support and structure: Associations with self-regulated learning, motivation, and problem behavior. *Learning and Instruction, 22*(6), 431–439. doi:10.1016/j.learninstruc.2012.04.002

Vermote, B., Aelterman, N., Beyers, W., Aper, L., Buysschaert, F., & Vansteenkiste, M. (2020). The role of teachers' motivation and mindsets in predicting a (de)motivating teaching style in higher education: A circumplex approach. *Motivation and Emotion, 44*(2), 270–294. doi:10.100711031-020-09827-5

Wang, B., Liu, Y., Qian, J., & Parker, S. K. (2021). Achieving effective remote working during the COVID-19 pandemic: A work design perspective. *Applied Psychology, 70*(1), 16–59. doi:10.1111/apps.12290 PMID:33230359

Watermeyer, R., Crick, T., Knight, C., & Goodall, J. (2021). COVID-19 and digital disruption in U.K. universities: Afflictions and affordances of emergency online migration. *Higher Education, 81*(3), 623–641. doi:10.100710734-020-00561-y PMID:32836334

ADDITIONAL READING

Collie, R. J. (2021). COVID-19 and teachers' somatic burden, stress, and emotional exhaustion: Examining the role of principal leadership and workplace buoyancy. *AERA Open*, *7*(1), 1–15. doi:10.1177/2332858420986187

Daniela, L. (Ed.). (2020). *Pedagogies of digital learning in higher education*. Routledge. doi:10.4324/9781003019466

Kitamura, Y., Omomo, T., & Katsuno, M. (Eds.). (2019). *Education in Japan: A comprehensive analysis of education reforms and practices* (Vol. 47). Springer. doi:10.1007/978-981-13-2632-5

Kubanyiova, M. (2009). Possible selves in language teacher development. In Z. Dörnyei & E. Ushioda (Eds.), *Motivation, language identity, and the L2 self* (pp. 314–332). Multilingual Matters. doi:10.21832/9781847691293-017

Nichols, M. (2020). *Transforming universities with digital distance education: The future of formal learning*. Routledge. doi:10.4324/9780429463952

Office of Planning, Evaluation and Policy Development. (2021). ED COVID-19 handbook, volume 3: Strategies for safe operation and addressing the impact of COVID-19 on higher education students, faculty, and staff. U.S. Department of Education.

Pacansky-Brock, M. (2012). *Best practices for teaching with emerging technologies*. Routledge. doi:10.4324/9780203095966

Richardson, P. W., Karabenick, S. A., & Watt, H. M. (Eds.). (2014). *Teacher motivation: Theory and practice*. Routledge. doi:10.4324/9780203119273

Stockwell, G. (2013). Technology and motivation in English-language teaching and learning. In E. Ushioda (Ed.), *International perspectives on motivation: Language learning and professional challenges* (pp. 156–175). Palgrave MacMillan. doi:10.1057/9781137000873_9

Tamim, R. M., Bernard, R. M., Borokhovski, E., Abrami, P. C., & Schmid, R. F. (2011). What forty years of research says about the impact of technology on learning: A second-order meta-analysis and validation study. *Review of Educational Research*, *81*(1), 4–28. doi:10.3102/0034654310393361

KEY TERMS AND DEFINITIONS

Affordances: The perceived benefits of a particular technology.

Embedded Design: A form of mixed-methods research in which both quantitative and qualitative forms of data collection are used in the same questionnaire or survey.

Emergency Remote Teaching: A method of teaching delivery due to a sudden emergency, conducted entirely long-distance via postal service correspondence or the internet.

Institutional Support: Aid provided by the organization where a teacher works that can include, but is not limited to, training, technological help, additional compensation, and services that make it easier for the teacher to do an effective job.

Learning Management System (LMS): A software application to facilitate the delivery of online courses. Common functions of this software are communication, material delivery, grading, and tracking.

Online Learning: A method of instruction facilitated by technology and the Internet where the student is not present in the physical classroom. Instruction can occur synchronously or asynchronously.

Teacher Lifestyle: The personal aspects of teachers' lives outside of their jobs.

Teacher Motivation: A desire to make decisions and take actions as a teacher moves through their training and careers.

Teaching Satisfaction: Enjoyment and contentment derived from the practice of teaching.

Technostress: Mental fatigue and strain brought about by the use of technology on a daily basis.

APPENDIX

Table 6. Traditional descriptive statistics for each item in the questionnaire

	n	*M*	*SD*	**Skewness**	**Kurtosis**
ISOI1	87	4.60	1.005	-.942	1.346
ISOI2	86	4.27	1.162	-.681	-.050
ISOI3	87	3.70	1.330	-.279	-.769
ISOI4	87	4.01	1.094	-.350	-.319
ISOI5	86	2.95	1.345	.027	-1.038
AFF1	86	4.09	1.476	-.546	-.742
AFF2	86	4.29	1.354	-.694	-.049
AFF3	86	4.50	1.234	-.730	.217
AFF4	87	4.24	1.210	-.601	.062
ISP1	87	2.94	1.528	.179	-1.365
ISP2	86	3.38	1.558	-.094	-1.189
ISP3	84	2.85	1.485	.431	-.806
ISP4	83	3.29	1.550	.124	-1.037
ISP5	86	3.53	1.508	-.089	-.988
TECH1	87	2.66	1.477	.686	-.481
TECH2	87	4.00	1.486	-.348	-.783
TECH3	87	4.52	1.477	-.798	-.399
TECH4	86	3.37	1.565	.111	-1.000
TECH5	86	3.05	1.586	.411	-.894
TLIF1	81	4.38	1.189	-1.246	1.479
TLIF2	87	4.36	1.347	-.885	.190
TLIF3	83	4.28	1.391	-.737	-.156
TLIF4	86	3.44	1.546	-.035	-1.099
TLIF5	86	4.02	1.346	-.221	-.655
TLIF6	86	3.51	1.650	.067	-1.187
OTM1	86	3.99	1.368	-.459	-.603
OTM2	86	4.94	1.010	-1.074	1.888
OTM3	83	4.53	1.223	-.993	1.044
OTM4	87	5.25	.967	-2.190	7.085
OTM5	87	5.02	1.034	-1.209	1.931

Note. ISOI = Instructor–Student Online Interaction; AFF = Affordances; ISP = Institutional Support; TECH = Technostress; TLIF = Teacher Lifestyle; OTM = Online Teaching Motivation. There were 35 missing data points overall. The original questionnaire is available upon request from Dr. Matthew Apple at mapple@fc.ritsumei.ac.jp.

Chapter 2
Pecha Kucha Presentations:
Digital Adaptation and Online Communication in ESP Higher Education

Soraya García-Sánchez
https://orcid.org/0000-0003-1095-9410
Universidad de Las Palmas de Gran Canaria, Spain

ABSTRACT

This comparative research analyses some reflections regarding the teaching and learning approaches designed to foster communicative English language skills under the modality of online education with real-time interaction and multimodal communicative mediation. Because of the global pandemic COVID-19, the higher educational community of three different subjects on English for Specific Purposes (ESP) modified their programs to full online education with different digital tools and interactive methods. A survey was used to analyze students' preferences regarding this abrupt change. Consequently, the delivery of communicative skills through mediated multimodal communication or interaction in English were explored with students' online speaking presentations, which followed the Pecha Kucha model. It is suggested that the multimodal Pecha Kucha speeches allowed participants to produce, receive, interact, and mediate their interpersonal communication with interactive comments, expressed synchronously via MS Teams or posted asynchronously on the forum via written or audio messages.

INTRODUCTION

Emergency circumstances, such as the ones experienced during the COVID-19 pandemic, have required rapid adaptation to fully online education, which, at the same time, have validated the need for digital literacy. Worldwide face-to-face educational communities shut down their buildings and were hastily transitioned to remote education, keeping in mind the course goals, skills, and evaluations required to accomplish both competences and content (König, Jäger-Biela & Glutsch, 2020; Zhao, Llorente & Gómez, 2021). For long, Computer- or Mobile-Assisted Language Learning (CALL/MALL) programs have allowed English language learners to improve their learning, enhance their linguistic skills, and have helped mediate global interaction between learners by means of technology (Gallardo del Puerto

DOI: 10.4018/978-1-7998-8717-1.ch002

& Gamboa, 2009; González-Lloret, 2003; Shayakhmetova, Mukharlyamova, Zhussupova & Beisembayeva, 2020). Learning a foreign language is a social and intercultural performance. It implies constant interaction with others.

English as a Foreign Language has been mostly performed face-to-face or in blended-learning environments that combine multimodal communicative onsite and offsite tasks with an ample array of Information and Communication Technologies (ICT). Furthermore, verbal and non-verbal communication are to be successfully delivered during any communication act. It seems necessary to gain further insight into English language courses, designed with a communicative approach and adapted to online education, which encourages learners to perform the communicative competence in English. Moreover, it is assumed that digital literacy is advanced in young higher education learners, who are more used to technologies and devices than their professors and teachers.

What this study seeks to determine is how this global transformation has also evidenced the digital literacy and digital pedagogy of learning communities in tertiary education. For this purpose, the Pecha Kucha (PK) presentation task, also known as a 20x20 (seconds x slides) speech or a lightning talk is the multimodal presentation style used in this study to develop students' online communicative mediation skills and interaction. Students were encouraged to prepare their speeches in 6.40 minutes with clear and concise information so that they could engage online. This research, therefore, aims at analyzing digital adaptation, multimodal-mediated interaction, and online communication in three English for Specific Purposes (ESP) courses in higher education in 2020 and 2021. The research questions are:

RQ1: What are the Spanish students' preferences regarding the correspondence between digital literacy and this abrupt online English language teaching-learning discourse in higher education?

RQ2: Have the Pecha Kucha presentations served as multimodal communicative tasks to engage in interpersonal interaction and online communicative mediation in English?

LITERATURE REVIEW

Digital Literacy for English Language Courses in Higher Education

Digital literacy and emerging applications are crucial for higher education learners who must have the attitude and the aptitude to be proficient when communicating information in different situations: personal, social and educational (Bhatt & MacKenzie, 2019; Coldwell-Neilson, 2018; Jan, 2018; Yu & Zadorozhnyy, 2021). This digital awareness resonates well with pedagogical and technological advances that are inevitably linked to English language education. Correspondingly, English language education is guided by practical, technological, and interactive negotiations so that communication in English can be confirmed, discussed, mediated, or resolved in onsite and offsite settings. As professionals in the field of education, professors have the responsibility to adapt and adopt the right measures to reach learners' realities and goals. As Evans et al. argued: "Pedagogical research has the potential to make significant contribution to the quality of learning and teaching" (Evans et al., 2020, p. 526). This educational excellence should address outstanding results regarding content and, more important, communicative skills in the English language learning community, which must also be advanced in digital skills to access global knowledge.

Digital literacy has been defined as "the ability to understand and use information in multiple formats from a wide range of sources when it is presented via computers" (Gilster, 1997, p. 1). Other studies have linked digital literacies to cognitive skills and professional purposes (Chan et al., 2017; Mishra et al., 2017). The study conducted by Sánchez-Caballé, Gisbert-Cervera and Steve-Món (2021) pinpointed that the digital competence is key in 21st century higher education. Furthermore, Spante et al.'s research review (2018) demonstrated that the digital competence is underpinned by digital literacy. While the latter is significantly attached to the various research goals in higher education and to the professional proficiency of teachers, the digital competence has been oriented to more policy reports and professional contexts.

(English) Language learners and teachers should be up to date with digital literacy skills so that CALL processes are successfully designed to enhance these abilities through interactive learning and technologies that foster real-time engagement. Roche's research (2017) stated that English for Academic Purposes (EAP) students accessing university with an explicit digital literacy focus reported a better understanding of academic and institutional practices, and less difficulty accessing course content. In another study, García-Sánchez (2016) emphasized that the physical space of a classroom can be adapted to a variety of digital spaces (combining synchronous and asynchronous education) through internet access and technologies that support ubiquitous learning. Accordingly, a narrow focus of digital literacy for educational ends in English language education must be identified when designing current programs, so that effective communicative skills are enhanced, while integrating technologies in the classroom (García-Sánchez, 2021; Meurant, 2010; Son, Park & Park, 2017). In this chapter, therefore, digital literacy is considered an indispensable ability in current English language education so that successful multimodal-mediated communication can be performed with adequate interactive technologies even in fully online learning environments (Bawden, 2008; García-Sánchez, 2012; Liang, 2021; Sindoni, 2014).

Designing English Language Courses in Higher Education

Building on my experience as a teacher and as an applied linguistics researcher, most communicative English language courses in higher education have three main directions: they are oriented to academic purposes (English for Academic Purposes -EAP), general language skills (English as a Foreign Language -EFL) and the specific professional fields of the students attending the courses (English for Specific Purposes -ESP). The latter plays a key role in facilitating English language acquisition while being in conversation with the core content of the learners' degrees (Architecture; Law; Social Work, Telecommunications Engineering…). Research abounds in this area motivating the frequent transformation of the content, the skills and the assessment of English language courses of tertiary level which are mostly planned under a blended-learning approach with inside and outside tasks that respond to learners' realities (Albiladi & Alshareed, 2019; Im & Kim, 2015; Rianto, 2020; Tarnopolsky, 2013; Zhang & Zhu, 2018).

Basöz and Erten (2018) found that willingness to communicate in English speaking tasks was moderate in Turkish tertiary education. Compared to written communication, students reported a lower level of willingness in speaking tasks. Similarly, other studies have focused on the necessary link between motivation or attitudes and English language learning results (Genc & Aydin, 2017; Ibrahim, 2010; Karabiyik, 2019), which somehow are related to an emotional-cognitive-skilled learning approach in the course design (Li, 2010; Miller & Gkonou, 2018; Ryan & Hendersin, 2018; Soland & Sandilos, 2021). This entails a satisfactory teaching-learning environment with clear communication between teachers and students, establishing goals, tasks, and feedback during the process.

Pecha Kucha: Online Communicative Interaction and Mediation in English

Pecha Kucha (PK) is originated from the Japanese "chit chat" or "casual talk" by architects Mark Dytham and Astrid Klein to address effective or lightning talks, supported by visual and time limited. The PK style comprises three key concepts: concise content, clear language, and attractive visuals that are restricted to 6.40 minutes or 20 seconds per slide (20 slides). Research has validated the effective use PK presentations in education (Beyer, 2011; Klentzin et al., 2010) and in developing public speaking skills (Coskun, 2017; Mabuan, 2017). A Pecha Kucha, or 20x20 presentation, is therefore an engaging method of sharing information online. It combines multimodal communication with concise delivery of information via 20 visual slides lasting 20 seconds each. This implies that the speech needs to be rehearsed to avoid reading out loud so that verbal and non-verbal communication as well as multimodal content are delivered in 6.40 minutes. Most importantly, the presenter must engage the audience with vivid speech.

PK presentations contribute to enhancing the communicative language skills of listening, speaking, reading, and writing since students must go over different steps of researching information (reading and listening), elaborating, organizing (writing) and practicing the speech (speaking techniques) to engage and interact with the audience (listening). An English language learning communicative approach has been based on the communicative language skills of listening, speaking, reading, and writing (Al Zoubi, 2018; Erdoğan, 2019; Sadiku, 2015). Today, with *The Latest edition of the Common European Framework of References for Languages, Companion Volume* (CEFR CV, 2020), communicative language skills have been transformed into the four macro-functions of the language, which are both considered activities and strategies for foreign language users: reception, production, interaction, and mediation (CEFR CV, 2020). *Reception* has to do with the input received by learners. It implies overall comprehension while engaging with others, while listening to their comments and questions, while reading a paragraph, or while watching an audio-visual document. *Production* addresses the output generated by learners when communicating messages in written and oral forms. *Interaction* has also been acknowledged as a paramount macro-function that encourages written and spoken collaborative exchanges either online or face-to-face. Finally, *mediation* is described as a macro-function that requires different techniques to build meaning between at least two speakers who have been unable to communicate messages. According to the CEFR CV, mediation is both an activity and a strategy that facilitates the interpretation of messages between two or more speakers or groups. As seen in Table 1, the four macro-functions of the CEFR CV correspond with activities and strategies to perform those communicative functions as active learners, which can be enhanced through the PK presentations.

Table 1. Macro-functions of the CEFR CV

COMMUNICATIVE FUNCTIONS	ACTIVITIES	STRATEGIES
RECEPTION	Oral comprehension or listening Audiovisual comprehension Reading comprehension	Identifying cues and inferring (Spoken, signed and written)
PRODUCTION	Oral production or speaking Written production or writing	Planning, compensating and monitoring and repair
INTERACTION	Oral interaction Written interaction Online interaction (vs. face-to-face)	Turn-taking, co-operating and asking for clarification
MEDIATION	Mediating texts Mediating concepts Mediating communication	Explaining a new concept (linking to previous knowledge, adapting language and breaking down complicated information) Simplifying a text (amplifying a dense text, streamlining a text)

Additionally, it is important to acknowledge that the action-oriented approach of the CEFR CV establishes that language learners are both users and social agents with an active role in their learning process so that the teaching proposal must be planned according to the students' real-life communicative needs (p. 29). Since learners are users and social agents, the action-oriented approach pursues the design of collaborative learning tasks with real-world applications for students. The PK presentations clearly respond to this purpose since active learners build their own PK presentations with the aim communicating their unique, communicative products.

Correspondingly, communication takes place when speaking and writing are produced by language learners with engaging utterances, arguments, or sentences that connect with others (listeners or readers). This requires interaction, either face-to-face or online, if the communicative task is produced onsite or online. Online communicative interaction together with mediation (of a text, of concepts, and of communication) are two descriptor scales added in the CEFR CV, which are of interest in this study because of their importance at the time of co-constructing meaning among participants. Likewise, compared to the previous 2001 CEFR version, the new scale categories of using telecommunications and giving information reinforce the importance of multimodal online communication in the CEFR CV.

Identifying the educational framework that combines the efficacy of digital literacy with the English language speaking tasks of the Pecha Kucha presentations in online settings is the purpose of the present study. Designing an English language course must combine the four macro-functions of the CEFR in either a face-to-face or an online learning environment. References to these macro-functions are paramount, since students should (1) produce an oral text that will be listened to by the educational community in an online platform, and (2) apply mediation strategies that deal with new content and communication. The participants come from similar ESP contexts oriented to their professional fields in Telecommunications Engineering, Social Work and Law as independent users at level B2. The multimodal Pecha Kucha presentations produced by these three groups would be discussed as examples of communicative interaction and mediation presented remotely.

METHODOLOGY

Participants and Setting

This qualitative-quantitative comparative research explores the teaching and learning processes implemented in three ESP compulsory subjects in higher education. It sought to determine successful approaches that combined digital literacy with multimodal online English language communication and mediated interaction after the COVID-19 global outbreak.

The number of students enrolled in these online ESP courses during the academic years 2019–2020 and 2020–2021 were 199 in total: 107 students in the third-year degree subject *English Applied to Social Work* (EASW), 4 of them Erasmus students from Italy and Sweden in the Degree of Social Work; 65 in the master's degree subject *Legal English* (LE) and 27 students in *Communicative Competences in English* (CCE), a compulsory subject in the fourth-year degree in Telecommunications Engineering. Of the total 199 students who did their Pecha Kucha presentation, 90 students volunteered to complete the anonymous survey: 44 students of EASW, 23 of LE and 23 of CCE.

The educational setting of these ESP subjects shared a communicative approach with different ESP content applied to their fields. EASW and CCE offered 6 ECTS in English (European Credit Transfer and Accumulation System) while LE offered 4.5 ECTS, which were presented in 15- and 7-week increments, respectively. The platform used for synchronous online sessions was *Microsoft Teams,* which was supported by the asynchronous digital space of *Moodle*. Interactive and communicative mediation tasks were encouraged in these courses, whose weekly plan was shared with the students at least one week in advance. Moreover, synchronous interaction was prompted through engaging lessons, debates, roleplays, reading comprehension exercises, vocabulary in context and questions, while asynchronous interaction and communicative written mediation were encouraged through online discussion forums together with topics and concepts applied to their professional fields.

Pecha Kucha Presentations: Interaction and Multimodal Communicative Mediation

As previously mentioned, the communicative task designed for interactive and oral communicative mediation was the speaking presentation, which followed the format of Pecha Kucha (PK). Delivering a PK presentation in a concise and decisive manner was a challenge for some students due to the information chosen, the structure and timing of their speeches, and the online delivery. It required various drills before the final product was delivered. This task also required paying attention to the four communicative functions of production, reception, interaction, and mediation (CEFR CV, 2020) so that learners could be accurate during their performances as communicators.

The instructions for the PK presentations were explained during the online synchronous sessions and then, posted on the platform. First, learners had a deadline to post the topic of their speech in the forum. It was required that each student's presentation topic was unique. Secondly, in the case of CCE, students had to prepare a Pecha Kucha (PK) presentation in pairs using remote communication, while EASW and LE students were offered the option of working individually or in pairs for their video PK presentations. In CCE, the PK presentations, which were recorded for evaluation purposes, were performed synchronously and in pairs via *MS Teams*. In EASW and LE, students recorded their asynchronous video PK presentations and posted them on the course forum. Finally, all the learners in the three groups were prompted to give and receive interactive peer-to-peer feedback, so that everyone provided and received some opinion, comment, or question from their peers either via immediate interactions performed synchronously via MS Teams, or via audio/written messages posted in the forum. This implied that two deadlines were necessary for the groups of EASW and LE: one to post their videos and one to post their comment or question, so that every presentation was addressed. It is important to acknowledge that all the learners in EASW, LE and CCE were distance participants who had previously coordinated their talk using a common multimedia *PowerPoint* visual aid to support their speech.

The assessment criteria for this speaking task were explained in class and organized in three main blocks. The first criteria (45%) were focused on the organization and content of the speech regarding vocabulary, use of English, purpose, techniques to open and close the speech, supporting ideas, and the correspondence between content, allotted time, and visuals. Items dealing with non-verbal communication and interaction was worth 15% of the total points. The last block (45%) corresponded with different items related to accurate speaking skills in English, such as vocal variation, clarity, intonation, pronunciation, fluency or preparation, and delivery, as shown in Figure 1.

Figure 1. Assessment criteria: PK speaking task

BLOCK 1 (45%)	BLOCK 2 (15%)	BLOCK 3 (40%)
Organization + Content (Intro technique) + Vocab + Use of English + clear purpose + supported ideas /examples + definite conclusions + allotted time + visuals	Body Language + Eye contact + Posture + Natural Approach + Interaction with others	Delivery + Enthusiasm + Vocal variation + Preparation (No Reading) + Effective delivery + Comprehension Pronunc. + Fluen. + Clarity + Intonation

Data Collection and Analysis

Over a three-month period, data was collected. The instruments and data used for this study were: 1) the online synchronous presentations in CCE and the asynchronous video presentations, in EASW and LE which followed the PK model, and which were posted on *Moodle*, 2) the communicative mediation messages for interaction, 3) the voluntary, anonymous survey and 4) the instructor's observations. The online survey, which was created with the *Microsoft* application "Forms", consisted of 10 questions dealing with students' reflections on the ESP courses and the changes towards immediate online education.

FINDINGS AND DISCUSSION

To analyze the results, qualitative-quantitative comparative methods were used. First, the questionnaire form, filled out by learners once the courses ended, reported on students' perceptions regarding face-to-face and remote learning environments to learn English. Second, multimodal communication to engage in real-time interaction and online communicative mediation was examined through the speaking task of the Pecha Kucha presentations. In EASW and LE, most students recorded their video PK presentations individually (all 100% of students in LE and 62% in EASW). About 48% of the latter chose the option of working in pairs at the time of creating their video presentation. In CCE, all students delivered their remote synchronous PK speeches in pairs through *MS Teams*.

RQ1. What are the Spanish students' preferences regarding the correspondence between digital literacy and this abrupt online English language teaching-learning discourse in higher education?

The data extracted from the survey was used to analyze the results for this research question. Once the three ESP courses finished, the first question of the online anonymous survey reported that most students (61% in EASW, 96% in LE and 82.6% in CCE) accomplished the language level goal of B2. Just a few students (2% in EASW, none in LE and 8.6% in CCE) considered having a C1 level. Correspondingly, one student in LE and another learner in CCE responded that they did not know their achieved language level, in contrast to 11 students in EASW who chose this dubitative option. Finally, 11% in EASW, none in LE, and 8.6% in CCE selected the option 'Other' to refer to another language level rather that B1, B2 or C1. So, in general terms, it seems that learners felt they progressed to the target level B2.

From question 2, it can be deduced that the mode of instruction preferred by most students was face-to-face (80% in EASW, 96% in LE and 87% in CCE) over online sessions (14% in EASW, none in LE and 5% in CCE). Only two learners selected the choice "do not know", as seen in Figure 2.

Figure 2. Students' preferences regarding lessons

Question 3 was oriented to register whether students had devoted more hours to their English language courses once the confinement and sudden online lessons began (after March 13th, 2020). The answers indicate a notable transformation on learners' workload, especially in EASW and LE, since 70% of students in EASW, 78% in LE, and 26% in CCE considered an increasing workload compared to a 20% of students in EASW, 17% in LE, and 30% in CCE who denied having encountered an augmented amount of work once they were fully working online.

Figure 3. Students' perceptions regarding workload

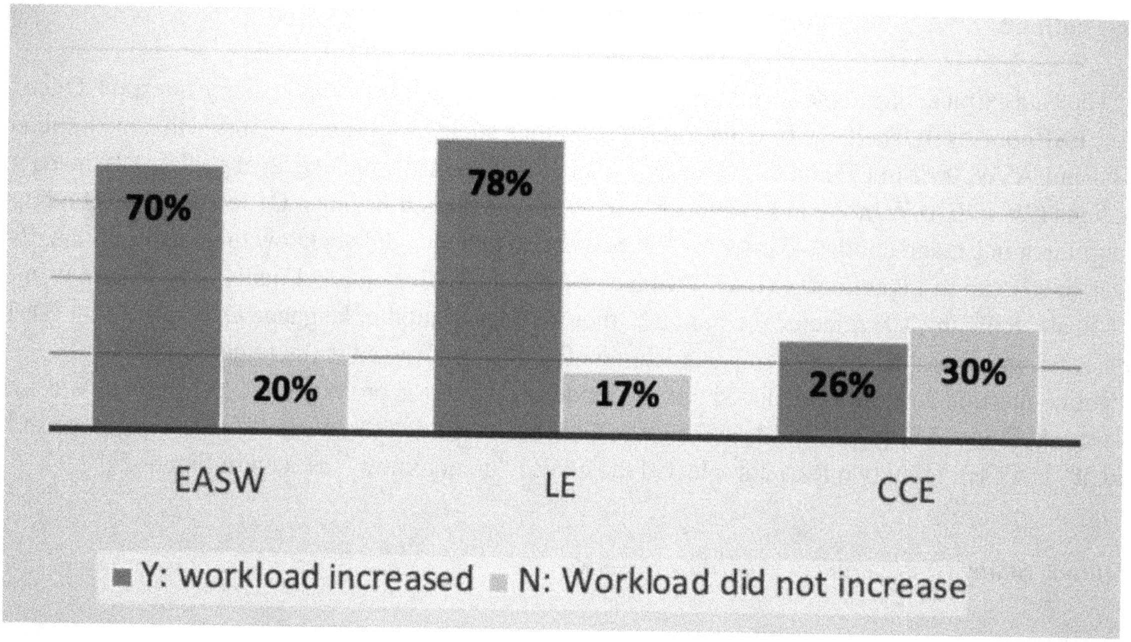

Question 4 enquired about whether the online weekly teaching-learning plan, which was posted on the *Moodle* platform at least one week in advance, helped students organize their learning. Most respondents confirmed that this outline was adequate and positive for the majority of participants: 89% in EASW; 74% in LE and 87% in CCE. It seems that the average weekly class workload was satisfactory for these ESP undergraduates.

Question 5 enquired whether students had any difficulties following the online sessions after the COVID-19 outbreak. On the one hand, about 64% of EASW students reported having faced some difficulties during synchronous online sessions, compared to 34% who felt comfortable (Figure 4). On the other hand, most students in LE and CCE replied not having had any problems (65% in LE and 69% in CCE) in contrast with a minor group who considered having had some complications (26% in LE and 14% in CCE).

Figure 4. Difficulties with online sessions

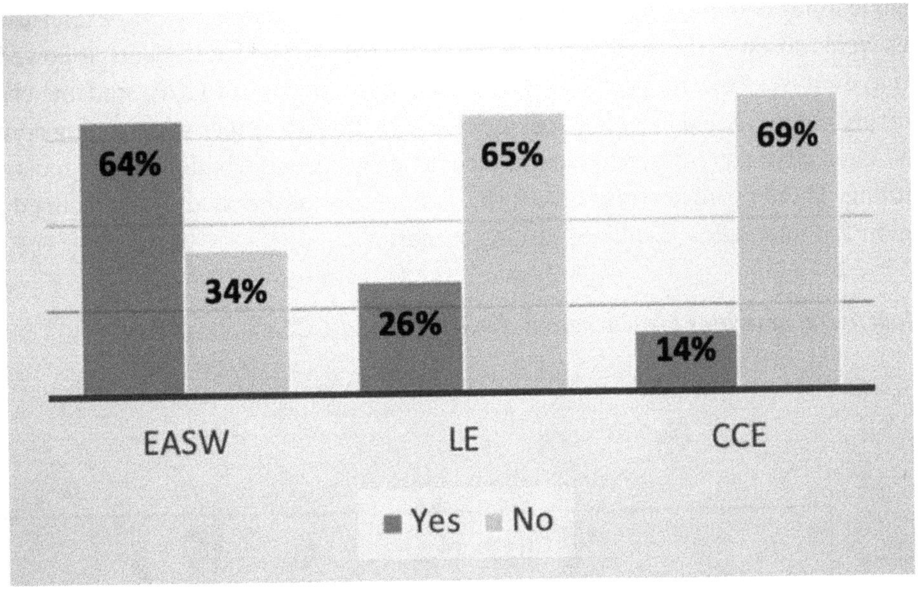

Due to the adaptation to online teaching-learning, there was a necessary transition to online assessment with similar tasks and exams modelled for face-to-face evaluation. Question 6 referred to the adequacy of the online evaluation tasks and the online exams for the subject programs. A similar percentage of students in all three groups (84% in EASW, 87% in LE, and 78% in CCE) reported that the adaptation to the online assessment was adequate, as shown in Figure 5.

Figure 5. Adequacy of online assessment

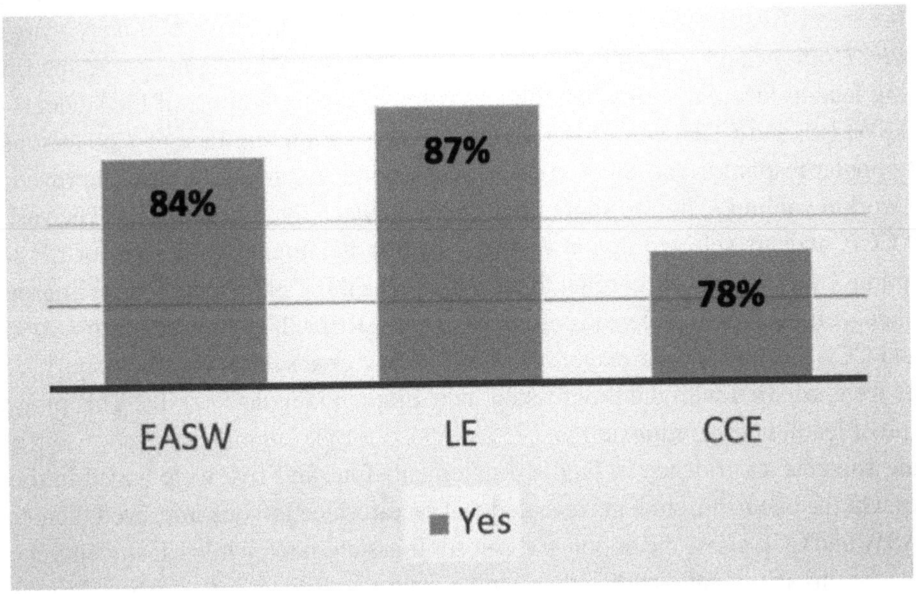

The next question (Question 7) reported on the most common activities or tasks students considered useful for their learning (Figure 6). Coincidently, from the options offered, listening exercises and interactive activities were chosen as the most useful activities for EASW and LE students, followed by reading and interactive exercises (second position). Interestingly, in the case of CCE, students chose face-to-face speaking presentations and listening activities (first position) together with reading comprehension exercises and interactive activities, and face-to-face debates (second position) as the most useful tasks for their learning. These results corresponded with the purpose of this study, which aimed at mediated communication and interaction in online learning scenarios.

Figure 6. Most useful activities for learners in EASW, LE and CCE

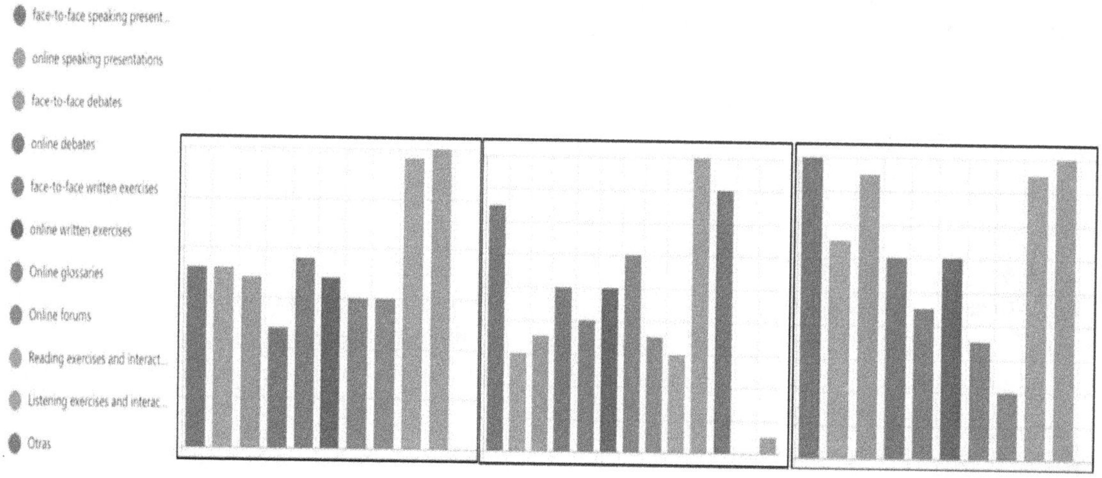

Question 8 addressed differences regarding face-to-face and online learning according to the participants. There were five statements that informants responded following the *Likert scale* from 1 to 5, being 1 *Totally Disagree* and 5 *Totally Agree*. The first statement, "I have improved my English skills, when working face-to-face," reported that the level of proficiency in most of the students of the three courses (EASW, LE, and CCE) was especially higher when attending face-to-face lessons, according to the most popular responses chosen (*4. Agree*). The second statement, "I have improved my English skills when working online," showed slight differences between the three courses. The vast majority of EASW and CCE students selected option *4. Agree* for this statement, while most of LE students who chose the option *3. Don't know*. According to the survey, the third statement, "I have improved my English skills when working face-to-face and online (NO DIFFERENCE)," showed more *4. Agree* responses in EASW and CCE. LE had similar responses in *5. Totally Agree* selected by the majority. So, it seems that students were satisfied with the progress on their English languageg skills. This progress was not linked to type of learning environment.

Regarding students' confidence in English, statements four and five were added in this question 8 of the survey. On the one hand, students revealed that face-to-face lessons improved their confidence in English: EASW and CCE chose the option *4. Agree* for this statement, while LE students chose option *5. Totally Agree* for this statement. On the other hand, whether online lessons improved English language learners' confidence, it was clear in the case of EASW (first chart in Figure 7) that more than a third of students chose *2. Disagree* and another third *4. Agree*, compared to LE who mostly felt that they did not know (option *3. Don't know*) or they agreed *4. Agree* and *5. Totally agree*. Similarly, more than half of students in CCE seemed to agree (*4. Agree*) with some progress in their confidence during online lessons, while less than a half was not sure about this statement.

Figure 7. Perceptions of EASW, LE and CCE students regarding English skills and confidence

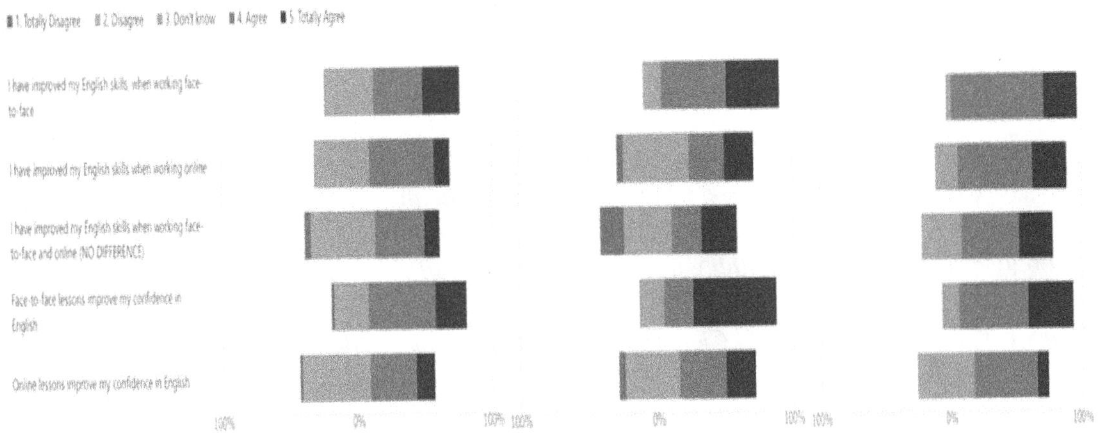

The responses to question 9 in the survey acknowledged the most frequent websites, platforms, applications, and social networks students specifically used for their classwork. In general terms, participants in the three courses added that the most common websites used were those oriented to the teaching-learning plan: *Microsoft Teams* or *Big Blue Bottom* for synchronous lessons, together with *Moodle* and the digital multimedia resources shared on the *Virtual Campus*. Also, there were some references to online dictionaries (monolingual and bilingual) as well as translators as sources that most informants especially used during their courses. The postgraduate students of LE also mentioned the dictionary *TheSaurus*.

The last question in the survey asked learners to provide suggestions or comments to improve any aspect of the teaching-learning plan, program and assessment of these ESP courses. In general terms it seems that the three groups felt satisfied with the adaptation of the 100% online teaching-learning situation with user-friendly applications and a corresponding workload that was shared and planned a week in advance. In EASW, learners' comments were especially oriented to the dynamics of the lessons and the interactive exchanges they could perform with other participants (through the forum and the PK presentations). Also, there were some comments addressing the need for extra practice on sentence structures for definitions and some more speaking tasks that could improve their confidence in public speaking. The students of LE had their contact hours planned from 15.00–21.00 from Monday to Friday. They especially struggled with the timetable set for this subject, which was from 19.00–21.00. Since this ESP subject required active participation and frequent interaction among participants, most students expressed that they would be more receptive and active contributors if this subject was planned in the early hours of their timetable, so that they were fresh to engage in online communication with the extra effort of doing it in English. They also positively reported on the task of the Pecha Kucha presentation and the dynamics of the online lessons, even though they clearly stated their preference for face-to-face education. Finally, the students of the telecommunications engineering degree (CCE) provided positive remarks regarding the overall smooth adaptation to online education with comments in favor of a balanced workload compared to face-to-face education, and to interactive engaging sessions (including the PK presentation format) that allowed them to think and perform communicative skills in English. Some comments offered by three students are shown below:

St. 1. I have no suggestions. I really liked the dynamics of the classes (EASW) and the Pecha Kucha presentations. The only thing I didn't like is doing it online, you lose a lot and there are many technical issues.

St. 2. I am very happy with the development of the classes (LE), the assignments and the evaluation. I have learned a lot. The most positive remark is the methodology used, it has been perfect and I can see the great work of the teacher. And as a suggestion, I would include something about Spanish law in the topics (for example, getting to know more about how to say the institutions and peculiarities of Spanish law in English). But otherwise, nothing to object. Thanks a lot!

St. 3. The truth is that this subject (CCE) is one of the best adapted to the sudden change we have experienced. You continue with the classes and the activities despite the difficulties, and also gave us facilities by noy adding extra work, and I really appreciate that. I have 5 more subjects and I have never worked so hard like this before. I really enjoyed your classes face-to-face, but I also did enjoy them online. I don't have suggestions other than keep it up!

In general terms, these English language students seem to have a preference for face-to-face education over 100% online education. The results corresponded with both the educational and emotional realities of each participant so that they could successfully demonstrate not only communicative skills in English but digital literacy. Likewise, the online discourse for English language teaching-learning, set for these three ESP courses, aimed at keeping some dynamics with communicative mediation and online interaction so that the participants could practice and feel engaged in synchronous conversations while being oriented/assessed accordingly (Hamutoğlu, Savaşçi & Sezen-Gültekin, 2019). The weekly learning plans posted at least a week in advance on the platform together with constructive feedback were key to promote collaboration and positive emotional-cognitive responses while coping with the remote learning challenges of the global pandemic (Miller & Gkonou, 2018; Ryan & Henderson, 2018; Soland & Sandilos, 2021). Additionally, it is important to acknowledge that the learners' favorite interactive tasks were based on speaking and listening practice, which reinforces the hypothesis that even though they were fully online, these tertiary education students engaged in communication and interaction, quite probably because of the tasks designed for their courses (e.g., Pecha Kucha presentations and online debates), which links to the second research question.

RQ2. Have the Pecha Kucha presentations served as multimodal communicative tasks to engage in real-time interaction and online communicative mediation in English?

One of the most prominent findings of this study has evidenced the assertion that online communicative skills can be performed in synchronous, real-time exchanges through verbal and non-verbal interaction and multimodal communicative mediation. Asynchronous interaction was also achieved through messages posted on the course forum. The task of the Pecha Kucha (PK) presentation, contemplated in this online student-centered learning environment, comprised a collection of new literacies that empowered students to engage in mediated interpersonal interactivity and multimodal online communication during the COVID-19 lockdown.

The findings suggest that the Pecha Kucha presentations engaged learners in building their own multimodal communicative products, which were shared by peers so that these ESP learners could simulate some necessary interaction while giving and receiving some comments. The PK presentations had a common structure: 1) starting with a greeting and a presentation of speakers, followed by a fact or engaging question; 2) adding an intro and development of topic with data, more questions for engagement, and attractive visuals (Figure 8), and 3) ending with a conclusion and a 'thank you' to engage with possible comments or questions from the class members/audience. It is inferred from the PK presentations that students adopted a responsible and motivating attitude towards the preparation, delivery and interaction of their multimodal speeches not only according to the time and content set, but also, according to making themselves understood with clear messages and comprehension of the content selected for the 6.40 minutes of the task. Some examples of PK presentations as multimodal communicative products are illustrated below:

Figure 8. Examples of PK presentations with visuals and the speakers

Similar to the findings presented by Satar (2015, 2016) and Garrison, Anderson and Archer (2010), the nature of social presence or interaction in online multimodal communication was key in these forced distance education programs since it aimed to establish some social and effective connections among language learners, which quite probably also improved their motivation and learning satisfaction. Also, mediated interpersonal interaction was reported via the communicative mediation messages posted on the forum or exchanged by the students in real-time conversations. Regarding the mediated interpersonal interaction corresponding with the PK presentations, there was a high number of interactive messages reported (268 in EASW and 246 in LE) as shown in Figure 9.

Figure 9. Mediated interpersonal interaction in EASW and LE on the forum

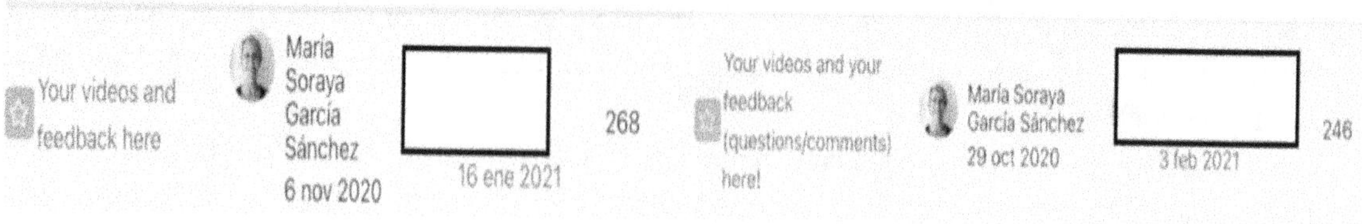

Accordingly, two examples of mediated interpersonal interaction, extracted from the LE forum, are shown below with the names of students anonymized (Table 2). Once learners posted their PK video presentations, they contributed to enhancing interactive messages that not only engaged in the discussion of each topic presented but allowed students to mediate between the communication, concepts and content delivered:

Table 2. Examples of mediated interpersonal interaction in LE

INTERACTION 1 between St.1 and St.2	INTERACTION 2 between St.3 and St.4
***St. 1.** Hello St1, the first thing I have to tell you is that it has been a very clear and straightforward presentation, congratulations! Now, I ask you the following question. Do you think this legal principle applies a lot in practice? Thanks so much for this great video!* ***St. 2.** Hi, St2, I'm glad you liked it! Thanks for your question, I think in our system we know this principle by the name of "teoría de los actos propios", and we learn about in public international law, so in this particular matter, yes, it applies a lot, but in our contract law it's not common to hear about it. We are used to look at our Civil Code and apply the rules written in it, although parties can draft contracts following their best interests. However, as far as I know, a party may allege in court that the other party is contradicting what they had stated previously. Furthermore, in commercial law, when a firm or a professional establishes the same condition among many contracts, a new general condition is born, and, subsequently, that firm or professional cannot go against that condition. In conclusion, even though it is not exactly the same principle in our system and the common law system, the essence is almost the same.*	***St. 3.** Hi everyone, Here is my video about "The age of smart cities and its regulation". Also, I post here some interesting links about smart cities: - https://eu-smartcities.eu/ - https://www.smartcityuk.com/roadshow-meeting-city-challenges - https://www.thesmartcityjournal.com/es/ - https://secmotic.com/smart-cities/* ***St. 4.** Hi St. 3, First at all, I really like your presentation! you look like a great European Parliament member xD. According to you final question, in my point of view, smart cities have an incredible impact in our quality of life. Personally, I think it is likely that it contributes to make our life easier and more comfortable with the time, as well as, provide sustainability, job opportunities and wellbeing. However, it is also to considerer the necessity of an innovative legislation, as I have seen in your video, and an elaborated plan in order to protect human rights in relation to the use of technology in life, which can only be achieved with a worldwide collaboration. Thank you very much, best wishes,* ***St. 3.** Hello St. 4! I'm glad that you liked my presentation. As you have said, smart cities contribute to make our life easier by transforming the traditional networks with the use of digital and telecommunication technologies but it's necessary a correct legal control in order to respect our fundamental rights. Thank you!*

In the case of CCE, the interactive messages were instantly produced, received, and mediated in synchronous verbal and non-verbal communication through the *MS Teams* platform as shown in Figure 10. The presenters shared their screen with the PK presentation they were explaining, followed by the exchanged views, comments, and questions of the audience.

Figure 10. PK presenters and mediated interpersonal interaction with verbal and non-verbal communication

Additionally, the findings resonate well with those of Peng, Zhang & Chen (2017) who corroborated that mediation of multimodal affordances are present in English language communicative education. PK presentations were potentially valuable products of online multimodal communication that combined the written content and the visuals added to the slides with verbal and non-verbal communication delivered by these remote English language learners. Likewise, as PK presentations were performed in computer-mediated contexts, multimodal interaction was produced in the form of speech, visuals, written or audio comments, and questions provided by these learners with the corresponding responses of the audience (Satar, 2015, 2016).

The PK presentations allowed these ESP students to produce, receive, interact, and mediate with specific vocabulary and communication thanks to a technology-supported pedagogy and a multimodal communicative approach. This fact is related to methodological innovations, adaptation, and transformation in English language education that has aimed to respond to students' needs.

Conclusively, as many studies have reported, strong affective and motivational conditions seem to have improved the learners' confidence to communicate accurately (Chou, 2018; Golonka et al., 2014; Kukulska-Hulme & Viberg, 2018). Even though the aforementioned barriers of the COVID-19 situation (e.g., more challenging communicative social exchanges), the online learning environment of these three ESP courses was maximized to replicate the dynamics usually practiced in the face-to-face-class with multimodal communicative mediation and interaction. It is suggested that the learning design of the Pecha Kucha presentations can be efficiently integrated into ESP language teaching-learning environments as to support English language acquisition, multimodal communication and mediated interpersonal interaction, even in in online learning environment.

CONCLUSIONS AND FUTURE RESEARCH

The COVID-19 pandemic has been a disruptive challenge for everyone. In less than 24 hours, buildings closed, and educators and learners adapted to full online education, keeping in mind the need for digital literacy and interactive communicative skills among participants. This chapter has examined ESP students' perceptions during these experiential circumstances, on the one hand, and their performance of linguistic skills and mediated interaction with the Pecha Kucha presentations, which served as multimodal communicative tasks for interpersonal interaction and online communicative mediation.

This transformation has evidenced the importance of human adaptation and of adopting the necessary emotional-cognitive-communicative skills in the foreign language classroom. The Pecha Kucha task was the speaking task model to move forward by facing new challenges with synchronous communication, mediation, and online interaction. The Pecha Kucha task has also fostered the development of new competencies that have been required for these ESP remote teaching-learning scenarios. Digital literacy and digital pedagogy have been enforced in these higher education communities, although there was a general preference for face-to-face lessons. Likewise, digital adaptation supported mediated interaction and online communication in the three English for Specific Purposes (ESP) courses of this research through the Pecha Kucha presentations.

Conclusively, online interaction, either between teacher and students or between learners themselves, has been achieved through multimodal synchronous and asynchronous communication technologies by means of chats, forums and real-time discussions and the Pecha Kucha presentations, in the target language. The inclusion of the two new CEFR scales (online conversation and discussion and goal-oriented transactions and collaborations) acknowledges the advances in online learning scenarios. Future lines of research could be extended to address willingness to communicate in real-time telecollaborative online learning environments and the importance of co-constructing meaning to build emotional-cognitive skills through verbal, non-verbal, and multimodal communication. Further pedagogical research practices in ESP need to be analyzed to ensure not only that the best instruction is provided but also, the best communicative learning results are achieved in this new digital classroom era.

REFERENCES

Al Zoubi, S. M. (2018). The impact of exposure to English language on language acquisition. *Journal of Applied Linguistics and Language Research, 5*(4), 151–162.

Albiladi, W. S., & Alshareef, K. K. (2019). Blended learning in English teaching and learning: A review of the current literature. *Journal of Language Teaching and Research, 10*(2), 232–238. doi:10.17507/jltr.1002.03

Basöz, T., & Erten, I. H. (2018). Investigating Tertiary Level EFL Learners' Willingness to Communicate in English. *English Language Teaching, 11*(3), 78–87. doi:10.5539/elt.v11n3p78

Basöz, T., & Erten, I. H. (2018). Investigating Tertiary Level EFL Learners' Willingness to Communicate in English. *English Language Teaching, 11*(3), 78–87. doi:10.5539/elt.v11n3p78

Bawden, D. (2008). Origins and concepts of digital literacy. *Digital literacies: Concepts, policies and practices, 30*(2008), 17-32.

Beyer, A. M. (2011). Improving student presentations: Pecha Kucha and just plain PowerPoint. *Teaching of Psychology, 38*(2), 122–126. doi:10.1177/0098628311401588

Bhatt, I., & MacKenzie, A. (2019). Just Google it! Digital literacy and the epistemology of ignorance. *Teaching in Higher Education*, *24*(3), 302–317. doi:10.1080/13562517.2018.1547276

Chan, B. S., Churchill, D., & Chiu, T. K. (2017). Digital literacy learning in higher education through digital storytelling approach. *Journal of International Education Research*, *13*(1), 1–16. doi:10.19030/jier.v13i1.9907

Chou, M. H. (2018). Speaking anxiety and strategy use for learning English as a foreign language in full and partial English-medium instruction contexts. *TESOL Quarterly*, *52*(3), 611–633. doi:10.1002/tesq.455

Coldwell-Neilson, J. (2018, November). Digital literacy expectations in higher education. In *Open oceans: Learning without borders: ASCILITE 2018 Conference Proceedings* (pp. 103-112). Geelong, Australia: ASCILITE.

Coskun, A. (2017). The Effect of Pecha Kucha Presentations on Students' English Public Speaking Anxiety. *Profile Issues in Teachers Professional Development*, *19*(_sup1), 11–22. doi:10.15446/profile.v19n_sup1.68495

Council of Europe. (2020). *Common European Framework of Reference for Languages: Learning, Teaching and Assessment – Companion Volume*. Council of Europe Publishing. Available at www.coe.int/lang-cefr

Erdoğan, V. (2019). Integrating 4C skills of 21st century into 4 language skills in EFL classes. *International Journal of Education and Research*, *7*(11), 113–124.

Evans, C., Kandiko Howson, C., Forsythe, A., & Edwards, C. (2021). What constitutes high quality higher education pedagogical research? *Assessment & Evaluation in Higher Education*, *46*(4), 525–546. doi:10.1080/02602938.2020.1790500

Gallardo del Puerto, F., & Gamboa, E. (2009). The evaluation of computer-mediated technology by second language teachers: Collaboration and interaction in CALL. *Educational Media International*, *46*(2), 137–152. doi:10.1080/09523980902933268

García-Sánchez, S. (2012). English in Class and on the Go: Multimodal U-Learning. *The EuroCALL Review*, *20*(2), 94–102. doi:10.4995/eurocall.2012.11381

García-Sánchez, S. (2016). Online metacognitive tasks for EFL distance learners. *Turkish Online Journal of Distance Education*, *17*(4), 76–90. doi:10.17718/tojde.60563

García-Sánchez, S. (2021). Ubiquitous Digital Literacy and English Language Education: A Systematic Review. Ubiquitous Learning. *International Journal (Toronto, Ont.)*, *15*(1), 37–50. doi:10.18848/1835-9795/CGP/v15i01/37-50

Garrison, D. R., Anderson, T., & Archer, W. (2010). The first decade of the community of inquiry framework: A retrospective. *The Internet and Higher Education*, *13*(1-2), 5–9. doi:10.1016/j.iheduc.2009.10.003

Genc, Z. S., & Aydin, F. (2017). An Analysis of Learners' Motivation and Attitudes toward Learning English Language at Tertiary Level in Turkish EFL Context. *English Language Teaching*, *10*(4), 35–44. doi:10.5539/elt.v10n4p35

Gilster, P. (1997). *Digital Literacy*. John Wiley & Sons, Inc.

Golonka, E. M., Bowles, A. R., Frank, V. M., Richardson, D. L., & Freynik, S. (2014). Technologies for foreign language learning: A review of technology types and their effectiveness. *Computer Assisted Language Learning*, *27*(1), 70–105. doi:10.1080/09588221.2012.700315

González-Lloret, M. (2003). Designing task-based CALL to promote interaction: En busca de esmeraldas. *Language Learning & Technology*, *7*(1), 86–104.

Hamutoğlu, N. B., Savaşçi, M., & Sezen-Gültekin, G. (2019). Digital literacy skills and attitudes towards e-learning. *Journal of Education and Future*, (16), 93–107. doi:10.30786/jef.509293

Ibrahim, A. I. (2010). ESP at the Tertiary Level: Current Situation, Application and Expectation. *English Language Teaching*, *3*(1), 200–204. doi:10.5539/elt.v3n1p200

Im, J. H., & Kim, J. (2015). Use of blended learning for effective implementation of English-medium instruction in a non-English higher education context. *International Education Studies*, *8*(11), 1–15. doi:10.5539/ies.v8n11p1

Jan, S. (2018). Investigating the Relationship between Students' Digital Literacy and Their Attitude towards Using ICT. *International Journal of Educational Technology*, *5*(2), 26–34.

Karabiyik, C. (2019). The Relationship between Student Engagement and Tertiary Level English Language Learners' Achievement. *International Online Journal of Education & Teaching*, *6*(2), 281–293.

Klentzin, J. C., Paladino, E. B., Johnston, B., & Devine, C. (2010). Pecha Kucha: Using "Lightning Talk" in University Instruction. *RSR. Reference Services Review*, *38*(1), 158–167. doi:10.1108/00907321011020798

König, J., Jäger-Biela, D. J., & Glutsch, N. (2020). Adapting to online teaching during COVID-19 school closure: Teacher education and teacher competence effects among early career teachers in Germany. *European Journal of Teacher Education*, *43*(4), 608–622. doi:10.1080/02619768.2020.1809650

Kukulska-Hulme, A., & Viberg, O. (2018). Mobile collaborative language learning: State of the art. *British Journal of Educational Technology*, *49*(2), 207–218. doi:10.1111/bjet.12580

Li, C. (2020). A positive psychology perspective on Chinese EFL students' trait emotional intelligence, foreign language enjoyment and EFL learning achievement. *Journal of Multilingual and Multicultural Development*, *41*(3), 246–263. doi:10.1080/01434632.2019.1614187

Liang, M. Y. (2021). Multilingual and multimodal mediation in online intercultural conversations: A translingual perspective. *Language Awareness*, *30*(3), 1–21. doi:10.1080/09658416.2021.1941069

Mabuan, R. A. (2017). Developing ESL/EFL Learners' Public Speaking Skills through Pecha Kucha Presentations. *English Review: Journal of English Education*, *6*(1), 1–10. doi:10.25134/erjee.v6i1.765

Meurant, R. C. (2010). The iPad and EFL digital literacy. In *Signal processing and multimedia* (pp. 224–234). Springer. doi:10.1007/978-3-642-17641-8_27

Miller, E. R., & Gkonou, C. (2018). Language teacher agency, emotion labor and emotional rewards in tertiary-level English language programs. *System*, *79*, 49–59. doi:10.1016/j.system.2018.03.002

Mishra, K. E., Wilder, K., & Mishra, A. K. (2017). Digital literacy in the marketing curriculum: Are female college students prepared for digital jobs? *Industry and Higher Education*, *31*(3), 204–211. doi:10.1177/0950422217697838

Peng, J. E., Zhang, L., & Chen, Y. (2017). The mediation of multimodal affordances on willingness to communicate in the English as a foreign language classroom. *TESOL Quarterly*, *51*(2), 302–331. doi:10.1002/tesq.298

Rianto, A. (2020). Blended Learning Application in Higher Education: EFL Learners' Perceptions, Problems, and Suggestions. *Indonesian Journal of English Language Teaching and Applied Linguistics*, *5*(1), 55–68. doi:10.21093/ijeltal.v5i1.574

Roche, T. B. (2017). Assessing the role of digital literacy in English for Academic Purposes university pathway programs. *Journal of Academic Language and Learning*, *11*(1), A71–A87.

Ryan, T., & Henderson, M. (2018). Feeling feedback: Students' emotional responses to educator feedback. *Assessment & Evaluation in Higher Education*, *43*(6), 880–892. doi:10.1080/02602938.2017.1416456

Sadiku, L. M. (2015). The importance of four skills reading, speaking, writing, listening in a lesson hour. *European Journal of Language and Literature*, *1*(1), 29–31. doi:10.26417/ejls.v1i1.p29-31

Sánchez-Caballé, A., Gisbert-Cervera, M., & Esteve-Món, F. (2021). La integración de la competencia digital en educación superior: Un estudio de caso de una universidad catalana. *Educar*, *57*(1), 241–258.

Satar, H. M. (2015). Sustaining multimodal language learner interactions online. *CALICO Journal*, *32*(3), 480–507. doi:10.1558/cj.v32i3.26508

Satar, H. M. (2016). Meaning-making in online language learner interactions via desktop videoconferencing. *ReCALL*, *28*(3), 305–325. doi:10.1017/S0958344016000100

Shayakhmetova, L., Mukharlyamova, L., Zhussupova, R., & Beisembayeva, Z. (2020). Developing Collaborative Academic Writing Skills in English in CALL Classroom. *International Journal of Higher Education*, *9*(8), 13–18. doi:10.5430/ijhe.v9n8p13

Sindoni, M. G. (2014). *Spoken and written discourse in online interactions: A multimodal approach*. Routledge. doi:10.4324/9780203587935

Soland, J., & Sandilos, L. E. (2021). English language learners, self-efficacy, and the achievement gap: Understanding the relationship between academic and social-emotional growth. *Journal of Education for Students Placed at Risk*, *26*(1), 20–44. doi:10.1080/10824669.2020.1787171

Son, J. B., Park, S. S., & Park, M. (2017). Digital literacy of language learners in two different contexts. *The JALT CALL Journal*, *13*(2), 77–96. doi:10.29140/jaltcall.v13n2.213

Spante, M., Hashemi, S. S., Lundin, M., & Algers, A. (2018). Digital competence and digital literacy in higher education research: Systematic review of concept use. *Cogent Education*, *5*(1), 1519143. doi:10.1080/2331186X.2018.1519143

Tarnopolsky, O. (2013). Developing ESP students English speaking, reading, listening, and writing skills in internet-assisted project work. *Journal of Teaching English for Specific and Academic Purposes, 1*(1), 11–20.

Yu, B., & Zadorozhnyy, A. (2021). Developing students' linguistic and digital literacy skills through the use of multimedia presentations. *ReCALL*, 1–15. doi:10.1017/S0958344021000136

Zhang, W., & Zhu, C. (2018). Comparing Learning Outcomes of Blended Learning and Traditional Face-to-Face Learning of University Students in ESL Courses. *International Journal on E-Learning, 17*(2), 251–273.

Zhao, Y., Llorente, A. M. P., & Gómez, M. C. S. (2021). Digital competence in higher education research: A systematic literature review. *Computers & Education, 168*, 104212. doi:10.1016/j.compedu.2021.104212

Chapter 3

Emergency Remote Teaching in Tertiary Education:

Issues Raised, Solutions Given, and Lessons Learned

Savvi Antoniou
Cyprus University of Technology, Cyprus

ABSTRACT

The recent pandemic has forced many language instructors to adjust their teaching practices since many of the methods used prior to COVID-19 could not be used remotely. The aim of this chapter is to share the experience of a language practitioner and 22 students and discuss how they managed to cope with this unprecedented situation. The issues raised, the solutions given, and the lessons learned at the end of this endeavor are documented and shared. Quantitative data were collected by a questionnaire addressed to the students at the end of this period. Qualitative data were collected by the practitioner's descriptive/reflective notes and by a semi-constructed interview of students. The results revealed that students' attitudes became more positive towards online learning at the end of this experience. The practitioner's adaptability, continuous self-training, and positive attitude towards change were proved to be determining factors linked to students' positive attitudes in the end.

INTRODUCTION

In spring 2020, the majority of schools, colleges, and universities were forced to move all their lessons from face-to-face to online. This unforeseen situation caused by the COVID-19 pandemic took almost everyone in the academic world by surprise. Instructors have suddenly found themselves with no other choice than online teaching. Many of them had no experience in the use of technology in teaching and they even had no interest in learning how to meaningfully integrate it into their classes before the pandemic; now, all of a sudden, they were entirely dependent on the use of technology (Godwin-Jones, 2020). This reluctance or resistance in incorporating technology into their class is in someway "legitimate" as "language teachers in higher education rarely have the status, the salary, the time, the encouragement,

DOI: 10.4018/978-1-7998-8717-1.ch003

or the opportunities to develop the critical engagement that would be required to genuinely transform professional practice" (Sadoux, 2021 p. 90). However, in a blink of an eye, instructors were asked to redesign their courses for synchronous, asynchronous remote delivery, or both, and many had absolutely no idea what these terms mean and how to proceed with this transition (Godwin-Jones, 2020). On the other side, there were instructors who had already been using technology in their classes or who were trained for it. While several countries had been providing language teachers with technological facilities and training, they failed to provide a sufficient level of skill development and motivation (Giannikas, 2019). Implementing technology in a language class is beneficial to the students but ineffective if the instructor does not know how to properly apply it (Giannikas, 2021). In addition to these, no teacher training program included a topic such as "how to deal with a pandemic" and such an emergency situation (MacIntyre et al., 2020).

A number of studies have been published since the beginning of the pandemic, but in those early days, there was not much published literature specifically examining experiences in the Higher Education (HE) sector with COVID-19 (also see Johnson et al., 2020). The early research conducted about "digital capabilities in HE has focused on the skills and experiences of students with little emphasis on teaching staff, therefore leaving a gap in need of filling at a fast pace, given the unprecedented scenario" (Munday 2021, p. 64). The move from face-to-face to online, required preparation and planning to ensure that time would not be wasted, and that every aspect of the experience would be considered and addressed (Cunico, 2021). Yet, time was something practitioners did not have. Systematic planning and preparation, based on current theories and practices, was not possible under the circumstances. Many language practitioners, without any point of reference, tried to do their best to cope with the new situation (Feldman, 2021, p.40)

This chapter describes the experience of a French language instructor and 22 students when lessons shifted online. Without any guidelines to follow, the language instructor documented and addressed the issues raised in those early days on emergency remote teaching. The chapter reports the difficulties that occurred, and the action plan the instructor followed in order to cope with this unprecedented situation. At the end of this endeavor, the students' attitudes and opinions were also documented. Results from data underline the importance of adaptability and maintaining a positive attitude in times of crisis and stress the fact that more targeted teacher training is necessary.

BACKGROUND

In an online teaching environment, one of the first decisions that need to be taken concerns the modes of teaching. Distance learning can involve synchronous learning, asynchronous learning, or a mixture of both. Each of them can contribute to the students' learning experience depending on which suits their learning style best. According to Higley (2013), in an online environment, synchronous learning involves lectures, discussions, and lesson presentations at a specific point in time. It supports interaction and collaboration, and students can ask questions in real-time. Synchronous online technology includes video-conferencing, webcasts, interactive learning models, and telephone conferences. In an asynchronous learning environment, students are able to actively participate in their own learning. There are "learning activities and expectations that require students to create, synthesize, explain, and apply the content or skills being taught" (Higley, 2013).

With the sudden shift to online teaching, language instructors had to decide what would be taught synchronously and what would be taught asynchronously and also decide on the material to use. In the case of language instructors who did not have any previous experience in online teaching, it is quite possible that, in addition, they did not even have the necessary material to use for online teaching. For instance, if the face-to-face lesson was based on material in a printed form, then this material could no longer be used in a distance mode of delivery. There is the possibility for this material to be uploaded in an e-platform or emailed to students, it is not possible, however, that students could have immediate feedback when following a distance learning method. In a remote environment, instant feedback can be automatically generated by the online activities the instructor chooses to integrate into the lesson. These activities can be ready-made, retrieved by various sides on the web, or created by the instructors themselves. Instant feedback can also be provided to students by synchronous online sessions or tutorials. This "reinforces their understanding of the content covered and the assigned tasks, discuss issues of concern, share ideas and knowledge, and interact with the instructor for questions or problems" (Papadima-Sophocleous & Loizides, 2016, p. 363).

The significance of tutorials was examined in Papadima-Sophocleous & Loizides (2006) and the authors underlined the benefits associated with the inclusion of synchronous weekly tutorials. According to them, these sessions provided students with the opportunity to have a meaningful interaction with the instructor and the other students. In their study, students did not work in isolation, but shared their learning experience. The data showed that this helped them feel reassured and part of a group. Besides timely and constructive feedback, and real-time collaboration (Racheva, 2018), synchronous distance learning stimulates active interaction and helps develop a stronger feeling of connection and engagement (Lin & Gao, 2020).

During quarantine, synchronous online teaching, which primarily involves video-conferencing, had tremendous potential to maintain a social connection (Reich et al., 2020). However, to enable social connection and have a kind of face-to-face interaction, the involved parties should be willing to turn on their cameras. In many cases, it was quite a challenge for the instructor to convince students to turn their cameras on, during synchronous tutorials class held via video-conferencing software, (Castelli & Sarvary, 2021) making the interaction more difficult.

The challenges raised with the pandemic were numerous and documented (Plutino & Polisca, 2021). The rapid transition left no time for preparation and there were many decisions that needed to be taken by the language instructor overnight (Schleicher, 2020). It is no surprise that both students and their instructors experienced stress and anxiety. Students' concerns were oriented towards the lack of academic support, the lack of adequate resources to support online teaching, the lack of socialization, and the lack of motivation in attending classes (Al-Maskari et al., 2021). Instructors' concerns were oriented towards the lack of training, the lack of familiarity, or comfort with digital pedagogy in online teaching. This was evidenced by the solution of many instructors that resorted to replicating a traditional lesson on a computer (Schleicher, 2020). Nevertheless, what the instructors actually wanted was to be better informed on how to support their students in this remote way as well as in best practices for themselves as they work and teach from home (Johnson et al., 2020).

Instructors across the globe were to cope with the education crisis and become acquainted with online teaching and learning, in one way or another. Hodges et al. (2020) describe online learning as "a form of distance education in which a course or program is intentionally designed in advance to be delivered fully online. Faculty use pedagogical strategies for instruction, student engagement, and assessment that are specific to learning in a virtual environment" (para. 18). Similarly, Bates (2020) argues that online learning is "a form of distance education in which a course or program is intentionally designed in advance to be delivered fully online. Faculty use pedagogical strategies for instruction, student engagement, and assessment that are specific to learning in a virtual environment" (para. 18). During the pandemic, the educational situation could only be described as "Emergency Remote Teaching". As Hodges et al. (2020) argue, this way of teaching and learning was neither planned nor designed to be online. It was an emergency situation which he describes as "a temporary shift of instructional delivery to an alternate delivery mode due to crisis circumstances".

It is clear that language instructors and their students were in a state of an emergency due to the pandemic, which differs from the description seen in Hodges et al. (2020) and Bates (2020). It was a shift of the delivery mode which "involves the use of fully remote teaching solutions for instruction or education that would otherwise be delivered face-to-face or as blended or hybrid courses and that will return to that format once the crisis or emergency has abated" (Hodges et al., 2020 para. 13). The situation in the early days of the pandemic was not online learning, it was Emergency Remote Teaching. Language instructors had to take the plunge and do their best in order to cope with the new situation, even if no one knew how long this situation would last.

As will be discussed further in the chapter, the French language instructor, and her 22 students tried to take the opportunity and get the most out of this situation, by exploring the possibilities of this new teaching mode. Before going online, the 4-hour French language course at the Cyprus University of Technology (CUT) Language Center (LC), was delivered twice a week onsite. The language practitioner was not experienced in Computer-Assisted Language Learning (CALL). The lesson was supported by technologically enhanced activities, but only in a basic form. These activities involved ready-made online activities retrieved from various websites, YouTube videos, and audio uploaded on Moodle, which is CUT's Learning Management System (LMS), and is used to support the course

As for the pedagogy followed, the onsite French language course was based on constructivism (see Piaget, 1968) that supports that, students have inherent knowledge from their past experiences and construct new knowledge based on what they have previously acquired. While in constructivism knowledge is actively constructed by the learner, constructionism asserts that constructivism occurs especially well when the learner is engaged in constructing something for others to see. Based on constructionism (Papert 1990) students need to be continuously engaged in their learning experience, and the outcome of the experience must be shared with others. Constructionism shares constructivism's main ideas and then adds that the "outcome of an educational activity must be meaningful" [and] "learning becomes meaningful when students are engaged in building a product that can be connected with a real-world problem" (Rob & Rob, 2018, p.227).

This can be succeeded by using Moodle, where the instructor can create a virtual class that facilitates contact and communication with the students and providing them the opportunity to share their learning experience by the use of forums, chats, and wikis. By using forums students can communicate with their fellow students and the instructor asynchronously. The chat system provides the opportunity for synchronized, real-time communication between the users on the course platform. The message system enables private communication between users. Another tool is wiki where students can work in groups in a collaborative manner (Oproiu, 2015).

The French-language course in question followed this pedagogy and was delivered by using activities involving real-life and contextualized situations, scenarios, and role-plays. To address the pandemic outbreak, the French language courses had to be shifted from onsite face-to-face mode to online mode. The instructor had to prepare for this emergency online remote teaching accordingly. Decisions about synchronous and asynchronous learning had to be immediately taken, students' anxiety had to be addressed straight away; the instructor's lack of training in online teaching and assessing had to also be dealt with as fast as possible. These were among the many issues raised when shifting online. The instructor's descriptive/reflective notes on this transition were recorded in action. The students' perspectives and views were documented with the use of an online survey and a semi-constructed interview conducted at the end of the semester.

METHOD

Participants

This study involved the case of a French-language instructor and her 22 students during the four weeks of online emergency teaching to the end of the semester. Out of 22 students, twenty took part in the survey and twelve in the semi-structured interview. Their age ranged from the early '20s to the late '30s. Both the instructor and the students had very limited experience in online teaching and learning respectively.

Research Design

For this research, Action Research design was adopted. It examines the experience of a French-language instructor and her 22 students during the four-week emergency online teaching and before the official end of the semester. The language instructor, followed Lewin's Action Research Model (1951) in terms of planning and conducting the lesson, observing the students' response to it and then reflecting upon the whole process. During this endeavor the following research questions were formed:

Q1: What were the issues raised when the lessons had to shift from face-to-face to online?

Q2: What strategies were adopted to cope with the new situation?

Q3: What were the lessons the participants and the instructor learned from this experience?

The study was conducted in March 2020, just after the pandemic outbreak. The case recorded the issues that were raised when the lesson switched from face-to-face to online delivery, the solutions that were given by the practitioner, and the lessons learned by the end of this experience.

With this case study, the author hopes to provide insights into the strategies that can be adopted to cope with this emergency situations. In addition to this, it is hoped to draw attention to the role of adaptability and positive attitudes in this particular context, as well as to tackle the lack of teacher training.

Data Collection Tools

Data were collected at the end of the spring semester 2020, including the instructor's descriptive/reflective notes. An observational protocol was adopted recording observation while observing combining descriptive and reflective notes (Creswell, 2009). Data were also collected quantitatively by the use of an end-of-semester evaluation questionnaire concerning the students' experience in learning French remotely. The Google forms Survey was used and was sent to the students at the end of the semester asking them to provide their opinions and reflections upon the four-week online experience.

In addition, a semi-constructed interview examined in more depth the students' opinions about their online learning experience. The interviews were transcribed verbatim.

Data Analysis

Descriptive statistics were used to analyze Quantitative data elicited from the online questionnaire the semi-constructed interview and the instructor's descriptive/reflective notes.

RESULTS

Descriptive/Reflective Notes

In the descriptive/reflective notes, the practitioner described the four-week online experience. She also reflected upon the methods and techniques she used during remote teaching. In the descriptive/reflective journal, there are five entries, one for each week's lessons and a final one for the two extra optional sessions. The practitioner's notes are personal and of a reflective nature, providing an overview of what happened during those weeks. This type of writing is also observed in Plutino & Polisca (2021), where their edited book was written in the same personal and reflective way.

Week 1

According to the practitioner's field notes, online teaching was asynchronously provided with the use of the institutional e-platform, namely Moodle, and synchronously with the use of a plugin named BigBlue-Button (BBB). BBB is a web conferencing system for online learning that supports real time sharing of slides (including whiteboard), audio, video, chat, emojis, breakout rooms, and screen. It also provides the possibility to record all content for later playback. (https://moodle.org/plugins/mod_bigbluebuttonbn). This system was chosen by the University for the synchronous online lessons and was already installed on the Moodle platform by the institution's ITs.

The practitioner created the link for the first online lesson using BBB (adding the time and the date of the online session) and added the link on the French course's Moodle page. Then the practitioner recorded an orientation video using Snagit–a Screen Capture and Recording Software–(https://www.techsmith.com/screen-capture.html), providing directions to the students on how to enter their first online lesson on BBB via Moodle. Since there were students who were not familiar with the Moodle platform, this video was sent to them using the Facebook Messenger app in a private group shared between the instructor and the students.

According to the practitioner's descriptive/reflective notes, when students entered the virtual class on BBB, the first thing the instructor observed was that they were worried and anxious about this new endeavor. A great portion of the first lesson's time was dedicated to reassuring students and urging them to maintain a positive attitude, supporting that this experience could only be beneficial for them. In the remaining time, the practitioner asked students to do a consolidating activity. This was a matching activity where students were given the two parts of a sentence in random order and students had to match them to create sentences. This activity had already been created by the practitioner on a word document and shared with the students via the BBB feature *screen sharing*. The practitioner asked students to carefully read the sentences and asked them to type their answers on the screen by turning on the multi-user whiteboard. This feature of BBB enables multiple users to type on the shared screen or whiteboard. According to the practitioner's notes, this method could not work because students were typing on each other's answers. In addition, this proved to be a very time-consuming process and so this method was quickly rejected. For the next consolidating activity, the practitioner asked students to type their answers in a private chat on BBB, between each student and the practitioner. According to the descriptive/reflective notes, this method was also quickly rejected. The reason for this was that the practitioner could not go over students' sentences and suggest corrections. This meant that she could not provide instant feedback to them as this would be very time-consuming.

At this point, the practitioner noted that interaction between her and the students was difficult. This was mainly due to the students' reluctance to use their cameras, even if the practitioner's camera was switched on. In the absence of visual contact, the practitioner was not able to be aware of the students' reactions and this made communication harder. The practitioner also noted that other methods and techniques had to be explored as the ones she used during the first week could serve neither the students' needs nor the courses' learning outcomes.

Week 2

For the second week, the practitioner decided to explore the benefits of asynchronous learning, observing how the students would perform having to work on their own, in their own time. They had one synchronous online session and then students had to work asynchronously for the second half of the week. According to the field notes, the practitioner had created and sent two videos before the online session. One of them involved again guidelines about how to enter the synchronous online session, sent to them by Facebook Messenger. In this way, students had easy-access instructions on how to access their synchronous online session. The second one was a detailed explanation about how the students were expected to work asynchronously explaining the activities they were expected to work on for the second half of the week. According to the field notes, the practitioner had already gathered a list of activities that the students were expected to work on, in their own time. These involved ready-made activities retrieved from various websites and providing students immediate feedback, with the purpose of consolidating the vocabulary recently introduced to them. This meant that at the end of each activity, the students could check whether their answers were right or wrong, and in the latter case, the right answers were shown to them. However, according to the practitioner's notes, these consolidating activities were in their majority, insufficient for the particular courses' learning outcomes. As the practitioner reflected on this subject, she noted: "These activities are not based on constructivism, they do not entail scenarios, real-life situations nor are they contextualized. There is a need for software to create my own online activities that will be enhanced with characteristics of constructivism." Moreover, as the activities already used were retrieved from various websites, the thematic coherence between them could not always be obtained.

Week 3

During the third week, students were able to access their online lesson on their own, without having the practitioner sending instructions. According to the practitioner's notes, during this week, the design of the structure of the course on Moodle was modified. Part of this modification was the addition of a number of interactive activities created by the French instructor with the use of Moodle Quiz (MQ). MQ is a tool provided by the Moodle platform that enables instructors to create their own activities, offering 21 different question types to choose from (Antoniou & Papadima-Sophocleous, in print). The practitioner created these new activities using MQ for teaching, consolidating, and formative assessment purposes.

These were enhanced with characteristics of constructivism. The course was redesigned in the Moodle platform. It was divided into themes, incorporating the new activities entailing real-life situations, role-plays, and scenarios. In her reflections, the practitioner recorded that the incorporation of more MQ activities not only serves the courses' learning outcomes but also the students' needs as they found the activities to be more interesting and motivating. The practitioner noted her interest in exploring more the MQ as it "offers a variety of activities and endless possibilities".

According to the practitioner's notes, students reached out more with the course changes than before. More and more questions of minor or major importance were being posted on the Facebook Messenger group. This was not observed during onsite lessons nor on the first and second week of online lessons. At that point, some students began to ask questions concerning the nature of their final assessment, mostly whether it would be conducted onsite or online.

Week 4

According to the reflective notes, the fourth week started with the students asking more questions about the courses' final assessment. They were informed that the university asked academic staff to create their course's final assessment online as the final exams could not be conducted onsite due to the pandemic restrictions. As most teaching and consolidating activities for the French course were already created with the use of the MQ, the practitioner decided to use MQ for the students' final assessment as well. The practitioner, aiming to gain more skills in using this particular tool, started experimenting even more with various types of activities offered by MQ; this allowed her to have a variety in the activities created. According to the reflective notes, students seemed more motivated and seemed to be enjoying the use of MQ in their learning.

At the end of the fourth week (the official end-of-lessons week), the practitioner created a Mock Exam with the use of MQ. Most of its activities reflected the learning and consolidating activities. Students were prompted to take the Mock Exam informing them that this was a sample of what the actual final exam would be. By already engaging in these types of activities in the Mock Exam, they were reassured concerning their final assessment.

Final Sessions

Even though the next two online sessions with the students were optional, the practitioner noted that the grand majority of the students were virtually present. According to the field notes, during these meetings, students asked several questions concerning their final assessment. In the first meeting, questions about the material they needed to revise were answered and there was also a detailed analysis and feedback of the Mock Exam. In the second meeting, more detailed directions about the final assessment were given to the students. Students were prompted to enter the video-conferencing using the BBB link created, before taking the exam. They were informed that free navigation would be enabled in the assessment, meaning that they could go back and forth within the online paper during the whole duration of the exam. The instructor underlined the fact that everyone's cameras were to be turned on and their working space around the keyboard had to be kept neat and without any notes nearby. Additionally, students were reassured that if any issues were to occur on the day of the exams, or if any questions about the test would arise, they could type their questions in the relevant space provided by BBB, namely in the *public chat*.

Finally, after the end of the lesson, the practitioner created a video using the screen recording program Snagit again containing all relevant information, and the students were prompted to watch it carefully.

The practitioner's final journal entry involved some reflections concerning the pedagogy of the activities created for the students' final assessment. Eleven testing activities for the final exam were created in total and the practitioner noted the aim of each activity and the MQ activity type used. The activities were enhanced with characteristics of constructivism, involving real-life situations, scenarios, authentic audio, and pictures. The activity types varied, images and audio were also included to make them more motivating and engaging. Here are the activities created, enhanced with scenarios of contextualized communicative situations:

1. You are visiting Paris next month. You decide to call the Novotel Hotel Gare de Lyon and make a room reservation in a hotel. Study the sentences and put the dialogue in the right order (Ordering question type)
2. A friend wants to go for a ski trip in the Alps and you help him fill in the French inscription form (Drag and drop into text question type).
3. You work part-time for a real-estate agency in Paris. Listen to the voicemail, study the three pictures of the apartments provided, and decide which apartment best fits the speaker's needs (Multiple Choice question type).
4. You are in the kitchen with your French-speaking friend in Paris. Read the first part of the dialogue and choose the second part to create full sentences (Matching Activity Type).
5. You are an Erasmus student in France. You decide to write an email to your French-speaking friend describing to him/her your new apartment (see the picture provided) (Essay question type).
6. Your French-speaking friend has emailed you his timetable but the information is not in the right order. Study the timetable and put the text in the right order (Ordering Activity type)
7. You are on a fashion runway; you see the models and you describe their outfits to your French-speaking friend. Study the pictures and the descriptions given and match the right description with the right person (Drag and drop matching question type).
8. You are at the train station Gare de Lyon in Paris. Listen to the announcements and fill in the right number of the trains and the time of departure (Embedded Answers (Cloze) question type).
9. Your French-speaking friend has just moved from Marseille to Dijon. She sends you an email describing her daily life. Read her email answer the following questions (Matching Activity type).
10. You are on holiday in Marseille, a city next to the sea. You decide to send an email to your French-speaking friend describing him/her, your days (Essay Question type).
11. You are an Erasmus student in Poitiers and your friend does not know how to move around the block. You decide to draw him a map and give him directions on how to find the students' residence, the university, the pharmacy, the market, and the gym (the map is provided) (Essay Question type).

In addition to the practitioner's notes, there is a survey and a semi-constructed interview. These two sets of data aimed to shed some light on the students' perspectives and opinions on the transition from face-to-face to online learning.

Questionnaire

The survey was collected at the end of the semester in the form of a Google Form Survey and aimed at gathering information about the students' attitudes, views, and perspectives towards the online version of the French language course. Out of a total of 22 students who took the course, 20 of them responded to the survey. The participants were asked to respond to twenty close-ended questions on their perceptions of the French online lessons. The answers were made up of a 5 Likert-type scale. The statements were graded as Strongly Disagree, Disagree, Neutral/Uncertain, Agree, Strongly Agree. There were 5 multiple-choice questions and 2 open-ended questions.

Students' ages were between 18 and 24; one student was 37. There were 7 male and 13 female students. There were 24 questions in total; there were questions about the students' attitudes and perspectives before going online, during online lessons, and after online lessons. There were also questions about their perception of the practitioner's contribution to this effort.

Close-Ended Questions

In the first section of the survey, students were asked about their initial willingness to take up the challenge and continue their lessons online. More than half (55%) were willing to take up the challenge, while (35%) were neutral. Only 10% stated that they were unwilling to continue online.

All students stated that videos sent before the online lessons to provide directions (as were to find the lesson on Moodle, what steps to follow, etc.) were helpful; the majority (90%) liked the fact that there was a fixed time for the online lessons. Eighty-five percent liked the way the Moodle platform was organized and all of them stated that the Mock Exam before the final assessment familiarised them with the final examination format, structure, and type of activities. All students also found that the group on Facebook Messenger shared with the instructor was very helpful. All students who attended the final two optional online meetings (80%) found them beneficial.

Concerning the practitioner's contribution to this experience, all students claimed that the instructor delivered the lessons successfully, adapted to the situation and the great majority believed that the support provided by the instructor was sufficient (95%).

The majority (80%) found this experience to be beneficial to them as a person and/or as a student; 20% of the students' attitude was neither positive nor negative.

When the students were asked if it was difficult for them to adapt to the new situation, half of them answered that it was not difficult (50%), less than half (35%) said that it was neither difficult nor easy, and 20% answered that it was difficult. The majority of the participants (85%) would likely recommend the online version of the French lesson, while 15% said that they would not.

Open Questions

Two open ended questions were included in the survey. A sample of 11 answers out of 19 given for the first question and 9 answers out of 16 for the second question, is presented in the table below.

Table 1.

Q1: Write in short what you liked or appreciated the most in learning French online
St1: The videos before the lecture and the recordings after the lecture ended. *St 3: That the instructor was sending our assignments checked right after the lesson and the videos she was uploading before the lesson. They were very helpful. St 5: I had the opportunity to prepare before class more easily.* *St 7: I liked the fact we had the lesson recorded so we could watch it again* *St 8: What I appreciated the most in learning French online was that we had the chance to attend(watch) the lesson again. If we had any questions or something we didn't understand well. Also, despite the difficulties of distance learning, the instructor had always been willing to help us with any questions we may have.* *St 9: Being able to watch the lesson again is the greatest advantage of online lessons.* *St 11: I appreciate the teacher's willingness to adapt so fast in the new situation and try different methods for the first 3 online lessons to see what's working for us and it's more beneficial! I also liked how the lessons were structured with the following online exercises, and additional materials for better understanding of each subject!* *St 12: The way she (the instructor) managed the lessons! The instructor was always on time and always prepared and willing to give many examples!! Without her French online lessons wouldn't be the same!!* *St 14: Not having to show up to classes since we could do everything from home and had sufficient material as well as support from our professor. It was a rather pleasant experience.* *St 16: The way that the instructor gave the lecture* *St 18: Our lecturer was very willing to help us with anything anytime.*
Q2: Write in short what you disliked in learning French online
St 1: Communication with each other *St 2: That we did not have the physical lecture* *St 4: Sometimes on an online lesson the connection was not good* *St 6: Wi-Fi connection* *St 7: If you don't feel the way the instructor wants to teach, it's hard to go straight online. Fortunately, this was not the case for us. I cannot find anything negative in our case.* *St 8: It is not like teaching in class.* *St 9: At the beginning I wasn't expecting the online class to work equally or even better than the physical class. The only thing that I disliked but only at the beginning it's that we didn't exercise the speaking (students reading in French in dialogues) but this is something that the teacher successfully managed throughout the next lessons. In conclusion learning French online it was a pleasure because, it was the most organized lesson I have had in this semester!* *St 10: That if I skip a lesson, it's required 24-48h to be able to watch it!* *St 12: The fact that we couldn't really participate in class that much (since it was either all students talking at once, giving their answers to the professor questions, or nobody speaking), didn't really develop our oral skills.*

In this section, students were asked to write what they liked or appreciated the most in learning French online and what they disliked. Almost all students liked the fact that the lesson was recorded and that they had the chance to watch it again, student 7 said "I liked the fact we had the lesson recorded so we could watch it again". The second most common answer on what they liked or appreciated in learning French online, involved the practitioner's contribution. Student 11 stated that the practitioner's "willingness to adapt quickly to this new situation and try different methods for the first three online lessons to see what's working for us and it's more beneficial". The student continued by stating that "I also liked how the lessons were structured with the following online exercises and additional materials for better understanding of each subject!" The variety of material available to the students was also noted by another student 14 who stated that the "… we had sufficient material as well as support from our professor". The practitioner's support was mentioned in other students' statements like student 8 who stated that "despite the difficulties of distance learning, she [the instructor] has always been willing to help us with any questions we may had" and student 18 who said that "Our lecturer was very willing to help us with anything anytime". student 12 claimed that "The instructor was always on time and always prepared and willing to give many examples! Without her, French online lessons wouldn't be the same" and student 14 stating that "It was a rather pleasant experience"

Concerning what they disliked about learning French online, unreliable, or bad internet connection was the answer most students gave. Student 1 stated that there was not much "communication with each other" and student 2 that they didn't like not having the physical presence in class, while student 8 stated that "it is not like teaching in class". Student 12 felt that online lessons didn't; help develop their oral skills "The fact that we couldn't really participate in class that much (since it was either all students talking at once, giving their answers to the professor questions, or nobody speaking), didn't really develop our oral skills". Student 10 stressed the fact that the lesson's recording took a lot of time to be uploaded by the system so they could watch it again stating that "if I skip a lesson, it's required 24-48h to be able to watch it". Student 8 stated fact that online teaching "is not like teaching in class". While 6 students did not write anything negative about the particular course, student 9 wrote "At the beginning I wasn't expecting the online class to work equally or even better than the physical class. The only thing that I disliked but only at the beginning it's that we didn't exercise the speaking (students reading in French in dialogues) but this is something that the teacher successfully managed throughout the next lessons. In conclusion learning French online it was a pleasure because, it was the most organized lesson I have had in this semester!" Finally, student 7 stated that it helped that the students knew the instructor and the way the lesson was conducted before going online "If you don't *feel* the way the instructor wants to teach, it's hard to go straight online. Fortunately, this was not the case for us. I cannot find anything negative in our case".

Semi-Structured Interview

An online semi-structured interview was carried out at the end of the online course by the practitioner. Twelve students willingly agreed to take part. Eleven out of 12 interviews were conducted via Skype, and 1 via Zoom. Their responses were recorded and transcribed verbatim. The semi-constructed interviews aimed at providing a more in-depth view of the students' answers given in the survey. The following table presents example quotes of the 12 students who accepted to be interviewed.

According to the answers students provided during the interviews all students were overall satisfied with the way French lessons were conducted online. At the beginning of this endeavor, eight students out of twelve claimed they were negative to this transition and did not want to continue their studies online. Four students were more positive but still worried about the outcome. Student 6 even said that she felt like a "guinea pig". However, in the next question, whether they would be more willing to take up an online course after their online learning experience than before, 11 out of 12 students stated that they were certainly more willing, and they would or probably would do it in the future.

As far as the French lesson per se, all students found Moodle to be very organized. Student 2 said: "The course was divided into weeks and subjects and this was really helpful" and student 3 said: "Moodle was very well organized; I knew where everything was." Similarly, student 4 said: "Moodle was organized, each week having its own subject," and student 6 and 8 provided a comparison between French and all the other online lessons she had, saying that "French lesson was the most organized online course I had".

When the students were asked whether there was factor that made French online learning course easier for them, almost all students talked about the variety of the activities provided on the courses Moodle page as well as the courses organization. The variety of the activities and the different types of activities provided to the students were viewed positively by them. Student 1 said that there were "many videos and images and activities to do anytime" Student 5 said that "I liked that there were many quizzes and many consolidating activities." In line with these two students, student 7 said: "Many activities that we could take any time as many times we wanted."

Table 2. Interviews

Questions	Example quotes
Q1: *Were you overall satisfied with the way French language course was conducted online?*	*St 1: Yes* *St 2: Yes, very satisfied* *St 9: Very satisfied* *St 12: Very much satisfied*
Q2: *Would you say that your attitude before going online was mostly positive or negative?*	*St 1: It was negative* *St 2: Towards positive. I wanted to give it a try* *St: 6: Negative. It was stressing. I felt like we were guinea pigs.* *St 7: Neutral. I didn't know what to expect* *St 12: Mostly curious than negative.*
Q3: *Did you find the course's page on Moodle organized?*	*St 2: The course was divided into weeks and subjects, and this was really helpful* *St 3: Moodle was very well organized; I knew where everything was.* *St 6: French lesson was the most organized online course I had* *St 8: Very organized. It was easier to navigate than other courses* *St 12: Extremely organized I hadn't been visiting Moodle before. But all the notes were there and organized. However, some extra material should have been deleted*
Q4: Where there any factor(s) that made online French lessons easier for you?	*St 1: many videos and images and activities to do anytime* *St 2: The lessons were being recorded and I could watch them again* *St 5: I liked that there were many quizzes and many consolidating activities* *St 7: Many activities that we could take any time as many times we wanted.*
Q5: Did you like it when you had the material (along with the preparation videos) uploaded on Moodle before the online session?	*St 3: Yes, because it was easier for me* *St 4: I wanted all the material uploaded before the online lesson because this was helping me be better prepared for the lesson.* *St 7: Yes, I wanted to be prepared before the session*
Q6: What were the disadvantages of French online course?	*St 2: Nothing. I wouldn't change anything* *St 8: I don't have anything negative to say* *St 10: I wanted be able to exercise more in speaking.*
Q7: Would you recommend the online version of the French lesson to other students?	*St 3: Yes, I would definitely recommend it* *St 4: I would recommend it even though I prefer learning face-to-face* *St 7: I would not recommend it because I personally prefer face-to-face lessons.* *St 12: I would recommend it only if the student is responsible and doesn't skip lessons*
Q8: Did remote online learning had any sort of impact on you, either positive or negative?	*St 4: I found out that I can actually manage online lessons. I didn't think I could.* *St 5: I am more positive now towards online learning than I was before* *St 8: I realized I could do more than I thought I was able to* *St 12: I learned that for every problem there is a solution and we (at the CUT) we found it and we were able to continue our studies.*

Student 12 said that both the course's organization and the variety of the consolidating activities provided and pushed them to "visit the course's Moodle page more often than before". However, the same student continues by stating that "there is still some extra material that I would prefer to have been deleted as it made the page look busy".

Of the 12 students who were interviewed, 10 indicated that they preferred having the material uploaded a day before the online session as this gave them time to prepare and take notes and helped them have a better understanding of the lesson. Student 4 said: "I wanted all the material uploaded before the online lesson because this was helping me be better prepared for the lesson."

When students were asked to give a negative trait of the French online lesson, 11 out of 12 specifically said that they would not change anything; student 10 said that she wanted to "be able to exercise more in speaking".

Nine out of twelve students said that they would recommend the online version of the French lesson. Student 12 clarified: "only if the student is responsible and does not skip lessons" and student 11 said, "I would recommend only the specific online lesson." Student 4 and student 9 said that they would recommend it, even though they still prefer face-to-face lessons in general. Student 7 said that she would not recommend it because online learning does not suit her learning style.

In the final question, students were asked to say whether online learning, in general, had any sort of impact on them, either positive or negative. All students agreed that the impact was positive as they gained experience in online learning. Student 8 said, "I realized I could do more than I thought I was able to." Student 12 said: "I learned that for every problem there is a solution and we, at the CUT, we had found it and we were able to continue our studies."

DISCUSSION

The present study has examined the experience of a French-language instructor and 22 students when they had to move from face-to-face to online. This small-scale study shed light on the methods and techniques a particular language practitioner used to make the transition as smooth as possible for the students and her efforts to compensate for the lack of experience in teaching remotely.

The results from the practitioner's descriptive/reflective notes indicate that even though the practitioner was not experienced in CALL nor in remote teaching, she adapted to the situation by continuously trying new methods and techniques, and reflecting upon their effectiveness. The present study shows that the practitioner's willingness to adapt and cope with the new situation let her seek self-training in remote teaching and in creating her own language activities. In attempting to exploit online resources, the French language practitioner observed that most of the websites were either generic in nature or not based on constructivism. This observation was also made in previous studies where authors were confronted by the same considerable shortcomings (Burston et al., 2016, p. 75).

For each week's lesson, the practitioner tried to provide students with instructions for learning, an input that would be either synchronous live session or asynchronous videos and audios, guided consolidating activities for students to complete, and opportunities for feedback to students. A process that echoes other studies (Visintini, 2021), which describe the practitioners' focus on adapting their teaching practices during emergency online teaching.

Students worried about their studies, and they were not very willing to go on with this transition. As all sets of data showed, the majority of students experienced stress and anxiety, especially during those early days of distance learning. This finding is also observed in Al-Maskari et al. (2021). In their report, it is indicated that 75% of students in HE institutions worldwide had experienced anxiety and unease due to the study suspension (p. 3).

The results from all data show that convincing students to turn their cameras on during synchronous sessions held via video-conferencing was a challenge. A reluctance on the part of the students was observed and this furthers the findings of a recent study on the same subject (Castelli & Sarvary, 2021). In Castelli & Sarvary (2021), 276 students were asked the reasons they preferred not turning their cameras on, and almost half of them indicated that they were worried about their appearance. However, having a visual of the students enables more direct communication and lowers the feeling of isolation as the social connection is maintained during quarantine (Reich et al., 2020).

Network connection is an important factor when lessons are conducted online. However, there were students whose poor connectivity made their effort to attend synchronous live sessions difficult and impacted students' academic concerns. Network connectivity issues can affect the quality of the students' learning and this finding was also observed in other studies exploring the issues raised when lessons had to go fully online (Al-Maskari et al., 2021; Mahdy, 2020; Visintini 2021).

The quality of students' learning can also be affected by the uncertainty on the part of the practitioner. The uncertainty comes from the lack of training in teaching in a remote environment, the lack of relevant literature, and the lack of support and training (Johnson et al., 2020; Schleicher, 2020). In this particular case, the practitioner tried to compensate for the lack of knowledge, skills and experience in remote teaching by seeking self-training a solution to which resorted many other academics (see Goria, 2021). The way this particular language practitioner acted, seeking self-training to cater for her students' needs in this new situation and embracing change echoes conclusions from other studies. Goria (2021) argues that despite the common belief that academics in higher education are unwilling to implement technology into their classes, during the pandemic outbreak in 2020 "Academics embraced the digital change, motivated by their awareness of the benefits of technology for responding to the new situation" (p. 48).

This study demonstrated a correlation between a positive attitude towards change and willingness to adapt by both the teacher and student. The findings suggest that the practitioner's positive attitude along with her organization had a positive impact on students. Similar research has shown the importance of adaptability in times of crisis and stresses the fact that "adaptability (the capacity to regulate one's thoughts, feelings, and behaviors in response to changing new, or uncertain situations) helps teachers to navigate change, novelty, and uncertainty at work" (Collie et al., 2020, p.1). Being able to adapt to any given situation and being willing to go for it, is an asset in today's fast-paced world; as Rosell-Aguilar puts it, *The readiness is all* (2021, p.77).

This experience helped students learn to be more open to new situations, as this experience changed their attitudes towards online learning, making them more willing to take up an online course after the end of this experience than they were before. On the other hand, five weeks into Emergency Remote Teaching, the practitioner acquired knowledge, skills, and experience in online teaching, trained herself in the creation of MQ online constructivist activities, and managed (according to the data) to keep her students motivated regarding French language learning. The outcome of this experience for both the particular practitioner and her students was surely positive.

The most significant lesson learned from this situation was the need for academics to continuously seek self-training to keep up with technological acceleration and new pedagogical trends. Adaptability and maintaining a positive attitude towards change proved to be key factors and of significant importance. Despite the major disruption in higher education, the response of the language practitioner in question has been positive and constructive, demonstrating her readiness to undertake new pedagogical paths. Opportunities for acquiring new skills, experience, and knowledge emerged and the language practitioner tried to make the most of this situation, and data prove she managed to do it. The process of the language practitioner's upskilling was speeded up by the pandemic who explored new ways of teaching and managed to become self-trained in creating her own language activities using Moodle Quiz (Antoniou & Papadima-Sophocleous, in print). This finding is in line with Visintini (2021) who argues that practitioners are "now familiar with webinar and conferencing tools, and have shifted to marking assessments online. These were all items that had been on our list of things to organize for a number of years but kept getting pushed back for various reasons (e.g. lack of time and resources, the false perception that languages can best be taught face-to-face, and that some language work is too complex to be marked online)" (p. 61). Through this unexpected situation, practitioners had the opportunity for a crash course in online teaching and in the use of technologies in their classes.

In this light, it is hoped that this book chapter might be of inspiration to other practitioners in continuously seeking self-training, creating more technologically enhanced lessons, and giving digital pedagogy the same respect as traditional face-to-face teaching.

CONCLUSION

In this study, the importance of adaptability and maintaining a positive attitude towards changes were underlined. The instructor's attitudes and the students' perspectives are linked to the decisions taken by the former and able to impact either positively or negatively the attitudes and thus the quality of learning of the latter. any studies have been published since the beginning of the pandemic about the teachers' response to this unprecedented situation and it is hoped that this study will further their findings and show that positive attitude, adaptability and continuous self-training can be of extreme importance in similar situations. It is hoped that more language practitioners will share their experience and provide best practices and ways to teach in a remote environment.

While "just get them (the students) through" became the mantra of some practitioners (Caspar, 2021. p. 116) and surely an occasional thought of others, this particular language practitioner and her 22 students decided to take this situation as an opportunity for growth. Although the results of this small-scale study cannot be generalized, it sheds light on how a particular language practitioner managed to cope with the rapid transition from face-to-face to remote emergency teaching, and the way students perceived this situation. The results of this study cannot confirm that this was the path chosen by other language practitioners to cope with the transition, and it cannot be proved that the methods and techniques used by the practitioner were the only ones that can be used in a similar situation. More examples of best practices are needed to explore how other language practitioners coped with this situation. Virtual realities are now part of our new normal (see Cunico, 2021) and language instructors must take advantage of the new skills, knowledge, and experience gained through the pandemic and emergency remote teaching. Institutions should now offer the opportunity to language practitioners to speak up, share their experiences and learn from each other.

While this situation in the educational world was often referred to as an educational crisis, it is the author's firm belief that this was a once in a lifetime opportunity; opportunity for fast-paced self-learning, for experimenting in a different teaching environment that otherwise would have never been possible in such a short time. It is the author's hope that this chapter will remind language practitioners that they were indeed able to rise to the challenge and managed to find the strength to overcome the issues raised during emergency times. Thus, it is now the time for universities to urge language practitioners to share their best practices and their innovative approaches to the academic world, to become a source of inspiration for others, and to push institutions to build a solid infrastructure for online teaching and assessing.

ACKNOWLEDGMENT

The author would like to thank the course's students for their participation in this study. A sincere thank you to Dr. Salomi Papadima-Sophocleous for her continuous support.

REFERENCES

Al-Maskari, A., Al-Riyami, T., & Kunjumuhammed, S. K. (2021). Students' academic and social concerns during COVID-19 pandemic. *Education and Information Technologies*. Advance online publication. doi:10.100710639-021-10592-2 PMID:34226817

Antoniou, S., & Papadima-Sophocleous, S. (2022). Using Moodle Quiz to Create Language Consolidating and Testing Activities. In A. El Shaban & R. Abobaker (Eds.), *Policies, Practices, and Protocols for the Implementation of Technology Into Language Learning* (pp. 20–53). IGI Global. doi:10.4018/978-1-7998-8267-1.ch002

Bates, T. (2020). *What should we be doing about online learning when social distancing ends?* Online Learning and Distance Education Resources. https://www.tonybates.ca/2020/04/07/what-should-we-be-doing-about-online-learning-when-social-distancing-ends/

Burston, J., Georgiadou, O., & Monville-Burston, M. (2016). Exploiting behaviorist and communicative action-based methodologies in CALL applications for the teaching of pronunciation in French as a foreign language. In S. Papadima-Sophocleous, L. Bradley & S. Thouësny (Eds), CALL communities and culture – short papers from EUROCALL 2016 (pp. 74-80). Research-publishing.net. doi:10.14705/rpnet.2016.eurocall2016.541

Caspar, S. (2021). Exploring the pandemic through language learning and multicultural studies. In A. Plutino & E. Polisca (Eds), Languages at work, competent multilinguals and the pedagogical challenges of COVID-19 (pp. 113-118). Research-publishing.net. doi:10.14705/rpnet.2021.49.1225

Castelli, F. R., & Sarvary, M. A. (2021). Why students do not turn on their video cameras during online classes and an equitable and inclusive plan to encourage them to do so. *Ecology and Evolution, 11*(8), 3565–3576. doi:10.1002/ece3.7123 PMID:33898009

Collie, R. J., Granziera, H., Martin, A. J., Burns, E. C., & Holliman, A. J. (2020). Adaptability among science teachers in schools: A multi-nation examination of its role in school outcomes. *Teaching and Teacher Education, 95*, 103148. doi:10.1016/j.tate.2020.103148

Creswell, J. W. (2009). Research Design Qualitative, Quantitative, and Mixed Methods Approaches. In Research Design Qualitative, Quantitative, and Mixed Methods Approaches (3rd ed.). Sage.

Cunico, S. (2021). Moving the year abroad online: ready, steady, go! In A. Plutino & E. Polisca (Eds.), Languages at work, competent multilinguals and the pedagogical challenges of COVID-19 (pp. 97-103). Research- publishing.net. doi:10.14705/rpnet.2021.49.1223

Feldman, P. (2021). Digital transformation in education: from vision to practice during the pandemic. In A. Plutino & E. Polisca (Eds.), Languages at work, competent multilinguals and the pedagogical challenges of COVID-19 (pp. 39-45). Research-publishing.net. doi:10.14705/rpnet.2021.49.1216

Giannikas, C. N. (2019). New Technologies and Language Teacher Education: Are We There Yet? *English Language Teacher Education and Development Journal, 22*, 53–59. http://www.elted.net/uploads/7/3/1/6/7316005/giannikas_vol._22.pdf

Giannikas, C. N. (2021). Interactive whiteboards in EFL from the Teachers' and students' perspective. *Research Papers in Language Teaching and Learning, 11*(1), 203–219.

Godwin-Jones, R. (2020). Building the porous classroom: An expanded model for blended language learning. *Language Learning & Technology, 24*(3), 1–18. http://hdl.handle.net/10125/44731

Goria, C. (2021). Reflections on the impact of COVID-19 on teaching and learning in the Faculty of Arts at the University of Nottingham. In A. Plutino & E. Polisca (Eds.), Languages at work, competent multilinguals and the pedagogical challenges of COVID-19 (pp. 47-55). Research-publishing.net. doi:10.14705/rpnet.2021.49.1217

Higley, M. (2013). Benefits of Synchronous and Asynchronous e-Learning: Advantages of Using Both Synchronous and Asynchronous Technologies in an Online Learning Environment. *eLearning Industry*. https://elearningindustry.com/benefits-of-synchronous-and-asynchronous-e-learning

Hodges, C., Moore, S., Lockee, B., Trust, T., & Bond, A. (2020). The difference between emergency remote teaching and online learning. *EDUCAUSE Review, 3*. https://er.educause.edu/articles/2020/3/the-difference-between-emergency-remoteteaching-and-online-learning

Johnson, N., Veletsianos, G., & Seaman, J. (2020). U.S. faculty and administrators' experiences and approaches in the early weeks of the COVID-19 pandemic. *Online Learning Journal, 24*(2), 6–21. doi:10.24059/olj.v24i2.2285

Lin, X., & Gao, L. (2020). Students' sense of community and perspectives of taking synchronous and asynchronous online courses. *Asian Journal of Distance Education, 15*(1), 169–179. http://www.asianjde.org

MacIntyre, P. D., Gregersen, T., & Mercer, S. (2020). Language teachers' coping strategies during the COVID-19 conversion to online teaching: Correlations with stress, wellbeing and negative emotions. *System, 94*, 102352. doi:10.1016/j.system.2020.102352

Mahdy, M. A. A. (2020). The Impact of COVID-19 Pandemic on the Academic Performance of Veterinary Medical Students. *Frontiers in Veterinary Science, 7*(October), 1–8. doi:10.3389/fvets.2020.594261 PMID:33134368

Munday, D. (2021). Teaching and learning post pandemic. In A. Plutino & E. Polisca (Eds.), Languages at work, competent multilinguals and the pedagogical challenges of COVID-19 (pp. 63-69). Research-publishing.net. doi:10.14705/rpnet.2021.49.1219

Oproiu, G. C. (2015). A Study about Using E-learning Platform (Moodle) in University Teaching Process. *Procedia - Social and Behavioral Sciences, 180*(November), 426–432. doi:10.1016/j.sbspro.2015.02.140

Papadima-Sophocleous, S., & Loizides, F. (2016). Exploring the benefits and disadvantages of introducing synchronous to asynchronous online technologies to facilitate flexibility in learning. In *CALL communities and culture – short papers from EUROCALL 2016* (Vol. 2016, pp. 363–368). Issue., doi:10.14705/rpnet.2016.eurocall2016.589

Papert, S. (1980). *Mindstorms: Children, Computers, and Powerful Ideas*. Basic Books.

Piaget, J. (1968). *Six Psychological Studies*. Vintage Books.

Plutino, A., & Polisca, E. (2021). Introduction. In A. Plutino & E. Polisca (Eds.), Languages at work, competent multilinguals and the pedagogical challenges of COVID-19 (pp. 1-7). Research-publishing.net. doi:10.14705/rpnet.2021.49.1213

Racheva, V. (2018). Social aspects of synchronous virtual learning environments. *AIP Conference Proceedings, 2048*, 020032. doi:10.1063/1.5082050

Reich, J., Buttimer, C., Fang, A., Hillaire, G., Hirsch, K., Larke, L., Littenberg-Tobias, J., Moussapour, R. M., Napier, A., Thompson, M., & Slama, R. (2020). *Remote Learning Guidance From State Education Agencies During the COVID-19 Pandemic: A First Look*. doi:10.35542/osf.io/437e2osf.io/437e2

Rob, M., & Rob, F. (2018). Dilemma between constructivism and constructionism: Leading to the development of a teaching-learning framework for student engagement and learning. *Journal of International Education in Business, 11*(2), 273–290. doi:10.1108/JIEB-01-2018-0002

Rosell-Aguilar, F. (2021). Locked down, but not isolated: Twitter collaboration among teachers in response to COVID-19. In A. Plutino & E. Polisca (Eds.), Languages at work, competent multilinguals and the pedagogical challenges of COVID-19 (pp. 71-77). Research-publishing.net. doi:10.14705/rpnet.2021.49.1220

Sadoux, M. (2021). How to flip it… never again? Towards agile models of work. In A. Plutino & E. Polisca (Eds.), Languages at work, competent multilinguals and the pedagogical challenges of COVID-19 (pp. 89-95). Research- publishing.net. doi:10.14705/rpnet.2021.49.1222

Schleicher, A. (2020). *Education disrupted deduction built. Spotlight: Quality education for all during COVID-19 crisis*. Organisation for Economic Co-operation and Development (OECD). https://hundred-cdn.s3.amazonaws.com/uploads/report/file/15/hundred_spotlight_covid-19_digital.pdf

Visintini, G. (2021). The "go digital" Bristol experience. In A. Plutino & E. Polisca (Eds.), Languages at work, competent multilinguals and the pedagogical challenges of COVID-19 (pp. 57-62). Research-publishing.net. doi:10.14705/rpnet.2021.49.1218

KEY TERMS AND DEFINITIONS

CALL: Computer-assisted language learning.

HE: Higher education.

LMS: Learning management system.

Moodle: Modular object-oriented dynamic learning environment.

MQ: Moodle quiz.

Chapter 4
Online Teaching Writing to University Students:
Negative Stereotypes Ruined

Tamara Kavytska
https://orcid.org/0000-0002-1528-9439
Taras Shevchenko National University of Kyiv, Ukraine

Viktoriia Drobotun
Taras Shevchenko National University of Kyiv, Ukraine

ABSTRACT

This chapter examines the emergency online writing instruction aimed at enhancing integrated cause-and-effect writing in tertiary school students. Specifically, the research compares two models of digital support in terms of their impact on the quality of cause-and-effect academic essays. The instruction relied on the integrated approach to writing instruction and the theory of online collaborative learning. The study was organized as experimental training with third-year university students (n=42) as participants who formed two experimental and two control groups. The study shows a generally positive impact of both digitally supported instruction models on the overall quality of cause-and-effect writing. However, different aspects of the indicated writing appeared unevenly affected by digital support of the online course. With the training efficacy of both digital support models confirmed, the general conclusion drawn from the research lies in the idea that only a targeted selection of online technologies can produce a significant enhancement of the skills under training.

INTRODUCTION

In the context of education, 2020 will go down in history as the year that turned the world into a global village of *emergency online learning* given the format of learning/teaching offered in response to a crisis. Neither traditional face-to-face nor blended educational patterns were congruous with the COVID-19 pandemic, so the teachers were forced to reshape the approaches and offer efficient online tools to provide

DOI: 10.4018/978-1-7998-8717-1.ch004

high standard teaching and learning in all educational settings. This kind of online educational activity was meaningfully different from well-planned online experiences in terms of course design, preparation, and development. The most crucial issue was time allotment, as it usually takes from six to nine months to design a fully online university course. Consequently, most educationalists worldwide were faced with the challenge of fast development of online courses that did not seem to meet the requirements of successful online teaching and learning.

The Ukrainian educational system, with its exceptional emphasis on face-to-face learning/teaching, appeared practically unprepared for a crisis. On the institutional level, there was no clear guidance regulating the teachers' and students' behaviour under new conditions; neither was there any institutional technical support to the instructors. On the personal level, the reluctance of teachers to shift online was observed due to several reasons. First, most lecturers complained about generally low level of ICT/apps literacy as well as of the lack of knowledge of online platforms and tools. Second, transferring of teaching materials into online platforms appeared extremely time- and effort-consuming, so the teachers' workload tripled with no financial compensation involved. And finally, most lecturers expressed doubts that online tools could enable effective teaching and fair assessment of productive skills.

The overall skepticism was expressed about teaching writing. Aware of the successful approaches and international achievements in online teaching writing (Dumford & Miller, 2018; Ellis, 2004; Kim, Mendenhall, & Johnson, 2010; Mort & Drury, 2012; Wingate & Dreiss, 2009), the instructors did realize that implementing best practices of online teaching writing presented in the literature would not be a 'copy & paste' process. On the one hand, writing is such a complex and varied activity that, as Cumming (2001) states, calls forth a multifaceted perspective on its teaching. On the other hand, there was clear understanding that target learning needs in writing should be addressed locally with accessible and effective online technologies involved.

With the abundance of research focusing on various aspects of online writing instruction (Hewett et al., 2015; Luna & Villalon, 2020; Warschauer, 2010), scarce research, to our knowledge, has offered a detailed and comprehensive examination of the emergency OWI. To fill in the gap, this chapter therefore *aims* to consider approaches and effective online tools and techniques applied for teaching cause-and-effect writing to the Linguistics majors in the emergency learning environment. Specifically, it compares the impact of two digital support models implemented in the OWI on the quality of the integrated cause-and-effect writing as well as on the learning outcomes in the writing course. The authors are particularly interested in examining whether OWI based on tools such as Teacher Tool and Paper Rater can considerably boost students' performance, motivation, and writing quality.

ONLINE WRITING INSTRUCTION IN THE PANDEMIC FRAMEWORK

In the 21st century, writing instruction has been undergoing radical transformations. With a variety of technology tools and multimedia platforms involved, it is no longer a paper-based activity (Westwood, 2008). A language class that does not use some form of technology is a rare case nowadays (Parvin & Salam, 2015). Writing instruction is no exception, so it is rapidly moving online across the globe. In the context of this study, online writing instruction (OWI) is conceptualized as

Writing instruction that occurs—at least partially if not fully—in a computer-based, Internet, or intranet instructional setting. It uses online/digital media to provide instruction; to talk about writing; or to

distribute, share, and/or collect writing-related materials. OWI can occur in either the synchronous or asynchronous modality using a variety of electronic media, platforms, and technologies (CCCC OWI Committee, 2011c, p. 2).

The OWI concept as well as its practice is far from being new in the global University setting. Scholarly attempts to present a structured and systematized research have been proliferating in the last two decades. However, despite numerous publications that give insight into both theoretical (Hewett et al., 2015) and practical (Alkhataba et. al., 2018; Adas & Bakir, 2013) aspects of the phenomenon, there are still a lot of doubts regarding the value of OWI over the face-to-face instruction (Amirsheibani & Iraji, 2014).

Stronger doubts are voiced about the effectiveness of OWI in the pandemic environment. While some researchers insist that remote learning is the necessity in the light of Covid-19 pandemic (Ali, 2020) and provide evidence of its positive impact on the writing skills (Clark et. al. 2020), the others claim that emergency online learning cannot provide the desired results, especially in the underdeveloped countries (Anwar & Adnan, 2020). In the developed countries, the sudden switch to remote learning had an immediate negative impact on the students who lack a private workspace in their home environments (Ponticiello, Simmons & Lee, 2021). Consequently, in OWI, these learners had to rely more on self-learning.

Does it mean that OWI in emergency environment cannot provide positive learning outcomes? To seek the answer to the question, the authors intend to find out to what extent the principles of OWI introduced by Hewett (2014) and generally accepted by the academic environments are applicable to emergency OWI. The primary principle of OWI – *inclusivity and accessibility* – is implemented in non-crisis education based on institutional preparatory planning, research, and consideration of all aspects such as staff training, access to technology, sustainable management, and support, etc. In emergency OWI, the educationalists had neither experience nor resources to implement the principle adequately, since a lot of students were unable to access the internet due to technical or financial issues (Wattoo et. al., 2020). Therefore, learning challenges related to socioeconomic issues were not promptly and adequately addressed in an emergency OWI environment.

Indispensable for successful OWI is the idea that an online writing course should *focus on writing instead of technology orientation* or teaching students how to use technologies. The proponents of a strong technology focus alongside with a writing focus stress, though, that constant updating of technologies is part of OWI (Alexander, 2006; Jukes, McCain & Crockett, 2010). The emergency OWI can hardly provide such an opportunity, so this type of instruction is likely to be supported through the technology which is accessible or considered sufficient for maintaining the course. Moreover, students and teachers should not waste a lot of time on becoming functionally literate in the selected technology since the diversity in online tools might become a distractor that prevents from investing more time and efforts in practicing writing.

A significant pedagogical argument related to OWI was voiced by CCCC OWI Committee (2011). On the one hand, the scholars of the committee warn against mechanical transferring of face-to-face writing pedagogies to the online setting. Instead, they insist on developing unique teaching and learning strategies that will address the writing skills of a particular online course. On the other hand, some migration or adaptation of appropriate writing theories and practices to the online setting is viewed as a necessary step (Warnock, 2009). In terms of presenting instructional materials for students to read and use in the process of writing, the onsite writing courses give preference to textbooks and handouts whereas the online setting introduces additions of visual as well as audio/video media materials etc. Such variety of instructional materials is rather beneficial as it can address a wider variety of student learning styles.

It is worth emphasizing that proper management and teacher's profile in OWI are major keys to success. In non-emergency setting, students and teachers are prepared by the institution for the unique technological and pedagogical features of the online course. The task is usually carried out by general technology or advising units through the institution's or any available LMS to keep teachers and students more connected within the course and fight a sense of aloneness which frequently accompanies OWI. In the pandemic environment, though, neither educators, nor students were prepared and managed properly by the institutions, as most of them were strongly focused on offline learning programmes and had no experience in organizing online courses. Moreover, online writing teachers in traditional OWI who usually volunteer to take up the course are provided with an appropriate OWI-focused training with an emphasis on course design, use of technology and assessment techniques (CCCC OWI Committee, 2011c). This appeared impossible under COVID-19 situation, so the burden of the course implementation, professional self-development and enhancing technological skills fell entirely on teachers. Consequently, the OWI teachers were gaining experience through trial and error, developing their skills literally on the go. However, as Hewett (2015a) claims, in non-crisis OWI courses, the most experienced teachers have also won their skills through trial and error.

Consequently, the level of the instructors' dissatisfaction about the workload and the institutional support regarding technology was high in most schools and universities across the globe. In most cases the anxiety of teachers in OWI classes related to the lack of technology skills and extreme time consumption. Although the research has not once stressed that teaching online can be more time-intensive (Allen & Seaman, 2010), it is only the pandemic that has finally ruined the myth that teaching and learning online is less time- and effort-consuming than teaching and learning on campus. High level of time-consumption in OWI courses is explained by the fact that they involve individual and focused teacher responses to students' writing that can hardly be automated. However, not only teachers but also students are faced with the time pressure in OWI courses. According to the research conducted by Griffin and Minter (2013), the literacy load – reading and producing texts - of the OWI classes appeared more than 2.75 times greater than in offline classes.

Partially, time pressure can be reduced by introducing more synchronous online classes to have a better balance between the teacher's instruction, collaborative learning, and independent writing practice. The modality, though, seems to be a cultural matter in the educational setting: some institutions focus on synchronous course tutorials whereas the others place an accent on asynchronous instruction. To date, there is no evidence whether the two online modes used in the OWI are equally effective; however, some researchers emphasize on student preference for video and audio communication during the course (Sommers, 2013).

In summary, most OWI principles that were developed by the scholars and writing practitioners and served as fundamental benchmarks of the instruction quality appeared unapplicable in the emergency environment. Therefore, this type of OWI requires deeper and more detailed examination to give a more professional response to new challenges.

Offline Writing Instruction Deficiencies Exported Online

Sudden and full digitalization of teaching writing due to the pandemic situation has prevented educationalists from an appropriate course implementation based on prior planning, selecting the technology to fit the course objectives as well as staff training. As a result, most teachers – especially those who came into the job when technology expertise was not a requirement – transferred their teaching beliefs and techniques of writing instruction from the onsite to online environment. Does it mean that it is the lack of technology skills that became the obstacle to effective OWI? The answer is far from being unambiguous.

The reason for this is the fact that even in face-to-face setting, writing appears a neglected skill across the globe (Graham & Rijlaarsdam, 2016). As the research reveals, major deficiencies of the onsite writing classes are related to insufficient time allotted for writing instruction (Brindle, Harris, Graham, & Hebert, 2016) and little emphasis on teaching students how to manage planning and revising as the necessary critical writing processes (Rietdijk et al., 2018). Irrespective whether it is L1 or L2 writing, the skill is the most cognitively complex and challenging among the language skills and thus requires a lot of instructional time which is significantly limited in many instances, (Graham, 2018). A lot of criticism has been voiced about the insufficient exposure of students to writing tasks in a typical classroom as well as about the lack of variety in the instructional practices (Brindle et al., 2016).

Another indicator of the deficiency of writing instruction in the onsite classroom is the prevailing absence of the technology use for writing. Given that most writing outside the classroom today is done digitally (Freedman et al., 2016), traditional offline instruction does not contribute to student motivation and task authenticity. Apart from those mentioned above, the other deficiencies of the classroom writing practices highlighted by the researchers boil down to the issues such as insufficient collaboration among students (De Smedt et al., 2016), inadequate classroom resources for teaching writing (Dockrell et al., 2016), infrequent formative assessment in the writing classroom (Rietdijk et al., 2018), low motivation for writing (Cutler & Graham, 2008).

Presumably, therefore, in the context of emergency demands to writing instruction brought about by the COVID-2019 pandemic, the teachers might have opted to use familiar methods and activities they employed in the face-to-face setting. Moreover, in the institutions with no online programs offered on a regular basis (Ukrainian universities, for instance), the teachers had to struggle with both technology and methodology issues.

Conceptualizing Approaches to Online Writing Instruction

Since contemporary higher education paradigm is shifting from knowledge-telling to knowledge-transformation model, writing instruction aims to use the approaches and techniques to enhance critical thinking and critical reading. In line with this goal is the *integrated* approach to teaching writing that incorporates the other language skills to enhance writing skills and create realistic communication in the language classroom (Wette, 2019). In the framework of this approach, integrated writing is frequently opted for by the teachers in the online environment as it makes it easier to use audio, video or textual materials while teaching writing. Processing information from sources of various modes is rather beneficial for the learners as they develop a multi-tasking ability which is indispensable for survival and success in the 21st-century professional setting.

Both cognitive and pedagogical values of integrated writing have been discussed by numerous research that provide evidence of positive impact of integration on writing skill development (Celik, 2019; Dunlop & Xhafer, 2016; Weston, 2015). The researchers claim that this type of writing enhances more thoughtful consideration and better understanding of ideas expressed in reading as well as develops rhetoric in learners (Calfee and Miller, 2005; Flower et al., 1990; Graham & Hebert, 2010).

What should be kept in mind while teaching integrated writing is that it is a cognitively demanding and complex problem-solving process with a non-linear pattern of thought generation or knowledge enhancement (Hajovski, et. al, 2018). If integration involves reading and writing, for instance, this pattern implies a shuttle-like text production with multiple recursive processes, such as reading comprehension, rereading, planning, organizing ideas etc. A chain of movements forth and back between reading and writing results in creating a significant cognitive dissonance in the process of text construction (Kavytska et. al., 2021). To partially eliminate the level of the cognitive dissonance mentioned above, the writing practitioners should be knowledgeable of the cognitive processes within the integrated writing. This will enable designing an instruction model that agrees with the cognitive model of writing under discussion. To date, the model of integrated writing, which is generally accepted by writing scholars and practitioners, comprises three major cognitive processes observed in the integrated writing from sources: 1) selecting relevant content from multiple texts; 2) organizing the content according to the writing goals; 3) connecting ideas from different sources and generating links between the ideas (Spivey & King, 1989; Spivey, 2001).

Apart from the integrated approach, this study relies on the theory of online collaborative learning (OCL). Proposed by Harasim (2012), the theory defines OCL as constructivist teaching that takes the form of instructor-led learning online. The theory places the emphasis on the facilities of the Internet to create learning environments that enhance collaboration and knowledge building through discourse instead of memorizing correct answers. Seeing the benefits of moving teaching and learning online, the author of the theory insists on a three-phase process of knowledge construction through discourse in a group: 1. Idea generating: the brainstorming phase, where divergent thoughts are gathered 2. Idea organizing: the phase where ideas are compared, analyzed, and categorized through discussion and argument 3. Intellectual convergence: the phase where intellectual synthesis and consensus occurs, including agreeing to disagree, usually through an assignment, essay, or other joint piece of work (Harasim, 2012). The OCL theory with adapted and applied by the authors of the chapter in the process of emergency OWI alongside with the integrated approach.

Integration Challenges of Cause-and-Effect Writing

The cause-and-effect rhetoric occupies a prominent place in academic discourse and writing. No less significant is it in social discourse and every-day communication. Since the purpose of the cause-and-effect writing is to reveal the relationship between various events and phenomena in terms of their reasons and consequences, it is viewed as one of the most cognitively demanding types of expository writing. The reason why this is the case is explained by the fact that determining causes and effects is usually a difficult and thought-provoking undertake: the connection between cause and effect is not always clear and evident (Nordquist, 2020). However, in terms of applying high-order cognitive processing such as understanding, application, analysis, creation, and evaluation, cause-and-effect writing demonstrates no difference from any other type of expository writing (Anderson & Krathwohl, 2001).

A specific challenge in cause-and-effect writing stems from the necessity for the students to differentiate between two types of causes: immediate and ultimate causes. Immediate causes are apparent as they are closest to the effect, and ultimate causes are somewhat removed and not so apparent and may perhaps even be hidden. Furthermore, ultimate causes may bring about effects which themselves become immediate causes, thus creating a *causal chain* (Rosa & Escholz, 1998). Additionally to identifying the type of cause, the writers are supposed to do a range of other cognitive tasks such as processing the information from reading or audio/video sources and selection of appropriate ideas for transforming them into a cause-and-effect written product.

On the organization level, students struggle how to select the appropriate model of organizing the essay. The existence of several variations of the two basic structural types – block and chain – of cause-and-effect essays turns the selection into a tricky dilemma (Oshima & Hogue, 2006). To reduce the level of cognitive load and anxiety, it is advisable that the students start with following a common and most widely spread pattern of essay organization. Based on the structure offered by Flachmann et.al (2003), the introduction presents the issue/phenomenon/event under analysis and clearly states the purpose of the analysis. The body of the essay then discusses all relevant causes and/or effects, moving from least to most influential or from most to least influential. Finally, the concluding section summarizes the various cause/effect relationships established in the body of the paper and clearly states the conclusions that can be drawn from those relationships.

In summary, major cognitive challenges that the learners are faced with in the process of cause-and-effect integrated writing are attributed to two facts: writers get a misleading or inadequate understanding of the cause-effect relationship presented in source texts; writers lack knowledge of cause-and-effect discourse type.

To further investigate the ways to deal with the challenges of the integrated cause-and-effect writing in the process of the online emergency learning, this chapter examines the impact of different technologies on the overall quality of writing as well as on its aspects, such as content integration, textual organization, and language. Therefore, the following hypotheses of the study have been formulated.

Hypothesis One: The selection of digital tools in the online writing course does not have a significant impact on the overall quality of the integrated cause-and-effect writing of tertiary school students.

Hypothesis Two: The selection of digital tools in the online writing course has an equal impact on all aspects of the integrated cause-and-effect writing of tertiary school students.

METHODOLOGY

Participants and Context

The participants of the study were 4 groups of the third-year students (a total of 42 learners) of Taras Shevchenko National University of Kyiv. The participants were doing an online writing course with the authors, with each author tutoring 2 groups. Aged between 19 and 23 the students are majoring in Turkish, Japanese and Korean as their first FL and English as the second FL. They formed two experimental groups (Group A and B) and 2 control groups (Group C and D). The participants were not assigned to groups randomly, since the OWI was part of a regular FL course. However, the groups were selected based on the criterion of the language proficiency matching. Noteworthy is the fact that neither instructors nor students had experience in online teaching or learning or profound technological expertise. Moreover, initially, the authors had negative perceptions of the OWI effectiveness.

Design

The study described in this chapter was organized as an experimental training within the OWI in the lockdown period. Carried out in the context of a university course, it aligned with the locally designed curriculum in terms of the content and writing skills taught. All writing activities were contextualized within the EFL course and did not promote cross-disciplinary connection. The writing skills, addressed in the process of teaching and assessment, were selected based on the curriculum developed and recommended by the University department. According to the curriculum that is built around the content and skills of the *Global: Level Advanced* (2016), a 3rd-year student is expected to complete a range of writing tasks that involve: writing a story; a book review; a report; several types of expository essays and an encyclopedia entry. Since the university focuses on face-to-face training in non-emergency environment, video conferencing was accepted as the most teacher- and student-friendly format with synchronous learning/teaching prevailing. On the initial stage of the study, the participants were asked to write a pre-training cause-and-effect essay; then, they were exposed to the online training (10 hours). All training components were identical in all groups except the technology variable: digital support used in teaching experimental and control groups was different. Finally, the post-training writing was offered to the groups and analyzed.

Material

Table 1. Source text analysis

Source Title & Type	No of Words & Origin	Content
A What Happens When a Language Dies and is Forgotten? (*Expository text*)	660: **By Trevor English** https://interestingengineering.com/	Languages die every year. The understanding of main reasons that lead to extinction helps save and protect languages. *Causes:* - a war or natural disaster wiped out the community; - cooperation with prosperous nation increased bilingualism; - limitation in usage (education and religion). *Effects:* - loss of a unique culture and perception of the world - loss of the memory of different histories - extinction of local resources - forgetting the language.
B Languages: Why we must save dying tongues (*Expository text*)	641: BBC	Hundreds of languages are teetering on the brink of extinction. *Causes:* -a socially, politically and economically dominant languages displaced the native ones; - a modern language helps to access jobs, education and opportunities; - a long history of persecution and restrictions encouraged pioneers to find ways out. *Effects:* - children were no longer learning the language; - new schools appeared; - IT technology created product to help language minority to communicate and research.
C. Why do languages die? (audio)	495: The Economist	It explains the notion of the dead language and dwells upon the dominant languages, Russian and Mandarin, in old times. *Causes:* -parents stop raising children to speak their native language; - multinational settlers to Palestine chose Hebrew as a language of communication among them; - some rulers banned native languages and imposed their own ones. *Effects:* - mastering the language of the developed and financially prosperous country became a key to success; - teenagers became bilingual and are ashamed to speak their native languages.

Two expository newspaper texts and a YouTube video (3:26 min) discussing the reasons and consequences of language disappearing were selected for the study (See Table 1). The sources thematically aligned with the course book topic, and after abridging both texts (See Appendix 1), their mean word length was

600 words. The text level difficulty, according to the online Text Analyzer and Automatic Readability Checker, fitted into CEFR level B2 upper intermediate. No lexical adaptations were introduced, since the vocabulary was within the course book unit being covered. After selecting relevant sources, the authors developed writing prompts for a cause-and-effect essay based on Calfee & Miller's (2005) strategies of developing prompts for integrated writing.

DIGITALIZING THE INSTRUCTION: FROM DIGITAL FEAR TO DIGITAL LOVE

OWI Model

The model described here aimed to boost both reading and writing skills as well as rhetorical knowledge, critical thinking, knowledge of both the writing process and the conventions of writing, along with the ability to present source material effectively with the appropriate integration of information. The intervention combined synchronous and asynchronous modes of learning and involved 3 phases (See Table 2) that aligned with the processes occurring in the integrated writing and online collaborative learning described above.

Table 2. The structure of the OWI

EXPERIMENTAL GROUPS	CONTROL GROUPS
Synchronous learning (video conferencing)	
Phase 1. *Selecting content from multiple sources and idea generating*	
Activities: Brainstorming (writing, speaking): summarizing; giving definitions; identifying relationship between events/ phenomena (e.g. cause-effect); "fast writing"/"one-minute speech" on the topic. *Digital tools*: TeacherTools.Digital, Zoom.	*Activities:* Brainstorming (writing, speaking): summarizing; giving definitions; identifying relationship between events/ phenomena (e.g. cause-effect); "fast writing"/"one-minute speech" on the topic. *Digital tools*: Mentimeter (Word Cloud, Multiple-Choice, Open-Ended options), Padlet, Zoom.
Phase 2. ***Organizing the content according to the writing goals***	
Activities: structural/ rhetorical transformation of ideas and texts (writing, speaking); making connections between ideas (structure/ language); vocabulary and syntax enhancement; *Digital tools:* TeacherTools.Digital, Zoom	*Activities:* structural/ rhetorical transformation of ideas and texts (writing, speaking); making connections between ideas (structure/ language); vocabulary and syntax enhancement; *Digital tools*: Padlet; Mentimeter; GoogleDocs; GoogleClassroom, Zoom.
Asynchronous learning	
Phase 3. ***Connecting ideas from sources and generating links between the ideas***	
Activities: coherence/cohesion enhancement; language transformation; editing. *Digital tools:* TeacherTools.Digital, PaperRater	*Activities:* coherence/cohesion enhancement; language transformation; editing. *Digital tools:* GoogleClassroom.

Below, the description of OWI models is given in detail.

Digital Support of the Writing Course

The authors' choice of the digital technology was dictated by the immediate necessity to maintain the writing instruction while physical learning space was out of reach. The tools were supposed to fit into a set of criteria: accessibility of the tool/platform; high task generation capacity; feedback generation capacity as well as the capacity to disable academic dishonesty; operational simplicity; functional diversity; compatibility with multiple devices, including a smartphone. Since the prevailing instructional mode within the institution was synchronous learning, both authors relied on Zoom conferencing in all groups; asynchronous learning was managed through Google Classroom and TeacherTool.Digital. Additionally, the instructors were looking for the tools that could motivate and engage students.

Control Groups: The More Tools, the Better?

The instruction in phase 1 aimed at teaching students to select relevant ideas from multiple sources and collaboratively generate knowledge based on shared and comprehensive understanding of the topic under study. The learners' prior knowledge of the topic was activated by engaging the students in active reflection through a variety of oral and writing brainstorming activities such as "fast writing"," one-minute speech" etc. Critical reading and understanding were enhanced through summarizing ideas from the sources, identifying logical relationship between events/ phenomena, and categorizing key concepts. This phase was carried out in the form of synchronous learning through Zoom conferencing with GoogleClassroom used as a course management platform. Additionally, the Mentimeter tool was embedded into Zoom.

A free plan product developed in Sweden in 2014, it has become one of the most popular interactive presentation platforms due to a well-developed interface and operational simplicity. A time-saver in the video conferencing class is the fact that no signing up is required from students: they participate in activities, using a link sent by a teacher. Mentimeter enables opting for a variety of activities by making use of the functions such as Multiple Choice, Word Cloud, Open Ended, Ranking, Scales and Questions and Answers, Quiz Competition, Contest Slides, and Advance Questions. A valuable feature of Mentimeter is that an instructor can easily moderate, guide audience, ask questions and share the gathered results. Visualizing students' responses in real time in the online class creates the feeling of a physical classroom, which adds to a positive psychological environment in the emergency learning setting.

The objective of phase 2 was to enhance the skills of organizing the content according to the writing goals. Students practise making appropriate logical and language connections between ideas through structural and rhetorical transformation (writing, speaking), vocabulary and syntax enhancement,

restating important and/or difficult sentences and paragraphs, etc. This phase was also implemented as a component of synchronous learning. Apart from the Mentimeter tool, both instructors in this phase made use of Padlet and GoogleDocs. Both tools are easily integrated with Google Classroom and can be accessed from different devices. Available in 29 languages and functioning as an interactive board, Padlet enables performing a number of tasks ranging from posts and messages to videos and portfolios. The tool is effective for collaborative writing and knowledge sharing as well as indispensable when it is necessary to engage the whole class in simultaneous writing with further screen sharing the students' posts by the teacher. Among the inconveniences of the platform is the absence of autofeedback function.

GoogleDocs is another effective tool for collaborative writing with the help of which the instructors can conquer the biggest criticism of online learning – passive, disengaged learning.

Phase 3 was implemented through asynchronous learning and targeted at enhancing the skills of connecting ideas from sources and generating links between the ideas. During this phase, the students received the writing prompt and were requested to synthesize and transform their knowledge into a cause-and-effect essay. Prior to performing the task, the students were encouraged to do some tasks to improve coherence/cohesion, language transformation, and editing. The management and digital support of the phase was carried out through GoogleClassroom.

Experimental Groups: Integrated Tool for Integrated Writing

The instructional model in the experimental groups is identical to that in the control groups, but the difference lies in the technology involved. The digital support in the experimental group was maintained through two basic tools: TeacherTools.Digital and PaperRater. The authors' idea behind selecting the tools was to optimize the instruction, using fewer multifunctional tools with powerful optimization capacities. Moreover, since the OWI aimed at enhancing integrated writing skills, the authors were looking for a platform that could provide teaching writing in the integration with reading, speaking, and listening enhancement. Both authors agreed that TeacherTools.Digital as the main course management platform met the requirement mentioned above. Developed in June 2020 in Japan, the platform is user-friendly and easy to access from various devices including a smartphone. It enables keeping track of students' performance and progress; creating interesting and interactive assignments; administering students' submissions and using auto-grading and auto-feedback options to reduce the teacher's time consumption by the OWI. The assignments panel comprises the following options: audio recording, video recording, written reports, speaking drill, text gap fill, text to test, video gap fill, multi choice, vocabulary test and content page. The advantageous function for teaching integrated writing is the opportunity to export a text, image, audio/video from Media Prompts and embed it into a writing prompt. The essential functions for the OWI include setting time (from 1 to 60 minutes) and word limits (990 words) as well as preventing plagiarism through disabling Copy & Paste function. Grammar Check and Essay Language (English, French, German, Spanish) are also among the platform's functions; however, coherence and cohesion are not subject to auto feedback.

PaperRator.com is another tool to involve even disengaged students in the process of OWI and thus to enhance students' outcomes. This tool is a completely automated service, which gives the feedback and analysis of any written task in real-time. The tool was integrated into the asynchronous module to motivate students to proofread their writing before submitting it for a final grade. It allows users to proofread 50 five-page submissions and guarantees ten plagiarism checks per month. There is also an option of identifying grammar and spelling errors, receiving writing suggestions and automated scoring. Moreover, to improve students' writing skills, the tool offers a detailed feedback and writing instructions on word choice, style and vocabulary, sentence length and variability, passive voice detection and others with references to the usage rules provided.

SOLUTIONS AND RECOMMENDATIONS

Product Quality Analysis

Two cause-and-effect essays (pre- and post-training writings) were analyzed against a set of criteria that are typically applicable to assessing integrated writing: content integration from sources; textual organization, and language. The writing products were assessed holistically, with the scaled adapted from Sole et al. (2013) and Kavytska et.al. (2021). To reduce the level of the students' anxiety in the emergency learning setting, the authors relied on a three-band scale with no detailed calibration of the rubric where levels "successful" and "adequate" were considered as satisfying in terms of meeting the OWI requirements.

The level of content integration was assessed based on the criteria, such as selection of information, integration, elaboration of information, textual organization, and comprehension errors (Segev-Miller, 2004; Spivey,1997). The scale is presented below (See Table 3).

Table 3. The scale of assessing content integration level

Integration level	Product description
Successful	Fully meets the task instruction, extracts relevant information from the ST and links it up in the text. Has an appropriate organization. Paraphrases or elaborates the ideas with no copying.
Adequate	Partially abides with the task. Contains brief statement of the most important ideas from each ST. Does not establish connections, might omit core information items. Paraphrases or elaborates the ideas with no copying.
Failed	Does not meet the task instruction. Faithfully copies the ideas in the order they appear in the ST. Does not adequately select or integrate the information. Has coherence problems.

Textual organization of cause-and-effect essays was evaluated based on the similar approach (See Table 4). The holistic scale reflects basic requirements to cause-and-effect writing (Oshima & Hogue, 2006).

Table 4. The scale of assessing textual organization of a cause-and-effect essay

Textual pattern	Product description
Successful	Introductory paragraph provides background information and makes a thesis that clearly indicates cause-effect focus and the essay's position. The essay focus consistently supports the thesis, with no irrelevant details. The body paragraphs (at least 3) discuss all relevant causes and effects and are arranged in a logical, purposeful manner, with smooth transitions to provide coherence and cohesion. The concluding paragraph summarizes causes and draws a conclusion from the analysis of the cause-effect relationship.
Adequate	Introductory paragraph provides background information and makes a thesis that clearly indicates cause-effect focus and the essay's position. The essay focus consistently supports the thesis, with very few irrelevant details. The body paragraphs (at least 3) discuss all relevant causes and effects and are arranged in a logical, purposeful manner, with smooth transitions to provide coherence and cohesion. The concluding paragraph summarizes causes but fails to draw a conclusion from the analysis of the cause-effect relationship.
Failed	Introductory paragraph provides background information and makes a thesis that may not clearly indicate cause-effect focus and the essay's position. The essay focus is mostly maintained through the essay, with numerous irrelevant details. The body paragraphs (at least 3) discuss all relevant causes and effects and are mostly arranged in a logical, purposeful manner but do not always provide coherence and cohesion. The concluding paragraph summarizes causes but fails to draw a conclusion from the analysis of the cause-effect relationship.

The scale assessing language focuses on the appropriate use of academic vocabulary, syntactic variety, grammar usage and spelling (See Table 5).

Table 5. The scale of assessing language

Level	Product description
Successful	Demonstrates an appropriate and varied academic vocabulary as well as diversity in syntax. The essay is devoid of misspellings, errors in grammar vocabulary, and style.
Adequate	Demonstrates an appropriate and varied academic vocabulary. Sentence variety is present but requires enhancement. The essay may contain some misspellings and errors in style that do not impact understanding or fluency.
Failed	Demonstrates an appropriate academic vocabulary. Sentence structure variety is lacking. The essay contains some misspellings and errors that hinder understanding or fluency.

The products were analyzed by the two authors of the chapter who carried out the instruction. The overall agreement between them was 86%, which indicates that the assessment procedure ensured the appropriate reliability.

RESULTS

Table 6 shows the summarized analysis of the level of content integration in students' pre-training and post-training cause-and-effect essays in both experimental and control groups. The analysis aligned with assessment procedure described above.

Table 6. Level of content integration in pre- and post-training writing

Pre-training writing			Post- training writing		
Experimental groups (n=20)					
Product category	**Number**	**Percentage**	**Product category**	**Number**	**Percentage**
Successful	3	15%	Successful	3	15%
Adequate	11	55%	Attempted	13	65%
Failed	6	30%	Failed	4	20%
Control groups (n=22)					
Successful	5	23%	Successful	5	23%
Adequate	9	41%	Attempted	11	50%
Failed	8	36%	Failed	6	27%

As it has been mentioned before, a pre-training prompt required writing a cause-and-effect essay and provided a graphic model of 2 structural types of the indicated essay: block and chain patterns. Although the students were not trained in cause-effect rhetoric, they possessed rather developed writing skills as they did a writing course prior to the lockdown: the course was implemented through face-to-face instruction with no digital support involved. The analysis of the pre-training essays in all groups reveals two commonalities: very few students (5 Of 42) opted for a block structural pattern of the essay and 14 students (66%) failed to integrate the content from 2 texts and a video and organize it into cause-effect writing. Copying appeared a frequent technique, as students highly depended on the sources. However, no written products demonstrated comprehension errors.

The post-training writing results show more considerable improvement in the experimental groups. 16 of 20 essays are categorized as 'successful' and 'adequate", as they present well-integrated ideas with no direct copying from the sources.

Compared to content integration, textual conventions of the essays were generally of higher level (See Table 7), with an average 19% of all texts written before training categorized as failed. After training, the share decreased to 0% in the experimental groups and to 4% in the control groups, which enables making a conclusion that textual organization skills are more affected by training compared to content integration skills.

Table 7. Level of textual organization in pre- and post-training

Pre-test writing			Post- test writing		
Experimental groups (n=20)					
Product category	**Number**	**Percentage**	**Product category**	**Number**	**Percentage**
Successful	5	25%	Successful	6	30%
Adequate	12	60%	Adequate	14	70%
Failed	3	15%	Failed	0	0%
Control groups (n=22)					
Successful	5	23%	Successful	5	23%
Adequate	12	54%	Adequate	16	73%
Failed	5	23%	Failed	1	4%

The failed essays display common deficiencies, such as: the body paragraphs contained numerous ideas irrelevant to the sources; the thesis was not consistently maintained through the essay; the concluding paragraph did not draw conclusions from causes and effects discussed in the sources.

Unexpected results were demonstrated by the 'Language' criterion (See Table 8). The improvement of language and mechanics in the experimental group was dramatic, with 100% of the after-training products meeting the requirements against 80% of pre-training works. This can be attributed to the effective self-editing capacities of the PaperRater and TeachersTool.Digital as well as to competent use of these tools by the experimental groups during asynchronous learning. No improvement of language and mechanics was observed in the control groups, which confirms the assumption that not all aspects of integrated writing are equally impacted by the appropriate selection of the digital support in the OWI.

Table 8. Language criterion in pre- and post-training writing

Pre-training writing			Post- training writing		
Experimental groups (n=20)					
Product category	**Number**	**Percentage**	**Product category**	**Number**	**Percentage**
Successful	3	15%	Successful	6	30%
Adequate	13	65%	Adequate	14	70%
Failed	4	20%	Failed	0	0%
Control groups (n=22)					
Successful	5	23%	Successful	5	23%
Adequate	14	41%	Adequate	14	41%
Failed	3	36%	Failed	3	36%

FUTURE RESEARCH DIRECTIONS

Given the existing gap in investigation of optimization capacities of various online tools in the context of OWI learning, the future research directions might focus on this research issue. The use of video/ audio input in the integrated writing prompts would also be valuable for the examination of teaching integrated writing online.

CONCLUSION

The chapter aimed at comparing two digitally supported OWI models implemented in the emergency learning environment due to the COVID-2019 pandemic. With the teachers who had no prior experience in online teaching or advanced technology expertise, the instruction on cause-and-effect integrated writing was carried out in the context of a university FL course as a combination of synchronous (video conferencing) and asynchronous modules. The paper specifically targeted at examining the impact of different technologies on three aspects of an integrated cause-and-effect essay. The instruction was based on the theoretical provisions of integrated approach to teaching writing and the theory of online collaborative learning with a view to offer opportunities for enhancing critical thinking, critical comprehension, and rhetoric.

This study shows a generally positive impact of both digitally supported OWI models on the overall of the cause-and-effect writing. Overall, our data support the formulated hypotheses. As for hypothesis one, it has been supported. The instruction in the experimental groups based on the involvement of TeacherTools.Digital and PaperRater has resulted in a higher level of improvement in the overall quality of the students' written products, with 90% of the essays assessed as successful and adequate against 78% in the control groups. Regarding hypothesis two, it has been partially supported. In all groups, the 'content integration' aspect appeared the least impacted by the technologies, which is an indicator that it is the most cognitively aspect in integrated writing. On the contrary, textual organization was the most influenced by the OWI: the number of the essays that meet the requirements in the experimental groups rose by 15% against 19% in the control group. Opposite results are observed with the 'language' aspect:

no impact on the language and mechanics has been recorded in the control groups whereas the most powerful impact is spotted in the experimental groups.

Therefore, though the data confirm the training efficacy of both digital support models, the general conclusion drawn from the research lies in the idea that only targeted selection of online technologies can produce significant enhancement of the skills under training. Additionally, it is advisable that the tools employed in the emergency learning should be user-friendly and possess a powerful optimization capacity in terms of time and effort consumption.

Regarding the authors' personal perceptions of the digital support in the OWI, more effective tools were considered those used in the experimental groups. Integrational feature of the platform enables saving time during synchronous video conferencing; it reduces the teacher's workload due to the autofeedback function and the opportunity to export the pre-existing tasks from the media library.

Finally, the authors of the chapter who had neither experience in online teaching, nor advanced technology expertise and were opponents of the OWI completed the course as ardent proponents of the digitally supported writing instruction.

REFERENCES

Adas, D., & Bakir, A. (2013). Writing Difficulties and New Solutions: Blended Learning as an Approach to Improve Writing Abilities. *International Journal of Humanities and Social Science*, *3*(9), 254–266.

Alexander, J. (2006). *Digital youth: Emerging literacies on the World Wide Web*. Hampton Press.

Ali, W. (2020). Online and remote learning in higher education institutes: A necessity in light of COVID pandemic. *High. Educ. Stud.*, *10*(3), 16–25. doi:10.5539/hes.v10n3p16

Alkhataba, A. H., Abdul-Hamid, S., & Bashir, I. (2018). Technology-Supported Online Writing: An Overview of Six Major Web 2.0 Tools for Collaborative-Online Writing. *Arab World English Journal*, *9*(1), 433–446. doi:10.24093/awej/vol9no1.30

Allen, I., & Seaman, J. (2010). *Class Differences: Online Education in the United States, 2010*. The Sloan Consortium. http://sloanconsortium.org/publications/survey/class_differences

Amirsheibani, M., Iraji, M. (2014). CALL and Teaching writing: Language teachers' attitude, an Iranian survey. *Procedia – Social and Behavioral Studies, 98, 258-266.*

Anderson, L. W., & Krathwohl, D. R. (2001). *A taxonomy for learning teaching and assessing: A revision of Bloom's taxonomy of educational objectives*. Longman.

Anwar, K., & Adnan, M. (2020). Online learning amid the COVID-19 pandemic: Students perspectives. *Journal of Pedagogical Research*, *1*(2), 45–51.

Ayan, E., & Seferoğlu, S. (2017). Using *Etherpad* for Online Collaborative Writing Activities and Learners with Different Language Learning Strategies. *Eurasian Journal of Applied Linguistics*, *3*(2), 205–233. doi:10.32601/ejal.461000

Brindle, M., Harris, K. R., Graham, S., & Hebert, M. (2016). Third and fourth grade teachers' classroom practices in writing: A national survey. *Reading and Writing*, *29*(5), 929–954. doi:10.100711145-015-9604-x

Calfee, R. C., & Miller, R. G. (2005). Breaking Ground: Constructing authentic reading-writing assessments for middle and secondary school students. In R. Indrisano & J. Paratore (Eds.), *Learning to Write, Writing to Learn: Theory and research in practice* (pp. 203–219). IRA.

CCCC OWI Committee for Effective Practices in Online Writing Instruction. (2011c). *The state of the art of OWI*. Retrieved from http://www.ncte.org/ library/NCTEFiles/Groups/CCCC/Committees/OWI_State-of-Art_Report_April_2011.pdf

Celik, B. (2019). Developing Writing Skills Through Reading. *International Journal of Social Sciences and Educational Studies*, *6*(1), 206–214.

Clark, C., Picton, I., & Lant, F. (2020). *"More time on my hands": Children and young people's writing during the COVID-19 lockdown in 2020*. National Literacy Trust.

Cumming, A. (2001). Learning to write in a second language: Two decades of research. *International Journal of English Studies*, *1*(2), 1–23.

Cutler, L., & Graham, S. (2008). Primary Grade Writing Instruction: A National Survey. *Journal of Educational Psychology*, *100*(4), 907–919. doi:10.1037/a0012656

Dockrell, J., Marshall, C., & Wyse, D. (2016). Teachers' reported practices for teaching writing in England. *Reading and Writing*, *29*(3), 409–434. doi:10.100711145-015-9605-9 PMID:26941477

Dumford, A. D., & Miller, A. L. (2018). Online learning in higher education: Exploring advantages and disadvantages of engagement. *Journal of Computing in Higher Education*, *30*(3), 452–465. doi:10.100712528-018-9179-z

Dunlop, D., & Xhafer, J. (2016). *Development of synthesizing skills in academic writing. Cambridge English: Research Notes, 64, 52-60.*

Ellis, R. A. (2004). Supporting genre-based literacy pedagogy with technology. In L. Ravelli & R. Ellis (Eds.), *Analysing academic writing: Contextualised frameworks* (pp. 210–232). Continuum.

Flachmann, K., Flachmann, M., Benander, K., & Smith, C. (2003). *The Brief Prose Reader*. Prentice Hall.

Flower, L., Stein, V., Ackerman, J., Kantz, M. J., McCormick, K., & Peck, W. C. (1990). Reading-to-write: Exploring a Cognitive and Social Process. Oxford University Press. Foundational Principles of Online Writing Instruction.

Freedman, S. W., Hull, G. A., Higgs, J. M., & Booten, K. P. (2016). Teaching writing in a digital and global age: Toward access, learning, and development for all. In D. H. Gitomer & C. A. Bell (Eds.), *Handbook of research on teaching* (5th ed., pp. 1389–1450). American Educational Research Association. doi:10.3102/978-0-935302-48-6_23

Graham, S. (2018). A revised writer(s)-within-community model of writing. *Educational Psychologist*, *53*(4), 258–279. doi:10.1080/00461520.2018.1481406

Graham, S., & Hebert, M. A. (2010). *Writing to read: Evidence for how writing can improve reading. A Carnegie corporation time to act report*. Alliance for Excellent Education.

Graham, S., & Rijlaarsdam, G. (2016). Writing education around the globe. *Reading and Writing, 29*(5), 781–792. doi:10.100711145-016-9640-1

Griffin, J., & Minter, D. (2013). The Rise of the Online Writing Classroom: Reflecting on the Material Conditions of College Composition Teaching. *College Composition and Communication, 65*(1), 140–161. https://www.jstor.org/stable/43490811

Hajovsky, D. B., Villeneuve, E. F., Reynolds, M. R., Niileksela, Ch. R., Mason, B. A., & Shudak, N. J. (2018). Cognitive ability influences on written expression: Evidence for developmental and sex-based differences in school-age children. *Journal of School Psychology, 67*, 104–118. doi:10.1016/j.jsp.2017.09.001 PMID:29571527

Harasim, L. (2012). *Learning theory and online technologies*. Routledge. doi:10.4324/9780203846933

Hewett, B. L. (2013). Fully online and hybrid writing instruction. In H. B. Hessler, A. R. Taggart, & K. Schick (Eds.), *A guide to composition pedagogies* (2nd ed., pp. 194–211). Oxford University Press.

Hewett, B. L. (2015a). *Reading to learn and writing to teach: Literacy strategies for online writing instruction*. Bedford/St. Martin's Press.

Hewett, B. L. (2015b). The online writing conference: A guide for teachers and tutors (Updated). Boston: Bedford/St. Martin's Press.

Hewett, B. L., & DePew, K. E. (2015). *Foundational practices of online writing instruction (Perspective on Writing)*. Parlor Press. doi:10.37514/PER-B.2015.0650

Jukes, I., McCain, T., & Crockett, L. (2010). Understanding the digital generation: Teaching and learning in the new digital landscape. 21st Century Fluency Project.

Kavytska, T., Shovkovyi, V., & Osidak, V. (2021). Source-Based Writing in Secondary School: Challenges and Accomplishments. In C. N. Giannikas (Ed.), *Teaching Practices and Equitable Learning in Children's Language Education* (pp. 63–83). IGI Global. doi:10.4018/978-1-7998-6487-5.ch004

Kim, C. M., Mendenhall, A., & Johnson, T. E. (2010). A design framework for an online English writing course. In Learning and instruction in the digital age (pp. 345-360). New York: Springer. doi:10.1007/978-1-4419-1551-1_21

Luna, M., Villalon, R., Mateos, M., & Martín, E. (2020). Improving university argumentative writing through an online training. *Journal of Writing Research, 12*(1), 233–262. doi:10.17239/jowr-2020.12.01.08

Moore, N. S., & Filling, M. L. (2012). iFeedback: Using video technology for improving student writing. *Journal of College Literacy and Learning*, 3–14.

Mort, P., & Drury, H. (2012). Supporting student academic literacy in the disciplines using genre-based online pedagogy. *Journal of Academic Language and Learning, 6*(3), A1–A15. https://journal.aall.org.au/

Nordquist, R. (2020). *Cause and Effect in Composition*. ThoughtCo. thoughtco.com/cause-and-effect-composition-1689834

Oshima, A., & Hogue, A. (2006). *Writing Academic English* (4th ed.). Pearson Longman.

Parvin, R. H., & Salam, S. F. (2015). The Effectiveness of Using Technology in English Language Classrooms in Government Primary Schools in Bangladesh. *Forum for International Research in Education, 2*(1), 1–5. doi:10.18275/fire201502011049

Ponticiello, M., Simmons, M., & Lee, J. S. (2021). The effects of the sudden switch to remote learning due to Covid-19 on HBCU students and faculty. In P. Zaphiris & A. Ioannou (Eds.), Lecture Notes in Computer Science: Vol. 12784. *Learning and Collaboration Technologies: New Challenges and Learning Experiences. HCII 2021*. Springer. doi:10.1007/978-3-030-77889-7_34

Rietdijk, S., van Weijen, D., Jassen, T., van den Bergh, H., & Rijlaarsdam, G. (2018). Teaching writing in primary education: Classroom practice, time, teachers' beliefs and skills. *Journal of Educational Psychology, 110*(5), 640–663. doi:10.1037/edu0000237

Rosa, A., & Eschholz, P. (1998). *Models for Writers* (6th ed.). St. Martin's Press.

Sommers, J. (2013). Response 2.0: Commentary on student writing for the new millennium. *Journal of College Literacy and Learning, 39*, 21–37.

Spivey, N. N. (2001). *Discourse synthesis: Process and product. In Discourse synthesis: Studies in historical and contemporary social epistemology*. Praeger.

Spivey, N. N., & King, J. R. (1989). Readers as writers composing from sources. *Reading Research Quarterly, 24*(1), 7–26. doi:10.1598/RRQ.24.1.1

Warnock, S. (2009). *Teaching writing online: How and why*. National Council of Teachers of English.

Warschauer, M. (2010). New Tools for Teaching Writing. *Language Learning & Technology, 14*(1), 3–8.

Wattoo, R. M., Latif, M., & Munir, N. (2020). Information Communication Technologies Hauling Out University Students' Effective Learning during COVID-19: A Qualitative Study. *Global Social Sciences Review, 3*(III), 351–357. doi:10.31703/gssr.2020(V-III).37

Weston, J.L. (2015). *The Impact of Strategy Instruction on Source-Based Writing* [Doctoral dissertation]. Arizona State University.

Westwood, P. (2008). *What teachers need to know about reading and writing difficulties*. Aust Council for Ed Research.

Wette, R. (2019). Embedded provision to develop source-based writing skills in a Year 1 health sciences course: How can the academic literacy developer contribute? *English for Specific Purposes, 56*, 35–49. doi:10.1016/j.esp.2019.07.002

Wingate, U., & Dreiss, C. A. (2009). Developing students' academic literacy: An online approach. *Journal of Academic Language and Learning, 3*(1), A14–A25. http://journal.aall.org.au

ADDITIONAL READING

Fox, S., & Mackeogh, K. (2003). Can E-Learning Promote Higher-Order Learning Without Tutor Overload? *Open Learning*, *18*(2), 121–134. doi:10.1080/02680510307410

Ibabe, I., & Jauregizar, J. (2010). Online Self-Assessment with Feedback and Metacognitive Knowledge. *Higher Education*, *59*(2), 243–258. doi:10.100710734-009-9245-6

Keck, C. (2014). Copying, paraphrasing, and academic writing development: A re-examination of L1 and L2 summarization practices. *Journal of Second Language Writing*, *25*(3), 4–22. doi:10.1016/j.jslw.2014.05.005

Kirkpatrick, L. C., & Klein, P. D. (2016). High-achieving high school students' strategies for writing from internet-based sources of information. *Journal of Writing Research*, *8*(1), 1–46. doi:10.17239/jowr-2016.08.01.01

List, A., & Alexander, P. A. (2017). The cognitive affective engagement model of multiple source use. *Educational Psychology*, *52*(3), 182–199. doi:10.1080/00461520.2017.1329014

McGreal, E., & Elliot, M. (2008). Technologies of Online Learning (E-learning). In T. Anderson (Ed.), *The theory and practice of online learning* (pp. 143–166). Au Press.

Scardamalia, M., & Bereiter, C. (1987). Knowledge telling and knowledge transforming in written composition. In S. Rosenberg (Ed.), Advances in Applied Psycholinguistics: Reading, writing and language learning (Vol. 2, pp. 142-171). Cambridge University Press.

Segev-Miller, R. (2007). Cognitive processes in discourse synthesis: The case of intertextual processing strategies. In G. Rijlaarsdam, M. Torrance, L. Van Waes, & D. Galbraith (Eds.), Writing and Cognition: Research and Applications (pp. 231–250). Elsevier.

KEY TERMS AND DEFINITIONS

Cause-and-Effect Writing: Writing that reveals the relationship between various events and phenomena in terms of their reasons and consequences; one of the most cognitively demanding types of expository writing.

Emergency Online Learning: Is the online format of learning/teaching offered in response to a crisis.

Integrated or Source-Based Writing Skills: Is the ability to critically read source texts and effectively integrate extracted ideas into a new written product.

Knowledge Transformation: Is a process of creating new knowledge which involves problem analysis and problem setting through problem solving activities in content and rhetorical domains.

Knowledge Transmission: Is the process of generating content without communicating it. Knowledge transmission can be compared to an everyday impromptu speech which does not involve such metacognitive strategies as goal setting, planning or revision.

Model of Integrated Writing: The model that comprises three major cognitive processes observed in the integrated writing from sources: 1) selecting relevant content from multiple texts; 2) organizing the content according to the writing goals; 3) connecting ideas from different sources and generating links between the ideas (Spivey & King, 1989; Spivey, 2001).

Online Collaborative Learning: Theory proposed by Harasim (2012). The theory defines as constructivist teaching that takes the form of instructor-led learning online. The theory places the emphasis on the facilities of the Internet to create learning environments that enhances collaboration and knowledge building through discourse instead of memorizing correct answers.

Online Writing Instruction (OWI): The instruction that occurs—at least partially if not fully—in a computer-based, internet, or intranet instructional setting.

Source-Based Writing Instruction: Provides scaffolding activities that allow students to integrate new context into existing knowledge through critical comprehension of source texts, recognition of the necessary text structures and accurate representation of the retrieved ideas in writing.

Chapter 5
University Students Going Online During the COVID-19 Pandemic:
Experiences From a Blended Delivery Course Model in Greece

Kia Karavas
National and Kapodistrian University of Athens, Greece

Trisevgeni Liontou
National and Kapodistrian University of Athens, Greece

ABSTRACT

Since March 2020, with the first outbreak of COVID-19, university education in Greece shifted to online teaching. Taking into account the principles of effective online teaching and with a view of making course content consistent, relevant, and meaningful to students, the authors of this chapter decided to transform a compulsory course of the Department of English Language and Literature into a blended course with elements of a remote flipped classroom. This chapter aims to present the decisions taken for the adjustment of the course and to present university students' evaluation of this course focusing their opinions of the revised course structure and challenges they faced while completing the course. The results revealed that although student response to fully online distance learning was not overwhelmingly positive, their response towards the flipped classroom model was. This points to the great potential the flipped classroom model can have for introducing pedagogies that combine distance learning with face-to-face teaching.

DOI: 10.4018/978-1-7998-8717-1.ch005

INTRODUCTION: THE COVID-19 PANDEMIC AND UNIVERSITY EDUCATION

The COVID-19 pandemic has posed extraordinary and unprecedented challenges for universities, their educators and students alike. Though the interruption of education has occurred previously in many local instances (e.g., in cases of war, civil unrest, famine or strikes), according to Williamson et al. (2020) it is "being experienced more acutely and affectively by educators, students and parents" at a global scale for the first time having affected more than 220 million tertiary-level students around the world" (p. 107).

The demands on academic staff and students have been –and continue to be– unparalleled. Both must manage work-life balance while teaching and learning in a largely unfamiliar way, in the midst of persistent uncertainty. Students have suddenly needed to direct and regulate their own learning and become digitally competent while instructors have had to switch to online teaching literally overnight regardless of their comfort level, familiarity, and training in digital pedagogies (Bozkurt et al., 2020, p. 3). According to the Organization for Economic Co-operation and Development's survey (Education Responses to COVID-19: Embracing Digital Learning and Online Collaboration 2020), some of the main challenges universities have to face were:

- Keeping an equilibrium between online courses and non-digital activities,
- Analyzing and focusing on students' emotional health by providing them with support throughout the process of learning,
- Taking into account the fact that not all students have access to the internet,
- And managing and monitoring their access to devices in order to effectively collaborate with them.

The International University Association, an independent NGO and global association of higher education institutions and organisations from more than 120 countries around the world, conducted a Global Survey on the impact of COVID-19 on higher education around the world from March 17 to April 2020 receiving replies from 427 universities (see Marinoni et al., 2020). The results revealed that at almost all HEIs, the COVID pandemic affected teaching and learning, with two-thirds of the participating universities reporting that classroom teaching has been replaced by distance teaching and learning. For about 25% of the Universities that participated in this survey, most activities were currently suspended but pertinent institutions were working on developing solutions to continue teaching and learning, through digital or self-study means. In other words, two-thirds of HEIs were able to move teaching online while one third was not. The European University Association (EUA) conducted a survey on "Digitally enhanced learning & teaching" in March 2020 which revealed that 95% of European Higher Education Institutions moved to distance online learning while 4% provided it in some faculties. The Irish National Digital Experience (INDEx) Survey (2020) also revealed that 70% of academics had never taught online pre-crisis, with similar figures in the UK. There is no reason to believe that experience levels were different in other European higher education systems.

More recently, UNESCO's Section for Higher Education conducted a survey from 15 December 2020 to 12 February 2021 of 57 member countries in order to provide an evidence-based overview of the current situation of the higher education system at national and global levels. All responding countries reported an increase in online, distance and hybrid learning. Digitalization of education has been found to be the major developing trend in the higher education system. More and more countries are shifting to an online or hybrid mode of teaching and learning due to the impact of the pandemic.

As far as Greece is concerned, a national lockdown was imposed on March 13 2020 when the first cases of COVID-19 were detected in various parts of the country. The Greek state responded immediately by amending its legal framework (Joint Ministerial Decision 16838) and allowing all universities in the country to move to distance online teaching (see Karalis & Raikou, 2020). It is worth highlighting that the Greek education system is among the most centralised in the OECD. The government sets out the general strategic goals of the system and the Ministry of Education and Religious Affairs (MofERA: https://www.minedu.gov.gr) shapes education policy, monitors its implementation and administers the education system. MofERA has responsibility for the entire education system from pre-primary to higher education. According to national policy, all teaching in public universities in Greece is to be conducted face to face while only up to 30% of any university course can be conducted online. Only the Hellenic Open University was allowed to offer distance education up until the recent crisis (Panitsides & Karapistola, 2020). With the publication of the Joint Ministerial Decision in March 2020, all Greek Universities made gigantic efforts to upgrade the available technological infrastructure (Learning Management Systems, buying unlimited time for the Webex, zoom and BBB platforms), and to train teaching personnel through webinars, online presentations and the development of detailed manuals on the use of online teleconferencing platforms, to facilitate the move to online teaching. By the end of March 2020, the majority of Greek Universities managed to offer more than 90% of their courses online (Raikou et al., 2020). Similarly, according to a review of 31 case studies conducted by Bozkurt et al. (2020), Greek higher education institutions had the capacity and quickly corresponded to the new imperatives but to a rather small scale. This said, the main challenges were to choose the right e-platforms, to quickly update the relevant technological infrastructure and mostly to train a percentage of professors in the use of the new software. According to Bozkurt et al., despite all the aforementioned difficulties, 96.35% of undergraduate courses were successfully able to continue through a combination of synchronous and asynchronous online instruction (Bozkurt et al., 2020, p. 57).

One of the most common educational methodologies used for distance learning at HEIs around the world during the lockdown period has been the Flipped Classroom model (Collado-Valero et al., 2021; Latorre--Cosculluela et al., 2020). According Collado-Valero et al. (2021) "the term Flipped Classroom reached its highest popularity during the lockdown, increasing its search frequency in Google Trends by up to 200% compared to the previous months" (p. 4). Given its potential for active and meaningful learning, for the development of learner autonomy, and the increased opportunities it offers for interactions between teachers and students, the flipped classroom methodology has recently gained a great level of attention in higher education along with the STEM courses (Jeong & González-Gómez, 2021) while a plethora of studies regarding the positive impact of the flipped classroom model on university students' performance and motivation have been published during the last year (Campillo-Ferrer & Miralles-Martínez, 2021; Gopalan et al., 2021; Haftador et al., 2021; Latorre-Cosculluela et al., 2020; Tang et al, 2020). It should be noted though that the implementation of the flipped classroom model is not widespread in Greek higher education, since up until now only two cases of implementation are mentioned (Rakitzi, et al., 2020; Plota & Karalis, 2019).

The COVID pandemic offered Greek HEIs the opportunity to experiment with different educational methodologies adapting new models of online and blended provision and using a variety of online learning tools. This was an opportunity not to be missed since the Greek Constitution and the MofERA allowed very limited use of blended, distance and online teaching in Greek public HEIs pro-COVID. In an effort to provide more active and meaningful learning experiences to our students during the lockdown period and to evaluate the effects of the novel flipped classroom methodology on student participation and motivation, during spring semester of the academic year 2019-2020, the authors of the present paper decided to plan, redesign and completely transform, a compulsory course of the undergraduate programme of studies of the Department of English Language and Literature entitled "Applied Linguistics to foreign language teaching and learning" offered in the fall semester of the academic year 2020-2021 into a blended course with elements of a remote flipped classroom. This chapter aims to present and justify the decisions taken for the adjustment of the course for distance online education adopting a flipped classroom methodology and to present university students' evaluation of this course focusing on a) their opinions of the revised course structure and challenges they faced while completing the course and b) their familiarity and attitudes towards online learning. In the present book chapter the findings of our study aim at providing valuable insights into emergency remote teaching practices in Higher Education in Greece by investigating whether and to what extent the aforementioned context actually facilitated and fostered students' engagement. Our findings are expected to shed light on the challenges university students and instructors alike faced while receiving synchronous and asynchronous instruction during the Covid-19 pandemic thereby contributing to enriching the discussion of the consequences and implications of Emergency Remote Teaching (ERT) and online learning for higher education pedagogy and their potential for the digital transformation of higher education.

LITERATURE REVIEW

University Students' Response to Emergency Remote Learning

Studies and surveys conducted during the past 12 months investigating university students' and instructors' response to new forms of learning as a result of the COVID-19 pandemic use terms and phrases such as: online learning, online education, distance education or e-learning interchangeably to describe the new educational landscape in HEIs. However, these terms do not quite capture what is being practiced during the sudden interruption of education. What we were all involved in and students experienced during lockdown can better be described as emergency remote teaching (ERT). Such an understanding is crucial as misconceptions in definitions would lead us to misconceptions in practices (Bozkurt & Sharma, 2020).

According to Hodges et al. (2020) "ERT involves the use of fully remote teaching solutions for instruction or education that would otherwise be delivered face-to-face or as blended or hybrid courses and that will return to that format once the crisis or emergency has abated" (p. 5). ERT is unplanned practice and represents a response to a crisis situation. It is a survival strategy in a time of crisis in which all resources, offline and online, are employed in order to offer some kind of continuity to learning.

Many studies have tried to investigate students' and instructors' attitudes, feelings, and responses towards emergency remote learning. According to Aboagye et al. (2020) among the main challenges that university students encountered during ERT were accessibility, connectivity, lack of appropriate devices alongside social issues represented by the lack of communication and interaction with teachers and peers. In a global survey on the impacts of the COVID-19 pandemic on the life of higher education students which involved 30,383 students from 62 countries in Europe, South America, Asia and Africa, Aristovnik et al. (2020) report that although students had adapted quite well to the new teaching and learning experience, they found it difficult to focus during online teaching in comparison to onsite one, that their workload had become larger or significantly larger and reported perceiving a worse study performance since the onsite classes had been cancelled. A large proportion of students in all three continents surveyed also reported problems with an underdeveloped Internet network, lack of and inexperience in using ICT equipment, and the fact that the only available devices for participating in online classes were mobile phones.

In a study investigating students' and university instructors' response and attitudes towards the shift to online learning during the COVID-19 pandemic in Romania (Coman et al., 2020) the results were rather discouraging. Students consider that the online process has less value than the traditional process, preferring the educational use of E-learning platforms in combination with traditional, face-to-face teaching/learning. Students also mentioned that they easily get distracted and lose focus during online instruction; they also mention environmental disruptors, lack of adequate learning space and isolation as factors inhibiting their online learning experiences. Similarly, in a survey of university students in Pakistan, the majority of the surveyed higher education students had reservations about online/digital learning and were struggling with their new learning environment. Lack of access to internet facilities, lack of proper interaction and contact with students and instructors and ineffective technology were among the major challenges faced by higher education students of Pakistan, according to Adnan and Kainat (2020).

On the other hand, in other countries students' perceptions of their new learning environment were positive. In South Korea, for example, Tae Eun Shima & Song Yi Leeb (2020) report that students expressed satisfaction with real-time emergency remote teaching because it made them feel as if they were taking one-on-one classes. They felt that remote learning actually helped them with their academic achievement due to a number of reasons including the fact that they could repeatedly review recorded class videos as well as focus better studying alone. In a similar vein, in a study of dentistry students in Poland (see Nijakowski et al., 2021), the majority of the surveyed students indicated that their learning efficiency increased during the pandemic. Additionally, they declared that the quality of subject teaching increased in comparison to the pre-pandemic period. They rated blended learning very highly, and most students stated that they would like to continue this form of education even after the COVID-19 pandemic has ended.

In Greece, a series of surveys were carried out with students of various departments of the University of Patras (see Karalis & Raikou, 2020; Karalis & Raikou, 2021; Kamarianos et al., 2020; Charissi et al., 2020) and the Democritus University of Thrace (Raikou et al., 2020) regarding their attitudes towards ERT and online learning. In all these studies, students expressed their satisfaction with the quick transition and the quality of online teaching. The majority of students reported feeling joy, pleasure and comfort about the new way of online education, while they also acknowledged the fact that they participated more in online classes, the content of the course was understandable and attendance was easy, the new mode of teaching was interesting, participation in class was great and communication with the teacher was at a satisfactory level. Most of the students did not have any difficulty in switching to online teaching, while they were very open to learn the new required skills and make new experiences. The only drawback reported by students was the lack of social interaction especially with their peers.

Thus on a global level, university students' responses to ERT and the shift to online learning have not been unanimously positive. Differences may be attributed to lack of or restricted access to technical infrastructure, lack of experience with pedagogies for distance learning, university instructors' competences, lack of digital skills and the requirements of specific fields of study. In Greece studies of university students' responses and attitudes to online learning in an ERT situation have been very few and have mainly been conducted by academics from the University of Patras. This study aims to contribute to the discussion of the experiences and attitudes of university students towards this 'emergency transition' to remote learning in Greece which until recently due to bureaucratic restrictions had limited experience in online education.

THE RISE OF BLENDED LEARING AND FLIPPED CLASSROOMS IN HEIS DURING THE COVID PANDEMIC

Blended learning and the flipped classroom methodology, was perhaps the most popular and effective methodology adopted for distance learning at HEIS around the world during the lockdown (Collado-Valero et al., 2021; Gopalan et al., 2021; Leong & González-Gómez, 2021; Latorre-Cosculluela et al., 2020). Although work on blended learning and the flipped classroom methodology is not new since studies on the effectiveness of blended learning appeared at least a decade ago (see Butler-Velegol, 2015; Baepler et al., 2014), during the covid pandemic blended learning became not only one of the best methodological options for HEIs but also one of the few alternatives (Collado-Valero et al., 2021).

Generally, blended learning refers to the integration of online teaching activities with traditional face-to-face class activities in a planned, systematic manner (Boelens et al., 2017). Blended learning combines online delivery of educational content with live instruction creating an interactively meaningful learning environment which allows for personalized learning and differentiated instruction (Kaur, 2013). According to Nahar & Chowdhury (2019) the implementation of blended learning tools in higher education institutions can result in significant improvements in the effectiveness, reach and cost of providing education in comparison to traditional learning approaches. These improvements can be so profound that they have the potential to change the overall competitiveness of the entire organization.

One type, or else, the offspring, of blended learning is the flipped classroom (Tang et al., 2020). According to Abeysekeraa & Dawson (2015) the flipped classroom can be defined "as a set of pedagogical approaches that: (1) move most information-transmission teaching out of class, (2) use class time for learning activities that are active and social and (3) require students to complete pre- and/or post-class activities to fully benefit from in-class work" (p. 3). The flipped classroom is considered an active educational methodology based on principles of cognitive constructivism and linked to Project-Based and Problem-Based Learning (Collado-Valero et al., 2021). The traditional classroom paradigm is redesigned (or inverted) with the flipped classroom since students learn course content outside the classroom through instructional online videos prepared by the instructor, slides and other teaching resources on online educational platforms while in-class time is used for active problem based learning, discussion of deeper issues, building conceptual understanding, collaborative tasks and practice activities that require students to engage concepts at a higher level in a group setting (Blair et al., 2016; Campillo-Ferrer & Miralles-Martínez, 2021; Latorre-Cosculluela et al., 2020; Tang et al., 2020). In- class time gives the instructor the opportunity to answer student questions, clarify issues and misunderstandings of course content, give feedback and re-examine key concepts (Baepler et al., 2014). According to Butler et al. (2015) within the flipped classroom model, in class time results in increased teacher-student and student-student interaction which can provide opportunities to students to develop higher order cognitive skills and to focus on applying and analyzing rather than memorizing material. Moreover, watching online videos outside class time allows students to absorb content in their own time and at their own convenience and pace allowing them to re-watch portions that were unclear to them (Butler et al., 2015) giving them, at the same time, a measure of control over their own learning (Blair et al., 2016).

A variation of the flipped classroom which involves replacing face to face class time with a tool of synchronous education is the remote flipped classroom (see Karalis & Raikou, 2021), a variation that was used in many HEIs worldwide during lockdown (Collado-Valero et al., 2021; Campillo-Ferrer & Miralles-Martínez, 2021; Haftador et al., 2021; Jeong & González-Gómez, 2021; Gopalan et al., 2021; Latorre-Cosculluela et al., 2020; Tang et al., 2020). In a remote flipped classroom, students study the lecture content out of class time (through videolectures, streaming videos, articles, multimedia based learning materials) and then meet with the instructor online through videoconferencing platforms (e.g. zoom, webex, Microsoft teams, etc.) and carry out activities aiming at consolidating, refining and extending their understanding of the lecture content. It should be stressed at this point that simply uploading material on a repository for remote study does not constitute a remote flipped classroom. Students must be explicitly guided into how to study and explore the material and must be assigned tasks to complete which encourage active and participatory learning. These tasks can be completed before the synchronous session with the instructor and their responses to the tasks can be discussed during the synchronous sessions. Alternatively, during the synchronous session students can be given collaborative or even collaborative jigsaw tasks tasks to complete (Haftador et al., 2021). According to Karalis and Raikou (2021) "through this intervention, not only a better understanding of the course content is sought, but also the development of collateral skills on the part of the students (indicatively: critical thinking, argumentation, collaboration, creativity)" (p. 23). Remote flipped classroom was the educational model adopted in the design of the course presented in this paper.

The flipped classroom model has been applied in various disciplines (e.g. science, technology, engineering, education, physiology) with success and research has shown promising results as regards its positive effects on student retention, student engagement and motivation, content understanding, the development of students' oral skills and digitals skills and student-teacher interaction (Baepler et al., 2014; Love et al., 2014; McLean et al., 2016). Means et al's (2013) review of empirical studies on online learning revealed that students in flipped classrooms achieve better learning outcomes than in traditional face to face classes and that student satisfaction with blended learning classes tends to be higher than in traditional classes. Latorre-Cosculluela et al's (2020) survey of 376 students from higher education of a Spanish University Institution who experienced the flipped classroom methodology during the academic year 2019-2020 revealed students' favorable appreciation regarding the benefits of the Flipped Classroom for developing skills for the 21st century (e.g. collaboration, communication, citizenship, critical thinking).

As far as the use of the flipped classroom in HEIs during the pandemic is concerned, Tang et al's (2020) survey of undergraduate engineering students at Chengdu University of Information Technology found that although students were dissatisfied with online learning and especially the lack of communication with the instructor, the combined model of online teaching with flipped classroom led to improved student learning outcomes and attention and more positive evaluation of courses by students. Campillo-Ferrer and Miralles-Martínez's (2021) study involved undergraduate students of primary education at the University of Murcia, Spain who had experienced flipped classroom model during the pandemic in the academic year 20/21. Their survey focused on students' self-perceived motivation and learning under the flipped classroom mode. Their data showed a positive evaluation of the approach by students, both in reported motivation and perception of learning. Gopalan et al. (2021) focused on graduate students of a physiology course who had experienced the remote flipped classroom model and their study set out to measure student perception of their adjustment to the new flipped classroom format, their confidence in completing the course successfully, and the usefulness of assessments and assignments in the remote flipped classroom. Results revealed that the flipped classroom model positively impacted student success, student adjustment to the remote teaching method increased significantly toward the end of the semester as did their confidence in completing the course in this teaching mode. Moreover, students expressed a positive response to the synchronous computerized exams and the formative group and individual assessments.

In one of the very few studies of the effect of the flipped classroom model in higher education in Greece, Karalis and Raikou (2021) found that undergraduate students at the University of Patras evaluated this mode of the course as approximately 30% better in comparison to the traditional one and they expressed clearly more positive views about it and reported that they spent more time studying the material compared to the time spent during a traditional lecture. According to Karalis and Raikou (2021) "all the elements of the remote flipped classroom (indicatively: better allocation of time, enhancement of cooperativeness, active participation, interaction among students and between students and instructors, opportunity to develop critical thinking) were considered as functional and were positively rated by the students'' (p. 34).

Given the opportunity that the pandemic granted university instructors in Greece to experiment with online methodologies and the promising results of the flipped classroom model in various HEIs around the world, the authors of this paper decided to carefully plan, redesign and adjust the content of a compulsory undergraduate course in the Department of English Language and Literature of the National and Kapodistrian University of Athens as a blended course with elements of a remote flipped classroom and investigate students' degree of satisfaction with the flipped classroom model and online learning more generally.

REDESIGNING THE APPLIED LINGUISTICS COURSE AS A BLENDED COURSE WITH ELEMENTS OF A REMOTE FLIPPED CLASSROOM

Applied Linguistics to Foreign Language Teaching and Learning is a core course in the undergraduate programme of studies of the Department of English Language and Literature of the National and Kapodistrian University of Athens. It is an essential component of the Pedagogic and Teaching Competence Programme (PPDE) that our Department offers. It is a degree requirement course and therefore compulsory for all undergraduate students as it is intended to provide them with qualifications to teach English as a 'foreign' or additional language.

The course is offered in the winter semester of each academic year to 3rd year students (around 300 students) who are divided into 3 sections by alphabetical order and taught by different instructors on the basis of a common curriculum and syllabus. Pre COVID, the course was delivered (as all courses in the Greek university) face to face in amphitheatres for three hours a week (the duration of the semester is 13 weeks) while the course was accompanied by an e-class (which is the university's learning management system), which serves as a bank of information for courses. More specifically, on the e-class platform students can access all the materials used during the face to face lectures (powerpoints, readings on the topic of sessions, multimedia resources and tasksheets). Through the e-class, announcements can be made (which are automatically sent to all registered students), students can send messages to course instructors while there is a separate section in which students can upload their assignments or homework tasks. The tasksheets developed for each lecture contained a number of practical tasks which served to link theory with practice and were completed after the lecture for homework. It should be noted that student attendance in university lectures in Greece is not compulsory. Students usually attend lectures at the beginning of the semester fairly systematically but attendance gradually dwindles as the semester proceeds.

The first lockdown (March 2020 to June 2020) took us all by surprise and instructors tried to transfer the usual face to face lectures via some sort of teleconferencing platform (zoom, Webex, BBB, Microsoft teams). In other words, during the ERT situation having absolutely no time to think about and plan for alternative online pedagogies instead of delivering lectures face to face, we delivered them face to screen. Being informed during the summer break of the almost certain second lockdown during the winter semester as a result of the second wave of the pandemic, the authors of this paper decided to carefully plan, redesign and adjust the content of the Applied Linguistics course (offered in the winter semester) as a blended course with elements of a remote flipped classroom. Our decision to transform the course for blended learning following the principles of a flipped classroom was based on a number of reasons. Firstly, we wanted to completely avoid using synchronous class time for delivering a rather "monotonous" lecture in which the instructor would simply speak in front of screen without knowing if and to what extent students were actually paying attention. Secondly, we wanted to provide students with a more participatory, active and meaningful learning experience while physically remote from each other. Thirdly, we wanted to experiment with a different form on online learning in order to judge its potential for implementation even after the end of the pandemic. The findings may be useful for a long-term appreciation of the knowledge and skills necessary for higher education students, and teacher students in particular, in order to be better prepared to deal with similar crisis situations in the following years.

In redesigning the course, we undertook an extensive literature review of online learning, blended learning and remote flipped classrooms. We took into serious account and tried to apply the principles of effective online learning (Cable & Cheung, 2017) and the eight instructional practices that are prominent in the higher education practitioner literature as contributors to more effective teaching and learning online (see Means & Neisler, 2021, p. 19). Namely,

1. including assignments that ask students to express what they have learned and what they still need to learn
2. Breaking up class activities into shorter pieces than in an in-person course
3. Administering frequent quizzes or other assessments techniques
4. Delivering live sessions in which students can ask questions and participate in discussions
5. Meeting in breakout groups during a live class
6. Sending personal messages to individual students about how they are doing in the course or making sure they can access course materials
7. Using real-world examples to illustrate course content
8. Working on group projects separately from the course meetings

Thus, for the purposes of our course, we decided to follow the remote flipped classroom model combining synchronous online sessions via the zoom platform with asynchronous sessions. In this new set up, the e-class for the course acted as the main "hub". The e-class for the course was organized week by week. Each week focused on a different topic and was made "visible" to students at the beginning of each week (Monday). Thus every Monday students were sent an announcement informing them about the new topic and the main learning outcomes. They were also given instructions on how to study asynchronously. By clicking on the topic students were presented with a videolecture link, the accompanying tasksheet, readings related to the topic and extra online resources for further study of the topic. The e-class was also used as a repository of learning resources and as a means of direct communication with students (announcements, guidelines on how to study the materials and social messages).

The purpose of the tasksheet accompanying each course topic was to enable in-depth comprehension of course content and to highlight the link between theory and practice. It consisted of various tasks (multiple matching and true-false tasks for assessing student comprehension of terms and principles presented in the videolecture, video observation tasks in which students viewed an extract of a videotaped classroom and answered related questions, samples of textbook materials which students were asked to analyse and evaluate on the basis of principles presented in the videolecture). The videotaped lectures were from the free open e-course programmes of our Department. In addition, two standalone e-modules (focusing on e-learning theories and 21st century education principles) were designed and offered. These modules contained various multimedia resources (e.g. powerpoint presentations, extracts from video-taped conference talks, videos from YouTube, links to relevant online resources, etc.) organized in a clear learning path (students were guided on what to view and study step by step). As students moved through the steps of the learning path (processing the information at every step) they were required to do specific tasks. Their responses to the tasks were also discussed during our synchronous online sessions.

Every two asynchronous sessions a synchronous online session was also delivered. The synchronous online 3-hour session always started with a discussion of the situation created by the pandemic and a discussion about students' well-being (how they were coping, what issues they faced, their health). The online sychronous sessions did not involve any lecturing in the traditional form but aimed at discussing student answers to the tasksheets, responding to student queries and discussing with students issues that arose during the completion of tasks while interacting with and supporting them. Students were also involved in collaborative practical tasks carried out in breakout rooms. The syllabus for the course was organized as shown in Table 1.

Throughout the term students were free to send e-mails to the instructors regarding any issues they faced while processing the content of the course and its structure. Student emails were responded to immediately.

One point worth highlighting before moving to the student evaluation of the course, is that student participation in synchronous sessions was overwhelming compared to their participation in face to face classes. Not only did the vast majority of students complete the assigned tasksheets but they also participated actively during the online sessions using the chat box mainly for expressing opinions and asking questions. Another important point to highlight before proceeding to students' evaluation of the course, is that, according to online discussions with students, the vast majority (over 80%) had no prior experience with online learning prior to the pandemic.

Since this setup offered a range of different online learning experiences to our students which they were not familiar with before the pandemic, an evaluation of students' attitudes and response to these new forms of learning was deemed necessary.

Table 1.

UNIT	TOPIC	MODE OF DELIVERY
1	**Introduction to the PPDE programme - Introduction to the course** (what is applied linguistics, how does it relate to other language related disciplines, what are the main concerns/areas of study of applied linguistics, what are the aims and objectives of this course)	Synchronous
2	**Theories of language** (what is a language theory, what is structuralism, what is functionalism, how have they affected language teaching)	Synchronous
3	**Competence-performance and Communicative competence** (what is proficiency and competence in a language, origins of communicative competence and its effect on language teaching, models of communicative competence, declarative and procedural knowledge)	Asynchronous (videolecture)
4	**Theories of Language Learning** what is behaviourism and what are its main principles, what is cognitivism, constructivism and interactionism, what are their main principles, how have they affected language teaching practices)	Asynchronous (videolecture)
	End of week 4- discussion of tasksheets	Synchronous
5	**E-learning theories** (review of main e-learning theories and of the ways they have affected foreign language education, practical applications)	Online module
6	**The good language learner and factors affecting the learning process** (individual differences in language learning, personality and cognitive variables, attitudes and motivation, learning strategies, learner autonomy, multiple intelligences	Asynchronous (videolecture)
	End of week 6- discussion of tasksheets	Synchronous
7	**An overview of methods and approaches** (what is a method and an approach, what are the components of a method, how they relate to theories of language and theories of language learning and language teaching, a historical account of different methods and approaches)	Asynchronous (videolecture)
8	**Curriculum and syllabus** (what is a curriculum, what is a syllabus, what is the Integrated Foreign Languages curriculum, steps in designing a language course)	Asynchronous (videolecture)
	End of week 8 – discussion of tasksheets	synchronous
9	**Examples of recent methods: Communicative language teaching and task based language teaching** what is a communicative syllabus, what are the main principles of the communicative approach and how does it differ from audiolingualism, what are the main principles of task based language teaching, what is a task, how do we design a task based lesson, what is intercultural competence)	Asynchronous (videolecture)
10	**Council of Europe work in modern foreign language learning** (language learning policies of the CoE and multilingualism, what is the CEFR, what is the ELP)	synchronous
	End of week 10- discussion of tasksheets	synchronous
11	**21st century language education: Towards a new paradigm** (communication and globalization in the 21st century, features of 21st century education, multimodality and multiliteracies	Online module
12	**Language education for multilingualism**	Asynchronous (videolecture)
13	**Discussion of tasksheets (21st century language education and multilingualism)** **Course overview/evaluation, Preparation for the final exam**	synchronous

RESEARCH METHODOLOGY

In order to investigate students' attitudes towards the new form of instruction adopted in the course of Applied Linguistics and their attitudes towards online learning more generally a detailed course evaluation questionnaire was designed and electronically administered via Google Forms to all students upon completion of the course. The questionnaire was an adaptation of the one administered by Tsagari et al. in March 2020. The research questions explored via the questionnaire were:

1. How did university students, following the applied linguistics course, respond to the transition from face-to-face to online lessons?
2. What were the attitudes of university students towards the blended learning course mode adopted?

In the first part of the questionnaire students were asked to express, based on a 5-point Likert scale, their level of satisfaction as regards the overall course aims & objectives, the content of weekly sessions, the organization and appropriacy of course material, the usefulness of weekly tasksheets and the usefulness of synchronous online sessions alongside the asynchronous ones. In the second part of the questionnaire students were asked to provide information about their online learning experiences before the pandemic by expressing their views on the differences and similarities between face-to-face and online lessons, attitudes towards online lessons (level of satisfaction, engagement, motivation, etc.), perceived level of personal involvement during synchronous sessions, positive and negative aspects of the blended course, etc. In order to ensure that the undertaken study was "ethically and morally acceptable" and did not breach participants' privacy rights (Dörnyei, 2007, p. 108), the anonymity and confidentiality of all participants was guaranteed since no question in the questionnaire asked for students' personal details (name, surname, student i.d. number). Respondents were also clearly informed about the voluntary nature of their participation and were welcomed to withdraw at any point if they felt uncomfortable or did not wish to continue with the completion of the questionnaire while a commitment was made by the researchers that collected data would be used solely for the purposes of research.

In designing the questionnaire every effort was made to make the items as meaningful to the respondents as possible, since experience and research in the field of questionnaire design have shown that if items are interesting and clearly relevant to the study, the response rate will increase (Gall et al., 2007, p. 432). Additionally, negative and double-barreled questions were avoided, since they could confuse respondents, who might agree with one aspect of the question but disagree with another (Gall et al., 2007, p. 430; Nachmias & Nachmias, 2007, p. 225). In order to deter respondents from following a response set, both positive and negative items were included (Wiersma, 2008, p. 174; Gall et al., 2007, p. 430). Finally, an effort was made to avoid biased or leading questions for the respondents not to be given any hints as to the type of answer most preferred or anticipated by the researchers (Brown & Rodgers, 2002, p. 143; Cohen et al., 2007, p. 248; Denscombe, 2007, p. 163).

FINDINGS: STUDENT RESPONSES TO THE QUESTIONNAIRE

The number of students enrolled in the course was 250. The number of students who responded to the questionnaire was 165 representing a 66% response rate. Collected data were subjected to statistical analysis using IBM SPSS 27.0.2 statistical package. Frequency distributions were calculated while all percentages are reported as valid percentages with missing data excluded. As Wiersma (2008, p. 198) explains, survey results typically include this kind of descriptive information, since such an approach enables the researcher to provide general information about respondents' central tendency when answering each question, and further show how responses disperse around the center. Due to the length limitations of the present chapter, and the amount of findings as regards each level of the rating scale (1-5), a decision was inevitably made to include a selection of research findings, focusing on the extreme ends of the scale, that is, Strongly disagree/Disagree (1-2) or Agree/Strongly agree (4-5).

The first part of the questionnaire (questions 1-10) focused on students' degree of satisfaction with the aims and content of the course and the way it was organized (see Table 1). In essence, these questions aim to evaluate students' response to the flipped classroom model that was adopted for the first time in this course. As can be seen in Table 1 below, students' response to the flipped classroom model was overwhelmingly positive since 83.6% of the respondents Agreed/Strongly agreed with the fact that the course aims and objectives were clear and straightforward while 85.4% and 86.4% respectively stated that the content of each weekly session met the aims and objectives of the course and that the course material (video-lectures, weekly tasksheets, additional multi-modal resources, etc.) was well-organized. As far as the usefulness of the synchronous sessions is concerned, the majority of students (78.8%) believed that these sessions and the clarifications provided facilitated their comprehension of course content.

Table 2. University students' beliefs about the course content

PART A: COURSE CONTENT				
(1: Strongly disagree-5: Strongly Agree)	1-2	3	4	5
1. The course aims and objectives were clear & straightforward.	2.4%	13.9%	22.1%	61.5%
2. The content of each weekly session met the aims and objectives of the course.	1.8%	12.7%	22.7%	62.7%
3. The course material (video-lectures, weekly tasksheets, additional multi-modal resources, etc.) was well-organized.	3.8%	9.8%	22.4%	64.0%
4. The course material (video-lectures, weekly tasksheets, additional multi-modal resources, etc.) facilitated the comprehension of course content.	5.5%	16.7%	18.2%	59.6%
5. In the synchronous online sessions useful clarifications on the course content were provided.	3.6%	17.6%	22.8%	56.0%
6. The synchronous online sessions helped me to better understand and process the course content.	6.2	17.0%	27.3%	49.5%

The second part of the questionnaire sought to investigate student responses to online learning more generally. It should be noted at this point, that the vast majority of courses that students participated in during the winter term consisted of 3hour lectures delivered through teleconferencing platforms.

As can be seen in Table 2 below, although the majority of students (78,1%) found the blended learning model adopted in the Applied Linguistics course interesting (see question 3), their experience of online learning during the lockdown period was not so positive. The vast majority of students (88.5%) stated that they made conscious efforts to learn as effectively as possible during the pandemic and most students (67,3%) felt confident in their ability to learn in an online distance learning environment. The majority (70.3%) also stated that attending online classes was their main priority and slightly fewer students (67,3%) felt that they performed well in their online classes. Although they enjoyed (70%) the flexibility offered by online learning, the convenience offered by videotaped lectures (70,9%) allowing them to process information at their own pace, and the usefulness of asking questions (which they would not feel comfortable asking in a face to face session) through the chat box (66,1%), more than half of the students (58,2%) stated that they still prefer face-to-face teaching to online teaching while around a quarter of the students (26,1%) were undecided as to which mode they preferred more. In fact, just over half of the students (53.9%) would rather do something else than to attend online classes. The majority of students (72.1%) felt overloaded with coursework during the ERT situation, they believed (67.3%) that the shift to online teaching impacted their academic progress and felt (63.7%) isolated from their classmates. Regarding students' degree of engagement in the online learning process, students were divided. Slightly over one third of the students (36.9%) felt disengaged while the other third (38.7%) felt engaged. The majority of students (65.8%) were also very concerned with the evaluation of their performance during the ERT situation while more than half of the students (57,8%) found it difficult to concentrate during online classes. For 41.8% of the students their concentration was impeded by distractions in their home environment. Their difficulty in concentrating may also be due to the fact that the majority (70.9%) acknowledged multitasking during the online lectures.

Table 3. University students' attitudes towards Online Learning

PART B: ONLINE LEARNING EXPERIENCES					
(1: Strongly disagree-5: Strongly Agree)	1	2	3	4	5
1. I am trying my best to learn effectively during the pandemic.	1.8%	2.4%	7.3%	30.9%	57.6%
2. I prefer the face-to-face teaching format to the remote one	4.2%	11.5%	26.1%	18.8%	39.3%
3. The blended course was interesting.	4.8%	10.3%	6.7%	43.6%	34.5%
4. I feel confident in my ability to learn remotely.	3.6%	10.9%	18.2%	41.2%	26.1%
5. I have been doing well in the course(s) this semester.	1.2%	2.4%	31.5%	43.6%	21.2%
6. I enjoy the more flexible class time during online learning.	6.1%	3.6%	20.0%	36.4%	33.9%
7. I appreciate the ability to return to the recorded lecture material and to go through it at my own pace	3.0%	5.5%	20.6%	33.3%	37.6%
8. The chat option in the platform allows me to ask questions which I would not be comfortable asking in front of the whole class.	8.5%	8.5%	17.0%	36.4%	29.7%
9. I feel disengaged in the remote/distance learning.	13.9%	24.8%	24.2%	23.6%	13.3%
10. My classes are not my highest priority these days.	37.6%	32.7%	13.3%	6.1%	10.3%
11. I feel that I have been left behind by the shift to remote learning.	3.6%	10.9%	18.2%	41.2%	26.1%
12. I would rather do anything else than attend online classes.	29.7%	24.2%	19.4%	16.4%	10.3%
13. I sometimes multitask during the online classes.	10.9%	6.1%	12.1%	46.1%	24.8%
14. I am feeling overloaded with coursework during the pandemic.	4.2%	8.5%	15.2%	27.3%	44.8%
15. I am unable to concentrate on online classes because of my home situation (e.g. other people around, childcare, family care, etc.).	18.2%	19.4%	20.6%	24.2%	17.6%
16. I feel physically isolated from my classmates.	14.5%	7.3%	14.5%	15.2%	48.5%
17. Visual contact with my teacher and classmates improves my mood.	4.2%	12.1%	23.0%	24.8%	32.1%
18. I worry how my activity during online classes and my performance will be evaluated.	17.0%	27.3%	-	28.5%	27.3%
19. I find it difficult to concentrate during the online classes.	21.2%	21.2%	-	30.9%	26.7%

DISCUSSION OF RESULTS

The results of students' evaluation of the course, and thus of the flipped classroom model, were overwhelmingly positive. The vast majority stated that they found the blended model interesting, they enjoyed the pre-recorded lectures, they found the chat box useful for asking questions they would not otherwise ask in a face to face session, they found the synchronous sessions useful in clarifying concepts and understanding course content. These findings are in accord with other studies that investigated university students' perceptions of the flipped classroom model during the pandemic (see Campillo-Ferrer & Miralles-Martínez, 2021; Gopalan et al., 2021; Tang et al., 2020) and are similar to students' evaluation of the flipped classroom model at the University of Patras in Greece (see Karalis & Raikou, 2021). In general, our students evaluation of the flipped classroom model coincide with Means et al's (2013) findings based on a review of empirical studies on online learning that student satisfaction with blended learning classes tends to be higher than in traditional classes.

However, our students did not express a high degree of satisfaction with online learning at university more generally. Although they enjoyed the flexibility offered by online learning, more than half of our students preferred the face to face format to the online one, they found it difficult to concentrate during the online classes (Agree/Strongly agree: 57.6%), they felt that they had been left behind by the shift to remote teaching (Agree/Strongly agree: 67.3%), while being physically isolated from their classmates (Agree/Strongly agree: 63.7%) and overloaded with coursework (Agree/Strongly agree: 72.1%). Moreover, the majority (Agree/Strongly agree: 65.8%) were concerned with the evaluation of their performance during the pandemic and slightly just over one third of our students felt engaged in the online learning process. Contrary to the studies of student perceptions of online learning in other Greek universities (see Charissi et al., 2020; Karalis & Raikou, 2021; Karalis & Raikou, 2020; Kamarianos et al., 2020), our student perceptions seem to coincide more with the results of global studies of students' response to online learning at universities (see Aboagye et al., 2020; Aristovnik et al., 2020) highlighting difficulties in concentration, engagement, social interactions with other students and in dealing with excessive workloads. Such emotions could be partly attributed to the overall emotional pressure and sense of uncertainty experienced by most individuals during the pandemic alongside university students' limited to non-existing experience with online teaching practices in Greek tertiary education before the pandemic.

CONCLUSION

The sudden shift to online learning led to a re-evaluation of teaching practices that were previously taken for granted and unquestioned at least at the higher education level in Greece where most teaching is face to face and lecture based (see Raikou et al., 2020). The pandemic allowed us to see the online learning environment not as a store for course materials where no actual learning took place but as a learning space which can be engaging and enriching and can promote more active and meaningful learning. The pandemic also offered us an excellent opportunity to move towards digitization and introduce more innovative pedagogical approaches in higher education using digital tools.

Our study aimed at providing valuable insights into emergency remote teaching practices in Higher Education in Greece by investigating whether and to what extent the combination of synchronous and asynchronous teaching through the flipped classroom model enhanced student motivation and engagement and provided students with a meaningful and enjoyable learning experience in the midst of the COVID-19 pandemic.

Although our student response to fully online distance learning was not overwhelmingly positive, their response towards the flipped classroom model was. This points to the great potential that the flipped classroom model can have for breaking the traditional lecture based teaching mold in which students are passive recipients of information and introduce pedagogies that combine distance learning with face to face teaching. The introduction of the flipped classroom model does not entail an end to in-person learning but a reconfiguration of in-person elements of learning to maximize their benefits. The flipped classroom model can enhance student participation and interest, can lead to greater classroom interaction and more active learning which Andrews and colleagues (2011) define when "an instructor stops lecturing and students work on a question or task designed to help them understand a concept" (p. 394). The use of the flipped classroom model in Greek HEI does not depend so much on instructors' willingness to change since the rigidity of bureaucracy which is an endemic feature of Greek education constrains the ability to change. The introduction of more flexible modes of teaching and learning which combine distance learning with in person learning depends to great extent on the willingness of the Ministry of Education and Religious Affairs to allow university instructors more autonomy to experiment and decide on the most effective pedagogical approaches for their students. Upon returning to 'normality', in the winter semester of 2021 all universities in Greece opened and returned to traditional lecture based teaching. The General Secretary for Higher Education claimed that all forms of distance or online learning at Greek HEIs as illegal and warned that any classes that were carried out either online or at a distance would not be accepted as "taught" classes. As a result, our plans for experimenting with the flipped classroom model in this and other courses that we teach, were diminished.

REFERENCES

Abeysekeraa, L., & Dawson, Ph. (2015). Motivation and cognitive load in the flipped classroom: Definition, rationale and a call for research. *Higher Education Research & Development*, *34*(1), 1–14. doi :10.1080/07294360.2014.934336

Aboagye, E., Yawson, J. A., & Appiah, K. N. (2020). COVID-19 and E-Learning: The Challenges of Students in Tertiary Institutions. *Educational Research for Social Change*, *2*, 1–8.

Adnan, M., & Kainat, A. (2020). Online learning amid the COVID-19 pandemic: Students' perspectives. *Journal of Pedagogical Sociology and Psychology*, *2*(2), 45–51. doi:10.33902/JPSP.2020261309

Andrews, T., Leonard, M., Colgrove, C. A., & Kalinowski, S. (2011). Active Learning Not Associated with Student Learning in a Random Sample of College Biology Courses. *CBE Life Sciences Education*, *10*(4), 394–405. doi:10.1187/cbe.11-07-0061 PMID:22135373

Aristovnik, A., Keržic, D., Ravšelj, D., Tomaževic, N., & Umek, L. (2020). Impacts of the COVID-19 Pandemic on Life of Higher Education Students: A Global Perspective. *Sustainability*, *12*(20), 8438. doi:10.3390u12208438

Baepler, P., Walker, J. D., & Driessen, M. (2014). It's not about seat time: Blending, flipping and efficiency in active learning classrooms. *Computers & Education*, *78*, 227–236. doi:10.1016/j.compedu.2014.06.006

Blair, E., Maharaj, C., & Primus, S. (2016). Performance and perception in the flipped classroom. *Education and Information Technologies*, *21*(6), 1465–1482. doi:10.100710639-015-9393-5

Boelens, R., De Wever, B., & Voet, M. (2017). Four key challenges to the design of blended learning: A systematic literature review. *Educational Research Review*, *22*, 1–18. doi:10.1016/j.edurev.2017.06.001

Bozkurt, A., Jung, I., Xiao, J., & Vladimirschi, V., Schuwer. R., Egorov, G., Lambert, S. R., Al-Freih, M., Pete, J., Olcott, D., Rodes, V., Aranciaga, I., Bali, M., Alvarez, Jr. A., Roberts, J., Pazurek, A., Raffaghelli, J. E., Panagiotou, N., Perrine de Coëtlogon, Shahadu, S., … Paskevicius, M. (2020). A global outlook to the interruption of education due to COVID-19 Pandemic: Navigating in a time of uncertainty and crisis. *Asian Journal of Distance Education*, *15*, 1–126.

Bozkurt, A., & Sharma, R. C. (2020). Emergency remote teaching in a time of global crisis due to CoronaVirus pandemic. *Asian Journal of Distance Education*, *15*, i–vi.

Brown, J., & Rodgers, T. (2002). *Doing Second Language Research*. Oxford University Press.

Butler-Velegol, S., Zappe, S. E., & Mahoney, E. (2015). The evolution of a flipped classroom: Evidence based recommendations. *Advances in Engineering Education*, 1–37.

Cable, J., & Cheung, C. (2017). Eight Principles of Effective Online Teaching: A Decade-Long Lessons Learned in Project Management Education. *PM World Journal*, *6*, 1–16.

Campillo-Ferrer, J.M. & Miralles-Martínez, P. (2021). Effectiveness of the flipped classroom model on students' self-reported motivation and learning during the COVID-19 pandemic. *Humanities and Social Sciences Communications*, 1-9.

Charissi, A., Tympa, E., & Karavida, V. (2020). Impact of the COVID-19 disruption on university students' perceptions and behavior. *European Journal of Education Studies*, *7*(11), 222–238. doi:10.46827/ejes.v7i11.3348

Cohen, L., Manion, L., & Morrison, K. (2007). *Research Methods in Education* (6th ed.). RoutledgeFalmer. doi:10.4324/9780203029053

Collado-Valero, J., Rodríguez-Infante, G., Romero-González, M., Gamboa-Ternero, S., Navarro-Soria, I., & Lavigne-Cerván, R. (2021). Flipped Classroom: Active Methodology for Sustainable Learning in Higher Education during Social Distancing Due to COVID-19. *Sustainability*, *13*(10), 5336. doi:10.3390u13105336

Coman, C., Tîru, L. G., Meses an-Schmitz, L., Stanciu, C., & Bularca, M. C. (2020). Online Teaching and Learning in Higher Education during the Coronavirus Pandemic: Students' Perspective. *Sustainability*, *12*(24), 10367. doi:10.3390u122410367

Denscombe, M. (2007). *The Good Research Guide*. Open University Press.

Dörnyei, Z. (2007). *Research Methods in Applied Linguistics: Quantitative, Qualitative, and Mixed Methodologies*. Oxford University Press.

European Universities Association. (2020). *European higher education in the Covid-19 crisis*. Available online at: https://eua.eu/downloads/publications/briefing_european%20higher%20education%20in%20the%20covid-19%20crisis.pdf

Gall, M., Borg, W., & Gall, J. (2007). *Educational Research: An Introduction* (8th ed.). Allyn & Bacon.

Gopalan, C., Butts-Wilmsmeyer, C., & Moran, V. (2021). Virtual flipped teaching during the COVID-19 pandemic. *Advances in Physiology Education, 45*(4), 670–678. doi:10.1152/advan.00061.2021 PMID:34498940

Haftador, A. M., Shirazi, F., & Mohebbi, Z. (2021). Online class or flipped-jigsaw learning? Which one promotes academic motivation during the COVID-19 pandemic? *BMC Medical Education, 21*(1), 499. doi:10.118612909-021-02929-9 PMID:34548075

Hodges, C., Moore, S., Lockee, B., Trust, T., & Bond, A. (2020). *The Difference between Emergency Remote Teaching and Online Learning*. Available online at: https://er.educause.edu/articles/2020/3/the-difference-between-emergency-remote-teaching-andonline-learning

International Association of Universities (2020). *Regional/National Perspectives on the Impact of COVID-19 on Higher Education*. Available online at: iau_covid-19_regional_perspectives_on_the_impact_of_covid-19_on_he_july_2020_.pdf

Irish National Digital Experience (INDEx) Survey: Findings from students and staff who teach in higher education. (2020). National Forum for the Enhancement of Teaching and Learning in Higher Education.

Jeong, J. S., & González-Gómez, D. (2021). A STEM Course Analysis During COVID-19: A Comparison Study in Performance and Affective Domain of PSTs Between F2F and F2S Flipped Classroom. *Frontiers in Psychology, 12*, 669855. doi:10.3389/fpsyg.2021.669855 PMID:34447329

Kamarianos, I., Adamopoulou, A., Lambropoulos, H., & Stamelos, G. (2020). Towards an understanding of university students' response in times of pandemic crisis. *European Journal of education. Studies, 7*, 20–40.

Karalis, Th., & Raikou, N. (2020). Teaching at the Times of COVID-19: Inferences and Implications for Higher Education Pedagogy. *International Journal of Academic Research in Business & Social Sciences, 10*(5), 479–493. doi:10.6007/IJARBSS/v10-i5/7219

Karalis, Th., & Raikou, N. (2021). Flipping the classroom remotely: Implementation of a flipped classroom course in higher education during the COVID-19 pandemic. *European Journal of Open Education and E-Learning Studies, 6*(2), 21–38. doi:10.46827/ejoe.v6i2.3809

Kaur, M. (2013). Blended Learning- its challenges and future. *Procedia: Social and Behavioral Sciences, 93*, 612–617. doi:10.1016/j.sbspro.2013.09.248

Latorre-Cosculluela, C., Suarez, C., Quiroga, S., Sobradiel-Sierra, N., Lozano-Blasco, R., & Rodríguez-Martínez, A. (2020). Flipped Classroom model before and during COVID-19: Using technology to develop 21st century skills. *Interactive Technology and Smart Education, 18*(2), 189–204. doi:10.1108/ITSE-08-2020-0137

Love, B., Hodge, A., Grandgenett, N., & Swift, A. W. (2014). Student learning and perceptions in a flipped linear algebra course. *International Journal of Mathematical Education in Science and Technology, 45*(3), 317–324. doi:10.1080/0020739X.2013.822582

Marinoni, G., van't Land, H. & Jensen, T. (2020). *The Impact of COVID-19 on higher education around the world.* IAU Global Survey Report. Available online at: iau_covid19_and_he_survey_report_final_may_2020.pdf

McLean, S., Attardi, S. M., Faden, L., & Goldszmidt, M. (2016). Flipped classrooms and student learning: Not just surface gains. *Advances in Physiology Education, 40*(1), 47–55. doi:10.1152/advan.00098.2015 PMID:26847257

Means, B., & Neisler, J. (2021). Teaching and Learning in the Time of COVID: The Student Perspective. *Online Learning Journal, 25*(1), 8–27. doi:10.24059/olj.v25i1.2496

Moore, M. G. (1997). Theory of transactional distance. In D. Keegan (Ed.), *Theoretical principles of distance education* (pp. 22–38). Routlege.

Nachmias, C., & Nachmias, D. (2007). *Research Methods in the Social Sciences* (7th ed.). Worth Publishers.

Nahar, K., & Chowdhury, R. (2019). Effectiveness of flipped classroom model in distance learning. *Proceedings of the AAEE2019 Conference.*

Nijakowski, N., Lehmann, A., Zdrojewski, J., Nowak, M., & Surdacka, A. (2021). The Effectiveness of the Blended Learning in Conservative Dentistry with Endodontics on the Basis of the Survey among 4th-Year Students during the COVID-19 Pandemic. *International Journal of Environmental Research and Public Health, 18*, 1–15.

OECD Policy Responses to Coronavirus (COVID-19). (2020). *Education responses to COVID-19: Embracing digital learning and online collaboration.* Available online at: https://www.oecd.org/coronavirus/policy-responses/education-responses-to-covid-19-embracing-digital-learning-and-online-collaboration-d75eb0e8/

Oppenheim, A. (2001). *Questionnaire design, interviewing and attitude measurement* (4th ed.). Continuum.

Panitsides, E. A., & Karapistola, A. (2020 in press). Enhancing the role of the Hellenic Open University as a Lifelong Learning Organization: Crossing the Rubicon into the e-learning era. In E. Sengupta, P. Blessinger, & M. Makhanya (Eds.), *Humanizing Higher Education: The Role of Technology*. Emerald.

Plota, D., & Karalis, T. (2019). Organization and implementation of a Flipped Classroom course in the Greek University context. *Educational Journal of the University of Patras UNESCO Chair, 6*, 53–61.

Raikou, N., Kaltsidis, Ch., Kedraka, K., & Karalis, Th. (2020). Teaching in Times of COVID-19 Pandemic in Two Peripheral Greek Universities: Lessons Learned from Students' Experiences and Opinions. *Research Journal of Education, 6*, 135–143.

Rakitzi, K., Botsoglou, K., & Roussakis, Y. (2020). Applying the Flipped Classroom Model to Higher Education: Students "take the floor". *Open Education, 16*, 132–144.

Shima, T. E., & Song, Y. L. (2020). College students' experience of emergency remote teaching due to COVID19. *Children and Youth Services Review, 119*, 1–7.

Studies in Distance Education. (1997). Theory of transactional distance. In D. Keegan (Ed.), Theoretical principles of distance education (pp. 22-38). Routledge.

Studies in Distance Education. (2013). The effectiveness of online and blended learning: A meta-analysis of the empirical literature. *Teachers College Record, 115*, 1–47.

Tang, T., Abuhmaid, A. M., Olaimat, M., Oudat, D. M., Aldhaeebi, M., & Bamanger, E. (2020). Efficiency of flipped classroom with online-based teaching under COVID-19. *Interactive Learning Environments*, 1–12.

Tsagari, D., Liontou, J., & Giannikas, C. N. (2020). *Language Educators Working Online during the COVID-19 Pandemic*. International Survey Questionnaire available online at: https://docs.google.com/forms/d/e/1FAIpQLSfAWizub856QxCX_k7bjBKwBKE5UMat5cfYKdxJ2-loaB2CmQ/viewform

UNESCO COVID-19 Education Response. (2021). *COVID-19: reopening and reimagining universities, survey on higher education through the UNESCO National Commissions*. UNESCO.

Wiersma, W. (2008). *Research Methods in Education: An Introduction* (9th ed.). Allyn & Bacon.

Williamson, B., Eynon, R., & Potter, J. (2020). Pandemic politics, pedagogies and practices: Digital technologies and distance education during the coronavirus emergency. *Learning, Media and Technology, 45*, 107–114.

Chapter 6
The Potential of a Telecollaborative Translation Course:
Virtual Exchange During the Pandemic and Beyond

Raphaelle Beecroft
Karlsruhe University of Education, Germany

Petra Bauer
Durham University, UK

ABSTRACT

Difficult global circumstances pose a challenge for face-to-face exchange in higher education level language pedagogy, creating the need for innovative digital alternatives which can be integrated into internationalisation strategies. This chapter presents such an endeavour merging translation and telecollaboration which fosters an interplay of intercultural and functional communicative competence. Combining approaches from translation studies and foreign language pedagogy, it is proposed that telecollaboration creates a plurilingual and pluricultural space within which participants from varying linguacultural backgrounds may collaborate on a common product – a translation. The translation process itself requires intercultural exchange in which participants engage in an immediate manner through online interaction. Preliminary results from a study focussing on a telecollaborative translation course implemented with Durham University German students and prospective English teachers from Karlsruhe University of Education, Germany are presented.

DOI: 10.4018/978-1-7998-8717-1.ch006

INTRODUCTION

The present chapter focusses on virtual exchange between university-level language students as a necessary and viable digital alternative to face-to-face exchange and collaboration. As part of this, the chapter postulates that collaborative translation taking place within the context of virtual exchange can foster the (intercultural) competences required of students of modern foreign languages, including future teachers of English. It does so by presenting and evaluating a telecollaborative translation course carried out with Durham University (UK) German students and prospective English teachers from Karlsruhe University of Education, Germany.

The chapter first delineates both the circumstances surrounding foreign language pedagogy in secondary and higher education settings in the UK as well as the competences which future language teachers in Germany are supposed to acquire during the course of their studies. It hereby focusses on intercultural, linguistic and media competences, discussing the challenges surrounding fostering these competences in a purely digital environment.

In a second step, the chapter presents virtual exchange as having the potential to provide a pedagogical framework opening up a space for the above-named competences to be fostered within digital teacher education and modern foreign language studies. The chapter then goes on to delineate the potentials of translation as one such collaborative task taking place within a virtual exchange format, emphasising the modern view of translation as a form of intercultural communication in itself. Employing insights from Translation Studies and foreign language pedagogy research, the chapter will provide an overview of the different understandings and levels of acceptance of pedagogical translation over the years, both from a theoretical and practical perspective.

Leading on from this, as a conclusion to the first, theoretical part of the chapter, it will be proposed that virtual exchange in the form of telecollaboration and translation can be combined to promote intercultural, linguistic and media competences in prospective teachers of English and students of German whilst creating a safe, productive, pluricultural and plurilingual space for students to meet each other and work on the common task – a translation – in order to further their studies and develop their competences in a pandemic and beyond.

The second part of the chapter then turns to the practical implementation of this proposal and will present the ‘TraDuKa’ telecollaborative translation course within its action-research methodological framework. In order to do so, the institutional frameworks, the requirements and the participant profiles of the two participating universities will be presented, as will be a timeline of the development of the course, charting its first implementation and challenges in a face-to-face format and its uncomplicated switch to a completely online format. The chapter describes the architecture and syllabus of the course as well as the digital and face-to-face organisation required to structure such an online bilateral cooperation.

From an empirical perspective, the chapter finally delineates the action-research, qualitative, longitudinal design of which the TraDuKa course is the object, detailing the research instruments employed to investigate the question of whether the content and architecture of the TraDuKa fosters the intercultural and linguistic competences required of future language teachers. The chapter ends with a presentation and discussion of selected results.

THE STATUS QUO – DIFFERING STARTING POINTS FOR A COMMON PROJECT

The following sub-chapter will present the different reasons for the development of the TraDuKa telecollaborative translation course against the backdrop of the current situational factors affecting the teaching and learning of German at Durham University, UK and of English at Karlsruhe University of Education, Germany respectively.

Modern Foreign Languages in the UK: The Case of German at the Secondary and Higher Education Level

In a 2016 survey by the European Commission, the UK was ranked last in knowledge of foreign languages in the adult population. Only 34.6% of the population aged 25-64 reported they knew one or more foreign languages, compared to the EU average of 64.6% (Eurostat, 2019). One of the most-cited reasons for the comparatively low level of language learning in British Modern Foreign Language learning are the changes to the National Curriculum over the past decades. (Higher Education Policy Institute 2020; British Council, 2020) This can be observed in the steady decline of GCSE entries in Modern Foreign Languages (MFL); German observed a drop after 2002 from a previously constant 22% to an all-time low of 7% in 2018 (Department for Education, 2020). Similarly, A-level subject entries declined, albeit more gradually, by two-thirds in the same time-span. (ibid.) This 'language crisis' (All-Party Parliamentary Group on Modern Languages, 2019) also has an effect on universities and subsequently the job market (cf. Confederation of British Industry & Pearson, 2019; The Times, 2019; Consumer News and Business Channel, 2019). Most university students, however, are interested in German mostly for the personal benefits of language learning (Gallagher-Brett, 2004), and more students than before are enrolling in non-degree seeking German modules at UK universities (Auswärtiges Amt, 2020). This raises the question of how the degree-seeking university courses can be adapted to meet expectations from students, employers and politics, while also combatting the negative effects of the changes to the national curriculum.

One successful answer to this question at Durham University was the introduction of an ab-initio strand to the German degree programme in 2014. This course, open to students with Grade A or above at A-Level in modern foreign languages, enables the participants to progress from being complete beginners to CEFR-level B2 at the end of the second year, when the students will go on their compulsory year abroad and finish their degree in the same final-year language classes with students who began their degree post-A-level, i.e. students with CEFR-level of B1. The course was designed with a strong emphasis on intercultural communication and understanding, a gradual progression from easier topics and tasks to more complex subject matters (cf. Hervey et al., 2006), and close collaboration with the lecturers of the supplementary 'content modules', which they take alongside the post-A-level students, to didacticize materials and provide additional exercises targeted towards the demands of the modules focussed on the analysis of cultural aspects / products from German speaking countries.

Of the up-to-15 students per year taking the ab-initio strand, on average 80% will continue to second year and from there most continue to the year abroad and the final year. Most of the students come from state schools or six form colleges, their ethnicity is mostly White English, Irish or other European, and 30% have a bilingual background (Internal Data). When enrolling into the programme, they usually have already studied two languages at A-Levels or, increasingly, EBacc. While most students enrol into the Modern Languages with Year Abroad programme, some students combine German with English, History or Anthropology in the Combined Hons Programme in Liberal Arts.

Overall, the ab-initio programme has proved to be very successful. However, it became apparent by the end of the second year that the students, whilst having reached the same level as the post-A-level students as far as acquisition of grammatical structures and translation skills is concerned, had mostly never visited a German-speaking country or had personal experience with German culture or German people, resulting in a lack of range of vocabulary and expressions as well as competence in intercultural communication compared to their post-A-level peers. The ab-initio programme likewise prepares the students for the compulsory Year Abroad in a German speaking country. The telecollaboration project between Durham University, UK, and Karlsruhe University of Education, Germany, was developed by the authors to address these specific concerns.

English Studies and Competence Development at Karlsruhe University of Education

At Karlsruhe University of Education, English can be studied as a subject for primary and lower secondary (up to year 10) education at the BA (3 years) and the MA (1-2 years) level. During their modular studies, students experience intensive pedagogical training relevant to their chosen age-group as well as seminars in the fields of linguistics, literary and cultural studies, whose contents are likewise reflected from a pedagogical perspective. The university provides opportunities for students to study abroad either in English-speaking countries or on English-speaking study programmes, or carry out an internship at an English-speaking school. However, a stay abroad is only compulsory in the Content and Language Integrated Learning teacher education programme, meaning that, for several reasons (financial, familiar, personal) only a relatively small proportion of prospective English teachers spend time in an English-speaking context outside of Germany.

Prospective English teachers must have taken English as a subject for their school-leaving *Abitur* exam, and are supposed to have, as a result of this, level B2 of the CEFR, a level which is sometimes exceeded in part due to time spent in an English-speaking country or in exposure to English through Informal Second Language Learning. Language practice is integrated in both the content and pedagogy-related courses and dealt with embedded in the context of the respective seminar.

As such, the English courses of study seek to foster pedagogical content and process (cf. Koehler & Mishra 2009) competences in their students, to enable these students to, in turn, later promote the content and process-related competences in their pupils. As the German modern foreign language context is increasingly laying its focus on teaching English for use in lingua franca contexts, amongst these competences, the most important is considered to be Intercultural Communicative Competence (ICC), based on Byram's (2021) model, with 'functional communicative competence' serving as a linguistic basis system at the service of ICC (Ministerium für Kultus und Sport, 2016) for teaching English with a lingua franca leaning.

The prospective English teachers' own ICC and functional communicative competence, which includes reading, writing, listening, speaking and mediation as well as the ability to employ linguistic items on a syntactical, lexical and phonological level must be fostered. At the same time however, they must be steered towards developing pedagogical competence by getting to know, experiencing and teaching according to fitting theoretical frameworks such as action-oriented foreign language teaching and its practical implementation in the form of task-based or supported foreign language teaching. Furthermore, the current pandemic has forced a long-necessary focus on the use of digital media in German (English) classrooms, meaning that the prospective teachers must, in addition, acquire technological competence in order to be able to be able to offer their future pupils contemporary and flexible learning opportunities. Here, the TPACK model developed by Mishra and Koehler in 2006 (Müller-Hartmann & Kurek, 2016, p. 133) which "refers to teacher competence as integrating technological, pedagogical and content knowledge" (ibid.), with "[t]he knowledge that lies at the intersection of these three different competencies account[ing] for the understanding of effective technology integration into teaching" (Rienties et al., 2020, p. 5) provides a useful framework for the promotion of the competences required of future English teachers.

The above-named competences are to be fostered even in the adverse circumstances presented by the current pandemic, which make both face-to-face teaching and the full experience of spending time in an English-speaking environment difficult. Prospective teachers of English as well as students of German in the UK must be given the chance to foster their ICC and functional communicative competence in an interactional, synchronous context and thus not be at a disadvantage in their degree due to the effects of the pandemic. Those responsible for teaching and learning in higher education have an obligation to develop pedagogical concepts which can be viable and valid both during and in the aftermath of the pandemic and which are not a secondary option to face-to-face teaching, but rather enhance it, providing students with a broader repertoire of concepts to experience and implement themselves later on in their career. The remaining chapter will present virtual exchange in the form of telecollaboration with translation at its core as one such possibility which took advantage of the new digital opportunities brought about by the pandemic.

BACKGROUND AND LITERATURE REVIEW

This sub-chapter will present the theoretical foundations of both telecollaboration as a form of virtual exchange and translation, culminating in a presentation of how the two can be combined to do justice to the competence requirements of both courses of study (Durham and Karlsruhe) described above.

Telecollaboration

In the literature, virtual exchange is broadly defined as

An umbrella term used to refer to the engagement of groups of learners in online language and intercultural interaction and collaboration with partners from other cultural contexts or geographical locations as an integrated part of course work, and under the guidance of educators and/or expert facilitators (O'Dowd, 2018 in Gutierrez & O'Dowd, 2021, p. 1)

It is usually considered to take place in the form of "bilingual-bicultural exchanges which involve two classes [...] studying each other's languacultures" (Gutierrez & O'Dowd, 2021, p.1) which are structured either as 'e-tandems' or telecollaboration (cf. O'Dowd, 2021, p. 214). Whereas e-tandems are realised through partner-based exchange with a focus on language acquisition, telecollaboration, which is the form of virtual exchange employed in the study at hand, takes place as a course usually integrated into a programme of study and has a broader scope of action, as described below:

In the telecollaborative model of virtual exchange, exchanges combine foreign language development with an emphasis on intercultural learning. These exchanges typically involve tasks where partners present aspects of their cultures to each other, compare their cultural practices and perspectives, or engage in discussions based on shared texts. Telecollaborative virtual exchanges are usually integrated into students' classes, with teachers supporting learners in their online interactions. (Gutierrez & O'Dowd, 2021, p. 2)

Regarding language teacher education, telecollaboration is increasingly being implemented in the field as it is considered as a framework for university courses which enable the participants to "first discover, then experience and, finally, reflect on the mutual relationship between technology and pedagogy in authentic linguistic and intercultural contexts" (Kurek & Müller-Hartmann 2017, p. 8). Furthermore, telecollaboration can be seen to create "'digital spaces' for collaborative learning" (Dooly, 2020, p. 102) in which pre-service "teachers are introduced to cross-cultural peer reflection and dialogic learning [...] and [...] are empirically exposed to new approaches they might then apply to their own teaching" (ibid.). Telecollaborative approaches thus merge collaborative learning and the fostering of intercultural communicative competence to "offer both a holistic and a highly contextualised approach to teacher training" (Kurek & Müller-Hartmann, 2017, p. 8).

Furthermore, although virtual exchange has been implemented in its different forms for more than 25 years (see, for example, Warschauer, 1996) (cf. O'Dowd, 2021, p. 214), it is currently gaining even more momentum in Modern Foreign Language university programmes in general due to an amalgamation of factors brought to a head by the current pandemic. Prior to the advent of COVID-19, universities were already considering virtual exchange formats as an "ideal addition to institutions' internationalisation at home programmes, and [...] as a useful complement to physical mobility programmes" (Gutierrez & O'Dowd, 2021, p. 2) as they were considered to offer [...] universities many benefits, including versatility, accessibility, and economic and environmental sustainability" (ibid.). Furthermore, it was recognised that, for financial, familiar and other personal reasons, not all students are able to take part in a semester at a university in another country and that there were not many further opportunities, in everyday modern language teaching in higher education, for communication with fellow students from different linguacultural backgrounds (cf. Rienties et al., 2020, pp. 2ff). Virtual exchange was, in this context, once again considered a valid alternative, creating a positive and proactive perspective which has been further intensified through the challenges presented by the ongoing COVID-19 pandemic.

Virtual exchange, and, more specifically, telecollaboration, having thus been recognised and embraced on both an institutional and practical level as a framework full of potential for fostering digital, collaborative and intercultural competences and even for replacing physical mobility, research in the field has, in recent years, turned to "establishing to what extent VE [Virtual Exchange] can achieve the learning goals which are expected of it" (O'Dowd, 2021, p. 217). This has, in the European context, been spearheaded by two initiatives, one being UNICollaboration, introduced in 2016, a "transdisciplinary organization for telecollaboration and Virtual Exchange [which] was launched to support the research and practice of VE in university education" (ibid., p. 214), and the other being "Evaluating and Upscaling Telecollaborative Teacher Education (EVALUATE) (2017-2019) [...] [,] a European Policy Experiment that studied the impact of VE on over 1000 students in initial teacher education across Europe" (ibid.).

As "the first large scale study designed to demonstrate the potential learning gains of a significant number of participants" (Hauck et al., 2020, p.8), the study generated many insights into the effects of virtual exchange. These include results on areas such as intercultural communicative competence, global citizenship and pragmatics (O'Dowd, 2018; O'Dowd & Dooly, 2020; Orsini-Jones & Lee, 2018) or virtual group formation and task design (Müller-Hartmann & Kurek, 2016) and digital-pedagogical competence development (Hauck et al., 2020).

These insights reveal that […] virtual exchange formats offer learners the opportunity to develop their communication skills, overcome anxiety, adapt to different communicative situations, and develop the knowledge, attitudes, and skills of the intercultural speaker (Byram, 1997 [2021]) – all in the context of their formal study programmes. Furthermore, the online modality of exchanges, combined with a formal educational context, offers participants the opportunity to learn media literacy and digital skills to appropriately consume and create content online, and to communicate and collaborate with international partners using diverse technological tools. (Gutierrez & O'Dowd, 2021, p. 2)

More specifically, on the one hand, the studies noted an increase in the development of foreign language communicative skills. Furthermore, virtual exchange provided an opportunity to communicate on a meaningful and relevant level, with this opportunity helping students to overcome language anxiety. On the other hand, various studies noted a development of intercultural communicative competence so central to modern foreign language pedagogy in relation to different affective factors. For one, students named an increase in factual cultural knowledge regarding, for example, social themes of relevance to the partner group. This was, however, also combined with "a growing awareness of cultural diversity and becoming aware of their partners' multiple identities and the need to avoid regarding cultures as monolithic" (O'Dowd, 2021, p. 218) which led to the students "to question some of their assumptions, reflect on their own beliefs and behaviours and see the complexity of intercultural relations rather than minimising difference, or seeing a binary relationship of "us" and "them""(Helm & Van der Velden, 2020, p. 38 in O'Dowd, 2021, p. 219). Furthermore, a feeling of being "better prepared to communicate and collaborate with people from different cultures" (O'Dowd, 2021, p. 219) was reported.

These positive effects can, however, only be brought about if the tasks employed within the telecollaboration are carefully designed and reflected. These tasks must be "interculturally challenging [...] [and] require [...] high levels of negotiation and collaboration (Helm & Van der Velden, 2019; The EVALUATE Group, 2019 in O'Dowd, 2021, p. 219) and present the students with "a range of collaborative hurdles and challenges which require them to find creative ways to collaborate and communicate successfully with their international partners" (O'Dowd, 2021, p. 219). In O'Dowd's (ibid.) words, "when tasks are carefully designed, VE can help push students out of their comfort zone and this is when skills and attitude development is most likely to take place". This 'careful design' entails, besides a focus on intercultural collaboration, a special consideration of "the interplay between tasks and tools" (Müller-Hartmann & Kurek, 2016, p. 137) employed to facilitate the virtual encounter and the tasks within it, as the tasks must be "appropriate to the medium used and [...] take into account the affordances ... of the modes available" (Hampel, 2006, p. 111 in Müller-Hartmann & Kurek, 2016, p. 137).

In light of this highlighted importance of developing tasks appropriate to the context and the goals of telecollaboration, in the next part of this literature review, the process of translation will be presented as a particularly well-fitting basis for reflected telecollaborative task design.

Translation as a Complex Telecollaborative Task

Translation Studies, emerging as an (inter)discipline in the 1950s and 1960s, has put a focus on developing and reflecting understandings of translation as a product, of the translation process and of the figure of the translator (cf. Munday, 2016). Within this context, during the 20th century, a shift can be seen from a 'narrow', reduced and purely (system)linguistic understanding of translation based on the assumption that signifiers from different languages, which correspond to one signified, are interchangeable, an understanding which reduces translation to an abstract, 're-coding' process (cf. Dizdar, 2006, p. 15; Rozmysłovicz, 2019, p. 53). This understanding furthermore portrays the process of translation as being contained within textual boundaries and is often described in terms of a vessel and transportation metaphor which depicts two riverbanks and a loaded freight vessel alternating between these two banks, with the vessel's load being transferred, unchanged, from one riverbank to another (cf. Dizdar, 2008, pp. 54f). As well as defining the translation product and process, this perspective has implications on the role of the translator, who is seen to act as a freight carrier, a ferryperson, or, in similar metaphors, as a messenger or a herald, whose only duty is to see that the freight or the message arrives intact at its destination (cf. Arrojo, 1997, pp. 25f; Dizdar 2006, p. 271; Siever, 2019, p. 73).

This understanding was, however, challenged first and foremost by Reiss and Vermeer's *Skopos* theory (Vermeer, 1978; Reiss & Vermeer, 1984) which caused a paradigm shift in Translation Studies through its functional approach (cf. Dizdar, 1999, p. 104; Munday, 2016, pp. 126ff) and first introduced the relevance of 'culture' to translation. Instead of focussing on the transfer of meaning from a 'source' to a 'target text' through equivalent linguistic units, "the approach positioned the goal of a translation (Skopos) at the forefront of the translation process and assigned the responsibility of reaching this goal to the translator" (Beecroft, 2015, p. 157). The context in which the translation was to be received was furthermore considered of utmost importance – this context being equated with 'culture', whose difference to the source text's culture had to be respected, with the goal of the translation being formulated against this backdrop. As such, Vermeer postulated translation as being an act of 'cultural transfer' (cf. Vermeer, 1984) and of intercultural communication (Vermeer, 1978; 1996) between two static, different source and target cultures, which came into contact with each other through the translation process (cf. Rozmysłovicz, 2019, pp. 53ff). This brought about a new understanding of the translator away from a passive messenger or ferryperson to someone who had responsibility for the translation process and above all, had to be 'culturally competent' in both the putative source and target cultures. Furthermore, the translator had to be able to mediate between these two 'cultures' in the act of translating in order to be able to reach the intended 'Skopos' for the 'target' culture (cf. Witte, 2000).

This dichotomous view of source culture and target culture is however, in recent literature, seen to replace the linguistic equivalence perspective with one of cultural equivalence (cf. Rozmysłovicz, 2019, pp. 58ff). As such, the role of 'culture' as well as the question of equivalence and difference both on a linguistic and sociocultural level in translation remains polemic and unresolved. However, concepts of transculturality (cf. Welsch, 1995) and hybridity (cf. Matz et al., 2014, p. 8) have recently being considered as a productive basis for describing the process of translation, with the product however, remaining on a level of representation of difference. This representation of difference at the product level is, however, negotiated with those involved in the process of translation (cf. Rozmysłovicz, 2019, p. 62), or within the translator themselves, now considered to be, not a messenger but a 'transcendental nomad' who, instead of crossing borders back and forth from a 'target' culture to a 'source' culture to transfer particular terms, uses their skills of interpretation and reflection across these borders to create a translation which they feel best represents their intentions (Siever, 2019, p. 79).

Translation has, during the 20th century, likewise been a source of controversy in foreign language pedagogy. The 'narrow' concept of translation, described above as equivalent linguistic transfer, was employed "in the service of grammar" (McLelland, 2020, p. 27) in the Grammar-Translation-Method (cf.

Cook, 2010, p. 9), up until the beginnings of the 20th century, and it was this understanding of translation which formed the basis for its rejection by the methods which followed. These, for different reasons based on the current pedagogical trends at the time of their emergence, however all centred around the primacy of monolingual teaching of the 'four skills' (reading, writing, listening, speaking) (cf. McLelland, 2020, p. 34) and the 'native-speaker ideal' (cf. Cook, 2010, p. 8, González-Davies, 2012, p. 3211) and thus had no room for translation in their implementations.

However, in the past ten years, a new understanding of translation has emerged within foreign language pedagogy which is much more in line with the discussions taking place within Translation Studies as well as with the current aim of foreign language pedagogy to promote intercultural communicative competence and further developments thereof. This welcome shift has come about due to internationalisation, globalisation and migration, which have, in turn, increased the linguacultural heterogeneity of classes of young learners, something which has been reflected in (European) language education policy in the Companion Volume to the Common European Framework of Reference for Languages (Council of Europe, 2018). The Companion Volume lists mediation, under which written translation also falls, as a "mode of communication" (Council of Europe, 2018, p. 32) alongside reception, production and interaction, thus affording it prominence. The Companion Volume furthermore takes the view of the language learner as a social agent who is no longer expected to conform to a putative native speaker ideal, but who much rather communicates through using their own plurilingual repertoire (cf. Bärenfänger et al. 2018, p. 10) upon which they build during their language learning process.

This has engendered a move to explore the implementation of a new understanding of translation "as a skill in itself and as a spontaneous or directed learning strategy capable of providing the means to act interculturally and to improve expertise [...] in learning contexts that involve languages and cultures in contact" (ibid., p. 3195).

These learning contexts are not the ones explicitly related to translator training and are thus referred to "Translation for Other Learning Contexts (TOLC)" (ibid., p. 3227), within which the study at hand likewise situates itself, although it is informed by developments within Translation Studies and translator training. One of these developments directly relevant to the study at hand is the concept of collaboration and, more specifically, telecollaboration in translator education. The process of translation itself, aided and altered by the various digital media and resources employed, requires collaboration. On a more abstract level, as described above, this collaboration is required on the one hand within the person of the translator themselves, who needs to, as a 'transcendental nomad', mediate between the different aspects of their linguacultural biography and plurilingual repertoire in order to create a translation. On the other hand, translation projects are more often than not carried out as "teamwork" (Marczak, 2017, p. 152), with the translator taking on "multiple roles" (ibid.) and having to "act creatively and flexibly [...] under the constraint of time" (ibid.). Based on a social-constructivist (Kiraly, 2000; González-Davies, 2017) view of (translator) education, collaboration can thus be seen as a "learning mode corresponding to the professional practices of translators and thus [...] promising to foster the development of [...] translator competence" (Kiraly, 2000 in Marczak, 2017, p. 152) as it "requires interaction [...] with a wide range of communities of practice and [...] must be perceived with regard to the social and cognitive processes and intercultural communication which it involves" (ibid.).

Research in telecollaboration in translator education (as proposed by Marczak, 2017; Krajka & Marczak, 2017) is, however still "scarce", (Marczak, 2017, p. 152), but, as a web-based resource, it can be seen to carry potential for creating a space for fostering those contemporary competences required of translators, which show parallels to those which must be promoted in pre-service teachers and Modern

Foreign Language students in general. As such, telecollaboration can be seen to "promote [...] learner autonomy and [to] create [...] a sense of responsibility for their own learning" (Marczak, 2017, p. 148), whereby "teamwork generates a synergy effect in that it fosters the acquisition of an amount of knowledge which goes beyond the sum of the knowledge already possessed by all learners involved in the collaborative experience" (ibid.).

On a specific competence level, translation tasks carried out within a telecollaborative setting have been proposed as fostering forms of organisational, intercultural and functional communicative competence relevant to both translator and teacher education as well as Modern Foreign Language students not yet oriented in a professional direction. Firstly, Marczak states that telecollaboration can help promote "service provision competence [...] as it comprises the ability to negotiate, clarify, plan, comply, work under pressure, work with partners in a group and self-evaluate" (2016, 8). Furthermore, students have to "define and evaluate translation problems, find adequate solutions as well as justify one's translation choices and decisions" (ibid.).

Regarding "language competence" (ibid.), telecollaborative tasks offer students "an opportunity to explore the language subsystems of grammar and lexis and conventions of the language in question, e.g., by examining samples of genuine communication in search of language patterns and changes which they undergo" (ibid.). Concerning "intercultural competence on the textual level" (ibid.), participants are able to "analyse the structure of a range of documents, the implicature of texts on the basis of the presuppositions, allusions or stereotypes which they contain" (ibid.), whilst "[t]ext analysis will also enable students to practise summarising the composition and content of documents, recognising culture-bound references and identifying the values and thought patterns which underpin the messages expressed" (ibid.). Furthermore, telecollaborative teams may "compose documents representative of selected text genres, or draft, rephrase, restructure, condense, and post-edit documents in pairs of languages" (ibid.). Engaging in such tasks thus has the potential to "shift away the focus from an over-emphasis on 'natural' cultural differences and instead raise students' awareness of how language and technology and culture are entwined in online intercultural competence per se" (O'Dowd, 2019, p. 26).

As such, against the backdrop of the advantages of telecollaboration, translation and telecollaboration in translator education described above, it is proposed that telecollaboration can be employed as a framework for incorporating Translation in Other Learning Contexts. Based on the category of mediation as described in the Companion Volume to the CEFR, it is furthermore claimed that telecollaboration can "facilitate a pluricultural space" (Council of Europe, 2018, p. 104) in which participants with diverging linguacultural backgrounds can come together to work on a common translation process. The translation tasks create a reason and an obligation to collaborate: together, the participants must, from a 'service provision'-perspective, develop telecollaborative strategies in order to be able to achieve the translation together. The translation, as a written product, requires a specific kind of translational functional communicative competence on the part of the participants whereby they must be able to select and justify their use of particular linguistic structures to each other on a precise, textual level. Furthermore, the translation requires an interpretation and reflection of meaning on an intercultural level, which the linguaculturally diverging participants negotiate amongst themselves to create a common text.

THE IMPLEMENTATION OF THE TraDuKa COURSE AND ITS ACTION-RESEARCH FRAMEWORK

Following on from the above discussion of the theoretical construct of telecollaborative translation tasks, the second part of the chapter will turn to the practical implementation of this proposal and will present the 'TraDuKa' telecollaborative translation course within its action-research methodological framework. In order to do so, the institutional frameworks, the requirements and the participant profiles of the two partner universities will be presented, as will be a timeline, in action-research terms, of the development cycles of the course, charting its first implementation and challenges in a face-to-face format, its uncomplicated switch to a completely online format and its continuing development regarding a possible return to face-to-face teaching.

Action-research was chosen as a methodological framework for the research accompanying the TraDuKa course. This was due to the goal of action-research, namely to "achieve change through a *synthesis* of research and action" (Townsend, 2013, p. 35) [italics in the original] in regard to context-related, practical issues (cf. ibid., p. 3) in "complex and messy settings" (ibid., p. 5) being deemed fitting for investigating a course which aimed to ensure or even enhance the quality of teaching under adverse conditions. Seeking to comprehend and build upon professional practice (cf. ibid., p. 3), the iterative nature of action-research cycles was thought to lend itself well to the repeated implementations of the TraDuKa course pre-, while- and post-pandemic.

The "complex and messy" (ibid., p. 5) setting named above can be attributed in the study at hand to the two groups of students from Karlsruhe University of Education, Germany and Durham University, UK, as well as their lecturers, the authors of this chapter who constituted the practitioner-researcher team shaping the action-research process. In the following, the institutional framework of the two groups involved will be described as well as, in order to define the sample of the study, the relevant demographics of the participating students.

At Karlsruhe University of Education, the TraDuKa course is offered as an undergraduate 'Research Seminar', which students must take at the end of their second or the beginning of their third year in Linguistics, Literary Studies and Cultural Studies, making up the 'English and its Areas of Research' module. The TraDuKa course is offered within the area of Linguistics and aims, as part of this, to provide students with a perspective on language use other than with regards to teaching English in the secondary or primary classroom.[1] Regarding assessment, students select one of the 'Research Seminars' in which to write a term paper on a subject deriving from the contents of the respective seminar. This term paper, written in English, constitutes the module mark. Topics have included translation quality assessment, the application of Skopos Theory to a chosen translation, machine translation and translation in foreign language pedagogy amongst others.

The following sample description is based on the participants of the two TraDuKa courses which form the 'action' of this action-research study: The first course carried out in a face-to-face and online setting from October 2019 to February 2020 (TraDuKa I), and the second course carried out in a purely online setting from October 2020 to February 2021 (TraDuKa II). 35 students from Karlsruhe University of Education and 12 Durham participants took part in TraDuKa I. 24 students from Karlsruhe University of Education and 12 students from Durham university took part in TraDuKa II. The Karlsruhe students were between 20 and 46 years of age[2] and all had a very good level of English, averaging at C1 level of the CEFR. They had not had any previous experience of translation, either theory or practice, at the higher education level.

At Durham University, the TraDuKa course is aimed at second year German continuing ab initio students with an initial level of German of B1+. It is firmly rooted within the translation part of the five-hour core language module and aims to expose the students to German language and culture and to enable interaction with German peers both at a formal level within the classroom and at an informal level outside the classroom setting. For Durham, the TraDuKa telecollaboration has the following four objectives in mind:

- Acquisition of Intercultural Communication and Competence
- Acquisition of Idiomatic Lexis and Expressions in German
- Improved Competence in German Grammar
- Acquisition of translational competence and the basics in translation theory.

The learning outcomes are formally assessed in three individual, formative translations into German, three individual, formative translations into English and one end of year summative translation exam consisting of one translation into German and one translation into English. This exam is worth 30% of overall mark for the module.

Action-research seeks to improve practice in professional communities, in this case in the educational, language pedagogy sector, through the practitioners' active shaping of and contribution to a process of action and reflection with the aim of improving practice in the practitioners' immediate settings (cf. Beecroft, 2019, p. 254). In the study at hand, the practitioners involved were the two authors of this chapter, who collaboratively taught and researched the TraDuKa courses, making them, as Stenhouse (1974 in Townsend, 2013, p. 35) claims "extended professional[s]" (cf. Beecroft, 2019, p. 254). Both practitioners have long-standing experience in the teaching of Modern Foreign Language in Higher Education and are keen to implement innovative teaching forms to support the current specific needs of their students and their institutions, which are reassessed regularly. In action-research terms, these would be deemed the 'focus' (the specific needs) and the 'action' (the innovative teaching forms) of the study – the focus representing the practitioners' identified need for change and the action the means employed to implement this change (cf. Townsend, 2013, p. 64). In the case of the study at hand, the need for change, based on the circumstances described at the beginning of this chapter, was identified as a wish to offer both student cohorts the opportunity for exchange on a linguacultural level. This was deemed necessary from, on the one hand, the perspective of the students' competence development regarding their particular requirements and on the other, against the backdrop of global events negatively influencing the possibility of physical mobility – beginning with Brexit and continuing with the COVID-19 pandemic. The 'action' of the study was thus to devise and implement a course which would provide a forum for exchange and collaboration on common linguistic tasks without necessarily including physical mobility and which could provide a viable or even enhanced alternative to physical mobility should this become impossible. This action, as well as the adjustment of the action according to the changing needs of the student cohorts influenced by global events, has, at the time of writing, been implemented in two cycles of action and reflection, the second building upon the first. The two cycles, which are adapted from models of action-research developed by Kemmis and McTaggart (1982), Elliot (1991) and Townsend (2013) form the beginning of a long-term action-research process forming the framework for longitudinal research on the TraDuKa course and will be described below.

The chosen action-research cycle design begins, in cycle I, with the **initial idea** of implementing a telecollaborative translation course between Durham University German students and prospective teachers of English at Karlsruhe University of Education, which was first discussed and agreed upon in 2017 but, due to other commitments on the part of the two initiators of the project, not put into practice straight away. Two years later, in 2019, a **planning and reconnaissance** phase took place in which a telecollaborative course was planned to begin in the following October. During this phase, the focus for each group was refined and the course parameters were adjusted to the respective institutional frameworks. The content of the course, based on the 'translation dossier' used by Durham university in the one-hour-per-week translation part of the course, which contains a wide range of different text-types (tourism, literary texts, instructions, non-fictional texts) to be translated either from German into English or vice-versa, with a strong focus on grammar and vocabulary and some input from translation theory, was agreed upon. Furthermore, the architecture of the first implementation of the course was designed: although the respective class-times partly coincided, working telecollaboratively as a group during this time was judged too complicated, the practitioners and the students not yet being as experienced with digital communication as they would become during the pandemic. Instead, it was decided that the students from Durham and Karlsruhe would telecollaborate outside of class in small groups using a digital medium of communication of their choice, working on the weekly translation assignment, which would then be discussed in separate face-to-face classes in Durham and Karlsruhe. **Action Step I** began in October 2019 when the participants were put into telecollaborative groups based on written descriptions of themselves which they had provided in advance. The first implementation of the TraDuKa course was then carried out, with a planned weekly telecollaborative exchange and face-to-face session, which came to a close with the end of the Karlsruhe semester in February 2020. The telecollaborative part of the TraDuKa course was followed by **Action Step II**, which comprised a voluntary study trip to Durham by the Karlsruhe students in February 2020, enabling the participants to meet and carry out translations in a face-to-face workshop context. An inter-institutional agreement was developed as a result of talks carried out during the visit.

The COVID-19 pandemic began just after the study trip to Durham and, as the course was to be carried out again beginning in October 2020, a further **reconnaissance** phase ensued, so that the action, the TraDuKa course itself, could be adapted both to pandemic circumstances and to reflect the feedback provided by the participants of the first implementation. This feedback first and foremost expressed the wish for the telecollaborative sessions to be made compulsory and to take place primarily during class time, so that more could be made of the exchange. Interestingly, this wish fitted in with the conditions exerted by the pandemic which caused all teaching to be transferred to online settings and thus proved simple to implement, something which would not have been the case had the course once again taken place in a face-to-face manner. This called for an **amended plan**, which saw the same content being implemented, with the addition of the translation of English and Baden-Württemberg (the German federal state in which Karlsruhe is situated) COVID-19 rules, but which afforded the TraDuKa course an altered architecture. In its second implementation, the next **action step** from October 2020 to February 2021, the TraDuKa course thus took place in an entirely online setting, using Big Blue Button, the videoconferencing platform employed by Karlsruhe University of Education. In order to be put into telecollaborative groups, this time the Durham students uploaded a video introducing themselves in German. The Karlsruhe participants were then able to request to be put in a group with a particular Durham participant with whom they felt that they would be able to work, and the students were then grouped on the basis of these requests. The TraDuKa course was then carried out online on a weekly basis, with the two groups coming together for a joint session twice a month, as luckily, the online class times could be synchronised in the amended plan. During these sessions, the mixed Durham and Karlsruhe student groups worked together in breakout rooms on the current translation, with each participant bringing a draft of a translation as a basis. The breakout telecollaborative sessions lasted about 40 minutes of the 60-minute unit, with the remaining 15-20 minutes being used as group discussion and reflection time. The participants were also free to meet up digitally outside of course-time. In order to enable more in-depth reflection, the Karlsruhe students were asked to, after every telecollaborative session, hand in their translation of the discussed text along with comments on their translation process in the form of a written think-aloud-protocol and to complete an online 'reflection diary' which contained questions on the telecollaborative process, digital communication and potential challenges faced when translating together. These instruments, as well as a semi-structured focus-group interview carried out just after the last telecollaborative session, provided the data for the accompanying ongoing research study. At the time of writing, the TraDuKa course once again finds itself in a **reconnaissance** phase, this time of the second, COVID-19 influenced cycle, where the feedback, provided in the form of the data revealed by research instruments described above, as well as the ever-changing pandemic circumstances will form the basis for the next cycle, which will begin again with an **amended plan**. The TraDuKa course has since then been presented as a best-practice example of virtual exchange in internal internationalisation round-tables as well as at online conferences around the globe.

Research Design

The final part of this chapter will present the research design integrated within the action-research framework and employed to investigate student perceptions of competence development as well as, in a later stage of the study, the student products for indicators of competence development brought about by their participation in the TraDuKa course.

The research is designed as a longitudinal study, investigating yearly iterations of the TraDuKa course in order to provide a process-oriented perspective on the course by charting its development as well as that of its participants over the course of time (cf. Flick, 2007, p. 183). Data will thus be gathered in every further implementation of the course. Due to the main object of research being the individual perspectives of the participants as well as the holistic analysis of their translated products investigated through the collection of open-ended, non-numerical data (cf. Kuckartz, 2014, p. 28), the study is based on a qualitative methodological paradigm.

The research question being investigated at this stage of the longitudinal study is thus: which areas of competence development can be observed in the participants' reflection of their experience of the second implementation of the TraDuKa course?

Findings

The findings presented in the following are gleaned from the qualitative content analysis (cf. Schreier 2012) of two sets of data collected from the Karlsruhe students: 75 responses to the reflection questions following on from the telecollaborative sessions and one semi-structured focus group interview (cf. Dörnyei, 2007, pp. 143ff) carried out with nine students at the end of the second implementation of the TraDuKa course in February 2021. The reflection questions focused on the areas of technology, ICC, the translation process as well as the development of the students' own learning process. The interview focused on the development of ICC in its different components.

Regarding the reflection questions, student responses were provided on average for four of the six telecollaborative sessions throughout the semester. It was possible to trace a development of the responses over this time. Both data-sets were coded according to concept-driven deductive categories (cf. Schreier, 2012, p. 84). The student responses were coded according to the categories: 'Communication and Technology' and 'Collaborative Translation Process'. Both the responses and the interviews were furthermore coded according to the categories of 'Development of Intercultural Communicative Competence' and 'Development of Functional Communicative Competence', with, however, data-driven, inductive categories being created where necessary in all areas (ibid.). As such, it was possible to chart perceived competence development in four dimensions:

Communication and Technology: Here, students commented on their developing perception of the functioning of the telecollaborative process enabled through technology. Communication was, at the beginning, perceived as being slower than in face-to-face contexts, and the process of joining breakout rooms for every meeting proved a challenge throughout the semester. As such, strategies were actively developed by the participants throughout the course to counteract this. These strategies included:

- Ensuring that a working camera and microphone were available. These were considered as essential to the communication process, with the chat function providing a sub-optimal alternative.
- Activating the 'shared notes' function available on Big Blue Button. This was deemed an effective tool for telecollaborative work.
- Working in small breakout room groups (3-4 students).

The Collaborative Translation Process: The collaborative translation process was perceived to be demanding and time-consuming but enriching due to the active negotiation of meaning created by the collaboration and required to create a translation. The completion of a translation as a joint endeavour was considered to be both gratifying and satisfying. The discussion and interpretation of particular concepts was seen to be particularly fruitful, both in terms of gaining semantic knowledge but also of language awareness – the participants realised that as first language speakers, they did not automatically know the meaning of a particular term and that they were thus not to consider each other as all-knowing 'experts' of 'their' language. At the same time, the participants noted that the first-language speakers of the language translated into in the respective translation were able to formulate text faster and more productively than the other participants and operationalised this observation as a group translation strategy.

The development of the participants' **Intercultural Communicative Competence** can be described through the following data-driven categories, formulated as the *savoirs* featured in Byram's (2021) model: relating to **savoir faire**, the participants noted that they were able to, throughout the course, overcome their fear of interacting with students from diverging linguacultural backgrounds. They felt that they were able to suspend disbelief relating to concepts and events which they had not heard of or experienced previously and which triggered a feeling of 'otherness' within them and, in their opinion, represented difference between the participants (**savoir être**). This included gaining knowledge (**savoir**) of the use of first names in the varying higher education contexts as well as the various living arrangements whilst studying. Furthermore, the participants noted that they were able to discuss and analyze common experiences against the backdrop of divergent linguacultural contexts (**savoir comprendre**), these experiences centering on higher education and the participants' shared experience of the COVID-19 pandemic. Interestingly, the participants named the pluricultural space created by the telecollaboration as the motor for this development, which was seen to increase with the progression of the course. The translation dimension was also cited, with the telecollaborative content however deemed to be the catalyst for a common interpretation, discussion and reflection of the translation of concepts identified as 'different' in the varying linguacultural contexts.

The participants furthermore noticed a progressive development of their **functional communicative competence**. Here, the inductive sub-categories included

- Improved sentence structure,
- Increased awareness of the participants' problems with grammatical items,
- Expansion of vocabulary
- A deeper insight into both German and English.

Conversely to the category of intercultural communicative competence, here the participants named the process of translation as being the catalyst for the development of their functional communicative competence, with the translation tasks increasing the participants' awareness of this category. This was first and foremost triggered by a shift, throughout the course, in the understanding of translation from translating word-for-word to conveying meaning through the use of other linguistic structures (cf. Rogers et al. 2020), which required the participants to make use of and expand their plurilingual repertoire. Telecollaboration was named as the framework which enabled the participants to develop strategies and support each other in doing this.

CONCLUSION AND LIMITATIONS

From these findings it is possible to see that the two components making up the TraDuKa course, telecollaboration and translation, were perceived to develop the above-named competences to different degrees. Telecollaboration was seen to primarily promote intercultural and technological competence whereas translation was considered conducive to developing functional communicative competence and an increased awareness of an understanding of translation away from the equivalent word-for-word transfer towards conveying meaning to reach a particular translatory goal. However, the participants also perceived both components as necessary, with the telecollaboration providing the support, discussion and reflection framework required to carry out the textual translation tasks. These translation tasks included representations of difference, which were, however, negotiated by the participants during the telecollaboration. Nevertheless, the use of two data-sets from the Karlsruhe perspective limits the scope of the study's findings to this group of participants' perceptions. It would be desirable to investigate the Durham participants' perceptions of the above-named competences as well as the participant translations themselves in order to gain more product related insights into the participants' competence development.

NEED FOR FURTHER RESEARCH

These findings provide the basis for further cycles of investigation, which will include an analysis of the Durham students' perceptions, the participants' think-aloud-protocols as well as of the translated products themselves, to allow for an investigation of the manifestation of competence development on a textual level. The TPACK dimension of the TraDuKa course, which was, in the described research cycle, only dealt with in one analysis category, will, in a further research cycle, be investigated further in order to provide insights into the participants' ability and willingness to work with digital media both in a higher education context and in their future careers as, for the Karlsruhe students, teachers of English.

ACKNOWLEDGMENT

The authors wish to thank Sebastian Straßburg (Durham University/Albert-Ludwigs-Universität Freiburg) for his invaluable assistance in editing this chapter.

REFERENCES

All-Party Parliamentary Group on Modern Languages (APPGML). (2019). *A National Recovery Programme for Languages*. https://university-council-modern-languages.org/wp-content/uploads/2020/05/languagesrecoveryprogrammeappgmfl-embargo4march.pdf

Arrojo, R. (1997). Pierre Menard und eine neue Definition des ‚Originals (J. Klemm, Trans.). In WolfM. (Ed.), *Übersetzungswissenschaft in Brasilien. Beiträge zum Status von „Original" und Übersetzung* (pp. 25–33). Stauffenburg.

Auswärtiges Amt. (2020). *Deutsch als Fremdsprache weltweit*. https://www.auswaertiges-amt.de/blob/2344738/b2a4e47fdb9e8e2739bab2565f8fe7c2/deutsch-als-fremdsprache-data.pdf

Bärenfänger, O., Harsch, C., Tesch, B., & Vogt, K. (2019). Reform, Remake, Retousche? Diskussion paper by the Deutsche Gesellschaft für Fremdsprachenforschung on the Companion to the CEFR (2018). *Zeitschrift für Fremdsprachenforschung*, *30*(1), 7–13.

Beecroft, R. (2013). From Intercultural Speaker to Intercultural Writer. Towards a New Understanding of Translation in Foreign Language Teaching. In D. Tsagari & G. Floros (Eds.), *Translation in language teaching and assessment*. Cambridge Scholars Publishing.

Beecroft, R. (2019). *The Performativity of the Intercultural Speaker: Mainstreaming Improvisational Tasks as an Action-Oriented Framework for the Lower Secondary Classroom. A Longitudinal, Mixed-Methods Action-Research Study* [Unpublished doctoral dissertation]. Heidelberg University of Education.

British Council. (2020). *Language Trends 2020: Language Teaching in Primary and Secondary Schools in England*. https://www.britishcouncil.org/research-policy-insight/research-reports/language-trends-2020

Byram, M. (2021). *Teaching and Assessing Intercultural Communicative Competence*. Multilingual Matters. doi:10.21832/9781800410251

Cook, G. (2010). *Translation in Language Teaching*. Oxford University Press.

Confederation of British Industry (CBI) & Pearson (2019). *Education and Learning for the Modern World: CBI/Pearson Education and Skills Survey Report 2019*. https://www.cbi.org.uk/media/3841/12546_tess_2019.pdf

Consumer News and Business Channel (CNBC). (2019) *Here are the Top Foreign Languages that UK Employers Want You to Have*. https://www.cnbc.com/2019/04/10/foreign-languages-that-uk-employers-want-you-to-have.html

Council of Europe. (2018). *Common European Framework of Reference for Languages: Learning, Teaching, Assessment. Companion Volume with New Descriptors*. rm.coe.int/cefr--companion--volume--with--new--descriptors--2018/1680787989

Department for Education. (2020). *Language Teaching in Schools (England)*. https://researchbriefings.files.parliament.uk/documents/CBP-7388/CBP-7388.pdf

Dizdar, D. (1999). Skopostheorie. In M. Snell-Hornby, H. G. Hönig, P. Kußmaul, & P. A. Schmitt (Eds.), *Handbuch Translation* (pp. 104–107). Stauffenburg.

Dizdar, D. (2006). *Translation. Um- und Irrwege*. Frank und Timme Verlag.

Dizdar, D. (2008). Translation zwischen den Disziplinen. *Natur und Geist. Forschungsmagazin der Johannes Gutenberg-Universität, 24*(2), 54–57.

Dooly, M. (2020). *Virtual Exchange in Teacher Education: Is there an Impact in Teacher Practice?* Academic Press.

Elliott, J. (1991). *Action Research for Educational Change*. Open University Press.

Eurostat. (2019). *Foreign Language Skills Statistics*. https://ec.europa.eu/eurostat/statistics-explained/index.php?title=Foreign_language_skills_statistics

Flick, U. (2007). *Qualitative Sozialforschung. Eine Einführung*. Rowohlt.

González-Davies, M. (2012). The Role of Translation in Other Learning Contexts: Towards Acting Interculturally. In S. Hubscher-Davidson & M. Borodo (Eds.), Global Trends in Translator and Interpreter Training: Mediation and Culture (Vol. 161). Academic Press.

González-Davies, M. (2017). The Use of Translation in an Integrated Plurilingual Approach to Language Learning: Teacher Strategies and Best Practices. *Journal of Spanish Language Teaching, 4*(2), 124–135. doi:10.1080/23247797.2017.1407168

Gutiérrez, B. F., & O'Dowd, R. (2021). Virtual Exchange. *Innovative Language Pedagogy Report*, 17.

Hampel, R. (2006). Rethinking Task Design for the Digital Age: A Framework for Language Teaching and Learning in a Synchronous Online Environment. *ReCALL, 18*(1), 105–121. doi:10.1017/S0958344006000711

Hauck, M., Müller-Hartmann, A., Rienties, B., & Rogaten, J. (2020). Approaches to Researching digital-pedagogical competence development in VE-based teacher education. *Journal of Virtual Exchange, 3*(SI), 5-35.

Higher Education Policy Institute. (2020). *Action Needed to Avert the Growing Crisis in Language Learning*. https://www.hepi.ac.uk/2020/01/09/action-needed-to-avert-the-growing-crisis-in-language-learning/

Kemmis, S., & McTaggart, R. (1982). *The Action Research Planner*. Deakin University Press.

Kiraly, D. (2000). *A Social Constructivist Approach to Translator Education. Empowerment from Theory to Practice*. St. Jerome.

Koehler, M., & Mishra, P. (2009). What is technological pedagogical content knowledge (TPACK)? *Contemporary Issues in Technology & Teacher Education*, *9*(1), 60–70.

Krajka, J., & Marczak, M. (2017). Telecollaboration Projects in Translator Education–Design, Implementation and Evaluation. In E. Smyrnova-Trybulska (Ed.), *Effective Development of Teachers' Skills in the Area of ICT and E-Learning*. University of Silesia - NOA.

Kuckartz, U. (2014). *Mixed Methods: Methodologie, Forschungsdesigns und Analyseverfahren*. Springer-Verlag.

Kurek, M., & Müller-Hartmann, A. (2017). Task design for telecollaborative exchanges: In search of new criteria. *System*, *64*, 7–20. doi:10.1016/j.system.2016.12.004

Marczak, M. (2016). *Students' Perspective on Web 2.0-Enhanced Telecollaboration as Added Value in Translator Education*. Research-publishing.net.

Marczak, M. (2017). Concordancer-Enhanced Reflection in Telecollaborative Translation Projects at University Level. *Między oryginałem a przekładem*, (38), 145-168.

Matz, F., Rogge, M., & Siepmann, P. (Eds.). (2014). *Transkulturelles Lernen im Fremdsprachenunterricht: Theorie und Praxis*. Peter Lang GmbH. doi:10.3726/978-3-653-04068-5

McLelland, N. (2020). Translation and Ideology in the History of Language Learning and Teaching: Changing Purposes, Practices and Prejudices in the Teaching and Learning of Modern Languages. *Zeitschrift für Fremdsprachenforschung*, *31*(1), 23–40.

MKS – Ministerium für Kultus, Jugend und Sport Baden-Württemberg. (Ed.). (2016). *Gemeinsamer Bildungsplan der Sekundarstufe I, Englisch als Fremdsprache*. www.bildungsplaene-bw.de/,Lde/LS/BP2016BW/ALLG/SEK1/E1

Müller-Hartmann, A., & Kurek, M. (2016). Virtual group formation and the process of task design in online intercultural exchanges. In R. O'Dowd & T. Lewis (Eds.), Online intercultural exchange (pp. 145-163). Routledge.

Munday, J. (2016). *Introducing translation studies: Theories and applications*. Routledge. doi:10.4324/9781315691862

O'Dowd, R. (2018). From Telecollaboration to Virtual Exchange: State of the Art and the Role of UNICollaboration in Moving Forward. *Journal of Virtual Exchange*, *1*, 1–23. doi:10.14705/rpnet.2018.jve.1

O'Dowd, R., & Dooly, M. (2020). Intercultural communicative competence development through telecollaboration and virtual exchange. In J. Jackson (Ed.), The Routledge Handbook of Language and Intercultural Communication (pp. 361-375). Routledge. doi:10.4324/9781003036210-28

O'Dowd, R. (2019). A Transnational Model of Virtual Exchange for Global Citizenship Education. *Language Teaching*, *53*(4), 477–490. doi:10.1017/S0261444819000077

O'Dowd, R. (2021). What do Students Learn in Virtual Exchange? A Qualitative Content Analysis of Learning Outcomes across Multiple Exchanges. *International Journal of Educational Research, 109*, 101804. doi:10.1016/j.ijer.2021.101804

Orsini-Jones, M., & Lee, F. (2018). *Intercultural Communicative Competence for Global Citizenship: Identifying cyberpragmatic rules of engagement in telecollaboration*. Springer. doi:10.1057/978-1-137-58103-7

Reiss, K., & Vermeer, H. (1984/2013). *Towards a General Theory of Translational Action: Skopos Theory Explained* (C. Nord, Trans.). St Jerome.

Rienties, B., Lewis, T., O'Dowd, R., Rets, I., & Rogaten, J. (2020). The impact of virtual exchange on TPACK and Foreign Language Competence: Reviewing a Large-Scale Implementation Across 23 Virtual Exchanges. *Computer Assisted Language Learning*, 1–27. doi:10.1080/09588221.2020.1737546

Rogers, M., White, M., Loughbridge, M., & Higgins, I. (2020). *Thinking German Translation. A Course in Translation Method: German to English*. Routledge.

Rozmysłowicz, T. (2019). Translation und Kulturelle Differenz. Kritik und Revision ihrer translationswissenschaftlichen Verhältnisestimmung. In L. Heller & T. Rozmysłowicz (Eds.), *Translation und Interkulturelle Kommunikation/Translation and Intercultural Communication: Beiträge zur Theorie, Empirie und Praxis kultureller Austauschprozesse/Theoretical, Empirical and Practical Perspectives on Cultural Exchanges* (Vol. 106, pp. 51–64). Frank & Timme Verlag.

Schreier, M. (2012). *Qualitative Content Analysis in Practice*. Sage Publications.

Siever, H. (2019). Metaphern für die Figur des Translators. In L. Heller & T. Rozmysłowicz (Eds.), *Translation und Interkulturelle Kommunikation/Translation and Intercultural Communication: Beiträge zur Theorie, Empirie und Praxis kultureller Austauschprozesse/Theoretical, Empirical and Practical Perspectives on Cultural Exchanges* (Vol. 106, pp. 65–88). Frank & Timme Verlag.

Stenhouse, L. (1975). *An Introduction to Curriculum Research and Development*. Heinemann.

The Times. (2019). *German is more Desirable than French for Employers*. https://www.thetimes.co.uk/article/german-is-more-desirable-than-french-for-employers-z7mbghm5t

Townsend, A. (2013). *Action research: The challenges of changing and researching practice: The challenges of understanding and changing practice*. McGraw-Hill Education.

Vermeer, H. J. (1978). Ein Rahmen für eine allgemeine Translationstheorie. *Lebende Sprachen, 3*, 99–102.

Vermeer, H.J. (1996). *Die Welt, in der wir übersetzen. Drei translatologische Überlegungen zu Realität, Vergleich und Prozess*. TextCONText.

Warschauer, M. (1996). *Telecollaboration in foreign language learning*. University of Hawai'i at Manoa: Second Language Teaching and Curriculum Center.

Welsch, W. (1995). Zur veränderten Verfaßtheit heutige Kulturen. *Zeitschrift für Kulturaustausch, 45*(1).

Witte, H. (2000). *Die Kulturkompetenz des Translators. Begriffliche Grundlegung und Didaktisierung*. Stauffenburg.

ADDITIONAL READING

Byram, M. (2021). *Teaching and Assessing Intercultural Communicative Competence*. Multilingual Matters. doi:10.21832/9781800410251

Cook, G. (2010). *Translation in Language Teaching*. Oxford University Press.

Munday, J. (2016). *Introducing translation studies: Theories and applications*. Routledge. doi:10.4324/9781315691862

O'Dowd, R., & Lewis, T. (Eds.). (2016). *Online Intercultural Exchange*. Routledge. doi:10.4324/9781315678931

Orsini-Jones, M., & Lee, F. (2018). *Intercultural Communicative Competence for Global Citizenship: Identifying cyberpragmatic rules of engagement in telecollaboration*. Springer. doi:10.1057/978-1-137-58103-7

Townsend, A. (2013). *Action research: The challenges of changing and researching practice: The challenges of understanding and changing practice*. McGraw-Hill Education.

KEY TERMS AND DEFINITIONS

Ab initio German Studies: The programme of study for students at Durham University (UK) with no 'A'-Level (school leaving certificate) in German.

Action-Research: A research framework which involves practitioners investigating their own practice through iterative cycles of planning, action, and reflection.

English Teacher Education: The teacher training programme at Karlsruhe University of Education (Germany) for prospective teachers of English at primary and secondary level.

Functional Communicative Competence: Knowledge of and ability to employ a particular linguistic system in interaction situations.

Intercultural Communicative Competence: The goal of modern foreign language pedagogy in Germany. It involves the development of learners into 'intercultural speakers' who are able to communicate and mediate between interlocutors of divergent linguacultural backgrounds.

Telecollaboration: Telecollaboration is a form of virtual exchange where two cohorts work together in online formats to solve complex tasks.

Translation in Other Learning Contexts: The study of the pedagogic implementation of translation in areas other than translator education.

Translation Studies: The branch of research which investigates translation, translation processes and the role of the translator from different (inter)-disciplinary perspectives.

Virtual Exchange: Virtual exchange is a general term for pedagogical online intercultural and linguistic exchange endeavours with partners in different geographical locations.

ENDNOTES

1 Although students may also choose to research the implementation of translation in the English classroom as a topic for their term paper.

2 In Germany, there is no differentiation between ‘regular’ and ‘mature’ students, and some students will have studied prior to embarking on teacher training or may desire a career change after having worked for a period of time or having taken the time out of a career for family reasons. This makes the age-range of the students at Karlsruhe University of Education very heterogeneous.

Chapter 7
Teacher Online ELT Experiences in a Rural Primary School in China During the COVID-19 Pandemic

Di Liang
https://orcid.org/0000-0001-9287-8344
The Pennsylvania State University, USA

Xingtan Cao
University of Ottawa, Canada

ABSTRACT

This study adopts narrative inquiry to report five English teachers' online teaching experiences in a rural primary school in China during the COVID-19 pandemic. From a sociocultural theoretical perspective, this study shows how the participating teachers navigated the transition in instructional mode and developed familiarity with online teaching over time. Using thematic analysis, the findings of this study reveal that the teachers showed anxiety toward online teaching, that they formed a virtual community of practice, that they incorporated lived experiences into online teaching, and that they called for professional development centered on online teaching and spoke to the changing needs for English teaching in the post-COVID era. Implications are provided regarding how the teachers could transfer face-to-face ELT to an online setting and how they could be better supported professionally by the school and their colleagues.

INTRODUCTION

Online teaching, the process to implement education via the internet on virtual platforms, is no longer a new concept to educators and students in the COVID-19 pandemic. In attune with the suggestions by the World Health Organization (WHO, 2021), local health officials in China (e.g., National Health

DOI: 10.4018/978-1-7998-8717-1.ch007

Commission of the PRC [NHC], 2020) recommended protective measures such as physical distancing, wearing a mask, avoiding crowds, limiting indoor gathering, frequent hands washing, and so forth, to reduce the spread of the Coronavirus. Under this advisory, a nationwide lockdown was implemented that shut down all indoor venues and activities, including schools (CGTN, 2021). As a result, teachers were required to shift from teaching face-to-face to teaching online with short notice (Moser et al, 2020).

The present study focuses on the shift of the instructional mode during the COVID-19 pandemic and discusses how it exerted influence over English Language Teaching (henceforth, ELT) in a rural primary school in a western province in China. This study is situated in two main contexts: ELT in China and the COVID-19 pandemic. In what follows, the authors describe the education system in China with an emphasis on English as a mandated subject and provide a brief account of the COVID-19 mitigating policies in China.

English as a Mandated Subject in the 9-Year Compulsory Education in China

Education in China can be divided into five phases (see Table 1). Primary school and junior high school constitute the 9-year compulsory education system in China. The *Compulsory Education Law of the People's Republic of China* passed in 1986 stated that attending the 9-year compulsory education is a civic obligation for all Chinese citizens (National People's Congress, 2019). The initial mandated subject areas in the 9-year compulsory education included Chinese language and literature, mathematics (both algebra and geometry), moral education, physical education, and music education; English was a latecomer to this group (Cao, 2018).

In 2001, the Ministry of Education (MOE) (2001) recommended integrating English as a mandated subject starting from grade 3. This recommendation came at a time after China had adopted the Reform and Opening-Up Policy for two decades. The boosting economy and open market modernized China; hence, China's education needed to keep up with this pace of modernization (Cao, 2018). According to the MOE (2001), "education should be geared to the needs of modernization, of the world and of the future" (para. 1). Therefore, English, a language spoken widely around the world, would enhance China's communication with the world (Liao, 2004). Since then, ELT has become a big component in primary, junior high, and senior high schools.

Table 1. Education system in China

Phase	Duration	Compulsory or not?
Kindergarten	3 years	No
Primary school	5 or 6 years	Yes
Junior high school	3 or 4 years	Yes
Senior high school	3 years	No
Colleges and universities	4 years	No

Source: (Cao, 2018)

The expansion of ELT in China brought about some issues. The first issue pertains to the shortage of qualified English teachers (Shu, 2004). When English first became a mandated subject, there was a nationwide shortfall of English teachers (Hu, 2005). To alleviate the situation, teacher training programs were provided to individual teachers who were interested in ELT; additionally, the enrollment capacity for English majors at the university level was expanded to recruit more ELT teacher candidates (Xiong & Xiong, 2017). Over the years, although more qualified teachers have joined the ELT team, the shortage of qualified English teachers remains salient in some rural areas in China (Chung & Mason, 2012; Li et al., 2020; Wei & Zhou, 2019).

The disparity in educational resources is another issue concerning the expansion of ELT in China. According to Hu (2003), "not all parts of China... have benefited equally from the efforts and resources invested in ELT" (p. 291). Consequently, "significant differences" in educational resources (e.g., instructional technology, textbooks, teaching strategies, etc.) exist "between major cities and small cities, between rural towns and countryside, between coastal and inland areas, between north and south, between key and non-key schools/universities" in China (Cortazzi & Jin, 1996, p. 61). In other words, compared to the schools in urban or coastal areas, the issue of disparity in educational resources impacts the schools in rural areas more negatively (Hu, 2002; H. L. Wong et al., 2014).

COVID-19 Mitigating Policies in China

On December 31st, 2019, the Wuhan Municipal Health Commission reported 27 cases of pneumonia in the city of Wuhan, Hubei Province, China (CGTN, 2021). Soon after, Wuhan saw a surge of cases in the beginning of 2020. By late January 2020, the then-mysterious pneumonia caused by the highly contagious virus, which later became known as COVID-19 Coronavirus, proliferated globally (WHO, 2020). On March 11th, 2020, the WHO characterized the crisis of COVID-19 Coronavirus as a pandemic (WHO, 2020).

In China, governments at all levels responded quickly to the situation: On January 23rd, 2020, one day before the Chinese New Year's Eve, a lockdown was ordered by the central government of China to the city of Wuhan (CGTN, 2021). Local governments in other provinces implemented lockdown policies two days after. On January 25th, 2020, China went into a nationwide lockdown. Along with the nationwide lockdown, K-12 schools and universities across the country opted for synchronous online instruction, which lasted for approximately three months (CGTN, 2021).

In this study, the authors intend to discuss how the aforementioned contextual themes – ELT in China, online teaching, and the COVID-19 pandemic – intersected. Hence, the authors elicited narrative experiences from five English teachers in a rural primary school in a western Chinese province to illuminate how their lives have been affected by the pandemic and how they navigated online teaching. To begin with, the authors review the scholarship of technology and ELT as well as the studies on ELT during the COVID-19 pandemic.

LITERATURE REVIEW

Prior to the mandated online instruction during the COVID-19 pandemic, ELT through technology-integrated methods has been explored to some extent, pointing to the fundamental pedagogical concept of Computer-Assisted Language Learning (CALL) (Chapelle, 2003). In this section, the authors provide a succinct look at the scholarship that studies technology and ELT and discuss how the emerging studies during the pandemic have contributed to this scholarship.

Technology and ELT

The advent of technology has provided advantages to transform teaching and learning (Billings & Mathison, 2011). Based on Jonassen et al.'s (2008) conceptualization, Gilakjani (2017) discusses that technology (1) supports learners' independent knowledge construction, (2) supports learners' seeking and accessing the necessary information to broaden their knowledge-base and worldviews, (3) provides learners with a real context where they could manipulate tools to tackle problems to gain valuable knowledge, (4) engages learners with their peers in an interactive learning environment, and (5) helps learners express what they know and reflect meta-cognitively on how they have come to know it – their meaning-making process. In sum, technology has a built-in potential for meaningful learning.

When it comes to ELT, technology has been implemented in different instructional modes to enhance English language learners' (ELLs) meaningful learning experiences. First, technology is commonly utilized in face-to-face learning. With the advancement of instructional technology in recent years, face-to-face ELT is enhanced by the teachers' strategic utilization of various multimedia learning materials (e.g., YouTube videos), Internet-based activities (e.g., Kahoot!), and audio-visual or multi-sensory devices (e.g., a tablet) (Solano et al., 2017; Zhao, 2003). Integrating instructional technology has been empirically proven to facilitate learners' comprehensibility of the subject matter and increase learner engagement (Eady & Lockyer, 2013; James, 2014; Mulyono, 2016). For example, Solano et al. (2017) found that ELLs in their study responded positively to the teacher's use of technological tools such as YouTube videos, podcasts, Padlet, and presentational slides. 90% of the participating students reported that they considered those tools "really productive for their learning process. They also affirmed that through the use of technology they can achieve better academic results" (p. 83). Hence, as the literature described, a technology-integrated classroom enriches ELLs' learning experiences.

Moreover, technology engenders a relatively new mode of ELT instruction: Flipped learning (Bergmann & Sams, 2012). As the name indicates, flipped learning refers to a reversed order of instruction where ELLs preview the multimedia learning materials online and complete homework prior to the face-to-face class, so in-class time can be used for meaningful interactive activities such as discussions, debates, hands-on projects, and so forth, where ELLs interact with the subject matter knowledge deeply and critically and apply what they learn in various tasks (e.g., Turan & Akdag-Cimen, 2020). This approach has been found to incentivize ELLs to learn autonomously (e.g., Choe & Seong, 2016; Yang, 2017), boost their confidence in learning and using the subject matter knowledge (e.g., Engin & Donanci, 2016), increase the level of ELLs' in-class engagement and interactions (e.g., Yang, 2017; Zainuddin, 2017), prolong their retention of the knowledge (e.g., Chen Hsieh et al., 2016), and improve their language skills (e.g., Abaeian & Samadi, 2016). In such an environment with a mix of online and face-to-face learning – namely, a blended learning environment (Bonk & Graham, 2012), learning has become a self-paced activity where ELLs are held accountable for their own learning process.

Lastly, technology equips online learning with flexibility. Considered an improved version of distance learning, online learning enables learning to happen in a different location from teaching and is often conducted synchronously or asynchronously (Moore et al., 2011). As it is a rather unconventional instructional mode, the implementation of online learning requires Internet-based technology and a system of lesson planning, teaching, tutoring, communication, and evaluation that tailors to bridge the distance between the teacher and the learners (Bozkurt, 2019). Because of its flexibility, online learning has been used widely in many subjects, including ELT (Vorobel & Kim, 2012). Although online learning has gained popularity in ELT and ELT-related research in recent years, it has become highly relevant in a global context during the COVID-19 pandemic (Kamal et al., 2021).

ELT During the COVID-19 Pandemic

Because of the school shutdowns and strict quarantine protocols, online learning has replaced any instructional modes with face-to-face components during the COVID-19 pandemic (Kamal et al., 2021). Focused on this predominant instructional mode and set in the COVID-19 era, a plethora of studies on ELT investigated various themes related to online learning during the pandemic.

For example, many studies pointed out that English teachers around the world faced tremendous pedagogical challenges as they were tasked with technology-based online instruction, including the lack of familiarity with the technology (e.g., Moorhouse, 2020), the difficulty of keeping students engaged (e.g., Adara & Najmudin, 2020), the ineffectiveness of teaching pronunciation and speaking (e.g., Bailey & Lee, 2020), the inconvenience of implementing assessments (e.g., Chung & Choi, 2021), and many other challenges. In light of the change in instructional mode, many studies documented how English teachers around the world explored technological tools for online teaching. Ways of using the technological tools include incorporating social media such as YouTube or Facebook in teaching to provide multimodal learning input for ELLs (e.g., Al-Shammari, 2020), implementing synchronous teaching on platforms such as Zoom and Google Meet (e.g., Basilaia & Kvavadze, 2020), giving assignments to students on interactive platforms such as Kahoot! and Google Classroom (e.g., Destianingsih & Satria, 2020), and attempting real-time communication after class on WhatsApp for attendance checking and answering questions from students as well as their parents (e.g., Asmara, 2020).

In addition to the studies listed here, the authors are aware that there are many other studies on ELT during the pandemic and that this body of literature is rapidly growing. Thus, the authors provided a brief review on a portion of the available studies rather than trying to exhaust this emerging scholarship. As far as the studies covered are concerned, the authors noticed that most of them were survey-based and did not have a theoretical underpinning. Hence, the authors of the present study hope to enrich this growing body of research by presenting a study with a well-developed theoretical framework and a different methodological approach.

PURPOSE OF THE STUDY

Informed by the scholarship in technology-integrated ELT and ELT studies conducted during the COVID-19 pandemic, the authors became interested in how English language teachers navigated online ELT in this trying time, more specifically, the teachers in rural settings. Under the nationwide lockdown, teachers in China were tasked with a deft transition from *teaching from a podium* to *teaching from a desk at home*. However, it was not an easy task, given that teachers would need to find an efficient way to transfer hard copies of teaching materials to digital versions, to develop instructional activities on virtual platforms, and to ensure their teaching be comprehensible to the students. Challenges as such were prominent in the schools nationwide, especially those in the rural areas, as rural schools in Chinese western provinces generally receive fewer resources and support compared to their urban, coastal counterparts (Hu, 2003, 2005; H. L. Wong et al., 2014); that is, the teachers in the rural setting face more pedagogical, professional, or personal challenges (Ma et al., 2018). During the pandemic, these challenges have been augmented while the teachers in rural areas were acclimating to online instruction. Therefore, this study was set in a rural primary school in a western Chinese province with a focus on the teachers' online teaching experiences.

The authors of this study asked this overarching question: *What were the teachers' online English teaching experiences in a rural primary school in China during the COVID-19 pandemic?* Under this general inquiry, the authors sought from the teachers' narrative experiences to answer the following sub-questions:

1. How did teachers' lived experiences (e.g., life, learning, and teaching experiences) inform their practices of teaching English online during the COVID-19 pandemic?
2. What were the challenges the teachers faced during teaching English online during the COVID-19 pandemic?
3. How did the teachers use available mediating artifacts to tackle those challenges and become accustomed to online teaching?

By presenting the teachers' narratives and answering these questions, the authors hope to draw attention to (1) how the teachers grew accustomed to online teaching, (2) the challenges they faced during the pandemic regarding transferring teaching from face-to-face to online instruction, (3) how they had risen to those challenges by using the relatively limited resources that were available to them, and (4) what professional supports they wished to have that could help them navigate online settings and transition more deftly from face-to-face teaching to online teaching. To this end, the authors hope to provide implications regarding how teachers from under-represented contexts could transfer language teaching from face-to-face to online settings and discuss how teachers could be better supported professionally and personally by the community, the school, colleagues, and other stakeholders.

THEORETICAL FRAMEWORK: A SOCIOCULTURAL THEORETICAL PERSPECTIVE

To many teachers, including the participating teachers in this study, the transition to teaching online was, to some extent, forced (Moorhouse, 2020), meaning that the teachers were not fully prepared or properly trained for teaching online fully; they were "learning the rope as we go" (Ms. Sun: Interview). For this reason, the authors considered teachers' adapting to online teaching as a learning process. During this process, teachers sought support from available mediating artifacts (e.g., instructions from the school, online materials, peer communication, etc.) to help them navigate online teaching during the COVID-19 pandemic (Darling-Hammond & Hyler, 2020). With this understanding, the authors understood such a process as the teachers' development resulting from mediation. Therefore, sociocultural theory (Vygotsky, 1978) is taken up in this study.

From a sociocultural theoretical perspective, a person's development of consciousness (e.g., learning particular behaviors and forms of knowledge) results from his or her participation in social activities and interaction with the physical or symbolic mediating artifacts (e.g., language, signs, concept, tangible materials, etc.) in the social surroundings (Johnson, 2006; Vygotsky, 1986). However, albeit interacting with the same set of artifacts, each person's development trajectory appears to be different. Vygotsky (1987) stated that a person might develop differently from each other, as each person interacts with the mediating artifacts in the social surroundings in a unique way that is informed by his or her lived experiences, personal history, and prior knowledge of the self and the world (Johnson & Golombek, 2003). Ergo, when a person's experiences and history are brought into contact with the social surroundings, a *social situation of development* is created. Vygotsky (1998) described social situation of development as "the unique, specific for a particular age, inimitable relationship" (p. 903) between a person and the social surroundings. In addition, social situation of development considers a person's interactions with capable peers in the society who are deemed as "the bearer of social-cultural experience" (Karabanova, 2010, p. 130). That is to say, a person's development is at the same time objective and subjective. To understand how a person develops in a social situation, Vygostky (1986) suggests locating the contradictions – the gap between what the person understands and what the social situation presents to him or her that is yet beyond his or her level of comprehensibility. To settle this contradiction, a person would seek mediation from social surroundings, including signs, artifacts, and other capable peers. In this way, a person's existing knowledge is enriched and reshaped through the mediating artifacts in the social surroundings; the newly acquired knowledge will then be gradually internalized by the individual, leading to a person's development of consciousness (Vygotsky, 1978).

In this study, the authors understood that the participating teachers experienced the same contradictions presented by the "forced" assignment of online teaching in the time of the COVID-19 pandemic. They also understood that each participating teacher learned how to fulfill this assignment on the go. Therefore, the authors utilized the theoretical concept of social situation of development to capture and examine the similarities and differences in how each teacher navigated online teaching. Under the sociocultural theoretical framework, the authors developed an interview protocol to elicit participating teachers' personal life, prior learning and teaching experiences, as well as their teaching experiences during the COVID-19 pandemic. The authors understood that "a sociocultural perspective recognizes the social as shaping the cognitive, and thus, it highlights the rich details of how teacher development emerges out of and is constructed by teachers within the settings and circumstances of their work" (Johnson, 2007, p. 186). Hence, once the teachers' narrative experiences were externalized, the authors continued to apply the sociocultural perspective to analyze the narratives in order to understand the participating teachers' social realities of online teaching in the time of the COVID-19 pandemic; more specifically, to understand (1) how each teacher's lived experiences informed one's online ELT practices and (2) how each teacher used available mediating artifacts to advance understanding of online teaching and get accustomed to this instructional mode.

METHODOLOGY

Research Context and Participants

Aiming to present English teachers' authentic experiences in online teaching during the COVID-19 pandemic, this study was conducted in a rural primary school in a western province in China. The town where the school is located is considered an impoverished area, according to its provincial government. The school has more than 100 years of history and is considered to be a renowned local educational institution. The school offers classes from Grade 1 to Grade 6 with a total enrollment of approximately 2,900 students. Currently, 138 teachers are working at this school, 12 of which are English teachers. After asking all 12 English teachers, five of them consented to participate in this study. All participating teachers have been working as English teachers for more than five years (see Table 2). Each teacher participated in a one-hour interview. The interview questions were designed to elicit participating teachers' experiences, understandings, and thoughts about online ELT in the rural setting in China during the pandemic.

Table 2. Demographic information on the participants

Teacher	Years of Teaching	Grades of Teaching
Ms. Zhao	7	6
Ms. Qian	13	5
Ms. Sun	21	6
Ms. Li	10	5
Ms. Wu	7	6

Note: All the teachers' names are pseudonyms.

Data Collection and Analysis

This study used narrative inquiry as the methodology to understand the participating teachers' authentic experiences (Golombek & Johnson, 2004) of teaching English online in the time of the COVID-19 pandemic. Narrative inquiry is defined as "the study of ways humans experience the world" (Clandinin & Connelly, 1991, p. 2) where "humans are storytelling organisms who, individually and socially, lead storied lives" (p. 2); that is, a person's experience shapes what and how the person comes to know about the world, life, and the self. According to Clandinin and Connelly (1994, 2000), building on Dewey's (1938) criteria of experience, experiences ought to be understood on a historical, personal, social, and contextual nexus. In educational research, narrative inquiry is believed to be a "powerful" (Witherell & Noddings, 1991, p. 280) research tool that allows researchers to learn from participants' experiences in order to "come to understand – ourselves, others, and even the subjects we teach and learn" (p. 279). When it comes to studying language teachers' experiences, narrative inquiry is described "as systematic exploration that is conducted by teachers and for teachers through their own stories and language" (Johnson & Golombek, 2002, p. 6). In other words, narratives can be used to externalize language teachers' experiences, which can be further used as orienting bases for inquiries, reflections, and imaginations as they pertain to the teachers' personal and professional lives.

For the reasons above, the authors chose to use narrative inquiry in this study. Situated in the sociocultural theoretical concept of social situation of development, an interview protocol was developed with questions to elicit from the participating teachers their personal and social experiences that reflected their social realities of teaching English online in the COVID-19 pandemic. Then, the authors used the protocol to conduct interviews respectively with each participating teacher. Data was transcribed after the interviews. Relevant sections in the data were translated from Chinese to English; the translation was proofread by the first author. Using thematic analysis (Braun & Clarke, 2012), the authors conducted two rounds of data analysis: In the first round, initial codes that "mirror participants' language and concepts" (Braun & Clarke, 2012, p. 61) were identified (e.g., "feeling anxious," "not knowing where to find teaching materials," "not being familiar with online teaching tools," etc.); in the ensuing round, the generated codes were reviewed by the authors "to identify areas of similarity and overlap between codes" (Braun & Clarke, 2012, p. 63). After reviewing, the authors subsumed the overlapping codes under four broad themes: "anxiety and uncertainty toward online teaching," "making lesson plans for online teaching," "forming a virtual community," and "looking into the future." Based on these broad themes, the authors wrote up narratives to reconstruct the teachers' authentic experiences.

FINDINGS

As narrative inquiry allows researchers to reconstruct or retell stories based on the data (Clandinin & Connelly, 1991; Witherell & Noddings, 1991), when presenting the findings, the authors chronologically organized participating teachers' narratives (Clandinin & Connelly, 1991; Witherell & Noddings, 1991) based on the broad themes emerged from the data (Liu & Xu, 2011). In this way, a *composite narrative* was created by weaving individual narratives together to reconstruct what the teachers' online English teaching experiences were in a rural primary school in China during the COVID-19 pandemic and show the developmental trajectory of them learning to do online teaching. In creating the composite narrative, first, the authors *timestamped* the narrative to indicate the time progression (e.g., "Day 1," "Day 6," etc.), to streamline the themes that emerged from each individual teacher's narrative, and to establish an idea of how the teachers developed in doing online teaching over time. Next, they *contextualized* the narrative with information that reflects each teacher's personal history, lived experiences, and prior knowledge to show how each teacher was mediated learning to do online teaching within her own social situation of development. Lastly, by drawing connections broadly among each individual teacher's narrative and identifying commonalities or differences in those narratives, the authors *imagined* how each teacher would interact with each other in the composite narrative (e.g., agreeing with each other). Using this structure, this study shows how the themes are expressed and discussed by the teachers and provides a contextualized account of the experiences of synchronous online ELT in a rural primary school in China during the COVID-19 pandemic.

Day 1: Anxiety and Uncertainty

Most teachers in this study exhibited anxiety and low self-confidence in using online instructional technology at the beginning of online teaching, which was primarily due to the haphazard nature of the shift in instructional mode as the teachers were given short notice. "Online teaching for us is as if a person is crossing a river by feeling their way by the stones," said Ms. Sun (Interview), who has been working in this school for nearly two decades. "Students did not even have the textbook with them when the outbreak started. We had to convert the content of the textbook to PowerPoint slides," Ms. Sun (Interview) added, indicating how unprepared they were with this sudden change to online teaching. Moreover, the fact that the school was not well equipped with technology contributed to the teachers' anxiety. Ms. Wu pointed out that the school had been planning to install computers, sound systems, projectors, and big screens in the classrooms, but the funding had been short to finish the installment, reflecting the reality that rural schools in general receive less funding for improving infrastructure from local government or private organizations than their counterparts in more developed regions (Hu, 2002; H. L. Wong et al., 2014). As a consequence, teachers were not well versed in the realm of instructional technology. They were not familiar with multimedia or online teaching resources; instead, they relied heavily on lecturing and tangible teaching props (e.g., flashcards, posters, handouts, etc.) in face-to-face teaching. On this note, Ms. Sun expressed her agitation for creating PowerPoint slides for online classes. In a face-to-face classroom, Ms. Sun would focus more on course delivery and classroom interaction, none of which requires PowerPoint slides in her practices. To Ms. Sun, creating PowerPoint slides was exhausting and "such a nuisance and distraction for teaching" (Ms. Sun: Interview). Ms. Qian shared the same opinion.

In addition to the familiarity with technology, some teachers expressed anxiety and concern that the parents might audit the online class with their children. Ms. Zhao confessed that she felt uneasy knowing that parents would sit next to their children listening to her lectures. Such an uncomfortable feeling was instigated by the change in the mode of communication between the teacher and the parents in the online environment: Normally, Ms. Zhao's interactions with the parents have been confined to updating the parents on their children's academic standings and in-class behaviors via WeChat, a real-time communication application; yet, on the online platform, the parents would be able to see more of Ms. Zhao – teaching, interacting with the students, and more. Online teaching seemingly shortened the distance between the teacher and the parents. As Ms. Zhao candidly said, "I feel like I am demystified" (Interview).

Some teachers felt uncertain about how to perform regular teaching duties in online teaching. For example, Ms. Wu was not sure about classroom management. In her view, face-to-face classes gave the teacher the advantage of managing the classroom via non-verbal cues, such as eye gaze, hand gestures, and body movements: Ms. Wu would use eye gazing for nominating students to speak or shutting down a non-sequitur in the back of the classroom. However, nuanced actions as such would be impossible for the teacher to convey or the students to capture on computer screens.

Unlike some of her colleagues who expressed anxiety or uncertainty toward online teaching, Ms. Li tended to seek the positive sides of such a new instructional mode. In her opinion, online classes provided teachers an opportunity to involve parents in students' learning journey to a greater extent than usual. For example, parents and their children would have the chance to collaborate on class projects. This way of thinking, interestingly, contradicted Ms. Zhao's hesitation in interacting with the parents. With a positive mindset, Ms. Li has been a leading voice – in her words, a "cheerleader" (Ms. Li: Interview) – in helping her fellow English language teachers navigate online instruction.

Day 6: Bringing Teaching Online

Survived a rather "hectic" (Ms. Sun: Interview) first week, teachers took some moments during the weekend to reflect on the challenges of online teaching and think about how to make online instruction more effective in the coming weeks. According to the teachers, the challenges they experienced include: (1) Students exhibited low motivation in learning; (2) students got distracted by irrelevant things that happened in their households; and (3) some students had trouble following teachers' instructions. In light of these challenges, some teachers felt the urgency of using available resources and technology to adapt the strategies they used in the face-to-face classroom to the online environment in order to increase the level of student engagement and the quality of online instruction.

To get students into learning mood, Ms. Zhao would usually start her class with a warm-up activity, focusing on vocabulary review. It would have been a straightforward activity if it were in a face-to-face class; Ms. Zhao had to be creative with transferring the warm-up activity online. She recalled that, when she was an English learner, she labeled objects at home with the corresponding English words to help memorize the words; Ms. Zhao decided to replicate this learning strategy. At the beginning of each class, Ms. Zhao would give students a short list of words – for example, "water," "red," and "soft" – and ask them to find the objects in their household that shared some sort of relation to those words – in the case of "water," "red," and "soft," a water bottle, a red wallet, and a sponge would work. Ms. Zhao would ask the students to take pictures of the objects and post them to a discussion thread she created on QZone, a social networking site. Then, Ms. Zhao would ask students to do a show-and-tell on the objects. She would wrap up the activity by having the whole class reading aloud the words. In this way, students were able to practice speaking and review the words visually, verbally, and kinetically.

Ms. Sun and Ms. Qian liked to write down important language points for the students on the whiteboard in the classroom. Ms. Qian said, "writing on the whiteboard provides students with a clear view of how the language should be used" (Interview). Ms. Sun agreed with Ms. Qian that, "For example, I can parse a sentence on the whiteboard, marking which part is the subject, which is the verb, and object, and other components. This is easier for students to comprehend than just listening to me talk" (Interview). Therefore, Ms. Sun and Ms. Qian took advantage of the virtual whiteboard function on the school-endorsed online teaching platform, DingTalk, and continued what they loved to do as if they were teaching face-to-face.

Ms. Wu believed that students getting distracted was partly because the teacher was not able to communicate with the students using paralinguistic or non-verbal cues effectively. In her opinion, those cues play an important part in classroom discourse: Paralinguistic cues (e.g., prosody, tone, pace, etc.) could help the teacher indicate important information (e.g., using stress or slowing down in talking); whereas, non-verbal cues (e.g., eye gaze, gesture, body movements, etc.) could help the teacher perform managerial tasks (e.g., using eye gaze to shut down side-talks in class) or provide additional instruction (e.g., using body movement to convey the meaning of a word). For paralinguistic cues, Ms. Wu simply exaggerated the way she talked in the online class. However, the subtle details of non-verbal cues were difficult for the students to capture via computer screens. While thinking about how to implement non-verbal cues in an online environment, Ms. Wu remembered that she had seen her daughter use an application on her cellphone to record facial or body movements and incarnate those expressions on an avatar; an idea hit her. Ms. Wu used the application, FaceRig, to pre-record some non-verbal expressions, such as an angry gaze, a turning-page motion, a tilted head, and many others; she used those expressions by holding up her cellphone to the camera during class when appropriate and achieved a somewhat comedic yet effective result.

On the note of bodily actions in teaching, Ms. Li has been keen on using drama to engage students in learning English. In the classroom, she would let students work in groups and use the learned vocabulary to make a short story; then, she would ask the groups to act out their stories. Ms. Li's love for drama originated from her own learning experience. When she was a learner of English, her teacher used a learning method that promoted learning English vocabulary through reading aloud and acting out the meaning of the word in a dramatic way. She enjoyed the performative aspect of this method very much; she also remembered that this method effectively attracted her interest in learning English, motivated her to participate in class activities, helped her overcome the unwillingness of speaking, and increased the retention of the language. Since then, Ms. Li has always liked drama for its vivid and bodily presentation of the language as well as its built-in potential for participation (R. Wong, 2014). Hence, Ms. Li attempted to transfer the drama experience to the online setting. By using an online teaching and conferencing platform, Tencent Meeting, Ms. Li divided students into groups by way of the breakout room feature; then, she gave each group a list of words; each group was given 20 minutes to improvise a story based on the words and discuss how to perform the story; students were encouraged to use their home space and household objects to help complete their performance; Ms. Li circulated from one group to another to facilitate their rehearsals; and lastly, all the groups came back to the main room to perform. While one group was performing, Ms. Li asked the others to give scores and feedback to the performing group via a polling application on their cellphones, WenJuanXing; by doing so, she was able to keep the rest of the class engaged. Ms. Li reported that this activity was of great success as students were very active and participatory.

Day 15: Setting up a Virtual Office

Online teaching deprived the teachers of working in the same space and meeting regularly. Teachers have been working individually at their home, and the weekly department meeting was put on halt since the onset of online instruction. However, after teaching for two weeks, teachers felt the need of resuming a collaborative working space in some way, shape, or form. As Ms. Sun put it, "we need more brains to figure out how to better cope with the situation" (Ms. Sun: Interview). Ms. Qian took the lead and set up a virtual office on the online conference platform, Tencent Meeting, where all the English teachers would meet for approximately an hour on Mondays, Wednesdays, and Fridays.

The virtual office benefited the teachers in several ways. First, it created a share-point of online teaching resources. Since most teachers in the group were not familiar with instructional technology, Ms. Zhao, who had some experiences, volunteered to share some online resources with the group. Ms. Li spoke highly of the generous sharing of useful tools (e.g., online dictionary – Youdao), videos (e.g., clips from animated movies in English on Youku Video), audios (e.g., a playlist of age-appropriate English songs on QQMusic), and interactive platforms (e.g., DingTalk, Tencent Meeting) by her colleague that helped her and other teachers enrich the content of online teaching and supported students' learning at home. More importantly, Ms. Li felt more confident about teaching online with the support from the virtual office.

Second, the virtual office provided space for teachers to bounce ideas for online teaching off each other. Ms. Li recounted that teachers became each other's "critical friend" (Ms. Li: Interview) by giving each other constructive feedback on lesson plans, brainstorming together feasible ideas for online teaching, and debating with each other whether an idea would work well. The mood overall in those meetings, described by Ms. Zhao, was "heated yet amicable" (Ms. Zhao: Interview). Ms. Qian acknowledged that the exchanges amongst colleagues were productive. As a product of the meetings, teachers established an online repository on Baidu Wangpan, a document-sharing cloud, of lesson plans for online instruction; every teacher contributed ideas to the lesson plans. Figuratively phrasing in a Chinese proverb, Ms. Qian remarked on the meetings that, "the fire will burn bigger when everyone contributes a piece of wood" (Ms. Qian: Interview).

Lastly, the virtual office offered the teachers the space for socializing during the pandemic. Ms. Wu said that the chitchats at the beginning of each meeting provided solace in isolation: "We just talked about our daily life, our kids, what shows we were binging, and what we cooked for dinner; we just focused on good and fun things" (Ms. Wu: Interview). Among them, Ms. Li has always had the spirit of positivity: Ms. Qian recalled that Ms. Li sent each teacher a hand-written letter with words of affirmation and encouragement every week throughout the duration of online teaching. "That kept me motivated, to be honest," said Ms. Qian. The virtual office surely bonded teachers, albeit the social distance.

Day 89: Online Teaching is the New Normal

As they reached the 3-month mark, all the teachers were well accustomed to online teaching, accepting it as the "new normal" (Ms. Zhao: Interview). In their experiences, such a "new normal" meant "no commuting to school" (Ms. Li: Interview), "teaching from my desk at home, instead of a podium" (Ms. Sun: Interview), "virtual interaction with the students and their parents" (Ms. Qian: Interview), "increased screen time searching for or developing teaching materials online" (Ms. Zhao: Interview), and "building a lesson on a variety of instructional technology" (Ms. Wu: Interview).

When asked about whether the online teaching during the pandemic has affected how they thought ELT should move forward in their school, all teachers shared similar perspectives. First, they agreed that teachers should be liberated from using the officially-acknowledged publications (e.g., Teachers' Handbook and the Work Book published with the textbook) as the only resources to inform lesson planning, activity developing, and teaching. During the pandemic, they saw the benefits of branching out to online resources and bringing useful content or strategies back to their teaching. For example, Ms. Wu followed several English teachers on social media, such as Douyin (Chinese version of TikTok), a short video social media platform, and Weibo, a short blog site, where she learned many "teaching hacks" (Ms. Wu: Interview) about online tools for English learning, activity designs, assessment ideas, and virtual classroom management tips. Moreover, the teachers experienced the benefits and convenience of teaching English with technology (e.g., built-in participatory potential, multimodal learning resources, vivid presentation of the language, etc.). For this reason, they hoped that the school could finish installing instructional technology in the classrooms and organize professional development on how to make good use of instructional technology.

DISCUSSION

Learning from the findings, teachers were agentive in creating social situation of development to navigate and grow accustomed to synchronous online teaching during the COVID-19 pandemic. In this section, the authors drew from teachers' narratives to answer research questions of this study and discuss implications as to how the teachers could transfer ELT from face-to-face to an online environment and how they would be better supported professionally by the school and their colleagues.

Valuing Lived Experiences

In their timely research on ELT in South Korea, Bailey and Lee (2020) found a positive correlation between teachers' prior experiences with instructional technology and their preparedness for online teaching during the COVID-19 pandemic, while teachers with no experiences with online teaching or teaching with technology were found to face more challenges, whether it be pedagogical or emotional. In this regard, based on the findings, the authors of this study suggest a broader view as to understand what constitutes a teacher's "prior experiences" that could inform one's online teaching practices.

Because of the lack of familiarity with instructional technology and online teaching experiences, teachers in this study faced pedagogical and emotional challenges. In facing the challenges, they were found to actively seek from their lived experiences, including experiences in life as well as prior learning and teaching experiences, to inspire their teaching practices in the online setting. That is, striving to understand how to do online ELT, the teachers brought their lived experiences into contact with the current situation to create their own social situation of development to tackle the challenges – or, in a sociocultural theoretical term, contradictions (e.g., what they wanted to do versus what they were able to do online) – and to facilitate their development in learning to teach online.

Upon answering the first research question, the authors noticed the following ways that the teachers used their lived experiences to inform online teaching practices. First, teachers replicated their positive English learning experiences from the past in the online classes (Davin et al., 2017). For instance, Ms. Zhao incorporated household objects in vocabulary review as she remembered that she used to memorize words that way, and Ms. Li brought drama online because she had a blast learning English through role-playing when she was a learner. Second, teachers transferred face-to-face learning experiences to the online setting by way of available technology. For example, Ms. Sun and Ms. Qian used DingTalk's whiteboard function to recreate whiteboard writing from a classroom; Ms. Zhao did the vocabulary warm-up activity with students via QZone. Finally, teachers were inspired by the seemingly trivial moments in their life: Ms. Wu got the idea of creating avatar emoticons with the help of FaceRig to mirror the non-verbal cues in a face-to-face class from her peek at her daughter playing with the application on the phone. In another example, some teachers tried out the "teaching hacks" they saw on social media in their online classes.

These examples show that teachers' lived experiences and social surroundings acted as mediating artifacts for enriching and developing their understanding of online teaching. Therefore, the authors argue that learning to do online teaching should be considered relational to and mediated by not only experiences with instructional technology or online teaching but also lived experiences. In this sense, when discussing what could inform a teacher's online teaching practices, "prior experiences" with online teaching or instructional technology are not deterministic; in fact, the teacher's lived experiences play an important role in the process and, thus, should be valued.

Building a Community of Practice

To answer the second and third research questions, the authors found that, rather than navigating online teaching independently, the teachers built a virtual office in which they collectively created a share-point of learning resources, a repository of lesson plans, and a space for socializing. From a sociocultural perspective, the authors considered this space a community of practice (CoP) (Lave & Wenger, 1991) in which teachers worked together to figure out how to do online teaching. As a sociocultural theoretical construct, CoP views individual learning process and social practice as co-constitutive of learning. Learning in such a community is manifested through the members' evolving degree of legitimate peripheral participation, which is gauged by members' level of engagement in the activities, familiarity of knowledge, and mastery of skills. That is to say, CoP created a social learning environment where individual discourse and learning plans interplayed with the community discourse and learning objectives.

The authors contend that building a CoP is helpful for facilitating teachers' learning and contributing to their level of readiness in the time of transition. In the context of this study, teachers learned about online teaching while transitioning from face-to-face instruction to online instruction. In the CoP they built, the teachers participated in activities such as interacting with online learning resources, debating the validity and feasibility of teaching ideas, and sharing confusions, struggles, and joys. The teachers reported in their narratives that being a part of these activities helped them get used to the new mode of teaching, increased their confidence about teaching online, and advanced their understanding of how to do online ELT. This outcome illuminates the central tenet to the sociocultural theoretical tradition: Personal (cognitive and psychological) development is concerned with how "external forms of social interaction become internalized psychological tools for thinking" (Johnson & Golombek, 2011, p. 1) and how the knowledge transforms from an interpersonal plane (e.g., social activities in a community) to an intrapersonal plane (e.g., internalization). In other words, personal development is in close relation to and interaction with social activities (Vygotsky, 1986). That is, personal development in CoP is a result of participating in social activities in the community (Haneda, 2006). In this sense, the authors understood that CoP benefited the teacher's social situation of development. Teachers brought into this CoP their own lived experiences about online teaching. When participating in the social activities, their experiences were validated (e.g., chats), questioned (e.g., feedback), or contested (e.g., debates), which created contradictions. Having perceived the contradictions, as the theoretical understanding of social situation of development predicts (Vygotsky, 1978), the teachers were motivated to seek mediation from social surroundings to advance their understanding of online teaching (e.g., taking advantage of the share-point of resources, receiving constructive feedback from colleagues on lesson plans, etc.) and, eventually, achieved personal development (e.g., implementing new online teaching tool in their own class). Therefore, the development of the teachers' understandings of how to do online ELT was afforded by their participation in the social activities in the CoP, their interactions with the available resources, and their mutually supportive relationships with other teachers in the community.

Professional Development on Online Teaching

The findings of this study also spoke to the necessity of professional development (PD). Specifically, the teachers in this study called for a PD that focuses on the concept and pedagogy of online teaching. As reported by the teachers, the school failed to adequately equip the classrooms with instructional technology or prepare the teachers for teaching online. This reflects the reality that, in general, teachers do not receive PD organized around the systematic instructions on how to design online lessons (Archambault et al., 2016). The COVID-19 pandemic has brought this inadequacy to the forefront. Thanks to the CoP they built, the teachers in this study were able to receive unofficial PD that incorporated the knowledge and lived experiences from capable colleagues and "teaching hacks" from social media on how to do online teaching. Despite the effectiveness of an unofficial, small-scale PD as such, it is important that a PD that addresses the challenges faced by the educators during such a trying time is organized at the school or district level to benefit a larger teacher population (Darling-Hammond & Hyler, 2020).

Given that the teachers in this study did not get to receive PD on online teaching, based on their narratives on what they hoped to have learned, the authors discuss in what ways PD could facilitate teachers' understanding of the concept of online teaching. From a sociocultural perspective, PD provides a venue for concept development (Johnson, 2009). According to Vygotsky (1986), concept development graduates a person's ability of thinking empirically to thinking abstractly by way of linking a person's everyday experiences with scientific concepts. In other words, concept development helps theorize and generalize a person's everyday experiences, which enables a person to "move beyond the limitations of everyday experiences" to "alternative circumstances and contexts" (Johnson & Golombek, 2011, p. 2) and grants a person a certain degree of maturity and freedom in thinking. In the context of this study, concept development for the teachers is to help them conceptualize what it means to teach English online. Concept development presupposes mediation, which can come in the forms of explicit instruction (Lantolf & Poehner, 2008), cultural artifacts, and social activities (Johnson & Golombek, 2011). For example, teachers can be prompted to share their understanding of online teaching by making connections with their own experiences (e.g., teaching during the pandemic, "teaching hacks" from social media). Then, teachers can learn about the theories and pedagogical strategies of online teaching through explicit instruction (e.g., lecture presentation). In this way, online teaching as a concept mediates teachers' thinking about how online teaching is different from teaching face-to-face and orients their actions toward developing a lesson with appropriate technology. Teachers can also participate in intervention activities (e.g., using a template to develop an online lesson) where they interact with mediating artifacts (e.g., handouts, lesson plan templates). By doing so, teachers can exercise, discuss, or reflect on the concept and strategies of online teaching. Through mediation, teachers will be inspired to transform their thinking as well as the ways of engaging in teaching and learning, manifesting a development in concept (Johnson, 2009; Lantolf, 2000). Hence, a well-organized PD on online teaching is crucial in helping enrich the teachers' knowledge-base, supporting them in meeting the challenges that they face, and providing them with strategies to cope with the increasingly technology-incorporated teaching of the post-COVID era (Bailey & Lee, 2020; Darling-Hammond & Hyler, 2020).

LIMITATION AND NEED FOR FUTURE RESEARCH

In this study, the authors present and discuss how English language teachers in a rural primary school in China navigated online teaching during the COVID-19 pandemic. Although the teachers brought up concerns about equity issues imposed by the transition to online teaching, the authors failed to pursue further into that direction. They did not elicit more information on how a change in the instructional mode in a rural school might instigate inequity. For example, teachers mentioned the school's limited access to instructional technology due to the lack of funding. This issue has existed for a long time (Van Dijk, 2006) and became salient during the time of COVID-19. However, regretfully, data in this study do not support an in-depth and critical discussion on the said issue, pointing to the authors' inadequate consideration for the scope of this study and the development of the interview protocol.

In light of this limitation, the authors suggest this study be considered as a springboard for future research on English teachers' experiences in rural educational settings. Future research can pay attention to not only the practical aspects of how to navigate the transition to online teaching but also, situated in the larger sociopolitical and socioeconomic contexts, the critical discussion of how the transition – or teaching with technology in general – might cause equity issues, such as accessibility of technology, training opportunities, emotional and mental burden, and so forth (see a special issue edited by Hartshorne et al., 2020). A discussion of the equity issues is critical that it could garner attention broadly from teachers, parents, educational scholars, policymakers, and other stakeholders, setting the stage for qualitative changes that could benefit students, schools, and communities-at-large in rural areas.

CONCLUDING REMARKS

Albeit being small in scale, this study sheds light on English teachers' rich narrative experiences of online teaching during the COVID-19 pandemic in a rural primary school in China. Upon analysis, the findings of this study point to the challenges created for the teachers by the intersectionality of online teaching and the COVID-19 pandemic. The findings also show the efforts that the teachers made to do online teaching with rather inadequate preparation time or support. Based on the findings, this study provides implications for how to support teachers in online teaching that could benefit English education in rural areas, which could also be applied to other subject areas in other educational settings. Considering the impact of the COVID-19 is still betiding, the authors hope that this study, along with other studies in this volume, could inspire a line of inquiry that examines phenomena and issues regarding the transition of instructional mode and online teaching in the midst or beyond the time of the pandemic.

REFERENCES

Abaeian, H., & Samadi, L. (2016). The effect of flipped classroom on Iranian EFL learners' L2 reading comprehension: Focusing on different proficiency levels. *Reading Comprehension, 3*(6), 10.

Adara, R. A., & Najmudin, O. (2020). Analysis on the differences in EFL learners' demotivating factors after COVID-19 pandemic. *TA'DIB, 23*(2), 225–236. doi:10.31958/jt.v23i2.2373

Al-Shammari, A. H. (2020). Social media and English language learning during Covid-19: KILAW students' use, attitude, and prospective. *Linguistics Journal, 14*(1), 259–275.

Archambault, L., Kennedy, K., Shelton, C., Dalal, M., McAllister, L., & Huyett, S. (2016). Incremental progress: Re-examining field experiences in K-12 online learning contexts in the United States. *Journal of Online Learning Research, 2*(3), 303–326.

Asmara, R. (2020). Teaching English in a virtual classroom using WhatsApp during COVID-19 pandemic. *Language and Educational Journal, 5*(1), 16–27. doi:10.52237/lej.v5i1.152

Bailey, D. R., & Lee, A. R. (2020). Learning from experience in the midst of COVID-19: Benefits, challenges, and strategies in online teaching. *Computer-Assisted Language Learning Electronic Journal, 21*(2), 176–196.

Basilaia, G., & Kvavadze, D. (2020). Transition to online education in schools during a SARS-CoV-2 Coronavirus (COVID-19) Pandemic in Georgia. *Pedagogical Research, 5*(4), 1–9. doi:10.29333/pr/7937

Bergmann, J., & Sams, A. (2012). Before you flip, consider this. *Phi Delta Kappan, 94*(2), 25–25. doi:10.1177/003172171209400206

Billings, E., & Mathison, C. (2011). I get to use an iPod in school? Using technology-based advance organizers to support the academic success of English Learners. *Journal of Science Education and Technology, 21*(4), 494–503. doi:10.100710956-011-9341-0

Bonk, C. J., & Graham, C. R. (2012). *The handbook of blended learning: Global perspectives, local designs*. Pfeiffer.

Bozkurt, A. (2019). From distance education to open and distance learning: A holistic evaluation of history, definitions, and theories. In S. Sisman-Ugur & G. Kurubacak (Eds.), *Handbook of research on learning in the age of transhumanism* (pp. 252–273). IGI Global. doi:10.4018/978-1-5225-8431-5.ch016

Cao, X. (2018). *Examining moral education: A comparative study between Quebec's ethics and religious culture program and China's moral education program* (Publication No. 28249235) [Master's thesis, McGill University]. ProQuest Dissertations Publishing.

CGTN. (2021). *The pandemic*. https://news.cgtn.com/event/2020/The-Pandemic/index.html

Chapelle, C. (2003). *English language learning and technology: Lectures on Applied Linguistics in the age of information and communication technology* (Vol. 7). John Benjamins Publishing. doi:10.1075/lllt.7

Chen Hsieh, J. S., Wu, W.-C. V., & Marek, M. W. (2016). Using the flipped classroom to enhance EFL learning. *Computer Assisted Language Learning*, *30*(1-2), 1–21. doi:10.1080/09588221.2015.1111910

Choe, E., & Seong, M. H. (2016). A case study of the flipped classroom in a Korean university general English course. *Journal of Pan-Pacific Association of Applied Linguistics*, *20*(2), 71–93.

Chung, C., & Mason, M. (2012). Why do primary school students drop out in poor, rural China? A portrait sketched in a remote mountain village. *International Journal of Educational Development*, *32*(4), 537–545. doi:10.1016/j.ijedudev.2012.02.012

Chung, S., & Choi, L. (2021). The development of sustainable assessment during the COVID-19 pandemic: The case of the English language program in South Korea. *Sustainability*, *13*(8), 1–13. doi:10.3390u13084499

Clandinin, D. J. (2006). Narrative inquiry: A methodology for studying lived experience. *Research Studies in Music Education*, *27*(1), 44–54. doi:10.1177/1321103X060270010301

Clandinin, D. J., & Connelly, F. M. (1991). Narrative and story in practice and research. In D. A. Schön (Ed.), *The reflective turn: Case studies in and on educational practice* (pp. 258–283). Teachers College Press.

Clandinin, D. J., & Connelly, F. M. (1994). Personal experience methods. In N. K. Denzin & Y. S. Lincoln (Eds.), *Handbook of qualitative research* (pp. 413–427). SAGE.

Clandinin, D. J., & Connelly, F. M. (2000). *Narrative inquiry*. John Wiley & Sons.

Cortazzi, M., & Jin, L. (1996). Cultures of learning: Language classrooms in China. In H. Coleman (Ed.), *Society and the language classroom* (pp. 169–206). CUP.

Darling-Hammond, L., & Hyler, M. E. (2020). Preparing educators for the time of COVID… and beyond. *European Journal of Teacher Education*, *43*(4), 457–465. doi:10.1080/02619768.2020.1816961

Davin, K. J., Chavoshan, I., & Donato, R. (2018). Images of past teachers: Present when you teach. *System*, *72*, 139–150. doi:10.1016/j.system.2017.12.001

Destianingsih, A., & Satria, A. (2020). Investigating students' needs for effective English online learning during Covid-19 for Polbeng students. *ELT-Lectura: Studies and Perspectives in English Language Teaching*, *7*(2), 147–153. doi:10.31849/elt-lectura.v7i2.4657

Dewey, J. (1938). *Experience and education*. Collier Books.

Eady, M. J., & Lockyer, L. (2013). Tools for learning: Technology and teaching strategies. Teach in the Primary School, 71-89.

Engin, M., & Donanci, S. (2016). Instructional videos as part of a 'flipped' approach in academic writing. *Learning and Teaching in Higher Education: Gulf Perspectives*, *13*(1), 73–80. Advance online publication. doi:10.18538/lthe.v13.n1.231

Gilakjani, A. P. (2017). A review of the literature on the integration of technology into the learning and teaching of English language skills. *International Journal of English Linguistics, 7*(5), 95–106. doi:10.5539/ijel.v7n5p95

Golombek, P., & Johnson, K. E. (2004). Narrative inquiry as a mediational space: Examining emotional and cognitive dissonance in second-language teachers' development. *Teachers and Teaching, 10*(3), 307–327. doi:10.1080/1354060042000204388

Haneda, M. (2006). Classrooms as communities of practice: A reevaluation. *TESOL Quarterly, 40*(4), 807–817. doi:10.2307/40264309

Hartshorne, R., Baumgartner, E., Kaplan-Rakowski, R., Mouza, C., & Ferdig, R. E. (2020). Special issue editorial: Preservice and inservice professional development during the COVID-19 pandemic. *Journal of Technology and Teacher Education, 28*(2), 137–147.

Hu, G. (2002). Recent important developments in secondary English-language teaching in the People's Republic of China. *Language, Culture and Curriculum, 15*(1), 30–49. doi:10.1080/07908310208666631

Hu, G. (2003). English language teaching in China: Regional differences and contributing factors. *Journal of Multilingual and Multicultural Development, 24*(4), 290–318. doi:10.1080/01434630308666503

Hu, G. (2005). English language education in China: Policies, progress, and problems. *Language Policy, 4*(1), 5–24. doi:10.100710993-004-6561-7

James, L. (2014). The integration of a computer-based early reading program to increase English language learners' literacy skills. *Teaching English with Technology, 14*(1), 9–22.

Johnson, K. E. (2006). The sociocultural turn and its challenges for second language teacher education. *TESOL Quarterly, 40*(1), 235–257. doi:10.2307/40264518

Johnson, K. E. (2007). Tracing teacher and student learning in teacher-authored narratives. *Teacher Development, 11*(2), 175–188. doi:10.1080/13664530701442879

Johnson, K. E. (2009). *Second language teacher education: A sociocultural perspective*. Routledge. doi:10.4324/9780203878033

Johnson, K. E., & Golombek, P. R. (2002). Inquiry into experience. In K. E. Johnson & P. R. Golombek (Eds.), *Teachers' narrative inquiry as professional development* (pp. 1–14). Cambridge University Press.

Johnson, K. E., & Golombek, P. R. (2003). "Seeing" teacher learning. *TESOL Quarterly, 37*(4), 729–737. doi:10.2307/3588221

Johnson, K. E., & Golombek, P. R. (2011). A sociocultural theoretical perspective on teacher professional development. In K. E. Johnson & P. R. Golombek (Eds.), *Research on second language teacher education: A sociocultural perspective on professional development* (pp. 1–12). Routledge. doi:10.4324/9780203844991

Jonassen, D., Howland, J., Marra, R. M., & Crismond, D. (2008). *How does technology facilitate learning? Meaningful Learning with Technology*. Pearson Allyn Bacon Prentice Hall.

Kamal, M. I., Zubanova, S., Isaeva, A., & Movchun, V. (2021). Distance learning impact on the English language teaching during COVID-19. *Education and Information Technologies*, *26*(6), 7307–7319. Advance online publication. doi:10.100710639-021-10588-y PMID:34075299

Karabanova, O. A. (2010). Social situation of child's development-the key concept in modern developmental psychology. *Psychology in Russia: State of the Art*, *3*(1), 130–153. doi:10.11621/pir.2010.0005

Lantolf, J. P. (2000). Introducing sociocultural theory. In J. P. Lantolf (Ed.), *Sociocultural theory and second language learning* (pp. 1–26). Oxford University Press.

Lantolf, J. P., & Poehner, M. E. (Eds.). (2008). *Sociocultural theory and the teaching of second languages*. Equinox.

Lave, J., & Wenger, E. (1991). *Situated learning: Legitimate peripheral participation*. Cambridge University Press. doi:10.1017/CBO9780511815355

Li, J., Shi, Z., & Xue, E. (2020). The problems, needs and strategies of rural teacher development at deep poverty areas in China: Rural schooling stakeholder perspectives. *International Journal of Educational Research*, *99*, 1–10. doi:10.1016/j.ijer.2019.101496

Liao, X. (2004). The need for communicative language teaching in China. *ELT Journal*, *58*(3), 270–273. doi:10.1093/elt/58.3.270

Ma, Y., Hou, X., Huang, J., Wang, W., Li, Y., Zhou, X., & Du, X. (2018). Educational inequality and achievement disparity: An empirical study of migrant children in China. *Children and Youth Services Review*, *87*, 145–153. doi:10.1016/j.childyouth.2018.02.026

Ministry of Education. (2001, November 19). *Jiaoyubu guanyu yinfa yiwujiaoyu kecheng shezhi shiyan fangan de tongzhi* [Announcement on the experimental plan of compulsory education curriculum]. http://www.moe.gov.cn/srcsite/A26/s7054/200111/t20011119_88602.html

Moore, J. L., Dickson-Deane, C., & Galyen, K. (2011). e-Learning, online learning, and distance learning environment: Are they the same? *Internet and Higher Education*, *14*(2), 129–135. doi:10.1016/j.iheduc.2010.10.001

Moorhouse, B. L. (2020). Adaptations to a face-to-face initial teacher education course "forced" online due to the COVID-19 pandemic. *Journal of Education for Teaching*, *46*(4), 609–611. Advance online publication. doi:10.1080/02607476.2020.1755205

Moser, K. M., Wei, T., & Brenner, D. (2021). Remote teaching during COVID-19: Implications from a national survey of language educators. *System*, *97*, 1–15. doi:10.1016/j.system.2020.102431

Mulyono, H. (2016). Using Quipper as an online platform for teaching and learning English as a foreign language. *Teaching English with Technology*, *16*(1), 59–70.

National Health Commission of the People's Republic of China. (2020, January 30). *Xinxing guanzhuang bingdu ganran de feiyan gongzhong fanghu zhinan* [Public protection handbook for the pneumonia caused by the novel coronavirus]. http://www.nhc.gov.cn/jkj/s7915/202001/bc661e49b5bc487dba182f-5c49ac445b.shtml

National People's Congress. (2019, January 7). *Zhonghua renmin gongheguo yiwujiaoyu fa* [Compulsory education law of the People's Republic of China]. http://www.npc.gov.cn/npc/c30834/201901/21b0be5b97e54c5088bff17903853a0d.shtml

Shu, D. (2004). *EFL in China: Problems and suggested solutions*. Shanghai Foreign Language Education Press., doi:10.1017/S0305741004000542

Solano, L., Cabrere, P., Ulehlova, E., & Espinoza, V. (2017). Exploring the use of educational technology in EFL teaching: A case study of primary education in the south region of Ecuador. *Teaching English with Technology*, *17*(2), 77–86.

Turan, Z., & Akdag-Cimen, B. (2020). Flipped classroom in English language teaching: A systematic review. *Computer Assisted Language Learning*, *33*(5-6), 590–606. doi:10.1080/09588221.2019.1584117

Van Dijk, J. A. (2006). Digital divide research, achievements, and shortcomings. *Poetics*, *34*(4-5), 221–235. doi:10.1016/j.poetic.2006.05.004

Vorobel, O., & Kim, D. (2012). Teaching at a distance: An overview of research. *CALICO Journal*, *29*(3), 548–562. doi:10.11139/cj.29.3.548-562

Vygotsky, L. S. (1978). *Mind in society: The development of higher psychological processes*. Harvard University Press.

Vygotsky, L. S. (1986). *Though and language* (A. Kozulin, Trans.). MIT Press.

Vygotsky, L. S. (1987). *The collected works of LS Vygotsky: The fundamentals of defectology* (Vol. 2). Springer Science & Business Media.

Vygotsky, L. S. (1998). The problem of age (M. J. Hall, Trans.). In RieberR. W. (Ed.), *The collected works of L.S. Vygotsky* (Vol. 5, pp. 187–205). Kluwer Academic/Plenum.

Wei, Y., & Zhou, S. (2019). Are better teachers more likely to move? Examining teacher mobility in rural China. *The Asia-Pacific Education Researcher*, *28*(2), 171–179. doi:10.100740299-018-0423-0

Witherall, C., & Noddings, N. (Eds.). (1991). *Stories lives tell: Narrative and dialogue in education*. Teachers College Press.

Wong, H. L., Shi, Y., Luo, R., Zhang, L., & Rozelle, S. (2014). Improving the health and education of elementary schoolchildren in rural China: Iron supplementation versus nutritional training for parents. *The Journal of Development Studies*, *50*(4), 502–519. doi:10.1080/00220388.2013.866223

Wong, R. M. H. (2014). An investigation of strategies for student motivation in the Chinese EFL context. *Innovation in Language Learning and Teaching*, *8*(2), 132–154. doi:10.1080/17501229.2013.777449

World Health Organization. (2020, April 27). *Archived: WHO timeline – COVID-19*. https://www.who.int/news/item/27-04-2020-who-timeline---covid-19

World Health Organization. (2021, July 1). *Coronavirus disease (COVID-19) advice for the public*. https://www.who.int/emergencies/diseases/novel-coronavirus-2019/advice-for-public

Xiong, T., & Xiong, X. (2017). The EFL teachers' perceptions of teacher identity: A survey of Zhuangang and Non-zhuangang primary school teachers in China. *English Language Teaching*, *10*(4), 100–110. doi:10.5539/elt.v10n4p100

Yang, C. C. R. (2017). An investigation of the use of the 'flipped classroom' pedagogy in secondary English language classrooms. *Journal of Information Technology Education: Innovations in Practice*, *16*(1).

Zainuddin, Z. (2017). First-year college students' experiences in the EFL flipped classroom: A case study in Indonesia. *International Journal of Instruction*, *10*(1), 133–150. doi:10.12973/iji.2017.1019a

Zhao, Y. (2013). Recent developments in technology and language learning: Literature review and meta-analysis. *CALICO Journal*, *21*(1), 7–27. doi:10.1558/cj.v21i1.7-27

KEY TERMS AND DEFINITIONS

Community of Practice (CoP): A concept developed by Jean Lave and Etienne Wenger that describes a group in which people with a shared objective come together to work collectively to achieve that objective.

Composite Narrative: An approach to presenting narrative data in which narrative from each individual participant is strategically interwoven to form a temporally and thematically coherent account.

Concept Development: A sociocultural theoretical construct that describes a person's development in understanding a certain concept resulted from instruction and mediation that connect the person's everyday experiences with scientific concepts.

Instructional Mode: A term used to describe the way a class is delivered, for example, face-to-face class, online class, and so forth.

Internalization: A theoretical construct central to Vygotskyan perspective that describes the learning process where a person appropriates mediational tools in social activities to transfer knowledge from an external-social domain to an internal-psychological domain.

Lived Experiences: Lived experiences represent a person's knowledge gained through interactions with and involvement in everyday activities, including social events, recreations, learning, working, and so forth.

Mediating Artifacts: A Vygotskyan concept that regards an array of psychological and physical tools (e.g., language, textbooks, computers) as mediational tools for a person's learning.

Professional Development (PD): A term used to describe the activity through which a person's professional identity, knowledge, and skills are upheld, advanced, or (re)shaped.

Social Situation of Development: A sociocultural theoretical concept that suggests a person's lived experiences and personal history in relation with the present contextual situation creates a social situation for a person's cognitive and psychological development.

Chapter 8
Teacher Practices Towards Providing Interaction During Online Education in K-8 Settings

Gizem Kara
Bahçeşehir University, Turkey

Melis Dilek
https://orcid.org/0000-0001-5678-931X
Bahçeşehir University, Turkey

Aysegul Liman Kaban
https://orcid.org/0000-0003-3813-2888
Bahcesehir University, Turkey

ABSTRACT

The purpose of the present study is to investigate what kind of practices teachers implement to offer interaction opportunities in online education in terms of learner-learner interaction, learner-instructor interaction, and learner-content interaction. The study has been carried out with 55 English teachers who have had online lessons during the COVID-19 pandemic, which has caused the closure of schools at every level until an unknown time. To collect data, a survey was implemented to English teachers who are teaching at K-8 levels and the results of the survey are analyzed quantitatively. The study has found that learner-learner interaction strategies are less implemented by the teachers in comparison to learner-content and learner-instructor interaction practices. Creating a positive learning environment is a building block for teachers to motivate learners in an online classroom setting.

DOI: 10.4018/978-1-7998-8717-1.ch008

INTRODUCTION

The Online teaching situation, also known as emergent online teaching, has surrounded the world since the COVID outbreak. Although massive online open courses had already become popular over the years, the situation students, teachers, and institutions are faced with nowadays is quite different due to the closure of schools of all levels and the quick transition to online education. Students have had to rearrange their habits to involve themselves in online learning environments, and even young learners have been struggling with challenges both in class and out of class. On the other hand, teachers have had to redesign their teaching materials, apply novel methods and techniques to be productive in online education to meet the needs of their learners. Especially in synchronous sessions, it became enormously important to form emotional bonds despite the physical distance with learners and to increase cognitive awareness during online sessions. Both students and teachers now have the responsibility to and need to keep the welcoming and warm classroom environment in their virtual learning settings as well as dealing with the technical and cognitive problems.

Interaction, especially with primary and secondary level learners, holds a crucial place in online education. Contrary to face-to-face classrooms, there are diverse challenges that teachers need to overcome in virtual environments to provide interaction in their sessions. Su et al. (2005) point out that interaction in online learning environments is crucial for student satisfaction and achievement. Previous research addresses the need for conducting more studies on the use of interaction in online learning environments to have a deeper understanding of the strengths and weaknesses of practices and to improve teaching and learning. The Community of Inquiry Framework by (Garrison et al., 1999) has guided many researchers who aim to explore distance education and online learning environment interactions. According to Arbaugh et al. (2008), the Community of Inquiry (CoI) framework can be used as a powerful and effective theoretical framework to examine online learning practices and it offers numerous opportunities to evaluate interaction and experiences in online learning environments. The community of inquiry framework asserts that in online environments, learning occurs through interaction which can be subdivided into three parts: teaching presence, social presence, and cognitive presence. The three types of presence correspond to learner-instructor interaction, learner-learner interaction, and learner-content interaction (Swan, 2006). That is why, it is of great importance to investigate the interaction practices provided by teachers in online environments to gain a better understanding of current practices under the circumstances brought by the pandemic and swift transition to online teaching in all levels from pre-school to higher education. Research on the current subject can provide insights into the interaction practices, strengths, and weaknesses of practices during online lessons and it also informs future researchers about the issues related to online learning environments.

LITERATURE REVIEW

COVID Outbreak

The world has witnessed a swift transition to online education since December 2019. Due to the COVID pandemic that affected many lives, institutions, and the world's economy, perhaps one of the most notable change has been experienced in education. "Education has been the bedrock of development of every nation; hence its sustainability is paramount to growth and development of all nations." (Owusu et al., 2020. p.89) However, many institutions and education systems have had to undergo rapid changes because of the lockdown and the growing number of affections among people. Now, all learners in different educational levels need to have their lessons from their homes using different video conferencing software such as Adobe Connect, Zoom, Microsoft Teams, and Google Meet. A research study conducted to investigate the challenges learners are faced with during the pandemic has revealed that some students are not able to join lessons; some of them are not studying and learning efficiently; and most importantly, they are not able to interact with peers and computer software effectively to manage their learning (Owusu et al., 2020).

The unexpected transmission required all practitioners to evaluate and adapt their techniques to achieve a high rate of success and interaction among learners. Given that now people have moved from traditional classrooms to virtual environments, teachers and institutions need to design and implement new techniques and methods to create an environment that is fruitful, interactive, and focuses on interaction, it would not be sufficient to manage only technical problems faced by teachers and learners (Tanık-Önal & Önal, 2020). The objectives of this study is to investigate the practices of the teachers throughout the pandemic.

The Community of Inquiry Framework

The Community of Inquiry (CoI) framework, which is developed by (Garrison et al., 1999), has been greatly beneficial for conceptualizing online learning. The research studies in the previous literature have shown that the CoI framework has been proven to be successful in terms of understanding virtual environments, practices, and learning in such environments (Mckerlich et al., 2011, Liman-Kaban, 2021). According to (Mckerlich et al., 2011), this framework is composed of three interconnected components: teaching presence, social presence, and cognitive presence. The notion of "presence" in the framework would be described as "a sense of active participation" and it turns the focus onto what learners create and how they contribute to their learning through several ways of communication in virtual learning environments (Saadatmand et al.,2018).

The design of the lesson, facilitating how and in which ways learners can learn best are components of teaching presence. Following such structure, teachers strive to improve learners' experience and endeavor to create meaningful learning environments. Yet, in online learning environments, what is required from teachers is not limited to providing learning opportunities. It requires teachers to establish a bond of relationship with the learners and guide them through their journey (Saadatmand et al.,2018). Social presence is explained as the ability of an individual to actively participate in the community they belong to. When learners are socially present in their online learning environments, they can connect with peers and they can meet their social and emotional needs as they exist in the community (Clarà et al., 2015). Being socially together with peers in a trusted and welcoming environment where everyone's ideas are valued and respected can contribute to both personal and affective bonds as well as creating a form of social acceptance (Swan et al., 2009). Lastly, the process or the cognitive journey learners go through can be clarified as cognitive presence. Cognitive presence enables learners to actively construct meaning and explore knowledge as they go through active "exploration, integration, application and continuous reflection in a community of inquiry" (Garrison, 2007, p.65). It "reflects higher-order knowledge acquisition and application" (Garrison et al., 1999, p.7). To sum up, the limitations of online learning environments may be decreased through building a sense of community in classrooms.

Interaction in Online Learning Environments

One of the issues that need to be debated and investigated is how the teachers will create opportunities for learner interaction and what kind of practices they should employ. During online education, students are not in a social environment as it was before and the interaction among teacher-learner, learner-learner is comparably less than it was in traditional education. The allocated time for interaction and teaching is limited and teachers still need to answer individual differences of learners from their screen. Moreover, teachers are expected to provide feedback to students, monitor and evaluate their progress as well as encouraging participation within a short time. As a result of all these new challenges, novel teaching practices should be implemented to increase interaction between learners and teachers to create a social environment. Furthermore, practices that are focused on a learner-centered approach should be implemented to allow learners to build on their knowledge and gain control of their tasks.

Interactivity in online courses can take several forms, such as interactivity between learner-learner, learner-instructor, and learner-content. "Building a blend of these three interaction types has been shown to improve motivation, satisfaction and achievement in online courses" (Mahle, 2011; Park & Choi, 2009 as cited in Dailey, 2018). Several studies in the literature show that allowing students to work in groups in online lessons rises peer learning and satisfaction. Interaction between students can be fostered by role-plays, discussions, or projects that require teamwork. Besides, the interaction set between learner and teacher stands as a key factor in online lessons as it promotes social presence. Hence, the feedback given by the teacher, the welcoming atmosphere of the lesson, and the accessibility of learning resources all contributes to the interactivity of online lessons.

A research study focused on the strategies and tools employed by teachers to develop a learner-centered environment demonstrated that such tools and strategies allowed teachers to know their students and was significantly beneficial for creating a social and supportive environment. Also, the study revealed that using web 2.0 tools provided collaboration and authentic learning opportunities (An & Mindrila, 2020). Another study on primary level students conducted by Zioga and Bikos (2019) demonstrated that using collaborative writing tools enhances learners writing skills positively and helped them build cooperation skills. The results of the study stress the importance and usefulness of collaborative tasks assigned to the learners in terms of enhancing their critical-thinking skills, a sense of community and belonging, negotiation, and co-construction in an online environment (Zioga & Bikos, 2019).

Advances in technology, a vast number of resources and tools available to individuals have made it is relatively easier for teachers to extend their use in their online lessons. Learners also feel more powerful and as a member of the community when their chance of interaction is increased in online lessons. Sun et al., (2008) point out that when interactivity is promoted, learner willingness to participate and communicate show a positive correlation. The results of the research study on the use of online games in English lessons are noteworthy because the study reveals that the use of games that push students to engage in competitive activities increases their motivation towards learning (Halim et al., 2020). Embedding gaming tools such as Kahoot! And Quizzes can change the atmosphere in online lessons and they can serve as a functional way of gathering student attention, increasing motivation, and assessing their performance.

With the changes in perceptions of learning and how it happens, learner-centered practices have become more prominent in the field. Plenty of research available in the literature on the perspectives and outcomes of learner-centered implementations in educational settings. Since the learner-centered approaches have been increasing the significance of the interaction and interactivity in learning environments, research suggests that interaction among learners and the teachers increases active processing leading to more meaningful learning (Sims, 2003). Literature also supports the positive impact of interaction on learners' learning process in both faces to face and online learning environments. Although there has been a notable le increase in online learning studies on how it can be improved to obtain the maximum benefit from the pandemic's drawbacks, there is a lot of research conducted to examine interaction and face to learning environments as well.

In the study conducted by Harrera et al. (2017) discussant activity consisting of discussions and debates was implemented to the participants who were university students in Europe. Participants were enrolled in discussion groups within the scope of a project and their learning situations were studied. The results showed that there is a significant relationship between interactive learning and satisfaction. In parallel with this study, Olmos et al. (2018) found out that using response systems in learning environments results in the active engagement of the learners leading to improvement in learning and high order processing of information.

As for interactivity and online learning, before the pandemic, they were predominantly used by adults to manage self-directed and cooperative learning with the applications of various online tools (Cercone, 2008). The study which was used Facebook and Google+ in online learning settings by Simandi (2017) stated that online learning environments are highly beneficial for community learning leading to collaborative and collaborative learning opportunities that have been getting more and more on-demand by educators. Not only computer and software environments but also online mobile learning settings also have a positive impact on learning. Contrary to the common belief on mobile phones' negative effect on learner's engagement in learning due to the distractive effects of applications, games and advertisement, Online Mobile learning especially for the language learning settings have a positive impact on learners' achievements by giving opportunities for interaction (Mellati et al., 2015).

However, when it comes to young learners and interaction opportunities in online learning environments, it has been noticed that limited amount of research available in the literature which mostly belongs to before pandemic period and young learners had not been engaged in fully online learning environments out of necessity. Having examined the literature on the positive impacts of interactivity on learning in both traditional and online learning settings, a requirement for the future study on teachers' perceptions on interaction and their methods are observed. Therefore, this study aims to investigate what kind of practices teachers implement to provide interaction in online lessons in terms of teacher-learner interaction, learner-learner interaction, and learner-content interaction. The research question of the study is as follows:

1. How do English teachers support interaction during emergency online education in K-8 settings?

METHODOLOGY

Research Design

This research study was conducted by applying a quantitative cross-sectional survey design creswell (2012) to investigate what kind of practices are employed by teachers to support learner-learner interaction, learner- instructor interaction, and learner-content interaction during online english lessons. In a cross-sectional research design, a researcher surveys participants to "examine attitudes, beliefs, opinions or practices." (p.377). In the present study quantitative data were collected with a survey which was given to the charter primary and secondary school efl teachers to investigate their practices and strategies to increase interaction opportunities in their virtual-classroom settings.

Setting and Procedures

The study took place in an online environment. Teachers were asked to fill in the survey regarding interaction practices on an online platform. Participation in the research study was voluntary and participants were free to withdraw from the research at any time. The responses given to the survey were analyzed by two researchers and duplicates were removed accordingly.

Participants

The participants of the research study are 55 English language teachers who are currently offering online lessons in K-8 schools, based in Turkey. The participants are chosen among teachers who are teaching at primary and secondary level mostly and they have an average of 4 to 6 hours of teaching sessions in a day. 45 of the teachers who participated in the survey are female and 10 of the participants are male. The teachers who participated in the study stated that they have a varying number of years of teaching between 1 and 23 years. 42 of the participants are using Zoom, 6 of them are using Microsoft Teams, 2 of them are using Adobe Connect, and 5 of them are using other video-conferencing tools to conduct online sessions. 10 teachers have 1 to 10 students, 28 teachers have 1 to 20 students and 19 teachers have 21 to 30 students in their online lessons. Among all participants, only 13 participants had online teaching experience before the COVID outbreak.

Data Collection

Participants were selected through convenience sampling to increase the opportunity for investigating the practices the participants implement. Data is collected employing an online survey with teachers. The survey aims to examine the interaction practices of teachers during online education. It consists of two parts: Personal Information and The Scale of Teacher Role Inventory.

Instruments

The instrument used in the present study is the Scale of Teacher Role Inventory (the STRI) developed by Huang (2017). The STRI is a 27-item and five-point-Likert scale that measures different roles of teachers not only in the context of online learning or blended learning but also across different instructional settings. And the instrument consists of three main factors that have been well validated: cognitive role of item 1–10, effective role of item 11–20, and finally managerial role of item 21–27 (Huang, 2017, p. 6). Previous studies showed that STRI is a highly reliable and valid instrument to examine teacher roles (Huang, 2017, p. 7). The Cronbach's Alpha value of the entire questionnaire was .955 and those of the three sub-roles were all above .891. In addition to the Scale of Teacher Role Inventory, to specify the strategies that teachers have been implemented in their virtual classrooms, strategies that were found from the study by Katlianik (2003) were included in the present study as well. The study is a dissertation thesis, and it was also published in indexed journals. Strategies for interactivity found in Katlianik's study (2003) included in STRI as additional items.

DATA ANALYSIS

To analyze the data collected from the participants, descriptive statistics were used through Excel and SPSS software. The questionnaire items comprising of three sub-groups such as learner-learner Interaction, learner-instructor interaction, and learner content interaction grouped and descriptive statistics of the data were calculated. They are shown in the form of charts.

Findings

Teachers' Strategies Regarding Learner-Learner Interaction

Table 1 shows the teacher's answers to the strategies regarding learner-learner interaction. The most used strategy implemented by the teacher is "providing equal opportunities for learners for participation in the lessons (m = 4.63, sd = 0.57). On the other hand, the "minimizing group size "strategy is the least rated one among the teachers (m = 2.36, sd = 1.16). Other items such as "i encourage students to discuss course-related content with other students in breakout rooms" and "i encourage students to give feedback to each other during the lesson" have relatively closer results (m = 3.50, sd = 1. 38), (m = 3.49, sd = 1.24).

Table 1. Learner-learner interaction

Question	Mean	Median	Standard Deviation
I establish clear rules for virtual classes.	4.43	5	0.73
I encourage students to explore ideas in pairs.	3.50	4	1.38
I encourage students to discuss course-related content with other students in breakout rooms.	3.14	4	1.50
I encourage students to give feedback to each other during the lesson.	3.49	4	1.24
I assign group activities/projects to students.	2.94	5	1.50
I keep students engaged and participating in role plays.	3.63	4	1.33
I reinforce the development of a sense of community among students.	4.23	4	0.89
I assign the presenter roles to children.	3.63	4	1.2
I provide equal opportunities for participation for students	4.63	5	0.57
I make ethical considerations.	4.47	5	0.96
I minimize class size.	2.36	2	1.16
I lead students to engage in in-class games.	4.43	5	0.94
I use interactive Web 2.0 tools to improve interaction among students.	4.09	4	1.08

Teachers' Strategies Regarding Learner-Instructor Interaction

Questions related to the learner- instructor interaction are shown in table 2. The item "I call students by their names" received the highest scores by the teachers (M = 4.92, SD = 0.97). "I provide private chat option" is the least chosen item by the participants. (M = 2.81, SD = 1.69). "Having names in the screen." (M = 4.87, SD = 0.57), "encouraging students to express their ideas" (M = 4.87, SD = 0.42) and "holding positive attitudes to the student to keep them motivated" (M = 4.87, SD = 0.42) are among the highly conveyed strategies among the teachers.

Table 2. Learner-instructor interaction

Question	Mean	Median	Standard Deviation
I use audios/songs to attract students' attention.	4.65	5	0.57
I make comments on students' work during the lesson.	4.36	5	0.96
I encourage students to express their feelings/ideas in English.	4.87	5	0.42
I give constant feedback to the students during the lesson.	4.50	5	0.73
I communicate with students about the course content through email.	2.90	3	1.62
I communicate with students about the course content through a chatbox.	3	3	1.45
I provide a private chat option.	2.81	3	1.69
I hold a positive attitude to the students to keep them motivated.	4.87	5	0.42
I respect students' privacy.	4.78	5	0.56
I remind students that I support them.	4.78	5	0.59
I keep my camera and microphone on during the lesson.	4.63	5	0.92
When addressing a student, I directly look at the camera to have an eye-contact with the student.	3.8	5	1.56
I use abbreviations and emoticons to create a friendly environment.	4.03	4	1.11
We have our names on the screen.	4.87	5	0.50
I call students by their names.	4.92	5	0.32
I try to adopt a facilitative approach over an instructional approach.	4.47	5	0.68

Teachers' Strategies Regarding Learner-Content Interaction

As shown in table 3, teachers mostly stated that they "provide clear instructions on how to participate in learning activities." (M = 4.85, SD = 4.35). The least rated item in the questionnaire is "I record all sessions and provide students access to them." (M = 2.47, SD = 1.55). "I use different colors, font s, size, etc. to highlight important points." (M = 4.76, SD =0.73) and "I use appropriate visuals and graphs to introduce content." (M = 4.76 SD =0.53) have the second-highest-rated items by the teachers.

Table 3. Learner-content interaction

Question	Mean	Mode	Median	Standard Deviation
I ensure interface accessibility and usability.	4.36	5	5	0.83
I recommend students reduce external-distractive factors during online lessons.	4.6	5	5	0.67
I avoid distractive medium designs and interface elements.	4.50	5	5	0.7
I promote using sound-isolating headphones.	3.56	5	4	1.49
I use different colors, font sizes, etc. to highlight important points.	4.76	5	5	0.73
I use appropriate visuals and graphs to introduce content.	4.76	5	5	0.53
I use interactive Web 2.0 tools to introduce content.	4.16	5	5	1.07
I use multimedia resources to help students to understand the content.	4.64	5	5	0.71
I recommend English websites/web pages to students to practice.	4.27	5	5	0.84
I help to guide the class towards understanding course topics in a way that helps students clarify their thinking.	4.72	5	5	0.52
I provide clear instructions on how to participate in learning activities	4.85	5	5	0.35
I utilize different types of supplementary materials to make content presentation powerful.	4.69	2.47	1	2
I record all sessions and provide the students with access to them.	2.47	1	2	1.55
I deny access to features not being used or being used inappropriately.	4.34	5	5	0.83
I let students see the progress/ structure of the lesson to raise their awareness of the content.	4.03	5	4	1.27

DISCUSSION AND CONCLUSION

The data collected from this study demonstrates that teachers convey varying interactive strategies in online classroom settings. Community of Inquiry (CoI) suggests that in an online learning environment, teacher presence, social presence and cognitive presence should be sustained to achieve high order skills and satisfy the needs. Especially in speaking activities, this need maximizes as they require meaningful involvement and interaction. Teachers should follow "Seven Principles of Good Practice for Undergraduate Education". In this framework, student-teacher contact, cooperation among students, active learning, prompting feedback, time on task, communication with high expectations, respecting diverse ways of learning are the essentials for effective implementation of the principles (Fiock, 2020). Regarding these principles, students and teachers should be offered a performance context where they can work together without interruption. The constraints such as technology usage and time also should be annihilated for the sake of effective communication. The results of observation show that the learning process is hampered by technical issues and time management issues. To adjust the online environment, training for both educators and administrators should be encouraged whilst students try to experience some technological tools to develop meaningful relationships with both the other students and the context itself. The presence of the teacher is crucial in creating an effective emergency remote teaching environment (Liman-Kaban, 2021). Students are more likely to find the course useful when the instructor is prepared and available, and offers a clear grading system. The study's participants also mentioned how much they enjoyed attending small group feedback sessions and receiving feedback on their course performance, which adds to the advantages of creating an online collaborative course with CoI. Teaching presence also requires teachers to establish a bond of relationship with the learners and guide them through their journey (Saatmand et al., 2018). To increase teacher presence, participants of the present study seem to approach the learners positively and try to create a positive learning environment as can be shown in the answers of the statement such as "I hold a positive attitude to the students to keep them motivated." (M = 4.87 SD 0.42). On the other hand, it is revealed that the majority of the teachers don't prefer having individual interaction with the learners. Providing private chat option (M = 3 SD = 1.45) and communicating with learners through email (M = 2.90 SD = 1.62) received less rates by the participants. One reason for such results may stem from participants' learning groups. A private chat option may not be plausible for the target learners. Having meaningful interactions with young learners through the chatbox and e-mail is difficult for the teachers working with young learners. One promising result inferred from the data is that teachers are aware of the importance of using web 2.0 tools in virtual classroom settings. In parallel with An and Mindralla (2020), most of the participants use web 2.0 tools to provide learning opportunities for the learners. (M = 4.16, SD = 1.16). Although using 2.0 tools seem to be internalized by the teachers, how to get aid from them seems to be less practiced by the teachers inferred from the results. As (Sun et al., 2008) point out that when interactivity is promoted, learner willingness to participate and communicate shows a positive correlation. When asked directly, most of the teachers' state that they use breakout rooms to minimize group size and increase learners' interaction with each other. However, results imply that fewer teachers try to implement authentic group work and project activities to decrease the group size and promote learner-learner interaction. (M = 2.94, SD = 1.50). The participants working in charter schools can be restricted with the pre-planned activities by the head of the departments leading to fewer activities prepared by the teachers themselves. It is also worth mentioning that most of the teachers' state that they give constant feedback to the learners (M = 4.50, SD = 073) which results in the active engagement of the learners (Olmos et al.,2018). However, feedbacks types that they implement in virtual classes need to be examined thoroughly with the related questions. According to Bozkurt et al. (2021), the effective use of digital tools in the process of accessing and processing information by learners and teachers is more about how and how they use these tools, rather than having them; therefore, it is essential that learners and teachers develop their digital literacy skills and increase their digital competencies by considering national and international frameworks.

In the study, only 13 of the participants have online lesson experience before the pandemics. It may be a reason for some of the strategies that haven't commonly been implemented by the teachers. As teachers gain more experience in online learning settings, the results of the study are expected to change.

In the study, the research question: "How do English teachers support interaction during online education in K-8 settings?" was examined. "Emergency remote teaching or re-engineered distance education should collaborate with different shareholders (e.g., psychologists, sociologists, therapists, etc.) to offer better and timely solutions" (Bozkurt & Sharma, 2020). Emergency remote teaching has many dimensions and it is not like remote teaching as there are various parameters. It is possible to state that social presence has gained importance in emergency remote teaching. If the teachers want to supply cognitive and teaching presence in their classes, the first think they need to supply is the social presence of the learners. Socially present students are the magic spell of the emergency remote teaching. Creating bonds between student to student, teacher to student, student to content, student to interface has gained importance as the students do not feel the power of being a member of the community. Strategies conveyed by English teachers sub-grouped under three categories such as learner-learner, learner- instructor, and learner-content interaction. It was revealed that teachers implement varying kinds of strategies for interaction such as giving priority to creating a positive learning environment in their teaching settings and creating clear rules for the online classes. Strategies for learner-learner interactions are less implemented by the teachers. The present study was conducted with 55 participants and the sample was restricted to K-8 teachers. There is a need for further research with a larger sample size and different target groups.

LIMITATIONS AND IMPLICATIONS

This study has potential limitations. Data for this study collected only through quantitative methods due to time restrictions. Qualitative methods blended with quantitative ones can be implemented to enhance the reliability and validity of the results. Also, the study is conducted with only K-8 teachers, the sample size is small to the generalizability of the results. Only descriptive statics are taken into account in the process of interpreting data, further analysis is required to reach more reliable conclusions regarding data.

In the future, similar studies with larger sample size and different target participants can be implemented. As this study, only presents cross-sectional results, longitudinal studies, examining participants changing strategies, and perceptions on the topic can be conducted by the researchers.

REFERENCES

An, Y., & Mindrila, D. (2020). Strategies and tools used for learner-centered instruction. *International Journal of Technology in Education and Science*, *4*(2), 133–143. doi:10.46328/ijtes.v4i2.74

Arbaugh, J. B., Cleveland-Innes, M., Diaz, S. R., Garrison, D. R., Ice, P., Richardson, J. C., & Swan, K. P. (2008). Developing a community of inquiry instrument: Testing a measure of the Community of Inquiry framework using a multi-institutional sample. *The Internet and Higher Education*, *11*(3-4), 133–136. doi:10.1016/j.iheduc.2008.06.003

Bodomo, A. (2006). Interactivity in web-based learning. *International Journal of Web-Based Learning and Teaching Technologies*, *1*(2), 18–30. doi:10.4018/jwltt.2006040102

Boyle, J. T., & Nicol, D. J. (2003). Using classroom communication systems to support interaction and discussion in large class settings. *Research in Learning Technology*, *11*(3), 43–57. doi:10.3402/rlt.v11i3.11284

Bozkurt, A., Hamutoğlu, N. B., Liman-Kaban, A., Taşçi, G., & Aykul, M. (2021). Dijital bilgi çağı: Dijital toplum, dijital dönüşüm, dijital eğitim ve dijital yeterlilikler. *Açıköğretim Uygulamaları ve Araştırmaları Dergisi*, *7*(2), 35–63. doi:10.51948/auad.911584

Bozkurt, A., & Sharma, R. C. (2020). Emergency remote teaching in a time of global crisis due to CoronaVirus pandemic. *Asian Journal of Distance Education*, *15*(1), i–vi. doi:10.5281/zenodo.3778083

Cercone, K. (2008). Characteristics of Adult Learners with Implications for Online Learning Design. *AACE Review*, *16*(2), 137-159. https://www.learntechlib.org/primary/p/24286/

Chickering, A. W., & Gamson, Z. F. (1987). Seven principles for good practice in undergraduate education. *AAHE Bulletin*, *3*, 7.

Clarà, M., Kelly, N., Mauri, T., & Danaher, P. A. (2015). Can massive communities of teachers facilitate collaborative reflection? Fractal design as a possible answer. *Asia-Pacific Journal of Teacher Education*, *45*(1), 86–98. doi:10.1080/1359866X.2015.1095280

Creswell, J. W. (2011). *Educational research: Planning, conducting, and evaluating quantitative and qualitative research* (4th ed.). Pearson.

Dailey-Hebert, A. (2018). Maximizing interactivity in online Learning: Moving beyond discussion boards. *Journal of Educators Online*, *15*(3), 1–15. https://files.eric.ed.gov/fulltext/EJ1199230.pdf. doi:10.9743/jeo.2018.15.3.8

Fandos-Herrera, C., Jiménez-Martínez, J., Orús, C., & Pina, J. M. (2017). Introducing the discussant role to stimulate debate in the classroom: Effects on interactivity, learning outcomes, satisfaction, and attitudes. *Studies in Higher Education*, *44*(2), 380–396. doi:10.1080/03075079.2017.1366437

Garrison, D. R. (2007). Online community of inquiry review: Social, cognitive, and teaching presence issues. *Journal of Asynchronous Learning Networks*, *11*(1), 61–72. https://files.eric.ed.gov/fulltext/EJ842688.pdf

Garrison, D. R., Anderson, T., & Archer, W. (1999). Critical inquiry in a text-based environment: Computer conferencing in higher education. *The Internet and Higher Education*, *2*(2–3), 87–105. doi:10.1016/S1096-7516(00)00016-6

Huang, Q. (2018). Examining teachers' roles in online learning. *The EuroCALL Review*, *26*(2), 3. doi:10.4995/eurocall.2018.9139

Katlianik, I. (2013). *Strategies for increasing the interactivity of children's synchronous learning in virtual environments* (Unpublished doctoral dissertation). University of Oxford.

Liman-Kaban, A. (2021). The Influence of Online CoI Presences on Learner Satisfaction in Higher Education. *Asian Journal of Distance Education*, *16*(1), 230–246. doi:10.5281/zenodo.5021228

Mckerlich, R., Riis, M., Anderson, T., & Eastman, B. (2011). Student perceptions of teaching presence, social presence, and cognitive presence in a virtual world. *Journal of Online Learning and Teaching*, *7*(3), 324–336.

Mellati, M., & Khademi, M. (2015). The impacts of distance interactivity on learners' achievements in online mobile language learning. *International Journal of Web-Based Learning and Teaching Technologies*, *10*(3), 19–35. doi:10.4018/ijwltt.2015070102

Owusu-Fordjour, C., Koomson, C. K., & Hanson, D. (2020). The impact of Covid-19 on learning -the perspective of the Ghanaian student. *European Journal of Educational Sciences*, *7*(3), 88–101. doi:10.5281/zenodo.3753586

Robinson, H. A., Sheffield, A., Phillips, A. S., & Moore, M. (2017). Introduction to teaching online: Usability evaluation of interactivity in an online social constructivist course. *TechTrends*, *61*(6), 533–540. doi:10.100711528-017-0187-z

Saadatmand, M., Uhlin, L., Hedberg, M., Åbjörnsson, L., & Kvarnström, M. (2017). Examining learners' interaction in an open online course through the Community of Inquiry Framework. *European Journal of Open, Distance and E-Learning, 20*(1), 61–79. https://files.eric.ed.gov/fulltext/EJ1187832.pdf

Shakir Azfar Abdul Halim, M., Hashim, H., & Md Yunus, M. (2020). Pupils' motivation and perceptions on ESL lessons through online quiz-games. *Journal of Education and E-Learning Research, 7*(3), 229–234. doi:10.20448/journal.509.2020.73.229.234

Simándi, S. (2017). Study circles in Online Learning Environment in the spirit of learning-centered approach. *Acta Technologica Dubnicae, 7*(2), 96–104. doi:10.1515/atd-2017-0017

Sims, R. (2003). Promises of interactivity: Aligning learner perceptions and expectations with strategies for flexible and online learning. *Distance Education, 24*(1), 87–103. doi:10.1080/01587910303050

Su, B., Bonk, C. J., Magjuka, R. J., Liu, X., & Lee, S. (2005). The Importance of Interaction in Web-Based Education: A Program-level Case Study of Online MBA Courses. *Journal of Interactive Online Learning, 4*(1), 1–19. http://www.ncolr.org/jiol/issues/pdf/4.1.1.pdf

Sun, P.-C., Tsai, R. J., Finger, G., Chen, Y.-Y., & Yeh, D. (2008). What drives a successful e-Learning? An empirical investigation of the critical factors influencing learner satisfaction. *Computers & Education, 50*(4), 1183–1202. doi:10.1016/j.compedu.2006.11.007

Swan, K. (2001). Virtual interaction: Design factors affecting student satisfaction and perceived learning in asynchronous online courses. *Distance Education, 22*(2), 306–331. doi:10.1080/0158791010220208

Swan, K., Garrison, D. R., & Richardson, J. C. (2009). A constructivist approach to online learning. *Information Technology and Constructivism in Higher Education*, 43–57.

Tanık-Önal, N., & Önal, N. (2020). Teaching science through distance education during the Covid-19COVID pandemic. *International Online Journal of Education & Teaching*, 7(4), 1898–1911. https://iojet.org/index.php/IOJET/article/view/1088

Zioga, C., & Bikos, K. (2020). Collaborative writing using Google Docs in primary education: Development of argumentative discourse. *Turkish Online Journal of Distance Education*, 133–142. doi:10.17718/tojde.690372

Chapter 9
Influence of Positive Student-Teacher Interaction on the Meaning-Making Process in Virtual Learning:
A Study in the Primary English Class

Agustin Reyes-Torres
University of Valencia, Spain

Ana García-Perera
University of Valencia, Spain

ABSTRACT

This chapter presents a study in a COVID virtual learning environment that focuses on the crucial role that teachers play to engage and to guide students to become meaning makers. To this end, the authors make use of the Pedagogy of Multiliteracies in the English Primary class to establish a positive students-teacher relationship as a determining factor to enhance the learning process. Qualitative research was conducted so as to explore to what extent these factors influence the meaning-making process. The findings are presented and elaborated upon in this chapter. The researchers worked with three different groups of students in a public school in Valencia (Spain) before and during the lockdown enforced by COVID-19. The analysis of the data obtained reveals that academic achievement and students' engagement are influenced by the quality of the student-teacher relationship and the teacher's role as a mediator of knowledge.

DOI: 10.4018/978-1-7998-8717-1.ch009

INTRODUCTION

While discovering which key factors make a difference in the process of learning a foreign language continues to be the aim of many scholars, the emergency caused by the COVID-19 pandemic has triggered the need for English Language Teaching programs to respond to the demand of distance education. In addition to adjusting to the digital environment and exploring how to transform online spaces into online learning spaces, in this chapter the authors discuss how the Pedagogy of Multiliteracies contributes to establish positive student-teacher relationships as a determining factor to enhance the learning experience both in class and in remote learning. How teachers relate and interact with students has a significant effect on students' progress and attitude towards the foreign language. This is still more relevant in the online space where fostering teaching presence is crucial to promote learning and to give a human feel to the information being presented (Richardson and Swam, 2003; Russel and Murphy-Judy, 2021). In this way, the Pedagogy of Multiliteracies offers a new perspective of viewing not only the teacher but also students and, as a result, the learning process. The teacher acts as a guide allowing students to be the principal constructor of their learning and promoting a trustful and positive relationship.

From a sociocultural perspective, the idea that language learning is not only a linguistic and cognitive activity but also a lived, participatory social practice within specific cultural contexts is an accepted principle of current second language acquisition studies such as Cognitive Linguistics, Functional Linguistics, the Dynamic System Theory and the Pedagogy of Multiliteracies. According to De Bot et al. (2007, p.7), what these theories have in common is that "they recognize the crucial role of the interaction of a multitude of variables at different levels: in communication, in constructing meaning, in learning a language and among the languages in the multilingual mind." This view is in fact regarded as an ecological approach that acknowledges that language learning, in this case, EFL, and the development of knowledge can be seen as an emergent, dynamic, open-ended and intersubjectively negotiated process (Kern, 2000; Reyes-Torres and Portalés-Raga, 2020). As the New London Group (1996) and Cope and Kalantzis (2015) highlight, learning is an active process of meaning-making. This idea is especially relevant under the current COVID-19 critical situation since in many cases EFL learners can only improve their command of the foreign language by practicing it and making sense of it in a digital context. However, being exposed to multiple pieces of information does not guarantee their learning or even basic comprehension unless all pieces can be ordered and processed coherently in a meaningful way. For this reason, a particular emphasis must be placed, first, on the role of the student as an active learner; second, on the role of the teacher as a guide and a facilitator of meaning, and third, on the social interaction established between students and teachers. Furthermore, because of COVID-19, this interaction must be done through online platforms and it is essential to give consideration to how to humanize online classes as a key element in virtual learning.

Accordingly, in order to achieve a better understanding of the influence that positive Student-Teacher relationships have in a virtual learning environment and the impact that teachers have in guiding students, this study presents the results of the qualitative research that the authors carried out with three groups of students from fifth and sixth grade over a period of almost four months from February to May in 2020. Whereas all this period was significant in order to develop positive student-teacher relationships and adjust to the online lessons, the research tasks were implemented during the last two weeks. The main difference between these groups of students was the teacher presence as a mediator and the kind of social interaction that the instructor established with them in class as well as in the online space. As will be shown, the implementation of the Pedagogy of Multiliteracies was a key factor to boost the meaning-making process. To this end, the authors worked with the picturebook ZOG (2010) by Julia Donaldson and Axel Scheffler, and the creation of a short film based on it. The combination of words and images of both resources constitutes an example of multimodal reading whereby students can get involved in an active process of constructing meaning (Sipe, 2008).

This chapter is divided into three main sections. First of all, the authors draw the theoretical framework by reviewing the rationale behind the Pedagogy of Multiliteracies (see New London Group, 1996) and paying attention to the different elements that take place in the process. Secondly, the research design is presented along with the results. For the purpose of this study, a qualitative interpretative investigation was conducted with a total of 65 students. Lastly, after assessing the outcomes, the authors reach several conclusions that validate their hypothesis: The process of meaning-making triggered by the implementation of the Pedagogy of Multiliteracies have a significant effect on Student-teacher relationships as well as on students' involvement and learning of EFL in a virtual environment. Thus, the aim of this chapter is, first, to explore the level of students' engagement depending on their relationship with the teacher and, second, to examine how applying the Pedagogy of Multiliteracies in online learning contributes to foster a healthy online teaching presence and enhances the meaning-making process. The research question we propose is: How does the Pedagogy of Multiliteracies affect the interaction between the teacher and learner in a virtual environment, and how does it enhance and promote meaningful learning experiences?

BACKGROUND

In light of the new digital contexts and the new challenges of the 21st century, new teaching methodologies such as the Pedagogy of Multiliteracies have emerged that conceive learning as an active process of producing meaning and highlight the role of the teacher as a facilitator in guiding students' literacy development (New London Group, 1996; Kern, 2000; Cope and Kalantzis, 2015; Paesani, Allen and Dupuy, 2016, Warner and Dupuy, 2018; Lacorte and Reyes-Torres, 2021). In this section, the authors review the rationale behind this Pedagogy and explain the elements that take place in the meaning-making process. First of all, it is important to underline the concept of education and learning with which this study will work. On the one hand, as Wessels (2015, p.2) points out,

Education is not about just presenting more adequate information in an effective manner; it is a process that must incorporate the developmental readiness of the student and must construct a bridge between the student's current way of understanding and the new way, thus providing a path on which to cross over.

Education should not be regarded as a way of filling an individual with knowledge; it must go beyond that, it has to be seen as an opportunity to contribute to the cognitive, social, personal and emotional development of students. On the other hand, learning must be understood as a process in which individuals make sense of knowledge, experience and relationships (Kern, 2000, Kucer 2014; Brisk 2015). On this regard, this paper foregrounds the idea of learning as a meaning-making process in which the learner is seen as an active constructor of it (Wells, 1986; New London Group 1996; Paesani *et al.*, 2016).

There are three different factors that are crucial in our approach to the process of learning: 1) student, 2) teacher and 3) knowledge. Students are regarded as cognitive agents who build up mental models of the world for themselves (Cope and Kalantzis, 2015). As learners, they are expected to have an active role in the construction of knowledge. Likewise, as we can see in figure 1 below, the role of the teacher is crucial in guiding students to become meaning-makers. Furthermore, the application of the Pedagogy of Multiliteracies and the use of ICT (Information and Communication Technology) enables teachers to bring together students and knowledge in a virtual learning environment. In this vein, the creation of positive student-teacher relationships and their social interactions contributes significantly to foster and enhance a meaningful connection between students and knowledge.

Figure 1. A model for the elements that takes place in the meaning making process

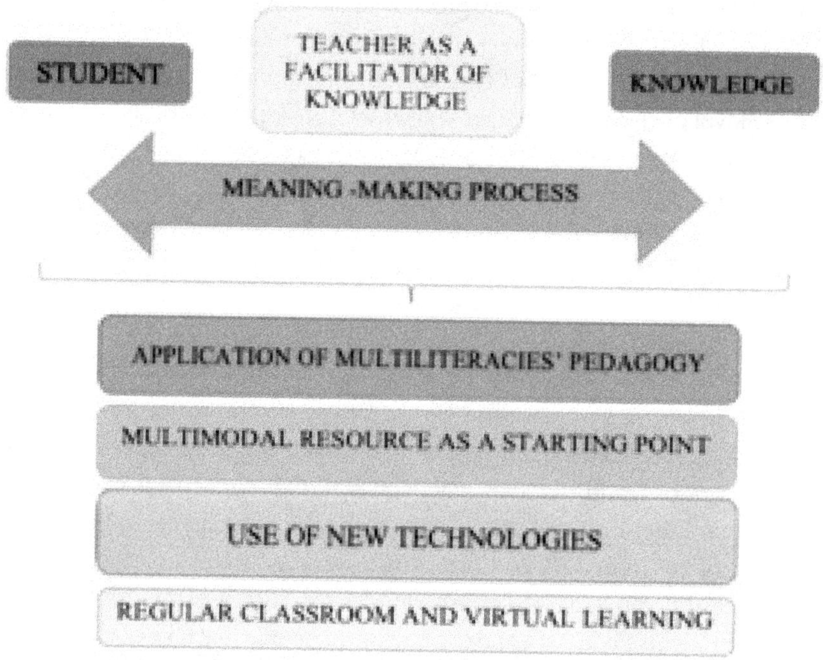

Taking everything into consideration, this literature review includes four subsections. The first one pays attention to the importance of multiliteracies pedagogy in our current society so as to provide meaningful learning experiences. The second one focuses on the students' active role in the construction of knowledge and the teacher's role as a facilitator of knowledge. The third subsection deepens in the student-teacher relationship as a determining factor in the meaning-making process. Finally, the last part gives consideration to the usefulness of ICTs in order to facilitate virtual learning and make this research possible.

The Pedagogy of Multiliteracies and Foreign Language Teaching

Literacy instruction has traditionally meant teaching and learning to read and write in standard forms of the language. Nevertheless, as the New London Group (1996) states, twenty-first century is characterized by the multiplicity of communication channels, which brings in turn an amendment of the notion of literacy. As Kucer (2014, p.3) puts it, "the emerging field of digital literacies is rapidly expanding our understanding of both the nature of text as well as text processing by drawing from work in media education and information and library sciences." Teaching in current society involves giving consideration to new literacies. Authors such as Kern (2000), Serafini (2014), Paesani et al. (2016) and Lacorte and Reyes-Torres (2021) agree with the fact that literacy development should embrace the ability to learn, not only how to speak, listen, view, read and write, but also how to think. Students should be able to interpret and construct meaning not only from written texts, but also from pictures, songs, spaces, advertisement, and so forth. Nowadays learners face a multiliteracies landscape in which they must acquire the thinking skills that will enable them to learn on their own, become meaning-makers and apply their linguistic knowledge to another knowledge base (Reyes-Torres, 2014; Menke and Paesani, 2019). In short, literacy has turned into multiliteracies –many literacies– and as a result, a multimodal approach should be incorporated in today's education (Kress, 2010; Serafini, 2014).

In the words of Warner & Dupuy (2018), contemporary multiliteracies paradigms underline the importance of situating language use within socially complex multimodal contexts. In the same line, Kern (2000) and Paesani et al. (2016) point out that the multimodal and multidimensional aspects of our current world should also be taken into consideration in language education. Learning a foreign language should significantly contribute to the personal, intercultural and social dimension of students as well as to the development of their capacity to construct meaning, reflect and express their ideas from multimodal resources. What students need is the kind of knowledge and skill that will enable them to make sense of their worlds, to determine their own interests, both individual and collective, and to express their views in a coherent and appropriate manner (Schodes, 1985; Reyes-Torres, 2012).

Consequently, in order to distinguish this understanding of literacy from the traditional one, the New London Group (1996) proposes the Multiliteracies Pedagogy (Cope and Kalantzis, 2015; López-Sánchez, 2009) which contains a Learning by Design approach that embraces the differences in contexts and the diverse patterns of communication that are currently emerging. Most importantly, it is an approach that can also be used as an instructional framework for teaching language, culture and literature as a whole in Foreign Language Teaching courses (Allen & Paesani, 2010; Warner and Dupuy, 2018; Reyes-Torres, Matilde-Portales and Bonilla-Tramoyeres, 2020). This means that it is no longer enough for literacy teaching to focus exclusively on vocabulary and grammar of the target language; teachers have to help learners to be capable of negotiating patterns of meaning from one context to another. As Kern (2000) points out, having an effective command of a second language goes beyond the use of vocabulary and linguistic structures in particular situations. In this respect, the Pedagogy of Multiliteracies reconcile the emphasis on verbal interaction of the communicative approach with the emphasis on the interaction between form, context, communicative functions and expressive functions, and the reciprocal connection between the academic learning at school and the real-world practical experiences (Warner and Dupuy, 2018). As will be shown, it proposes a Knowledge Processes Framework (KPF) that is made up of four pedagogical components: (1) Experiencing; (2) Conceptualizing; (3) Analyzing; (4) Applying (New London Group, 1996; Cope and Kalantzis, 2015).

This KPF serves as a guide and is neither hierarchical nor sequential; in fact, elements of each of the acts may overlap and take place in any moment during the learning process (NLG 1996; Allen & Paesani, 2010; Reyes-Torres and Portalés-Raga, 2020). As Menke and Paesani (2019) and Cope and Kalantzis (2015) explain, each process contributes to engage learners in the acts of meaning design:

- Experiencing aims to engage learners in authentic lessons that incorporate both spontaneous reflection and lived experiences. The initial purpose of the teacher is to activate students' mind by carrying out a situated practice, for example, through an initial discussion of the topics and multimodal features of the picturebooks that they are about to read.
- Conceptualizing. As its name suggests, it consists of guiding students in learning a selection of concepts or contents –linguistic, visual, literary, subject-oriented, specific metalanguage– that appear in a text and from which they can reach other perspectives and access new reflections. The aim is to have students get acquainted with them in order to use those in the process of constructing new knowledge.
- Analyzing aims to develop formal reasoning, learn how to support or rebut alternative arguments and gradually develop a critical mind. The goal is to guide students to reflect on a text, discuss any given message from another perspective and comment on the potential relationship between language use and social contexts.
- Applying. According to Cope and Kalantzis (2015, p. 32), "knowledge is not (just) the stuff that ends up in our minds. It is what we do and make. Learning is a consequence of a series of knowledge actions." This act aims to provide learners with tasks that enable them to transform and put into practice everything they have learned. This is indeed a fundamental stage in the process of becoming multiliterate. By constructing meaning using available cognitive, conceptual and sociocultural features, students are actively engaged in generating and applying knowledge

As a final point, the implementation of this KPF places students at the center of learning and allows them to improve their communicative competence while at the same time become meaning-makers of different sign modes such as print, sound, color and images, acquiring thus a cross-cultural and critical understanding of multiliteracies (López-Sánchez, 2009). In sum, through the use of the multiliteracies approach and multimodal resources, it is possible to create a supportive learning environment, virtually as well as in the regular face-to-face classrooms, in which students become capable of producing meaning and thinking critically in the EFL lesson.

Students' Role as Meaning Makers and Teachers' Role as Facilitators

As Wells (1986) highlights, knowledge cannot be transmitted, it can only be constructed. From this perspective, learning is a process in which students are expected to adopt an active role and teachers are responsible for creating a learning path and engaging them in this process. This is, in essence, the basis of constructivism. Learning requires the transformation of existing knowledge (Vygotsky, 1978; Block, 2003; Reyes-Torres, 2019).

As Rosenblatt (1986), puts it, meaning does not reside ready-made in the text or in the reader but happens during the transaction between reader and text. In this respect, children need time to examine and carefully interpret the ways in which words and pictures relate to each other in an aesthetic way. Each learner, therefore, establishes a different relationship with a text or a multimodal resource, and it is out of inquiry that this interaction contributes positively to the development of active, creative and critical learners. Rosenblatt (1986) defines this kind of relationship as the transactional theory in which reading is a key factor that brings meaning to a text in order to extract further meaning from it. Reading is thus understood as a complex, non-linear, self-correcting transaction between reader and text in which each reader makes a particular interpretation of the text due to their prior knowledge and their personal background. According to Weaver (1994), these schemata depend on a variety of social factors: cultural, ethnic, and socioeconomic background; age and educational attainment; interests and values and so forth. No two readers are identical, the result of their transaction cannot be the same (Rosenblatt, 1986).

Throughout the four different acts of the Pedagogy of Multiliteracies, students are able to establish this kind of relationship with the text. During the learning and reading processes, they progressively construct knowledge, and finally, almost subconsciously, they become meaning-makers. Nevertheless, despite this active role that learners play, the multiliteracies pedagogy requires a complex involvement of the teacher. As already mentioned, teachers are responsible for bringing together the reader and the multimodal text. They are the ones who must implement the KPF, engage learners and initiate, foster and make possible the whole meaning-making process.

The teacher is viewed then as a facilitator that assists students who in turn are the primary creators of their learning. As Dewaele (2020) points out, a good teacher, like a good conductor, knows exactly what his or her students are able to do; and the aim of the conductor is not to shine, but to help the orchestra to be outstanding. Similarly, for Kern (2000), the challenge for foreign language teachers is to provide a scaffold for their students' learning with their own knowledge and experience. Scaffolding is originally a Vygostkyan concept. It is based on the idea of providing supportive assistance to the learner within a leaner's Zone of Proximal Development (ZPD). The ZPD is defined as "the distance between what a student can do with and without help" (Vygotsky 1978). It is during this process, according to Vygotsky, that a teacher can make a difference. Through teacher prompting the learner builds up knowledge using what they already know and internalize new information. It is true that even though teachers should provide clarity and support, the students are the ultimate agents in charge of constructing knowledge. In short, teachers play the role of clarifier, challenger and mediator at the same time. They are commissioned to guide students to develop enough capabilities to think by themselves, start linking ideas and gradually provide them with the tools they need to initiate the process of meaning-making.

Moreover, this role of teachers as mediators becomes even more important in technological learning environments and especially so in an English digital classroom of Elementary Education. Because students are used to face-to-face interactions, sitting in the classroom next to their teachers, and being surrounded by their classmates, virtual learning and the new digital scenarios may make them feel disoriented or even provoke discomfort. It is for this reason that the role of the teacher becomes so significant in order to humanize an online course and develop teaching and social presence through student-teacher interaction (Russel and Murphy-Judy, 2021). Teachers have to be there, offering the same guidance and support as they normally offer when they are in school. Therefore, the role of the teacher is central and becomes even more indispensable in digital learning environments, as they have to offer students appropriate scaffolding and build a positive relationship with them

Student-Teacher Positive Relationships in Online Space

The transition from face-to-face to online teaching represents a substantial change not only for many teachers, but also for the students, so there is increasing interest in the way this transition impacts their relationship. In this regard, numerous studies highlight positive student-teacher interaction as crucial for teaching and learning at any level of education both in class and in remote learning (Pianta, 1999; Dewaele, 2012; Wang 2015; Pacansky-Brock, 2015; Varga 2017). While learning has been regarded as a meaning-making process, humans can be defined as meaning-seekers who learn in relation with other human beings. Relationships define humans. Every human being is expected not only to grow but also to thrive through their interaction with others. Authors such as Moskowitz and Dewaele (2021) consider the affective quality of the student-teacher interactions a key factor for students in their school engagement, wellbeing and academic success. Likewise, the way teachers communicate plays a critical role. Teachers who are friendly and positive develop better relationships with their students. According to Vadillio (1999), "the teacher of the foreign language should have a profound competence of different aspects of the target language in addition to owning some personal qualities like warmth, tolerance and communication skills" (quoted in Yunus et al., 2016, p.64). Moreover, Pianta (1999) refers to positive student-teacher relationships as an emotional and academic support that exists between students and teachers; "it is a form of relationship that is characterized by mutual acceptance, understanding, warmth, closeness, trust, respect, care and cooperation" (Pianta, 1999, p.263). Finally, for Varga, positive relationships are the ones that include teachers who think about their practice and search for ways to improve it. These teachers give students power and choice during their lessons. Furthermore, they make their students feel a sense of belonging. As Moskowitz & Dewaele (2021) state, the importance of student perceptions of teachers impacts the online space, too, where FL acquisition is often facilitated by learners' positive attitudes about their teacher.

In this line of thought, Hampel and Stickler (2015, p. 65) emphasize that "language teaching online is a socio-constructivist endeavor." It is not just about focusing on technology but about creating the conditions that enable students to engage with the contents and participate actively. Moreover, as Murphy (2015, p. 47) states there is widespread acceptance that language teaching differs from other disciplines in that the language is both the subject of, and vehicle for, instruction. Likewise, language learning, particularly online, makes significant affective demands. Consequently, as Russel and Murphy-Judy explain (2021, p. 132), in order to be proficient at online language teaching, instructors must acquire a broad base of knowledge across different domains: knowing how to teach language, knowing how to teach online, knowing how to use educational technologies and knowing how to humanize the virtual learning environment. Thus, there is a need to provide teachers and educators with appropriate and ongoing training support in order for them not only to become digitally competent, but most importantly, to help them become pedagogically aware of why and how ICT can enhance the creation of positive student-teacher online relationships. If children do not feel comfortable with teachers, if children do not get on well with them, if a positive relationship between teacher and student is not established, teachers are not going to be able to offer them a meaningful online learning experience. On the contrary, when students relate to an online instructor as something more than an expert on the foreign language and begin to conceive themselves as part of a larger community, they are more likely to be motivated and willing to learn (Richarson and Swam, 2003). These ideas can be compressed in the words of veteran educator James Comer (2005): "No significant learning occurs without a significant relationship" (quoted in Wessels, 2015, p.2). And this is what this study wants to echo and hand over to challenge the readers. According to Dewaele (2020), students and teachers maintain a place not only in each other's lives, but in each other's minds, and the student-teacher relationship is social and emotional by nature both in face to face and in virtual learning. There is no doubt that when teachers' actions and words demonstrate that they care for their students, students are more likely to perform well. The emotional connection is therefore one of the most determining factors to establish a positive relationship.

Lastly, teachers also need to maintain classroom management in the online space. If the teaching objectives are clear and if the learning path is well designed, there's a strong likelihood that students will engage in the meaning-making process. The goal is to use ICT to create a calm and supportive remote learning environment in which students can express their own opinions, feel free to interact and make mistakes. In such an interactive setting, the aim for teachers is not only to provide tasks and promote participation, but also to create a virtual scenario where students can still experience individualized and responsive attention. As Murphy (2015) argues, teachers have to transform existing teaching skills in order to create the kind of structured, non-threatening, inclusive online learning space which learners need in order to explore, exchange information, connect and apply ideas and successfully develop their language skills.

ICT and Virtual Learning

Until now, primary students had rarely imagined that their homes could become their learning classroom, but today a wide range of technological tools and resources are used to create content for remote teaching and learning. As a result of the COVID-19 landscape, the introduction of digital technologies as an educational tool has transformed and redefined language learning and teaching. Today a multitude of online spaces are available and ICTs constitute the most efficient way, first, to bridge the gap that the COVID-19 situation has created between teachers and students and, second, to act as a driving force of the meaning-making process. This is the main reason why drawing the attention to the role of technology has become so essential in this study.

Few will dispute the claim that social network sites, online games, video-sharing sites and gadgets such as iPods, iPads and mobile phones have become an essential aspect in students' everyday lives. While most children and teenagers may regard the digital environment as fun contexts just to play and for entertainment purposes, these gadgets offer not only new and varied ways of joy, but also new ways of communication and learning. As Cope & Kalantzis (2015, p.11) explain, "computer-mediated learning environments herald the long-awaited widespread realization of constructivist." Likewise, Pandian & Baboo (2015, p. 232) remark that "the pathways of literacy in the students' digital life clearly demand that we re-examine the practices of literacy in schools to enable children to engage and get involved with learning activities in creative and productive ways." Online environments offer great potential for real world communicative experiences, socializing, both within a class but also with the wider world. Students can work with their peers (in pairs or in larger groups); they can interact with their teacher; learners of an L2 can communicate with L1 speakers of the language in their own or another country. However, they need guidance in doing so. Furthermore, the benefits for students related to the general use of technology include increased motivation, engagement in the learning process and more active processing, resulting in higher-order thinking skills and better recall (Stepp-Greany, 2002). Finally, Warschauer and Kern (2000), highlight communication, empowerment and learning as three common factors of student motivation provided by a technology enhanced settings.

Taking everything into account, ICT provide diverse resources to work more efficiently and can afford greater educational experiences along with offering new channels for learners to build up their knowledge. One of the drawbacks, however, could be that students' engagement and concentration is much lower than in a regular face-to-face classroom. Students at home could be distracted easily. In addition to this one, the absence of body language can cause miscommunication – silences, for example, can be interpreted wrongly (Stickler et al., 2007). As a result, social presence has to be created in different ways compared with face-to-face encounters, and users have to become familiar with new patterns of communication. Therefore, the role of the teacher as a guide become completely necessary, and even more paramount. The materials and the tasks provided must be consciously planned in order to design a clear learning path, afford successful language learning experiences despite the distance and create a constructive learner–teacher relationship.

In brief, the meaning-making process constitutes a mechanism that requires different pieces in order to be put into action. This mechanism embraces four different elements: teacher, student, the multiliteracies pedagogy and ICTs. The combination of all four along with positive students-teacher relationships make possible a new way of approaching teaching and learning in virtual environments.

RESEARCH DESIGN

Methodology and Procedure

As previously mentioned, due to the COVID-19 crisis, this research has been carried out in a virtual learning environment. The researchers have used a qualitative approach to explore, first, how the multiliteracies pedagogy fosters interaction and positive relationships between teachers and students in a regular classroom and, second, how this, in turn, has an impact on learners' meaning-making process in the online space. To this end, this study is based on an interpretative paradigm which seeks to analyze and understand the data provided by the participants (Creswell, 2009).

The following table 1 summarizes the procedure that has been followed to conduct the research. It also gives a precise overview of timing.

Table 1. Steps of the study

Steps	Timing
1) Research and teaching period starts	3rd February 2020
2) Creation of positive relationships with students in the classroom environment	3rd February – 13th March
3) Selection of participants	13th March – 22th March
4) Adaptation of the study to COVID-19 emergency situation	23rd March – 28th March
5) Development of virtual tasks and research instruments	28th March – 20th April
6) Collection of data	20th April – 1st May
7) Data analysis	2nd May – 22nd May
8) Interpretation and evaluation of results	22nd May – 30th May
9) Drawing conclusions	30th May – 5th June

This research encompassed a long process formed by different lineal stages; once the permission to conduct it was obtained and the research objectives were established, the following step was the selection of the different groups that will take part in the study. Participants were chosen taking into consideration the characteristics of the students, the relationship that they had with the teacher and their level of English. The next step consisted of adapting the work to be able to carry it out during virtual learning. Therefore, all the tasks and instruments that would help the research to gather and analyze the data had to be reconsidered. After this, the final phase focused on assessing the results so as to be capable of drawing the corresponding conclusions of the research.

Context and Participants

The study was carried out with students of *CEIP Campanar*, a state-elementary school located in the city of Valencia. The participants were students in 5th and 6th grade. As Table 2 shows, three different groups participated in this research: two groups from Year 5 (that were 5th-A, 5th-B; and one group from Year 6, concretely 6th-A. Group A in 5th grade consisted of 25 students, but only 23 of them were enrolled in the English lesson. As for group 5th-B, there were 19 students who selected English. Regarding the 27 students in group 6th-A, two of them studied French as a second language and two of them followed a completely different curriculum. Therefore, 23 students participated in this research group. In total, there were 65 students involved in the investigation.

It should be noted that even though the participants were from different grades, they had a similar level of English and cognitive skills. They were chosen because of the relationship that the teacher-researcher had developed with them previously inside the school. The researcher had taught 5th-A and 6th-A students for six weeks, whilst students from group 5th-B barely knew her and therefore, no such relationship nor interaction had been established. All these factors are mainly what made these participants ideal candidates with whom to carry out this study and determine, first, to what extent the implementation of the Pedagogy of Multiliteracies contributed to the development of the student-teacher relationship and interaction in the English classroom and, second, if it had an influence on their engagement and in the process of meaning-making in a virtual learning environment.

Table 2. Participants selected

Groups involved	Students involved	Main aspects
Group 1: 5th B **Year 5**	19 students	· No relationship was created during the face-to-face classroom period. · During the virtual learning period, they had to work on their own, without any kind of interaction with the teacher.
Group 2: 5th A **Year 5**	23 students	· A positive relationship was created during the face-to-face classroom period. · During the virtual learning period, they had to work on their own, without any kind of interaction with the teacher.
Group 3: 6th A **Year 6**	23 students	· A positive relationship was created during the face-to-face classroom period. · During the virtual learning environment, teacher implemented the Pedagogy of Multiliteracies and provided students with guidance and interaction in the process of meaning-making throughout the didactic unit.

Research Instruments

Taking into consideration all the learning variables of this study, the main instrument that was used to collect sufficient data was a didactic sequence that consisted of nine tasks that were designed based on the picturebook *ZOG* (2010). Each of these tasks was developed following the Pedagogy of Multiliteracies approach in which students, regardless of their group, are expected to have an active role and get involved in the four acts of the Knowledge Processes Framework discussed before: experiencing, conceptualizing, analyzing and applying

ZOG, written by Julia Donaldson and illustrated by Axel Scheffler, conveys a story in which the protagonist is a keen dragon, named ZOG, who goes to school and always wants to win a golden star. Each year, Madam Dragon teaches him and his classmates different things to become an incredible dragon: how to fly, how to roar, how to blow, how to capture a princess or how to fight with a knight. However, ZOG is not really good at it. Luckily for him, when he is confronting failure, a girl with a medical kit appears every time and patches him up. Eventually, she will help him understand that they are not forced to be what the world expects of them. In fact, although she turns out to be a princess she announces that she does not wish to be rescued, but to pursue her vocation, become a doctor and help people all around the world. ZOG, on his part, wants to be her ambulance. In the end, each character finds what they are meant to be and do.

During the nine tasks, the teacher-researcher acted as a guide with students in group 3, but she rarely interacted during the process with groups 1 and 2. As all the tasks were carried out during virtual learning, students were required to use ICT to do the tasks and teacher interaction was provided through different video recordings. Thank to these videos, the teacher was able to engage, introduce and mediate in the process of working with the picturebook and the different tasks.

- Task 1 was based on exploring the cover and engage students in the story. They were encouraged to interpret and describe with their own words what they saw.
- Task 2 consisted of getting students involved in the story and understanding the beginning of it so that they looked forward to continuing the reading.
- In Task 3, they continued the reading of ZOG and were asked to organize it in different parts.
- Task 4 went deeper in the analysis of specific lexical concepts. New vocabulary words were shown and students were asked to make connections between text and pictures.
- Task 5 focused on guiding students in a reflection process. In the same way that the forest in ZOG is seen as dragons' school, students could become aware that their homes had turned into a school and they had learnt so many things in this new environment.
- Throughout Task 6, students continued reflecting on the story and were prompted to guess how it ends. Once they had commented on it, they were ready to find out what finally happened. Afterwards, they answered some questions in order to elaborate their interpretation about the different events.
- In the same way that ZOG and Princess Pearl express their dreams in the second part of the story, Task 7 aimed to motivate students to think about their future. Students were prompted to think big, reflect about their strengths and talk about what they want to be.
- Task 8 aimed to encourage students to go back to the story so as to pay attention to some specific concepts and reflect more in-depth about them.
- Task 9 consisted of fostering students' ability to use the thoughts and ideas that they had developed throughout the previous tasks and apply them in a real-word situation. In this case, dealing with COVID-19 crisis had leaded many of them to become more aware of the importance of ZOG's job and the risk of getting infected bringing people to the hospital. Students were asked to write a letter encouraging ZOG during those hard circumstances.

The following Table 3 presents an outline of the nine tasks, their main learning outcomes and their connection with the four pedagogical acts of the KPF. Due to the fact that each knowledge process can take place in any moment, it shows the ones that are expected to occur regarding the type of the task designed.

Table 3. Outline of the nine tasks

Task	Name	Learning outcomes	Knowledge process
1	Brainstorming about the cover	To describe what they see and express their own ideas about the cover	Experiencing
2	Let's discover Zog story	To engage in the story and relate with it	Experiencing
3	Put in order the different parts of the story	To remember the line of argument of the story	Experiencing
4	Guess the meaning going back to the story	To focus on different parts of the story and learn new vocabulary	Conceptualizing
5	What have you learnt at home school?	To identify their learnings in such a difficult situation	Analyzing / Applying
6	Focus, reflect and guess the end of the story	To interpret the story properly and give a coherent guess	Analyzing
7	Let's think about our dreams	To imagine and create a mental picture of themselves in the future	Analyzing / Applying
8	Let's see the relationship between the text and the pictures.	To have a holistic idea of everything that take place in a picturebook	Conceptualizing / Analyzing
9	Letter to encourage Zog with his job	To mix their own ideas and the new knowledge acquired and write a motivational letter.	Applying

RESULTS

The data analyzed generated findings in two different areas: first, the level of students' engagement depending on their relationship with the teacher; and second, how implementing the Pedagogy of Multiliteracies promotes a healthy online teaching presence and enhances the meaning-making process in a virtual learning environment. Hence, on the one hand, taking into consideration each group and the number of students who were engaged in the nine tasks, those other students who disengaged during the process and those who did not even complete any work at all, the authors can conclude that it is indisputable that there is a strong correspondence between students' involvement and students-teacher relationships.

Tables 4, 5 and 6 below show an overview of students' engagement in group 1(5th-B), group 2 (5th-A) and group 3 (6th-A).

Table 4. Engagement results in group 1: students in 5th-B

	TASKS								
STUDENTS 6TH A	1	2	3	4	5	6	7	8	9
Student 1									
Student 2	X	X	X	X	X	X	X	X	X
Student 3	X	X	X	X	X	X	X	X	X
Student 4									
Student 5									
Student 6	X	X	X	X	X	X	X	X	X
Student 7	X	X	X	X	X	X	X	X	X
Student 8	X	X	X	X	X	X	X	X	X
Student 9	X	X	X	X	X	X	X	X	X
Student 10									
Student 11	X	X	X	X	X	X	X	X	X
Student 12	X	X	X	X	X	X	X	X	X
Student 13	X	X	X	X	X	X	X	X	X
Student 14									
Student 15	X	X	X	X	X	X	X	X	X
Student 16									
Student 17									
Student 18	X	X	X	X	X	X	X	X	X
Student 19	X	X	X	X	X	X	X	X	X
Student 20	X	X	X	X	X	X	X	X	X
Student 21									
Student 22	X	X	X	X	X	X	X	X	X
Student 23	X	X	X	X	X	X	X	X	X

STUDENT WHO WERE ENGAGED FROM THE BEGINNING TO THE END

15/23

STUDENT WHO DISENGAGED DURING THE PROCCESS

0/23

STUDENT WHO WERE NOT ENGAGED AT ALL

8/23

Table 5. Engagement results in group 2: students in 5thA

	TASKS								
STUDENTS 5TH A	1	2	3	4	5	6	7	8	9
Student 1	X	X	X	X	X	X	X	X	X
Student 2	X	X	X	X	X				
Student 3	X	X	X	X	X	X	X	X	X
Student 4	X	X	X	X	X	X	X	X	X
Student 5									
Student 6	X	X	X		X		X	X	
Student 7	X	X	X	X	X	X	X	X	X
Student 8									
Student 9									
Student 10	X	X	X	X	X	X	X	X	X
Student 11	X	X	X						
Student 12									
Student 13	X	X	X	X	X				
Student 14	X	X	X	X	X				
Student 15	X	X	X						
Student 16									
Student 17	X	X	X	X	X	X	X	X	X
Student 18	X	X	X						
Student 19	X	X	X	X	X	X	X	X	X
Student 20	X	X	X	X	X	X	X	X	X
Student 21	X	X	X	X	X	X	X	X	X
Student 22	X	X	X	X	X	X	X	X	X
Student 23	X	X	X	X	X	X	X	X	X

STUDENT WHO WERE ENGAGED FROM THE BEGINNING TO THE END

11/23

STUDENT WHO DISENGAGED DURING THE PROCESS

7/23

STUDENT WHO WERE NOT ENGAGED AT ALL

5/23

Table 6. Engagement results in group 3: students in 6thA

	TASKS								
STUDENTS 6TH A	1	2	3	4	5	6	7	8	9
Student 1									
Student 2	X	X	X	X	X	X	X	X	X
Student 3	X	X	X	X	X	X	X	X	X
Student 4									
Student 5									
Student 6	X	X	X	X	X	X	X	X	X
Student 7	X	X	X	X	X	X	X	X	X
Student 8	X	X	X	X	X	X	X	X	X
Student 9	X	X	X	X	X	X	X	X	X
Student 10									
Student 11	X	X	X	X	X	X	X	X	X
Student 12	X	X	X	X	X	X	X	X	X
Student 13	X	X	X	X	X	X	X	X	X
Student 14									
Student 15	X	X	X	X	X	X	X	X	X
Student 16									
Student 17									
Student 18	X	X	X	X	X	X	X	X	X
Student 19	X	X	X	X	X	X	X	X	X
Student 20	X	X	X	X	X	X	X	X	X
Student 21									
Student 22	X	X	X	X	X	X	X	X	X
Student 23	X	X	X	X	X	X	X	X	X

STUDENT WHO WERE ENGAGED FROM THE BEGINNING TO THE END

15/23

STUDENT WHO DISENGAGED DURING THE PROCESS

0/23

STUDENT WHO WERE NOT ENGAGED AT ALL

8/23

In the first group (5th-B), in which teacher and students barely knew each other, just three students completed all the tasks; by contrast, in the third group (6th A), fifteen out of twenty-three students were engaged from the beginning to the end. Thus, these results confirm that the implementation of multiliteracies pedagogy enhances the creation of positive student-teacher relationships in a regular face-to-face classroom and has a direct impact on students' involvement in a virtual learning environment. The students who have continuous interaction with their teacher show a higher degree of involvement to complete the tasks provided and are more motivated to learn.

Moreover, these tables also reveal that the number of disengaged students during the process is significantly higher when they did not have any help and mediation from the teacher. As we can see in table 5, in group 2 there were seven students whose involvement gradually decreased during the process and they did not complete all the tasks. However, as table 6 shows, students in group 3, that was guided, were involved in all nine tasks.

On the other hand, with regard to the previous findings, four different rubrics were created in order to examine more closely how implementing the Pedagogy of Multiliteracies and the KPF enhance the meaning-making process. As will be shown, these rubrics in Table 7, 8, 9 and 10 are in line with the four pedagogical acts – experiencing, conceptualizing, analyzing and applying– and have allowed us to assess students' responses and analyze their ability to interact with the picturebook *ZOG* and develop their thoughts.

Table 7. Rubric to determine the level of achievement in the experiencing process

EXPERIENCING TASKS	1 ☹	2	3	4 ☺
AIMS: ***-Fostering students expressive and communicative abilities*** ***-Activate students' minds*** ***-Experiencing between the known and the new***	They have described what they see in a simple way and they haven't paid attention to the story at all.	The student describes what he/she sees in a more complex way and his/her involvement in the story is adequate.	The student interprets, reads the picture and describes it with their ideas briefly and the engagement is good.	The student interprets, reads the picture and describes it with elaborate ideas and thoughts. His/her engagement is high and can remember perfectly the main parts of the story.

Table 8. Rubric to determine the level of achievement in the conceptualizing process

CONCEPTUALIZING TASKS	1 ☹	2	3	4 ☺
AIMS: ***-Guiding student to become aware of the visual and linguistic elements that take place in the story*** ***-Seeing to what extend these elements help them to construct meaning***	The student doesn't pay attention to any elements. Therefore, he/she is not able to identify any concrete meanings and he/she doesn't become aware of the relationship between the text and the pictures.	The student pays attention to some elements and he/she is able to identify some meanings. In contrast, he/she might not become aware of the relationship between the text and the pictures.	The student pays attention to the different elements, he/she is able to identity some concrete meanings and he/she becomes slightly aware of the relationship between text and the pictures.	The student pays attention to the different elements and he/she is able to identity most concrete meanings. Besides, he/she becomes astutely aware of the relationship between the text and the pictures.

Table 9. Rubric to determine the level of achievement in the analyzing process

ANALYZING GOALS	1 ☹	2	3	☺
-Guiding students to create meaning and reflect about it from another perspective	The student is not able to analyze meaning, neither develop a critical mind nor reflect about themselves.	The student begins to analyze meaning but he/she is not able to develop a critical mind and reflect about themselves.	The student is able to analyze meaning, develop a critical mind and reflect about themselves.	The student is able to analyze meaning in a meaningful way, reflect about themselves and develop a critical mind.

Table 10. Rubric to determine the level of achievement in the applying process

APPLYING GOALS	1 ☹	2	3	4 ☺
-Apply linguistic and cultural knowledge collected during the tasks. ***-Transfer what they have learnt and put it into practice with a real situation***	They have not constructed any knowledge and consequently, they are not able at all to transfer and adapt it in a real word situation.	They have constructed some knowledge, but they are not able to transfer and adapt it in a real word situation.	They have constructed some knowledge and they are slightly able to transfer the knowledge constructed in a real word situation.	They are able to transfer and adapt the knowledge constructed in a real word situation in a meaningful way.

The results of the rubrics display that the level of achievement of students in group 3 (6th-A) was very satisfactory. Seventeen of them achieved level 3 or 4 and only six of them reached a level 1 or 2. Accordingly, their progress and their ability for meaning making was much higher than students in the other groups.

Furthermore, in addition to the findings achieved from the rubrics, a focus group was made with 10 students just from 6th-A so as to provide more specific evidence of how the meaning-making process develops throughout all the tasks and all the processes. The answers of those 10 students were analyzed and classified applying a conceptual map made with different categories and codes that we can see in table 11.

Table 11. Definition of categories and codes

Categories Multiliteracies	Codes	Definition
Experiencing	(AM)	Activate students Minds
	(DLA)	Development of Linguistic Abilities
	(EKN)	Experiencing between the known and the new
Conceptualizing	(AVLE)	Awareness of Visual and Linguistic Elements
	(RTP)	Relationship between Text and Pictures
Analyzing	(PITP)	Personal Interpretations of Text and Pictures
	(DCM)	Development of Critical Minds
Applying	(ALK)	Application of Linguistic Knowledge
	(TMRS)	Transfer Meaning Constructed to Real Situation

Although, as it was already mentioned, the four pedagogical components of the KPF could emerge in any task and at any moment during the learning process, in order to provide readable and coherent results, table 12 below is an example of the data collected from Task 1. In this case, it shows students (S) responses in relation with the process of "experiencing" based on the picturebook ZOG.

Table 12. Category and codes of the process of "experiencing"

Category: Experiencing	
Units of meaning – Group 3 (6th A)	
Task 1 **(Description of the cover)** 6th A→ S6: "I can see six little dragons and one big dragon." 6th → S7: "I can see two brown birds. One is flying and the other one is on a tree. There are seven dragons. It's colors are orange, blue, yellow, pink, brown and two greens. I see a lot of trees." 6th → S9: "I can see a lot of dragons with different colours." 6th → S18: "I also see many trees in the forest and a cave in the corner." 6th → S19: "I think the wheather is sunny with clouds."	**(AM)** Activate students Minds
Task 1 **(Description of the cover)** 6th A→ S6: "I can see a snail with its shell on top of a grey rock." 6th → S12: "I see a rabbit in the background." 6th → S15: "In this picture, I can see a large green dragon that explains to a smaller red dragon on blackboard." 6th → S18: "And finally, I see a rabbit on the grass."	**(DCA)** Attempt to use Language Abilities
Task 1 **(Description of the cover)** 6th → S9: "I think the girl in the blackboard is a princess." 6th → S12: "Look at the teacher dragon." 6th → S13: "They are celebrating something." 6th → S15: "I think it is a teacher who teaches." 6th → S23: "I think the big dragon is a teacher. The forest is the school ".	**(EKN)** Experiencing between the Known and the New

As students' answers show, encouraging them to describe the cover of the picturebook activates their minds. Colors, shapes, sizes and the different elements that appear on the cover caught their attention and helped them to describe it and express their ideas. Many of the comments indicate how students are already anticipating that one of the topics is connected with dragons teaching and learning. Similarly, during the second task students learned about the first part of the story and this is what increased their willingness to continue reading. In general, each of the tasks offered students an opportunity to use their linguistic abilities and put into practice sentence stems such as "I think" or "In this picture, I can see" or connectors such as "finally". In addition to this, the relationship between what they knew and what they discovered was fascinating. They were able to construct a bridge and use their experiences. For instance, some students were capable of relating the drawing on the blackboard with the characteristics of a princess. Furthermore, taking into consideration the background (blackboard, a big dragon and small ones), some of them regarded the green dragon as a teacher and the forest as a school.

In conclusion, the data analyzed shows that if a positive relationship is not established, students do not even try to carry out the tasks provided, and hence, no knowledge can be constructed. Furthermore, apart from student-teacher relationships, the data obtained indicates that the multiliteracies pedagogy helps students to become meaning-makers and that the role of the teacher is crucial in the process of constructing meaning and even more important in a virtual learning environment. Thus, it is possible to affirm that factors such as academic achievement and student engagement are influenced by the quality of the student-teacher relationships and the teacher's role as a mediator of knowledge.

FUTURE RESEARCH

This chapter is expected to help teachers to become more aware of the need to enhance their relationship with learners in such a way that they deliberately scaffold an engaging meaning-making process both in class and in a remote setting. Nevertheless, there are several limitations of this study that can be addressed in future research. Due to the fact that the investigation was carried out during virtual learning and no kind of control was implemented, parent's involvement and help with the different tasks could have an effect on students' answers and their construction of knowledge. It is impossible to know how much help they received. Therefore, it would be interesting to carry out this research in a face-to-face classroom environment where all tasks are completed during school time.

Additionally, future research should consider the length of the study. If the study had occurred for more than three months, would the influence of student-teacher relationships be even more evident? It is likely that the results could vary. Likewise, the same study could be applied in a regular classroom and several conclusions could be drawn with regard to the differences between virtual learning and a regular one. Finally, another possibility to enrich this research is implementing the same methodology across multiple grade levels, especially the younger grades because they normally form stronger bonds with their teachers and therefore, the relationship between them could be more meaningful. This could offer a holistic overview of the benefits of positive relationships throughout different years of schooling.

CONCLUSION

A change in the concept of education cannot take place if this change does not start with a change in teachers' perspectives and their way of regarding themselves. As Clifford (1987) predicted: "technology will not replace teachers in the future, but rather teachers who use technology will probably replace teachers who do not" (quoted in Blake, 2013, p. 14). Current changes and COVID-19 circumstances particularly are prompting teachers to get acquainted with new ways and new methods to teach. How teachers see the world and how they relate to it have a great impact on how they get involved in their job, how they teach new generation and hence, how this world could change for the better. Therefore, the role of the teacher is completely essential. As Arnold (2020, p. xx) points out: "Teachers who are highly motivated will work to find the best ways to teach the language and to relate to their students. When teachers show interest in their students, have empathy with them, reduce their anxiety, and contribute to their feeling of confidence, they will have more positive results with their teaching."

All this comes to show that unforgettable language learning experiences can take place in the online space if positive student-teacher relationships are promoted. No one can love if he or she is not loved; therefore, only if teachers love what they do and show affection to their students, will they be able to guide learners to love the beauty of learning. It has been proved that the way teachers relate with their students has an impact on how they construct knowledge and on their growth on an academic and personal level. Whatever the educational challenges are that lie ahead, the interaction between teachers and students that the Pedagogy of Multiliteracies facilitates through a process of meaning-making design is indeed a determining factor in a virtual learning environment.

REFERENCES

Allen, H. W., & Paesani, K. (2010). Exploring the Feasibility of a Pedagogy of Multiliteracies in Introductory Foreign Language Courses. *Journal of Linguistics and Language Teaching*, *2*, 119–142.

Arnold, J. (2020). Foreword. In The emotional rollercoaster of language teaching (pp. xix-xx). Bristol: Multilingual Matters.

Brisk, M. (2015). *Engaging Students Literacies. Genre-based pedagogy for K-5 classrooms*. Routledge.

Blake, R. J. (2013). *Brave New Digital Classroom. Technology and Foreign Language Learning*. Georgetown University Press.

Block, D. (2003). *The Social Turn in Second Language Acquisition*. Georgetown University Press.

Creswell, J. W. (2009). *Research Design. Qualitative, quantitative and Mixed Methods Approaches*. Sage Publications.

Cope, B., & Kalantzis, M. (2015). *A Pedagogy of Multiliteracies. Learning by design*. Palgrave and Macmillan.

De Bot, K., Wander, L., & Verspoor, M. (2007). A Dynamic Systems Theory Approach to Second Language Acquisition. *Bilingualism: Language and Cognition*, *10*(1), 7–21. doi:10.1017/S1366728906002732

Dewaele, J.-M. (2020). If classroom emotions were music, teachers would be conductors and learners would be members of the orchestra. In O. Mentz & K. Papaja (Eds.), *Focus on Language. Challenging language learning and language teaching in peace and global education* (pp. 8–10). Lit Verlag.

Dewaele, J.-M. (2012). Affect and Language Teaching. In *The Encyclopedia of Applied Linguistics*. University of London.

Donalson, J., & Scheffler, A. (2010). *ZOG*. Scholastic Children's Books Euston House.

Kern, R. (2000). *Literacy and language teaching*. Oxford University Press.

Kress, G. R. (2010). *Multimodality: A social semiotic approach to contemporary communication*. Routledge.

Kucer, S. (2014). *Dimensions of Literacy: A Conceptual Base for Teaching, Reading and Writing in School Settings*. Routledge. doi:10.4324/9780203428405

Lacorte, M., & Reyes-Torres, A. (2021). *Didáctica del español como 2/L en el siglo XXI*. Madrid: Arco Libros.

López-Sánchez, A. (2009). Re-writing the goals of foreign language teaching: The achievement of multiple literacies and symbolic competence. *International Journal of Learning*, *16*(10), 29–37. doi:10.18848/1447-9494/CGP/v16i10/46632

Menke, M. R., & Paesani, K. (2019). Analysing Foreign Language Instructional Materials through the Lens of Multiliteracies Framework. *Language, Culture and Curriculum*, *32*(1), 34–49. doi:10.1080/07908318.2018.1461898

Moskowitz, S., & Dewaele, J.-M. (2021). Is teacher happiness contagious? A study of the link between perceptions of language teacher happiness and student attitudes. *Innovation in Language Learning and Teaching*, *15*(2), 117–130. doi:10.1080/17501229.2019.1707205

Murphy, L. (2015). Online Language Teaching: The Learner's Perspective. In R. Hampel & U. Stickler (Eds.), *Developing Online Language Teaching. New Language Learning and Teaching Environments*. Palgrave Macmillan., doi:10.1057/9781137412263_4

New London Group. (1996). A pedagogy of multiliteracies: Designing social futures. *Harvard Educational Review*, *66*(1), 60–93. doi:10.17763/haer.66.1.17370n67v22j160u

Paesani, K., Allen, H. W., & Dupuy, B. (2016). *Multiliteracies Framework for Collegiate Foreign Language Teaching*. Pearson.

Pandian, A., & Baboo, S. B. (2015). Digital Lifeworlds and Designers of Literacy Practices in Malaysian Schools. In B. Cope & M. Kalantzis (Eds.), *A Pedagogy of Multiliteracies. Learning by Design* (pp. 231–255). Palgrave Macmillan. doi:10.1057/9781137539724_13

Pianta, R. C. (1999). *Enhancing relationships between children and teachers*. American. Psychological Association. doi:10.1037/10314-000

Reyes-Torres, A. (2012). Literature in the foreign language syllabus: Engaging the student through active learning. *Tejuelo*, *15*, 9–16.

Reyes-Torres, A. (2014). Literacy Education: The first step towards Literary Competence. In A. Reyes-Torres, L. Villacañas & B. Soler (Eds.), Thinking Through Children's Literature in the Classroom. (pp. 42-52). Cambridge: Cambridge Scholars Publishing.

Reyes-Torres, A. (2019). Literatura. In J. Muñoz-Basols, E. Gironzetti, & M. Lacorte (Eds.), *The Routledge Handbook of Spanish Language Teaching* (pp. 628–640). Routledge.

Reyes-Torres, A., Portalés-Raga, M., & Bonilla-Tramoyeres, P. (2020). Multimodalidad e innovación metodológica en la enseñanza del inglés: El álbum ilustrado como recurso literario y visual para el desarrollo del conocimiento. *Revista Nebrija de Lingüística Aplicada a la Enseñanza de Lenguas, 14*(28), 54–77.

Reyes-Torres, A., & Portalés-Raga, M. (2020). A Multimodal Approach to Foster the Multiliteracies Pedagogy in the Teaching of EFL through Picturebooks: *The Snow Lion. Atlantis (Palma de Mallorca), 42*(1), 1–26. doi:10.28914/Atlantis-2020-42.1.06

Richardson, J. C., & Swan, K. (2003). Examining social presence in online courses in relation to students' perceived learning and satisfaction. *Journal of Asynchronous Learning Networks, 7*(1), 68–88.

Rosenblatt, L. M. (1986). The Aesthetic Transaction. *Journal of Aesthetic Education, 20*(4), 122–128. doi:10.2307/3332615

Russell, V., & Murphy-Judy, K. (2021). *Teaching Language Online: A Guide for Designing, Developing, and Delivering Online, Blended, and Flipped Language Courses.* New York: Routledge.

Scholes, R. (1985). *Textual Power: Literary Theory and the Teaching of English.* Yale University Press.

Stepp-Greany, J. (2002). Student perceptions on language learning in a technological environment: Implications for the new millennium. *Language Learning & Technology, 6*(1), 165–180.

Serafini, F. (2014). *Reading the visual: An introduction to teaching multimodal literacy.* Teachers College Press.

Sipe, L. (2008). *Storytime. Young Children's Literary Understanding in the Classroom.* Teachers College Press.

Stickler, U., Batstone, C., Duensing, A., & Heins, B. (2007). Distant classmates: Speech and silence in online and telephone language tutorials. *European Journal of Open, Distance and E-Learning, 2007*(2).

Stickler, U., & Hampel, R. (2015). Transforming Teaching: New Skills for Online Language Learning Spaces. In R. Hampel & U. Stickler (Eds.), *Developing Online Language Teaching. New Language Learning and Teaching Environments.* Palgrave Macmillan. doi:10.1057/9781137412263_5

Varga, M. (2017). *The Effects of Teacher-Student Relationships on the Academic Engagement of Students.* Maryland Shared Open Access Repository.

Vygotsky, L. S. (1978). Mind in Society: The Development of Higher Psychological Processes. In M. Cole, V. John-Steiner, S. Scribner, & E. Souberman (Eds.). Harvard University Press.

Wang, A. (2015). Facilitating participation: Teacher roles in a multiuser virtual learning environment. *Language Learning & Technology, 19*(2), 156–176.

Warner, C., & Dupuy, B. (2018). Moving toward Multiliteracies in Foreign Language Teaching: Past and present perspectives ... and beyond. *Foreign Language Annals*, *51*(1), 116–128. doi:10.1111/flan.12316

Warschauer, M., & Kern, R. (Eds.). (2000). *Network-based language teaching: Concepts and practice*. Cambridge University Press. doi:10.1017/CBO9781139524735

Weaver, C. (1994). *Reading Process and Practice from Socio-psycholinguistics to Whole Language*. Heinemann.

Wessels, F. (2015). The critical role of relationship education. *Hervormde Teologiese Studies*, *71*(3), 2702. Advance online publication. doi:10.4102/hts.v71i3.2702

Wells, G. (1986). *The Meaning Makers: Children learning language and using language to learn*. Hodder and Stoughton.

Yunus, M. M., Osman, W. S., & Ishak, N. M. (2011). Teacher-student relationship factor affecting motivation and academic achievement in ESL classroom. *Procedia: Social and Behavioral Sciences*, *15*, 2637–2641. doi:10.1016/j.sbspro.2011.04.161

ADDITIONAL READING

Cooper, J. D., Kiger, N., Robinson, M., & Slansky, J. A. (2018). *Literacy: Helping Children Construct Meaning*. Cengage Learning.

De Dios Martínez Agudo, J. (Ed.). (2018). *Emotions in second language teaching. Theory, research and teacher education*. Springer. doi:10.1007/978-3-319-75438-3

Dewaele, J.-M., Witney, J., Saito, K., & Dewaele, L. (2018). Foreign language enjoyment and anxiety in the FL classroom: The effect of teacher and learner variables. *Language Teaching Research*, *22*(6), 676–697. doi:10.1177/1362168817692161

Mercer, S. (2016). Seeing the world through your eyes: Empathy in language learning and teaching. In P. MacIntyre, T. Gregersen, & S. Mercer (Eds.), *Positive Psychology in SLA*. Multilingual Matters. doi:10.21832/9781783095360-004

Tishman, S. (2018). *The Art and Practice of Learning Through Observation*. Routledge.

Van Manen, M. (2017). *Tact of Teaching: The meaning of pedagogical thoughtfulness*. S.l.: Routledge.

Warschauer, M. (2015). *Learning in the Cloud: How (and Why) to Transform Schools with Digital Media*. Teachers College Press.

Wu, J., Hughes, J. N., & Kwok, O. (2010). Teacher–student relationship quality type in elementary grades: Effects on trajectories for achievement and engagement. *Journal of School Psychology*, *48*(5), 357–387. doi:10.1016/j.jsp.2010.06.004 PMID:20728688

KEY TERMS AND DEFINITIONS

Literacy: A dynamic and multidimensional concept whose main aim is to provide twenty-first century learners with the language skills, visual thinking strategies and dialogic attitudes that are necessary to develop the knowledge that allows them to grasp and evaluate information, organize ideas, exchange perspectives, construct meaning and reflect critically on a variety of sociocultural contexts.

Meaning Making: A process by which individuals interpret situations, events, objects, or discourses, in the light of their previous knowledge and experience. It requires an active role and involves identities and emotions.

Multimodality: A complex entity that occurs in both print and digital settings [and] uses a variety of cultural and semiotic resources to articulate, represent, represent, and communicate a variety of narratives, concepts, or information.

Student-Teacher Relationships: A key component of students' academic and emotional development that may affect the social and learning environments of classrooms and schools.

Virtual Learning Environment: an online platform that allows the process of teaching and learning replacing the educational processes from classrooms to the internet.

Chapter 10
Digital Literacy in Language Education: The COVID-19 Era of Cyprus

Christina Nicole Giannikas
https://orcid.org/0000-0002-5653-6803
Cyprus University of Technology, Cyprus

Dina Tsagari
Oslo Met, Norway

Trisevgeni Liontou
National and Kapodistrian University of Athens, Greece

ABSTRACT

The abrupt shift to online learning and teaching shocked the majority of the language education community who had to become familiar with online tools, resources, and adjust their teaching approaches overnight. Beyond the state of alarm, it is now evident that a nexus between innovation and ICT exists. The pandemic has highlighted the critical role of technology in language education. As part of a larger study, this chapter focuses on language education in Cyprus and examines the issues facing language teachers' digital literacy and competence through the lens of complex and unpredictable adaptive systems. The data displayed and discussed in the chapter contradicts teachers' confidence of their digital literacy and competence of delivering language lessons online and what was applied in practice, and concludes by making specific recommendations at policy making, pedagogical, and research levels.

INTRODUCTION

On March 11, 2020, the World Health Organization (WHO) declared the COVID-19 outbreak as a pandemic. Cyprus responded with an instant national lockdown in order to prevent the spread. In schools there were closures and teachers were recalled to recreate school-specific action plans for distance synchronous

DOI: 10.4018/978-1-7998-8717-1.ch010

and asynchronous learning options within 5-7 days (https://www.cedefop.europa.eu). The abrupt shift to online learning and teaching shocked the majority of the language education community who had to become familiar with online tools, resources, and adjust their teaching approaches overnight (Giannikas, 2020). Beyond the state of alarm, it is now evident that a nexus between innovation and ICT exists. The pandemic has highlighted the critical role of technology in language education. However, the successful integration of technologies and digital tools mainly depends on the teacher's knowledge and literacy to apply them effectively and meaningfully within the learning environment. In other words, teachers are those who are obliged to decide which tools, as a means of instruction, would assist them in language teaching and how to use the chosen technology in delivering the content. This is a timely process, one that cannot be developed overnight. One's competence is associated with the skills teachers have developed during their training and practice, which evidently prompts them to apply certain tools. Most importantly, digital literacy implies that language teachers have developed the ability and the know-how to reach teaching objectives in their contexts (Guzmán & Marín, 2011) and guide students effectively within the digital environment. Therefore, we cannot merely speak of the abilities to assess and retrieve information, but should additionally develop skills to sufficiently use this information, transform it into knowledge, and share it with students (Sánchez-Cruzado, Santiago Campión & Sánchez-Compaña, 2021). As will be discussed further in this chapter, the switch to online learning environments and the concept of digital literacy is perplexing; however, it has been seen as the only solution at the start of the pandemic in a number of contexts. Nonetheless, the educational system at large has shown limitations regarding school policies, and the state of practitioners' digital competence this past year of living with the pandemic. The pressure of the lack of training and preparation has resurfaced, as the majority of the educational community reached the conclusion that technology and digital tools can help solve numerous problems of the teaching–learning process such as lack of interest and motivation, encouraging cooperative work, social awareness, autonomy, and helping students become digitally literate for educational purposes (Sánchez-Cruzado et al, 2021; Altuna Urdín & Martínez de Morentin de Goñi y Amenabar Perurena, 2017). Unfortunately, well into the 21st century, technology is still not properly established in the day-to-day teaching approaches, and this was verified by all the teachers' and students' struggles during the lockdown. As part of a larger study, this book chapter focuses on language education in Cyprus and examines the issues facing language teachers' digital literacy and competence through the lens of complex and unpredictable adaptive systems. More specifically, the authors have focused on the following research questions:

Q1: What are the digital literacy levels of English language teachers?
Q2: What perceptions do English teachers have about digital literacy?
Q3: Do teachers' digital literacy perceptions agree to what was applied in practice?

The data displayed and discussed in the chapter contradicts teachers' confidence of their digital literacy and competence of delivering language lessons online and what was applied in practice, and concludes by making specific recommendations at policy making, pedagogical and research level.

BACKGROUND

Before the pandemic, the education system in Cyprus was based on onsite learning and the substantial integration of technology, in public schools especially, was close to absent (Hall, et al. 2020). Before the pandemic, there was no sign of a framework for remote learning, as far as public schools were concerned (Giannikas, 2021). Therefore, it is safe to assume that the Cypriot education system was caught off-guard, as it was not prepared to deploy a full distance education plan. Nonetheless, the Minister of Education of the Republic of Cyprus, Prodromos Prodromou, had claimed in the Spring of 2020 that the vast majority of teachers in Cyprus are ready to implement distance learning. Specifically, the Minister argued that "we need to face our reservations and our hesitations regarding this new system, together" (https://cyprus-mail.com/2020/10/29/distance-learning-the-way-to-go-says-education-minister/). The Ministry announced school and university closures as a precautionary measure to contain the spread of COVID-19, and more than 110,000 teachers and students joined and had access to the Distance Education System developed, especially, by the Ministry. To facilitate the transition to online teaching, the Ministry has claimed to have implemented key actions which include (MOEC, 2020):

- Internet connection to all households for children to participate in distance learning;
- 2,000 tablets have been provided to schools for use in the distance learning program;
- The Ministry of Education launched a new website (), as one useful guide for distance learning;
- Free use of MS TEAMS (Office365) for all students and teachers;
- Asynchronous training for all teachers on how to use the virtual classrooms.

Supportive educational material was uploaded onto the Ministry's website. Public and private television channels also supported overall efforts by broadcasting lessons and other educational programmes, especially for younger age groups. The gradual lifting of the COVID-19 restrictions began on 4 May, 2020, where, according to the government plan for reopening schools, priority was given to the final year of upper secondary education. Students were divided into two groups and physically attended school lessons on a weekly rotation basis. Primary and lower secondary education schools did not fall far behind as they reopened on 21 May 2020, on the same weekly rotation basis. Students who were in the first and second year of upper secondary education did not return to school that year and continued their distance learning (https://www.cadefop.europa.eu/en/news-and-press/news/cyprus-responses-covid-19-outbreak).

RESEARCH METHODOLOGY

The main aim of the chapter is to draw attention to the practitioner's practices and needs in order to propose an appropriate training path that will effectively meet the challenges of developing digital literacy.

Data Collection Tools

The participants of the study completed an online survey, which was selected as a method of collecting language professionals' views. The aim of creating the tool in question was to produce data that are valid, robust, and meaningful, therefore, prior to dissemination the survey was piloted and feedback was used in order to develop the content and verify the quality, validity and the usability of the survey. The pilot prompted participants to: 1) determine whether the questions appear reasonable for acquiring the necessary data; 2) ensure the questions are all focussed on the issue; 3) assess whether the questions posed imply the desired outcome to be achieved by the specific data collection tool; 4) address whether the questions posed reflect the response of the entire target population (also see Ball, 2019).

After the survey was edited as per the feedback received it disseminated to the target audience in English, and was created on Google Forms with built-in features to facilitate data collection and analysis (see: https://forms.gle/kx2a5AK7hiXnBVeY6). The survey contained 47 questions which consisted of:

- Yes/no or other dichotomous questions
- Open-ended text responses (long answer and short answer)
- Multiple choice – select exactly 1 of n (select a single answer).
- Multiple choice – select as many as k of n (select variable number of answers)
- Likert and semantic differential questions
- Open-ended questions
- Horizontal-scale, vertical-scale, drop-down, side-by-side formats.

The survey addressed the following: 1) Demographic Information, 2) Digital Confidence 3) Online Teaching Methods and Practices/Assessment, 4) Resources 5) Transfer from Onsite to Online, and 6) Teacher Education Needs. The survey was estimated to take approximately 30 minutes to complete, and reached a wide audience via email requests. The email sent to individual respondents contained information regarding the purpose of the study and the link to the online survey. Participants were sent a follow-up reminder email with the survey link within a 3-week period.

All participants remained anonymous and it was made clear that the entering of information to the survey questions and submission of their response signified consent for their data to be used by the researchers and authors of this chapter. The descriptive analysis conducted on Google forms facilitated the process of data analysis. Initially Microsoft Excel was used for straightforward functionality. The researchers also adopted a coding process for the open-ended responses, which involved the manual allocation of categories to practitioners' comments. Further statistical analysis used multiple spearman correlations between variables of interest.

The Participants

As part of a larger study, there was a sample of 45 participants based in the Republic of Cyprus, with the vast majority of the participants being female (86%). The data showed that the majority of the participants were secondary school English teachers (27%), followed by Higher/further education and private institution instructors (25% each sector), and 11% were primary school English teachers, as can be seen in detail in Table 1:

Table 1. Participants' place of work

Place of Work	N	%
Primary School	5	11%
Secondary School	12	27%
Higher/Further Education	11	25%
Language School/Institution	11	25%
Freelance teacher	3	7%
Freelance teacher trainer	1	2%
Other	1	2%

Almost half of the participants had been teaching for 11-20 years (48%) and 80% were postgraduate degree holders. Furthermore, according to the data a high percentage of 69% claim to have received training to teach online, nonetheless the vast majority claim to have no previous experience of online teaching, whereas only 27% claimed to *sometimes* teach online. Just over half of the participants (57%) claim to have *never* taught blended courses, 27% stated that they sometimes teach blended courses, while 16% teach blended courses *very often*. The training the participants have received to participate in any online or blended courses can be seen in Table 2:

Table 2. Online language teacher training

Type of training	N	%
Self-training (i.e. attending webinars, watching videos, reading online activities etc.)	23	72%
Training provided by my institution	10	31%
Training provided by specialized training institutions	10	31%
Informal training by colleagues	11	34%

The data further showed that 87% of the respondents transferred all their teaching online, and 86% stated that it was mandatory that they do so. More specifically, there was a negative correlation between teachers reporting that it was mandatory in their school/institution to transition the face-to-face courses/classes to an online platform and them working at a primary school, $\rho(44) = -.484$, $p = .010$. There was a positive correlation between teachers reporting that it was mandatory in their school/institution to transition the face-to-face courses/classes to an online platform and them reporting that they have received training on how to teach online, $\rho(42) = .610$, $p < .0005$. All participants were given a week to make this change, and no variables correlated with the number of days the teachers were given to prepare their courses/classes to go online.

FINDINGS

Digital Confidence

This section of the chapter presents the findings of the study with a focus on the data gathered from the case of the Republic of Cyprus.

According to the statistical data analysis, 60% of the respondents were confident in their ability to implement the existing curriculum in an online environment, however there was a negative correlation between teachers feeling confident in their ability to implement the existing curriculum in an online environment and them working at a primary school, $\rho(44) = -.457, p = .021$. However, there was a positive correlation between teachers feeling confident in their ability to implement existing curriculum in an online environment and them reporting that they have received training on how to teach online, $\rho(42) = .459, p = .025$. Additionally, 57% of the respondents stated they were confident in applying various online teaching approaches, 52% were confident using digital tools in their online teaching environment, and 47% stated they were confident in helping their students develop their digital knowledge. Furthermore, there was a positive correlation between teachers feeling confident in their ability to use different methods of teaching online and them reporting that they have taught blended courses before, $\rho(44) = .526, p = .003$. There was a positive correlation between teachers feeling confident in their ability to use different methods of teaching online and them reporting that they have received training on how to teach online, $\rho(42) = .480, p = .015$. These facts are also displayed in Tables 3 and 4:

Table 3. Teachers' confidence in their ability to implement the curriculum online

Confidence in my ability to implement existing curriculum in an online	N	%
To a lesser extent confident	3	7%
2	8	18%
3	7	16%
4	13	30%
Very confident	13	30%

Table 4. Teachers' confidence in their online teaching methods

Confidence in my ability to use different methods of teaching online	N	%
To a lesser extent confident	4	9%
2	5	11%
3	10	23%
4	17	39%
Very confident	8	18%

According to the data regarding the use of digital tools, only 27% stated that they were very confident in the use of digital tools. There was a positive correlation between teachers feeling confident in their ability to use different digital tools for teaching purposes and them reporting that they have taught blended courses before, $\rho(44) = .565$, $p = .001$. Furthermore, only 27% of the respondents claimed that they were confident in their ability to assist students with digital tools, while putting their digital knowledge to use. There was a positive correlation between teachers feeling confident in their ability to help students develop new digital knowledge and skills and them reporting that they have taught online before COVID-19, $\rho(44) = .449$, $p = .025$. There was a positive correlation between teachers feeling confident in their ability to help students develop new digital knowledge and skills and them reporting that they have taught blended courses before, $\rho(44) = .515$, $p = .004$.

Online Teaching Methods and Practices

The following survey questions prompted respondents to elaborate regarding their online teaching practices. One of the most serious issues that arose within the education community during the lockdown caused by the pandemic was the students' interactive and social learning activity. According to the data, 77% were to a lesser extent confident in this domain. There was a positive correlation between teachers feeling confident in their ability to promote online cooperation among students and them reporting that they have taught blended courses before, $\rho(44) = .477$, $p = .012$. A high percentage of 73% to a lesser extent confident in managing online collaboration among students. According to the statistical results, there was a positive correlation between teachers feeling confident in their ability to manage online cooperation among students and them reporting that they have taught blended courses before, $\rho(44) = .463$, $p = .018$.

The respondents were also asked about the material they used during their online teaching. Regarding the use of textbooks, 65% were to a lesser extent confident about their ability to apply digital tools in order to enhance textbook-based content, and no variables correlated with teachers' responses. The teachers' confidence plummeted when it came to using online student assessment to modify instruction, as only 7% felt confident to do so. According to the statistical analysis, there was a negative correlation between teachers feeling confident in their ability to use online student assessment to modify instruction and them working at a primary school, $\rho(44) = -.528$, $p = .003$. There was a positive correlation between teachers feeling confident in their ability to use online student assessment to modify instruction and them reporting that they have taught blended courses before, $\rho(44) = .452$, $p = .023$.

The survey prompted responses on relevant activities teachers encouraged their students to take part in online, as displayed in Table 5:

Table 5. Online activities teachers encourage

Encouraging students to engage in:	N	%
Pair work	15	35%
Group work	18	42%
Independent study	37	86%
Self-assessment	28	65%
Peer assessment	8	19%
Teacher assessment	0	0%

According to the statistical analysis, no variables correlated with teachers encouraging their students to engage in pair work, in independent study, in self-assessment, in peer-assessment and teacher assessment. There was a positive correlation between teachers encouraging their students to engage in group work and them reporting that they have taught blended courses before, $\rho(43) = .510$, $p = .005$. Additionally, 73% of the respondents have observed changes in their teaching since transferring online. However, the majority of respondents (69%) also indicated that their online teaching reflects their classroom teaching.

Resources

The data showed that the respondents used a variety of resources, with 86% applying their own ideas in the online learning environment, 73% used online resources, 39% collaborated with colleagues to get hold of resources, 34% were provided with guidelines from their institution and a low 23% sought advice from a colleague with online teaching experience. There was a positive correlation between teachers reporting that they have used their own ideas when making the transition to online teaching and them reporting that they have received self-training, $\rho(32) = .604$, $p = .003$. No variables correlated 1) with teachers reporting that they have used resources they found online when making the transition to online teaching, 2) with teachers reporting that they have sought advice from someone with more online teaching experience, and 3) with teachers reporting that they have been working closely with some of their colleagues when making the transition to online teaching. The data also indicate that 73% of the teachers used online resources prior to COVID-19. Furthermore, 64% of the teachers have stated that they plan to continue to use the *new* material when they return to the classroom.

Transfer from Onsite to Online

According to the data gathered, 57% of the teachers have indicated a positive experience to the transfer from onsite to online teaching. Nonetheless, 75% of the respondents claim that the educational leadership in their context was not ready for the education emergency. Furthermore, 79% of the respondents indicated that the educational leadership did not provide teachers with guidance and support for online teaching. The data also shows that 73% of the respondents were not provided with the necessary equipment to carry out online teaching. Table 6 displays the vision the institutions held regarding online learning, which could help readers comprehend the background of online learning among important stakeholders within the Republic of Cyprus. To be specific, and according to the highest percentages, 51% claim to have received very little support when shifting their teaching to an online environment; 30% claimed that the available infrastructure was taken into account; while 28% stated that specific objectives of the implementation of online learning had been set. According to the statistical analysis, there was a positive correlation between teachers reporting that very little has been done to support them in shifting to online teaching in their institution and them working in the public sector, $\rho(43) = .447$, $p = .030$.

Table 6. Institutions' vision of online learning

Specifically, in our institution:	N	%
A strong vision towards online learning is present	10	23%
Professional development for online learning is supported	11	26%
Specific objectives of the implementation of the online learning have been set	12	28%
The available ICT infrastructure is taken into account	13	30%
Attention is paid to the processes of changing to online learning	10	23%
A professional development strategy towards online learning has been adopted	6	14%
Very little has been done to support us in shifting to online teaching	22	51%
Other	0	0%

Furthermore, the respondents shed light on the other side of the screen, specifically the equipment the students were provided with in order to embark upon their ERT journey. The data show that the majority of the respondents taught students who did not have the necessary equipment (i.e. laptop, quality internet connection, etc.). Furthermore, 48% of the respondents claim that their students were not willing to attend their online classes. Teachers were divided, as 41% stated in the surveys that their students received guidelines on how to access the online platforms, a percentage very close to that of those who referred to their students' unwillingness to join the online classes. Teachers also demolish the myth of the tech savvy student as 61% stated that their learners were not familiar with digital tools for educational purposes. According to the statistical analysis, there was a negative correlation between teachers agreeing that their students are familiar with online tools for educational purposes and them working in the public sector, $\rho(44) = -.579$, $p < .0005$. Additionally, just over half the respondents (52%) stated that their students were cooperative during their online classes, and 63% stated that there were positive outcomes through online education; these are high numbers to result from an emergency situation.

Teacher Education

Regarding teachers' professional development and training prior to COVID-19, 52% stated that they attended online teacher training webinars, 59% attended professional development in educational technologies held by various teaching communities. According to the statistical analysis, there was a negative correlation between teachers reporting that before COVID-19, they used to participate in teacher communities for professional development in educational technology and them working at a primary school, $\rho(44) = -.430$, $p = .041$. The data also showed that 36% of the teachers participated in eTwinning, Erasmus+ exchange programs, and 86% of the teachers stated that they search online for ideas on how to improve their teaching. There was a positive correlation between teachers reporting that before COVID-19, they used to search online for ideas to improve their teaching practices and them reporting that they have received training on how to teach online, $\rho(42) = .463$, $p = .023$. Finally, as high as 80% of the participants of the study stated that they sampled various digital tools for classroom use. There was a positive correlation between teachers reporting that before COVID-19, they used to try out various digital tools for classroom use and them reporting that they have received training on how to teach online, $\rho(42) = .462$, $p = .023$. Despite the indication of high use and acceptance of educational technology, the participants indicated the need additional training in online teaching as displayed in Table 7:

Table 7. Feeling for the need of training in online teaching

Do you feel you need training in online teaching?	N	%
No	6	14%
Maybe	17	39%
Yes	21	48%

There was, however, a negative correlation between teachers feeling they need training in online teaching and higher qualifications of teachers, $\rho(44) = -.430$, $p = .041$.

The vast majority of the respondents preferred that their trainers were certified professionals (73%). The respondents specified the needed areas of additional training, as seen in Table 8. The highest needs lie in 1) Practical approaches to assessing learners online (78%), 2) Practical suggestions on online teaching practices (69%) and 3) Technical knowledge on using different online platforms (61%).

Table 8. Needs for additional training

Training needs	N	%
Technical knowledge on using different online platforms	22	61%
Online courses on specific teaching practices	19	53%
Practical approaches to assessing learners online	28	78%
A demonstration on how to pedagogically convert an onsite lesson into an online on	20	56%
Practical suggestions on online teaching practices	25	69%
Participation in teacher communities/events for professional development	19	53%

SOLUTIONS AND RECOMMENDATIONS

As the COVID-19 pandemic lockdown affected almost all aspects of society and everyday life, the entire globe needed to adjust and learn to organise their professional and personal life in a new way. This chapter displays our investigation on how early language educators adapted to online teaching during COVID-19 school closures in March 2020. Our research questions were concerned with how teachers dealt with challenges in these unknown territories and what factors could account for how they faced such challenges. According to the analysis of the survey, the participants' performance displays useful insights about areas of strength and weakness in their online teaching that potentially can be used to support individual future trainees in areas of teaching. The data show a representation of reality, where language professionals indicate the steps taken to rapidly transfer their teaching online, the lack of training and infrastructure and the confusion of one's ability to keep their heads above water when it comes to developing the necessary digital literacy.

More specifically, according to the data, there was confusion and hesitation during the process of transferring online, as teachers stated confidence regarding the use of digital tools, but hesitation when it came to applying them for pedagogical purposes, such as group work, feedback etc. The findings indicate that even though teachers were highly qualified, as the vast majority held postgraduate degrees, they were inhibited by their fears of using technology and digital tools, unaware of the fact that "digital learning needs to be pedagogically led, and thus the key differences for success are the identification of digital competencies that teachers need and the provision of training to help them acquire their competences" (Carrier & Nye, 2017, p. 209). The lack of training brought limitations to the execution of the transfer and the teachers' disbelief in the process and the outcomes of their new professional norm. There was a haze, and dare we say, misunderstanding of the use of digital tools and digital pedagogy as teachers and students stated they were confident using the tools for educational purposes, but when it came to teaching approaches that held a social and communicative element there was hesitation. Most importantly, the social and communicative elements that are not only vital to any language lessons, in any shape or form, but are also essential in times of emergency isolation and restrictions were compromised as teachers were unaware on how to apply teaching approaches in the remote learning environment that would embrace social and communicative learning. Furthermore, the findings suggest that the issue of resources also brought distress. According to the data, most of the respondents felt the need to create their own material and use EFL websites in order to work online, considering this to be in accordance with remote teaching. There was confusion regarding textbooks and the confusion of how they can be applied in an online environment, this confusion may be the reason why the majority of teachers turned to online EFL websites. This could be seen as a positive outcome, as the majority states that they would be using these resources when they return to the classroom, combined with their text-books.

The findings of the study confirm that we cannot expect teachers to instantly revise curriculum, teaching approaches, resources, and their pedagogical perspectives as they are being rushed online. Nonetheless, after the experience they have had and knowing what we now know, we cannot continue as normal. Our normal has changed. It would be unrealistic to expect to avoid upheaval entirely, nonetheless, as the data have shown, teachers need teacher education and need to become digitally literate in order to gain the confidence they deserve to cope in an ever changing world. There may be changes to the workstreams of teachers, administrators and others who support education as there is a need to learn and test out these new ways. This does not need to be negative, but it can give us hope that the field of education is working towards something solid and of high quality. While the data of this study indicates that the teachers were aware of important differences between teaching online and onsite, it must be mentioned that the teaching approaches in question are not fundamentally different as online education also supports teaching principles of good quality education.

CONCLUSION

The findings of the present study highlight the need for increased training and knowledge around digital literacies for a smooth adoption of the new norm in language education in Cyprus and beyond. The lack of or limited digital literacies among practitioners in the specific context raises doubts regarding effectiveness of remote/online teaching functions in the way it was handled in the time of the COVID-19 crisis. The research described above can significantly influence the way educational leadership supports practitioners, evaluate their own online teaching, shed light on the needs of the current teaching situation in Cyprus, the lack of preparation beyond the familiar and the lack of understanding of digital literacy. Furthermore, objectives related to student learning online should be clarified, and teachers, teacher educators and policy makers should account for relevant competences needed for effective use of digital tools during further partial school closure and re-openings. This chapter has revealed specific factors in the area of teacher competence, digital literacy and teacher education that impact practitioners' successful mastery of new challenges such as the one faced during the lockdowns of 2020. It also highlights the need to develop teacher competences in teaching in the digital era and preparing for it in initial teacher education and their further professional development. Preparing practitioners for digitalisation in their teaching is a chance that teacher education cannot neglect. Despite the promising findings of this study, the limitations should also be discussed. First, the results only reflect responses from the online survey the participants completed. Interviews were not conducted as the response rate for interviews were low due to the challenging times the teachers were facing during the start of the pandemic. There were planned follow-up questions, however, these were not possible after the researchers received the completed surveys.

The COVID-19 school closures and the rushed solution to ERT has highlighted the need for teacher education aligned with the digital times and schools' flexibility to unforeseen circumstances. A movement towards preparation, digital awareness and inclusive process of training that would empower language educators to work confidently and effectively. Such a change requires a shift to a more emancipatory underpinning philosophy of teacher education, which can confront the pedagogy of the present technical paradigm. The education community learned valuable lessons in this time, and it is our opinion that we need to take advantage of the lessons learned to equip teachers for an on-going crisis and take the opportunity for re-imagining to occur. By challenging the current crisis and skill-based orientation of teacher education programs, teacher educators in Cyprus and beyond can begin to embrace the constructs alluded to in this chapter.

ACKNOWLEDGMENT

The authors of the chapter would like to wholeheartedly thank the language educators across the globe who took part in the study.

*This research received no specific grant from any funding agency in the public, commercial, or not-for-profit sectors.

REFERENCES

Altuna, J., Martínez de Morentin, J. I., & Amenábar, N. (2017). Teaching and Learning Theories and Internet Resources: Its Confluence in Primary Schools. *Estudios Sobre Educación, 33*, 145–167.

Archambault, L. (2011). The Practitioner's Perspective on Teacher Education: Preparing for the K-12 Online Classroom. *Journal of Technology and Teacher Education, 19*(1), 73–91.

Carey, K. (2020). Is everybody ready for the big migration to online college? Actually, no. *The New York Times*. https://www.nytimes.com

Carrier, M., & Nye, A. (2017). Carrier M. and Nye A. (2017). Empowering Teachers for the Digital Future. What do 21st century Teachers need? In M. Carrier, R. M. Damerow, & K. M. Bailey (Eds.), *Empowering Teachers for the Digital Future: Research, Theory, and Practice*. Routledge.

Giannikas, C. N. (2020). Prioritizing when Education is in Crisis: The language teacher. *Humanising Language Teaching, 22*(3).

Giannikas, C. N. (2021). *Sending our Teachers into the Wild: What we learned about preparedness during COVID-19. Hellenic Association of the Study of English (HASE) Colloquium.*

Godbey, S. (2018). Testing Future Teachers: A Quantitative Exploration of Factors Impacting the Information Literacy of Teacher Education Students. *College & Research Libraries, 79*(5), 611–623. doi:10.5860/crl.79.5.611

Groff, J., & Mouza, C. (2008). A Framework for Addressing Challenges to Classroom Technology Use. *AACE Journal, 16*, 21–46.

Guzmán Ibarra, I., & Marín Uribe, R. (2011). La Competencia y las Competencias Docentes: Reflexiones sobre el concepto y la Evaluación. *Revista Electrónica Interuniversitaria de Formación del Profesorado*, 151-172.

Hall, A. K., Nousiainen, M. T., Campisi, P. J., Dagnone, D., Frank, J. P., Kroeker, K. I., Brzezina, S., Purdy, E., & Oswald, A. (2020). Training disrupted: Practical tips for supporting competency-based medical education during the COVID-19 pandemic. *Medical Teacher, 42*(7), 756–761. doi:10.1080/0142159X.2020.1766669 PMID:32450049

Hodges, C., Moore, S., Lockee, B., Trust, T., & Bond, A. (2020). The difference between emergency remote teaching and online learning, *EDUCAUSE Review*. Available at: https://er.educause.edu/articles/2020/3/the-difference-between-emergency-remote-teachingand-online-learning

Imbernón, F., Silva, P., & Guzmán, C. (2011). Competencias en los procesos de enseñanza-aprendizaje virtual y semipresencial [Teaching skills in virtual and blended learning environments]. *Comunicar, 36*(36), 107–114. doi:10.3916/C36-2011-03-01

Jandrić, P., Hayes, D., Truelove, I., Levinson, P., Mayo, P., Ryberg, T., Monzó, L. D., Allen, Q., Stewart, P. A., Carr, P. R., Jackson, L., Bridges, S., Escaño, C., Grauslund, D., Mañero, J., Lukoko, H. O., Bryant, P., Fuentes-Martinez, A., Gibbons, A., ... Hayes, S. (2020). Teaching in The Age of Covid-19. *Postdigital Science and Education, 2*(3), 1069–1230. doi:10.100742438-020-00169-6

Jewitt, C., Clark, W., & Hadjithoma-Garstka, C. (2011). The use of learning platforms to organise learning in English primary and secondary schools. *Learning, Media and Technology, 36*(4), 335–348. doi:10.1080/17439884.2011.621955

Lau, W.W.F., & Yuen, A.H.K. (2014). Developing and Validating of a Perceived ICT Literacy Scale for Junior Secondary School Students: Pedagogical and Educational Contributions. *Computers and Education, 78*, 1–9. doi:10.1016/j.compedu.2014.04.016

Leu, D., O'Byrne, W., Zawilinski, L., McVerry, J., & Everett-Cacopardo, H. (2009). Expanding the New Literacies Conversation. *Educational Researcher, 38*(4), 264–269. doi:10.3102/0013189X09336676

Li, Q., & Ma, X. (2010). A Meta-analysis of the Effects of Computer Technology on School Students' Mathematics Learning. *Educational Psychology Review, 22*(3), 215–243. doi:10.100710648-010-9125-8

Madalińska-Michalak, J., O'Doherty, T., & Flores, M.A. (2018). Teachers and teacher education in uncertain times. *European Journal of Teacher Education*. . doi:10.1080/02619768.2018.1532024

Moore-Adams, B. L., Monty Jones, W., & Cohen, J. (2016). Learning to Teach Online: A Systematic Review of the Literature on K-12 Teacher Preparation for Teaching Online. *Distance Education, 37*(3), 333–348. doi:10.1080/01587919.2016.1232158

OECD. (2019). *OECD Skills Outlook 2019: Thriving in a Digital World.* OECD Publishing., doi:10.1787/df80bc12-

OECD. (2020). *Keeping the Internet up and running in times of crisis.* OECD Publishing.

Rice, K., & Dawley, L. (2009). The Status of Professional Development for K-12 Online Teachers: Insights and Implications. *Journal of Technology and Teacher Education, 17*(4), 523–545.

Sánchez-Cruzado, C., Santiago Campión, R., & Sánchez-Compaña, M. T. (2021). Teacher Digital Literacy: The Indisputable Challenge after COVID-19. *Sustainability, 13*(4), 1858. doi:10.3390u13041858

Chapter 11
Accommodating New Challenges:
EFL Student Teacher and Teacher Trainer Attitudes Towards Transferring Teacher-Training Online

Georgios Neokleous
https://orcid.org/0000-0002-4941-3071
Norwegian University of Science and Technology, Norway

ABSTRACT

The importance of technology was cemented amidst the COVID-19 pandemic with virtual learning environments (VLEs) and social networking sites being adopted as education switched to distance learning and meetings took place online. Despite research focusing on learning in times of COVID-19, the effectiveness of transferring language teaching from face-to-face to online settings in teacher education programs remains underexplored. The purpose of this chapter is to delve deeper into student teachers and their instructors' attitudes to explore how the field of language teaching adapted to changes that have derived from the pandemic. The overarching research question the study attempted to address was: What are the pre-service teacher attitudes and their instructors toward digital learning of EFL teacher-training amidst the global pandemic? The findings offer insights into how to adequately prepare and design online teaching and activities for teacher training programs in the future.

INTRODUCTION

The changing nature of literacy initiated by the advent of digital technologies and the impact they can have on education in primary schools was identified in the mid-90s (New London Group, 1996). Research at the time argued that the ability to use digital technologies competently and creatively should be reworked into national curricula. Recently, this possibility was further strengthened in European countries when digital competence had been acknowledged as one of the eight key competences for Lifelong Learning

DOI: 10.4018/978-1-7998-8717-1.ch011

by the European Union. As the European Commission (2003) stated, "Digital literacy is…a prerequisite for creativity, innovation and entrepreneurship and without it citizens can neither participate fully in society nor acquire the skills and knowledge necessary to live in the 21st century" (p. 3).

The meaning of the word digital has grown over the last three decades, while today it is used to describe various internet-connected hardware and software, content available online to download or stream, online and virtual environments (Bloch, 2021; Reedy & Parker, 2018). A clear portrayal as to how digital our lives have become is illustrated with the introduction of the term *Internet of things* that describes our digital interaction with networked everyday objects embedded but also our interaction between them (Xia *et al.*, 2012). The latter rings particularly true as children are growing up in a world that is progressively prescribed by technologized environments. The prominent role technology exerts in our lives was identified the past decade in the literature (Bloch, 2021; Lankshear & Knobel, 2011; Reedy & Parker, 2018; White, 2015) with digital literacy being described as "a survival skill" (Eshet, 2004, p. 102). However, according to Vuorikari *et al.* (2016), 44.5% of the European Union population between 16 and 74 years old do not have sufficient digital skills to participate in society and in the economy. Therefore, digital literacy should constitute a quintessential component in today's education and one of the important parameters for a successful society. Because of the multifaceted and dynamic nature of our digital lives, the question with which educators are faced is how to accommodate this tendency in the language teaching classroom to adequately prepare students meet the 21st-century literacy skills in order to facilitate their transition into an interconnected digital world.

The importance of digital competence was cemented amidst the global pandemic of COVID-19 as it has changed how teachers proceed with conducting teaching and learning activities making recourse to platforms and available social networking sites (e.g., Google classroom, Facebook). Online education became ubiquitous as a result of the COVID-19 pandemic and most educational courses were redesigned to provide student teachers with opportunities to learn and teach online. The global pandemic necessitated the emergency transfer of physical teaching to online classes. the effectiveness of shifting from inside classroom learning to online learning (König *et al.*, 2020). This chapter attempts to unearth perception change of student teachers after online teaching and the challenges they encountered using an online platform during this process.

In fact, following a review of the literature on the topic, its purpose is to delve deeper into student teachers and their instructors' attitudes to explore how the field of EFL teacher training adapted to changes that have derived from the pandemic. To shed more light on the topic, from the teacher-training perspective, the present chapter focuses on thirty-nine pre-service teacher attitudes toward digital learning of two university teacher-training courses that moved online during the fall semester of 2020 and the spring semester of 2021. The overarching research question the study attempted to address was: 1) What are the student teachers' and their teacher trainers' attitudes toward digital training of EFL teacher-training amidst the global pandemic? The findings of the study aim to offer insights into how to adequately prepare and design online teaching and activities for teacher training programs in the future. In addition, the results would provide insight into designing relevant training programs whose aim would be to adequately prepare EFL teachers deliver lessons in synchronous online teaching mode that would also consider the student voice.

BACKGROUND

Digital Literacy in the 21st Century

The emphasis on new perspectives on literacy with a new set of 21st-century skills has been identified as quintessential during the past decade (Ba *et al.*, 2002; Ferrari, 2012; Lankshear & Knobel, 2011; Tompkins, 2018). The UNESCO Broadband Commission for Sustainable Development (2017) report identified digital literacy as one of the essential skills that learners should acquire from an early age because "digital technologies now underpin effective participation in key areas of life and work…The skills and competencies needed to make use of digital technology and benefit from its growing power and functionality have never been more essential" (p. 4).

The importance of digital literacy has made its impact in the curricula of certain countries. Indeed, fostering digital literacy has been one of the recent objectives of governments and educational institutions (Chetty *et al.*, 2018). National curricula in countries such as Norway, Australia, and Singapore have proceeded to implement policies that aimed at fostering and strengthening digital literacy (ACARA, 2016; Norwegian Directorate of Education and Training, 2020; Singapore Ministry of Education, 2020). Norway is often perceived as an example as to how the national curriculum promotes digital literacy. Digital literacy has been identified as the fifth basic competence along with reading, writing, arithmetic, and oral skills at every subject and grade (Norwegian Directorate of Education and Training, 2020). Teachers are encouraged to enhance their teaching practices and approaches with the integration of digital tools, 2.0 technologies, and devices to foster digital competence (Tompkins, 2018). The main rationale behind this idea is to pave the way for digital inclusion as 21st century living, and employability dictates advanced knowledge of digital skills (Greener, 2009; Coiro, Knobel, Lankshear & Leu, 2014).

The growth associated with technology is also evidenced in the definition of the term digital literacy that has evolved throughout the years. Being digitally literate encompasses an assortment of complex skills (cognitive, sociological, motoric, and emotional) that move beyond the technical ability to employ a software, an application, or a tool. The current definition has come to encompass the different competencies and capabilities required to live, learn, and work in a digital society. Taking this into consideration, White (2015) defined digital literacy as "the knowledge, skills, abilities, confidence and competence required to develop our usage of digital technologies. Development of critical thinking, creativity, responsibility and productivity is facilitated and encouraged, allowing us to use digital technologies for living, learning and work" (p. 18).

Advantages of Using Digital Tools in the Classroom

The advent of digital technologies has permeated schools and classrooms (Tompkins, 2018). While most language teaching is carried out in person, research has highlighted the potential of teaching English beyond a formal classroom through the means of digital devices and interfaces (Sundqvist & Sylvén, 2016; Tompkins, 2018). The use of ICT in EFL teaching has proved to "lead to increased student learning and improved teaching methods" (Papadima-Sophocleous, Giannikas, & Kakoulli-Constantinou, 2014, p. 296). Recent research has also shown that digital teaching outside the classroom contributed to ameliorating EFL students' proficiency and cross-cultural communication (Al-Maroof & Al-Emran, 2018; Gatcho & Hajan, 2019; Lee, 2019, Lee, 2020; Lee & Lee, 2019).

Fostering digital literacy opens new possibilities for collaboration not only between students but also between teacher-learners while it also provides the opportunity for authentic materials to be used in the classroom (Tompkins, 2018). Using authentic materials in the classroom provides students with the opportunity to experience from different social groups and familiarize themselves with different accents. Furthermore, being able to understand and follow authentic materials used in the classroom boosts the children's confidence and helps them develop positive attitudes toward language learning. and feel more confident to engage with the language. Research has shown that in early primary EFL classrooms teaching literacy through technology and digital media can strengthen the development of early reading skills in similar settings (Castillo & Wagner, 2018).

While mastering how to use technologies can be challenging for some, research studies have shown that providing a link to practical daily applications, being in an environment that is reassuring, and having peer and social support can speed up and facilitate the learning process (Merriam *et al.*, 2007; Tsai *et al.*, 2017). A great advantage of technology is its abundant opportunities it presents to extend digital literacy practice beyond the walls of the classroom. It offers the possibility to work on projects/tasks/activities integrating different digital tools on the internet and continue to develop digital literacy skills further. As technology affords a broad range of opportunities for literacy practices outside the classroom, students become more autonomous and independent and assume ownership of their own learning (McDougall *et al.*, 2018; Tompkins, 2018). Most importantly, such opportunities fostered EFL learners' self-confidence and autonomy (Atmojo & Nugroho, 2020; Zhang, 2020). Azmi (2017) and Hussain (2018) asserted that the use of ICT in the language classroom affects the increase of students' autonomous learning, motivation, and performance in EFL learning.

There were also some drawbacks that could have an impact on the smooth implementation of online classes. For example, for some students who may not have online access or who have had limited experience with online learning tools, such as Google classroom and Zoom, this transition might be difficult and challenging (Fedynich, 2013; Wedenoja, 2020). In addition, Kim (2020) argued that "online learning may not give sufficient or appropriate opportunities to involve young children who need more interactions and hands-on activities to focus and learn compared to adult learners" (p. 147). These children's quality of online teaching can be optimized through adequate support and guidance offered by the teachers. However, teachers need to be skillful and efficient in their use of digital tools adopted in the classroom. Their attitudes and skills toward technology constitute an important factor in the teaching experience with technology of the students (Konca *et al.* 2016; Kim, 2020).

Studies on Teacher Use of Digital Literacy

Implementing digital literacy activities can be quite challenging and the COVID-19 pandemic with classes moving online necessitated the need for teachers to be digitally literate. Schools not only need to be able to offer the necessary equipment and infrastructure, but teachers also need to be technologically savvy and flexible to navigate, support, and provide new spaces for learning. Current research highlights the need to adequately prepare EFL primary school teachers as most of them have had limited experience with digital technologies and their pedagogical purposes (Cote & Milliner, 2018; Terenko & Ogienko, 2020; Tompkins, 2018;). Among the different types of remote teaching, video conferencing platforms, such as Zoom and Teams, have become a common practice for many EFL instructors. This emergency switch has not been smooth for all countries because of poor connectivity, lack of technological hardware and infrastructure, instructors' lack of adequate digital competence, and ability to meet the students' and courses' needs and objectives. For instance, Eryansyah *et al.*'s (2019) study among pre-service EFL teachers in Indonesia revealed that because of the dearth of infrastructure but also insufficient teacher training, some of the EFL learners did not develop their digital literacy skills. Research has contended that to participate in e-learning students but also their instructors need to be digitally literate for efficient and quality teaching. (Cheung, 2021; Tang & Chaw, 2016). Terenko and Ogienko's (2020) study showed that for the efficiency of online learning, the provision of educational support for teachers and students can play a key role in ensuring a smooth learning process.

A study by Raman and Yamat (2014) among EFL teachers revealed that their teaching experience and age could play a decisive role in their technology use in the classroom. As the study elaborated, their teaching is rooted in the traditional teacher-fronted instruction approach that affects the adoption of new methods. The participants ascribed their hesitancy to provide technology-enhanced lessons to the lack of training with and knowledge of new tools and applications. Similarly, a recent study by Sánchez-Cruzado *et al.* (2021) amongst 4883 teachers of different education levels revealed participants' low-self perceptions of their digital skills with only 1.7% of those surveyed reporting a high level of digital competence. In addition, Sánchez-Cruzado *et al.*'s (2021) study showed that teachers need to be adequately competent to prepare students detect and redirect the dangers of online environments. König's *et al.*'s (2020) study revealed that teacher's digital competence is pivotal in teachers adapting to online teaching.

Student Attitudes towards Digital Literacy

While a substantial number of studies were conducted on digital literacy in teaching and learning English from the teacher perspective (Churchill, 2016; Kleemans & Eggnik, 2016; Neumann, Finger, & Neumann, 2017), very few studies attempted to unearth the student voice and examine what primary learners believe digital literacy entails (Geer & Sweeney, 2012; Neokleous, 2019; Turula, 2017). Neokleous' (2019) study delving deeper into the young learner perspective revealed that the 14 participants acknowledged the potential of technology and highly valued its integration in the classroom. As it transpired from their interviews, technology offered several collaboration opportunities, fostered active learning, created authentic learning situations, and harnessed higher order thinking skills. In sync with Neokleous' (2019) findings, a recent study by Mudra (2020) revealed that the use of web 2.0 technologies and social networks culminated in improving the students' EFL reading, writing, listening, and speaking skills as they sustained their motivation. These findings were also corroborated by earlier studies undertaken by Vikneswaran and Krish (2015) and Kabilan *et al.* (2010).

Moreover, Turula's (2017) study also unraveled the underlying problems that young learner participants faced in their digital literacy instruction including the lack of availability of digital tools and access to certain platforms and their teachers' lack of adequate expertise. A recent study by Eryansyah *et al.* (2019) revealed that students did not develop sufficiently their digital literacy in settings where students do not have adequate internet coverage. The young learner participants were also critical about the ensuing costs of using digital tools in the classroom but also about the complexity of some of the materials.

During the COVID-19 pandemic, Terenko and Ogienko's (2020) study revealed that most of the student participants positively evaluated the digital learning experience, and the findings of the study displayed an increase in students' motivation for learning and their cognitive activity. Studies exploring the young learner attitudes on transferring EFL teaching online generated positive responses as it was reported to encourage their learning efficacy (Atmojo & Nugroho, 2020). Most significantly, students who are strong believers in the digitalization of learning can convince teachers who are open to new ways of teaching and aspire towards student-centred environments into incorporating technology into the classroom (Greener, 2009). However, while university students are often perceived to have an extensive knowledge of digital technologies, Vázquez-Cano *et al.*'s (2020) argued that the tools which students use, and with which are familiar are rather limited.

Implementing Online Teaching in the Classroom

While studies revealed students' preference for online teaching and findings noted an increase in motivation and cognitive activity, researchers caveated about the lack of the practical experience in teacher-education programs (Sepulveda-Escobar & Morrison, 2020). Preparing prospective teachers requires a practical component in their training where students could apply in practice what they have learned. Its importance was underlined early in the literature as it was believed to shape the teachers' identity and future work (Caires, Almeida, & Vieira 2012). To mitigate this, several approaches have been used that would offer a satisfactory alternative to practicum including the use of peer learning whereby students taught each other (Donitsa-Schmidt & Ramot, 2020; Flores & Gago 2020). Ulvik, Helleve, and Smith (2018) argued that the practical component of teacher education is difficult to be materialized in online circumstances. However, recent research studies exploring the implications of online teacher education as a new mode of delivery noted that remoting teacher education offers the possibility to develop, enhance and complement other skills of the face-to-face teacher preparation (Silva *et al.*, 2019)

Another issue that teacher training courses had to tackle was the fostering of a sense of belongingness that was challenging to achieve via remote teaching. Both the teachers and the students valued the importance of establishing a sense of community which was an element they deemed fruitful and contributing to meaningful learning during their face-to-face teaching. The use of digital video tools enabled the interaction between students not only during teaching hours but also engaging outside the established hours (Carrillo & Flores, 2020). Sepulveda-Escobar and Morrison's (2020) study in Chile echoed the importance attributed to interaction and belongingness with the teacher participants indicating the lack of indirect interaction as a factor having a detrimental effect on their learning. Studies revealed that one of the key challenges that teachers faced during online teaching was the maintenance of social contact with students and their parents (Eickelmann & Drossel, 2020).

Moving classes online has also proved particularly challenging for language instructors because, in most cases, their teaching is based on the principles of communicative language teaching (CLT) and relies on interactions between them and their students. While EFL teachers seemed to acknowledge the benefits associated with technology integration in their classes (Huang *et al.*, 2019), they were often reluctant to adopt technology integration because of lack of confidence or sufficient training (Bai & Lo, 2018).

Teaching Online during the Pandemic

The global pandemic took place amid recent calls for a digitization of education that would result in better preparing students meet 21st-century needs (König *et al.*, 2020). The need was deemed quintessential particularly since findings from the International Computer and Information Literacy Study (ICILS) indicated "underachievement in digital competence" (European Commission 2019, p. 11).

The COVID-19 lockdown necessitated the importance of introducing experienced teachers to the benefits that technology-enhanced classrooms can bring and the ways in which they can optimize their students' learning experience through the use of a variety of digital tools. The COVID-19 outbreak has also increased digital inequalities further. Flores and Gago (2020) found that constraints in terms of internet accessibility can affect online teaching and learning. The high cost of equipping schools with the technology-based infrastructures made transferring teaching online a burden for some countries. Evidently, schools and teachers who had already software resources available and were familiar with their use in class were advantaged during the COVID-19 lockdown (König *et al.*, 2020). Recent reports also revealed that many European countries lag behind in terms of the infrastructure and knowledge required to move to the digitization of education (Fraillon *et al.*, 2019).

While accessibility and infrastructure are key parameters, research studies emphasize the need to integrate training programs that would prepare programs and teachers to teach digital literacy (Gómez-Trigueros *et al.*, 2019; König *et al.*, 202; Tompkins, 2018; Záhorec, Hašková & Munk, 2019). Undisputedly, to keep up with the pace of technology and to make advantage of the unlimited possibilities it can offer to optimizing the learning experience, schools and institutions need to provide up-to-date training for their teachers. Some teachers are often reluctant to change and prefer to stick to principles that they have been using for years (Gómez-Trigueros, Ruiz-Bañuls & Ortega-Sánchez, 2019; Záhorec *et al.*, 2019). This resistance is often attributed to a lack of confidence as they are challenged with tools, software, and applications they have never used (Chaudron, 2015). To mitigate this, pre- and in-service teacher-training programs could assist teachers build their confidence, understand the value that technology can have in the classroom, and instil student-centred classroom environments in ways that technology could only offer (Coiro *et al.*, 2014; Tompkins, 2018).

For this to be materialized, however, adequate training was deemed a requirement as it would shed light on the ways in which technology can be used. For instance, Llerena-Izquierdo and Ayala-Carabajo's (2021) study described an online training space that was created during the COVID-19 lockdown whose objective was to familiarize university professors with digital tools. While pinpointing the challenges that this process entailed, the participants revealed that the online training enhanced their ICT skills and their ability to digitally interact and collaborate with their students. Similarly, Rony and Awal's (2020) study displayed a significant change of mindset and perception amongst teachers regarding online teaching, training, class conduction and assessment.

METHODOLOGY

The study builds on recent research focusing on learning in times of COVID-19 unearthing teacher and student perspectives. However, the effectiveness of transferring language teaching from face-to-face to online settings in teacher education programs remains rather underexplored. To shed more light on the topic, from the teacher-training perspective, the purpose of this chapter is to delve deeper into student teachers and their trainers' attitudes in an attempt to explore how the field of language teaching adapted to changes that have derived from the pandemic. The overarching research question the study attempted to address was: 1) What are the student teachers' and their teacher trainers' attitudes toward digital learning of EFL teacher-training amidst the global pandemic?

Data Collection Strategies

To address the research question, a qualitative approach design was adopted. Data were collected through digital observations of two EFL teacher-training classrooms that moved their lessons online and semi-structured interviews with thirty-nine student teachers and the two teacher trainers. The thirty- nine teacher trainees were in-service teachers that were enrolled in a teacher-training program at a university in Norway and the two teacher trainers were their instructors. The chapter explores the perceptions of two groups of student teachers and their two teacher trainers in an EFL teacher training course in Norway. The first group consisted of twenty-three first year students and their instructor and the second group comprised sixteen fourth year students and their instructor. The first-year course focuses on EFL instruction for primary school children in grades 5-10. It introduces student teachers to EFL pedagogical approaches on vocabulary and grammar teaching. The fourth-year course covers current linguistic methodologies, trends, and approaches to EFL acquisition in multicultural and multilingual settings.

The researcher joined six of the online sessions of each class in different periods throughout the fall semester of 2020 for the fourth-year course and the spring semester of 2021 for the first-year course. Torill taught the first-year class and Thomas the fourth-year group. The names used for the two teacher trainers are pseudonyms. Torill's class consisted of 31 students while Thomas' class consisted of 17 students. Thirty-nine students were at the end of the semester interviewed. Semi-structured interviews allowed comparison while at the same time they provided opportunities for queries that arose from the observation data or during the interview to be clarified. Interview and observation protocols were developed to contribute to the consistency of the data collected as they assisted the researcher in maintaining a clear focus during the interviews and the digital observations. Notes taken during the observations were later written up as field notes and encompassed the third data collection strategy. The interviews enabled the student teacher and teacher trainer participants to delve deeper into their general attitudes towards digital learning of EFL teacher training, which was the focus of the overarching research question. The observations aided the researcher to gather an understanding as to how the participants experience and interact online learning. Most significantly, they enabled the researcher to capture the reality of online learning and identify classroom instances on which student teachers and teacher trainers could elaborate and justify their actions.

While the sample for the study is a purposeful one and might not be generalized, the researcher maintains that, since data were collected from two different years of study, the findings provide an adequate understanding of the insights that might reflect Norwegian EFL student teacher and teacher trainer attitudes. Also, as the observations were conducted over a span of a semester, the research is believed to present a sufficient portrayal of the attitudes on the topic. Participant information is summarized in the table below:

Table 1. Participant information

	Classroom 1	**Classroom 2**
Study program	EFL teacher training	EFL teacher training
Teacher trainer	Torill	Thomas
Year of study	1st year	4th year
Number of student teachers interviewed	25	14
Total number of student teachers	31	17
Academic year observed	Fall semester 2020	Spring semester 2021

Data Analysis

As already mentioned, the present chapter focuses on thirty-nine student teacher attitudes toward digital learning of two university teacher-training courses that shifted to a virtual format during the fall semester of 2020 and the spring semester of 2021. Data were collected through online classroom observations and the use of semi-structured interviews. Field notes taken during the digital observations constituted the third data collection strategy.

An interpretational approach was employed to answer the research questions, while triangulation was used to validate the findings. Gall, Gall, and Borg (1999) defined interpretational analysis as a process which "involves a systematic set of procedures to code and classify qualitative data to ensure that the important constructs, themes, and patterns emerge" (p. 315). Applying the interpretational principles to this study, individual interviews with the student teachers and the two teacher trainers were transcribed and coded using Saldaña's (2009) two coding cycle methods. The purpose was to identify the participants' attitudes towards digital learning of their teacher-training course. The participants' views and perceptions on the topic, therefore, produced the codes for the research questions. The observational protocol notes along with the field notes were also coded to identify the ways in which the participants experienced and interacted during online teaching. Most significantly, as these data collection strategies were coded first, they enabled the possibility of pinpointing specific themes that emerged on which student teachers and teacher trainers could elaborate and justify. Codes to the three data collection strategies were highlighted using colour pens. Whenever a reference to a theme surfaced, it was color-coded with each individual colour representing a theme. Of course, during the Second Cycle Coding, these segments were further refined and subdivided. To comply with the issues raised by the decision to conduct interviews, all ethical considerations were considered. The Pseudonyms are also used throughout the study. The following section delves deeper into student teacher and teacher trainer attitudes regarding online teaching based on their experience during the COVID-19 pandemic.

FINDINGS

The consensus among student teachers and teacher trainers regarding remote teaching was relatively positive. The two teacher trainers and twenty-seven out of the thirty-nine student teachers interviewed acknowledged significant benefits to remote teaching. The benefits the participants identified can be grouped into three categories: a) enhancing digital literacy skills, b) introducing them to new tools that can be of use in the future, and c) promoting independent learning skills and autonomy. However, the participants also cautioned about the potential drawbacks of teacher training classes conducted in their entirety online. Such possibility would a) affect their personal development as teachers and b) deprive them of interaction and collaboration opportunities as both challenges culminated in a difficulty of putting into practice pedagogical concepts. The two graphs below summarize the main findings of the study. The first graph outlines the benefits both groups associated with online teaching and the second graph the challenges encountered during this experience.

Figure 1. Student teachers' and teacher trainers' attitudes towards online teaching: The benefits

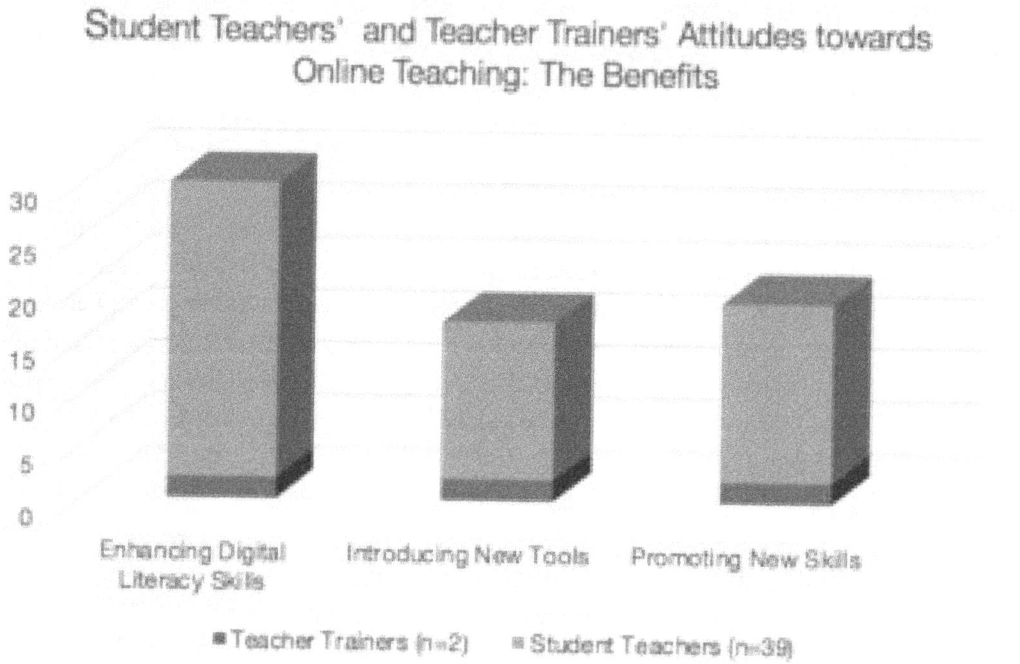

Figure 2. Student teachers' and teacher trainers' attitudes towards online teaching: The challenges

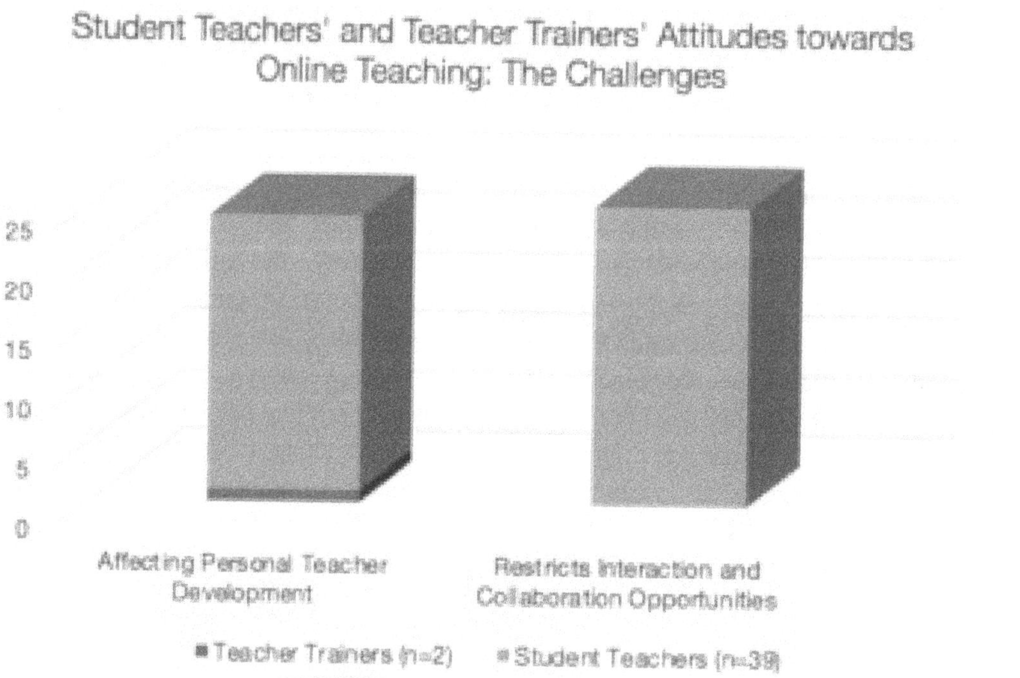

The main findings of the study are presented in the section below.

Benefits of Online Teaching

Enhancing Digital Literacy Skills

Eleven student teachers interviewed from Thomas' class acknowledged that the use of different web tools that their teacher trainer used during their teaching enabled them to foster their digital literacy skills. As four of the interviewees elaborated, they were not familiar with the majority of the tools that were used by their teacher. For these four students, being introduced to tools such as Glogster and Bubbl.us contributed to their understanding of how "we actually think that we know technology by heart when in fact we don't really know much". Because the latest version of the Norwegian curriculum for the subject of English (Norwegian Directorate of Education and Training, 2020) encourages teachers to implement different forms of technology, the four students described this experience as "enriching" as during their teaching practice they mostly relied on "just a couple of tools". As they elaborated, introducing variety to a digital lesson was often also achieved with the choice of tools the teachers made. Consequently, the various tools that their teacher trainer opted to integrate in their classes contributed to "enhancing variety" in their own lessons with four interviewees describing it as an important "motivating factor".

However, two student teachers cautioned that the integration of some of the digital tools that their teacher chose to employ resulted in "significant stress" because they were not "familiar" and "savvy" to operate them and follow the pace of the rest of the class. For these students, the time devoted to familiarizing themselves with new digital tools generated a feeling of anxiety and because of this it often negatively affected the fostering of their digital literacy skills. As they continued in their interviews, they would have preferred their teacher trainer to post a list of the tools beforehand so that they can familiarize themselves prior to the scheduled time of the class. The stress and frustration that some of the student teachers had undergone due to the unfamiliarity with the tools used in the lesson were also noted during the observations. Yet, despite the difficulty the use of some of these tools engendered, the student teachers in question appreciated the opportunity that remote teaching offered as it enabled them to understand the different functions various web tools can fulfil in the classroom.

When asked to comment on similar difficulties, Thomas articulated that using new tools "is the only way of strengthening students' literacy skills" and this possibility was what cemented his instructional decisions. Elaborating on the rationale behind his decision, Thomas argued that the impossibility of face-to-face interaction prompted him to seek opportunities to incorporate interaction possibilities through the medium of a range of web tools. As he pointed out, Thomas "favoured group work activities and while at first…feared this might not be possible through remote teaching, I have managed to find tools that could offer this". In fact, Thomas and the eleven student teachers interviewed from this classroom articulated that switching online furnished them with the opportunity to further enhance their digital literacy skills. What six of the student teachers and Thomas identified as "surprising" was their ability to develop their digital skills "faster than expected" but also "on their own…while playing around" as Thomas elaborated.

Similarly, seventeen student teachers from Torill's classroom maintained that the online classes offered them the opportunity to enhance their digital literacy skills. As they stressed in their interviews, they appreciated their teacher trainer's efforts to implement a number of different tools that would render the lesson "more interesting". While Thomas described himself as "digitally competent", Torill expressed a sense of insecurity experienced during the planning process of her online lessons and described the process as "frightening". She ascribed these feelings to her inexperience with using digital tools previously but also to potential technical issues that might have emerged and would have been "challenging" to address. Torill cited her ability to tackle some of the technological issues that emerged as "a sign that my skills have improved". Growing accustomed to the "challenges of online teaching" made her more confident and "not afraid" to tackle the technical issues that they encountered during this process.

Introducing New Tools

As already briefly mentioned, along with enhancing both the teacher trainers' and the student teachers' literacy skills, remote teaching has also provided them with the opportunity to be introduced to and familiarize themselves with new web tools and applications that could prove useful for their classrooms. While initially more familiar with meeting technology platforms Zoom and Teams, the two semesters that required online teaching prompted them to "mix things up" as Thomas indicated, "so that students won't get bored". The desire to introduce variety "behind the screen routine", as Torill indicated, encouraged teachers to seek a range of tools that would "energize class" and conduct in digital format some of the learning activities that would have been done in class.

Similarly, fifteen student teachers from the two classrooms acknowledged this possibility that virtual teaching offered. Five students pinpointed that they were "impressed" by some of the web tools that were used during the semester and were eager to use them during their own practice. As six students further elaborated, being able to gain a first-hand experience as to how some of these tools operated made them feel more confident in how to effectively use them themselves or "plan a lesson around them". While their teacher trainers, the six students continued, often provided them with online tools that could be integrated in their EFL lessons, some of the recommendations and practices that their teachers offered relied on "pure descriptions" that lacked "a practical demonstration". The experience of remote teaching offered them the opportunity to navigate and operate some of these tools, and as a result, this further boosted their confidence in using them in the future. In addition, Torill identified that being introduced to a range of tools contributed to fostering a more "personalized teaching" as these were suited to the different needs of their students.

Having at one's disposal such a wide variety would enable them to cater to their students' learning preferences by selecting the applications and tools that are more appropriate to the students' technology skills and which accommodate their individual needs. For instance, Thomas argued, for learners that "pick up new knowledge with the help of visual cues", mind mapping and brainstorming tools could optimize their learning experience. Similarly, for auditory learners, the integration of audio-editing and text-to-speech software can enhance their language acquisition. As seven student teachers articulated, remote teaching constituted "the perfect opportunity" to understand the impact digital tools can have on learners' EFL development and the ways in which it could cater to different learner needs. While also expressing the same belief, the two teacher trainers also underlined the positive impact it had on their own digital literacy.

Promoting New Skills

Apart from building on their digital literacy skills, seventeen student teachers highlighted the role online teaching can play in also strengthening important life skills. As some of the tasks required individual work, fourteen students argued that remote learning enhanced their independent learning and their time management skills. In addition, online teaching fostered a sense of autonomy that "would have been otherwise difficult". As ten student teachers argued, getting them to take risks and assigning individual tasks that had to be completed both synchronously and asynchronously resulted in adopting "a more serious approach to teaching". Prompted to elaborate on what qualifies as "a serious approach to teaching", the ten students highlighted the ability to develop an independent, proactive approach to their learning.

Echoing their students' feelings, Torill and Thomas postulated that one of their objectives for the semester was the promotion of learner autonomy. For the two teacher trainers, encouraging the development of such skills ensures "a successful 21st century learner" that would be capable of "organizing and carrying out tasks with critical thinking and problem-solving skills". As it was evident in their interviews, autonomous learning was for the two instructors inextricably linked with critical thinking and problem-solving. By taking charge of their own learning, Thomas commented, students would be required to evaluate choices and make decisions that would lead to the best possible outcome. For this to be materialized, he continued, students would have to inevitably harness the two skills.

Challenges of Online Teaching

Affecting Personal Teacher Development

While acknowledging the benefits that online teaching entails, the student teachers caveated about the drawbacks that this practice would generate. Twenty-three students were concerned that the lack of practicum experience in a classroom setting would have a negative impact on their development as teachers. As the twenty-three interviewees elaborated, their practicum not only enabled them to put into practice some of the pedagogical theories they learned during the semester, it also led to more "in depth considerations of how things are done and how certain things can be addressed".

The twenty-three interviewees acknowledged that online conditions are different from face-to-face teaching. For this reason, some of the teaching tasks that student teachers had to complete in groups online either via Zoom or Teams felt that they did not reflect actual classroom conditions. As a result, nineteen students argued that they "did not get the best out of this experience". The latter rang particularly true as the interviewees from Thomas' class postulated when a new teaching approach was introduced. Indeed, as already mentioned, the fourth-year group delved deeper into multilingual approaches to teaching and during the semester, the student teachers were introduced for the very first time to the pedagogical concept of translanguaging. Having not being familiarized with the concept in their previous years of study, the fifteen interviewees mentioned that they felt that they were "not able to internalize the concept" because of the absence of an actual classroom setting where they could see it "in action". Online teaching rendered their classroom "more theoretical" as seven out of the fifteen fourth-year student teachers argued, and this resulted in "not adequately grasping a new teaching approach" that they could use in their own class. Consequently, six of the interviewees continued, they believed that they did not "develop as teachers" during the period of online teaching.

Similarly, as he admitted, Thomas shared the same concern with his group of student teachers, particularly since the content of the class introduced concepts that "they have not encountered previously". Thomas described the reliance on "theoretical considerations at the expense of practical applications because of the impossibility of physical teaching…a challenge that was difficult to overcome". As he elaborated, he had to change instructional practices to better reflect the online classroom environment and often ended up relying on "on-the-spot strategies", which was not what he initially wanted with most of them, however, still being "inefficient". During the observations, a sense of frustration on the part of the student teachers was noted with a number of questions being addressed to the teacher trainer as some of the student teachers had trouble understanding the topic of the lesson. On the other hand, Torill did not express any concerns whether online teaching could have a negative impact on the student teachers' personal development. In her interview, she exemplified that through remote teaching professional development can be "successfully attained" as participants can maintain "higher retention levels" of the topics covered while at the same time enhance their technological skills.

Restricts Interaction and Collaboration Opportunities

Along with the lack of gaining hands-on experience in the teaching field and the possibility of applying theories learned in practice, twenty-five student teachers articulated that online teaching stripped them away from interaction and collaboration opportunities. While the eleven students interviewed from Thomas' class praised their teacher for the number of group work activities and projects they conducted in class, they still underlined that this experience did not accurately reflect interaction and collaboration "as expected". As they elaborated, "group work activities allow us…[students] to interact with each other and practice the language". Interacting in groups was pinpointed by twenty-five students as the greatest benefit that their pre-COVID teaching with their instructor offered. Particularly, as they continued, in foreign language teaching where students should take advantage of practicing and engaging in exchanges in the target language. The element of collaboration constituted a factor that motivated and which, during online teaching they "cherished" as one of the students identified.

For the fourth-year participants, the lack of interaction and collaboration opportunities was believed to have a detrimental effect on familiarizing themselves with the new topics that their teacher trainer introduced. As already mentioned, the concept of translanguaging was the focus of their classes and as six of the students pinpointed, not being able to discuss and exchange ideas as to how this pedagogical approach could be implemented in Norwegian classrooms rendered the "accessibility of the content covered" "more difficult". Because the topic was perceived as "somewhat challenging", eight students felt that their teacher trainer opted for "extensive, lengthy descriptions" of the concept that deprived them from interaction opportunities that could assist in shedding more light on how multilingual approaches to teaching can be implemented in different settings that the student teachers have encountered during their practicum. A similar concern was also echoed by the first-year group of student teachers as eight of them went on to describe the lack of interaction amongst them as "one of the greatest disadvantages". As they continued, the difficulty of putting into practice some of the teaching approaches they were being taught in a physical classroom could have been mitigated by integrating digital interaction and collaboration opportunities.

However, while twenty-five students highlighted in their interviews the lack of interaction and collaboration opportunities, the two teacher trainers positively evaluated the possibility of remote teaching establishing interaction and collaboration. In fact, Thomas postulated that this semester the choice of tools and activities were based on "the criterion of engaging students and providing them a platform to express themselves". He continued by admitting that "remote teaching provided more interaction and collaboration opportunities…than in the past". To enable this, Torill argued that she had carefully chosen to integrate tools that promoted an active learning environment. Similarly, Thomas abided by the same principles as for him a collaborative classroom constitutes "an active learning environment" that further enables students to harness their creativity but also "practice some of the teaching tips" their instructors provided.

DISCUSSION

As it readily transpired from the interviews, the student teachers and their instructors positively evaluated the opportunities remote teaching offered as it enhanced their digital literacy skills, introduced them to new tools, and promoted independent learning skills and autonomy. At the same time, however, the teacher trainers also believed that online learning affected their personal development. Furthermore, the student teachers postulated that it deprived them of interaction and collaboration opportunities that would enable them to internalize some of the new concepts to which they had been introduced.

More strikingly, the findings revealed a discrepancy regarding the perception student teachers and their instructors had on the interaction and collaboration opportunities that their online classes offered. As exemplified in the section above, the online learning conditions for both courses did not provide the interaction opportunities that face-to-face teaching offered and the student teachers went on to identify this as "a major drawback", as one of the participants exemplified, of the current mode of delivery. On the other hand, teacher trainers presented a different perspective. The two teacher trainers evaluated their lessons as being "more interactive and collaborative" than was the case pre-COVID. In fact, as they elaborated, they argued that the inclusion of web tools prompted a variety of collaborative teaching and learning "that had not been the case previously". The student teachers, however, did not share this sentiment as they anticipated a higher amount of interaction taking place through digital tools. The importance of collaboration in online settings was mirrored in a recent study conducted by Sepulveda-Escobar and Morrison (2020).

In particular, this belief was dominant amongst the fourth-year group whose learning objectives included the introduction of multilingual approaches to teaching. Because these were concepts with which the student teachers were not familiar, they maintained that interaction and collaboration opportunities would have assisted them in further delineating the ways in which these approaches could be implemented in the EFL classroom. In fact, what the student teachers seemed to prefer in terms of interaction was the possibility of practicing these new approaches even in a fictional digital classroom setting consisting of their classmates who would have assumed the role of their learners. As they went on to elaborate, because of the impossibility of physical teaching and "the materialization of an actual classroom setting", their instructors designed and conducted classes that were heavily teacher fronted that as two students exemplified "at times…[it] complicated things".

As it emerged from the data, for student teachers, it was of paramount importance to enable the practical application of theoretical considerations they were being taught. As they stressed in their interviews, they felt that remote teaching negatively impacted the implementation of the practical element of their courses since they became more theoretical in nature. Since the student teachers did not have the opportunity to undertake in-classroom practicum, they argued that their classes should have strengthened and focused on practical applications either through a digital classroom setting or through the provision of videos that described how a particular approach translates and could be applied in the classroom. Elaborating on how interaction and collaboration could have been reinforced, ten student teachers suggested microteaching activities that would allow them to not only experiment with, but also get feedback on whether they have understood the principles of the novice pedagogical approaches.

It can be argued that the challenges that the student teachers identified in their interviews about remote teaching are inextricably linked with the impact this mode of delivery had on the practical directions and implications of their course. The fourth-year group was accustomed to an approach to teaching that enabled them to put into practice the theoretical foundations and see them, as six of the student teachers identified, "in action". On the other hand, the first-year group expected a more prominent focus on the pedagogical implementation and the practical considerations of the themes and topics covered. The dearth of similar approaches in their online classes generated dissatisfaction with the student teachers identifying it as "an omission" on the part of their instructors. The student teachers' expectation was to gain extensive practical experience that they could use in their own classrooms to support learner development. Familiarizing themselves with teaching tips and activities that would enable them to plan and teach well-structured lessons and to adapt and cater to the needs of their own learners constituted their priority. Its lack thereof comprised the main reason behind their source of frustration of their remote teaching experience.

However, while the student teacher participants expressed their dissatisfaction with the format their digital teaching adopted, the two teacher trainers asserted that their lessons offered interaction and collaboration possibilities. As the two teacher trainers postulated, they resorted to the use of tools that would promote group work in the classroom. The participatory approach was perceived by the participants of the study as a key factor in teacher training programs. Despite their teacher trainers employing applications and tools that enhanced student engagement, the student teachers interviewed acknowledged the lack of interpersonal interactions and engagement as having a significant impact on the way they perceived and experienced their learning. From their perspectives, the lack of interpersonal interaction could have a detrimental effect to their learning experience.

Five of the student teachers interviewed postulated the difference in classroom dynamics that online interaction entailed. Despite activities requiring students to communicate digitally, they considered that the lesson "did not feel learner-centered" while they also claimed that to make the most of these tools, their instructors should have undergone "additional ICT training". While recent studies have underlined that online learning encourages student-centered learning (e.g., Atmojo & Nugroho, 2020; Lasfeto, 2020; Zhang, 2020), there were also concerns over establishing sufficient interaction echoed in studies conducted by Peachey (2017), Mumford and Dikilitas (2020). Further difficulties of establishing online interaction amongst students was also reported in recent research conducted in underdeveloped countries (e.g., Adnan & Anwar, 2020).

Digital interaction and communication did not seem to fulfil and replicate face to face engagement and was described by the student teachers as "a barrier" to their personal teacher development. What seemed to matter for the student teachers was the quality and not the quantity of interaction in the classroom. Research has illustrated that interpersonal interaction has generally been demonstrated to lead to better student outcomes (Mehall, 2020; Pacquette, 2016). In fact, Mehall (2020) calls for "purposeful interpersonal interaction…any high quality, organic, and valid communication exchange between two or more participants of the learning process that directly relates to the achievement of established learning outcomes or to the building of social relationships" (p. 185).

The discrepancy the study identified could be ascribed to the insufficient understanding or the lack of clear instructions on the part of the teacher trainers as to how the different tools operate and the different tasks they could perform. As discussed in the findings section, some of the student teachers expressed a preference for an introduction in advance of the tools used in the lessons. Understanding the usage and the ways in which digital tools could support learning and meet the desired objectives could ameliorate the students' digital classroom experience. Furthermore, to lessen discrepancies and improve the satisfaction and motivation levels in an online class, course instructors should strive and collect feedback from their students so that their views and attitudes about teaching could be in sync, and thus optimize the learning experience. As this study revealed, inconsistencies in perception could culminate in great dissatisfaction amongst learners and potentially provide a source of demotivation (Sepulveda-Escobar & Morrison, 2020).

Given the predominant role technology exerts and its impact in national curricula, teacher education programs should strive to adequately prepare prospective teachers how to enhance language learning through the use of tools and applications. As the COVID-19 pandemic has illustrated, in certain cases the education sector was found unprepared to tackle the challenges of digitization. What initially described as a temporary solution, remote teaching can fulfil and execute a critical role in education post-pandemic. For this reason, teacher education programs need to display and illustrate the positive impact and benefits a technology-enhanced lesson can have without necessarily been perceived as the last resort. The rapid move to online learning and a hybrid model of education needs to take full advantage of what technology could offer to students with sufficient training, adequate preparation, and infrastructure, but also shared views between teachers and students as what this entails.

LIMITATIONS OF THE STUDY

While the findings of the study offer an insight into the attitudes of teacher trainers and student teachers towards remote teaching, they cannot be generalized since the number of participants in this study was relatively low but also because the study focused on one semester of teaching. As the study gathered data from two different groups and study programs, however, they do provide an adequate understanding of the insights that might reflect Norwegian EFL student teacher and teacher trainer attitudes on the benefits and challenges they associate with online learning. Of course, as the study solely focused on one classroom from each group renders the generalization of the findings rather difficult. They offer a starting point for future teacher trainers in Norway but also outside the country on how to best utilize the online setting for active and engaged learning where students can learn and develop.

Additional longitudinal studies should be conducted to shed light on the development and expectations of the learning processes of student teachers and teacher trainers in similar situations. The studies could aim to build a common understanding of instructional approaches with clear emphasis on frequent student>instructor communication. Such studies focusing on both students and their instructors would offer a deeper understanding as to how the teacher training learning experience could be optimized but would also assist them in becoming expert remote teachers.

FUTURE RESEARCH DIRECTIONS

The pandemic has revealed that students can be more adept at using digital tools than their teachers while in certain cases some teachers might not feel comfortable using digital tools in the classroom (Sadaf & Gezer, 2020). Future research should also take into account the student voice. Studies conducted among young learners that would shed light on the way students perceive online learning while it would also contribute towards optimizing their learning experience. The findings from research conducted among students and teachers from the same classroom would pinpoint the elements that work for both and would make learning more accessible. Individual action research projects would also enable the materialization of the latter.

A digitally literate person should possess a deeper understanding of how to engage with technology in compelling ways that harness creativity, critical and analytical thinking, collaboration, and communication. Digital tools should not be used just for the sake of it simply because the learners might find the lesson more entertaining. The purpose of integrating them in the classroom should solely rely on how they can be used in an educational context. For this reason, teacher training should provide teachers but also students with rigorous and systematic training to meet the needs that arose in today's educational world. Teacher-training programs should design and integrate courses that familiarize pre- but also in-service teachers with the current trends and what being digitally literate entails. These courses should be annually reviewed and revised so that teachers can tackle the challenges emanating from the rapidly and ever-changing technological world.

CONCLUSION

Although the student teacher's experiences and their instructors presented in this study shared similarities with those of other participants around the world during the pandemic (e.g., Flores and Gago, 2020 in Portugal; Moorhouse, 2020 in Korea; Bao, 2020 in China), additional research would assist in further delineating the ways in which remote teaching for teacher education programs can be optimized. The purpose of integrating them in the classroom should solely rely on how they can be used in an educational context. As the data revealed the discrepancy that emerged between the conceptualization of a lesson and its actual implementation in the classroom, a clear purpose behind each task that would promote students' digital literacy skills, but which would also deepen their knowledge in the field should be prioritized. An effective digital lesson could also enable students develop personal strengths and skills alongside enhancing their digital literacy. However, often, students are more adept at using digital tools than their teachers and in certain cases some teachers might not feel comfortable using digital tools in the classroom (Lasfeto, 2020; Llerena-Izquierdo & Ayala-Carabajo's, 2021). In addition, the results would be useful in designing relevant training programmes whose aim would be to adequately prepare EFL teachers deliver lessons in synchronous online teaching mode that would also take into account the student voice.

Because of the ever-evolving nature of technology, such courses need to be offered to in-service teachers to provide a smoother transition between new forms and trends so that teachers do not feel uncomfortable integrating novice software and tools and students are sufficiently trained as tomorrow's digital citizens. Classrooms need not only to reflect the needs and practices of the real world, they should also pave the way for innovative, critically thoughtful, and socially purposeful methods and approaches that would facilitate everyday life as well.

REFERENCES

ACARA. (2016). *Australian curriculum, assessment and reporting authority*. Retrieved from http:// www. australiancurriculum.edu.au/

Adnan, M., & Anwar, K. (2020). Online learning amid the COVID-19 Pandemic: Students' perspectives. *Online Submission*, *2*(1), 45–51. doi:10.33902/JPSP.2020261309

Al-Maroof, R. A. S., & Al-Emran, M. (2018). Students acceptance of Google classroom: An exploratory study using PLS-SEM approach. *International Journal of Emerging Technologies in Learning*, *13*(06), 112–123. doi:10.3991/ijet.v13i06.8275

Atmojo, A. E. P., & Nugroho, A. (2020). EFL classes must go online! Teaching activities and challenges during COVID-19 pandemic in Indonesia. *Register Journal*, *13*(1), 49–76. doi:10.18326/rgt.v13i1.49-76

Azmi, N. (2017). The benefits of using ICT in the EFL classroom: From perceived utility to potential challenges. *Journal of Educational and Social Research*, *7*(1), 111–118. doi:10.5901/jesr.2017.v7n1p111

Ba, H., Tally, W., & Tsikalas, K. (2002). Investigating children's emerging digital literacies. *The Journal of Technology, Learning, and Assessment*, *1*(4), 5–48.

Bai, B., & Lo, C. K. (2018). The barriers of technology integration in Hong Kong primary school English education: Preliminary findings and recommendations for future practices. *International Journal of Languages. Literatura y Lingüística*, *4*(4), 290–297.

Bao, W. (2020). COVID-19 and online teaching in higher education: A case study of Peking University. *Human Behavior and Emerging Technologies*, *2*(2), 113–115. doi:10.1002/hbe2.191 PMID:32510042

Bloch, J. (2021). *Creating digital literacy spaces for multilingual writers*. Multilingual Matters.

Broadband Commission for Sustainable Development. (2017). *Working group on education: Digital skills for life and work*. UNESCO.

Buchholz, B. A., DeHart, J., & Moorman, G. (2020). Digital citizenship during a global pandemic: Moving beyond digital literacy. *Journal of Adolescent & Adult Literacy*, *64*(1), 11–17. doi:10.1002/jaal.1076 PMID:32834710

Caires, S., Almeida, L., & Vieira, D. (2012). Becoming a teacher: Student teachers' experiences and perceptions about teaching practice. *European Journal of Teacher Education*, *35*(2), 163–178. doi:10.1080/02619768.2011.643395

Carrillo, C., & Flores, M. A. (2020). COVID-19 and teacher education: A literature review of online teaching and learning practices. *European Journal of Teacher Education*, *43*(4), 466–487. doi:10.1080/02619768.2020.1821184

Castillo, N. M., & Wagner, D. A. (2018). Supporting home language reading through technology in rural South Africa. *International Review of Education.* Retrieved from https://repository.upenn.edu/literacyorg_articles/36/?utm_source=repository.upenn.edu%2Fliteracyorg_articles%2F36&utm_medium=PDF&utm_campaign=PDFCoverPages

Chaudron, S. (2015). *Young children (0-8) and digital technology, a qualitative study across Europe*. JRC Science for Policy Report.

Chetty, K., Qigui, L., Gcora, N., Josie, J., Wenwei, L., & Fang, C. (2018). Bridging the digital divide: measuring digital literacy. *Economics: The Open-Access, Open-Assessment E-Journal*, *12*, 1–20.

Cheung, A. (2021). Language teaching during a pandemic: A case study of zoom use by a secondary ESL teacher in Hong Kong. *RELC Journal.* Retrieved from https://journals.sagepub.com/doi/pdf/10.1177/0033688220981784

Churchill, N. (2016). *Digital storytelling as a means of supporting digital literacy learning in an upper primary-school English language classroom* (Doctoral thesis). Edith Cowan University, Joondalup, Australia. Retrieved from https://ro.ecu.edu.au/theses/1774

Coiro, J., Knobel, M., Lankshear, C., & Leu, D. J. (Eds.). (2014). *Handbook of research on new literacies.* Routledge. doi:10.4324/9781410618894

Cote, T., & Milliner, B. (2018). A survey of EFL teachers' digital literacy: A report from a Japanese university. *Teaching English with Technology, 18*(4), 71–89.

Donitsa-Schmidt, S., & Ramot, R. (2020). Opportunities and challenges: Teacher education in Israel in the Covid-19 pandemic. *Journal of Education for Teaching, 46*(4), 586–595. doi:10.1080/02607476.2020.1799708

Eickelmann, B., & Drossel, K. (2020). *Schule auf Distanz. Perspektiven und Empfehlungen für den neuen Schulalltag. Eine repräsentative Befragung von Lehrkräften in Deutschland* [Distance education. Perspectives and recommendations for the new everyday school life. A representative survey of teachers in Germany]. Retrieved from https://www.vodafone-stiftung.de/umfrage-co ronakrise-lehrer/

Eryansyah, E., Erlina, E., Fiftinova, F., & Nurweni, A. (2019). EFL students' needs of digital literacy to meet the demands of 21st century skills. *Indonesian Research Journal in Education, 3*(2), 442–460.

Eshet, Y. (2004). Digital literacy: A conceptual framework for survival skills in the digital era. *Journal of Educational Multimedia and Hypermedia, 13*(1), 93–106.

European Commission. (2003). *e-Learning: Designing tomorrow's education-A mid-term report.* Retrieved from http://www.elearningeuropa.info/extras/pdf/mid_term_e n.pdf

European Commission. (2019). *Call for digital innovation hubs on artificial intelligence.* Retrieved from https://ec.europa.eu/digital-single-market/en/news/call-digital-innovation-hubs-artificial-intelligence

Fedynich, L. V. (2013). Teaching beyond the classroom walls: The pros and cons of cyber learning. *Journal of Instructional Pedagogies, 13*, 1–7.

Ferrari, A. (2012). *Digital competence in practice: An analysis of frameworks.* Institute for Prospective Technological Studies, European Commission. Retrieved from http://www.ifap.ru/library/book522. pdf

Flores, M. A., & Gago, M. (2020). Teacher education in times of COVID-19 pandemic in Portugal: National, institutional and pedagogical responses. *Journal of Education for Teaching, 46*(1), 1–10.

Fraillon, J., Ainley, J., Schulz, W., Duckworth, D., & Friedman, T. (2019). *IEA international computer and information literacy study 2018 assessment framework.* Springer. doi:10.1007/978-3-030-19389-8

Gatcho, A. R. G., & Hajan, B. H. (2019). Check your Face (Book) on page…": Unpacking the pedagogical potentialities of English teachers' wall posts. *Online Submission, 13*(1), 1–9. doi:10.21512/lc.v13i1.5253

Geer, R., & Sweeney, T. A. (2012). Students' voices about learning with technology. *Journal of Social Sciences*, *8*(2), 294–303. doi:10.3844/jssp.2012.294.303

Gómez-Trigueros, I. M., Ruiz-Bañuls, M., & Ortega-Sánchez, D. (2019). Digital literacy of teachers in training: Moving from icts (information and communication technologies) to lkts (learning and knowledge technologies). *Education Sciences*, *9*(4), 274–284. doi:10.3390/educsci9040274

Greener, S. (2009). e-Modeling--Helping Learners to Develop Sound e-Learning Behaviours. *Electronic Journal of e-Learning, 7*(3), 265-272.

Huang, F., Teo, T., & Zhou, M. (2019). Factors affecting Chinese English as a foreign language teachers' technology acceptance: A qualitative study. *Journal of Educational Computing Research*, *57*(1), 83–105. doi:10.1177/0735633117746168

Huber, E., & Shalavin, C. (2018). Surveying the digital literacy landscape for academic and professional staff in higher education. In M. Campbell, J. Willems, C. Adachi, D. Blake, I. Doherty, S. Krishnan, S. Macfarlane, L. Ngo, M. O'Donnell, S. Palmer, L. Riddell, I. Story, H. Suri & J. Tai (Eds.), *Annual conference of the Australasian society for computers in learning in tertiary education: ASCILITE 2018: Conference Proceedings* (pp. 151-158). ASCILITE.

Hussain, Z. (2018). The effects of ICT-based learning on students 'vocabulary mastery in junior high schools in Bandung. *International Journal of Education and Literacy Studies*, *10*(2), 149–156.

Kabilan, M. K., Ahmad, N., & Abidin, M. J. Z. (2010). Facebook: An online environment for learning of English in institutions of higher education? *Internet and Higher Education*, *13*(4), 179–187. doi:10.1016/j.iheduc.2010.07.003

Kim, J. (2020). Learning and teaching online during Covid-19: Experiences of student teachers in an early childhood education practicum. *International Journal of Early Childhood*, *52*(2), 145–158. doi:10.100713158-020-00272-6 PMID:32836369

Kleemans, M., & Eggink, G. (2016). Understanding news: The impact of media literacy education on teenagers' news literacy. *Journal of Education*, *5*(1), 75–88.

Konca, A. S., Ozel, E., & Zelyurt, H. (2016). Attitudes of Preschool Teachers towards Using Information and Communication Technologies (ICT). *International Journal of Research in Education and Science*, *2*(1), 10–15. doi:10.21890/ijres.21816

König, J., Jäger-Biela, D. J., & Glutsch, N. (2020). Adapting to online teaching during COVID-19 school closure: Teacher education and teacher competence effects among early career teachers in Germany. *European Journal of Teacher Education*, *43*(4), 608–622. doi:10.1080/02619768.2020.1809650

Lankshear, C., & Knobel, M. (2011). *New literacies*. McGraw-Hill Education.

Lasfeto, D. (2020). The relationship between self-directed learning and students' social interaction in online learning environment. *Journal of e-Learning and Knowledge Society*, *16*(2), 34-41.

Lee, J. S. (2019). Informal digital learning of English and second language vocabulary outcomes: Can quantity conquer quality? *British Journal of Educational Technology*, *50*(2), 767–778. doi:10.1111/bjet.12599

Lee, J. S. (2020). Informal digital learning of English and strategic competence for cross-cultural communication: Perception of varieties of English as a mediator. *ReCALL, 32*(1), 47–62. doi:10.1017/S0958344019000181

Lee, J. S., & Lee, K. (2019). Informal digital learning of English and English as an international language: The path less traveled. *British Journal of Educational Technology, 50*(3), 1447–1461. doi:10.1111/bjet.12652

Llerena-Izquierdo, J., & Ayala-Carabajo, R. (2021). University teacher training during the COVID-19 emergency: The role of online teaching-learning tools. In *International Conference on Information Technology & Systems* (pp. 90-99). Cham: Springer. 10.1007/978-3-030-68418-1_10

López-Meneses, E., Sirignano, F. M., Vázquez-Cano, E., & Ramírez-Hurtado, J. M. (2020). University students' digital competence in three areas of the DigCom 2.1 model: A comparative study at three European universities. *Australasian Journal of Educational Technology, 36*(3), 69–88. doi:10.14742/ajet.5583

McDougall, J., Readman, M., & Wilkinson, P. (2018). The uses of (digital) literacy. *Learning, Media and Technology, 43*(3), 263–279. doi:10.1080/17439884.2018.1462206

Mehall, S. (2020). Purposeful Interpersonal Interaction in Online Learning: What Is It and How Is It Measured? *Online Learning, 24*(1), 182–204. doi:10.24059/olj.v24i1.2002

Merriam, S. B., Caffarella, R. S., & Baumgartner, L. M. (2007). *Learning in adulthood: A comprehensive guide*. Jossey-Bass.

Moorhouse, B. L. (2020). Adaptations to a face-to-face initial teacher education course 'forced'online due to the COVID-19 pandemic. *Journal of Education for Teaching, 46*(4), 609–611. doi:10.1080/02607476.2020.1755205

Mudra, H. (2020). Digital literacy among young learners: How do EFL teachers and learners view its benefits and barriers? *Teaching English with Technology, 20*(3), 3–24.

Mumford, S., & Dikilitaş, K. (2020). Pre-service language teachers reflection development through online interaction in a hybrid learning course. *Computers & Education, 144*, 103706. doi:10.1016/j.compedu.2019.103706

Neumann, M. M., Finger, G., & Neumann, D. L. (2017). A conceptual framework for emergent digital literacy. *Early Childhood Education Journal, 45*(4), 471–479. doi:10.100710643-016-0792-z

New London Group. (1996). A pedagogy of multiliteracies: Designing social futures. *Harvard Educational Review, 66*(1), 60–92. doi:10.17763/haer.66.1.17370n67v22j160u

Norwegian Directorate of Education and Training. (2020). *English subject curriculum*. Retrieved from https://www.udir.no/lk20/eng01-04?lang=eng

Papadima-Sophocleous, S., Giannikas, C. N., & Kakoulli-Constantinou, E. (2014). ICT in EFL: The global effect of new technologies in the language classroom. In *Proceedings of the 2014 EUROCALL Conference CALL Design: Principles and Practice* (pp. 296-300). Research-publishing. net. 10.14705/rpnet.2014.000234

Paquette, P. (2016). Instructing the instructors: Training instructors to use social presence cues in online courses. *The Journal of Educators Online, 13*(1), 80–108. doi:10.9743/JEO.2016.1.4

Peachey, N. (2017). Synchronous online teaching. In M. Carrier, R. M. Damerow, & K. M. Bailey (Eds.), *Digital language learning and teaching* (pp. 143–155). Routledge. doi:10.4324/9781315523293-12

Raman, K., & Yamat, H. (2014). Barriers teachers face in integrating ICT during English lessons: A case study. *Malaysian Online Journal of Educational Technology, 2*(3), 11–19.

Reedy, K., & Parker, J. (2018). *Digital literacy unpacked.* Facet. doi:10.29085/9781783301997

Rony, H. A. Z., & Awal, S. T. (2019). University teachers' training on online teaching-Learning using Online Platform during COVID-19: A case study. *Bangladesh Education Journal, 18*(2), 57–65.

Sadaf, A., & Gezer, T. (2020). Exploring factors that influence teachers' intentions to integrate digital literacy using the decomposed theory of planned behavior. *Journal of Digital Learning in Teacher Education, 36*(2), 124–145. doi:10.1080/21532974.2020.1719244

Saldaña, J. (2009). *The coding manual for qualitative researchers.* SAGE.

Sánchez-Cruzado, C., Santiago Campión, R., & Sánchez-Compaña, M. (2021). Teacher digital literacy: The indisputable challenge after COVID-19. *Sustainability, 13*(4), 1858. doi:10.3390u13041858

Sepulveda-Escobar, P., & Morrison, A. (2020). Online teaching placement during the COVID-19 pandemic in Chile: Challenges and opportunities. *European Journal of Teacher Education, 43*(4), 587–607. doi:10.1080/02619768.2020.1820981

Silva, J. S., Usart, M. U., Lázaro-Cantabrana, J. L. L. C., Silva, J., Usart, M., & Lázaro-Cantabrana, J. L. (2019). Teacher's digital competence among final year Pedagogy students in Chile and Uruguay. *Comunicar. Media Education Research Journal, 27*(2), 33–43.

Singapore Ministry of Education. (2020). *Refreshing our curriculum.* Retrieved from https://www.moe.gov.sg/microsites/cos2020/index.html

Sundqvist, P., & Sylvén, L. K. (2016). *Extramural English in teaching and learning: From theory and research to practice.* Springer. doi:10.1057/978-1-137-46048-6

Tang, C. M., & Chaw, L. Y. (2016). Digital literacy: A prerequisite for effective learning in a blended learning environment? *Electronic Journal of E-learning, 14*(1), 54–65.

Tejedor, S., Cervi, L., Pérez-Escoda, A., & Jumbo, F. T. (2020). Digital literacy and higher education during COVID-19 lockdown: Spain, Italy, and Ecuador. *Publications, 8*(4), 48–65. doi:10.3390/publications8040048

Terenko, O., & Ogienko, O. (2020). How to teach pedagogy courses online at university in COVID-19 pandemic: Search for answers. *Romanian Journal for Multidimensional Education/Revista Romaneasca pentru Educatie Multidimensionala, 12,* 173-179.

Tompkins, G. (2018). *Literacy for the 21st century: A balanced approach* (7th ed.). Pearson.

Tsai, H. Y. S., Shillair, R., & Cotten, S. R. (2017). Social support and "playing around" an examination of how older adults acquire digital literacy with tablet computers. *Journal of Applied Gerontology*, *36*(1), 29–55. doi:10.1177/0733464815609440 PMID:26491029

Turula, A. (2017). Learner autonomy as a social construct in the context of Italki. *Teaching English with Technology*, *17*(2), 3–28.

Ulvik, M., Helleve, I., & Smith, K. (2018). What and how student teachers learn during their practicum as a foundation for further professional development. *Professional Development in Education*, *44*(5), 638–649. doi:10.1080/19415257.2017.1388271

Vázquez-Cano, E., León Urrutia, M., Parra-González, M. E., & López Meneses, E. (2020). Analysis of interpersonal competences in the use of ICT in the Spanish University Context. *Sustainability*, *12*(2), 476–488. doi:10.3390u12020476

Vikneswaran, T., & Krish, P. (2016). Utilising social networking sites to improve writing: A case study with Chinese students in Malaysia. *Technology, Pedagogy and Education*, *25*(3), 287–300. doi:10.1080/1475939X.2015.1030441

Vuorikari, R., Punie, Y., Carretero, G. S., & Van Den Brande, G. (2016). *DigComp 2.0: The digital competence framework for citizens. Update Phase 1: The conceptual reference model*. Publication Office of the European Union.

Wedenoja, L. (2020). *What to expect when you weren't expecting online classes*. Rockefeller Institute of Government. Retrieved from https://rockinst.org/blog/what-to-expect-when-you-werent-expecting-online-classes/

White, J. (2015). *Digital literacy skills for FE teachers*. Sage. doi:10.4135/9781473909571

Xia, F., Yang, L. T., Wang, L., & Vinel, A. (2012). Internet of things. *International Journal of Communication Systems*, *25*(9), 1101–1102. doi:10.1002/dac.2417

Záhorec, J., Hašková, A., & Munk, M. (2019). Teachers' professional digital literacy skills and their upgrade. *European Journal of Contemporary Education*, *8*(2), 378–393.

Zhang, R. (2020). Exploring blended learning experiences through the community of inquiry framework. *ELT Journal*, *24*(1), 38–53.

Chapter 12
Engendering WTC in Online Learning Spaces:
Peer Connectivity Is More Important Than We May Think

Amelia Yarwood
Kanda University of International Studies, Japan

Phillip A. Bennett
Kanda University of International Studies, Japan

ABSTRACT

Since 2020, language learning environments have had to swiftly transition from traditional face-to-face learning to remote learning contexts. This chapter interrogates factors related to students' willingness to communicate (WTC) in online-mediated discussions in a Japanese university classroom. Using a self-determination theory framework to conduct a thematic analysis of data collected from focus group discussions and the written reflections of English L2 learners (N=19), three main factors were found to contribute to a lack of WTC. Two of the three are unique to online learning: disruptive environmental factors and a thwarting of relatedness between classmates. The third factor, a perceived lack of communicative ability, although not unique to online learning, was amplified by the online environment. In order to address these factors, which contribute to a lack of WTC, a number of teaching interventions aimed at fostering communicative online classrooms are introduced.

INTRODUCTION

The role of technology in language classrooms the world over has undergone a significant change since early 2020, when institutions were confronted with the unprecedented task of moving to online classrooms following the global pandemic. For classrooms which relied on communicative pedagogical approaches, they faced the daunting task of creating safe, social spaces online for facilitating a free flow of dialogue between students. However, communicating in a synchronous classroom through video-

DOI: 10.4018/978-1-7998-8717-1.ch012

conferencing platforms and other online communication tools is subject to challenges outside of those present in traditional face-to-face learning environments, especially in terms of learners' Willingness To Communicate (WTC).

WTC originally emerged as an affective construct applied to L2 communication by MacIntrye and Charos (1996) following its conception in L1 communication studies. In its original form, WTC was viewed as a personality construct (McCroskey & Baer, 1985; McCroskey & Richmond, 1987) measuring individuals' willingness to communicate during interpersonal encounters. Since then, it has evolved to include an array of dynamic contextual factors (MacIntyre & Legatto, 2011; Yashima, 2002; Yashima, MacIntyre & Ikeda, 2018) often found in the L2 speaker's situated environment. Additionally, factors such as perceived communicative competence (Joe, Hiver & Al-Hoorie, 2017), communicative apprehension (Yashima, 2012), and self-evaluation (King, 2013; Gregersen, MacIntyre & Meza, 2014; MacIntyre & Doucette, 2010) are viewed as integral influences on WTC.

When looking at the field of TESOL in Asia over the last two decades, the WTC of East Asian learners has been somewhat controversial. In particular, Shao and Gao (2016) investigated the question of whether or not "East Asian learners' "unwillingness to communicate" was a result of "long-standing prejudice and hackneyed Eastern-Western stereotypes" (p.116). Based on a summary of publications over the past two decades, they concluded that East Asian language learners' unwillingness to communicate "cannot be solely accounted for by cultural reasons and have to be understood in relation to a variety of cultural, historical, and social conditions and processes" (Shao & Gao, 2016, p. 119). With this in mind, the authors believe it to be important to define and distinguish nonverbal communication in the online classroom.

Nonverbal communication in the classroom is often referred to as silence; however, researchers have differentiated between silence and reticence. As Bao (2019) details, reticence stems from deficiencies in communicative competence, which results in the avoidance of participation. At its severity, reticence can be thought of as a verbal paralysis resulting in a complete loss of autonomy: where students perceive themselves in a learning environment that is akin to drifting in a gravity-less void. On the other hand, silence can be utilised as a powerful communicative tool to show agreement, disagreement, respect, moments of reflection, or even a scheme to negotiate power (Bao, 2019; King; 2013; Shao & Gao, 2016; Ellwood & Nakane, 2009). Bao goes on to state that one of the distinctions between reticence and silence is "a question of motives." In this way, silence can be utilised as a form of interpersonal discourse to fulfil a communicative function; it can be used as a form of supportive control, giving space and adequate time for others to gather their thoughts and form a reply. In the case of reticence, the motive is often to save face when dealing with communicative apprehension. As previously mentioned, distinctions that can be made between reticence and silence, however, research that shows there are intersections between the two, generated from shyness or due to communication breakdown.

In this chapter, the authors investigate the factors that contribute to the suppression of English learners' WTC in online-mediated discussions. Silence and reticence are demonstrated in the data, but will be shown to be shaped by three contextual factors - physical, digital and psychological -within the learner's situated environments.

BACKGROUND

What is Willingness to Communicate?

WTC was originally focused on L1 use (McCroskey & Baer, 1985). In terms of L2 communication (L2 here is used as a placeholder for communication in a language other than individuals' first language/s) the concept was expanded upon by MacIntyre et al. (1998) over a decade later. While they agree with findings—both empirical and anecdotal—that WTC can be trait-like (McCroskey & Baer, 1985), MacIntyre et al. (1998) draw focus to the situational variables that influence communicative behaviours, thereby giving equal weight to both personality and the intergroup climate as the foundation of WTC. They approach the concept of L2 WTC, stating that "WTC strongly implies a behavioural intention" where a person plans to speak up when the opportunity arises (p. 548). The authors further emphasise that "the most immediate cause of behaviour is the intention to engage in a behaviour and the person's actual control over his or her actions...intention must combine with opportunity to produce behaviour" (MacIntyre et al., 1998, p.548). An example of this is students raising their hand to answer a question, and although they might not be called on, they still had the intention to speak. Furthermore, teachers sometimes unconsciously demonstrate teaching behaviours that suppress students' WTC (Ryan & Deci, 2017). In other words, even though the intention and willingness to communicate exists, factors within the classroom environment can prevent communication from taking place or WTC is simply not noticed or recognised.

As shown, WTC in L2 behaviour is situational (i.e., influenced by a learning environment) and not solely an extension of their innate L1 WTC traits. As Ryan and Deci (2017, p. 546) state, "...L2 use carries a number of intergroup issues, with social and political implications, that are usually irrelevant to L1 use". They conclude that WTC in an L2 is not necessarily based on the language ability of a person, but rather on a number of factors that change depending on time, place, social, and personal contexts. Instances of these manifest in face-to-face classroom environments: teacher-led versus group-based communicative activities (Fushino, 2010), and in online environments (e.g., Wi-Fi connectivity issues, camera use, time limits in *breakout rooms*, familiarity with software/apps, etc.). To understand the dynamic factors which influence WTC, the authors believe that focus thus needs to be localized to specific student populations within individual teaching and learning contexts.

WTC in Japan

Over the past two decades the WTC of East Asian learners have been problematised. In particular, an examination of the claim that Confucian heritage cultures can lead to learners experiencing communicative apprehension, i.e., having their WTC impeded, (Shao & Gao, 2014; Ellwood & Nakane, 2009). Despite the cultural factors that do impact students' WTC, there are a number of studies that have shown these factors to be overly generalised (Shao & Gao, 2014). In Japan specifically, the interplay between group-level contextual factors and individual characteristics, including personality and proficiency, were found to account for differences in WTC (King, 2013; Yashima 2002; Yashima et al., 2018).

As mentioned earlier, the distinction between reticence and silence is one of motives (Bao, 2019): where reticence is the inability to participate in communication, and silence is an agentic communicative act. Additionally, with a simple shift in perspective, an observation can be made that problematises how Western students are not silent enough (see Ellwood & Nakane, 2009). What the research elucidates is that Japanese learners, despite their observed nonverbal manners, do desire to participate through oral speech in L2 activities (Yarwood, 2019b; Mynard et al., 2020). Furthermore, an investigation of students' needs and motives rather than observations are of significant importance for pedagogical changes to future language teaching and learning.

Self-Determination Theory and WTC in Online Classrooms

Self-Determination Theory (SDT) has been employed as a framework for exploring student wellbeing and thriving in teaching and learning environments for decades (Ryan & Deci, 2017). The basic premise of SDT lies in the psychological need individuals have for a sense of autonomy, relatedness, and competence. Self-awareness, often through reflective acts, are considered the foundation of agentic behaviours, and it is through self-awareness that individuals are able to self-organise in ways that are consistent with their values and self-endorsed motivations (Ryan & Deci, 2017).

In traditional classroom settings, SDT has been proposed as a core model for addressing language learner agency (Noels, 2009; Yarwood et al., 2019a), L2 WTC (Joe et al., 2017), and supportive classroom climates (Black & Deci, 2000; Joe et al., 2017). However, with the rise of technology being used in language classrooms, and the tendency for online spaces to amplify the difference between 'participating' (characterised by written artifacts) in a class and 'interacting' (characterised by collaborative knowledge building) (Delahunty & Jones, 2014), SDT approaches could also provide a framework to understand WTC in online classrooms.

Research has consistently suggested that students have experienced dissatisfaction with social presence and interactions (Delahunty & Jones, 2014; Bowers & Kumar, 2015; Butz & Stupnisky, 2017; Wang et al., 2019) in their online learning experiences, which in a communicative L2 classroom would only serve to undermine feelings of relatedness and WTC. Wang et al. (2019) suggest that the physical and psychological distance created by the reduced proximity between individuals and their interlocutors is the primary factor in thwarting relatedness during online communicative situations. In their review of the literature on online interactions, Delahunty & Jones (2014) summarised that the "intangible social space of the virtual classroom" tended to be mediated by learners' perceived competence and the quality of interaction between peers, while simultaneously acknowledging that not all learners craved the same sense of community. Despite this, there have been a number of studies that have found that technology-mediated communication can enable learners to interact with each other in social and collaborative ways (Sato & Ballinger, 2016; Peeters, 2019; Lee, 2019; Lee & Lee, 2020) both in and outside the digital classroom. Social factors in these studies highlight how relatedness in the form of interpersonal relationships are greatly mediated by the online contexts.

While a number of studies have focused on asynchronous contexts, there are only a few studies that look into synchronous online learning (Freiermuth & Haung, 2012; Jung et al., 2019). There is significant room for further inquiry on synchronous online language learning contexts; our chapter aims to contribute to that discussion by investigating the role that online spaces have on students' relatedness-needs and WTC.

RAISING AWARENESS IN ONLINE LANGUAGE CLASSROOMS

Background to the Study

In 2019, a team of educators at a medium-sized foreign language university in Japan gathered to participate in an SDT-inspired, action-research project. The aim of this project was to support students' use of English in the university' s self-access learning centre (SALC) through classroom discussions that were designed to raise awareness of learners' beliefs, needs, and strategy usage (Yarwood et al., 2019a). The results showed that the discussion intervention promoted stronger peer communities within the physical classroom. Additionally, discussions within the peer communities fostered self-awareness and more positive perceptions of their speaking competence. Combined, these factors appeared to work in tandem to encourage agentic English use in the SALC for several of the participants.

The spread of COVID saw the university, like many others, manoeuvre to an online platform. Concerns regarding the nature of online interactions in communicative language classrooms were expressed, and strategies to overcome the perceived limitations were discussed among staff. Following the modest success of the intervention in face-to-face classrooms (Yarwood et al., 2019a), modifications were made; a 1st Year Foundational Literacies class was used as a trial for the online iteration of the intervention. The rationale for its implementation included the belief that by actively engaging with the discussion prompts, students would co-construct an understanding of how they learn, using their L2 in both traditional class and in an unfamiliar online classroom. Through these interactions, students' self-awareness of their needs, competencies and communicative behaviours would ideally grow, and be foster by their peers.-

The Intervention

The intervention took place twice a week during the initial segment of each synchronous class. A 10-minute warm-up discussion was conducted in Zoom Breakout rooms with groups of four students. The discussion prompts used were generated by the first author to elicit shared experiences, opinions and strategies for a number of classroom and self-directed learning issues (For a full explanation, see Yarwood et al, 2019a). Each discussion prompt had a main question or statement followed by several follow-up questions to further broaden students' perspectives and scaffold the discussion where necessary (Image 1). Classroom prompts were categorised based on their applicability to a general class environment—irrespective of medium—and the interactions within. Meanwhile, self-directed learning prompts encompassed learner strategies, beliefs, and the learning behaviours that took place outside of physical or digital classroom settings.

Figure 1. An example of a self-directed learning prompt

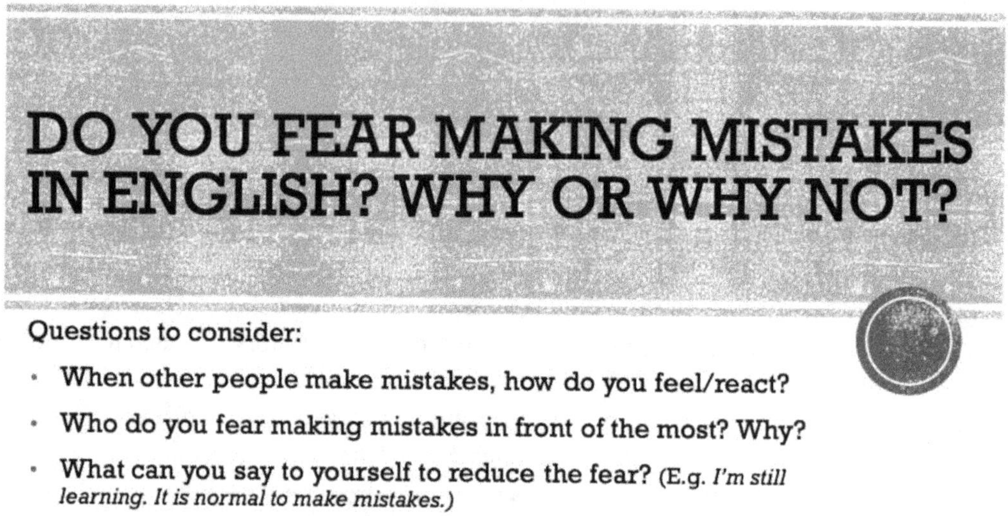

Two primary modifications were made to the original intervention. The first was the addition of online (Zoom) related discussion prompts (Image 2). In total, 19 self-directed learning, 8 online-specific, and 6 general classroom-based prompts were used over the course of a full academic year. Online-specific prompts were defined as prompts that related to the use of and/or interactions within these online environments.

Figure 2. An example of an online-specific prompt

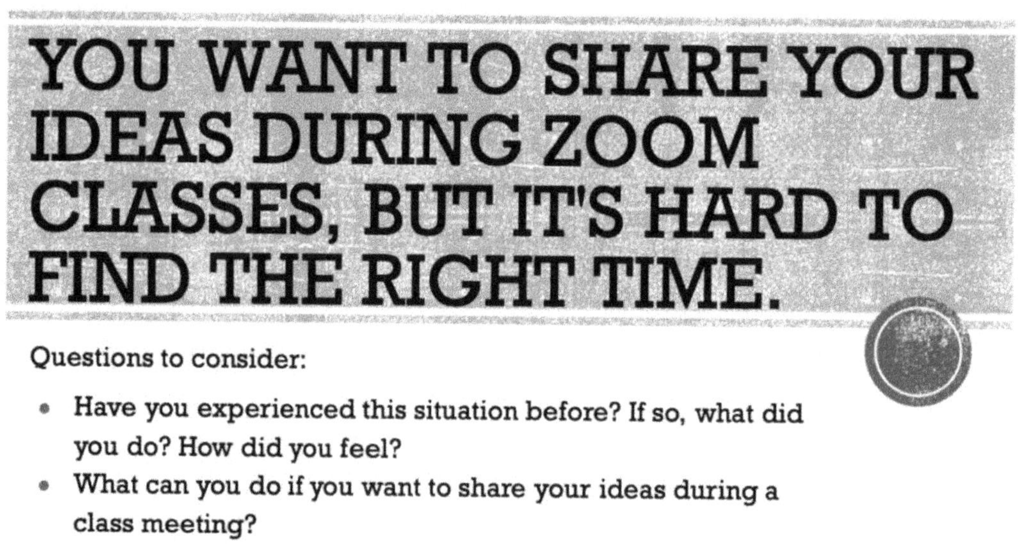

A short reflection written in English and submitted via Google Forms directly after the intervention constituted the second of the two modifications. From the students' perspective, the aim of the reflection was to solidify any new realisations gained from the discussions, while simultaneously allowing them to share potential frustrations with their teachers. The inclusion of the written reflection thereby carried with it a two-fold purpose. First, it provided a timely understanding of how the discussions were influencing the learner' s awareness of their own strengths, weaknesses and learning needs. Second, it was used to help inform prompt selections for subsequent classes.

Students were invited to write their reflection as a journal entry in which they could share any thoughts they had. To guide their writing, the follow questions were included as optional cues:

1. How did your discussion go today?
2. What did you think about the discussion topic?
3. How does this topic connect to your own experience?
4. Did you learn anything new or surprising during your discussion?

Data Collection and Analysis

Data collection took place in two stages during each semester. First, written discussion reflections submitted via Google Forms (N=70) were collected from the 19 members of the class. Meanwhile, the second stage of data collection was derived from students who volunteered to participate in focus groups (N=10) held at the end of the Spring and Autumn semesters. The focus groups lasted for 30 minutes and were primarily conducted in English. Japanese was offered as an alternative to ensure the participants could express themselves without language barriers. Pseudonyms were assigned and audio recordings were transcribed. In cases where Japanese was used, it was translated by the first author before undergoing a bilingual speaker check. All relevant data was assigned descriptive codes (Saldañas, 2013) which were informed by SDT, WTC, and online factors. Thematic analysis took place in line with the primary research question: What are the suppressors of students' WTC in online-mediated discussions?

RESULTS AND DISCUSSION

Based on our findings, there were three main issues that resulted in reduced WTC in online settings. First, there were technical and environmental factors unique to remote learning that led to learner reticence. Specifically, issues with Wi-Fi connectivity caused audio and video disruptions to student participation in discussions. Additional technical issues, such as a lack of an understanding of computers for problem-solving and critical thinking (Cote & Milliner, 2017) led to frustration with online learning that curtailed students' WTC. Moreover, the physical environment where students remotely attended class led to numerous distractions, i.e. ambient noise, (e.g., at home, in public areas, etc.) and a lack of personal discipline (students checking their phones during class).

Second, and to a much greater degree, the lack of a sense of connectivity, i.e., a thwarting of relatedness, led to silence. A significant number of students stated that not meeting their classmates in person made it difficult for them to communicate during class. Students also asserted that their classmates' reluctance to turn on their cameras and/or microphones (which might or might not have been due to technical issues) exacerbated an already existing learner reticence. Additionally, a lack of interaction with peers outside of class, for example, when moving around campus or during extracurricular activities due to being isolated at home, resulted in the thwarting of their sense of relatedness, leading to an agentic use of silence.

As mentioned above, based on findings (Yarwood et al, 2019b; Mynard, 2020) and experiences *a priori*, learners' perceived lack of language ability appears to suppress their WTC. Instead of attempting to communicate with peers, students were reluctant to speak in fear of making mistakes; incidentally, along with the feeling of embarrassment, they avoided communication in class. In other words, there was no evidence of actual negative experiences of learners' mistakes influencing their reticence, but rather the fear of the actualisation of such occurrences. In regard to students who expressed a general sense of shyness or communicative apprehension, a sense of connectivity with their peers appeared to contribute to the dissipation of their shyness or fear to speak; however, this didn't necessarily resolve all WTC issues.

Finally, the notion of confidence did not appear to be a significant factor, as we assumed, in apprehension to communicate. What we found was that students lacked confidence in their perceived linguistic and communicative ability rather than their confidence in the act of speaking. Next we' ll discuss remote learning issues which impacted learners' WTC.

Remote Learning Issues

Technical Issues

A recurrent theme that was out of students' control were Wi-Fi connectivity issues; poor connections acted as an impediment to the flow of communication. Lag obstructed opportunities for student participation by closing active turns before students could interject or catch what was said:

...When my house wifi is not working, the time lag screen and voice [occur], so I can' t catch up [with the] talking contents. – Hana, Spring discussion reflection

I think it is difficult to improve my English skills online, because there are many Wi-Fi problems. – Tamaki, Spring discussion reflection

Problems can expand beyond just missing opportunities to speak, as information deficit may additionally occlude opportunities for students to actively participate in discussions. While not confined to online environments, the possibility of disruptions and distractions one experiences can be daunting. It is not uncommon to be distracted by an insect or even zoning out into space while lost in a daydream. However, in face-to-face settings, teachers may notice such distractions and confirm whether students are following what was said, or a distracted student could easily ask their peers to help catch up on what was missed. Conversely, in an online classroom teachers may not be aware that a student is experiencing connectivity issues, and our findings revealed a complete absence of references to students seeking help from classmates after experiencing technical difficulties. Additionally, being at the mercy of their bandwidth, this loss of agency to remedy the connectivity issues may result in negative affective issues which are not ideal for effective learning.

Environmental Issues

Connectivity issues weren't the only issue in online learning; another issue was the location where students attended class. Due to circumstances beyond the control of students, it appeared that some learners' surroundings may not have been conducive to learning:

Today' s discussion was terrible, because my house so noisy and I can't tell my opinion well. Today' s topic is easy to understand. I couldn't hear other opinions because of my house was noisy. – Soichiro, Autumn discussion reflection

As expressed by the student above, learning at home made the class "terrible" due to their noisy environment; even though the topic was "easy to understand", it was difficult for the student to communicate effectively. Such instances can result in student disengagement from lessons, leading to demotivation (Ushioda & Dörnyei, 2011) and ultimately negatively impact their WTC. It is likely that the pandemic led to a rather particular and possibly unfortunate situation where students and their family members may have also been operating from home; multiple users simultaneously using the Internet could cause the aforementioned connectivity issues. Based on our findings, the spaces in which students attend an online class unequivocally plays a critical role not only in students' WTC, but fundamentally dictates the capability and capacity to communicate, regardless of their motives.

Additionally, there was a general lack of computer literacy: the ability to interact with a computer at an adequate level for creation, communication, and collaboration (see Vasilache, 2016; Murray & Blyth, 2011). Students also expressed a deficit of digital literacy due to insufficient troubleshooting knowledge. We believe this led to frustration with remote learning that curtailed students' WTC as suggested in the students' comments:

I don' t know well yet about how to using a iPad, so I think online is more difficult. – Hana, Spring discussion reflection

In today' s discussion, some of my friends had mechanical trouble so we couldn' t go well. – Tamaki, Spring discussion reflection

Based on studies conducted over the past 10 years, computer and digital literacy issues in Japanese universities have been evident. The literature suggests the issues - sans smartphones - stems from a deficiency in public schools' ability to satisfy Japan's national educational curriculum (Lockley, 2011; Murray & Blyth, 2011; Cote & Milliner, 2017). It is possible that with more developed computer and digital literacy, as well as the implementation of using smartphones as a pedagogical tool, silence and reticence issues could be better mediated. Next, we will shift the primary focus away from the technological and environmental impacts of online education to the learners themselves.

Self-Regulation Issues

In addition to environmental issues that were out of students' control, students also reported that aspects of their learning environment were a distraction, which required them to self-regulate their behaviour. While studying online during the 2020 pandemic, students were generally confined to their home environment. For many students, attending a class from the (un)comfort of their personal classroom—whether it be their dining room table, desk, or bed— disrupted the students' engagement in classes:

We all think it is a little difficult to stay focused, because there are a lot of distractions in my room... – Tamaki, Spring discussion reflection

...When I study online class in home, I relax. So I can' t focus. – Kie, Spring discussion reflection

As shown, students had difficulty focusing in class, which led to disengagement and subsequently affects WTC during lessons. However, a number of students were aware of the issue and came up with solutions to maintain engagement:

There are many obstacles at home. The most different point is that there are no people around me at home. I can concentrate better when there are people around me, so I can solve this problem by turning on the camera during the class. – Mayu, Spring discussion reflection

All of my group mates said we should stretch our bodies and drink something if we cannot stay focus while studying online. – Anon, Spring discussion reflection

Discussed above are how environmental issues unique to learning online manifested in silence and lack of WTC of students. Although some of these environmental issues were somewhat unique to lockdowns (i.e., learning while family members were also learning/working in the same environment), such situations may be commonplace in remote-learning contexts. Consequently, these technical and environmental issues at a deeper level impeded the relatedness between learners, which was a significantly more prominent factor regarding silence and their WTC.

Relatedness

The sense of connection developed between classmates plays a significant role in the interactions they have with each other. In traditional classroom environments, freedom of movement before, during, and after classes; the ability to engage in side-conversations, and physical proximity are just a few of the factors that encourage positive relationships between peers. Several of our participants acknowledged the importance of these non-class related interactions:

Because we haven't met directly yet so it is natural not to feel close to our classmates. I think doing homework together or talking with our classmates in our free time is good for making closer connections. – Anon, Spring Discussion Reflection

I think we don't close well because we just talk about study on zoom. We haven't meet directly and [had a] conversation. Therefore, I think we have to talk with classmates in Japanese using LINE or talk on the phone. – Hana, Spring discussion Reflection

Looking at these two comments, it is apparent that the students perceive online classes as limiting their ability to interact freely with their classmates in a way that promotes deeper connections. For freshman students in particular, university life is where they expect to make new friends and enjoy the learning process. These quintessential experiences which are grounded so completely in physical campus spaces are evidenced by the students' insistence that "to feel close" to each other requires being able to "meet directly" in order to "do homework together" or discussing topics that are unrelated to study or the use of English. In this way, the affordances provided by campuses and classrooms have functioned as part of learners' proximal social contexts (Ryan & Deci, 2017), in which notions of optimal communicative interactions have been established in relation to physical proximity. These notions of what is best for communicative interactions have been in place since the beginning of their educational careers; it is unsurprising that adapting to online learning spaces disrupts their sense of relatedness.

Compared to traditional classrooms, communication in online environments is significantly limited with teachers mediating many of the opportunities, thereby reducing learners' autonomy to decide where, when and with whom they wish to communicate with. It is perhaps unalarming then that an overwhelming majority of students in this study expressed a desire to return to traditional settings. Many of the comments gathered revealed a prevalent mindset had formed among the students that placed an importance on face-to-face interactions:

For me, my most memorable discussion topic is "You don't feel close to your classmates" because at that discussion, we just talked about our online class and class on campus. And we all want to see each other on campus and we feel that online class may make us not close to each other. – Hisako, Autumn focus group

Our group's opinion was we can't share our emotions and feelings online. Actually it is true because I can't keep conversation easily online. I'd like to talk with my classmates directly. – Anon, Spring discussion reflection

As implied earlier, the lack of physical proximity in online interactions appeared to go against what learners are used to, requiring a recalibration in their understanding of what it means to be a member of a language class capable of sharing "emotions and feelings online". In a way, students need to set new psychological horizons (Ryan & Deci, 2017) in which they envision new modes of communication, engagement, and interactions that don't prioritise a physical presence over a digital one. Envisioning new modes of communication and how to engage actively in these new spaces may require classroom environments to undergo a social and cultural change. However, this change cannot occur without learners first becoming aware of their language-learning needs and determining which actions they can intentionally employ to affect this cultural revolution around online classroom communication.

One aspect of envisioning the possibilities of active communication in online settings is considering the immediate, physical settings students join online spaces from before attending to aspects of the digital space. Joining online classes from distracting private locations or which fail to put students into a communicative mindset may have a negative effect on peer connectivity, as suggested by the following statements:

We all think it is a little difficult to stay focused, because there are a lot of distractions in my room. Sometimes I feel bored, but I try to stay focused. – Tamaki, Spring discussion reflection

All of our members lose focus in the class which we don't have to turn on the camera. So I realised that we need the eyes to see us if we want to concentrate on our studies. – Hana, Spring discussion reflection

The last comment in particular reveals how in addition to the physical settings, learners also make deliberate decisions about the platform functions they use to participate in discussions. The need for accountability in order to concentrate on communicative tasks provides a small insight into the minds of the students, and the above comment was not the only one that linked the turning off of web cameras to a lack of engagement with class tasks, or the enabling of distracted behaviours:

I become sleepy when I [am] studying online and I can see the smartphone all time. If I should turn on the camera while I [am] studying, I'm not able to sleep because everyone can see me. I have to turn off the smartphone. – Hana, Spring discussion reflection

I agree with the topic [on focusing during online classes] because there are many obstacles at home. The most different point is that there are no people around me at home. I can concentrate better when there are people around me, so I can solve this problem by turning on the camera during the class. – Mayu, Spring discussion reflection

Being unable to see interlocutors creates additional factors that may thwart positive-relationship building. Just as body language can signal disinterest, it is possible that the act of turning off cameras signalled an intention to disengage. Furthermore, without a clear view of conversational partners, a sense of hesitancy may develop in which students avoid speaking to those they perceive as being uninterested, resulting in agentic silence. For language learners, initiating a conversation in an L2 requires courage; starting a conversation with a screen devoid of reactions and visual cues just makes it all the more difficult. Sadly, silence in the form of deliberate disengagement facilitated by static images appeared to have persisted throughout the entire academic year:

But I think only English class I want to see my classmates in university because [as] Saki said, in second semester almost all classmate turn off camera [so] I couldn't see anyone. But I think I want to talk to my classmates. Well, I want to see [them]. So I think I want to take English class in university. – Rina, Autumn focus group

It is clear from this statement, that group cohesion and feelings of affiliation were thwarted in online classroom discussions - whether influenced by shyness or apathy and this resulted in volitional silence. While hesitancy to engage in dialogue could be perceived as reticence, ongoing observations from one student, which spanned the duration of the intervention, suggest that students perceived linguistic competence may not have played as great a role in subverting WTC:

Today's discussion was not great. Some of them were still too shy to talk. I tried to guide them but it didn't work. I said you could speak Japanese if you don't know how to speak in English but still no answers. The whole atmosphere was a little bit embarrassing as always. – Miho, Spring discussion reflection

Miho's comment highlights how an offer to use L1 were insufficient to elicit WTC. In addition, her persistent attempts to guide her peers in their discussion were frequently rejected:

There were two new students so I introduced myself. No one reacted. It was bad start but I thought they are shy. So I started to share my ideas but no one reacted. I said, "Anyone want to answer the next question?" They kept quiet. I got mad a little bit. I just wanted them to react and say something. – Miho, Autumn discussion reflection

This was not always the case. During later discussion reflections Miho explained that while her classmates were shy, sometimes when she took charge, they did demonstrate WTC. The need for a leader during class discussions appeared as a salient feature in Miho's comments:

I have to be the leader, to just tell them what we should do and just lead them and give a topic to [use in the] discussion.

From these findings, it is possible that initial interactions bring with them a degree of shyness that stems from being with peers of unknown qualities. These unknowns could be exacerbated by individuals' unwillingness to show their faces or take risks in front of "strangers". Disengagement can become habitual: the longer an individual acts in a disengaged manner, the harder it is to summon the courage to re-enter an established communicative routine. Moreover, the communicative apprehension generated by these interactional situations may prevent learners from asking questions to get to know each other or exchanging ideas - the groundwork for relatedness. The cultural phenomenon of deferral to a leader or seniority during communicative tasks may also have a role to play in the silence witnessed in many of the online discussions. In the case of Miho and her peers, once a relationship had been established, and the other students accepted Miho as a leader, she was able to elicit responses from them. However, the downside of this habit formation meant that unless Miho prompted, verbal engagement was not self-initiated.

Competence

While relatedness and cultural factors may be primary factors in suppressing WTC, there was evidence of students demonstrating reticence due to doubts in their ability to answer questions accurately or without mistakes. Despite consistent exposure to a variety of discussion topics related to their own learning and some familiarity with their peers, this lack of confidence appeared to persist into the second semester with multiple students expressing similar thoughts as to why active speaking did not take place during small group discussions:

Today's discussion theme was silence during the small group discussion. I noticed that there was a lot of silence. I think the embarrassment of making mistakes causes silence. It is important to speak without fear or making mistakes. – Tamaki, Autumn discussion reflection

We could start discussion smoothly. But there were silence a little it. I [thought] the reason of silence is that we cannot answer the question and don't have confidence. If I don't know how to answer the question, I would be silence. But I think it is bad, so I would try to answer the question as soon as possible. – Momiji, Autumn discussion reflection

Here we see linguistic or communicative competency entwine with learners' lack of confidence. These forms of reticence occurred for several reasons including, a perceived lack of vocabulary or ability to express ideas in an understandable manner, a lack of familiarity with the topic, or difficulties in elaborating on their ideas.

The first of these competency concerns manifested in a general hesitancy to actively communicate in part due to the responsibility for successful communication being self-imposed:

Because I couldn't explain something that I thought [to] myself, so they couldn't understand it [my opinion] – Momiji, Autumn reflection discussion

It was not good because I made silent time, so I should have told that I need more time to think. I feel fear when speaking English because my English skills are poor and I worry about other people's reactions. – Mayu, Autumn reflection discussion

While students' concerns of being understood are valid, the self-imposed responsibility for ensuring understanding goes against the co-constructed nature of dialogue in society in which conversational partners should work together to successfully communicate.

To mitigate this perceived lack of communicative competence, students expressed the desire for time to carefully formulate their ideas and structure them prior to output opportunities. While understandable, this desire for time to construct mistake-free utterances may only serve to reinforce feelings of communicative apprehension when confronted with spontaneous interactions or conversational tangents. Rather than spending time to construct utterances, students would benefit from using preparation time to brainstorm their ideas about in-class discussion topics since in addition to a perceived lack of linguistic resources, several of the discussion reflections across the academic year revealed that difficulties in generating or elaborating on ideas posed a significant barrier to engaging with peers in the online discussions. As one student stated:

If I don't know how to answer the question, I would be silent. But I think it is bad, so I should try to answer as soon as possible. – Momiji, Autumn discussion reflection

Rather than assuming students don't have opinions and experiences to share about topics directly related to their learning, it is possible that the lack of "ideas" derives from a fear of not having an appropriate response. This conclusion was evidenced by students who expressed that not knowing "how to answer the question" would result in self-imposed silence. Alternatively, expanding on the ideas already presented, may have posed a hurdle for many students:

I cannot talk because I don't have an idea, so it was difficult. Our ideas are mostly same, so we cannot extend discussion. – Taiga, Spring discussion reflection

意見が対立したり、あとオンライン授業に関するトピックの時は結構デイスカッションが盛り上がった。なんか、*if everyone says same opinion, the discussion is over.* うん、そう。対立意見あれば、盛り上がれる。*[When there are different opinions, like in the topic about online classes, then we are all pumped. Like, if everyone says same opinion, the discussion is over. Yeah, so if the opinions are different, we can get excited.] – Risako, Autumn focus group*

As suggested, discussions in which each participant has a similar thought can create problems for language learners who haven't developed a repertoire of strategies necessary for expanding on a single topic. Providing a variety of responses may certainly be preferable, but without exposure to new perspectives through personal experience, media or research, it is not likely students would be able to produce such diverse responses. Competencies in rephrasing, summarising, questioning, and experience-sharing would provide learners with a greater repertoire to pull from in order to bring vitality to otherwise monotonous discussions.

IMPLICATIONS

As our study shows, an intention and willingness to communicate exists within the students, and while the desire to communicate in face-to-face situations was overwhelming, there was no evidence to suggest that WTC did not exist in online contexts. However, situational factors involving technology, perceived communicative competence and group cohesion presented themselves as potential suppressors of WTC in online contexts. To deal with these undoubtedly intertwined factors, we would like to propose that forms of technological training, as well as online communication training be fully integrated into online curricula. As MacIntyre (1988) suggested, intention must combine with opportunities to produce communicative behaviours in L2 learners. However, without the knowledge, strategies, and safe environments in which to practice their new skills, learners may not be equipped to create their own opportunities, irrespective of their communicative intentions. The development of skills needed to take initiative are therefore crucial (Yashima et al., 2018) for enhancing WTC. Due to the unique nature of each classroom, the training options outlined here should be considered, explored and modified based on practitioner's own localised contexts, technological expertise and student characteristics.

Technology Training

New technology brings with it challenges for learners and practitioners alike. As demonstrated previously, technological issues can and do cause misunderstandings or limit the information learners have access to. As such, the authors would like to raise practitioners' awareness about the possible limitations of devices and the communicative platforms or apps associated with them: video-conferencing, direct messaging software, etc. Utilising different forms of technology in conjunction with others (e.g., viewing a web browser while in Zoom) or even navigating the functions within a specific platform (e.g., Zoom's chat, camera, screen share, etc.) can prove frustrating. Therefore, it would be in the best interests of students and practitioners to understand the limitations of the technology they have access to while co-constructing viable, context-specific strategies to ease these limitations. To this end, the implementation of group assignments that focus on technology-use and promote out-of-class contact should be included as an integral component to an online curriculum that aims to be effective in encouraging WTC. In this study, while students were cognisant of the benefits of communicating with each other outside of class using social media and direct messaging apps, to the authors' knowledge, they did not take the initiative to do so. Group assignments that take advantage of popular messaging platforms could be designed to encourage in-group troubleshooting for dealing with the limitations of assigned devices, software, platforms and apps. Once relationships in which students are able to rely on each other for support are established, it may become easier for them to reach out to their peers for help with not only technology, but with communicative tasks as well.

Addressing a separate technological factor, despite being aware of the positive influence cameras have on their ability to learn in class, cameras were frequently turned off. So, it is suggested that practitioners design learning activities that approach camera use for both language teaching and awareness-raising purposes. For example, a simple 'compare and contrast' activity where students have a conversation with their cameras off and then again with their cameras on; students can then list the advantages and disadvantages camera use has when speaking with an interlocutor. Cameras can also be used as a pedagogical tool for doing activities that incorporate body language and facial expressions such as charades. The main benefits of these activities are in establishing cameras as devices for generating feelings of accountability and connectedness through visual cues.

Each of these suggestions still need to be modified and trialled in individual contexts. However, it is believed that these suggestions can provide learners with a greater awareness of the role technology plays in their WTC. Without an understanding of how communication is mediated through the technology they are using, learners may be ill-equipped to deal with potential problems by themselves. However, through the co-construction of shared digital knowledge, learners can collaboratively overcome any issues that arise in online learning spaces, while concurrently developing a safe, supportive online classroom culture.

Communication Training

Our results showed that students' self-imposed responsibility to contribute to peer-to-peer discussions in a mistake-free and original manner undermined WTC. Additionally, the desire to respond in ways perceived as acceptable (by what criteria is still to be explored), suggests that learners' perception of L2 communication is somewhat removed from the co-constructed nature of L2 communication espoused by the sociocultural turn in modern language education. Educators may thus need to be aware of any potential conceptual differences in how they view communicative tasks and how the students perceive them. In online contexts, this conception must be even more clearly defined as technology heavily mediates interactions by augmenting some forms of communication and limiting others.

Online platforms have a range of functions including chat, emoticon and screen sharing; learners can be trained to use each in optimal ways to facilitate the sharing of ideas and opinions. For example, in situations where learners find themselves unable to translate their ideas into their L2, the chat function could be used to share the words they want to use in order for collaborative learning to take place. The physical evidence of ideas and opinions left behind in the chat could also be used as reference points for later discussions. This means that learners would be able to reuse the words and expressions used to assist in increasing their sense of linguistic competency. For language learners struggling to find the vocabulary and grammar necessary to express their ideas, screen-sharing images as examples or using the annotation capabilities of the various conferencing platforms could support their output. At the very least, it can provide a stimulus for groups to co-construct meaning.

Should technical or device limitations prevent camera usage, then the chat functions along with emoticons could act as a go-between to demonstrate a learner's active engagement with either what is being discussed, or to signal confusion, agreement or amusement. Such acts, even when cameras are actively being used, are non-face threatening and should be promoted to supplement learners' WTC. Additionally, such low-risk behaviours in online discussions could bolster the speaker's enthusiasm to speak since the use of these functions could be considered the online equivalent of active listening body language. For students who perceive communicative competence to be low, these simple strategies could provide them with both a sense of safety and confidence in their ability to actively participate.

Finally, strategic use of chat functions and emoticons carries with it additional benefits in terms of relatedness. Should learners view their peers as being active respondents to their speech acts, those views may generate feelings of affiliation, thereby contributing to a positive culture of language learning and use within the online classroom.

CONCLUSION

Students' futures will be increasingly online; therefore, language learning classrooms should adapt to the benefit of students' ability to communicate effectively and be aware of the affordances and limitations at hand. In this study, it was found that the major factors related to WTC were dynamic and situational. Physical and digital influences on remote learning environments were detrimental to students' ability to participate in classes. These remote learning environments in turn affected learners' sense of relatedness by reducing the sense of physical and social proximity resulting in volition silence. Students' perception of their language ability was also shown to be detrimental to their ability to participate in classes.

Unfortunately, some of the technical setbacks of learning online cannot be remedied as well as certain situational dispositions. However, through activities that not only raise intervention-awareness, but utilise technology and the environment, students' WTC can be activated in class. Regarding learners' perceived confidence, these interventions primarily focus on support through the teaching of conversational strategies - notably strategies unique to online communication. Said strategies serve to highlight the benefits of peer-support (e.g., leadership, encouragement, troubleshooting technological issues, and the co-constructed learning environments) of the language-learning classroom as a place to make and learn from mistakes, rather than a place to avoid them. Furthermore, the benefits of supportive peer networks are not specific to online environments; learning online, however, greatly thwarted group cohesion, which manifested in a reduction of learners' WTC.

Despite the presence of factors that suppressed WTC, the authors believe that with adequate support and scaffolding aimed at facilitating relatedness between students - both in and out of class - students can experience a sense of belonging, competency, and awareness which will engender higher levels of WTC.

REFERENCES

Bao, D. (2019). The place of silence in second language acquisition. *English Language Teaching & Research*, *1*(1), 26–42. doi:10.33474/eltar-j.v1i1.4771

Bennett, P. A., & Yarwood, A. (2021). A Case for Scaffolding Self-reflection. *Pan SIG Journal*, *6*(1), 55–64.

Black, A. E., & Deci, E. L. (2000). The effects of instructors' autonomy support and students' autonomous motivation on learning organic chemistry: A self-determination theory perspective. *Science Education*, *84*(6), 740–756. doi:10.1002/1098-237X(200011)84:6<740::AID-SCE4>3.0.CO;2-3

Bowers, J., & Kumar, P. (2015). Students' perceptions of teaching and social presence: A comparative analysis of face-to-face and online learning environments. *International Journal of Web-Based Learning and Teaching Technologies, 10*(1), 27–44. doi:10.4018/ijwltt.2015010103

Butz, N. T., & Stupnisky, R. H. (2017). Improving student relatedness through an online discussion intervention: The application of self-determination theory in synchronous hybrid programs. *Computers & Education, 114*, 117–138. doi:10.1016/j.compedu.2017.06.006

Cote, T. J., & Milliner, B. (2017). Preparing Japanese Students' Digital Literacy for Study Abroad: Is More Training Needed? *The JALT CALL Journal, 13*(3), 187–197. doi:10.29140/jaltcall.v13n3.218

Delahunty, J., Verenikina, I., & Jones, P. (2014). Socio-emotional connections: Identity, belonging and learning in online interactions. A literature review. *Technology, Pedagogy and Education, 23*(2), 243–265. doi:10.1080/1475939X.2013.813405

Dörnyei, Z., & Ushioda, E. (2011). *Teaching and researching: Motivation*. Routledge.

Ellwood, C., & Nakane, I. (2009). Privileging of speech in EAP and mainstream university classrooms: A critical evaluation of participation. *TESOL Quarterly, 43*(2), 203–230. doi:10.1002/j.1545-7249.2009.tb00165.x

Freiermuth, M. R., & Huang, H. C. (2012). Bringing Japan and Taiwan closer electronically: A look at an intercultural online synchronic chat task and its effect on motivation. *Language Teaching Research, 16*(1), 61–88. doi:10.1177/1362168811423341

Fushino, K. (2010). Causal relationships between communication confidence, beliefs about group work, and willingness to communicate in foreign language group work. *TESOL Quarterly, 44*(4), 700–724. doi:10.5054/tq.2010.235993

Gregersen, T., MacIntyre, P. D., & Meza, M. D. (2014). The motion of emotion: Idiodynamic case studies of learners' foreign language anxiety. *Modern Language Journal, 98*(2), 574–588. doi:10.1111/modl.12084

Joe, H. K., Hiver, P., & Al-Hoorie, A. H. (2017). Classroom social climate, self-determined motivation, willingness to communicate, and achievement: A study of structural relationships in instructed second language settings. *Learning and Individual Differences, 53*, 133–144. doi:10.1016/j.lindif.2016.11.005

Jung, Y., Kim, Y., Lee, H., Cathey, R., Carver, J., & Skalicky, S. (2019). Learner perception of multimodal synchronous computer-mediated communication in foreign language classrooms. *Language Teaching Research, 23*(3), 287–309. doi:10.1177/1362168817731910

Kato, S., & Mynard, J. (2015). *Reflective dialogue: Advising in language learning*. Routledge. doi:10.4324/9781315739649

King, J. (2013). *Silence in the second language classroom*. Palgrave Macmillan. doi:10.1057/9781137301482

Lee, J. S. (2019). EFL students' views of willingness to communicate in the extramural digital context. *Computer Assisted Language Learning, 32*(7), 692–712. doi:10.1080/09588221.2018.1535509

Lee, J. S., & Lee, K. (2020). Affective factors, virtual intercultural experiences, and L2 willingness to communicate in in-class, out-of-class, and digital settings. *Language Teaching Research*, *24*(6), 813–833. doi:10.1177/1362168819831408

Lockley, T. (2011). Japanese students' experience of ICT and other technology prior to university: A survey. *The JALT CALL Journal*, *7*(1), 93–102. doi:10.29140/jaltcall.v7n1.110

MacIntyre, P. D., & Charos, C. (1996). Personality, attitudes, and affect as predictors of second language communication. *Journal of Language and Social Psychology*, *15*(1), 3–26. doi:10.1177/0261927X960151001

MacIntyre, P. D., & Doucette, J. (2010). Willingness to communicate and action control. *System*, *38*(2), 161–171. doi:10.1016/j.system.2009.12.013

MacIntyre, P. D., & Legatto, J. J. (2011). A dynamic system approach to willingness to communicate: Developing an idiodynamic method to capture rapidly changing affect. *Applied Linguistics*, *32*(2), 149–171. doi:10.1093/applin/amq037

MacIntyre, P. D., Clément, R., Dörnyei, Z., & Noels, K. A. (1998). Conceptualizing willingness to communicate in a L2: A situational model of L2 confidence and affiliation. *Modern Language Journal*, *82*(4), 545–562. doi:10.1111/j.1540-4781.1998.tb05543.x

McCroskey, J. C., & Baer, J. E. (1985). *Willingness to communicate: The construct and its measurement.* Paper presented at the annual convention of the speech communication association, Denver, CO.

McCroskey, J. C., & Richmond, V. P. (1987). Willingness to communicate. In J. C. McCroskey & J. A. Daly (Eds.), *Personality and interpersonal communication* (pp. 129–155). Sage.

Murray, A., & Blyth, A. (2011). A survey of Japanese university students' computer literacy levels. *The JALT CALL Journal*, *7*(3), 307–318. doi:10.29140/jaltcall.v7n3.124

Mynard, J., Burke, M., Hooper, D., Kushida, B., Lyon, P., Sampson, R., & Taw, P. (2020). *Dynamics of a social language learning community: Beliefs, membership and identity*. Multilingual Matters.

Myskow, G., Bennett, P. A., Yoshimura, H., Gruendel, K., Marutani, T., Hano, K., & Li, T. (2018). Fostering collaborative autonomy: The roles of cooperative and collaborative learning. *Relay Journal*, *1*(2), 360–381. doi:10.37237/relay/010212

Noels, K. A. (2009). The Internalisation of Language Learning into the Self and Social Identity. In *Motivation, language identity and the L2 self* (pp. 295–313). Multilingual Matters. doi:10.21832/9781847691293-016

Peeters, W. (2019). The peer interaction process on Facebook: A social network analysis of learners' online conversations. *Education and Information Technologies*, *24*(5), 1–28. doi:10.100710639-019-09914-2

Ryan, R. M., & Deci, E. L. (2017). *Self-determination theory: Basic psychological needs in motivation, development, and wellness*. Guilford Publications. doi:10.1521/978.14625/28806

Saldaña, J. (2013). *The coding manual for qualitative researchers*. Sage Publications.

Sato, M., & Ballinger, S. (2016). *Peer interaction and second language learning: Pedagogical potential and research agenda*. John Benjamins. doi:10.1075/lllt.45

Shao, Q., & Gao, X. A. (2016). Reticence and willingness to communicate (WTC) of East Asian language learners. *System, 63*, 115–120. doi:10.1016/j.system.2016.10.001

Dornyei, Z., & Ushioda, E. (2011). *Teaching and researching motivation.* Longman.

Vasilache, S. (2016). Student perspectives of computer literacy education in an international environment. *Universal Journal of Educational Research, 4*(6), 1426–1431.

Wang, C., Hsu, H., & Bonem, E, M., Moss, J, D., Yu S., Nelson D, B., & Levesque-Bristol, C. (2019). Need satisfaction and need dissatisfaction: A comparative study of online and face-to-face learning contexts. *Computers in Human Behavior, 95*, 114–125.

Yarwood, A., Rose-Wainstock, C., & Lees, M. (2019a). Fostering English-use in a SALC through a discussion-based classroom intervention. *Studies in Self-Access Learning Journal, 10*(4), 256–378.

Yarwood, A., & Lorentzen, A., Wallingford, & A., Wongsarnpigoon, I. (2019b). Exploring Basic Psychological Needs in a Language Learning Center. Part 2: The autonomy-supportive nature and limitations of a SALC. *Relay Journal, 2*(1), 236–250.

Yashima, T. (2002). Willingness to communicate in a second language: The Japanese EFL context. *Modern Language Journal, 86*(1), 54–66.

Yashima, T. (2012). Willingness to communicate: Momentary volition that results in L2 behaviour. In S. Mercer, S. Ryan, & M. Williams (Eds.), *Psychology for language learning: Insights from research, theory and practice* (pp. 119–135). Palgrave Macmillan.

Yashima, T., MacIntyre, P. D., & Ikeda, M. (2018). Situated willingness to communicate in an L2: Interplay of individual characteristics and context. *Language Teaching Research, 22*(1), 115–137.

KEY TERMS AND DEFINITIONS

Communicative Apprehension: The hesitancy to speak in an L2 due to a fear of mistakes.

Competence: The feeling of effectiveness and mastery in doing an action (e.g., speaking in an L2).

Online Classrooms: A learning environment that takes place via video conferencing platforms and possibly supported by learning management systems, and other software.

Relatedness: The connection an individual feels with members of a group.

Reticence: The result of a communication breakdown and/or a deficit of communicative competence ranging from a choice to avoid communication to the complete inability to participate in communicative L2 activities.

Self-Determination Theory (SDT): A theory of human motivation developed by Ryan & Deci over the past 40 years, stating that three basic psychological needs (autonomy, relatedness, and competence) must be met for individuals to flourish.

Silence: The result of a self-endorsed, non-verbal communication strategy.

Willingness to Communicate (WTC): Autonomous verbal communication in a language learning classroom.

Chapter 13
Exploring the Shaping of English Language Teacher Practices While Working With Refugees and Asylum Seekers During the COVID-19 Pandemic

Gary Motteram
University of Manchester, UK

Susan Dawson
University of Manchester, UK

Richard Fay
University of Manchester, UK

Andres Mora
Caritas Refugee Education, UK

Francesco Leoni
Caritas Refugee Education, UK

ABSTRACT

This chapter reports on a project which began during the first wave of the COVID-19 pandemic in the UK. The project supported a group of UK-based ESOL (English for Speakers of Other Languages) teachers and volunteers as the pandemic forced them to move from face-to-face to online teaching with refugees and asylum seekers. Using an ecological perspective, the authors explored the different possibilities for action that the teachers and volunteers perceive in the ever-changing pandemic environment and consider how language teacher practices and the achievement of organisational aims have been shaped, and in turn are shaping, online teaching. It concludes by considering how the practices developed for online teaching might now shape teaching as it returns, to a large extent, to face-to-face.

DOI: 10.4018/978-1-7998-8717-1.ch013

INTRODUCTION

The Covid-19 pandemic has changed the world in many ways, including teaching of all types in all parts of the world. For many teachers, this meant a rapid move into an online world that many had not previously experienced, or experienced so intensely, and a steep learning curve to come to terms with the nature of online teaching. This chapter reports a project that started in June 2020 whilst the UK was experiencing the first wave of the global COVID-19 pandemic. It involved teachers and volunteers working for a charity, Caritas Refugee Education, which amongst other things provides support services and education to refugees and asylum seekers who live in the Greater Manchester area of the UK. These English to Speakers of Other Languages (ESOL) colleagues were supported by language teacher education specialists at the Manchester Institute of Education (MIE), University of Manchester, UK.

Caritas Refugee Education (CRE) works alongside refugees and asylum seekers residing in the north-west region of the UK, to support their well-being and processes of settling in the UK. They do this by providing English language courses delivered in a welcoming community environment, mentoring into further education and employment, and wrap-around well-being services. Students typically come from a variety of backgrounds, both demographically, professionally and in terms of their life experiences. About 50% of them come from East Africa (primarily Sudan, Ethiopia, and Eritrea) and a further 45% come from the Middle East (Syria, Yemen, Lebanon, and Iran) (Leoni & Mora, 2021). The remainder come from diverse contexts including Central and South America, and West Africa. Some of them have little to no formal education of any kind, while others have professional or academic qualifications from their home countries and have worked in skilled roles before coming to the UK.

MIE has a long history of teacher education for Teachers English to Speakers of Other Languages (TESOL). Members of the team have a particular interest in online teaching. For a number of years now, they have been working on exploring ways of supporting teachers at a distance using mobile technologies. As many of the CRE students had limited access to technology and low quality internet access, it was thought that practices learned through these earlier projects might be useful. We had also undertaken a recent project with teachers who are refugees living in Jordan (Motteram, Dawson & Al-Masri, 2020) and engaged in earlier years in projects with EAL (English as an Additional Language) teachers (Beaumont & O'Brien, 2000). Institution colleagues also have experience in other areas relevant to this project including ecological thinking as applied to the shaping influences on educational and other developing practices (e.g., Fay & Stelma, 2016; Stelma & Fay, 2014, 2019; Stelma, Fay & Zhou, 2013; Stelma & Kostoulas, 2021); and language education and refugees (e.g., Holmes, Fay & Andrews, 2017).

BACKGROUND

Defining Our Terms

The terms *asylum seeker*, *immigrant*, *migrant*, and *refugee* are often used interchangeably, and/or confusingly, thereby obscuring differences usefully identified in the movements of people around the world. And with additional terms such as *people of refugee background* now being promoted, the terminological arena is somewhat congested (Douglas, Cetron & Spiegel, 2019). The imprecise, unclear, or inappropriate use of terms can also lead to misrepresentation of the realities in receiving countries. In this article, while acknowledging the disparity of definitions and the often political associations of the different terms, we use asylum seekers and refugees. These are the terms most commonly used by practitioners in the UK ESOL (English to Speakers of Other Languages) sector and by Caritas Refugee Education, the charity where the language teacher participants in this study are based.

ESOL for Refugees in the UK

In the UK, funding of language support for refugees started in 1966, and was directed initially at schools' provision (NALDIC, 2015). Early support, termed Section 11 funding because it was a part of Home Office legislation, was provided to local authorities and was initially used to set up local language centres, or withdrawal classes in mainstream schools. Following criticism of this provision, in 1986 language centres and withdrawal became in-class language support. In 1999, Section 11 funding was replaced by the Department for Education and Employment (DfEE) Ethnic Minority Achievement Grant (EMAG), but in 2003, this became part of mainstream school funding and specific language provision has largely disappeared (Simpson (2019).

Usually referred to as English to Speakers of Other Languages (ESOL), provision for adults has always been much less certain and has become "a fragmented field" (Simpson, 2012, cited in Simpson, 2019, p. 28). Funding has decreased overall and is targeted at specific initiatives like skills provision following on from *Skills for Life* set up and run by New Labour, which included a specific ESOL provision, or around certain groups, e.g., the Syrian Refugees Resettlement Programme, or the Ex-Gratia Scheme for Afghan interpreters (Gov.uk, 2020).

An important part of the provision for ESOL in the UK has been the charity sector, increasingly picking up on the shortfall in the further and adult education sector as funding has been reduced. The involvement of charities started in the 1960s and 1970s and was a part of the growth of social movements around that time and went alongside the provision of language classes for children described above (Podziewska, 2014). As is emphasised in most writing in this area (Furlong & Hunt, 2009; Simpson, 2012), the informal sector fills in gaps when the state sector providers have no capacity, or offer flexibility to groups who cannot for various reasons attend funded classes, as Simpson (2012) argues:

Small charities or faith-based organisations often seem to be the only organisations which are able to meet the needs of those who cannot access more mainstream provision. (p. 39)

This provision varies in quality, but the best provision can be the best form of responsive, respectful and community engaged offering (Podziewska, 2014).

Technological Perspectives

The use of technology for language learning has been an important contributor to our understandings of technology use in education. The broad needs of people learning languages to explore different skills—speaking, listening, reading and writing—has meant that a language teacher who is interested in this area needs to develop a broad range of skills with different digital tools (Motteram, 2013). Developing this wide range of skills can be seen as a barrier, alongside long-held beliefs that technology does not 'improve' learning.

Many teachers have developed their skills; however, a lot depends on the opportunities that are available in different contexts. It was recognised in the further education sector that digital skills of both teachers and the students needed enhancing (Blunkett, Halfon & Pember, 2021) and the Education and Training Foundation have created guidance and other materials to enhance skills (https://www.et-foundation.co.uk/supporting/edtech-support/).

We also see the influence of demographics, where more teachers now belong to a generation that are referred to as 'digital residents' (White & Cornu, 2011). We can come across some very high-tech classrooms in almost any part of the world, but there are a lot more places where access is either limited or non-existent. Because so many ESOL classrooms are a part of the non-formal sector, they are not likely to be highly equipped (El-Metoui & Graham-Brown (2021).

Another part of the context that needs to be considered is learners' access to technologies in their personal lives, in terms of both hardware and software, as well as access to the internet. We need to be aware of the fact that in terms of their age profile, they may be seen as digital residents, but the varied backgrounds of refugees and asylum seekers means that general levels of digital literacy may vary greatly. There is a need to develop the relevant digital literacies to access services in the countries where they now reside. In countries like the UK, without this access, and the skills to manipulate them, basic services are often not accessible. Vollmer (2020).

Ecological Perspectives

In this chapter, we use an ecological perspective as both a conceptual lens and an analytical tool to explore the teachers' developing understanding of their online language teaching practices during the pandemic. This perspective draws on the work of educational psychologists such as Gibson (1979), Bronfenbrenner (1979), and Young, DePalma & Garrett (2002) who were concerned with understanding the relationship between an individual and their environment. More directly it builds on the work of Stelma and colleagues (Fay & Stelma, 2016; Stelma & Fay, 2014, 2019; Stelma, Fay & Zhou, 2013; Stelma & Kostoulas, 2021) who have continued to develop ideas and concepts initially proposed by these educational psychologists. In particular, it uses the constructs of shaping influences, affordances and intentionalities to explore what shapes the CRE teachers' different approaches and attitudes towards the use of technology in the online environment, and how in turn, that online environment shapes teaching and learning during the ongoing pandemic.

In this chapter, following the lead of the aforementioned work by Gibson (1979), Bronfenbrenner (1979), and Young, DePalma and Garrett (2002), we focus on the mutuality between an individual and their environment, and between a group and the environment. This mutual relationship is a bilateral, ongoing and complex process where an individual and / or group interacts with their environment and both shapes, and is shaped, by that environment. In the case of the CRE ecology, this mutuality, as it pertains to this chapter, is illustrated in Figure 1 which emphasises our focus on teachers, volunteers and students in CRE within the UK context rather than present the full, interconnected ecology. These teachers, volunteers, and students are both shaped by, and in turn shape, the aims, objectives, ethos, and practices of CRE, which in turn is shaped by, and shapes, the broader UK and more local Manchester refugee context.

Figure 1. The ecology of CRE

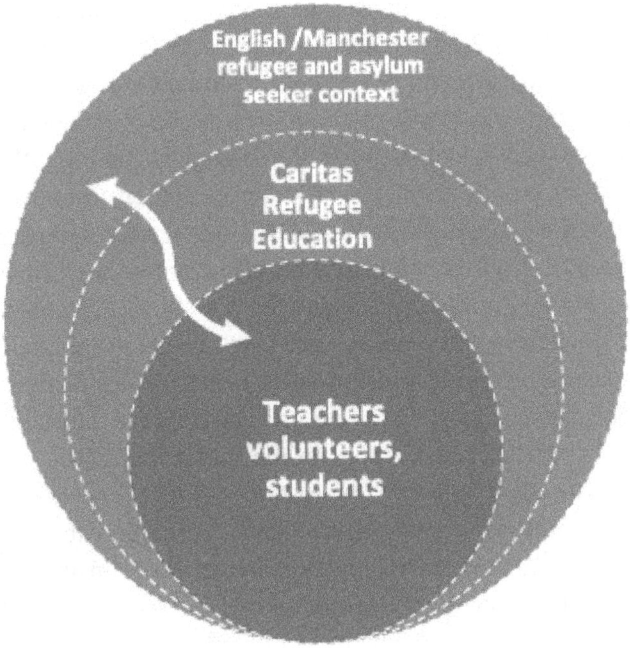

With the onset of the global pandemic, Covid-19 becomes a further shaping influence on English language teacher practices within the pandemic environment (Figure 2). In this new environment, with all teaching and learning being rapidly moved online, technology becomes a potential affordance for CRE to continue to meet its goals.

Figure 2. The ecology of CRE during the pandemic

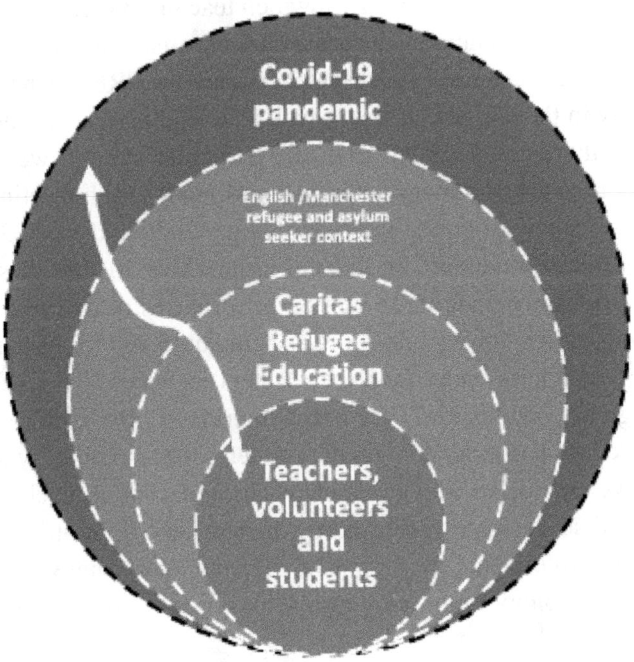

Affordances, as used in this chapter, refer to the possibilities for action that an individual and /or group perceive in their environment. Affordances are more than objectively described properties in an environment; for a property in the environment to be an affordance or action possibility, the individual and /or group must have the ability to use it and perceive its potential for action (Young, DePalma & Garret, 2002). More specifically, affordances, or action possibilities, can be understood in relation to an individual or group of language teachers' goals and purposes. In ecological thinking, the term intentionalities is used when individuals and /or groups act on the affordances perceived in their environment to pursue their goals (Stelma, Onat-Stelma, Lee & Kostoulas, 2016). These intentionalities take on a critical edge when an individual or group begins to problematise the affordances they perceive. This involves taking a critical look at the roots of those affordances and at the possible ideologies and social, historical and cultural contexts within which these affordances arise (Stelma, Onat-Stelma, Lee & Kostoulas, 2016). Being critically intentional leads to being transformative of the environment in which one is living and working and pursuing goals that challenge the *status quo* and improve the quality of life for those within that environment; in the case of the current study, for the students of CRE.

In this chapter, we are concerned with how the practices of teachers at CRE were shaped by, and in turn shaped, their environment during the ongoing pandemic. We explore the different shaping influences on their practices and in particular, how technology was perceived as an affordance enabling them to be intentional and purposeful in their pursuit of their individual and collective goals. We explore the extent to which they are critical in their work and how these critical intentionalities might transform the lives of their students. This exploration was driven by the following research questions:

1. How have teaching practices been shaped throughout the pandemic?
2. How have teachers' attitudes to teaching online been shaped throughout the pandemic?

Research Methodology

To answer these research questions, we engaged in a longitudinal, qualitative study. The ongoing study began in June 2020 and seeks to capture the way in which teaching practices have been, and are being, shaped throughout the continuing pandemic. The research design itself has also been shaped by the mutual collaboration and exchange between the MIE researchers and the CRE teachers. The MIE researchers have participated regularly in the online classes, as well as attending teacher meetings, where different challenges and pedagogical solutions arising from the particular context were shared and discussed. These meetings were recorded and summary notes were written for each meeting. The MIE researchers also carried out two sets of semi-structured interviews (June 2020 and April 2021) with the teachers, volunteer teachers, and administrative staff, and a focus group (May 2021) with students. The interviews aimed to capture how participants made sense of their experiences of teaching at CRE throughout the pandemic with particular focus on how technology was being used and for what reasons. The first round of interviews (June 2020) sought to understand the teachers' beliefs about teaching and their attitudes to, and uses of technology pre-pandemic. These initial interviews also explored the experiences of the teachers in the early weeks of the pandemic with the sudden shift to online, synchronous teaching. The second round of interviews, conducted after a year of synchronous online teaching (April 2021), focused on the main challenges and successes experienced by the teachers, their attitudes towards, and uses of technology, and their own professional development over the year. There were also forward-looking questions about the role technology might play as teaching moved to a more hybrid form combining online and face-to-face classes in Covid-secure classrooms. The data extracts and discussion below are based primarily on these two sets of interview data with the teachers (see Table 1 below). All names are pseudonyms.

Table 1. The research participants

Name	Role at CRE	Started volunteering in CRE	Started paid work in CRE
Tayeb	Education Coordinator + teacher	August 2016	October 2016
Arthur	Deputy Education Coordinator + teacher		July 2017
Petra	Teacher	July 2019	January 2020
Neila	Teacher		September 2019
Zorah	Teacher	Sept. 2017	September 2018

The data has been analysed through the ecological lens of shaping influences as described above. Analysis was carried out collaboratively between the MIE researchers, with input and checking from colleagues at CRE. Thus, each researcher analysed the data from an ecological perspective, and then we came together to discuss the analysis. In this way, our analysis was discussed and refined. Initial analysis has also been shared with the CRE teachers and the broader academic community via seminars and conference presentations. In the analysis process, we looked at the teachers' purposeful actions (intentionalities) as they pursued their goals of providing quality English language lessons for their learners and at their perception of the affordances of technology in doing so. We considered how their pedagogy and their practice was shaped throughout the pandemic.

Findings

We present the results emerging from this analysis below in two main ways. Firstly, we present two vignettes: one of the Educational Coordinator, Tayeb, and the other a relatively new teacher to CRE, Petra. These vignettes provide a holistic insight of how an individual teacher is both shaped by, and in turn shapes, their environment. It highlights the affordances they perceive in that environment and their purposeful actions to achieve their goals. We then outline the main shaping influences on the CRE teachers as they move from the pre-pandemic face-to-face classroom, through an online only model to a more hybrid model of teaching and learning in Covid-secure classrooms.

Tayeb's Vignette

Tayeb has a background in development, having studied the topic as an undergraduate. His course included a year at the University of Manchester in the Global Development Institute. Tayeb has been involved in education for over ten years, starting off as a teaching assistant working in special education needs, working as an Erasmus Plus organiser and then just before joining CRE worked in a pupil referral unit. He joined CRE as a volunteer, then became the Education Coordinator in 2016. He helped set up the current education centre. His own views about how teaching should be carried out and his use of technology in teaching and learning throughout his career shaped the way the teaching rooms were set up, and he intentionally sought funding and partnerships to provide interactive whiteboards in these rooms. CRE has also been shaped by Tayeb's belief that a whole-person approach, as presented in the work of Carl Rogers, should be a guiding principle for the practice at CRE. This extended to his recruitment policy of other teachers and volunteers. This belief also shaped his search for affordances that would enable CRE to maintain its classes online in the early days of the pandemic. Online classes enabled CRE to maintain contact with the students and support them, as well as maintain the language classes *per se*. While Tayeb saw technology as an intrinsic part of his teaching, moving online was also initially a challenge, but, at the same time, offered a range of affordances for providing student pyscho-social support that he believes positively shaped the services overall. His desire is to maintain the additional added value that online offered and use these practices to reach out to other parts of the refugee community who cannot normally access the classes, for a variety of reasons.

Petra's Vignette

Petra had come to CRE as a newly qualified ESOL teacher six months before the pandemic forced all teaching and learning online. The ethos and aims of CRE aligned with her own personal intentionality of providing a welcome for the most marginalised in society. Her pedagogy was shaped by her belief that everyone has something to contribute; learners can also be teachers. Before lockdown, technology played a mostly incidental role in her classes; she used the affordances of PowerPoint to show images and text shaped by her belief in the power of both to bring responses from the learners, but little else. Driven by the collective intentionality of the CRE teachers to continue providing both quality teaching, well-being support and community to the students, she explored the affordances of Zoom and other Apps for her classes, maintaining her pedagogical beliefs and seeking new ways to do the old things. Planning and delivery of lessons were shaped by her perception of the action possibilities of different Apps, and the realities of her students' language levels, digital literacy, internet access and device use. The nature of online teaching as a more intense and less spontaneous experience shaped her approach to lesson planning and she became more purposeful in her structuring of lessons through constant questioning of why she was doing certain things and what goals they could help achieve. She intentionally sought ways of recreating and adapting activities to work in an online setting. With the move to Covid friendly classrooms, this purposefulness in searching for action possibilities in her environment to fulfil her personal goals and collective goals of the CRE teachers continue to shape her approach to teaching and learning.

The CRE Ecology

CRE was initially an organic response to the lack of English provision for asylum seekers and refugees in the local area and the perceived importance of the English language for their integration into society and their psycho-social well-being (Tayeb, Intv 1). The wider, transformative agenda of Caritas is to increase the potential and quality of life of its clients (Caritas, n.d) and for refugees and asylum seekers this includes helping them navigate the UK asylum determination process and supporting them as they deal with the trauma of their recent past. These broader intentionalities to provide holistic support prompted them:

To provide English in a community environment that was in itself therapeutic and where they could have peer engagement, where they could relate to staff members. (Tayeb, Intv 1)

For Tayeb, as illustrated in his vignette, the most prominent shaping influence on the creation of this therapeutic environment was the person-centred approach of Carl Rogers (1951). He intentionally sought:

Staff members who buy into that, and who present those qualities themselves, and who are approachable, and who do see the sort of humanitarian and psychosocial dimension of what this work is. (Tayeb, Intv 1)

A Manchester based Trinity TESOL course, whose trainees do their teaching practice at CRE, provides another affordance for achieving this goal. All the current teachers at CRE, bar Tayeb, are graduates of this course and all are motivated by more than the desire to "just teach English" (Zorah, June 2020). Petra's vignette illustrated her aspiration to provide welcome for the more marginalised in our society. She intentionally applied for a job at CRE, "because it aligns very much with this sort of thing that I'm interested in doing anyway" (Petra, Intv 1). CRE provided the affordance for her to pursue that goal. This intentionality to contribute to increasing the quality of life of the CRE students through teaching English was also cited by Neila as a reason for working at CRE:

I really want to work there, because I want to teach. I want to help these people as much as I can, and I think teaching English is a way I can help them. And yeah, it just means more to me than teaching English. (Neila, Intv 1)

The transformative agenda of CRE and the critical intentionalities of the individual teachers in their desire to reduce inequalities and provide the tools their students need to move forward in their new lives shape the way in which English language teaching is both envisioned and envisaged at CRE.

Responding to the First Pandemic Lockdown

It is these critical intentionalities of the CRE teachers that shaped their response to the changing environment of the first lockdown. Led by Tayeb, who had sought advice from friends and family in countries that had locked down before the UK, Zoom, Google Classroom and WhatsApp were chosen because of their perceived affordances to enable the teachers to continue providing synchronous classes and support students' learning and well-being. The video conferencing tool Zoom was picked because it was thought by others to be "reliable" (Tayeb, Intv 1) and it met the required needs of the classes at CRE. The choice of Google Classroom was shaped by its specific affordances of being able to send materials to specific groups of students, and for the materials to be stored for future use. It is also free and if students have Gmail accounts, contributions to materials can be monitored. The final choice was WhatsApp as a communication tool. This was based on the affordance that it was a familiar tool as the community were using it to keep in touch with each other and their families back at home.

The decision to move classes online through Zoom contrasted with the decision of most other English language providers in the area:

A lot of the higher education colleges have, in the first few months, and some of them still today, will just post lessons online, for example, and not having that interaction, not having, you know an actual class that people could attend. (Arthur, Intv.2)

According to Tayeb, this approach would not have worked with their learners or enabled them the wider well-being support that CRE sought to provide:

With a lot of our learners who come from of range of backgrounds, some who have not gone into formal schooling, a lot of whom tech issues ... not just tech literacy, but I suppose tech poverty and a lack of access to computers, it just didn't seem like a wise way ... plus, also, as we've been mentioning here, with this big emphasis on psychosocial well being, you don't really get that from the lack of human interaction. (Tayeb, Intv 1)

As with the rest of the world, the switch to online teaching was sudden: "we only had a week to adapt to the whole new concept of teaching online" (Zorah, Intv 1). One teacher had some experience of teaching one-to-one online, but the majority had no experience. As exemplified by Petra's vignette above, different technologies were used for different purposes in the pre-pandemic era, but the use, and frequency of use, varied from teacher to teacher. Neila, similarly to Petra said that technology played a small role in her practice:

[I'm] more of a paper and pen kind of teacher, and face-to-face I never even had the Internet on in the lessons. It was just a PowerPoint. (Neila, Intv 2)

For Tayeb, the use of technology was more normalised:

I've always integrated technology. I don't think I've ever done a lesson since I started as a teacher without some sort of tech there, without projecting via my computer materials I'd found. (Tayeb, Intv 1)

Despite the mixed experiences of using technology and of teaching online, the teachers were very intentional about their move to synchronous online classes. This was shaped by their purposeful commitment to their learners and recognition of their circumstances and how those might be further impacted by Covid: "we can't just leave them [the students] in the lurch, you know. Life's difficult already for them" (Petra, Intv 1). We can see the group-environment mutuality here as they seek to shape the pandemic environment in a positive way for their learners, rather than be shaped by it. As Petra (Intv 1) says, their response as teachers could have been "that sounds way too hard, I don't really want to do that or I'm not used to it or I've never taught online". Instead, there is a collective pursuit here of their goals as they shape each other and encourage each other to give it a go:

I think there's an openness, maybe an entrepreneurial spirit almost of, you know, just let, let's give it a try, you know, let's try this. So, it kind of felt like we were on the front of the reaction, you know, that was like, well, how can we engage still, and this felt like the best thing to do. (Petra, Intv 1)

Their collective identity underpins their purposefulness as they resist the status quo and continue to pursue their transformative agenda through moving forward in a clearly intentional way.

The Shaping Influence of the CRE Learners' Characteristics

As suggested above (for example, Figures 1 & 2), the broader ecology of CRE as situated in the UK asylum seeker and refugee context and the characteristics of its clients has been a major shaping influence on the agenda and practices of CRE. The pandemic brought to the fore different aspects of that ecology, in particular the personal environment of the students. As Tayeb explained:

I think also a challenge is the living circumstances, right. It's now no longer just where they live, but it's where they study, it's where everything takes place. A lot of the living environments that these individuals are in, whether it's asylum accommodation through NAS, or whether it's through really low quality private rental environments, whether it's overcrowded where there's issues of mould and there's just poor unhygienic conditions around them, that poses all sorts of challenges to them. (Tayeb, Intv. 2)

This was echoed by other teachers, who spoke of the "chaotic" environment of the learners and their difficulty in finding a space to learn (Petra, Intv. 1). For some learners, having to learn online coupled with the pandemic meant they dropped out of lessons for a time. The CRE teachers were quick to follow-up on these students and frequently the reason was that circumstances had overwhelmed them: "it just turns out they've just had some sort of episode, and you know they've not been able to cope". (Arthur, Intv. 2).

Access to Technology and Internet

Their circumstances and living conditions also posed other challenges: refugees and asylum seekers have very limited funds, which means many had no, or perhaps only sporadic, internet access, with some hot-spotting from a friend's Wi-Fi where possible, or drifting in and out of class as the internet access ebbed and flowed. Most had never experienced online learning. CRE perceived various affordances in the environment to help with some of the practical issues, for example, redirecting money previously used on bus passes to buy data for students, although this did not cover all the needs. They also used the affordances of their Arabic speaking Education Administrator to do one-to-one tutorials with students to help them access Zoom and talk through the practical requirements and etiquette of online classes.

At the beginning of the pandemic, very few students had access to a laptop or computer, so the majority were accessing their classes on a mobile phone. This reality shaped the way that teachers approached their planning and delivery of classes and was cited as the biggest challenge by all of the teachers in the first interviews:

The students being on phones. That's the biggest thing, the size of the screen. What can they physically see? I have to expand things, zoom in, a reading task could take like three or four slides by the time they've managed to read it all. Something simple in the classroom, like a matching activity becomes really complicated on the phones. So basically, I approach it from that angle, more of a technological angle of what can we physically do. (Neila, Intv. 1)

How to teach quality classes that were accessible on a mobile phone led the teachers to explore the affordances of different Apps and strategies that would work for students, such as increasing the font size, creating pdfs and sending them in WhatsApp "which means that they can scroll up and down rather than trying to fit everything on one screen" (Petra Intv. 1). Although these things seemed "kind of peripheral to teaching" (Petra Intv. 2), they were key features of teaching CRE students in an online environment.

Digital Literacy and Language Levels

All the teachers suggested a correlation between language level and technical ability, with the lower language levels being the most challenging to teach online.

So the high levels, I would say that the more technologically capable they are, the more satisfying the lesson because ... we can really stretch them. Even things like you know, take a screenshot of this and then take that into the breakout room and share it. All that sort of thing, you know, that would take a whole lesson for me to try and explain in the lower levels, so we can get a lot more done when they are technically more capable (Petra Intv. 1)

The teachers identified two main action possibilities for supporting the lower levels. The first was the use of volunteers. While CRE had always used volunteer teachers, the ease of being able to join a class on Zoom rather than travel to a physical location increased the number and geographical spread of volunteers. Volunteers became particularly important in the lower levels as they facilitated the use of breakout rooms, quizzes, Padlets, crosswords and so on. As one teacher said:

Before we had the volunteers, we couldn't even do breakout rooms with the lower levels because they just didn't know how to press the buttons. And also, if they were in there on their own, I don't know what they'd be doing, they need someone there to help them and guide them. (Neila, Intv 1)

Another affordance came again through the Arabic speaking Education Administrator who annotated screenshots of different Zoom functions and Apps in Arabic for the lower level students. Again, the group-environment mutuality is evident here and we see the purposeful action of the teachers in pursuing their individual and collective goals to meet the needs and expectations of their students.

As the pandemic has continued, the students too have become more adept at using the different functions of Zoom and are now shaping their learning environment by helping each other and taking the role that previously the teacher or volunteers needed to take. Petra describes this as one of the successes of the past year:

I think some of my successes have been sort of feeling like the learners really sort of embrace the technology, you know, I sort of felt really pleased, you know, if I go into a breakout room, someone's already sharing their screen, and they're halfway through the questions. (Petra, Intv. 2)

This growth in their digital skills has also enabled learners to access the wider services they need that are now predominantly online.

Being Shaped as Teachers

As illustrated above, the CRE teachers quickly identified and acted on the possibilities of Zoom at the start of the pandemic in order to continue to fulfil their collective goal of providing for the language and psychosocial needs of their clients. We also noted that they had little collective experience of teaching online. From an ecological perspective, a property in the environment becomes an affordance when it is both perceived as a possibility for action and there is potential for it to be used in order to achieve a goal or purpose (Young, DePalma & Garrett, 2002). The first round of interviews highlighted the lack of perceived action possibilities, or what we might term perceived constraints in the environment.

This lack of action possibilities was identified by a focus on certain teaching and learning activities such as drilling and phonics work with the lower levels. Zorah (Intv. 2) said, "that's not been too positive because it's not been possible to have those kinds of lessons in place, just because of the online things". Writing skills were also cited by all teachers as being problematic because of the perceived lack of ability to be able to monitor and check, particularly with the lower levels. As Petra explained:

I find that quite frustrating because I don't actually know what they're doing ...even if I say, okay, we're going to do spelling now. Everyone, get your pen, get your paper, we're going to do some writing. And you can see some of them just sitting there like that, and you know they're not doing it. (Petra, Intv. 1)

Where affordances were perceived, there was still a sense of loss of being able to use the techniques and strategies they were familiar with in the face-to-face context. For one teacher this concerned the whiteboard:

I miss the whiteboard, just being able to quickly write something, go somewhere else for five minutes, and I know they have a whiteboard [in Zoom], but by the time you've stopped sharing your screen [the PowerPoint], got it [the Zoom whiteboard] up, written it all down, it loses that momentum. (Neila, Intv. 1)

There was also a concern that the new affordances were not as effective as the previous ones and not able to achieve the purpose they wanted:

There is one thing actually that's very different that bothers me. In classroom lessons, they always have something to take away, like some paper with exercises and stuff they can read at home. And online, that's been a struggle because we have Google classroom, but they don't really use it. So, I've now started asking them to take screenshots or photos of certain bits of the screen. But I don't know how effective that is." (Neila, Intv.1)

Giving feedback on written work was also something of a struggle and despite using the affordances of sending photographs in WhatsApp, the process was not as efficient as physically writing on a piece of paper during the class:

Collecting the work and delivering the feedback can be quite a time-consuming process to get the students to write something on a piece of paper, take a photograph, send it to you, and then you've got to find some way of you know annotating it or marking it and getting it back to them. (Arthur, Intv. 2)

When speaking about their experiences in the first round of interviews they used terms such as stressful, intense, less natural, more stage-managed, more rigorous, more carefully planned. All the teachers spoke of the way that online teaching had shaped their approach to lesson planning. Some spoke of "less room to manoeuvre, or be creative, or wing it" (Arthur Intv. 1) and there being "less gap, there's less space for things to happen" (Petra Intv.1). Tayeb contrasted his identity as a face-to-face teacher who is more like a showman who manages and responds to the atmosphere in the class with a more detailed thought through way of delivering the lesson in the online environment.

I think, in an online context, you have to be a lot more precise and tight with your sort of teaching, and making sure that it's like sequenced correctly, the timings of activity, the flow of activities, right, so you have to be a lot more thoughtful I think in your lesson planning, because you can't just like draw on being a showman like you can in a face-to-face environment and read the atmosphere there and go okay, we're sort of done with this part, we need to move on to this other element. Now you don't have like those sort of intuitive readings of the situation. (Tayeb, Intv 2)

As time went on and as the teachers became more perceptive of the action possibilities in the online environment, they grew in confidence and began to shape the online environment they were working in. Teachers' attitudes towards the online environment also changed. In his first interview, Arthur stated a positive dislike for online teaching "I'll be honest with you, the benefits are very few, I really, I don't like teaching online at all" (Arthur Int. 1). This changed to a recognition of the possibilities online teaching offered "I can't believe I'm actually saying this, there are actually some ways in which online teaching is superior to face to face" (Arthur Intv 2).

This was also reflected in their approaches to the imminent move back to the physical classroom, albeit a Covid-secure classroom with social distancing in place. Through the individual / group-environment mutuality during the pandemic they had become more resilient teachers, perhaps more perceptive in their pursuit of affordances, as they had both shaped and been shaped by that environment. Petra reflects on how her approach to teaching is now shaped more fully by a purposeful and informed pursuit of her goals by "always asking yourself, why do I want to do this, what's it achieving, and then if I can't achieve it the old way, how can I do it in the new way" (Petra, Intv. 2). Rather than seeing a lack of action possibilities, once those aims are clarified and justified, she actively seeks affordances that will enable her to achieve them.

For Tayeb, the experience of the pandemic shaped his whole approach to the way ... could deliver not only its language classes, but the way it could also achieve its wider goals moving forward. He could see the affordances of the online possibilities to deliver these goals in a more creative and innovative way.

I think it's been informative, and it's changed entirely my views on it ...now I'm sort of looking at online in a different way, it's sort of not even related to the pandemic, and it's not a substitute for something. It's actually a way to sort of innovate and ... create a service and get it out to people in an entirely different way. (Tayeb Intv. 2)

One aspect of their work that has been enhanced by the move online is their ability to canvas ideas and feedback from students. Tayeb reflects on how these possibilities were always present, they had just not perceived them in the past and "it's mad that it took a pandemic for us to see that" (Tayeb, Intv 2). The pandemic has enabled them to find new possibilities that will continue to enhance their ability to improve the quality of life for those they seek to serve through Caritas.

The Shaping Influence of Collaboration

One unexpected yet very welcome innovation to arise from the pandemic has been a greater sense of collaboration between the teachers through weekly Zoom meetings among themselves and with the university researchers. Again, Tayeb suggests that this possibility was always present, they had just not seen it before the pandemic:

We always wanted to create sort of more peer support amongst the teachers themselves, and to have a more tightly knit community within that and to learn from one another. And we just couldn't do it because of the constraints of funding and geographical constraints of asking teachers to come in for this time, whereas you know all along we could have been doing Zoom sessions like we do every Friday. (Tayeb, Intv. 2)

There is a sense in which these collaborative sessions also enable them to shape each other and to collectively identify and pursue the different affordances in their environment for their particular teaching context.

The collaborations that we've done, it's given us sort of an insight into how other teachers are coping with it, how they are doing, what their ideas are, and so going about it in a sort of collaborative way, has sort of helped this process along, and it's made me really confident now to be teaching online. (Zorah, Intv. 2)

One of the tangible outputs of these meetings and collaboration has been the development of a Toolkit that specifically addresses teaching and learning online with students who have few resources and are generally learning through a mobile phone.

Discussion

The chapter has presented an analysis of the interview data from an ecological perspective. The critical intentionality of providing language education within a supportive environment that takes a whole-person approach to language teaching shaped the way the teachers have responded to the evolving pandemic environment. There is evidence of their individual and collective purposefulness to transform the lives of their students, helping each of them to achieve their own goals through improving their English language skills. The realities of the living conditions, language abilities, digital literacies and access to technology and the internet of their asylum seeker and refugee students profoundly shaped their search for and perception of the different action possibilities available to them. This has transformed not only the way in which they now deliver English language classes, but the holistic service that they offer their students.

Because of the forced move online at the beginning of the pandemic, digital technologies have played a key role in the shaping of the teachers' practices and their response to the pandemic. We could argue that technologies have become increasingly normalised (Bax, 2011) in teachers' lives as the desire to meet students' needs have encouraged a greater understanding and insight into the affordances of the different technologies provided initially by Caritas. Teachers have intentionally sought new ways and new tools to meet the needs of the students. There is also an expressed desire to continue to make effective use of technology as they move back into the face-to-face classroom.

While most of the teachers expressed doubts about how the move online would work, particularly in the first interviews in June 2020, they continued to innovate both individually and then sharing ideas in their meetings about the lessons they were developing. Lesson ideas were taken up by other teachers and adapted to the needs of the different classes. The management team also re-shaped student support, finding more systematic ways of keeping track of students who were not coping. The teaching practices could be argued to have followed a quite natural progression in initially trying to replicate their face-to-face practice online, however, their practice was also shaped by the access limitations of their students. In this they were supported by the academic advisors at the Manchester Institute of Education. The overall impact of this development of practice can be seen in the development of the online toolkit, which is a repository of a number of different lessons that have been developed by the teachers: https://refugeeeducationtoolkit.org/.

As discussed in the literature, the charity sector is able to be much more flexible and innovative in its approach to its provision. We see evidence of this in a number of ways in the findings. Funding and links to other organisations meant that the initial set up of the school was rather different from the local state sector. CRE were able to move quickly online and while there were challenges for many of the students, the affordances of online meant that they could reach out to groups of students in the community that they had not been able to reach out to before. They could also make more effective use of a greater number of volunteers, who could offer more time because they did not have to travel to the face-to-face classes and volunteers did not have to be regionally based. Some volunteers during the pandemic were based in London. CRE are hoping to continue to provide online classes to students who have not been able to access the face-to-face classes in the past.

The psycho-social support services that have always been a feature of the whole person ethos of CRE have also been able to be more effectively managed and deployed during the pandemic. Tayeb reports a four-fold increase in welfare referrals from 2020-2021 (from 5-20 referrals), for example. Being able to focus more effectively on providing psycho-social support, probably exacerbated by the conditions of the pandemic and also being mindful of students' needs in lessons come across clearly in the findings. Looking for ways to enable students to meet up, as they would do, in the face-to-face space is also an important activity that they focused on. It could be argued that the teachers became more aware of the living situation of the students, their lack of access to internet data and suitable technology to access the classes, as well as their living conditions, in shared houses with no quiet space to access their classrooms. The needs of students to develop their digital literacies, to be able to find and access materials online, to interact with those materials and then return them to the teachers. The teachers report a missing element with online was being able to monitor the students' work effectively. Not being able to see what the students were doing and the reluctance of students to be able to send written work for marking.

This study has focussed on a particular sector and student profile, but the findings have several implications for language learning in challenging and resource-limited contexts. It has shown the need to work with both the technology and the digital literacy that students have as a starting point. This is particularly important where students are learning through mobile phones, which is a very different experience to learning through a device with a larger screen. Teachers need to be sensitive to this and design materials, tasks and activities that work on a small screen (Hashim, Md. Yunus, Amin Embi, & Mohamed Ozir, 2017; Rias & Ismail, 2010). There is also a need to scaffold and develop digital literacy skills so that students feel skilled and comfortable in using the technology needed so they can focus on learning the language and not be alienated by the technology. This can be more challenging for lower levels, and just as in the physical classroom teachers often scaffold students' understanding of the classroom language needed to be able to fully participate in the class, so in the online class, there is a need to help students understand not just new phrases such as 'share your screen' but support their technical ability to do that. This is where the use of screenshots and L1 support can be helpful. This approach can also help develop skills which are essential to surviving an increasingly online world and increase the employability of students.

Another implication is the vital role that volunteers can play in these online environments. Where volunteers are not available, there might be the possibility to use students who have a higher level of language and / or digital literacy skills. In teaching environment that has more resources, team teaching or the use of teaching assistants might be helpful in this regard.

FUTURE RESEARCH DIRECTIONS

The link between CRE and MIE is ongoing and with plans for CRE colleagues to provide input on to the MIE MA TESOL course units. There will also be volunteering opportunities for the MA students and staff. We are exploring the setting up and running of a regular online class to provide access to lessons to families who come directly to the UK on the community sponsorship programme. We would be looking to research the design and development of this course and to extend its use to refugees who are on their way to the UK. Furthermore, we would also be looking to link up with colleagues working on similar projects in Greece and in Jordan.

CONCLUSION

The ecological analysis used in this chapter has illustrated how a small group of teachers working within a very specific political, economic and social environment have both shaped and been shaped by the ongoing pandemic environment with regards to their language teaching practice. It has looked at the different action possibilities they perceived within their environment, especially technological ones, and the purposefulness with which they have acted on those to meet the needs of their clients and grow the reach of and improve the services they offer. It has also suggested ways in which the teaching practices that have been shaped by the pandemic environment in the UK refugee and asylum seeker context might also be applied in the wider language teaching context, especially in Education in Emergencies and other challenging and low resource contexts.

REFERENCES

Bax, S. (2011). Normalisation Revisited: The Effective Use of Technology in Language Education. *International Journal of Computer-Assisted Language Learning and Teaching*, *1*(2), 1–15. doi:10.4018/ijcallt.2011040101

Beaumont, M., & O'Brien, T. (Eds.). (2000). *Collaborative research in 2nd language education*. Trentham Books.

Blunkett, D., Halfon, R., & Pember, S. (2021). *Skills for Life: A new strategy for English, Maths, ESOL and Digital: Learning from the past to improve the future: Next stage 2021-2031*. Further Education Trust for Leadership (FETL). https://dera.ioe.ac.uk//37498/

Bronfenbrenner, U. (1979). *The ecology of human development: experiments by nature and design*. Harvard University Press.

Chamorro, G., Garrido-Hornos, M., & Vázquez-Amador, M. (2021). Exploring ESOL teachers' perspectives on the language learning experiences, challenges, and motivations of refugees and asylum seekers in the UK. *International Review of Applied Linguistics in Language Teaching*. Advance online publication. doi:10.1515/iral-2020-0155

Douglas, P., Cetron, M., & Spiegel, P. (2019). Definitions matter: Migrants, immigrants, asylum seekers and refugees. *Journal of Travel Medicine, 26*(2). Advance online publication. doi:10.1093/jtm/taz005 PMID:30753575

El-Metoui, L., & Graham-Brown, N. (2021). Emerging from the pandemic: reflections for the ESOL sector. *The ESOL Journal, 32*(1), 7-19. https://www.ingentaconnect.com/content/natecla/esol/2021/00000032/00000001/art00003

Fay, R., & Stelma, J. (2016). Criticality, intentionality and intercultural action. In M. Dasli & A. Diaz (Eds.), *The Critical Turn in Language and Intercultural Communication Pedagogy: Theory, Research and Practice* (pp. 126–140). Routledge.

Furlong, C., & Hunt, J. (2009). *ESOL in Wales: Learning from the voluntary sector*. Welsh Assembly and NIACE, Cymru.

Gibson, J. J. (1979). *The ecological approach to visual perception*. Houghton Mifflin.

Gov.UK. (2020). *More Afghan interpreters to move to the UK as scheme extends*. https://www.gov.uk/government/news/more-afghan-interpreters-to-move-to-the-uk-as-scheme-extends

Hashim, H., Md. Yunus, M., Amin Embi, M., & Mohamed Ozir, N. A. (2017). Mobile-assisted Language Learning (MALL) for ESL Learners: A Review of Affordances and Constraints. *Sains Humanika, 9*(1-5). Advance online publication. doi:10.11113h.v9n1-5.1175

Holmes, P., Fay, R., & Andrews, J. (Eds.). (2017). Special issue - Education and migration: Languages foregrounded. Language and Intercultural Communication, 17(4).

Leoni, F., & Mora, A. (2021). *Caritas Refugee Education End of Year Report (2020-21)*. Caritas.

Motteram, G. (Ed.). (2013). *Innovations in learning technologies for English language teaching*. The British Council.

Motteram, G., Dawson, S., & Al-Masri, N. (2020). WhatsApp supported language teacher development: A case study in the Zataari refugee camp. *Education and Information Technologies, 25*(6), 5731–5751. Advance online publication. doi:10.100710639-020-10233-0 PMID:32837232

NALDIC. (2015). *How the EAL needs of bilingual learners in English schools are funded*. Research and information, NALDIC, EAL Funding. https://www.naldic.org.uk/research-and-information/eal-funding/

Podziewska, J. (2014). The volunteer ethos and the utopian impulse in the ESOL classroom. *Language Issues, 25*(1), 23–28.

Rias, R. M., & Ismail, F. (2010). Designing interfaces in a mobile environment: An implementation on a programming language. *2010 International Conference on User Science and Engineering (i-USEr)*, 232-237. doi: 10.1109/IUSER.2010.5716758

Rogers, C. R. (1951). *Client-centered Therapy, Its Current Practice, Implications, and Theory*. Houghton Mifflin.

Simpson, J. (2012). "Bits here and there" — Fragmented ESOL provision in Leeds. *Language Issues, 23*(2), 33–45.

Simpson, J. (2019). Policy and adult migrant language education in the UK. In M. Cook & R. Peutrell (Eds.), *Brokering Britain, education citizens* (pp. 25-41). Blue Ridge Summit: Multilingual Matters. doi:10.21832/9781788924634

Stelma, J., & Fay, R. (2014). Intentionality and developing researcher competence on a UK master's course: An ecological perspective on research education. *Studies in Higher Education, 39*(4), 517-533.

Stelma, J., & Fay, R. (2019). An ecological perspective on critical action for language education. In A. Kostoulas (Ed.), *Challenging Boundaries in Language Education* (pp. 51–70). Springer.

Stelma, J., Fay, R., & Zhou, X. (2013). Developing intentionality and researching multilingually: An ecological and methodological perspective. *International Journal of Applied Linguistics, 23*(3), 300–315.

Stelma, J., & Kostoulas, A. (2021). *The Intentional Dynamics of TESOL*. De Gruyter Mouton.

Stelma, J., Onat-Stelma, Z., Lee, W., & Kostoulas, A. (2016). Intentional dynamics in TESOL: An ecological perspective. *Working Papers in TESOL and Applied Linguistics, 15*(1), 14-23. https://tesolal.columbia.edu/article/intentional-dynamics-in-tesol/

Vollmer, S. M. (2020) *The Digital Literacy Practices of Newly Arrived Syrian Refugees: a Spatio-Visual Linguistic Ethnography* (PhD thesis). University of Leeds.

White, D. S., & Le Cornu, A. (2011). Visitors and Residents: A new typology for online engagement. *First Monday, 16*(9). https://doi.org/10.5210/fm.v16i9.317

Young, M. F., DePalma, A., & Garrett, S. (2002). Situations, interaction, process and affordances: An ecological psychology perspective. *Instructional Science, 30*(1), 47–63.

Chapter 14
Language Teachers' Health:
Emotions and Wellbeing in the COVID-19 Pandemic

Cristina Pardo-Ballester
https://orcid.org/0000-0001-9494-2717
Iowa State University, USA

ABSTRACT

This chapter documents language teachers' emotions and wellbeing from the emergency online transition in Spring 2020 due to the Covid-19 pandemic to the end of Spring 2021. It also looks at how language teachers within the United States perceive the future of teaching languages. 175 educators responded to an anonymous online survey composed of various types of items such as multiple-choice, binary format, selection of multiple answers, and open-ended. Cronbach's alpha was .717 for 114 items and sub items. Descriptive statistics and repeated measures t-tests were computed to investigate teaching strategies and psychological consequences during the Covid-19 pandemic. The goals of this chapter are twofold: (1) to identify emotions and wellbeing issues that may be affecting language faculties and their success at their United States institutions and (2) to offer general recommendations to high-level administrators that draw upon language teachers' perceptions and factors that hinder L2 development in language programs.

INTRODUCTION

While most teachers are aware of the importance of students' wellbeing in the learning process (Cohen, Hoy & Dull, 2020; Hapsari, 2021; Maican & Cocorada, 2021; Pardo-Ballester, 2020; Rossomondo, 2020; Russell 2020), there exists less clarity around the awareness of instructors' wellbeing within the remote teaching environment (Anderson, Bousselot, Katz-Buoincontro, & Todd, 2021; MacIntyre, Gregersen, & Mercer, 2020; Hartshorn & McMurry, 2020). Recently, universities have shown increasing attention on the importance of instructors' wellbeing through multiple communication channels such as emails, newsletters, meetings, or general announcements. Research in this area shows that language teachers also suffer from stress, depression, and anxiety (Hartshorn & McMurry, 2020; MacIntyre, Gregersen

DOI: 10.4018/978-1-7998-8717-1.ch014

& Mercer, 2020; Moser, Wei, & Brenner, 2021; Proietti Ergun & Dewaele, 2021; Gregersen, Mercer & MacIntyre, 2021) due to the pandemic, but also due to different stressors related to their work situation (Pardo-Ballester, 2021a).

Today, language teachers are better prepared to design courses and teach different formats from teaching face-to-face (F2F) with a wide range of digital resources (Sosulski, 2020; Ji Xu, Deiffell & Angus, 2021) to more sophisticated and dedicated courses delivered with hybrid, flipped, or online models. The pandemic has prepared us to learn new strategies by focusing on students' learning and on the actual process of learning a language. We succeeded in doing what we were trained to do. Even those language teachers who never thought of teaching online will now consider this model for personal or pedagogical reasons (Moser et al., 2021; Yi Xu et al., 2021). However, even though the language faculty is better prepared for distance learning, we should have the same autonomy deciding the model of the courses we teach as the autonomy we have when selecting online tools. Some teachers will prefer F2F teaching or blended learning in order to feel the sense of belonging within a language department and maintain social connections with their colleagues and their students. Others will opt for distance learning for reasons such as research, commuting, or difficulties with mobility due to disability issues (Pardo-Ballester, 2021a).

The focus of this chapter is on an under-investigated setting of higher education and language teachers' psychological consequences, namely emotions and wellbeing, which is subsumed here under the broader field of "health" on four counts: before the Covid-19 pandemic, the onset, during the pandemic, and the future without a pandemic. Even though there have been studies on the beginning of the pandemic with a focus on the transition to emergency online teaching and on the need to create digital communities during the pandemic (Lomicka, 2020), there is a scarcity of studies about prior experience with distance education before the pandemic (Moser et al., 2021). This chapter documents language teachers' emotions and wellbeing from the emergency online transition in Spring 2020 due to the Covid-19 pandemic to the end of Spring 2021. It also looks at how language teachers within the United States perceive the future of teaching languages. Therefore, the goals of this chapter are twofold: (1) to identify emotions and wellbeing issues that may be affecting language faculties and their success at their United States institutions and (2) to offer general recommendations to high-level administrators that draw upon language teachers' perceptions and factors that hinder L2 development in language programs.

BACKGROUND

Emotions and Wellbeing

MacIntyre et al. (2020) cited Lazarus' work from 1996 and 2006 to define stress as "a psychological reaction to environmental conditions (stressors) that produce a variety of effects including physical arousal and threats to wellbeing" (p.2). Every profession has its stressors, but MacIntyre et al. (2020) have stated that even before the pandemic, being a teacher 'was listed as one of the most stressful professions' (p.2). Some of the stressors mentioned are heavy workload, heavy administrative responsibilities, time spent learning new methods and making changes, complex relationships with school administrators or colleagues, losing control of the class, and others. In addition, the language teacher also suffers from causes specific to teaching a language, such as the emotions related to teaching a foreign language, the fear about the teacher's language ability, dealing with the anxiety of their learners, or even the fact that language teachers spend a lot of energy when teaching.

Due to the fast-spreading and growing nature of COVID-19, language teachers were forced to reconstruct their courses and quickly adapt to an online format, which created more stressors such as overwhelming uncertainty regarding the pandemic and dealing with anxiety-ridden students and parents who were struggling to adapt to this new reality (Anderson, et al., 2021; Hartshorn & McMurry, 2020; MacIntyre et al., 2020; Moser et al., 2021). Teachers had to deal with these novel issues in addition to the stressors present before the pandemic (MacIntyre et al., 2020; Yi Xu et al., 2021). Some of the factors that affected the language educators' experiences were technology and Internet issues, socioeconomic differences among learners, and learners' age and motivation. As Moser et al. (2021) stated in their investigation, language teachers at the K-12 level perceived that teaching a foreign language was less important than teaching other subjects such as math, history, or other subjects. Moser et al. (2021) cited the Education Commission of the States (2020) to inform that the federal government mandated testing waivers so that students could focus on the more important content, even though teaching foreign languages is considered a core subject. This policy greatly discouraged coursework completion and progress. As Moser et al. (2021) indicated postsecondary educators are not constrained by these same policies and difficulties and faced significantly fewer challenges.

According to Butler and Kern (2016), "wellbeing is not simply the absence of negative function, but rather is something more. That is, a lack of negative affect, depression, loneliness, insecurity, and illness is not the same as the presence of positive affect, happiness, social connection, trust, and wellness" (McIntyre et al., 2020, p.4). Even though some language teachers were not happy before the pandemic, there are no doubts about the new stressors and coping mechanisms that came with the problematic switch to online teaching. This sudden shift left MacIntyre et al. (2020) wondering how language teachers were coping with these new problems in their lives. Their research is essential for many reasons, with one being that it is crucial to understand how the stress educators experience ultimately affects the students. Additionally, teachers' disengagement adversely affects students, which is exacerbated by secondary traumatic stress, in which teachers experience stress through caring for students with trauma (Anderson et al., 2021).

MacIntyre et al. (2020) analyzed the wellbeing of 634 language educators worldwide during the onset of the pandemic. Their participants taught at the elementary, secondary, and post-secondary levels. Their instrument was an online survey derived from various more-extended tools such as the PERMA profiler, the WHO-5 Index of wellbeing, the health Index, the stress index, and others. According to individual circumstances, language educators coped with the pandemic and its challenges (Hartshorn & McMurry, 2020). In MacIntyre et al. (2020), coping strategies were categorized as either approach or avoidant. For example, the strategy of accepting the situation or keeping a positive attitude are approach strategies, but denying the pandemic, giving up, or using alcohol or other drugs were considered avoidant strategies. It was found that the majority of the 634 respondents relied on approach strategies more than avoidant strategies. However, those with minimal stress generally relied on approach strategies, whereas those under the most pressure turned to avoidant coping strategies. The negative emotions researched in their study were anxiety, anger, stress, sadness, and loneliness. Generally, educators who relied upon avoidant coping strategies experienced even increased negative emotions, demonstrating an emotional cost of coping for individuals who resort to avoidant coping strategies. Overall, teachers used various coping mechanisms to mitigate the negative emotions that came with the pandemic and existing stressors.

The social distancing measures significantly impacted education. The feelings of separation, isolation, and loneliness caused the social distancing measures that affected learners' and teachers' mental and emotional health. The anxiety surrounding COVID-19 created many problems in education, most notably poor academic performance and compromised physical and psychological health (Hartshorn & McMurry, 2020). Language teachers have identified the negative emotions of stress and anxiety coming from the workplace where they were either concerned about their feelings of contracting the virus from a classroom setting (Pardo-Ballester, 2021b) or potentially being the one who could bring the virus into the school (Gregersen et al., 2021). Language educators have reported fear for their and others' health, of being affected by self-isolation, and by dealing with their work while perhaps also homeschooling their own children (Gregersen et al., 2021; MacIntyre et al., 2020; Hartshorn & McMurry, 2020). Teachers in different studies also reported their worries about financial insecurity, job security, and the future of their employment as their student numbers were significantly reduced, thus reducing their teaching load and income (Gregersen et al., 2021; Hartshorn & McMurry, 2020; Moser et al., 2021).

Other scholars have reported that language teachers were concerned for their students' learning progress because they felt they were not learning at the same pace as before the pandemic. Hartshorn and McMurry's (2020) study analyzed the experience of 153 international students learning English as a Second Language (ESL) and 41 ESL teachers from the intensive English program at Brigham Young University. The students in this study were involved in a 15-week intensive English program that included 18 hours (weekly) of comprehensive coursework. Teachers were very concerned about their students' wellbeing and wanted their students to continue to make language progress. Additionally, many teachers acknowledged how difficult it must be for their students to have limited social interaction and how this ultimately affected their mental health and academic performance. They were seven weeks into the program before F2F instruction was discontinued. It was also found that while students improved their speaking and writing skills despite the emergency remote format, the improvement in speaking was much lower than writing, and it was low compared to previous semesters without the effect of a pandemic.

The COVID-19 pandemic has disrupted education systems globally and has left teachers with an abundance of stress after being forced to change their curriculum and retain student engagement virtually (Anderson et al., 2021). Teachers do their job better when they have the option to select the delivery format of the course they teach (Pardo-Ballester, 2021a; Yi Xu et al., 2021). To effectively deliver an online course, an educator needs to have knowledge and skills in online language pedagogy (Russell, 2020). Because of this experience, Moser et al. (2021) investigated how prior online teaching experience affected remote language teaching and found that previous online teaching experience positively correlated to teacher satisfaction as this experience aided instructors in overcoming various challenges.

Moreover, according to Gregersen et al. (2021), teachers' resilience and happiness are associated with positive experiences considering the pandemic as an opportunity for learning new skills by adapting their courses to a new format. Additionally, Yi Xu et al. (2021) found in their investigation that teachers increased self-confidence with unique abilities and their students' response to their instruction. They positively predicted some teachers' intentions to pursue online teaching in the future. Other researchers have stated that the more experience an educator had in teaching an online language course, the more positive the learner experiences were (Proietti & Dewaele, 2021; Moser et al., 2021).

Through an online survey, Yi Xu et al. (2021) asked 662 U.S.-based college foreign language educators about their perceived usefulness of online courses, self-confidence, technology access, stress, student readiness, and intentions to use online formats in post-pandemic times. 57.2% of respondents agreed or strongly agreed, and 24.8% disagreed or strongly disagreed with teaching language classes 100% online in the future. The one factor that seemed to influence educators' decisions on teaching online in the future was stress. Stress experience affected their perceived value of online teaching and their self-confidence. Instructors' perception of student readiness also affected their perceived value and self-confidence. Many of these educators reported that their negative experience with online teaching thus far caused them to believe that remote options should never be used in place of face-to-face language instruction if possible. They pointed to the difficulty in creating fluid communication and facilitating connections with and between students as a significant influencer in their opinions. Another reason for respondents' reluctance to continue online teaching is that online instruction was not compatible with their teaching style. Many believed that it increased stress from the extra effort it took to generate student engagement and maximize learning.

The previous investigation echoed the study of Moser et al. (2021) that asked 377 language educators about pandemic-related teaching and its effect on future and existing practices. Most educators saw their courses as significantly less detailed and with less management support while necessitating more adjustments to interact with the students and needing to encourage synchronous interaction. Many educators also indicated problems outside of their control, such as student accountability, motivation, interest, and technological challenges. Though educators with prior online teaching experience rate course design similar to that of educators without this experience, those without experience have less confidence in their students' performance and learning. Those with prior experience were also generally more comfortable with the online format as they were accustomed to technological tools and the hybrid setting.

Overall, the pandemic has brought on changes that will have a lasting impact. By understanding how language teachers cope with stressors, it is hoped that in the future, there will be a greater emphasis on supporting educators when they are facing adversity (MacIntyre et al., 2020). Additionally, educators need to receive proper training to prepare them how to deliver online courses effectively. It is necessary to also include increased technology training in all aspects and even increasing technology use in a face-to-face classroom. The benefits of this could be that students and instructors will be more prepared if the need to move remotely arises (Moser et al., 2021).

Lessons Learned from Remote Learning: Flexibility and Compassion

Even though the pandemic has caused negative impacts on teachers' emotions and wellbeing, the reality is that we all have learned to cope with our current teaching situations. Additionally, many teachers without a computer-assisted language learning (CALL) background have improved their teaching strategies after their experience teaching online (Anderson et al., 2021). Given the lessons learned during the pandemic, it is evident that language instructors now are better prepared to offer different teaching formats (online, hybrid & flipped) and offer students the flexibility to choose the format that is most suitable for them (Pardo-Ballester, 2021a; Yi Xu et al., 2021).

During the pandemic, instructional designers, language teachers, language directors, language coordinators, presidents, and provosts learned quickly that flexibility and compassion were key to finish the Spring 2020 semester and continue teaching during this pandemic time. There are reflections posted on blogs or academic journals about how different people with administrative duties at private or public institutions moved forward during the COVID-19 outbreak (Sosulski, 2020; Rossomondo, 2020). Those reflections inform us about the difficulty of the emergency transition for remote teaching and the steps that followed. Directors of Language centers, course designers, and IT departments were crucial to getting ahead and informing about the necessary technologies like videoconferences via Zoom, WebEx,

Microsoft Teams, and Google Meet to teach synchronously, or other tools for learning asynchronously via VoiceThread, Vocaroo, and Vozme (Pardo-Ballester, 2020). Language teachers received necessary information about technology to teach conversation, listening, grammar or classes focused on content. Those people with higher administrative ranks needed to protect the health of everyone, ensuring that the Spring semester would be completed, while providing students and faculty the vital support and training they needed to make remote teaching possible (Sosulski, 2020). That is why language educators participated in workshops or had more meetings than usual to ensure fairness for our students who were sent home in the middle of a course.

Flexibility and compassion were the keys, demonstrated by many educators (Rossomondo, 2020). Attendance and participation conducted synchronously were difficult to control because some students could be in quarantine. Therefore, we were flexible, tolerant, and organized our courses the best that we could to keep interacting with our students and helping them to learn the language and content (Pardo-Ballester, 2020). Grades were often inflated, and all requests for accommodations and extensions were granted as well. Students did not fail a language course based on attendance and thus the feedback from students was overwhelmingly positive about remote learning (Rossomondo, 2020). The reality is that we did the best we could, and the workload was heavy for many educators who learned new techniques and worried about their students' anxiety and stress (Moser et al., 2021; Gregersen et al., 2021).

Teachers also suffered from anxiety, stress, and sadness for many other reasons, but there is a lack of reflections or published articles informing us about what administrators specifically did for their educators when the teachers' health was not stable (Pardo-Ballester, 2021b). The teacher's job is to educate, control the class, engage with students, and receive excellent feedback from students via evaluations. However, when they are not at their best due to psychological issues, they still have to move forward. It is unusual to stop teaching suddenly, but we teachers had to bite the bullet and keep teaching. Students are aware of teachers' problems when they react with anger for not doing their homework or not understanding a reading assignment, especially if this happens often. However, students typically are not aware of their teachers' emotions such as sadness, because we often are trying to stay strong and do our jobs. When good teachers are experiencing emotional stress, they sometimes put on an invisible shield for protection while in action. Teachers can be flexible and compassionate towards students, but we do not ask students to do the same for us. However, we can talk about our situations to our superiors in order to find alternative solutions together.

RESEARCH QUESTIONS

This study aims to answer the following research questions:

1. What type of teaching strategies did language teachers have before the pandemic?
2. Did language teachers perceive a change in their teaching strategies due to the emergency remote teaching?
3. What coping strategies do language teachers use in pandemic times?
4. With more work than before the pandemic and without new teaching strategies on language assessment, how did the pandemic affect teachers' mental health when assessing students? What are the language teachers' perceptions about language assessment in post-pandemic times?

5. Do language teachers experience significantly different psychological consequences of COVID-19 with regard to:
   a. Before the pandemic and at the beginning of the pandemic (Spring 2020)
   b. During the pandemic (Fall 2020 & Spring 2021)
   c. What did language teachers do to stay positive?

METHODOLOGY

An exploratory mixed method approach was adopted in this study (Cresswell & Plano Clark, 2018).

Participants

One hundred seventy-five world language teachers in higher education within the United States fully or partially completed an online questionnaire. Participant background information is shown in Table 1: 123 were females, 46 males, four selected the option "I prefer not saying," and two participants skipped the gender question. Participants reported teaching 21 target languages. The five top languages were English as a Second Language (ESL), French, German, Portuguese, and Spanish. Spanish was the target language with the higher percentage reported. The number of Spanish respondents could have been due to how this data was first collected via email to this author's contacts in institutions across the country. The majority of the author's connections teach Spanish as the primary target language. The teaching experience was varied. Thirteen educators reported more than 30 years of teaching experience, 25 selected less than five years of experience, and 29 indicated more than 15 years of teaching experience. The higher number of participants was 37 with more than 20 years of experience, followed by 35 participants with more than ten years and the same number with more than five years of experience.

When asked about the type of position they hold at their institution, 14 reported holding an Assistant Professor position, and seven of those had administrative responsibilities, such as directing or coordinating a language program. Twenty-three participants reported holding an Associate Professor position; 10 of those participants had administrative duties such as chair or director of language section or program. Nineteen were Full Professors, and eight of them had managerial responsibilities. Only tenured or tenure-track participants reported foreign language CALL as one of their research areas. Fifty hold a non-tenure-track position and identified as lecturers, including two who were language coordinators, nine participants were Assistant Teaching Professors, 10 had an Associate Teaching Professor position, and one participant reported to be staff without any more information, so this participant could have an advisor position or any other staff position covering courses when in need. Of the 45 participants who reported being a Teaching Assistant, 35 identified themselves as pursuing a Ph.D. degree and seven a Master's degree, three of them did not specify the type of degree pursuing. Less than 10% of participants hold a technology-related degree: five participants (1.87%) indicated having a degree in curriculum and instructional technology, and 17 (6.34%) had a degree in Applied Linguistics and technology.

Table 1. Background information of participants

Category	Level	n	Percent [a]
Gender	Female Male Not saying	123 46 4	71.10 26.59 2.31
Target language	Spanish German French ESL Portuguese	109 13 14 10 9	59.23 7.06 7.6 5.43 4.89
Years of teaching experience	More than 30 More than 20 More than 15 More than 10 More than 5 Less than 5	13 37 29 35 35 25	7.47 21.26 16.67 20.11 20.11 14.37
Type of position	Tenure track or tenured Non-tenure track Graduate Teaching Instructor Another type	56 70 45 3	32.18 40.22 25.86 1.72
Type of degrees	Curriculum and instructional technology Applied linguistics and technology Applied linguistics without expertise in technology Literature with a focus on a foreign language I keep up with technology to help students learning the language I use the traditional slides, transparency, smartboard, videos, and LMS	5 17 37 92 64 53	1.87 6.34 13.81 34.33 23.88 19.78
Institution	Public university research 1. My department has a graduate program Public university research 1. My department does not have a graduate program. Private university research 1 with a graduate program. Public university research 2. My department has a graduate program. Public university research 2. My department does not offer a graduate program. Private university research 2. My department offers a graduate program. Private university research 2. My department does not offer a graduate program. Community college Private liberal arts college Other types	72 17 3 8 5 1 2 6 9 4	56 13 2 6 4 1 2 5 11 3

Note: There are a few missing data points for the categories: types of positions, years of teaching experience, and institutions. Participants reported multiple options in the target language, type of degrees, and institutions. [a] N=175

Instrument and Data Collection

This researcher designed an online survey for data collection. The items were designed using the book *Tools for Teaching* by Barbara G. Davis (1993) and Moser et al. (2021) that inform about teaching strategies for college and university teaching and teaching practices respectfully. Questions about coping strategies, stress, and wellbeing were developed following the article from MacIntyre et al. (2020). The questions were first piloted with four Spanish professors located in the United States to ensure items were easily understood and items were appropriate to all types of language teachers regardless teaching experience. Some items of the questionnaire were deleted, and some were adapted after the piloting. The survey is composed of fifty-four items, but one item was not taken into consideration because even though it was adapted after piloting, for some respondents it was not clear. A skip pattern option was set in the survey so that respondents were only asked to complete some items if they confirmed or refuted

some statements about psychological emotions. The items are: a) multiple-choice items with a 5-point Likert scale; b) items with the option to select multiple answers created up to 15 sub items within one question. Moreover, one of the options offered the opportunity to comment, giving participants the chance to share information not included in selecting responses; c) items with a binary format (yes or no); and d) one open-ended question. Cronbach's alpha for internal consistency among the self-reported items for teaching strategies (before and in post-times pandemic), coping strategies during the pandemic, and teachers' perceptions about language assessment was 0.717 for 114 items and sub items.
The anonymous online survey consisted of various types of questions:

1. Ten items were about demographic information and contextual information.
2. Twelve items asked about their perceptions on teaching strategies or practices and their stress levels before the pandemic.
3. Twenty-four questions dealt with the situation during the pandemic from March 2020 to April 2021. This section informs about their research production during the pandemic and their psychological and mental health within different pandemic periods, such as reasons for staying positive during the pandemic.
4. Seven items looked at perceptions of teaching foreign languages once the pandemic is controlled: students' engagement, students' preference for language learning, testing methods, and more options for students to succeed in a language course.

The anonymous online survey was administered via Qualtrics between April 5 and April 14, 2021. Twenty-five colleagues located in a variety of institutions were asked to share the anonymous link with colleagues. The survey was also distributed to subscribers of the Computer-Assisted Language Instruction Consortium (CALICO) and subscribers of the Distance Learning group from the American Council on the Teaching of Foreign Languages (ACTFL), calling for participation from language instructors at the university level within the United States.

Data Analysis

Survey response items were analyzed via SPSS using dichotomous variables (1 for marking an option and 0 if the option is not marked). To address the first four research questions regarding language teachers' strategies before and during the pandemic, coping strategies during the pandemic, and future teaching practices on post-pandemic times, descriptive statistics of items were calculated. Repeated measures t-tests were performed to answer research questions 5a and 5b to evaluate if the COVID-19 crisis affected language teachers in different times and to investigate if there was a change in their responses. Descriptive statistics were computed to answer research question 5c about strategies to stay positive during the pandemic.

RESULTS

Teaching Practices and Strategies Before the Pandemic

Descriptive statistics were computed for learning about the different formats that teachers were familiar with before the pandemic. One hundred fifty-seven responded to seven items related to different models for teaching languages. Results from descriptive statistics revealed the lack of preparation to teach remotely online. The highest number of the survey respondents (M=.82, SD=.384) stated to be familiar with teaching F2F using online exercises from a publisher (Pearson, McGraw Hill, Wiley, etc.). More than half of our participants reported being used to teach F2F without technology (M=.59, SD=.494). Less than half reported to be familiar teaching with the flipped model (M=43, SD=.497). What is most concerning, however, are the high numbers from teachers who were not accustomed to teaching hybrid with F2F and synchronous teaching online (78%, M=.22, SD=413) or hybrid with F2F and asynchronous teaching online (75%, M=.25, SD=.437). Similar results appeared from not being familiar with teaching synchronously online (73%, M=.27, SD= .444) or asynchronously online (70%, M=.30, SD= .459).

In order to learn a foreign language, it is essential to interact with other students, with native speakers, and with the help of one's professors to develop second language skills. Teachers expose learners to a variety of input when teaching, and they model activities before asking students to work on them. Teachers make pedagogical choices when teaching a second language, but there are teachers with more or less experience, and depending on their training and years of experience, there will be differences in a lesson's comprehensibility. Table 2 summarizes the descriptive statistics of the items selected for teaching strategies. Item 3 asked participants to select all practices that they did before the pandemic to evaluate whether students understood the lessons taught. Almost all teachers selected classroom discussions in class (M=.91, SD=.285), followed by communicating via email (M=.69, SD=.464), student self-reflection (M=.63, SD=.485), and mid-semester questionnaire (M=.59, SD=.492). Fewer teachers reported using an end-of-semester questionnaire (M=.51, SD=.502), or weekly journal entries (M=.18, SD=.383), or they would quiz their students using audience response software such as Kahoot (M=.46, SD=.500) or electronic discussion outside of class (M=.38, SD=.487). This suggests that teachers generally relied on traditional practices within the F2F instruction, and technology was not often used, even by half of the teachers in or outside of the classroom.

Item 4 concentrates on what was done to reduce students' anxiety and enhance their performance in tests, quizzes or another type of assessment. The majority of the participants explain the format of the exam before the test (M=.87, SD=.334). They also have review sessions before major exams (M=.82, SD=.388), advise students on how to study or how to prepare for an exam (M=.80, SD=.398), and answer their emails and post information on the platform (M=.78, SD=.412). More than half of teachers selected the option to give more than one examination (M=.61, SD=.488). They also asked students how they could help them feel less anxious (M=.54, SD=.388), encouraged students to study in groups (M=.56, SD=.498), and avoided pop quizzes (M=.51, SD=.514). Fewer of the participants distributed practice exams or posted them online (M=.40, SD=.491), scheduled extra office hours before a test (M=.39, SD=.488), included one or more extra credit question on the exam (M=.31, SD=.464), gave students the opportunity to comment on the test (M=.20, SD=.398), or handed out essay questions in advance (M=.21, SD=.408). A very small portion gave another strategy for reducing anxiety during assessments (M=.15, SD=.354). Their responses were to drop the lowest grade, re-take the first test, offer low-stakes formative assessments that do not weigh as much as other assessments, emphasize task-based language learning (TBLL) presentations using multimedia, give writing assignments outside of the class period, have group projects and final projects. Two educators could not comment because the semester of the pandemic was their first semester teaching. Very few teachers reported making the first exam very easy

Table 2. Descriptive statistics of teaching strategies items

Statements	N	M	SD
3.1 Student self-reflection	158	.63	.485
3.2 Mid-semester questionnaire	158	.59	.492
3.3 End-of-semester questionnaire	158	.51	.502
3.4 Weekly journal entries	158	.18	.383
3.5 Communicate via email	158	.69	.464
3.6 Classroom discussions in class	158	.91	.285
3.7 Electronic discussions outside of class	158	.38	.487
3.8 Quiz them using audience response software such as Kahoot, Quizizz, …	158	.46	.500
4.1 Ask students how I could help them feel less anxious	158	.54	.500
4.2 Avoid pop quizzes	158	.51	.514
4.3 Review sessions before major exams	158	.82	.388
4.4 Advise them on how to study or prepare for an exam	158	.80	.398
4.5 Make the first exam very easy	158	.06	.233
4.6 Give more than one examination	158	.61	.488
4.7 Encourage students to study in groups	158	.56	.498
4.8 Schedule extra office hours before a test	158	.39	.488
4.9 Answer their emails and post information on the platform…	158	.78	.412
4.10 Before an exam, explain the format to students	158	.87	.334
4.11 Distribute practice exams or post them online	158	.40	.491
4.12 Include one or more extra-credit questions on the exam	158	.31	.464
4.13 Give students the opportunity to comment on the test	158	.20	.398
4.14 Hand out essay questions in advance	158	.21	.408
5.1 Give students the opportunity to comment on the test	158	.40	.491
5.2 Post grades promptly	158	.81	.393
5.3 Use some class time to discuss the overall results	158	.83	.377
5.4 Schedule extra office hours after posting grades	158	.22	.413
5.5 Offer extra credit to improve the current grade for a specific assessment	158	.20	.403
5.6 Give students a second chance to learn by administering …a second test…	158	.17	.377
6.1 Enthusiasm about the subject I teach	158	.94	.233
6.2 Organization of the course	158	.92	.267
6.3 Good rapport with students	158	.92	.276
6.4 Use of appropriate and understandable examples	158	.90	.295
6.5 Make students active participants in learning	158	.95	.221
6.6 Help students set achievable goals for themselves	157	.54	.500
6.7 Hold high but realistic expectations for your students	157	.81	.394
6.8 Tell students what they need to do to succeed in my course	157	.89	.320
6.9 Avoid creating intense competition among students	157	.66	.477
6.10 Respond to their work	157	.94	.245
7.1 I varied my teaching methods (role-playing, debates, brainstorming, ...)	134	.97	.171
7.2 I let students have some say in choosing what will be studied	134	.33	.471
7.3 I worked from students' strengths and interests	134	.72	.449
7.4 I increased the difficulty of the material as the semester progresses	134	.57	.496
7.5 Another strategy	134	.12	.325
8.1 I assigned the reading at least two sessions before it will be discussed	134	.58	.495
8.2 I assigned study questions	142	.63	.485
8.3 I asked students to write a one-word journal or one-word sentence	142	.15	.356
8.4 I asked non-threatening questions about the reading	142	.65	.477
8.5 I used class time as a reading period	142	.32	.470
8.6 Another strategy	142	.16	.370
9.1 I give students feedback as quickly as possible	136	.96	.206
9.2 I reward success using positive comments	136	.72	.450
9.3 I introduce students to the good work done by their peers	136	.39	.489

(M=.06, SD=.233). Descriptive data suggests that educators are aware of students' anxiety when taking tests and the majority of them are concerned about their language achievement while maintaining the standards. This suggestion is supported by item 5 data. This item asked teachers about their actions after administering a test or another type of assessment. The majority of the participants reported using some class time to discuss the overall results (M=.83, SD=.377) and posting grades promptly (M=.81, SD=.393). Less than half gave students the opportunity to comment on the test (M=.40, SD=.491). Less than one-fourth scheduled extra office hours after posting grades (M=.22, SD=.413), or offered extra credit to improve their current grade for a specific assessment (M=.20, SD=.403), or gave students a second chance to learn by administering and grading a second test with different questions (M= .17, SD=.377).

Motivation is key for language acquisition, and language educators are aware of the importance of motivation (Larsen-Freeman, & Long, 1994). Items 6 and 7 were related to the teachers' practices and the organization of their courses to motivate students. Means values for motivation are very high for most of the statements when teaching before the pandemic. Language teachers perceived that in order to motivate students they need to offer a variety of teaching methods such as role playing, debates, brainstorming, games, or discussions (M=.97, SD=.171), making students active participants in learning (M=.95, SD=.221), and responding to their work (M=.94, SD=.245). Moreover, they need to be enthusiastic about the subject they are teaching (M=.94, SD=.233), have a good rapport with students (M=.92, SD=.276) and organize their courses (M=.92, SD=.267). In addition, they need to use appropriate and understandable examples (M=.90, SD=.295), inform students what they need to do to succeed in their courses (M=.89, SD=.320), and hold high but realistic expectations for their students (M=.81, SD=.394). More than half of the educators considered it important to avoid creating intense competition among students (M=.66, SD=.477) and to help students set achievable goals for themselves (M=.54, SD=.500). When organizing the course to motivate students, almost three fourths of the participants claimed that they work from students' strengths and interests (M=.72, SD=.449), and more than half of the participants increased the difficulty of the material as the semester progressed (M=.57, SD=.496). More than one third of the participants let students have some say in choosing what they will study (M=.33, SD=.471). Moreover, when asking them to give other strategies, they responded with collaboration, interaction, real-world practice in the target language, conducting a needs analysis at the beginning of class, co-creating the syllabus together, and using Project Based Language Learning (PBLL) and Question Formulation Technique (Right Question Institute; https://rightquestion.org/).

According to the data, the participants asked non-threatening questions about the readings (M=.65, SD=.477), assigned study questions (M=.63, SD=.485), and assigned the reading at least two sessions before the assignment was discussed (M=.58, SD=.495). More than one fourth of the participants used class time as a reading period (M=.32, SD=.470). Less than one fourth of educators asked students to write a one-word journal or one-word sentence (M=.15, SD=.356). Other strategies reported were teaching reading strategies, doing pre-reading advance organizers to assist students with reading assignments, having pre-class discussions, submitting reading notes for completion of credit, assigning reading according to their interests, giving reading quizzes and chapter summaries, providing videos or audios related to the readings, introducing vocabulary, and discussing the context of the story (M=.16, SD=.370). Almost all our respondents gave students feedback as quickly as possible (M=.96, SD=.206). Almost three fourths of the participants rewarded success using positive comments (M=.72, SD=.450), and less than half responded to introduce students to the good work done by their peers (M=.39, SD=.489).

Teaching Strategies' Improvement After Experiencing the Impact of the Pandemic

The mean of item 26 was 1.19 (1=Yes, 2=No) with a standard deviation of .397. Only 28 participants (19.44%) responded to not having improved their teaching skills because they already had online teaching experience. Therefore, 116 participants improved their teaching skills (80.56%). This means that most respondents were positive about improving their teaching practices after teaching online in Spring 2020, Fall 2020 and/or in Spring 2021. Further analysis from item 33 revealed how their teaching practices improved due to the emergency online transition. The majority of respondents learned about new tools to teach online (M=.87, SD=.340), and they learned to teach with the online format (M=.70, SD=.458). They recognized that their digital resources were greater than before and that they adapted their F2F class to online synchronously (M=.69, SD=.463). Almost half of the participants carefully considered what students said via questionnaires or during class (M=.49, SD=.503), and more than half gave encouragement to students who were performing poorly (M=.57, SD= .497). Almost one fourth of participants indicated that they now know how to teach with the hybrid format (M=.24, SD=.427). Less than one fourth of participants perceived that teaching online synchronously reduced students' anxiety about tests (M=.21, SD=.408). They also learned the new strategy of requesting students' oral or written paraphrases about a lecture or a reading assignment (M=.22, SD=.416) and asked students to provide a summary of the reading (M=.18; SD=.389). Some educators were aware of students' temptations for cheating, so they used take-home exams (M=.20, SD=.403). A very small portion of participating teachers said they recorded their online classes to review their performance and improve their teaching (M=.18, SD=.389). Some participants commented on another reason for improving their teaching strategies (M=.19, SD=. 396). Some comments were related to the advantages of teaching online and doing many things online, which were not possible F2F. They mentioned the use of Zoom during class and the copious feedback and explanations on essays. Moreover, they pre-recorded lectures or mini-lectures to have more time in class for discussion and interaction. Finally, they eliminated exams and switched to mini projects, final projects or even to a project-based curriculum.

Coping Strategies during the Pandemic

The majority of teachers relied on communicating with their students (M=.87, SD=.343) as one of the coping strategies during the transition over the emergency online teaching or social distancing during F2F instruction. Almost three fourths of participants kept a positive attitude (M=.74, SD=.438) and were flexible with their students turning in assignments (M=.71, SD=.456). They were humble and honestly told their students that they were also learning in the process (M=.67, SD=.473). More than half of the participants were confident with their capacity for adapting to the new environment (M=.61, SD=.490) and they were motivated to learn more about online teaching (M=.55, SD=.500). Other coping strategies that were reported were: 1) fostering a digital community (M=.46, SD=.500), 2) having efficient Internet (M=.44, SD=.498), 3) trusting students' technical skills (M=.31, SD=.463), 4) letting students learn the language at their own pace (M=.18, SD=.383), and 5) fostering language learning by letting students watch the video lessons more than once (M=.10, SD= .300). What follows summarizes the participants' comments to the coping strategies item from the last sub item 'Another response. Please explain' (M=.06, SD=. 234).

Teachers' Perceptions about Language Assessment

Participants were asked if grades were inflated due to the current pandemic situation. Only 35% (50 out of 142 respondents) did not feel grades were inflated (M=1.35, SD=.479), but the remainder of the educators confirmed the idea of grade inflation. More than half of the teachers who confirmed grade inflation thought it was due to taking online quizzes or giving open book tests (M=.62, SD=.489), or even feeling sorry for some distressed students with mental health problems (M=.60, SD=.492). Almost half of the teachers reported that eliminating materials from the course (M=.47, SD=.502) led to grade inflation. More than one-fourth of educators felt they needed to help students who came to class daily (M=.33, SD=.473) and to encourage them to keep taking language courses (M=.30, SD=.459). One-fourth of respondents agreed that students looked for new strategies to improve their grades (M=.25, SD=.437). Educators commented about grade inflation and their comments were grouped into six themes:

1. Pressure from their institution urging faculty to be more lenient in terms of grades due to the multiple challenges associated with the pandemic crisis.
2. Students experiencing a difficult situation: Understand the hardships that students are facing due to the pandemic and the importance to keep moving forward when students are fragile.
3. Forced to help students even after suspected plagiarism with open books, online translators or by not using a camera for the final oral examination.
4. Motivation: Teachers gave points for every assignment or discussion that they asked students to do. They also motivated them by giving extra chances to turn in late work or resubmit assignments with low grades.
5. Changing the curriculum: Tests were eliminated and grades were based on oral presentations or other type of assignments.
6. Working hard with students and feeling sorry for not being able to be with them physically or excusing them for the Internet connection problems.

Language educators were asked to agree or disagree with some testing methods that they would plan to use in the future (1= strongly disagree up to 5 = strongly agree). They agree or strongly agree with traditional testing methods such as using oral presentations (M=4.39, SD=.876), oral exams (M=4.13, SD=1.04), essay questions to assess comprehension and interpret material (M=4.07, SD=1.07), and multiple-choice or short answer questions for assessing students' specific knowledge (M=4.04, SD=1.00). The mean was lower for matching tests for recognition of vocabulary and definitions (M=3.57, SD=1.23). When asked for testing methods where students work together as a team and collaborate to achieve a grade, language teachers did not approve the use of paired testing to work on a single essay exam (M=2.89, SD=1.18). In a previous section 'Teaching practices and strategies before the pandemic,' educators agreed that motivation is important in language acquisition and almost all participants agree with making students active participants in class (M=.95, SD=221). In item 7, they also confirmed that before the pandemic they varied their teaching methods with role-playing, debates, discussions… (M=.97, SD=.171). This suggests that educators are aware that interaction and collaboration are essential for language learning. However, their teaching practices are not aligned with their assessments.

One hundred and thirty-one educators agreed or disagreed with some statements for assessing students once the pandemic is over. They were moderately positive about quizzing students using audience response software such as Kahoot, Quizizz, Top Hat, Poll Everywhere and others (M=3.67, SD=1.21) or distributing practice exams or posting them online (M=3.45, SD=1.34). More than one-fourth of teachers agree to letting students have some say in choosing what will be studied (M=3.34, SD=1.24). They were impartial about the idea to include one or more extra-credit question on the exams (M=3.01, SD=1.34). Language teachers disagree with removing attendance from the grading criteria (M=2.20, SD=1.27) and agree or completely agree with advising students on how to study or prepare for an exam (M=4.53, SD=.930). These results suggest that educators would like to continue with the same methods as before the pandemic. They will use some technology for assessing and for offering students the opportunity to have access to the material online, but attendance will continue to be part of the grading criteria in the curriculum.

Psychological Consequences of COVID-19

I conducted a paired-sample t-test to explore whether the pandemic significantly affected the language teachers' health. compared the data of item 24, which asked if before the pandemic they were stressed due to their job, and item 20 that asked if they were distressed or had mental health problems at the beginning of the pandemic (Spring 2020) due to the emergency online transition. Results of this comparison indicated that the crisis significantly affected teachers' health. 142 participants were compared: before the pandemic (M=1.44, SD=.498) to Spring 2020 (M=.1.61, SD=.490), t (141) -3.089, p=0.002 (two-tailed). The mean increased in their responses (M=.169) with a 95% confidence interval ranging from -.277 to -.061. Results from Cohen's d (.652) revealed the comparison of effect sizes from before the pandemic to the beginning of the pandemic was medium following Cohen's (1992) guidelines.

The second repeated measures techniques compared the effect of the pandemic in Fall 2020 and Spring 2021. Items 28 and 31 have the same content as item 20 but indicates different semesters. Once again, results indicated that there was a significant increase of health problems from Fall 2020 to Spring 2021 but with a relatively smaller valid sample size compared to the first t-test computed before Spring 2020 and Spring 2020. Thirty-one respondents were compared in Fall 2020 (M=1.64, SD=.482) and Spring 2021 (M=1.32, SD=.475), t (30) -3.780, p=0.00069 (two-tailed). The mean decreased (M=-.323) with a 95% confidence interval ranging from -.497 to -.148. The comparison of effect sizes from Fall 2020 to Spring 2021 was small (Cohen's d .475).

Nine items explored the reasons for not diminishing the distress level or mental health problems during Fall 2020. Two of those items offered the opportunity to explain their personal situation. Thirty teachers selected multiple answers. The majority of them were distressed for having more work than usual (M=.87, SD=.346). More than half of the respondents were not satisfied teaching online (M=.60, SD=.498) and the same number (60%) selected due to their personal situations. Their personal situations were health issues (anxiety, depression, low self-esteem, and getting COVID-19), having children learning at home, financial problems, and immigration issues. Results revealed that more than half were teaching with a modality they were familiar with (67%, M=. 33, SD=.479) and almost three fourths were familiar with the teaching tools (73%, M=.27, SD=.450). Six teachers were distressed from losing a relative or good friend due to COVID-19 (M=.20, SD=.407). Six respondents (M=.20, SD=.407) also explained that they were worried about family in the healthcare business, dramatic changes in their living situation and unexpected extra financial burdens due to the pandemic, negative feedback from committees and spending too much time and energy teaching. One teacher stated:

'Teaching a course I had never taught before and having to create a lot of materials for it. Grading in digital format proved to be very time-consuming. Also, Academic Dishonesty was rampant in online work.'

Seven items looked at reasons for being distressed or having mental health issues during the spring 2021. Twenty-one teachers selected one or more reasons for their distress. The highest number of participants decided to comment on their reason for having health problems (M=.67, SD=. 483). Their comments were grouped into five themes: They commented about teaching (low self-confidence about meeting students' needs through synchronous remote teaching, poor connectivity, being worn out from interacting on Zoom, grading by hand, lack of control over cheating due to online teaching, and dislike of the hybrid model). The second theme was personal problems, i.e. dealing with kids at home while teaching, family stress or problems related with partner. The third theme was about health; teachers suffered from anxiety or were worried about their health or the health of their dependents. Others commented about the workload related to service within their institution. The final theme was related to humanity. Specifically, one teacher stated:

'I am discouraged by how many people deny Covid-19 is real, refuse to wear masks and keep distant, and are vaccine hesitant. It has reduced by faith in humanity to see how uncivil people have been.'

The second highest numbers were being behind with research and having heavy workload (M=.57, SD=.507). Other problems reported were being distressed about promotion or job security and being worn out teaching hybrid with small group-size of asynchronous sessions (M=43, SD=.507). A low number of educators were scared about COVID and people spreading it in Spring 2021 and Summer 2021 (M=.19, SD=.402). This suggests that 81% were not concerned about spreading the virus. No one reported fearing that social distancing will continue in Fall 2021.

One hundred and forty-six language educators responded in item 34 to report about their power to stay positive during the crisis. Teachers declared doing exercise (M=.77, SD=.424), being grateful for many things such as health, family, or having a job… (M=.74, SD=.440), being resilient (M=.68, SD=.469), learning new things (M=.59, SD= .494), caring for themselves (M=.59, SD=.494), eating healthy (M=.56, SD=.498), connecting digitally with their friends (M=.54, SD=.500), having a positive attitude about life (M=.50, SD=.502), spending more time with their families (M=.42, SD=.496), and meditating (M=.31,SD=.463). Twenty-one teachers confirmed working remotely with their psychologist (M=.14, SD=352) and 22 commented other reasons for staying positive. Their responses are summarized into six themes:

1. Taking anti-depressants or medications for anxiety.
2. Their religious faith.
3. Staying connected and working with colleagues.
4. Informally mentoring minority and first-generation students and appreciating students for whom they have become teachers.
5. Having a more flexible schedule allowing teachers to set personal and work goals, and using the extra time to work harder.
6. Finding pleasure in small things, such as eating chocolate and playing with pets, shopping and looking for bargains, watching TV, creative writing and journaling, and making donations to support progressive political and charitable organizations.

FUTURE RESEARCH DIRECTIONS

Additional research is needed on language attendance and assessment, particularly in the areas of group collaboration or class discussion. There is a gap between language teachers' instruction and assessing their students with the same techniques used in the classroom. Empirical studies could be conducted to uncover the misalignment between teaching and assessment. Changes to policies within language programs could be beneficial for student learning and for teachers' mental health by preventing negative effects when assessing students.

CONCLUSION

Regarding the lack of preparation to teaching remotely, the findings in this study are aligned with those of Moser et al. (2021) and Xi Lu et al. (2021) about language teachers not having any teaching experience teaching hybrid or online models before the pandemic. Findings also suggest that when teaching F2F prior to the crisis, instructors relied on traditional practices and half of our participants did not include technology in or outside of the classroom. These results are expected because in order to teach hybrid or online courses, teachers need a different pedagogy (Blake, 2012; Russell, 2020). It is essential to motivate students and put them together in pairs or groups to collaborate (Russell, 2020). Results from before the pandemic also revealed that language teachers knew how to handle anxiety issues when teaching in the classroom and when administering assessments.

Even though the pandemic brought distress and teachers were not prepared for the emergency remote teaching, previous studies reported that teachers have learned from the experience and that teachers now are prepared for teaching using technology and know more about designing and teaching in different formats. Results from descriptive statistics showed that 81% (116 participants out of 144) improved their teaching experience due to the pandemic. They learned how to use new digital tools and new models. Moreover, 70% reported learning to teach synchronously online due to the pandemic and before the pandemic 73% (115 participants out of 157) declared not knowing how to teach a language course with the model synchronously online. Findings of this study are consistent with those of previous studies (Pardo-Ballester, 2021a; Sosulski, 2020; Xi Lu et al., 2021).

Furthermore, qualitative data indicated that most teachers were patient and had compassion for their students. They were also flexible with students turning in assignments and found new strategies to teach online such as eliminating exams and using final projects or oral presentations. Results from qualitative data showed consistency with Rossomondo (2020), and Sosulski, (2020). Language teachers also indicated flexibility with their own agendas, not just flexibility with their students. This finding was not reported in other studies.

Findings from quantitative data showed that 87% of educators were very communicative with their students, 74% had a positive attitude while teaching, and 61% of teachers have confidence to adapt their teaching to the new environment. In addition, 46% of teachers stated they were fostering the digital community. Following MacIntyre et al. (2020), these coping strategies were categorized as approach strategies and as in their study, findings indicated that the majority of our respondents relied on approach strategies instead of avoidant strategies.

Results in this study indicated that 35% (50 teachers out of 142) inflated students' grades for different reasons: feeling sorry for their situations, pressure from their administrators, plagiarism, to motivate students, and a change of the language curriculum. Our findings are also consistent with previous investigations about grade inflation (Pardo-Ballester, 2020; Rossomondo, 2020). In addition, even if grade inflation is an issue that was present before the pandemic, findings of the current study suggest that grade inflation was a new strategy that teachers and administrators adopted to compensate students who were suffering the effects of the pandemic.

Findings about language assessment indicated that only 25% (31 teachers out of 122) indicated that in the future they are willing to use paired testing to work on a single essay exam. Considering that, 97% (130 participants of 134) of participants recognized using collaboration and interaction as a teaching method before the pandemic, the low frequency of teachers willing to test students with collaborative work suggest that teaching practices are not aligned with assessment. Teachers could also foster collaborative assessment as professionals do across the world. When teaching a second language, many language educators prepare students for their workplace (King Ramirez & Lafford, 2018). If collaboration is key for language acquisition, why do language teachers often refuse to use collaboration in testing? Some respondents in our study commented on the use of oral presentations or projects instead of using exams, and the new change in their curriculum worked during the pandemic. So, why do we want to go back to our outdated assessment practices when the pandemic is over?

Attendance has also been an important element for language assessment. Findings in the current study suggest that teachers will keep using attendance in their classes and it will be part of their grading system. This finding was not consistent with Rossomondo's reflection (2020) about updating their curriculum in which students could fail for lack of attendance. She described the courses in the Spanish program to be offered in formats that require F2F meetings, and they had a strict attendance policy. In their program, they value class participation, which accounts for 20% of the final grade and there is no way to make up for it in case of absence. She described that flexibility had not been a driving principle in their program.

Regarding the teachers' health, this study reports a statistically significant difference between language teachers' stress level before the pandemic and at the beginning of the pandemic. Findings are consistent with several studies (McIntyre et al., 2020; Moser et al., 2021; Anderson et al., 2021, Gregersen et al., 2021) with language teachers suffering stress in the Spring 2020. Moreover, the significant difference found before the pandemic and at the beginning of the pandemic is consistent with Moser et al.'s study (2021) about the stress and concern that teachers suffered due to the educational and emotional wellbeing of their students. The current findings are also aligned with Hartshorn & McMurry's (2020) study that confirmed the teachers' distress due to overload teaching, adaptation to remote teaching, and other type of stressors such as worries for their families and their job security. It is noteworthy that this study also revealed a significant difference of the distress level or mental health problems during Fall 2020 and Spring 2021. In the Fall 2020, teachers reported that their health problems were related to their teaching responsibilities, financial problems, dissatisfaction teaching online, and the loss of a relative or friend due to COVID-19. The stress was higher in the Fall 2020 than in the Spring 2021. For example, in the Spring 2021, teachers stated to be worn out teaching with Zoom, concerned about their job promotion or security, but none of 31 respondents were concerned about social distance in Fall 2021. In addition, the majority of teachers were not even concerned about the spreading of COVID-19. These findings, to my knowledge, have not been reported in any other studies.

Language teachers suffered from health problems due to the stressors of the pandemic and other stressors prior the crisis, but even when their workload increased and they were concerned for their family's health, they were very successful in teaching their courses remotely. Moreover, in the Fall 2020 and Spring 2021, they taught their courses with online or hybrid models with more preparation.

In those situations, they reported communicating with their students and encouraging them to do their assignments. In general, they did their teaching job well, but the health of some teachers was vulnerable when they could not control plagiarism and did not have support from their administrators. These health issues continued until the end of the course due to the model they were forced to teach. As Proietti Ergun and Dewaele (2021) found, when teachers have experience teaching online, learners have experiences that are more positive. They also found that language teachers with high levels of wellbeing are likely to be more successful teachers and can better face obstacles. Their study sheds light on data and prompts policy makers and stakeholders to give more autonomy to language teachers to select a teaching model that matches their preference in order to enable teachers to be more successful.

REFERENCES

Anderson, R. C., Bousselot, T., Katz-Buoincontro, J., & Todd, J. (2021). Generating buoyancy in a sea of uncertainty: Teachers creativity and well-being during the Covid-19 pandemic. *Frontiers in Psychology, 11*, 1–17. doi:10.3389/fpsyg.2020.614774 PMID:33536979

Blake, R. (2012). Best practices in online learning: Is it for everyone? In F. Rubio & J. Thoms (Eds.), *Issues in Language Program Direction: Hybrid language teaching and learning: Exploring theoretical, pedagogical and curricular issues* (pp. 10–26). Heinle & Heinle.

Cohen, A., Hoy, L., & Dull, B. (2020). A descriptive study of COVID-19 related experiences and perspectives of a national sample of college students in spring 2020. *The Journal of Adolescent Health, 67*(3), 369–375. doi:10.1016/j.jadohealth.2020.06.009 PMID:32593564

Cohen, J. (1992). A power primer. *Psychological Bulletin, 112*(1), 155–159. doi:10.1037/0033-2909.112.1.155 PMID:19565683

Cresswell, J. W., & Plano Clark, V. (2018). Designing and conducting mixed methods research. *Sage (Atlanta, Ga.).*

Davis, G. B. (1993). *Tools for Teaching*. Jossey-Bass.

Education Commission of the States. (2020). *State education policy tracking*. https://www.ecs.org/state-education-policy-tracking/

Gregersen, T., Mercer, S., & MacIntyre, P. D. (2021). Language Teacher Perspectives on Stress and Coping. *Foreign Language Annals*, 1–19. doi:10.1111/flan.12544

Hapsari, C. T. (2021). Distance learning in the time of Covid-19: Exploring students' anxiety. *ELT FORUM, 10*(1), 40–49. doi:10.15294/elt.v10i1.45756

Hartshorn, K. J., & McMurry, B. L. (2020). The effects of the COVID-19 pandemic on ESL learners and TESOL practitioners in the United States. *International Journal of TESOL Studies*, 2(2), 140–156. doi:10.46451/ijts.2020.09.11

King Ramirez, C., & Lafford, B. (2018). Introduction. In Transferable skills for the 21st century: Preparing students for the workplace through world languages for specific purposes (pp.1-20). Sabio Books.

Larsen-Freeman, D., & Long, M. (1994). *Introducción al estudio de la adquisición de segundas lenguas*. Gredos.

Lomicka, L. (2020). Creating and sustaining virtual language communities. *Foreign Language Annals*, *53*(2), 306–313. doi:10.1111/flan.12456

MacIntyre, P. D., Gregersen, T., & Mercer, S. (2020). Language teachers' strategies during the Covid-19 conversion to online teaching: Correlations with stress, wellbeing and negative emotions. *System*, *94*, 102352. Advance online publication. doi:10.1016/j.system.2020.102352

Moser, K. M., Wei, T., & Brenner, D. (2021). Remote teaching during COVID-19: Implications from a national survey of language educators. *System*, *97*, 102431. Advance online publication. doi:10.1016/j.system.2020.102431

Pardo-Ballester, C. (2020). Coronavirus y el futuro de la educación de lenguas extranjeras a nivel universitario. *Puente Atlántico del siglo XXI*, 1-7.

Pardo-Ballester, C. (2021a). El pasado, presente y futuro de la enseñanza de ELE. *Cuadernos de Aldeuu*, *35*, 335–358.

Pardo-Ballester, C. (2021b). Curso de interpretación en línea para acomodar nuevas demandas y desafíos. *Puente Atlántico del siglo XXI*, 1-7.

Proietti Ergun, A. L., & Dewaele, J.-D. (2021). Do well-being and resilience predict the foreign language teaching enjoyment of teachers of Italian? *System*, *99*, 102506. Advance online publication. doi:10.1016/j.system.2021.102506

Rossomondo, A. (2020). Flexibility is the watchword. *Second Language Research & Practice*, *1*(1), 164–167. http://hdl.handle.net/10125/69850

Russell, V. (2020). Language anxiety and the online learner. *Foreign Language Annals*, *53*(2), 338–352. doi:10.1111/flan.12461

Sosulski, M. (2020). Responding to COVID-19: A chief academic officer's perspective. *Second Language Research & Practice*, *1*(1), 139–143. http://hdl.handle.net/10125/69845

Yi Xu, L. J., Deifell, E., & Angus, K. (2021). Emergency Remote Language Teaching and U.S. - Based College-Level World Language Educators' Intention to Adopt Online Teaching in Post-pandemic Times. *Modern Language Journal*, *105*(2), 1–23.

ADDITIONAL READING

Back, M., Golembeski, K., Gutiérrez, A., Macko, T., Miller, S., & Pelletier, D. L. (2021). "We were told that the content we delivered was not as important": disconnect and disparities in world language student teaching during COVID-19. *System*, *103*, 102679. Advance online publication. doi:10.1016/j.system.2021.102679

Jin, L., Deifell, E., & Angus, K. (2021). Emergency Remote Language Teaching and U.S.-Based College-Level World Language Educators' Intention to Adopt Online Teaching in Postpandemic Times. *Modern Language Journal, 105*(2), 412–434. doi:10.1111/modl.12712

Sulis, G., Mercer, S., Mairitsch, A., Babic, S., & Shin, S. (2021). Pre-service language teacher wellbeing as a complex dynamic system. *System, 103*, 102642. Advance online publication. doi:10.1016/j.system.2021.102642

Zhang, C., Yan, X., & Wang, J. (2021). EFL Teachers' Online Assessment Practices During the COVID-19 Pandemic: Changes and Mediating Factors. *The Asia-Pacific Education Researcher, 30*(6), 499–507. doi:10.100740299-021-00589-3

KEY TERMS AND DEFINITIONS

Collaboration: It is the process of working with another person or more people to complete a task. In the area of language teaching, collaboration is a strategy that many educators use for engaging learners to produce output and learn the language. Students collaborate with others during a variety of tasks such as discussion, role-plays, games, or projects.

Language Assessment: A term used interchangeably with the word 'testing'; it is the process of evaluating the language ability of the language learners in order to learn how much they understood from the teacher knowledge and materials used when teaching. Language assessment or testing is a complex field of applied linguistics that deals with the process of test development.

Needs Analysis: It is the process of analyzing the needs of a specific field of study. For example, a language teacher distributes an online questionnaire to learners to learn about their perceptions about topics, tasks, or tests included in a course. Results from the questionnaire can guide the educator to make changes in the syllabus and course.

Stress: It is a negative feeling that changes one's state of mind. Feeling tired, angry, anxious or nervous are reactions to an exterior condition such as too much work or fear of unknown situations.

Wellbeing: It is the mental state for feeling happy, healthy, protected, and at ease with oneself. This mental state can change suddenly due to unexpected situations.

Chapter 15
Building a K-12 Educator Community of Learners During Emergency Remote Learning

Melanie M. Wong
https://orcid.org/0000-0003-4171-0896
University of British Columbia, Canada

ABSTRACT

Due to the recent COVID-19 pandemic, the ways that Kindergarten to Grade 12 (K-12) educators support their English Language Learners (ELLs) have changed. These circumstances have brought on unprecedented challenges as educators attempt to make learning relevant and learn a new digital terrain. The lingering question is how teacher leaders can support colleagues to teach during global crises and post-pandemic times. This autoethnography explores experiences of a K-12 teacher leader. Using multiliteracies and learning by design, the knowledge processes employed are explored. Using digital technologies, such as Microsoft Skype, educators were able to collaborate as a community of learners to exchange teaching ideas and best ELL practices at daily K-12 teacher drop-in sessions.

INTRODUCTION

In March 2020, the students in the Canadian school district I work at were sitting in their seats in busy Kindergarten to Grade Twelve (K-12) classrooms. The notion of not having face to face classes or not being able to congregate in the same space had never entered our minds. However, as a worldwide pandemic has hit and it has become apparent that this is the new reality for K-12 educators. It also becomes obvious that we need to reconsider how we "bring school" to our students. Many school districts were attempting to shift to online platforms in order to deliver curriculum. Although there were technology inequities when considering access, where access to digital technologies is not equal across school divisions or homes (see Warschauer & Matuchniak, 2010). These are the times we live in and K-12 educators have been forced to "rethink" and "reimagine" learning during a global pandemic.

DOI: 10.4018/978-1-7998-8717-1.ch015

However, questions emerge with regards to how to support our diverse learners such as our English Language Learners (ELLs). In particular, how school districts can support their teachers to support these ELL students in times when we are not physically able to meet with our students. The following paper explores my experiences in a school district administrator role, a teacher leader. I was one of two ELL Strategists (teacher leaders) supporting teachers in a large school district in Western Canada. My role was to work with teachers to build their capacity to better support their K-12 ELL students. Part of this role included creating professional learning opportunities for teachers, meeting with teachers to plan or make recommendations on how to best support their students, and team teaching in classrooms. I will use an autoethnographic approach (Adams et al., 2015; Ellis, 2020) to explore the creation of a K-12 teacher community of learners (see Dufour et al., 2008) in an emergency remote learning space. An autoethnography "uses a researcher's personal experience to describe and critique cultural beliefs, practices and experiences…shows people in the process of figuring out what to do, how to live, and the meaning of their struggles" (Adams et al., 2015, p. 1-2). I choose to do an autoethnography because my experiences although not unique during remote learning provide a better understanding into the learning experiences of K-12 educators during remote learning. In particular, I will focus on the pedagogical moves, the knowledge processes (Cope & Kalantzis, 2015), I used to design both this particular teacher learning experience and suggested/modelled ELL student tasks. The purpose of this autoethnography is to illuminate an example of a K-12 teacher community of learners which was created using the affordances of digital technologies and also highlight how teacher leaders might support their K-12 colleagues to better program for their ELL students. This learning space was significant because it illustrates both a need for researchers to conduct further research in emergency remote learning and technology-enhanced environments but also a need for practitioners to rethink the ways K-12 ELL educators are supported during a pandemic, post-pandemic and global crises. This book chapter is organized as follows: 1) there will be a detailed discussion of learning by design theory (Cope & Kalantzis, 2015), my concept the *known,* and related literature; 2) an exploration of Teacher Collaboration Model literature; 3) a description of the research methodology; 4) my autoethnography, creating an emergency remote learning community of learners, will be explored; 5) a discussion of the potential implications for practice and future research; and 6) concluding remarks. In the next section, I will discuss the literature starting with a brief discussion of learning by design (Cope & Kalantzis, 2015).

BACKGROUND: LEARNING BY DESIGN

Prior to entering into my autoethnographic discussion, I want to provide a foundational literature discussion. When the New London Group (1996) introduced the concept of multiliteracies, they presented an argument that is still relevant more than two decades later. They argued that traditional language-based approaches to literacy instruction were limited and did not encompass the continued changes in the global landscape, which includes communication changes. The New London Group's (1996) argument was that literacy pedagogy needed to account for the "… challenges of cultural and linguistic diversity" (dialects, languages and registers) and also the "… newly prominent modes and technologies of communication; and changing text usage in restructured workplaces" such as new literacies (e.g., YouTube literacies, Minecraft literacies) (p. 62). The multiliteracies framework (Cope & Kalantzis, 2009, 2015; New London Group, 1996, 2000), comprises of three components of the Multiliteracies argument: the "why," "what," and "how" of Multiliteracies. For this autoethnographic study, I will be focusing on the "how."

Cope and Kalantzis (2009, 2015) extended on the work theorized by the New London Group (1996, 2000) by expanding and building on the "how" of multiliteracies. They emphasized that the multiliteracies approach comprises of a process of teaching and learning that goes back and forth, between and across, various knowledge processes and pedagogical moves. When designing tasks, teachers will design a sequence of learning activities (Cope & Kalantzis, 2015). Pedagogical moves are the choices that an individual makes when designing a learning activity. As teachers design tasks and consider their pedagogical moves, a potential framework to use is to consider the four components of the multiliteracies pedagogies, as articulated by the New London Group (2000). Cope and Kalantzis (2009; 2015) extended on these four components of the multiliteracies pedagogy: situated practice (*experiencing*), overt instruction (*conceptualizing*), critical framing (*analyzing*), and transformed practices *(applying)*. As they apply these notions to curriculum practices (the "how" of multiliteracies), they translate these notions into what they term knowledge processes. Knowledge processes are activities an individual does in order to know (Cope & Kalantzis, 2015). Knowledge processes also describe a range of ways of making knowledge. For example, when a student draws on previous experiences this is what Cope and Kalantzis refer to as *experiencing the known*. However, it is argued that no matter what terms are used to categorize learning activity types, the crucial idea in a multiliteracies and learning by design approach is that learning involves this notion of "weaving" across different pedagogical moves.

When looking at this notion of design and how teachers design sequences of activities for learning, two questions arise in the process of pedagogical design: which activities to use and in what order?" (Cope & Kalantzis, 2015, p. 17). They add that this concept of learning by design is a classification of activity types; for the purposes of this autoethnography, such a classification is a very helpful conceptual framework, especially when examining and analyzing a teacher collaborative learning environment during emergency remote learning (see below in Table 1 for a summary of the Knowledge Processes). The following conceptual framework helped me to better understand the pedagogical moves that I made when designing and establishing an emergency remote community of learners. In particular, it helps to better understand how I sequenced activities of learning. Unlike other frameworks, it provides a breakdown of the pedagogical moves I made and helps to provide a better understanding of this learning experience.

Table 1. Knowledge processes (Cope & Kalantzis, 2015)

Knowledge Processes	Definition
Experiencing the Known	Incorporating opportunities for students to draw on their previous experiences or the "familiar."
Experiencing the New	Introducing a learner to a topic that is less familiar. Learning occurs with these activity types when it is scaffolded.
Conceptualizing by Naming	Defining and learning to use abstract and generalized terms. This activity type also includes categorizing similar and differences and labeling a diagram.
Conceptualizing by Theory	Asking a learner to link the concept name into the language of generalization (e.g., concept maps, putting concepts together, drawing a diagram).
Analyzing Functionally	When a learner is reasoning, drawing inferential and deductive conclusions, establishing cause and effect.
Analyzing Critically	When a learner critically considers human interests and intentions- their own and other people's (e.g., identify the gaps).
Applying Appropriately	When a learner applies knowledge in the "usual" way to see whether it works in a predictable way in a conventional context. (e.g., solving a math problem)
Applying Creatively	Using knowledge you have learned and applying it into another context.

TAPPING INTO THE KNOWN

As I will discuss further in my autoethnography, the concept of the *known* is crucial for all learners (adult and children). In my own research, I have explored the learning experiences of K-12 learners in technology-enhanced classrooms, in particular this notion of the *known* and the implications it has on school-sanctioned learning (see Wong, 2021). I would argue this work has significance for the autoethnographic work presented here as I assert that teachers need to be aware of their students' *known*, this is particularly crucial during a global pandemic. There have been many challenges that are prevalent due to the ongoing pandemic including being unable to provide face to face instruction to children and having to utilize a variety of digital technologies to support learning. Becoming more aware of the students' *known* can help teachers better navigate these challenges.

Prior literature of Kindergarten to Grade 12 (K-12) ELL students has illuminated the rich and engaging learning experiences that occurred in what I term, interstitial (non-sanctioned) learning spaces (Wong, 2019). Interstitial learning spaces are those learning spaces including the back of the classroom, hallway, or out-of-school spaces. What is noted in the literature is that K-12 students (including ELLs) are engaging in writing fan fiction (Black, 2008), online chatrooms (Lam, 2004, 2009), virtual online worlds (Black & Reich, 2012), watching or creating videos on YouTube (Lange, 2014), interacting in World of Warcraft (Nardi, 2019), and creating pixelated block worlds in Minecraft (Abrams, 2016). However, although we are aware of many of the interstitial learning experiences, little is known about the implications these interstitial experiences might have in school-sanctioned learning spaces. Furthermore, research in the area of K-12 ELL students using technology is limited. Here we know that ELL students are using iPads as a tool to express meaning and support literacy development (Hutchison et al., 2012); creating digital stories (using sound, text, and images) which enable students to share their narratives (Johnson & Kendrick, 2017); using SMART boards to support vocabulary development (Wong, 2014); coding in the classroom using programming environments such as Scratch (Maloney et al., 2010); and engaging in video gaming, such as Minecraft (Abrams, 2016). However, literature in this area has on occasion shined a bright light on the technology rather than the learning experiences that occur. For example, studies have focused on the technology, such as an iPad, and have not addressed the pedagogical implications nor the actual learning experiences that occurred as a result of teacher task design. These studies have focused solely on the technology rather than the learning. There is an urgency for researchers to address how tasks are designed and how technologies have been used as a tool to support the learning experiences that occur in these digital learning spaces. Hence, in my ethnographic case study of a Grade 6 technology-enhanced classroom, I sought to better understand the learning experiences that occurred as a result of teacher task design. Of particular significance, my study noted that students tapped into what I termed, the *known,* when completing their school-sanctioned assignments (Wong, 2021). The New London Group (1996) defined lifeworld as "spaces for community life where local and specific meanings can be made" (p. 70). In these community lifeworlds, K-12 students are increasingly engaging in digital interstitial learning spaces, which include the various interstitial learning spaces I have already discussed above such as Fan Fiction websites and online chatrooms. However, these lifeworlds also include those interstitial learning spaces that are not digital such as home and religious communities. The New London Group argued in order for learning to be relevant, the learning processes that are used need to "recruit" rather than erase or ignore the different subjectivities, which the New London Group defined as interests, intentions, commitments and purposes that students bring to the classroom. Here, different subjectivities needed to mesh with curriculum and with the "attendant languages, discourses and registers, and use these as resources for learning" (p. 72). Hence, schools need to incorporate opportunities for students to bring in [recruit and mobilize] their multiple lifeworld knowledge and experiences (practices), their different subjectivities. Therefore, I define the *known* to include learner's lifeworld practices, their subjectivities, attendant languages, discourses, registers (that is, their communicative repertoires), and their understandings acquired in their multiple lifeworlds (Wong, 2021). These are the resources for learning that a learner might access if provided with opportunities to do so by their teacher. The *known* has the potential to impact the learning that occurs in another learning space (whether school-sanctioned or not). This *known* is unique to each person; it is individual and shaped by the multiple community lifeworld experiences an individual might have. I argue that the *known* is crucial during times of a pandemic where teachers and teacher leaders are unable to physically see their students (child learner and K-12 colleagues). In terms of the child learner, this *known* can be drawn on as resources for learning when creating tasks and designing learning opportunities which will be undertaken with the support of a parent or caregiving. When you intentionally design opportunities for the *known* to be incorporated into learning tasks, learning becomes more meaningful. For example, when students are able to engage in the knowledge processes of *experiencing the known* and *applying creatively,* they are able to draw on their *known* to support the completion of a school-sanctioned task. However, as I will discuss in my autoethnography, opportunities also need to be created so that teachers can draw on their own *known,* such as their understandings of what is good pedagogy for ELL students or what works in their Face 2 Face classrooms when supporting ELL students, in order to more effectively support their students and design lessons that are meaningful.

TEACHER COLLABORATIVE LEARNING MODELS

In terms of teacher education, there has been a multitude of research addressing how to best support and teach educators (e.g., Friend & Cook, 2002; Honigsfeld & Dove, 2010; Honigsfeld & Dove, 2019; Laal & Laal, 2011; Nevin, et al., 2009; Villa et al., 2008). These studies have looked at a wide range of social contexts and also topics. Most relevant to this particular autoethnography is the literature that addresses supporting English Language Learners (ELLs) and how teacher leaders can encourage and foster professional conversation with their colleagues and growth in teacher practice. Several models have been explored in the literature. However, I will briefly highlight only the relevant literature to this autoethnography.

In Honigsfeld and Dove's (2010) work they have argued that teachers should collaborate to better support ELLs; these researchers argue for a co-teaching model in classrooms. In these co-teaching environments, teachers are intentionally working together to support the various needs in their classrooms. Usually these co-teaching experiences involve an ELL teacher co-teaching with a general education teacher. These types of collaborative co-teaching environments improve the learning for students and also for teachers. The following autoethnography highlights the importance of teacher collaboration between a teacher leader and their colleagues and how when teachers are involved in professional conversation it can potentially encourage growth in teacher practice.

It has been argued that "[partnerships] between teachers of English as a second language and general educators can differentiate instruction for students whose first language is not English. All educators can collaborate with multicultural experts who can help differentiate instruction for students who have ethically and racially diverse heritages" (Nevin, et al., 2009, p. 570). Literature in the area of K-12 collaborative teaching has highlighted different approaches, one of significant interest to this autoethnography is the approach of collaborative consultation between classroom teachers and other teachers with a particular expertise (e.g., content knowledge, pedagogy knowledge) (see Friend & Cook, 2002; Villa et al., 2008). Laal and Laal (2011) asserted that collaboration has become a trend in the twenty-first century. The emphasis has been from independence to community. This collaborative learning approach to teaching and learning includes groups of learners working together to complete a task, solve a problem or create a product.

With these collaborative learning models, there is often an opportunity for teacher leaders to support this process. These teacher leaders may include those subject-area specialists mentioned earlier (see Nevin, et al., 2009), where teachers of English as a second language will collaborate with general teachers to differentiate instruction for students whose first language is not English. Teacher leaders are argued to understand the process of learning to teach and have a mastery of learning to teach which distinguishes them from other educators (see Henning et al., 2019). Therefore, teacher leaders will create an environment in which they are always learning. It is contended that teacher leaders can foster/generate innovative new experiences in order for co-teaching to occur. Such collaborative work is asserted by Henning and colleagues to benefit teachers "because the new design will push mentor teachers to develop their abilities with both reflection-in-action and reflection-on-action" (p. 150).

In related literature is the notion of a Virtual Exchange (VE) which is described as an umbrella that refers to "the engagement of groups of students in sustained online intercultural interaction and collaboration with international partners under the guidance of their teachers" (O'Dowd & Dooly, 2021, p. 1). O'Dowd and Dooly's work explored the impact of VE on educators' teaching practice and continued development as professionals. The data in this research indicated that teachers involved in these exchanges felt that the experiences had an impact on their own personal practice, perspectives and opportunities with regards to teaching and learning. This finding is partly significant for this autoethnography because it justifies why virtual collaborations/exchanges are crucial to support teacher development. It was also argued that these VE experiences offered increased collaboration between teachers. Another significant finding was that the teacher educators involved in these VE experiences were able to develop their professional skills including their abilities to collaborate online and developed innovative teaching practices. I would argue this is significant for this particular autoethnography where I (as the teacher educator) could potentially have opportunities to develop my own professional skills. Therefore, this autoethnography is extending on this literature and furthering our understandings with regards to this significant area of research.

An alternative way to view and describe professional communities of learners is to consider the Community of Inquiry (CoI) framework as it is argued to describe a collaborative and constructive approach to thinking and learning (Garrison, 2015). Garrison contends that this CoI framework provides a theoretical framework to use when studying and better understanding purposeful learning environments. The following framework accomplishes this by considering the three interdependent elements: cognitive, social and teaching presence. The CoI framework was initially developed to better understand and study online learning but it is however not limited to these learning spaces. Garrison argues that the CoI framework makes use of technological affordances to create opportunities for "sustained discourse where the breadth of access to information can be fused with the depth of collaborative inquiry" (p. 54). Here, educators can potentially take advantage of the connectiveness of the digital world and actively be learners in both collaborative thinking and learning experiences; which is similar to what I will describe in my autoethnography in an emergency remote learning community of learners. In this emergency remote learning community of learners, educators are utilizing the affordances of the digital world to collaboratively think and learn. Increasingly this type of collaboration in the digital world is prevalent and important for teachers working in virtual environments and also in times of global crises where teachers are unable to teach or meet face to face.

One way to engage in collaborative learning is for schools and teacher leaders to create professional learning communities (PLCs) (see Dufour et al., 2008). This PLC model has been taken up largely in K-12 contexts including the school district that I worked at. In this model, Dufour and colleagues describe how PLCs focus on a commitment to student learning. During these conversations, teachers collaboratively focus on learning and a "shared purpose, vision, collective commitments and goals…[a] PLC is composed of collaborative teams whose members work independently to achieve common goals- goals linked to the purpose of learning for all- for which members are held mutually accountable" (Dufour et al., 2008, p. 15). These environments encourage collaboration between teachers and also purposeful conversation between educators. As I will discuss further in this autoethnography, these PLCs can occur in emergency remote learning environments. Using the affordances of digital technologies, a collaborative space was created that invited both teacher educators and teachers to engage in intentional discussions about how to best support their ELL students.

RESEARCH METHODOLOGY

As Ellis (2004) explains autoethnography "refers to writing about the personal and its relationship to culture" (p. 37). Philips and Kara (2020) describes how autoethnographies centre around descriptions and observations of the researcher's thoughts, behaviours and experiences. The focus of autoethnographies are on "culture and society rather than the author and the individual life…In autoethnography, 'a personal story'…informs sociological understanding" (p. 34). I would also assert that the autoethnographic approach taken in this book chapter illuminates one potential learning experience that teacher educators and teachers might engage in during pandemics, post-pandemic or global crises. It illustrates how the affordances of digital technologies when intentionally used can invite the creation of a community of learners and effective collaboration among educators. There have been several notable autoethnographies done previously that have informed the following autoethnography. However, I want to highlight one done by Canagarajah (2012) which focuses on his navigation of differing teaching practices and professional cultures. In particular his autoethnography provides insights to those in the profession with regards to how the various communities that he belonged to played an important role in shaping his professional identity. Unlike other research methods, this autoethnography, as Canagarajah mentioned was his intent, allowed the reader to "generate additional comparisons and interpretations from alternative perspectives" (p. 260); I believe this is one of the strengths of an autoethnography and one reason why this particular research methodology was used here. It also informs are sociological understandings (as Philips and Kara (2020) argue) and provides a deeper understanding with regards to a particular experience. In my case, this autoethnography will deepen our understandings about how an emergency remote learning community of learners was created.

My data included personal written reflections and digital artifacts (created by me) (e.g., emails, resources I created to share with teachers etc.) collected over an emergency remote learning period of time (March 2020 until June 2020). The knowledge processes (see Table 1) that I have employed were analyzed using thematic analysis (Saldãna, 2016). By using thematic analysis, I gained a better understanding of the themes and the pedagogical moves that I used when designing this emergency remote learning community of learners. I did multiple levels of coding to better understanding the knowledge processes that I employed in my model task design.

Below I will begin my autoethnographic discussion, it is my intent to illuminate a learning experience that supported K-12 ELL teachers during an emergency remote learning time. Further implications will be discussed with regards to post-pandemic learning opportunities and how such a learning experience might occur and benefit K-12 ELL educators.

CREATING AN EMERGENCY REMOTE LEARNING COMMUNITY OF LEARNERS

After spring break we were meeting in Microsoft Skype to have a school district ELL team meeting. Our government had called a state of emergency less than 10 days previous. As a result, our 247 schools were now in an emergency remote learning environment. Only days prior to this state of emergency, COVID-19 had only been a "name," an unknown illness that had shut down parts of Asia and infected passengers on a cruise ship. Although global headlines were making their way on to our televisions and social media feeds, COVID-19 was not a reality yet. However, there had already been impeding fear. In my role as a teacher leader supporting all schools with their ELL programming, I had already had two COVID-19 scares. One scare occurred at a teacher professional development event, where a teacher had emerged during a group discussion to inform me that she had taught a child that had been confirmed to have COVID-19 and she had symptoms. Another scare occurred at a school where I was informed that a child had been removed from a classroom due to a family member testing positive for COVID-19. These incidents had made COVID-19 real.

After receiving the message that schools were closed to face to face learning, many teachers struggled to find child care for their own children. This had resulted in extra constraints for these teachers as they were juggling both work and caring for their own children. The school district had explicitly indicated that teachers were not to bring their children to work. Therefore, many teachers were working from home, taking personal days to accommodate the new evolving situation. During emergency remote learning, it became common to have children interrupt meetings or teachers expressing their frustrations openly about navigating childcare issues and work. Also, although all of the teachers were given a school laptop, many of my colleagues were using older laptop models and were not due for an upgrade yet. As a result, some teachers struggled to log into various applications (e.g., on Skype some teachers were unable to talk because their laptop microphones did not work).

Teachers had spent the three days prior to spring break working from home. The previous two days had consisted of working from a school district building. Teachers were asked to develop a plan for learning. At the end of the second day, I was sent home because it was deemed to be too dangerous to work with others in the same space. In these three days prior to spring break, as a teacher leader, I had met with several schools sitting at my kitchen table. In one meeting, an entire school staff and I had met using the virtual classroom environment, Bongo. This school staff had panicked about how to support their high ELL population. Many of the teachers on this staff were newer to the practice. Although we also had many experienced teachers on staff. Some currently used digital technologies in the classroom, while others were reluctant based on their own personal comfort. During my session with these teachers, I had shared some ideas from my experiences using technology to support ELLs. The previous night I had stayed up late researching new ideas to share with these teachers. Technology, I knew, was constantly evolving. In another conversation with a middle school, the staff had expressed a worry about how they could program effectively for large range of ELL students. In this middle school, they had a number of students who were recent immigrants to the country. The English language proficiency level of these students was low. As it was, teachers were already struggling with how to support these students during in person learning. Parent support was also limited as these parents worked long hours and were often unable to support their students at home with their learning. Teachers at this middle school were more experienced educators but were also reluctant to use technology in their classrooms. Therefore, during this meeting, I shared some ideas about flexible groupings and how teachers could regroup their students during the day to effectively target their learning needs.

After these online sessions, I spent my spring break reflecting and developing ideas that might support our ELL students more intentionally in remote learning environments. It was during one of my moments of reflection I came up with the idea of K-12 teacher drop-in sessions in Skype hosted by ELL Strategists, (myself) and my team partner. Drawing on the work that was already occurring in the school district around professional learning communities (Dufour et al., 2008), I thought we could capitalize on these ongoing conversations but move them into an online learning space. I also saw a potential opportunity to create a school-sanctioned learning space (Wong, 2019) which invited teachers to step out of the "traditional" school-sanctioned learning space and try new ways of teaching and learning in a digital world. I knew from my conversations with teachers that they were at various levels of comfort when it came to implementing digital technologies.

I worked for a large school district in Western Canada, our ELL student population was approximately 30 000 children, with students coming from all over the world. In my five years working in this position, I had supported almost all of the 247 schools. I had planned with numerous teachers, consulted with colleagues about struggling students, and implemented countless unit plans. My doctoral studies had created an interest in "living the work," applying what I knew was sound pedagogy from the research into practice. Therefore, I had intentionally taken what I knew about ELL research and put it into practice. During one of my early courses in my Master's program, I recalled a discussion with a professor who had noted that it took over 40 years for research to enter into practice. I wondered about this "barrier," and why teachers were not taking the research and integrating it into practice. There were several reasons for this, I noted. First, research was not always accessible to teachers. Journals are often written for researchers. The register is not always accessible nor are the actual journals. Second, teachers are negotiating a number of barriers including working in classrooms that have become increasingly diverse and complex. These educators are often on "survival mode," applying strategies that are not necessarily informed by the literature but rather applied because they are convenient and work with their context and students. With this global pandemic, I saw a greater need to apply research into practice. I felt this was an opportunity to share my knowledge and learnings from my years of study with regards to ELL and technology to support the K-12 students in our school district.

During this ELL team meeting, I proposed my K-12 teacher drop-in idea. Like all school district initiatives, it needed to be approved by our senior leadership group. I will admit I was never good with following the rules and often bended them to make it work especially if it was good for students. However, I was hopeful it would be considered since it would provide a space for teachers to collaborate and plan together. It was approved after several days, much to my delight and disappointment (I felt it should have been approved earlier). As soon as I was given formal approval. I began the process of composing an email to be sent out to each school representative, which we called "ELL Designates." Below is the first email I sent my teacher colleagues and schools (see Figure 1).

Figure 1. ELL designate email (April 16, 2020)

Subject: K-12 Teachers--- Consulting with ELL Strategists
Date: Thursday, April 16, 2020 at 12:46:05 PM Mountain Daylight Time
From: Author
To: Author

Dear Colleagues/ELL Designates,

Please share this email with staff members (Teachers and EAs) that might be interested.

As we transition into online learning, the ELL team is offering informal drop in sessions (1 hour in length) to consult with ELL Strategists with regards to supporting K-12 ELL students in a digital environment. The following times for the upcoming week are below with a link to the virtual room (there will be other times in the future):

- Monday April 20, 2020 1:00pm-2:00pm Join Skype Meeting
- Wednesday April 22, 2020 10:00am-11:00 am Join Skype Meeting
- Friday April 24, 2020 10:00am-11:00am Join Skype Meeting

If you are unable to attend these times or if you would like to have a group meeting with an ELL Strategist, please send your email requests to Melanie (email address) or [ELL Strategist #2] (email address) and they can arrange an alternative time with you. **We request that you please send your questions before hand so that we can have a more targeted conversation.** This also could be a great opportunity for you to network with other colleagues and share great practices that are already occurring.

Thank you!
All the best,
[ELL Strategist #2] and Melanie

In Figure 1, I am inviting my colleagues to join a community of learners. In this email it highlights several knowledge processes (Cope & Kalantzis, 2015) that I utilized in my creation of this K-12 educator community of learners. "As we transition into online learning, the ELL team is offering informal drop-in sessions (1 hour in length) to consult with ELL strategists with regards to supporting K-12 ELL students in a digital environment," in this example I am employing the knowledge process of *experiencing the new,* where I was introducing the learners (teachers) to a topic that was less familiar, teaching online. By creating a K-12 teacher drop-in learning space, teachers were also invited to enter into a learning experience that was scaffolded. I was also employing the knowledge process of *experiencing the known.* Teachers were familiar with the notion of consulting with an ELL strategist at their schools. By sending this email, I was attempting to create a learning space that invited teachers to start a discussion.

BRINGING IN THE KNOWN

It was Monday April 20 and it was the first K-12 teacher drop-in. Over the past week, I had noted challenges working from home. Virtual meetings had become a fascinating show of persistence; virtual meetings included family members making appearances to pets interrupting meetings. In my case, my dog had gotten upset during a particularly long meeting and had decided to destroy the wall. However, in addition to the social challenges, technology had become a dominant issue. The work laptop I had been given was due for an upgrade in June. I had frequent blue screens and "green" webcam challenges (where my webcam would transmit a green image). I had also been forced to upgrade my personal wifi network to a mesh wifi system to accommodate the increased usage of internet in my home.

Schools were also struggling with ensuring all students had access to technology and internet. Many of these students, who did not have access to technology, were ELL students. In addition to technology issues, there were language challenges communicating with these families. As my school district was a technology-enhanced one, technology was able to be provided to the majority of our families. School laptops were repurposed and sent home to families to use during the emergency remote learning. Local internet companies were also stepping up to provide broadband internet to families that could not afford. Unlike many other school districts in our province, we were quite prepared for remote learning. We had a multitude of technologies including a learning management system (Desire 2 Learn), Google Suites and other technologies. However, although there was access to technologies, the obstacle was providing professional development to support teachers to use these technologies and also getting teachers to use the technology that was available. The literature has noted that although technology tools are increasingly present in the K-12 classroom, they may not be used (e.g., Blackwell et al., 2014). A variety of reasons have been documented in the literature, but prominent among them is the teacher's lack of knowledge or training. Fullan (2013) asserts there has been "digital disappointment" (p. 36): although countless school districts and governments have attempted to take up this idea of a "21st century skills mantra . . . it turns out that inspiration is not much of the basis for action," and therefore digital technologies are not being taken up in classrooms (p. 36). Hence, this emergency remote learning was an opportunity to perhaps shift this mindset and get teachers to use the available technologies to support their learners especially their ELL ones.

An additional challenge for teachers had been navigating live Google Meets with their students, in particular the younger learners. I had been invited to a Google Meet for grade 2 students. The teacher was an experienced educator and he used technology on a regular basis. However, this emergency remote learning environment had posed many challenges for him as an experienced teacher (which we had discussed during meetings afterwards). During this particular Google Meet, classroom management had been quite difficult. First, as students were younger, parents were sitting with their children during the live meet, supporting these children with the technology. Therefore, this teacher was now also navigating parent questions during his Google Meets. Second, this was a new environment for these learners and naturally these grade 2 students were finding many opportunities to try out the features in this space. Unfortunately, this included typing inappropriate messages in the Google chat or using the microphone and camera to interrupt the teacher when he was teaching. In other Google Meets I had attended with students that were older, I noted similar challenges with teachers having to remove students from Google Meets due to inappropriate behaviour.

In addition to the live meet challenges, teachers were also having difficulties communicating with families, some families had not responded after students went into emergency remote learning. In one instance, a grade 9 teacher had contacted me concerned that one of her ELL students had not attended Google Meets or answered her emails or phone calls. She was worried about this student. The family had many challenges including an ongoing divorce and financial issues. During my phone conversation with this teacher, we brainstormed ideas to support the student. In the end, we concluded it might be best to request a "welfare check" and have the police visit the family home to ensure the student was safe. These were only some of the challenges that my colleagues were facing on a regular basis.

It was already 1:00 p.m. and much to my surprise we had a full house in Microsoft Skype. There were 47 participants. Our session started off slow. Teachers were quiet and probably adjusting to using Microsoft Skype. Many teachers probably also came in to listen and did not speak. However, several had mentioned in the text chat function that their microphones and cameras did not work so they would be typing their questions, another challenge during emergency remote learning. We had a range of participants today including teachers teaching various grade levels. I was familiar with many of my colleagues in attendance as I had worked in so many classrooms across the school district. Many of these teachers were experienced teachers, teaching more than 5 years. However, we also had newer teachers who were at the beginning of their careers. The majority of the teachers taught in high populated ELL schools.

To start the conversation off, I shared my screen and some teaching ideas. The previous evening I had come across a website that had translated at home activities for families; it was a choice board activity. Families were able to choose a literacy-based activity to do (e.g., "Watch a TV show and name the characters, plot and setting") (see ESL at Home, 2020). I talked about how we could share these activities with families whom English was not their first language. Here I employed the knowledge process of *experiencing the new* and *experiencing the known* again. Many of the teachers in our school district were familiar with the idea of a choice board. However, I was also encouraging these teachers to *apply creatively,* where teachers applied this familiar (or not in some cases hence the employment of the knowledge process *experiencing the new*) to another learning context (emergency remote learning) to support their ELL students. After sharing a few more resources, teachers began to present their issues. Many of them typing in the chat box or using the microphone (if possible) to tell us their challenges. One teacher asked how to support beginner ELL students online. I shared my screen again and reviewed some resources. In particular I employed the knowledge process of *experiencing the known*. During my many school visits, I often suggested that teachers create an ELL bin (or binder) that contained activities that beginner ELL students could work on. K-12 classrooms are busy places. These classrooms have learners with a variety of learning needs. Individual ELL bins were customized to the student's learning needs (e.g., if they were working on letter sounds, there would be these activities included). I suggested that this teacher consider creating a digital version of this ELL bin, a folder in Desire 2 Learn (D2L) or Google Classroom, and fill it with activities for the student to do at their level. Here, I was also employing the knowledge process of *applying creatively* by encouraging this teacher to take a familiar idea they had learned in one context and apply it into another context.

VIRTUAL FIELD TRIPS

It was a warm May day. I was now conducting my meetings working at my stand up desk. Working from home had also presented ergonomic challenges. I had figured out the best way to support my back was to stand when I was working. In a recent conversation with a teacher, she had commented on how difficult it had been to engage her students in an online learning environment. She was a beginner teacher.

During our conversation, I had made several suggestions such as bringing in guest speakers or taking the learning offline (where students would take pictures of various different patterns in their neighbourhood and share these during a Google Meet). This teacher was not unique in her challenges, many teachers (with varying degrees of experience) faced similar challenges.

After a month of conducting sessions, we were now getting the hang of doing this. To better meet the needs of our teachers, we had created times for specific grade level consultations. As these sessions were well attended, we decided to do grade level specific meetings. By doing this, we could also focus on planning for specific students and also curriculum. For example, we met with Grade 1 and 2 teachers in the morning and then Grade 3 and 4 teachers in the afternoon. At this meeting on a May day, we were meeting with Grade 1 and 2 teachers. The majority of teachers at this meeting were regular attendees. Some of the teachers were beginner teachers and others more experienced. These teachers worked a various schools across the city (some with no ELL students and others with many). It had become a routine to come prepared with ideas just in case our teachers were reluctant to speak. This strategy helped to generate conversation and teachers usually contributed to the discussion after we "broke the ice." The initial awkward silence of Microsoft Skype, as a result of teachers being reluctant to speak, was filled now with myself or my team partner sharing teaching ideas. I usually researched online the night before and brought something interesting to share the following day. I tried to bring in ideas that were grade level specific and connected to the curriculum that was being studied. It had become a daily habit to lay on the couch and search for ideas on my phone, emailing these ideas to my work email account. During these evening sessions, I thought about the curriculum a teacher might be teaching and tried to connect the dots. My mind was also focused on what was best for our ELL students.

The overwhelming theme of our K-12 drop-in discussions consisted of teachers trying to figure out how to support students with lower English language proficiency levels. Besides language barriers with students, parents were also unable to communicate and interpreters had been requested to support these families. Many of our recent sessions had been dedicated to this discussion where I would often talk about explicit language teaching and creating opportunities for oral language practice and vocabulary development. During these sessions I employed knowledge processes such as *experiencing the new* and *applying appropriately* and *creatively,* where I introduced new ideas and then we applied this new knowledge in some of the usual ways and also into new contexts (an online learning environment). What I had learned from my brief time in an emergency remote learning environment, it was about "flipping the switch," considering how you might do this particular activity offline and finding the digital tools to make it happen virtually. Did it look different? Yes, it did. However, the learning intentions were still the same. Ultimately it came down to reading the research about teaching beginner level ELL students and thinking about how this learning experience might be translated into an online environment.

Today at the beginning of our morning session, I shared the idea of taking virtual field trips. If teachers were intentional, virtual field trips were an opportunity to differentiate the learning for ELL students (at various English language proficiency levels). I had read a recent article in the news about the panda exhibit at the local Zoo and how it had gone virtual (see CBC Calgary, 2020). As a result of the pandemic, the pandas were leaving due to a shortage in food. The Zoo was unable to secure enough bamboo to feed the pandas. I shared this article with these teachers and as a group we talked about how this might be an opportunity to work on oral language skills or writing skills which we knew from the ELL literature was good practice (see Gibbons, 2015). For example, students could go on a virtual field trip at home with their families (e.g., to the zoo or a museum). The teacher would provide a variety of sentence frames and key vocabulary words to use during this activity. The summative activity would be having students record a FlipGrid video. In this FlipGrid video, students would be encouraged to use the sentence frames and key vocabulary words provided by the teacher to describe what they saw during their virtual field trip. When analyzing this learning experience, there were several pedagogical moves made on my part when designing this potential/model task for students. First, I brought in the notion of field trips (*experiencing the known*); this was a part of the students' *known.* I also employed the knowledge processes of *experiencing the new* and *conceptualizing by theory* and *naming,* where students and their families would go on a field trip and experience a new topic; they would be introduced to something less familiar. Their task would be to identify key vocabulary words and summarize what they had experienced during this learning experience in a Flipgrid video. The K-12 teachers who took up this activity with their ELL students would be applying my idea into their own context (both *experiencing the new* and *applying creatively* and *appropriately).* However, I hoped these teachers would consider their own context and *apply creatively*, adapting the idea/lesson into something that worked for all their learners. In this example, as the teacher leader, I was intentionally employing a variety of knowledge processes to encourage my K-12 teaching colleagues to consider how they might be able to support their ELL students in creative ways in an emergency remote learning environment. During this conversation, teachers also asked questions and contemplated different ways they could adjust the task to work in their own classroom contexts. For example, one teacher commented that her class composition consisted of more advanced students. She wondered how she could adjust this lesson to work better with her students. We talked about ways to extend this activity. Perhaps students could choose a virtual field trip location and share these locations with the class through a presentation. I also suggested using the technology to invite guest speakers into the classroom. I gave the example of when I brought a guest speaker into my face to face classroom. In this example, I recalled how I asked a chemistry professor to come to my classroom. The reason why I did this was because my students had an interest in this particular topic and it had been a part of our classroom inquiry. With this activity, my students interviewed the chemistry professor and asked him questions. This activity extended my students' understandings of this area and challenged them further. As I mentioned to this teacher during this K-12 teacher drop in session, it was also possible to move this type of activity into an online classroom due to the affordances of digital technologies. In this particular recall of a face to face classroom experience, I was activating the knowledge process of *experiencing the known* and bringing in my own experiences and then *applying* this *known creatively* in a new context, an emergency remote learning environment.

CREATING AN IDENTITY TEXT

In a third K-12 teacher drop-in in late May and we were meeting with a group of grade 5 and 6 teachers. The last few drop-in sessions had gone relatively smoothly. Although on one occasion when we were meeting with high school teachers, I had experienced network login issues on my work computer, many other teachers had also had similar issues. I had been forced to drive to a nearby school and sit in the parking lot to facilitate the drop-in discussion. Overall, we had a steady flow of teachers attending. Sessions ranged between 10 to 40 participants depending on the grade level. As I mentioned previously, we had a range of teachers who attended on a regular basis. Many were beginner teachers, however we also had experienced teachers attend as well. We tried to move these sessions to different times to accommodate the various teaching schedules.

During this grade 5 and 6 teacher session, I had already answered questions about skill development and teaching reading strategies such as annotating texts and pre-reading strategies. I had shared my screen multiple times and used didactic pedagogy to explicitly teach my colleagues how to use these resources in the classroom (*experiencing the new*). For example, while showing one resource I walked the teachers through how to use this with their students. "I would model this pre-reading strategy by reading this book. While I am reading it, I will use a think aloud strategy to model what good readers do. I know this is good practice because according to our ministry of education ESL assessment tools, this is what beginner level ELL students need."

Later in the conversation, a teacher asked if there was a way to engage ELL parents in the learning. During my time as a teacher leader, I often reminded teachers about the importance of maintaining the first language and the importance of using this language to support English language development (see Chiumak-Horbatsch, 2012). I had even facilitated family engagement sessions at the local library on this exact topic. Therefore, I took this opportunity to discuss the idea of creating a dual language text. Sharing my screen I showed this teacher, Scribjab (Scribjab, 2020) and Storybooks Canada (Storybooks Canada, 2020), websites that had books in various languages. I suggested that this might be an opportunity during remote learning to have parents create an Identity Text (Cummins & Early, 2011) with their child. In this suggested Identity Text task design, I employed many different knowledge processes (*experiencing the new and the known* and *applying creatively*). However, what is prevalent in this discussion and perhaps the most important part of my role as a teacher leader was encouraging my K-12 colleagues to consider bringing in their students' *known* (Wong, 2020). One of the challenges with emergency remote learning is that teachers were not able to see their students physically. However, there was also many opportunities for parent engagement and bringing in a child's *known* to support school-sanctioned tasks.

Perhaps one of the main issues teachers faced during this time in emergency remote learning, besides parent engagement, was the lack of connection with their students. Many colleagues commented during these teacher drop in sessions that they struggled with not being able to check in with their students informally on a regular basis. Some teachers had started to call their students on the phone daily. Teachers also worried their students were not getting enough to eat. These teachers had connected with local organizations and they were arranging for hampers to be delivered to these students' homes.

Another challenge was the long work hours, perhaps longer compared to the usual. As many of my colleagues had never taught in online environments, they were spending hours figuring out the technology or planning their lessons. Teaching online also meant we were connected 24/7. The only way to communicate was via digital technologies where teachers were expected to check their emails on a regular basis for school district updates and emails from students. One teacher commented during a drop in sessions that she had never worked so hard during her 30 year teaching career. Many colleagues were looking into early retirement options. Emergency remote learning had presented challenges for my colleagues and myself.

DISCUSSION AND IMPLICATIONS FOR PRACTICE

The following autoethnography explored my experiences as a teacher leader during emergency remote learning. I created a K-12 teacher community of learners during emergency remote learning. Using the affordances of digital technologies, my colleagues and I were able to meet and discuss how to best support our ELL students in a Microsoft Skype learning space. Therefore, a professional learning community

(PLC) (Dufour et al., 2008) was created online. As Dufour and his colleagues elaborated on in their work, there needs to be a collaborative culture cultivated in order for a PLC to be formed. They argue that district level leadership, which I was a part of, needs to "create a network of schools [and teachers that are] engaged in improvement initiatives so they can learn from one another" (p. 339). Here, by creating this community of learners online, it provided an opportunity to create a "network of schools and teachers." It is argued that in order for teacher leaders to build a mentoring culture, the teacher leader needs to develop a vision for teacher development, which in this case was a K-12 teacher community of learners that shared ideas and best ELL teaching practices (Henning et al., 2019). It is also asserted that teacher leaders should be focused on "facilitating their abilities to design and implement instructional innovation" (p. 151). Here, in this school-sanctioned learning space, I employed a variety of knowledge processes when building the capacity of my K-12 colleagues and in my sample/model ELL student task design. Most notable was my usage of the knowledge processes, *experiencing the new, experiencing the known* and *applying creatively.* I often didactically taught my colleagues how to teach certain skills and competencies to their ELL students in a digital environment. I also intentionally employed such knowledge processes as *experiencing the new and known* and *applying creatively* to encourage my colleagues to create opportunities to encourage: 1) potential parent involvement (e.g., creating identity texts) and 2) students to bring in their *known* (e.g., field trip experiences, ELL digital bins) into an emergency remote learning environment. However, I would argue from this K-12 teacher drop-in learning experience, there are several important implications for teacher leaders who are supporting teachers with their ELL students. First, by using the affordances of digital technologies, I was able to create a network of teachers; this has many implications for K-12 teachers post pandemic. Although, I have left my school district role, this notion of an online community of learners has continued. My former colleagues are hosting regular drop-in sessions for teachers; this allows for teachers at different schools to connect. It is convenient and teachers can log in during lunch or after school without leaving their school buildings. Using a variety of knowledge processes (such as *experiencing the new, experiencing the known and applying creatively and appropriately)*, teacher leaders can cultivate a mentoring culture (Henning et al., 2019), one that invites their colleagues to participate and take up research driven practices. Second, in this community of learners, I modelled a variety of ways teachers can incorporate opportunities to bring in students' *known* into school-sanctioned tasks. As I have already noted in my own research, students when invited by teachers will activate a variety of knowledge processes such as *experiencing the known* and *applying creatively* to bring in their *known* to support the completion of school sanctioned activities (e.g., using YouTube to find an idea for a business project) (see Wong, 2021). However, I would also argue that it is important for teacher leaders to consider their K-12 colleague's *known* when engaging in collaborative learning opportunities, as this *known* is the starting place for discussions leading to innovative task design. A teacher leader or an instructional coach provides "...support to staff to build... and strengthen technical skill" (Hall & Simeral, 2017, p. 151) and also this *known.*

LIMITATIONS

A potential limitation of this autoethnography was that I was unable to include interview data from the teacher participants at the K-12 drop-in sessions. It would have enriched our understanding of what knowledge processes were activated by the teacher participants and whether or not my pedagogical moves were impacting the student learning experiences. Another potential limitation was how I was able to interview students to better understand the learning experiences that occurred as a result of their teachers' task design. These interviews would have added to our understanding of the learning experiences in a K-12 teacher community of learners.

CONCLUSION

The following emergency remote learning experience highlights opportunities for teacher leaders to use the affordances of digital technologies to support teachers with their ELL programming. In these school-sanctioned learning spaces (Wong, 2019), teacher educators and teachers are able to engage in collaborative learning opportunities. This autoethnography also calls for further research to be done with regards to how teacher leaders can better support their teachers to support K-12 ELL students in post-pandemic and global crises.

ACKNOWLEDGMENT

I want to thank my former colleagues in my school district for attending my K-12 drop-in sessions but also participating in this virtual community of leaners.

REFERENCES

Abrams, S. S. (2016). Emotionally crafted experiences: Layering literacies in Minecraft. *The Reading Teacher*, *70*(4), 501–506. doi:10.1002/trtr.1515

Adams, T. E., Jones, S. H., & Ellis, C. (2015). Autoethnography: Understanding qualitative research. Oxford.

Black, R. W. (2008). *Adolescents and online fan fiction*. Peter Lang.

Black, R. W., & Reich, S. M. (2012). Culture and community in a virtual world for young children. In C. Steinkuehler, K. Squire, & S. Barab (Eds.), *Games, learning and society learning and meaning in the digital age* (pp. 210–228). Cambridge University Press. doi:10.1017/CBO9781139031127.018

Calgary, C. B. C. (2020). *Calgary zoo to ship giant pandas back to China early due to difficulty getting bamboo during pandemic*. Retrieved February 13, 2021 from, https://www.cbc.ca/news/canada/calgary/giant-pandas-calgary-zoo-1.5566027

Canagarajah, A. S. (2012). Teacher development in a global profession: An Autoethnography. *TESOL Quarterly*, *46*(2), 258–279. doi:10.1002/tesq.18

Chiumak-Horbatsch, R. (2012). *Linguistically appropriate practice: A guide for working with young immigrant children*. University of Toronto Press.

Cope, B., & Kalantzis, M. (2009). "Multiliteracies": New literacies, new learning. *Pedagogies*, *4*(3), 164–195. doi:10.1080/15544800903076044

Cope, B., & Kalantzis, M. (2015). The things you do to know: An introduction to the pedagogy of multiliteracies. In B. Cope & M. Kalantzis (Eds.), *A pedagogy of multiliteracies: Learning by Design* (pp. 1–36). Palgrave Macmillan. doi:10.1057/9781137539724_1

Cummins, J., & Early, M. (2011). Introduction. In J. Cummins & M. Early (Eds.), *Identity texts: The collaborative creation of power in multilingual schools* (pp. 3–19). Trentham Books.

Dufour, R., Dufour, R., & Eaker, R. (2008). *Revisiting professional learning communities at work: New insights for improving schools.* Solution Tree Press.

Ellis, C. (2020). *Revision: Autoethnographic reflections on life and work.* Routledge. ESL at Home. Retrieved February 13, 2021 from, https://eslathome.edublogs.org

Friend, M., & Cook, L. (2002). *Interaction: Collaboration skills for school professionals* (4th ed.). Allyn and Bacon.

Garrison, D. R. (2015). *Thinking collaboratively: Learning in a community of inquiry.* Taylor & Francis Group. doi:10.4324/9781315740751

Gibbons, P. (2015). *Scaffolding language, scaffolding learning: Teaching English language learners in the mainstream classroom* (2nd ed.). Heinemann.

Hall, P., & Simeral, A. (2017). *Creating a culture of reflective practice: Building capacity of schoolwide success.* Association for Supervision & Curriculum Development.

Henning, J. E., Gut, D. M., & Beam, P. C. (2019). *Building mentoring capacity in teacher education:A guide to clinically-based practice.* Routledge.

Honigsfeld, A., & Dove, M. (2010). *Collaboration and co-teaching: Strategies for English learners.* Corwin.

Hutchison, A., Beschorner, B., & Schimidt-Crawford, D. (2012). Exploring the use of the ipad for literacy learning. *The Reading Teacher, 66*(1), 15–23. doi:10.1002/TRTR.01090

Johnson, L., & Kendrick, M. (2017). "Impossible is nothing": Expressing difficult knowledge through digital storytelling. *Journal of Adolescent & Adult Literacy, 60*(6), 667–675. doi:10.1002/jaal.624

Laal, M., & Laal, M. (2011). Collaborative Learning: What is it? *Procedia: Social and Behavioral Sciences, 31*, 491–495. doi:10.1016/j.sbspro.2011.12.092

Lam, W. S. E. (2004). Second language socialization in a bilingual chat room: Global and local considerations. *Language Learning & Technology, 8*(3), 44–65.

Lam, W. S. E. (2009). Multiliteracies on Instant Messaging in Negotiating Local, Translocal, and Transnational Affiliations: A Case of an Adolescent Immigrant. *Reading Research Quarterly, 44*(4), 377–397. doi:10.1598/RRQ.44.4.5

Lange, P. G. (2014). *Kids on YouTube: Technical identities and digital literacies.* Left Coast Press.

Maloney, J., Resnick, M., Rusk, N., Silverman, B., & Eastmond, E. (2010). The scratch programming language and environment. *ACM Transactions on Computing Education, 10*(4), 1–15. doi:10.1145/1868358.1868363

Nardi, B. A. (2019). *My life as a night elf priest: An anthropological account of world of warcraft*. The University of Michigan Press.

Nevin, A. I., Thousand, J. S., & Villa, R. A. (2009). Collaborative teaching for teacher educators-What does the research say? *Teaching and Teacher Education*, *25*(4), 569–574. doi:10.1016/j.tate.2009.02.009

O'Doyd, R., & Dooly, M. (2021). Exploring teachers' professional development through participation in virtual exchange. *ReCALL*, 1–16.

Scribjab. (2021). Retrieved on February 13, 2021 from, http://www.scribjab.com

Storybooks Canada. (2021). Retrieved on February 13, 2021 from, https://storybookscanada.ca//

The New London Group. (1996). A pedagogy of multiliteracies: Designing social futures. *Harvard Educational Review*, *66*, 60–92.

The New London Group. (2000). A pedagogy of multiliteracies designing social futures. In B. Cope & M. Kalantzis (Eds.), *Multiliteracies: Literacy learning and the design of social futures* (pp. 9–37). Routledge.

Villa, R., Thousand, J., & Nevin, A. (2008). *A guide to co-teaching: Practical tips for facilitating student learning* (2nd ed.). Corwin Press.

Warchauer, M., & Mauchniak, T. (2010). New technology and digital worlds: Analyzing evidence of equity in access, use and outcomes. *Review of Research in Education*, *34*(1), 179–225.

Wong, M. M. (2014). Smart virtual word walls: Moving away from the traditional into the digital. *English in Texas*, *44*(1), 27–29.

Wong, M. M. (2019). "S:ay what you want…:" Rap battles in a technology-enhanced classroom. *Canadian Modern Language Review*, *72*(2), 169–182. https://doi.org/10.3138/cmlr.2018-0155

Wong, M. M. (2021). Silly putty: Mobilization of the known across technology-enhanced learning spaces. *Language and Literature*, *23*(3), 146–164.

Wong, M. M. W. (2020). *Mobilizing knowledge processes and lifeworld practices across learning spaces: Exploring grade 6 English language learners' inquiry-based learning experiences in a technology-enhanced classroom* [Unpublished doctoral dissertation]. University of British Columbia. https://open.library.ubc.ca/cIRcle/collections/ubctheses/24/items/1.0395371

Chapter 16
Understanding Teacher Burnout Coping Strategies During a Global Pandemic

Caleb J. Powers
Middlebury Institute of International Studies at Monterey, USA

ABSTRACT

In the beginning of 2020, the impromptu conversion to distance learning forced administrators to consider alternatives to providing quality education which often neglected to consider the toll asked of the teachers. Subsequently, these conditions contributed to an unprecedented surge in teacher burnout. This chapter explores the strategies of 165 U.S. world language teachers for coping with teacher burnout during the pandemic: 76.7% of respondents indicated an increase in burnout after the pandemic started. The most alarming trends in the data are the reduction of access to certain coping strategies, the degradation of effective strategies into ineffective ones, and the severe reduction of the time and energy available to engage in these strategies. These data indicate that teacher burnout should be a priority concern to prevent any further damage to our education systems.

This chapter explores the strategies of 165 U.S. world language teachers for coping with teacher burnout during the COVID-19 pandemic. Survey and interview data were collected to address two research questions: (1) How has the pandemic affected these teachers' levels of burnout; and (2) Have they made changes to their coping strategies? The data indicate a significant increase in levels of teacher burnout among world language teachers while working during the pandemic. The most alarming trends in the data are the reduction of access to certain coping strategies, the degradation of effective strategies into ineffective ones, and the severe reduction of the time and energy available to engage in these strategies.

DOI: 10.4018/978-1-7998-8717-1.ch016

INTRODUCTION

Teachers have long gone underappreciated and under-supported for the critical, society-advancing work they undertake within their classrooms (Thirumurthy et al., 2007). Every day, educators engage in the gratifying work that is teaching but over time, unresolved complications in our education systems have accumulated and caused larger-scale issues. For example, teachers must face unfair expectations and negative perceptions from the public alongside being the topic of many heated political conversations (DeWitt, 2019). These issues have negatively impacted the quality of education that students receive (Bahrami & Moradkhani, 2019) and have adversely altered the reputation of the teaching profession (Anderson et al., 2009). Because of the pandemic that unfolded in the beginning months of 2020, many points of contention in American education systems were highlighted by the impromptu and compulsory conversion to distance learning. This grueling transition forced administrators to consider many possible methods of providing quality education, but their plans sometimes neglected to consider the toll asked of the teachers who enact administrators' visions.

Even before the coronavirus pandemic, burnout was a major concern within the teaching profession (Gold, 1985), and now the conditions of working during a global health crisis have contributed to an unprecedented surge in teacher burnout. These data indicate that teacher burnout should be a priority concern for both teachers and administrators alike to prevent any further damage to our education systems.

LITERATURE REVIEW

What is Teacher Burnout?

Burnout has been studied in many contexts, mostly in the caregiving and service industries, and so there is not one agreed-upon definition of burnout (Gold, 1985). Freudenberger (1974) was the first to define the term as:

Feelings of failure and being worn or wrung out, resulting from an overload of claims on energy, on personal resources, or on the spiritual strength of the worker...or a loss of interest by workers in the persons with whom they work...and as psychological distancing from work. (Friedman, 1991, p. 325)

Maslach and Leiter (1997) described burnout in education as a deterioration of engagement that transforms meaningful work into an unpleasant chore. Maslach (1998) later developed a multidimensional perspective on burnout to account for the complexity of the subject, which states that this workplace syndrome is "an individual stress experience embedded in a context of complex social relationships, and it involves the person's conception of both self and others" (p. 69). This multidimensional perspective is important to consider especially in the present context as the global pandemic has contributed to the complexity of the situation.

Why Should We Study Teacher Burnout?

Through their daily tasks, teachers operate in several roles (mentor, caregiver, disciplinarian, etc.) and over the years, more responsibilities have been delegated to them (Davis, 2001). Teachers must prepare course materials, care for the wellbeing of their students, volunteer for additional professional duties, teach classes, evaluate students' work, and much more. And now, with the global pandemic that overturned the profession, teachers are expected to learn how to teach simultaneously in-person and online (Clapsaddle et al., 2021) while also managing hygiene protocols and social distance measures (World Health Organization, 2020). Even before the pandemic, this kind of increase in responsibilities had created "adverse and stressful classroom and school conditions [which] have led to increased emotional and physical disabilities among teachers and other school personnel" (Moe, 1979; as cited in Gold, 1985, p. 210). We must also consider the fact that the teaching profession was already characterized as having "*high* levels of burnout and emotional exhaustion," which means any increase in pressures that may lead to burnout is concerning (Chang, 2009, p. 193, emphasis in original).

These increasingly adverse conditions also lead to *attrition*, which is when teachers leave the profession indefinitely (Carver-Thomas & Darling-Hammond, 2019). The workload required of teachers has become overwhelming for many and, in fact, has been a leading cause of attrition globally for years (Geiger & Pivovarova, 2018). High turnover of teachers affects the quality of education in the classroom and causes administrative issues with understaffed schools (Chang, 2009), meaning the consequences of leaving teacher burnout unaddressed carry a heavy toll. It is imperative to learn how to better understand and prevent teacher burnout, because teaching under burnout conditions is not sustainable and continues to create detrimental issues every day in our education systems.

Causes of Teacher Burnout

The issue of teacher burnout is complex and has roots in multiple levels of our education systems; therefore, it is important to consider the causes of burnout from both the individual and the organizational perspectives. The individual perspective on teacher burnout considers the factors that describe an educator with a "higher propensity to burn out" (Friedman, 1991, p. 325). For example, Chang (2009) explains that motivated and invested employees are more likely to burn out if they experience a difference between their expected results and their reality. Many other personality factors, such as self-esteem, levels of expectation, and coping methods of processing emotion, also impact burnout levels (Friedman, 1991). Other factors in this perspective have less conclusive impacts on burnout and require more research (e.g., age, gender, marital status, level of education, and years of experience) (Chang, 2009; Gold, 1985; Farber, 1984; Kahn et al., 2006).

The organizational perspective relates to the environment in which a teacher works and the variables within that environment that contribute to burnout. Although the individual perspective does influence burnout to a degree, the "main cause for the majority of cases of burnout is environmental" (Friedman, 1991, pp. 325–326). Friedman adds that an organization's culture and social/professional support networks are very influential in the levels of burnout faculty members experience. The leadership styles of the administrative team and institutional alignment with employee's career expectations also influence employees' levels of burnout (Friedman, 1991).

There are several factors to consider within the pedagogical environment of a teacher that can lead to burnout, such as the quality of the classroom, "teacher-pupil ratio, grade level taught, types of exceptional children taught, and workload," the latter being the "most salient element that contributed to burnout" (Chang, 2009, p. 196). Teaching requires substantial *emotional labor*, or "what employees perform when they are required to feel, or at least project the appearance of feeling certain emotions as they engage in job-relevant interactions" (Chang, 2009, p. 203). Perpetually having to engage in emotional labor leads to emotional exhaustion. To best address the pressing issue of teacher burnout, we must consider both the individual and organizational perspectives.

Manifestations of Burnout

It is imperative to be capable of identifying common manifestations of burnout so that adequate intervention and support can be provided to struggling teachers. By *manifestations*, the researcher means the ways in which the symptoms of burnout, both obvious and subtle, make themselves visible. There are manifestations related to *emotional vitality*, which is the limited energy teachers use to engage in emotional labor and the depletion of this energy is the most noticeable manifestation of burnout; Common examples are "intense reactions of anger, anxiety, restlessness, depression, tiredness, boredom, cynicism, guilt feelings, psychosomatic symptoms, and in extreme cases, nervous breakdown" (Friedman, 1991, p. 325). The symptoms of burnout can appear similar to those of depression, such as "feelings of hopelessness, helplessness, emptiness, and sadness" (Gold, 1985, p. 210). A burned-out teacher might exhibit *emotional exhaustion* if they have "depleted [their] emotional resources," leaving them feeling fatigued and debilitated, causing them to be less responsive to the needs of their students (Chang, 2009, p. 196). Emotional exhaustion can also manifest as "a loss of motivation and commitment" (p. 195). Changes in self-confidence and self-perceived efficacy are also indicators of teacher burnout (Friedman, 1991; Chang, 2009; Pines, 2002).

Another relevant manifestation is that of *depersonalization* or *isolation,* which is when an employee "actively ignores the service recipients in an attempt to put distance between them and oneself" or a "detached attitude" between colleagues (Chang, 2009, p. 197). It is unclear as to whether we should consider depersonalization a symptom of burnout or a coping strategy to prevent it. The profession of teaching is already an isolating experience as many educators work day-to-day separated from other adults (Fullan, 2001), and even though burned-out teachers perceive it as a preventative measure, isolation can actually cause teachers to become "frustrated, bored, and depleted as they privately struggle with their anxieties" (Chang, 2009, p. 193). One teacher may exhibit many of these manifestations or just a few, but all of them should be considered signs of a potentially burned-out teacher.

Coping Strategies

Burnout can be a terminal diagnosis for educators who feel like their best option is to leave the profession altogether; however, it can also be a temporary emotional status for teachers. In fact, Friedman and Farber (1992) found that even though teachers report feelings of burnout, they indicate that they would still want to enter the profession if they were to restart their careers. For burned-out teachers to persevere, however, they must employ coping strategies to aid them with their daily responsibilities. A *coping strategy* is what Lazarus and Folkman (1984) define as "constantly changing cognitive and behavioral efforts to manage specific external and/or internal demands that are appraised as taking or exceeding the resources of the person" (p. 141). Teachers can experience burnout when they do not have adequate coping resources or if the rewards do not outweigh their work demands and stressors (Blasé, 1982).

There are many coping strategies that teachers use to address their burnout. Lazarus and Folkman (1984) list the most common of them: confrontation, distancing, self-control, seeking social support, accepting responsibility, escape-avoidance, problem solving, and positive reappraisal. There are two main types of coping strategies: *action-focused*, where the root of the issue is addressed, and *emotion-focused*, where one regulates, avoids, or distracts oneself from emotion (Martínez et al., 2020). Research shows that proactive coping and employing emotion-focused and problem-focused coping strategies aid in the prevention of burnout (Greenglass, 2002; Lazarus, 2006). There are several variables to consider when determining which coping strategies would best address a burned-out teachers' symptoms.

Burnout During COVID-19

It is important to study how teachers have coped with burnout specifically during the COVID-19 pandemic because the exceptional challenges they have faced may have altered their use of coping mechanisms.

The Horace Mann Educators Corporation surveyed 1,240 American teachers who work in K-12 public schools. They found that 77% of teachers work more than they did the year prior (2019) and 60% are less satisfied with their jobs (Johnson Hess, 2020). A more recent study conducted by the Center for State and Local Government Excellence (SLGE) found that 54% of their respondents (494 K-12 public school educators) experienced feelings of burnout, 63% felt stressed, and 47% felt anxious (SLGE, 2021). Other research has shown that the COVID-19 pandemic has exacerbated the feelings of teacher burnout (Ali, 2020) and isolation among teachers (Walker, 2020). Educators must deal with the physical and mental health distractions of their families and themselves while also facing unprecedented challenges in the workplace (Johnson Hess, 2020). According to the Horace Mann study, approximately 27% of American teachers are considering quitting out of concern for their health (Johnson Hess, 2020). That number was even higher in the SLGE study (38%) (SLGE, 2021). Some have left the profession altogether. According to a RAND Corporation survey, "about 44% of teachers who left voluntarily during COVID-19 cited the pandemic as the primary reason for their exit (Jagannathan, 2021).

Some teachers have been frustrated with the lack of transparency or flexibility of their administrations' plans for their schools (Olsen & Sexton, 2009) or they may feel blindsided by the sudden shift toward distance learning (Fagell, 2020). As many educators have only recently joined the conversation on distance learning, several have voiced "feelings of concern that they are less effective teachers when teaching remotely" (Sokal et al., 2020a, p. 2) and many have reminded us of the inequities our students might face in these digital learning environments (Sokal et al. 2020b). Sokal et al. (2020a, 2020b, 2020c) published a series of studies focusing on burnout in Canadian schools during the first COVID-19 wave. Their research found that some recommended coping strategies, such as talking with "partners/families, peers, and friends; therapies such as counselling, instruction in technology; and sleep" are being perceived by burned-out teachers as additional sources of stress and as an additional burden of responsibility (2020c, p. 72). Since demotivation and feeling overwhelmed are common symptoms of burnout, it may seem daunting or exceptionally overwhelming to embark on the often-unpaid labor required to escape burnout.

By reading about how other teachers' coping strategies have changed, world language teachers who are burned out (or approaching burnout) can benefit from learning what has worked for their peers. The results may also be applicable for teaching during future emergency situations or may even contribute to the prevention of teacher burnout in general (Holmes et al., 2020).

In this chapter, the researcher attempts to explore the feelings associated with the COVID-19 pandemic in more detail, answering the following questions:

How has the global COVID-19 pandemic affected world language educators' levels of teacher burnout? Are any observed differences statistically significant?

Have these educators changed how they cope with burnout during the pandemic, and if so, how?

RESEARCH METHODOLOGY

Context and Participants

The purpose of this research was to study the context of working as a world language educator in the United States during the 2020 global COVID-19 pandemic. This research was conducted in two parts: first was a questionnaire portion, then an interview portion. To obtain survey participants, snowball sampling was employed by sharing the survey via email with 300 individuals in the researcher's professional network.

Data Collection Instruments

Questionnaire

The questionnaire (Appendix 1) began with an item verifying that the participants fit within the target audience of world languages teachers located in the United States who taught during the pandemic. This initial question prevented the collection of irrelevant responses. The first section of the questionnaire gathered data on the participants' personal backgrounds, teaching experience and contexts. In section B of the questionnaire, participants reflected on their teaching experiences prior to March 2020. They were asked to select a number on a seven-point Likert scale to indicate their average weekly level of burnout, to indicate which burnout symptoms they experienced, and which coping strategies they used. Section C followed the same pattern as section B, but the time frame focused on the participants' experiences after the U.S. lockdown in March 2020. In responding to the second half of section C, participants also provided a timeline describing the changes to the delivery of education at their institutions, some recommendations for other educators in similar contexts, and an explanation of how they have perceived their changes in burnout coping strategies, if any. The final item on the questionnaire asked for volunteers to participate in the interview portion of this study.

Interviews

For the second phase, the researcher conducted semi-structured interviews with a representative sample of participants. For each 30-minute interview, six prepared questions were asked to gather data on the potential changes to participants' coping strategies, examples of burnout, burnout triggers during the pandemic, and advice for other world language educators. For each interviewee, two to five additional questions were prepared that clarified some of their responses to the questionnaire items. The questions can be seen in Appendix 2.

Procedures

The questionnaire was administered online via Google Forms. To select questionnaire participants, the snowball sampling approach was used by sharing the questionnaire via email with colleagues, peers, and past professors asking them to forward the questionnaire to their colleagues. While the U.S. lockdown started in March of 2020, this data collection took place from March to April 2021. Thus, the respondents provided data based on a year of experiencing pandemic conditions.

The interviews were conducted via Zoom and were recorded using the Zoom record feature. The participants for the interview portion of this research self-nominated in the questionnaire, of which 48.5% (n = 80) indicated they were interested in participating in an interview. To choose which respondents would be interviewed, the researcher analyzed the candidates' languages taught, experience levels, teaching contexts, and differences in the burnout levels they reported as having before and after the pandemic started to select a sample that was representative of the diversity of the entire respondent population. When possible, the school-affiliated emails provided by the volunteering respondents were used to attempt to diversify the geographic contexts in which the interviewees work. Of the 80 interview candidates, 7 of them were interviewed. The responses to the questionnaire and interviews were coded for coping strategies.

FINDINGS AND DISCUSSION

In the first phase, the questionnaire was distributed via email to 300 individuals in the researcher's professional network of whom 172 responded. Of those responses, 7 were invalid due to the respondent not being a world language teacher in the United States, or due to the submission of multiple responses. Therefore, the number of valid responses was 165, yielding a rate of return of 55%. The average age of the participants was 47.3 years old (SD = 11.6) and the average teaching experience was 17.8 years (SD = 9.4). (One respondent preferred not to provide their age.) Thirty-five percent of respondents indicated that they were native speakers of the language(s) they teach, 57% are non-native speakers of the language(s) they teach, and 8.5% of them the researcher classified as 'mixed,' meaning they teach both their first and additional languages. Figure 1 illustrates the various languages taught by the respondents.

Figure 1. Languages taught by participants

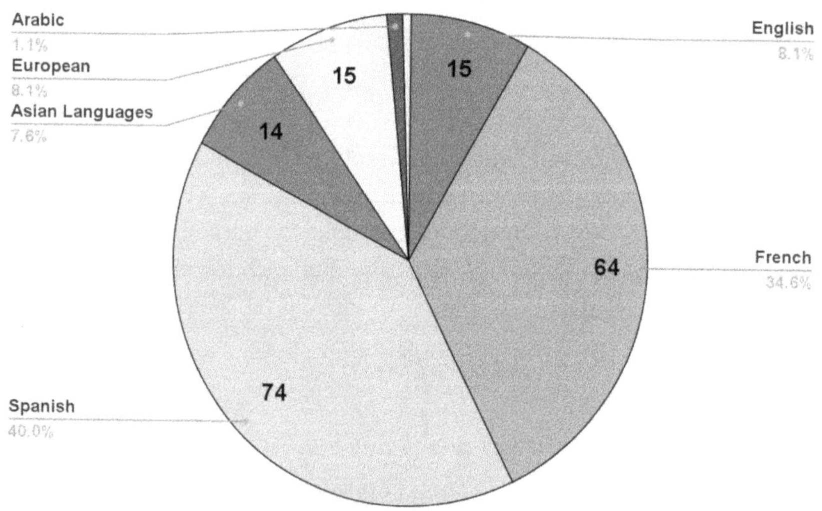

Of the 165 respondents, roughly 75% teach French and/or Spanish, while the remaining 25% teach English as a second language, Asian languages (Mandarin, Japanese, or Korean), other European languages (German, Latin, Italian, Portuguese, Norwegian), Arabic (1.2%), or American Sign Language (0.6%). Table 1 displays the highest levels of education of the respondents. Table 2 provides the contexts in which the participants work.

Table 1. Highest level of education

Highest Level of Education	Number of Respondents
Teaching Certification	29 (17.6%)
Bachelor's Degree	30 (18.2%)
Master's Degree	98 (59.4%)
Post-Graduate Degree	31 (18.8%)
Currently Working Toward Next Level	4 (2.4%)

Table 2. Participants' teaching contexts

Teaching Context	Number of Participants
K-12	114 (69.1%)
Undergraduate University or Community College	50 (30.3%)
Post-Graduate School	18 (10.9%)
Adult School	5 (3.0%)
Intensive Language Program	6 (3.6%)
International School	4 (2.4%)
Private Language School	6 (3.6%)
Private Tutoring	5 (3.0%)

Comparing Manifestations of Burnout

Respondents to the survey indicated which symptoms of burnout they were experiencing pre- and post-pandemic. (Since the pandemic is ongoing as of this writing, *post-pandemic* is being used here to refer to any time after the U.S. began lockdown in March 2020.) Of the nine common manifestations of burnout prompted in the questionnaire, results showed that there was an increase from pre-pandemic to post-pandemic for every single manifestation. These data are illustrated in Table 3.

Table 3. Self-reported pre- and post-pandemic symptoms of burnout

Range of Increase	Symptoms of Burnout	Pre-Pandemic	Post-Pandemic
Most Increase Least Increase	Depersonalized/Isolated	13 (7.9%)	67 (40.6%)
	Emotionally Exhausted	62 (37.6%)	112 (67.9%)
	Unmotivated/Uncommitted	25 (15.2%)	68 (41.2%)
	Intense Emotional Swings	13 (7.9%)	50 (30.3%)
	Depressed/Hopeless	16 (9.7%)	46 (27.9%)
	Fatigued	115 (69.7%)	143 (86.7%)
	Stressed/Anxious	87 (52.7%)	114 (69.1%)
	Cynical/Negative	34 (20.1%)	60 (36.4%)
	Self-Conscious/Ineffective	41 (24.8%)	66 (40.0%)

Addressing the first research question of how teachers have been affected, these data show that the manifestations of teacher burnout appear in more educators while teaching under the conditions of a global pandemic than compared to an average year. It is important to consider that some of the respondents may have exhibited these manifestations but did not consider them as being related to their teacher burnout. For example, Participant 7 noted that they suffered from depression and anxiety before the pandemic, while another respondent said, "I actually feel more depressed, and I think it might be the pandemic and not the teaching" (Participant 135). Regardless of their cause, these emotional symptoms may lead to even more teacher burnout and, therefore, must be addressed.

Comparing Levels of Burnout

Before the U.S. lockdown in March 2020, the majority of the questionnaire respondents indicated that their average weekly burnout levels were somewhere between 2 and 5 (on a scale of 1–7, where 1= few symptoms of burnout and 7= completely burned out). After the start of the pandemic, the majority of the respondents reported that their average weekly levels of burnout were between 5 and 7. In fact, 76.7% of respondents indicated an increase in burnout after the pandemic started. The questionnaire responses indicated a change in respondents' perceptions of burnout pre- and post-pandemic. These results are represented in Figure 2. These data address the first research question and indicate that teaching during a global pandemic increases teachers' average levels of burnout.

Figure 2. Self-reported pre- vs. post-pandemic ratings of burnout

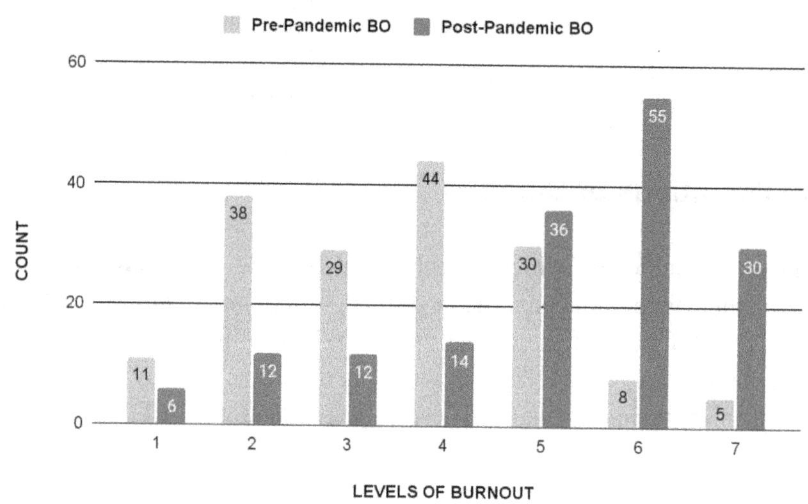

The data displayed in Figure 2 can also be described using means and standard deviations of the ratings on the 7-point Likert scale. For the pre-pandemic ratings, the mean was 3.53 and the standard deviation was 1.46. For the post-pandemic ratings, the mean was 5.1 and the standard deviation was 1.64. To address the research question regarding a possible significant difference between the respondents' pre-pandemic and post-pandemic ratings of burnout, a paired-samples t-test was conducted using an online statistical calculator (T-Test Calculator for 2 Dependent Means, 2021). Alpha was set at 0.01 and a two-tailed test was used. A t-value of 11.588911 was obtained ($p < 0.00001$). Thus, it is clear that the difference between the pre-pandemic and post-pandemic ratings of burnout were statistically significant.

Comparing Coping Strategies

Given the increases in reported burnout symptoms, it is important to analyze how, if at all, the participants' coping strategies changed. One of the main purposes of this study was to investigate the coping strategies employed by world language educators to understand which strategies were most commonly engaged and to identify potential strategies that may ease feelings of burnout.

Table 4. Comparing burnout difference and strategy difference

	Increased Burnout	Neutral Burnout	Decreased Burnout
Increased Strategies	62 (37.6%)	5 (3.0%)	3 (1.8%)
Neutral Strategies	32 (19.4%)	8 (4.8%)	2 (1.2%)
Decreased Strategies	33 (20.0%)	12 (7.3%)	8 (4.8%)

Table 4 illustrates that roughly half of the respondents whose burnout levels increased also increased their use of coping strategies. However, the other half of those respondents who had self-reported increased levels of burnout decreased or maintained the number of coping strategies they employed. These data indicate that when a teacher's level of burnout increases, they may be more likely to increase the number of strategies employed, but also may make no change or decrease that number. In the following sections, the differences in use of coping strategies reported by the participants and some possible implications will be discussed.

Increased Strategies

The strategies that were used by *more* respondents after the pandemic had begun are sequenced in order of largest to smallest increase in Table 5. An increase in use of these coping strategies could potentially mean that respondents sought out new strategies that were more feasible while confined in their homes during the pandemic. Most of these strategies are individualistic, meaning they can be instigated and carried out by a teacher without the approval or supervision of an administrator. Additionally, many of these strategies can be implemented in a very short amount of time with little to no preparation. For example, meditation and music therapy can take place during short breaks between classes. We must also consider that respondents may have selected a strategy merely because it accurately reflected their actuality, without reflecting on whether or not they intentionally engage in this strategy to address their teacher burnout. For example, the rise in use of isolation could be an unintended happenstance of working remotely from home.

Table 5. Strategies with more uses post-pandemic

Range of Increase	Strategy	Pre-Pandemic	Post-Pandemic
Most Increase	Leave the profession/ significantly reduce teaching time	3 (1.8%)	16 (9.7%)
	Isolation or psychological disengagement	18 (10.9%)	29 (17.6%)
	Diet and exercise	106 (64.2%)	117 (70.9%)
	Say "no" to new opportunities	71 (43.0%)	81 (49.1%)
	Meditation and Mindfulness	68 (41.2%)	76 (46.1%)
	Music therapy	39 (23.6%)	44 (26.7%)
	Counseling external to your place of work	30 (18.2%)	32 (19.4%)
Least Increase	Attend trainings on emotional intelligence	22 (13.3%)	23 (13.9%)

Of these strategies, diet and exercise were popular coping mechanisms of choice for 64.3% of respondents before the pandemic and 70.9% after the pandemic started. In fact, 28 respondents took the time to elaborate on how their exercise habits impacted their burnout levels in an optional comment section on the questionnaire. Interviewee 1, someone who did not exercise much before the pandemic, boasted about how they saw a considerable change in their romantic partner's mentality after the partner joined a socially distanced exercise group. This drastic change convinced Interviewee 1 to join the group as well and to consider exercise as an effective coping strategy. Conversely, a handful of respondents (n = 8) actually indicated they have been exercising less due to a lack of time, energy, personal safety, or access to a gym.

Another trend in the data shows that 10 respondents considered reducing their responsibilities or leaving the profession altogether. After ten years of teaching at a university, Participant 11 decided to pursue private tutoring full time. Participant 166 acknowledged that they were privileged enough to take a sabbatical to avoid their impending burnout, whereas others might not be so lucky. Other teachers, such as Participants 62, 97, and 154 have strategically chosen to reduce the amount of time they spend on certain responsibilities, such as grading, lesson preparation, committee participation, or the number of courses they teach. It is unclear as to whether or not these reductions in responsibilities contribute to the aforementioned degradation of the quality of education their students receive. Unfortunately, the stress of teaching during a pandemic has led educators, both experienced and novice, to leave the profession completely. Participant 29, who has been teaching for 33 years, noted that after they decided they would retire at the end of the Spring 2021 semester, they saw a reduction in stress and an improvement in their mindfulness. Participant 38, who is 36 years old and has been teaching French for 11 years, said, "I completely gave up on my career as a teacher. I want to leave the profession ASAP." In our discussion, Interviewee 1 disclosed that, for one week near the beginning of the lockdown, they considered quitting their teaching and administrative positions and reconsidering their career. Though this feeling only lasted one week, Interviewee 1 affirmed that it was a compelling thought. These data align with the research that shows that teacher burnout often leads to attrition (Vanderslice, 2010) and support the claim that, if left unaddressed, teacher burnout will continue to deter world language teachers from continuing a career in education.

Since teaching has long been described as an "egg crate" profession due to the isolation many teachers experience (Lortie, 1975), it could be expected that depersonalization and isolation might be common among respondents. The questionnaire results show an increase from 10.9% to 17.6% of respondents feeling isolated. A few participants indicated that activities that used to be communal are now solitary (e.g., daily walks, lunch breaks) and that their isolation from their colleagues contributed to their burnout.

Some educators, like Participant 47, intentionally isolate because time with colleagues is not as effective a strategy as it used to be or contributes to their emotional exhaustion. Interviewee 6, who serves as her on-campus student dorm's "den mother," admitted to using the back entrances to the school buildings to avoid interacting with her students. She explained that by entering through the common areas, she would be obligated to enforce social distancing measures that she herself did not believe in. Her view is that the administration has perverted her role as teacher to that of a police officer whose primary duty is to punish offenders: "We've gone overboard, and we haven't taken into account what the psychological and the social impact will be." Socializing is a large part of the job of a teacher (e.g., teachers' lounge interactions, pre-class chatting, bonding with colleagues), but the strategy of isolating is a crucial reminder that the same strategies will not be effective at reducing burnout for all teachers. For some educators, it is an escape from being overwhelmed; for others, it is the source.

Decreased Strategies

Table 6 illustrates the strategies that were used by *fewer* respondents after the pandemic had begun and are sequenced in order of largest to smallest decrease in responses. A reduction in use of these strategies could be due to several factors such as perceived efficacy, reduction of access, or lack of time or energy. It should be noted that these strategies all require other participants or a significant amount of time or energy.

Table 6. Self-reported strategies with fewer uses post-pandemic

Range of Decrease	Strategy	Pre-Pandemic	Post-Pandemic
Most Decrease	Take on more responsibilities and/or leadership positions	43 (26.1%)	18 (10.9%)
	Discussions with colleagues and supervisors	97 (58.8%)	91 (55.2%)
	Participate in stress management programs	18 (10.9%)	15 (9.1%)
	Crafts and other non-professional hobbies	64 (38.8%)	62 (37.6%)
Least Decrease	Practice and learn new time management strategies	38 (23.0%)	36 (21.8%)

For example, to use discussions with colleagues as an effective coping strategy, it is required that a teacher has a colleague or supervisor who is available and willing to devote the time and emotional capital to a conversation. This requirement has become less probable especially for educators who are teaching remotely and have fewer face-to-face interactions with their colleagues. Interviewee 2, a relatively new faculty member at their institution, explained that they did not feel comfortable verbalizing their feelings of burnout (or concerns for student safety) out of fear of causing social turmoil among their colleagues. However, discussions with others are not ineffective or improbable for all. In fact, 11 respondents commented about how socializing has benefited them particularly when educators are so isolated.

Other strategies might require administrative approval or require an exorbitant amount of energy on the part of the burned-out teacher (e.g., learning time management strategies, hobbies, assuming additional responsibilities) while others require a nonnegotiable and lengthier time commitment (e.g., participating in stress management programs, taking on a leadership position). It would require a secondary study to fully understand the participants' motivations behind the coping strategies they use. Some teachers have used the pandemic as an opportunity to reassess their curriculum and professional development. Participant 28 said they found it "ironically invigorating" to "mobilize" their stress and anxiety to revise their department's curriculum and assessment strategies. Similarly, Participant 36 has participated in webinars on engagement strategies for distance learning and found more of a sense of control in the virtual classroom. However, Participant 100 and other teachers report that webinars are exhausting since they contribute to screen-time and that the abundance of choices can be overwhelming as they are now unlimited by geography.

Additional Strategies

There were several coping strategies that participants reported using that were not included as options in the questionnaire. In the additional comments section of the questionnaire, 12 participants mentioned a mindset of acceptance. This acceptance manifested differently among the participants. For some, it was an acceptance of what they were capable of doing at that time. For example, Participant 29 commented, "I give myself permission to not expect myself to be the 'best' teacher. This year is hard, and we just have to keep doing what we can and tossing what we can't out the door." For Participant 88, their perspective considered the challenging context in which they teach: "In normal times, success is being more cutting edge. In these times, success is just doing the job and offering students the chance to learn if they apply themselves." Similarly, Participant 110 adjusted their expectations of their students: "I am learning to assign LESS, do LESS, expect LESS, go SLOWER, [and] repeat MORE" (capitalization in original).

Similar to the trend of acceptance is a shift in priorities and boundaries. Teachers, like Participants 33 and 102, have been actively focusing on their work-life balance, allocating more time to personal care and leisure activities. Interviewee 5 stated:

Teaching is no longer a priority. In fact, my job is no longer a priority. I just do the minimum amount of work so that I don't get in trouble. I focus on my own life. I have hobbies, sports, family, and friends. That's what's important to me.

Others, like Participants 70 and 169, indicated that they work less outside of contract hours. Since teaching is not an hourly profession, it can be easy to work past one's contracted teaching hours. To avoid burnout, some participants reported that they 'clock out,' or set clear boundaries of when they would work and when they would not work. For some participants, this boundary means ignoring emails until work time, or not engaging students outside of class time. A popular strategy reported by a number of participants was having work-free weekends; unless a task was *absolutely* necessary, it could wait until Monday morning. Similarly, many respondents, like Participant 95, said they do not work after a certain hour in the evening, even if their duties were not complete, and this strategy soothed their symptoms of burnout.

Understanding boundaries is important because many participants voiced that if they are not working, they have feelings of guilt or feel like there is always something more they could work on. Having defined boundaries is especially crucial for educators who are teaching remotely from home, as it can be a challenge to relax and work in the same space (Ciolfi et al., 2020; Cook, 2020). Participant 54 explained, "Stepping away from work has to be more intentional now that work is at home and there is no physical difference in surroundings." Additionally, six respondents indicated that taking short breaks throughout the workday is beneficial in easing their feelings of burnout. Some teachers, like Participant 91, take afternoon breaks to exercise and enjoy outdoor activities, and then return to work in the evenings. Participants 67 and 144 explained in the questionnaire that because they no longer commute to work, they have more time in their schedules to take wellness breaks or to go on hikes in the middle of the week.

Complementary to breaks from work are breaks from the screen. Eight respondents commented that they participate in offline hobbies or work specifically to reduce their screen time. Participant 81 has adopted the practice of blocking out an hour a day to paint or draw. Participant 36 emphasized how impactful it can be to plan collaboration or work off-screen. Other educators, such as Participant 19 and Interviewee 6, indicated that they take breaks from social media or from watching the news, as engagement with these media only contributes to feelings of frustration or being overwhelmed.

In the questionnaire responses and interviews, many other forms of coping strategies were discussed (e.g., animal therapy, a good night's rest, alcohol, and drugs). However, it is beyond the scope of this chapter to discuss all coping strategies mentioned in the questionnaire or contributed by participants.

Changes to Coping Strategies

Using Strategies More

Five respondents indicated that they have intentionally been implementing coping strategies more often. Participant 46 commented, "I've had to ramp [my coping strategies] up significantly to stay afloat." Participants 60 and 80 use their strategies "more frequently" and "more consistently," respectively. Participant 170 illustrates the stark difference in how their coping applications have changed: "Prior to the pandemic, I would need strategies occasionally [during] more stressful periods... [After the pandemic started], I have had to consistently apply as many strategies as I can to survive." Similarly, Participant 66 stated, "[My coping strategies] have become more intentional and intense, given that I have more 'time' to be much more 'aware' of my burnout symptoms." In fact, three respondents mentioned that their awareness of their symptoms of burnout had increased during the pandemic: "I am more aware of my burnout and have learned to control it better" (Participant 18). In contrast, four respondents indicated in the comments section that they either saw no change in the application of their coping strategies or were not aware of how their strategies had changed. Interestingly, 15 respondents indicated that they had no strategies at all.

Using Strategies Less

Lack of Time or Energy. For many educators, it is a struggle to find the time or energy to nurse their burnout symptoms. Four respondents indicated that their abundance of work responsibilities contributed to this lack of time or energy. Pre-pandemic, Participant 9, who teaches at home with their two young children, reported using four coping strategies, but only two post-pandemic: "The lack of time and energy is the main issue for me at the moment." Participant 2 likewise said:

The idea of making more time to take care of myself just seems like another thing that will cause me to get further behind or to be less able to manage everything that is required of me at this time.

Similarly, Participant 55 reported not having enough energy to address their burnout, even though they recognized that coping strategies would help.

Ineffective Strategies: Nine respondents mentioned in the comments that their coping strategies are no longer effective. Participants 2 and 128 say that even though they are applying strategies more consistently than they ever have, their strategies have become less effective over time. Without the support of their coping strategies, some teachers feel helpless and as if "nothing seems to work" (Participant 41). Several respondents indicated that this ineffectiveness is due to the unprecedented challenges teachers have faced during this pandemic. Participant 48 said their strategies "aren't effective because the factors causing burnout are too strong" and Participant 119 added, "I'm doing more to take care of myself, but it's not always that effective given the very stressful task we're given."

Loss of Access to Strategies: Due to the enforced social distancing measures, certain coping strategies teachers might have used were no longer available. Some strategies that were mentioned were massages, dinner parties, yoga classes, religious ceremonies, and band rehearsals. "Unfortunately, any opportunity to implement stress relief strategies or burnout prevention activities I may have had before the pandemic sort of went away once the confinement started," explained Participant 10. Such a sudden loss of access to coping techniques could have contributed to the increased feelings of burnout among respondents. Therefore, it is important to consider access issues when recommending coping strategies to burned-out teachers.

LIMITATIONS

As with all research, there are certain limitations that must be considered with the present study. Firstly, the self-reported data about how teachers coped prior to the pandemic were gathered around a year into the U.S. lockdown, meaning time could affect the validity of these data. Since the data are based on self-report, it is possible those who did not participate would have responded differently. Neither the Maslach Burnout Inventory (MBI) nor any other validated burnout assessment instrument were used because the focus of the study was on coping strategies, which are not included in the MBI. However, this could affect the validity of the reported burnout data due to the quantity of questionnaire items (i.e., The present questionnaire had only nine burnout-specific items, whereas the MBI has 22).

FUTURE RESEARCH DIRECTIONS

There is a need for more research on the prevention of teacher burnout. Sokal et al. (2020c) recommend a more "nuanced examination of resources" because "not all resources are perceived as equally supportive and not all intended resources are interpreted as benefits at all by teachers" (Sokal et al., 2020c, p. 72). It is important to note that the present chapter only addresses the prevention of teacher burnout from the individual perspective. There is a need for more research on the prevention of teacher burnout from the organizational perspective. Additionally, the questionnaire and interviews of the present study gathered world language teachers' recommendations to their administrations and other burned-out teachers that remain to be analyzed. Furthermore, no data was gathered to understand the participants' motivations when deciding which coping strategies they chose to employ, therefore a secondary study would be beneficial. Finally, it would be useful to assess which of the present coping strategies are proven effective in addressing the symptoms of burnout, but doing so was beyond the scope of this study.

CONCLUSION

Teacher burnout is a complex and ubiquitous issue that impacts the field of education in ways that affect the quality of education provided to learners and that deter professionals from entering and remaining in the teaching profession. The COVID-19 pandemic and its impact on education have contributed to the alteration of world language teachers' implementation of coping strategies by reducing access to certain strategies, by rendering once effective strategies ineffective, and by severely reducing the time and energy available to engage in strategies. It is crucial to understand the coping strategies that prevent or reduce teacher burnout so that we may help better educate burned-out teachers.

ACKNOWLEDGMENT

This research received no specific grant from any funding agency in the public, commercial, or not-for-profit sectors. This research would not have been possible without the contributions of the 165 participants who volunteered their time during an exceptionally challenging year. And finally, thank you to all burned-out teachers for doing your best.

REFERENCES

Ali, S. S. (2020). *Educators teaching online and in person at the same time feel burned out.* NBC News.com. https://www.nbcnews.com/news/us-news/educators-teaching-online-person-same-time-feel-burned-out-n1243296

Anderson, A., Evans, R., Kozak, R., & Peterson, B. (2009). Improving the perception of public education. *HORIZON: Issues Challenging Education, 28.*

Bahrami, M., & Moradkhani, S. (2019). A comparison of public school and private institute EFL teachers' burnout. *Technology of Education Journal, 13*(3), 626–637. doi:10.22061/jte.2018.3542.1890

Blasé, J. J. (1982). A social–psychological grounded theory of teacher stress and burnout. *Educational Administration Quarterly, 18*(4), 93–113. doi:10.1177/0013161X82018004008

Carver-Thomas, D., & Darling-Hammond, L. (2019). The trouble with teacher turnover: How teacher attrition affects students and schools. Education Policy Analysis Archives, 27(36). doi:10.14507/epaa.27.3699

Chang, M.-L. (2009). An appraisal perspective of teacher burnout: Examining the emotional work of teachers. *Educational Psychology Review, 21*(3), 193–218. doi:10.100710648-009-9106-y

Ciolfi, L., Gray, B., & Pinatti de Carvalho, A. F. (2020). Making home work places. *Proceedings of the 18th European Conference on Computer-Supported Cooperative Work: The International Venue on Practice-centered Computing on the Design of Cooperation Technologies—Exploratory Papers, Reports of the European Society for Socially Embedded Technologies.* https://ulir.ul.ie/handle/10344/897

Clapsaddle, S., Smith, R., & Bratberg, W. (2021). "I'm having the quaran-time of my life": Modeling emergency remote instruction to teacher candidates during the COVID-19 crisis with a HyFlex-multi option approach. In E. Langran & L. Archambault (Eds.), *Proceedings of Society for Information Technology & Teacher Education International Conference* (pp. 133–137). Association for the Advancement of Computing in Education (AACE). https://www.learntechlib.org/primary/p/219124/

Cook, D. (2020). The freedom trap: Digital nomads and the use of disciplining practices to manage work/leisure boundaries. *Information Technology & Tourism*, *22*(3), 355–390. doi:10.100740558-020-00172-4

Davis, H. A. (2001). The quality and impact of relationships between elementary school students and teachers. *Contemporary Educational Psychology*, *26*(4), 431–453. doi:10.1006/ceps.2000.1068 PMID:11681827

DeWitt, P. (2019). *12 Critical issues facing education in 2020*. EducationWeek. https://www.edweek.org/leadership/opinion-12-critical-issues-facing-education-in-2020/2019/12?s_kwcid=AL!6416!3!486544088589!b!!g!!&utm_source=goog&utm_medium=cpc&utm_campaign=ew+dynamic+recent%20&ccid=dynamic+ads+recent+articles&ccag=recent+articles+dynamic&cckw=&cccv=dynamic+ad&gclid=CjwKCAjw6qqDBhB-EiwACBs6x3Mi-JO4sYfO_KW16kIBEKOkatOVhdUgFsaWMLrrSCDdjy3v-EHPF1BoCnM8QAvD_BwE

Fagell, P. L. (2020). Career confidential: Distance learning frustrations. *Kappan*, *102*(3), 66–67. doi:10.1177/0031721720970708

Farber, B. A. (1984). Stress and burnout in suburban teachers. *The Journal of Educational Research*, *77*(6), 325–331. doi:10.1080/00220671.1984.10885550

Freudenberger, H. J. (1974). Staff burnout. *The Journal of Social Issues*, *30*(1), 159–164. doi:10.1111/j.1540-4560.1974.tb00706.x

Friedman, I. A. (1991). High- and low-burnout schools: School culture aspects of teacher burnout. *The Journal of Educational Research*, *84*(6), 325–333. doi:10.1080/00220671.1991.9941813

Friedman, I. A., & Farber, B. A. (1992). Professional self-concept as a predictor of teacher burnout. *The Journal of Educational Research*, *86*(1), 28–35. doi:10.1080/00220671.1992.9941824

Fullan, M. (2001). *The new meaning of educational change*. Teachers College. doi:10.4324/9780203986561

Geiger, T., & Pivovarova, M. (2018). The effects of working conditions on teacher retention. *Teachers and Teaching*, *24*(6), 604–625. doi:10.1080/13540602.2018.1457524

Gold, Y. (1985). Burnout: Causes and solutions. *The Clearing House: A Journal of Educational Strategies, Issues and Ideas*, *58*(5), 210–212. doi:10.1080/00098655.1985.9955539

Greenglass, E. R. (2002). Proactive coping and quality of life management. In E. Frydenberg (Ed.), *Beyond coping: Meeting goals, visions, and challenges*. Oxford University Press., doi:10.1093/med:psych/9780198508144.003.0003

Holmes, E., O'Connor, R., Perry, V., Tracey, I., Wessly, S., Arseneault, L., & Ballard, C. (2020). Multidisciplinary research priorities for the COVID-19 pandemic: A call for action for mental health sciences. *The Lancet. Psychiatry*, *7*(6), 547–560. doi:10.1016/S2215-0366(20)30168-1 PMID:32304649

Jagannathan, M. (2021, March 1). *Teachers were already leaving the profession due to stress–then COVID-19 hit.* MarketWatch.com. https://www.marketwatch.com/story/teachers-were-already-leaving-the-profession-due-to-stress-then-covid-19-hit-11614025213

Johnson Hess, A. (2020, December 14). *27% of teachers are considering quitting because of Covid, survey finds.* CNBC.com. https://www.cnbc.com/2020/12/14/27percent-of-teachers-are-considering-quitting-because-of-covid-survey.html

Kahn, J. H., Schneider, K. T., Jenkins-Henkelman, T. M., & Moyle, L. L. (2006). Emotional social support and job burnout among high-school teachers: Is it all due to dispositional affectivity? *Journal of Organizational Behavior, 27*(6), 793–807. doi:10.1002/job.397

Lazarus, R. S. (2006). Emotions and interpersonal relationships: Toward a person-centered conceptualization of emotions and coping. *Journal of Personality, 74*(1), 9–46. doi:10.1111/j.1467-6494.2005.00368.x PMID:16451225

Lazarus, R. S., & Folkman, S. (1984). *Stress, appraisal and coping.* Springer. https://books.google.com/books?hl=en&lr=&id=i-ySQQuUpr8C&oi=fnd&pg=PR5&dq=Lazarus,+R.+S.,+%26+Folkman,+S.+(1984).+Stress,+appraisal+and+coping.+New+York:+Springer.&ots=DgFRkufgUf&sig=NGhfIg0t2xfz1FpR01rALRqgljM#v=onepage&q=Lazarus%2C%20R.%20S.%2C%20%26%20Folkman%2C%20S.%20(1984).%20Stress%2C%20appraisal%20and%20coping.%20New%20York%3A%20Springer.&f=false

Lortie, D. (1975). *Schoolteacher: A sociological study.* University of Chicago Press. https://www.jstor.org/stable/2777575

Martínez, J. P., Méndez, I., Ruiz-Esteban, C., Fernández-Sogorb, A., & García-Fernández, J. M. (2020). Profiles of burnout, coping strategies and depressive symptomatology. *Frontiers in Psychology, 11*(591), 591. Advance online publication. doi:10.3389/fpsyg.2020.00591 PMID:32300323

Maslach, C. (1998). A multidimensional theory of burnout. In C. L. Cooper (Ed.), *Theories of organizational stress.* https://books.google.com/books?hl=en&lr=&id=ahfJ16b-BdUC&oi=fnd&pg=PA68&dq=Maslach,+C.+(1998).+A+multidimensional+theory+of+burnout.+In+C.+L.+Cooper+(Ed.),+Theories+of+organizational+stress,+68%E2%80%9385.&ots=O-cnQIsyAY&sig=rLsoYWYlMgfFmhXi6kptsb0L27c#v=onepage&q&f=false

Maslach, C., & Leiter, M. P. (1997). *The truth about burnout: How organizations cause personal stress and what to do about it.* Jossey-Bass. https://books.google.com/books?hl=en&lr=&id=uzomWhbqcCAC&oi=fnd&pg=PR7&dq=Maslach,+C.,+%26+Leiter,+M.+P.+(1997).+The+truth+about+burnout:+How+organizations+cause+personal+stress+and+what+to+do+about+it.+Jossey-Bass.&ots=9B7rnuPFWz&sig=7ZM2OjzfSWAM-AFGe_pwF_Uy_og#v=onepage&q&f=false

Olsen, B., & Sexton, D. (2009). Threat rigidity, school reform, and how teachers view their work inside current educational policy contexts. *American Educational Research Journal, 46*(1), 9–44. doi:10.3102/0002831208320573

Pines, A. M. (2002). Teacher burnout: A psychodynamic existential perspective. *Teachers and Teaching, 8*(2), 121–140. doi:10.1080/13540600220127331

SLGE (The Center for State and Local Government Excellence at ICMA-RC). (2021, February). *Survey findings: K-12 public school employee views on finances, employment outlook, and safety concerns due to COVID-19.* The Center for State and Local Government Excellence at ICMA-RC. https://slge.org/assets/uploads/2021/02/2021-slge-cv19-k12-report.pdf

Sokal, L. J., Eblie Trudel, L. G., & Babb, J. C. (2020a). Canadian teachers' attitudes toward change, efficacy, and burnout during the COVID-19 pandemic. *International Journal of Educational Research Open, 1*, 100016. doi:10.1016/j.ijedro.2020.100016

Sokal, L. J., Eblie Trudel, L. G., & Babb, J. C. (2020b). *How to prevent teacher burnout during the coronavirus pandemic.* The Conversation Canada. Retrieved from https://theconversation.com/how-to-prevent-teacher-burnout-during-the-coronavirus-pandemic-139353

Sokal, L. J., Eblie Trudel, L. G., & Babb, J. C. (2020c). Supporting teachers in times of change: The job demands-resources model and teacher burnout during the COVID-19 pandemic. *International Journal of Contemporary Education, 3*(2), 67–74. doi:10.11114/ijce.v3i2.4931

T-Test Calculator for 2 Dependent Means. (2021, October 12). Retrieved from https://www.socscistatistics.com/tests/ttestdependent/default2.aspx

Thirumurthy, V., Szecsi, T., Hardin, B. J., & Koo, R. D. (2007). Honoring teachers: A world of perspectives. *Journal of Early Childhood Teacher Education, 28*(2), 181–198. doi:10.1080/10901020701366764

Vanderslice, R. (2010). Abc's of keeping the best: Attrition, burnout, and climate. *Childhood Education, 86*(5), 298–301. doi:10.1080/00094056.2010.10521412

Walker, T. (2020). Helping students and educators recover from COVID-19 trauma. *NEA Today.* https://www. nea. org/advocating-for-change/new-from-nea/helping-students-and-educators-recover-covid-19-trauma

World Health Organization. (2020). *Coronavirus disease (COVID-19): Schools.* https://www.who.int/news-room/q-a-detail/coronavirus-disease-covid-19-schools

KEY TERMS AND DEFINITIONS

Attrition: The significant reduction in work time or complete desertion of one's profession.

Burnout Symptom: A noticeable change in one's interpersonal composure or professional attitude as a result of experiencing burnout.

Coping Strategy: A method of addressing the internal and/or external demands on resources in order to mitigate burnout symptoms.

Emotional Labor: The performance of displaying emotion, or feigning emotion, while engaging in social interactions in the workplace.

Global Pandemic: A worldwide health crisis involving the uncontrolled outbreak of a disease.

Lockdown: The state-mandated temporary closure of businesses and order for civilians to remain in their homes and practice social distancing measures.

Post-Pandemic: The period of time starting immediately after the beginning of the state-mandated lockdown.

Teacher Burnout: A depletion of emotional and physical energy and/or reduction in professional efficacy due to an overexertion of resources.

APPENDIX 1

Questionnaire

Thank you for agreeing to participate in this brief questionnaire. Your responses will contribute to my study to understand how world language educators' levels of teacher burnout have been affected by the global COVID-19 pandemic. Please share this questionnaire with your colleagues who teach world languages.
Section A: Background

A1) Age: (Open Response)
A2) First language(s): (Open Response)
A3) Years of teaching experience: (Open Response)
A4) Highest level of education: (Multiple Choice)
- High School Diploma
- Teaching certification/credentials
- Associate's Degree
- Bachelor's Degree
- Master's Degree
- Doctorate

A5) Language(s) you currently teach or have taught in the past 5 years: (Open Response)
A6) Context(s) in which you currently teach or have taught in the past 5 years (Select all that apply):
- Primary (K-12)
- Secondary (Undergraduate University or Community College)
- Post-Secondary (MA/PhD graduate programs)
- Adult School
- Intensive Language Program
- International School
- Private Language School
- Other

A7) If the contexts above do not accurately reflect your teaching context, please elaborate here. (Open Response)

Section B: Pre-Pandemic Burnout

For this research, I will be using the following definitions of burnout: "feelings of failure and being worn or wrung out, resulting from an overload of claims on energy, on personal resources, or on the spiritual strength of the worker…or a loss of interest by workers in the persons with whom they work...and as psychological distancing from work" (Friedman, 1991, p. 325). Burnout is "an erosion of engagement that what started out as important, meaningful, and challenging work becomes unpleasant, unfulfilling, and meaningless" (Maslach & Leiter, 1997).

B1) Reflecting on your teaching experience before March 2020, how would you have rated your average weekly level of teacher burnout during a typical semester? (7-point Likert scale)

B2) Which, if any, of the following burnout symptoms did you regularly experience before the pandemic started? "I felt..."

- Intense emotional swings
- Emotionally exhausted
- Fatigued or drained or energy
- Stressed out or anxious
- Unmotivated or uncommitted
- Cynical or negative
- Depressed or hopeless
- Depersonalized or isolated from my peers
- Self-conscious or ineffective
- Other

B3) Which, if any, of the following burnout management/prevention strategies did you engage in *before* the pandemic started? (Select all that apply)

- Attend training(s) on emotional intelligence
- Participate in stress management programs
- Isolation or psychological disengagement
- Take on more responsibilities and/or leadership positions
- Leave the profession/ significantly reduce teaching time
- Meditation and mindfulness
- Discussions with colleagues and supervisors
- Counseling external to your place of work
- Music therapy (can also be informal use of music to soothe oneself).
- Say 'no' to new opportunities
- Practice and learn new time management strategies
- Diet and Exercise
- Crafts and other non-professional hobbies
- Other

B4) Do you have any other comments on this section of the questionnaire? (Open Response)

Section C: Burnout During the Pandemic

For this section, please focus on your experiences after the global shutdown in March 2020.

C1) Reflecting on your teaching experience since March 2020, how would you rate your current average weekly level of teacher burnout? (7-point Likert scale)

C2) Which, if any, of the following burnout symptoms do you regularly experience since the pandemic started? "I feel..."

- Intense emotional swings
- Emotionally exhausted
- Fatigued or drained or energy
- Stressed out or anxious
- Unmotivated or uncommitted
- Cynical or negative
- Depressed or hopeless

- Depersonalized or isolated from my peers
- Self-conscious or ineffective
- Other

C3) Which, if any, of the following burnout prevention strategies have you engaged in since the pandemic started? (Select all that apply)

- Attend training(s) on emotional intelligence
- Participate in stress management programs
- Isolation or psychological disengagement
- Take on more responsibilities and/or leadership positions
- Leave the profession/ significantly reduce teaching time
- Meditation and mindfulness
- Discussions with colleagues and supervisors
- Counseling external to your place of work
- Music therapy (can also be informal use of music to soothe oneself).
- Say 'no' to new opportunities
- Practice and learn new time management strategies
- Diet and Exercise
- Crafts and other non-professional hobbies
- Other

C4) Can you please provide a detailed timeline of your institution(s)' teaching context since January 2020? (*Ex. in-person Jan-March 13, 2020; distance learning via Zoom March 23–May 2021*) (Open Response)

C5) Reflecting on the timeline you provided above, what is one practice/habit/change you would recommend to administrators or other world language educators to lessen burnout in a context similar to yours? (Open Response)

C6) How, if at all, have your teacher burnout prevention strategies changed since the pandemic started? (Open Response)

C7) Do you have any other comments on this section of the questionnaire? (Open Response)

Section D: Interview Participation

D1) Would you be willing to participate in a brief interview (15–30 minutes) via Zoom? Your participation in the interview portion of this research project is completely optional and your rejection of this offer will not affect your participation in the questionnaire portion of this research. You will be given a pseudonym and your name will remain confidential.

D2) You have indicated that you are willing to participate in a brief interview. In order to set up this meeting, please provide your name and email address. You will be given a pseudonym and your name will remain confidential.

Name and Email Address:

APPENDIX 2

Semi-Structured Interview Questions

1. Can you give me an example of a time when you were burned out or close to burnout? What manifestations made you aware that you were burned out?
2. What was one aspect about teaching during a pandemic that led to feelings of burnout? How did you manage it?
3. How, if at all, have your colleagues/administrators helped you manage your levels of teacher burnout? Did it help?
4. In the questionnaire, you mentioned ____. Can you elaborate on that?
5. What advice do you have for other world language educators regarding teaching during a pandemic?
6. Do you have any other comments or concerns about teacher burnout and your experiences teaching during a global pandemic?

Compilation of References

Abaeian, H., & Samadi, L. (2016). The effect of flipped classroom on Iranian EFL learners' L2 reading comprehension: Focusing on different proficiency levels. *Reading Comprehension*, *3*(6), 10.

Abeysekeraa, L., & Dawson, Ph. (2015). Motivation and cognitive load in the flipped classroom: Definition, rationale and a call for research. *Higher Education Research & Development*, *34*(1), 1–14. doi:10.1080/07294360.2014.934336

Aboagye, E., Yawson, J. A., & Appiah, K. N. (2020). COVID-19 and E-Learning: The Challenges of Students in Tertiary Institutions. *Educational Research for Social Change*, *2*, 1–8.

Abós, Á., Sevil, J., Martín-Albo, J., Aibar, A., & García-González, L. (2018). Validation evidence of the Motivation for Teaching Scale in secondary education. *The Spanish Journal of Psychology*, *21*(9), 1–12. doi:10.1017jp.2018.11 PMID:29633687

Abrams, S. S. (2016). Emotionally crafted experiences: Layering literacies in Minecraft. *The Reading Teacher*, *70*(4), 501–506. doi:10.1002/trtr.1515

ACARA. (2016). *Australian curriculum, assessment and reporting authority*. Retrieved from http://www. australiancurriculum.edu.au/

Adams, T. E., Jones, S. H., & Ellis, C. (2015). Autoethnography: Understanding qualitative research. Oxford.

Adara, R. A., & Najmudin, O. (2020). Analysis on the differences in EFL learners' demotivating factors after COVID-19 pandemic. *TA'DIB*, *23*(2), 225–236. doi:10.31958/jt.v23i2.2373

Adas, D., & Bakir, A. (2013). Writing Difficulties and New Solutions: Blended Learning as an Approach to Improve Writing Abilities. *International Journal of Humanities and Social Science*, *3*(9), 254–266.

Adnan, M., & Kainat, A. (2020). Online learning amid the COVID-19 pandemic: Students' perspectives. *Journal of Pedagogical Sociology and Psychology*, *2*(2), 45–51. doi:10.33902/JPSP.2020261309

Al Zoubi, S. M. (2018). The impact of exposure to English language on language acquisition. *Journal of Applied Linguistics and Language Research*, *5*(4), 151–162.

Albiladi, W. S., & Alshareef, K. K. (2019). Blended learning in English teaching and learning: A review of the current literature. *Journal of Language Teaching and Research*, *10*(2), 232–238. doi:10.17507/jltr.1002.03

Alexander, J. (2006). *Digital youth: Emerging literacies on the World Wide Web*. Hampton Press.

Alghamdi, J., & Holland, C. (2020). A comparative analysis of policies, strategies and programmes for information and communication technology integration in education in the Kingdom of Saudi Arabia and the republic of Ireland. *Education and Information Technologies*, *25*(6), 4721–4745. doi:10.100710639-020-10169-5

Ali, S. S. (2020). *Educators teaching online and in person at the same time feel burned out.* NBC News.com. https://www.nbcnews.com/news/us-news/educators-teaching-online-person-same-time-feel-burned-out-n1243296

Ali, W. (2020). Online and remote learning in higher education institutes: A necessity in light of COVID pandemic. *High. Educ. Stud., 10*(3), 16–25. doi:10.5539/hes.v10n3p16

Alkhataba, A. H., Abdul-Hamid, S., & Bashir, I. (2018). Technology-Supported Online Writing: An Overview of Six Major Web 2.0 Tools for Collaborative-Online Writing. *Arab World English Journal, 9*(1), 433–446. doi:10.24093/awej/vol9no1.30

Allen, I., & Seaman, J. (2010). *Class Differences: Online Education in the United States, 2010.* The Sloan Consortium. http://sloanconsortium.org/publications/survey/class_differences

Allen, H. W., & Paesani, K. (2010). Exploring the Feasibility of a Pedagogy of Multiliteracies in Introductory Foreign Language Courses. *Journal of Linguistics and Language Teaching, 2*, 119–142.

All-Party Parliamentary Group on Modern Languages (APPGML). (2019). *A National Recovery Programme for Languages.* https://university-council-modern-languages.org/wp-content/uploads/2020/05/languagesrecoveryprogrammeappgmfl-embargo4march.pdf

Al-Maroof, R. A. S., & Al-Emran, M. (2018). Students acceptance of Google classroom: An exploratory study using PLS-SEM approach. *International Journal of Emerging Technologies in Learning, 13*(06), 112–123. doi:10.3991/ijet.v13i06.8275

Al-Maskari, A., Al-Riyami, T., & Kunjumuhammed, S. K. (2021). Students' academic and social concerns during COVID-19 pandemic. *Education and Information Technologies.* Advance online publication. doi:10.100710639-021-10592-2 PMID:34226817

Al-Shammari, A. H. (2020). Social media and English language learning during Covid-19: KILAW students' use, attitude, and prospective. *Linguistics Journal, 14*(1), 259–275.

Alsuelmi, A. (2021). *Perceptions of faculty members on the value of distance education at two different types of institutions of higher education in The Kingdom of Saudi Arabia* [Doctoral dissertation, Kansas State University]. K-State Electronic Theses, Dissertations, and Reports.

Altuna, J., Martínez de Morentin, J. I., & Amenábar, N. (2017). Teaching and Learning Theories and Internet Resources: Its Confluence in Primary Schools. *Estudios Sobre Educación, 33*, 145–167.

American Federation of Teachers. (2017). *Educator quality of work life survey.* https://www.aft.org/sites/default/files/2017_eqwl_survey_web.pdf

Amirsheibani, M., Iraji, M. (2014). CALL and Teaching writing: Language teachers' attitude, an Iranian survey. *Procedia – Social and Behavioral Studies, 98, 258-266.*

Anderson, A., Evans, R., Kozak, R., & Peterson, B. (2009). Improving the perception of public education. *HORIZON: Issues Challenging Education, 28.*

Anderson, L. W., & Krathwohl, D. R. (2001). *A taxonomy for learning teaching and assessing: A revision of Bloom's taxonomy of educational objectives*. Longman.

Anderson, R. C., Bousselot, T., Katz-Buoincontro, J., & Todd, J. (2021). Generating buoyancy in a sea of uncertainty: Teachers creativity and well-being during the Covid-19 pandemic. *Frontiers in Psychology, 11*, 1–17. doi:10.3389/fpsyg.2020.614774 PMID:33536979

Andrews, T., Leonard, M., Colgrove, C. A., & Kalinowski, S. (2011). Active Learning Not Associated with Student Learning in a Random Sample of College Biology Courses. *CBE Life Sciences Education, 10*(4), 394–405. doi:10.1187/cbe.11-07-0061 PMID:22135373

Andrich, D. (1978). Scaling attitude items constructed and scored in the Likert tradition. *Educational and Psychological Measurement, 38*(3), 665–680. doi:10.1177/001316447803800308

Antoniou, S., & Papadima-Sophocleous, S. (2022). Using Moodle Quiz to Create Language Consolidating and Testing Activities. In A. El Shaban & R. Abobaker (Eds.), *Policies, Practices, and Protocols for the Implementation of Technology Into Language Learning* (pp. 20–53). IGI Global. doi:10.4018/978-1-7998-8267-1.ch002

Anwar, K., & Adnan, M. (2020). Online learning amid the COVID-19 pandemic: Students perspectives. *Journal of Pedagogical Research, 1*(2), 45–51.

An, Y., & Mindrila, D. (2020). Strategies and tools used for learner-centered instruction. *International Journal of Technology in Education and Science, 4*(2), 133–143. doi:10.46328/ijtes.v4i2.74

Aoki, K. (2010). The use of ICT and e-learning in higher education in Japan. *World Academy of Science, Engineering and Technology, 42*, 854–858.

Apple, M. T., & Mills, D. (2021). *"Like a hamster on a spinning wheel": University instructor reactions to a year of teaching online* [Manuscript in preparation].

Arbaugh, J. B., Cleveland-Innes, M., Diaz, S. R., Garrison, D. R., Ice, P., Richardson, J. C., & Swan, K. P. (2008). Developing a community of inquiry instrument: Testing a measure of the Community of Inquiry framework using a multi-institutional sample. *The Internet and Higher Education, 11*(3-4), 133–136. doi:10.1016/j.iheduc.2008.06.003

Archambault, L. (2011). The Practitioner's Perspective on Teacher Education: Preparing for the K-12 Online Classroom. *Journal of Technology and Teacher Education, 19*(1), 73–91.

Archambault, L., Kennedy, K., Shelton, C., Dalal, M., McAllister, L., & Huyett, S. (2016). Incremental progress: Re-examining field experiences in K-12 online learning contexts in the United States. *Journal of Online Learning Research, 2*(3), 303–326.

Aristovnik, A., Keržic, D., Ravšelj, D., Tomaževic, N., & Umek, L. (2020). Impacts of the COVID-19 Pandemic on Life of Higher Education Students: A Global Perspective. *Sustainability, 12*(20), 8438. doi:10.3390u12208438

Arnold, J. (2020). Foreword. In The emotional rollercoaster of language teaching (pp. xix-xx). Bristol: Multilingual Matters.

Arrojo, R. (1997). Pierre Menard und eine neue Definition des ‚Originals (J. Klemm, Trans.). In WolfM. (Ed.), *Übersetzungswissenschaft in Brasilien. Beiträge zum Status von „Original" und Übersetzung* (pp. 25–33). Stauffenburg.

Asmara, R. (2020). Teaching English in a virtual classroom using WhatsApp during COVID-19 pandemic. *Language and Educational Journal, 5*(1), 16–27. doi:10.52237/lej.v5i1.152

Atmojo, A. E. P., & Nugroho, A. (2020). EFL classes must go online! Teaching activities and challenges during COVID-19 pandemic in Indonesia. *Register Journal, 13*(1), 49–76. doi:10.18326/rgt.v13i1.49-76

Auswärtiges Amt. (2020). *Deutsch als Fremdsprache weltweit.* https://www.auswaertiges-amt.de/blob/2344738/b2a4e47fd-b9e8e2739bab2565f8fe7c2/deutsch-als-fremdsprache-data.pdf

Ayan, E., & Seferoğlu, S. (2017). Using *Etherpad* for Online Collaborative Writing Activities and Learners with Different Language Learning Strategies. *Eurasian Journal of Applied Linguistics, 3*(2), 205–233. doi:10.32601/ejal.461000

Azmi, N. (2017). The benefits of using ICT in the EFL classroom: From perceived utility to potential challenges. *Journal of Educational and Social Research, 7*(1), 111–118. doi:10.5901/jesr.2017.v7n1p111

Baepler, P., Walker, J. D., & Driessen, M. (2014). It's not about seat time: Blending, flipping and efficiency in active learning classrooms. *Computers & Education, 78*, 227–236. doi:10.1016/j.compedu.2014.06.006

Ba, H., Tally, W., & Tsikalas, K. (2002). Investigating children's emerging digital literacies. *The Journal of Technology, Learning, and Assessment, 1*(4), 5–48.

Bahrami, M., & Moradkhani, S. (2019). A comparison of public school and private institute EFL teachers' burnout. *Technology of Education Journal, 13*(3), 626–637. doi:10.22061/jte.2018.3542.1890

Bai, B., & Lo, C. K. (2018). The barriers of technology integration in Hong Kong primary school English education: Preliminary findings and recommendations for future practices. *International Journal of Languages. Literatura y Lingüística, 4*(4), 290–297.

Bailey, D. R., & Lee, A. R. (2020). Learning from experience in the midst of COVID-19: Benefits, challenges, and strategies in online teaching. *Computer-Assisted Language Learning Electronic Journal, 21*(2), 176–196.

Banegas, D. J., & Manzur Busleimán, G. I. (2014). Motivating factors in online language teacher education in southern Argentina. *Computers & Education, 76*, 131–142. doi:10.1016/j.compedu.2014.03.014

Bao, D. (2019). The place of silence in second language acquisition. *English Language Teaching & Research, 1*(1), 26–42. doi:10.33474/eltar-j.v1i1.4771

Bao, W. (2020). COVID-19 and online teaching in higher education: A case study of Peking University. *Human Behavior and Emerging Technologies, 2*(2), 113–115. doi:10.1002/hbe2.191 PMID:32510042

Bärenfänger, O., Harsch, C., Tesch, B., & Vogt, K. (2019). Reform, Remake, Retousche? Diskussion paper by the Deutsche Gesellschaft für Fremdsprachenforschung on the Companion to the CEFR (2018). *Zeitschrift für Fremdsprachenforschung, 30*(1), 7–13.

Basilaia, G., & Kvavadze, D. (2020). Transition to online education in schools during a SARS-CoV-2 Coronavirus (COVID-19) Pandemic in Georgia. *Pedagogical Research, 5*(4), 1–9. doi:10.29333/pr/7937

Basöz, T., & Erten, I. H. (2018). Investigating Tertiary Level EFL Learners' Willingness to Communicate in English. *English Language Teaching, 11*(3), 78–87. doi:10.5539/elt.v11n3p78

Bates, T. (2020). *What should we be doing about online learning when social distancing ends?* Online Learning and Distance Education Resources. https://www.tonybates.ca/2020/04/07/what-should-we-be-doing-about-online-learning-when-social-distancing-ends/

Bawden, D. (2008). Origins and concepts of digital literacy. *Digital literacies: Concepts, policies and practices, 30*(2008), 17-32.

Bax, S. (2011). Normalisation Revisited: The Effective Use of Technology in Language Education. *International Journal of Computer-Assisted Language Learning and Teaching, 1*(2), 1–15. doi:10.4018/ijcallt.2011040101

Beardsley, M., Albó, L., Aragón, P., & Hernández-Leo, D. (2021). Emergency education effects on teacher abilities and motivation to use digital technologies. *British Journal of Educational Technology, 52*(4), 1455–1477. doi:10.1111/bjet.13101

Beaumont, M., & O'Brien, T. (Eds.). (2000). *Collaborative research in 2nd language education*. Trentham Books.

Beecroft, R. (2019). *The Performativity of the Intercultural Speaker: Mainstreaming Improvisational Tasks as an Action-Oriented Framework for the Lower Secondary Classroom. A Longitudinal, Mixed-Methods Action-Research Study* [Unpublished doctoral dissertation]. Heidelberg University of Education.

Beecroft, R. (2013). From Intercultural Speaker to Intercultural Writer. Towards a New Understanding of Translation in Foreign Language Teaching. In D. Tsagari & G. Floros (Eds.), *Translation in language teaching and assessment.* Cambridge Scholars Publishing.

Bennett, P. A., & Yarwood, A. (2021). A Case for Scaffolding Self-reflection. *Pan SIG Journal, 6*(1), 55–64.

Benson, P. (2011). Language learning and teaching beyond the classroom: An introduction to the field. In P. Benson & H. Reinders (Eds.), *Beyond the Language Classroom* (pp. 7–16). Palgrave Macmillan. doi:10.1057/9780230306790_2

Bergmann, J., & Sams, A. (2012). Before you flip, consider this. *Phi Delta Kappan, 94*(2), 25–25. doi:10.1177/003172171209400206

Betts, K. S. (1998). An institutional overview: Factors influencing faculty participation in distance learning in postsecondary education in the United States: An institutional study. *Online Journal of Distance Learning Administration, 1*(3). https://www.westga.edu/~distance/betts13.html

Beyer, A. M. (2011). Improving student presentations: Pecha Kucha and just plain PowerPoint. *Teaching of Psychology, 38*(2), 122–126. doi:10.1177/0098628311401588

Bhatt, I., & MacKenzie, A. (2019). Just Google it! Digital literacy and the epistemology of ignorance. *Teaching in Higher Education, 24*(3), 302–317. doi:10.1080/13562517.2018.1547276

Bidwell, L. M., Grether, S. T., & Pedersen, J. (2021). Disruption and difficulty: Student and faculty perceptions of the transition to online learning in the COVID-19 pandemic. In J. M. Ryan (Ed.), *COVID-19: Social consequences and cultural adaptations* (Vol. 2, pp. 31–46). Routledge.

Billings, E., & Mathison, C. (2011). I get to use an iPod in school? Using technology-based advance organizers to support the academic success of English Learners. *Journal of Science Education and Technology, 21*(4), 494–503. doi:10.100710956-011-9341-0

Black, A. E., & Deci, E. L. (2000). The effects of instructors' autonomy support and students' autonomous motivation on learning organic chemistry: A self-determination theory perspective. *Science Education, 84*(6), 740–756. doi:10.1002/1098-237X(200011)84:6<740::AID-SCE4>3.0.CO;2-3

Black, R. W. (2008). *Adolescents and online fan fiction.* Peter Lang.

Black, R. W., & Reich, S. M. (2012). Culture and community in a virtual world for young children. In C. Steinkuehler, K. Squire, & S. Barab (Eds.), *Games, learning and society learning and meaning in the digital age* (pp. 210–228). Cambridge University Press. doi:10.1017/CBO9781139031127.018

Blair, E., Maharaj, C., & Primus, S. (2016). Performance and perception in the flipped classroom. *Education and Information Technologies, 21*(6), 1465–1482. doi:10.100710639-015-9393-5

Blake, R. (2012). Best practices in online learning: Is it for everyone? In F. Rubio & J. Thoms (Eds.), *Issues in Language Program Direction: Hybrid language teaching and learning: Exploring theoretical, pedagogical and curricular issues* (pp. 10–26). Heinle & Heinle.

Blake, R. J. (2013). *Brave New Digital Classroom. Technology and Foreign Language Learning.* Georgetown University Press.

Blasé, J. J. (1982). A social–psychological grounded theory of teacher stress and burnout. *Educational Administration Quarterly*, *18*(4), 93–113. doi:10.1177/0013161X82018004008

Bloch, J. (2021). *Creating digital literacy spaces for multilingual writers.* Multilingual Matters.

Block, D. (2003). *The Social Turn in Second Language Acquisition.* Georgetown University Press.

Blundell, G. E., Castañeda, D. A., & Lee, J. (2020). A multi-institutional study of factors influencing faculty satisfaction with online teaching and learning. *Online Learning Journal*, *24*(4), 229–253. doi:10.24059/olj.v24i4.2175

Blunkett, D., Halfon, R., & Pember, S. (2021). *Skills for Life: A new strategy for English, Maths, ESOL and Digital: Learning from the past to improve the future: Next stage 2021-2031.* Further Education Trust for Leadership (FETL). https://dera.ioe.ac.uk//37498/

Bodomo, A. (2006). Interactivity in web-based learning. *International Journal of Web-Based Learning and Teaching Technologies*, *1*(2), 18–30. doi:10.4018/jwltt.2006040102

Boelens, R., De Wever, B., & Voet, M. (2017). Four key challenges to the design of blended learning: A systematic literature review. *Educational Research Review*, *22*, 1–18. doi:10.1016/j.edurev.2017.06.001

Bolliger, D. U., Inan, F. A., & Wasilik, O. (2014). Development and validation of the Online Instructor Satisfaction Measure (OISM). *Journal of Educational Technology & Society*, *17*(2), 183–195.

Bolliger, D. U., & Wasilik, O. (2009). Factors influencing faculty satisfaction with online teaching and learning in higher education. *Distance Education*, *30*(1), 103–116. doi:10.1080/01587910902845949

Bonk, C. J., & Graham, C. R. (2012). *The handbook of blended learning: Global perspectives, local designs.* Pfeiffer.

Bower, B. L. (2001). Distance education: Facing the faculty challenge. *Online Journal of Distance Learning Administration*, *4*(2), 1–6.

Bowers, J., & Kumar, P. (2015). Students' perceptions of teaching and social presence: A comparative analysis of face-to-face and online learning environments. *International Journal of Web-Based Learning and Teaching Technologies*, *10*(1), 27–44. doi:10.4018/ijwltt.2015010103

Boyle, J. T., & Nicol, D. J. (2003). Using classroom communication systems to support interaction and discussion in large class settings. *Research in Learning Technology*, *11*(3), 43–57. doi:10.3402/rlt.v11i3.11284

Bozkurt, A. (2019). From distance education to open and distance learning: A holistic evaluation of history, definitions, and theories. In S. Sisman-Ugur & G. Kurubacak (Eds.), *Handbook of research on learning in the age of transhumanism* (pp. 252–273). IGI Global. doi:10.4018/978-1-5225-8431-5.ch016

Bozkurt, A., Hamutoğlu, N. B., Liman-Kaban, A., Taşçi, G., & Aykul, M. (2021). Dijital bilgi çağı: Dijital toplum, dijital dönüşüm, dijital eğitim ve dijital yeterlilikler. *Açıköğretim Uygulamaları ve Araştırmaları Dergisi*, *7*(2), 35–63. doi:10.51948/auad.911584

Bozkurt, A., Jung, I., Xiao, J., & Vladimirschi, V., Schuwer. R., Egorov, G., Lambert, S. R., Al-Freih, M., Pete, J., Olcott, D., Rodes, V., Aranciaga, I., Bali, M., Alvarez, Jr. A., Roberts, J., Pazurek, A., Raffaghelli, J. E., Panagiotou, N., Perrine de Coëtlogon, Shahadu, S., … Paskevicius, M. (2020). A global outlook to the interruption of education due to COVID-19 Pandemic: Navigating in a time of uncertainty and crisis. *Asian Journal of Distance Education*, *15*, 1–126.

Bozkurt, A., & Sharma, R. C. (2020). Emergency remote teaching in a time of global crisis due to CoronaVirus pandemic. *Asian Journal of Distance Education*, *15*, i–vi.

Brindle, M., Harris, K. R., Graham, S., & Hebert, M. (2016). Third and fourth grade teachers' classroom practices in writing: A national survey. *Reading and Writing, 29*(5), 929–954. doi:10.100711145-015-9604-x

Brisk, M. (2015). *Engaging Students Literacies. Genre-based pedagogy for K-5 classrooms.* Routledge.

British Council. (2020). *Language Trends 2020: Language Teaching in Primary and Secondary Schools in England.* https://www.britishcouncil.org/research-policy-insight/research-reports/language-trends-2020

Broadband Commission for Sustainable Development. (2017). *Working group on education: Digital skills for life and work.* UNESCO.

Bronfenbrenner, U. (1979). *The ecology of human development: experiments by nature and design.* Harvard University Press.

Brown, J. D. (2001). *Using surveys in language programs.* Cambridge University Press.

Brown, J. D. (2009). Open-response items in questionnaires. In J. Heigham & R. A. Croker (Eds.), *Qualitative research in applied linguistics: A practical introduction* (pp. 200–219). Palgrave MacMillan. doi:10.1057/9780230239517_10

Brown, J., & Rodgers, T. (2002). *Doing Second Language Research.* Oxford University Press.

Buchholz, B. A., DeHart, J., & Moorman, G. (2020). Digital citizenship during a global pandemic: Moving beyond digital literacy. *Journal of Adolescent & Adult Literacy, 64*(1), 11–17. doi:10.1002/jaal.1076 PMID:32834710

Burston, J., Georgiadou, O., & Monville-Burston, M. (2016). Exploiting behaviorist and communicative action-based methodologies in CALL applications for the teaching of pronunciation in French as a foreign language. In S. Papadima-Sophocleous, L. Bradley & S. Thouësny (Eds), CALL communities and culture – short papers from EUROCALL 2016 (pp. 74-80). Research-publishing.net. doi:10.14705/rpnet.2016.eurocall2016.541

Butler-Velegol, S., Zappe, S. E., & Mahoney, E. (2015). The evolution of a flipped classroom: Evidence based recommendations. *Advances in Engineering Education*, 1–37.

Butz, N. T., & Stupnisky, R. H. (2017). Improving student relatedness through an online discussion intervention: The application of self-determination theory in synchronous hybrid programs. *Computers & Education, 114*, 117–138. doi:10.1016/j.compedu.2017.06.006

Byram, M. (2021). *Teaching and Assessing Intercultural Communicative Competence.* Multilingual Matters. doi:10.21832/9781800410251

Cable, J., & Cheung, C. (2017). Eight Principles of Effective Online Teaching: A Decade-Long Lessons Learned in Project Management Education. *PM World Journal, 6*, 1–16.

Caires, S., Almeida, L., & Vieira, D. (2012). Becoming a teacher: Student teachers' experiences and perceptions about teaching practice. *European Journal of Teacher Education, 35*(2), 163–178. doi:10.1080/02619768.2011.643395

Calfee, R. C., & Miller, R. G. (2005). Breaking Ground: Constructing authentic reading-writing assessments for middle and secondary school students. In R. Indrisano & J. Paratore (Eds.), *Learning to Write, Writing to Learn: Theory and research in practice* (pp. 203–219). IRA.

Calgary, C. B. C. (2020). *Calgary zoo to ship giant pandas back to China early due to difficulty getting bamboo during pandemic.* Retrieved February 13, 2021 from, https://www.cbc.ca/news/canada/calgary/giant-pandas-calgary-zoo-1.5566027

Campillo-Ferrer, J.M. & Miralles-Martínez, P. (2021). Effectiveness of the flipped classroom model on students' self-reported motivation and learning during the COVID-19 pandemic. *Humanities and Social Sciences Communications*, 1-9.

Canagarajah, A. S. (2012). Teacher development in a global profession: An Autoethnography. *TESOL Quarterly*, *46*(2), 258–279. doi:10.1002/tesq.18

Cao, X. (2018). *Examining moral education: A comparative study between Quebec's ethics and religious culture program and China's moral education program* (Publication No. 28249235) [Master's thesis, McGill University]. ProQuest Dissertations Publishing.

Carey, K. (2020). Is everybody ready for the big migration to online college? Actually, no. *The New York Times*. https://www.nytimes.com

Carrier, M., & Nye, A. (2017). Carrier M. and Nye A. (2017). Empowering Teachers for the Digital Future. What do 21st century Teachers need? In M. Carrier, R. M. Damerow, & K. M. Bailey (Eds.), *Empowering Teachers for the Digital Future: Research, Theory, and Practice*. Routledge.

Carrillo, C., & Flores, M. A. (2020). COVID-19 and teacher education: A literature review of online teaching and learning practices. *European Journal of Teacher Education*, *43*(4), 466–487. doi:10.1080/02619768.2020.1821184

Carver-Thomas, D., & Darling-Hammond, L. (2019). The trouble with teacher turnover: How teacher attrition affects students and schools. Education Policy Analysis Archives, 27(36). doi:10.14507/epaa.27.3699

Caspar, S. (2021). Exploring the pandemic through language learning and multicultural studies. In A. Plutino & E. Polisca (Eds), Languages at work, competent multilinguals and the pedagogical challenges of COVID-19 (pp. 113-118). Research-publishing.net. doi:10.14705/rpnet.2021.49.1225

Castelli, F. R., & Sarvary, M. A. (2021). Why students do not turn on their video cameras during online classes and an equitable and inclusive plan to encourage them to do so. *Ecology and Evolution*, *11*(8), 3565–3576. doi:10.1002/ece3.7123 PMID:33898009

Castillo, N. M., & Wagner, D. A. (2018). Supporting home language reading through technology in rural South Africa. *International Review of Education*. Retrieved from https://repository.upenn.edu/literacyorg_articles/36/?utm_source=repository.upenn.edu%2Fliteracyorg_articles%2F36&utm_medium=PDF&utm_campaign=PDFCoverPages

CCCC OWI Committee for Effective Practices in Online Writing Instruction. (2011c). *The state of the art of OWI*. Retrieved from http://www.ncte.org/ library/NCTEFiles/Groups/CCCC/Committees/OWI_State-of-Art_Report_April_2011.pdf

Celik, B. (2019). Developing Writing Skills Through Reading. *International Journal of Social Sciences and Educational Studies*, *6*(1), 206–214.

Cercone, K. (2008). Characteristics of Adult Learners with Implications for Online Learning Design. *AACE Review*, *16*(2), 137-159. https://www.learntechlib.org/primary/p/24286/

CGTN. (2021). *The pandemic*. https://news.cgtn.com/event/2020/The-Pandemic/index.html

Chamorro, G., Garrido-Hornos, M., & Vázquez-Amador, M. (2021). Exploring ESOL teachers' perspectives on the language learning experiences, challenges, and motivations of refugees and asylum seekers in the UK. *International Review of Applied Linguistics in Language Teaching*. Advance online publication. doi:10.1515/iral-2020-0155

Chan, B. S., Churchill, D., & Chiu, T. K. (2017). Digital literacy learning in higher education through digital storytelling approach. *Journal of International Education Research*, *13*(1), 1–16. doi:10.19030/jier.v13i1.9907

Chang, M.-L. (2009). An appraisal perspective of teacher burnout: Examining the emotional work of teachers. *Educational Psychology Review*, *21*(3), 193–218. doi:10.100710648-009-9106-y

Chapelle, C. (2003). *English language learning and technology: Lectures on Applied Linguistics in the age of information and communication technology* (Vol. 7). John Benjamins Publishing. doi:10.1075/lllt.7

Charissi, A., Tympa, E., & Karavida, V. (2020). Impact of the COVID-19 disruption on university students' perceptions and behavior. *European Journal of Education Studies, 7*(11), 222–238. doi:10.46827/ejes.v7i11.3348

Chaudron, S. (2015). *Young children (0-8) and digital technology, a qualitative study across Europe*. JRC Science for Policy Report.

Chen Hsieh, J. S., Wu, W.-C. V., & Marek, M. W. (2016). Using the flipped classroom to enhance EFL learning. *Computer Assisted Language Learning, 30*(1-2), 1–21. doi:10.1080/09588221.2015.1111910

Chetty, K., Qigui, L., Gcora, N., Josie, J., Wenwei, L., & Fang, C. (2018). Bridging the digital divide: measuring digital literacy. *Economics: The Open-Access, Open-Assessment E-Journal, 12*, 1–20.

Cheung, A. (2021). Language teaching during a pandemic: A case study of zoom use by a secondary ESL teacher in Hong Kong. *RELC Journal*. Retrieved from https://journals.sagepub.com/doi/pdf/10.1177/0033688220981784

Chickering, A. W., & Gamson, Z. F. (1987). Seven principles for good practice in undergraduate education. *AAHE Bulletin, 3*, 7.

Chiumak-Horbatsch, R. (2012). *Linguistically appropriate practice: A guide for working with young immigrant children*. University of Toronto Press.

Choe, E., & Seong, M. H. (2016). A case study of the flipped classroom in a Korean university general English course. *Journal of Pan-Pacific Association of Applied Linguistics, 20*(2), 71–93.

Chou, M. H. (2018). Speaking anxiety and strategy use for learning English as a foreign language in full and partial English-medium instruction contexts. *TESOL Quarterly, 52*(3), 611–633. doi:10.1002/tesq.455

Chung, C., & Mason, M. (2012). Why do primary school students drop out in poor, rural China? A portrait sketched in a remote mountain village. *International Journal of Educational Development, 32*(4), 537–545. doi:10.1016/j.ijedudev.2012.02.012

Chung, S., & Choi, L. (2021). The development of sustainable assessment during the COVID-19 pandemic: The case of the English language program in South Korea. *Sustainability, 13*(8), 1–13. doi:10.3390u13084499

Churchill, N. (2016). *Digital storytelling as a means of supporting digital literacy learning in an upper primary-school English language classroom* (Doctoral thesis). Edith Cowan University, Joondalup, Australia. Retrieved from https://ro.ecu.edu.au/theses/1774

Ciolfi, L., Gray, B., & Pinatti de Carvalho, A. F. (2020). Making home work places. *Proceedings of the 18th European Conference on Computer-Supported Cooperative Work: The International Venue on Practice-centered Computing on the Design of Cooperation Technologies—Exploratory Papers, Reports of the European Society for Socially Embedded Technologies.* https://ulir.ul.ie/handle/10344/897

Clandinin, D. J. (2006). Narrative inquiry: A methodology for studying lived experience. *Research Studies in Music Education, 27*(1), 44–54. doi:10.1177/1321103X060270010301

Clandinin, D. J., & Connelly, F. M. (1991). Narrative and story in practice and research. In D. A. Schön (Ed.), *The reflective turn: Case studies in and on educational practice* (pp. 258–283). Teachers College Press.

Clandinin, D. J., & Connelly, F. M. (1994). Personal experience methods. In N. K. Denzin & Y. S. Lincoln (Eds.), *Handbook of qualitative research* (pp. 413–427). SAGE.

Clandinin, D. J., & Connelly, F. M. (2000). *Narrative inquiry*. John Wiley & Sons.

Clapsaddle, S., Smith, R., & Bratberg, W. (2021). "I'm having the quaran-time of my life": Modeling emergency remote instruction to teacher candidates during the COVID-19 crisis with a HyFlex-multi option approach. In E. Langran & L. Archambault (Eds.), *Proceedings of Society for Information Technology & Teacher Education International Conference* (pp. 133–137). Association for the Advancement of Computing in Education (AACE). https://www.learntechlib.org/primary/p/219124/

Clarà, M., Kelly, N., Mauri, T., & Danaher, P. A. (2015). Can massive communities of teachers facilitate collaborative reflection? Fractal design as a possible answer. *Asia-Pacific Journal of Teacher Education*, *45*(1), 86–98. doi:10.1080/1359866X.2015.1095280

Clark, C., Picton, I., & Lant, F. (2020). *"More time on my hands": Children and young people's writing during the COVID-19 lockdown in 2020*. National Literacy Trust.

Cohen, A., Hoy, L., & Dull, B. (2020). A descriptive study of COVID-19 related experiences and perspectives of a national sample of college students in spring 2020. *The Journal of Adolescent Health*, *67*(3), 369–375. doi:10.1016/j.jadohealth.2020.06.009 PMID:32593564

Cohen, J. (1992). A power primer. *Psychological Bulletin*, *112*(1), 155–159. doi:10.1037/0033-2909.112.1.155 PMID:19565683

Cohen, L., Manion, L., & Morrison, K. (2007). *Research Methods in Education* (6th ed.). Routledge-Falmer. doi:10.4324/9780203029053

Coiro, J., Knobel, M., Lankshear, C., & Leu, D. J. (Eds.). (2014). *Handbook of research on new literacies*. Routledge. doi:10.4324/9781410618894

Coldwell-Neilson, J. (2018, November). Digital literacy expectations in higher education. In *Open oceans: Learning without borders: ASCILITE 2018 Conference Proceedings* (pp. 103-112). Geelong, Australia: ASCILITE.

Collado-Valero, J., Rodríguez-Infante, G., Romero-González, M., Gamboa-Ternero, S., Navarro-Soria, I., & Lavigne-Cerván, R. (2021). Flipped Classroom: Active Methodology for Sustainable Learning in Higher Education during Social Distancing Due to COVID-19. *Sustainability*, *13*(10), 5336. doi:10.3390u13105336

Collie, R. J., Granziera, H., Martin, A. J., Burns, E. C., & Holliman, A. J. (2020). Adaptability among science teachers in schools: A multi-nation examination of its role in school outcomes. *Teaching and Teacher Education*, *95*, 103148. doi:10.1016/j.tate.2020.103148

Coman, C., Tîru, L. G., Meses an-Schmitz, L., Stanciu, C., & Bularca, M. C. (2020). Online Teaching and Learning in Higher Education during the Coronavirus Pandemic: Students' Perspective. *Sustainability*, *12*(24), 10367. doi:10.3390u122410367

Confederation of British Industry (CBI) & Pearson (2019). *Education and Learning for the Modern World: CBI/Pearson Education and Skills Survey Report 2019*. https://www.cbi.org.uk/media/3841/12546_tess_2019.pdf

Consumer News and Business Channel (CNBC). (2019) *Here are the Top Foreign Languages that UK Employers Want You to Have*. https://www.cnbc.com/2019/04/10/foreign-languages-that-uk-employers-want-you-to-have.html

Cook, D. (2020). The freedom trap: Digital nomads and the use of disciplining practices to manage work/leisure boundaries. *Information Technology & Tourism*, *22*(3), 355–390. doi:10.100740558-020-00172-4

Cook, G. (2010). *Translation in Language Teaching*. Oxford University Press.

Cope, B., & Kalantzis, M. (2009). "Multiliteracies": New literacies, new learning. *Pedagogies*, *4*(3), 164–195. doi:10.1080/15544800903076044

Cope, B., & Kalantzis, M. (2015). *A Pedagogy of Multiliteracies. Learning by design*. Palgrave and Macmillan.

Cope, B., & Kalantzis, M. (2015). The things you do to know: An introduction to the pedagogy of multiliteracies. In B. Cope & M. Kalantzis (Eds.), *A pedagogy of multiliteracies: Learning by Design* (pp. 1–36). Palgrave Macmillan. doi:10.1057/9781137539724_1

Cortazzi, M., & Jin, L. (1996). Cultures of learning: Language classrooms in China. In H. Coleman (Ed.), *Society and the language classroom* (pp. 169–206). CUP.

Coskun, A. (2017). The Effect of Pecha Kucha Presentations on Students' English Public Speaking Anxiety. *Profile Issues in Teachers Professional Development*, *19*(_sup1), 11–22. doi:10.15446/profile.v19n_sup1.68495

Cote, T. J., & Milliner, B. (2017). Preparing Japanese Students' Digital Literacy for Study Abroad: Is More Training Needed? *The JALT CALL Journal*, *13*(3), 187–197. doi:10.29140/jaltcall.v13n3.218

Cote, T., & Milliner, B. (2018). A survey of EFL teachers' digital literacy: A report from a Japanese university. *Teaching English with Technology*, *18*(4), 71–89.

Cotterall, S., & Reinders, H. (2001). Fortress or bridge? Learners' perceptions and practice in self access language learning. *Tesolanz*, *8*, 23–38.

Council of Europe. (2018). *Common European Framework of Reference for Languages: Learning, Teaching, Assessment. Companion Volume with New Descriptors*. rm.coe.int/cefr--companion--volume--with--new--descriptors--2018/1680787989

Council of Europe. (2020). *Common European Framework of Reference for Languages: Learning, Teaching and Assessment – Companion Volume*. Council of Europe Publishing. Available at www.coe.int/lang-cefr

Cresswell, J. W., & Plano Clark, V. (2018). Designing and conducting mixed methods research. *Sage (Atlanta, Ga.)*.

Creswell, J. W. (2009). Research Design Qualitative, Quantitative, and Mixed Methods Approaches. In Research Design Qualitative, Quantitative, and Mixed Methods Approaches (3rd ed.). Sage.

Creswell, J. W. (2003). Research design: Qualitative, quantitative, and mixed method approaches. *Sage (Atlanta, Ga.)*.

Creswell, J. W. (2009). *Research Design. Qualitative, quantitative and Mixed Methods Approaches*. Sage Publications.

Creswell, J. W. (2011). *Educational research: Planning, conducting, and evaluating quantitative and qualitative research* (4th ed.). Pearson.

Cumming, A. (2001). Learning to write in a second language: Two decades of research. *International Journal of English Studies*, *1*(2), 1–23.

Cummins, J., & Early, M. (2011). Introduction. In J. Cummins & M. Early (Eds.), *Identity texts: The collaborative creation of power in multilingual schools* (pp. 3–19). Trentham Books.

Cunico, S. (2021). Moving the year abroad online: ready, steady, go! In A. Plutino & E. Polisca (Eds.), Languages at work, competent multilinguals and the pedagogical challenges of COVID-19 (pp. 97-103). Research- publishing.net. doi:10.14705/rpnet.2021.49.1223

Cutler, L., & Graham, S. (2008). Primary Grade Writing Instruction: A National Survey. *Journal of Educational Psychology*, *100*(4), 907–919. doi:10.1037/a0012656

Dailey-Hebert, A. (2018). Maximizing interactivity in online Learning: Moving beyond discussion boards. *Journal of Educators Online, 15*(3), 1–15. https://files.eric.ed.gov/fulltext/EJ1199230.pdf. doi:10.9743/jeo.2018.15.3.8

Darling-Hammond, L., & Hyler, M. E. (2020). Preparing educators for the time of COVID… and beyond. *European Journal of Teacher Education, 43*(4), 457–465. doi:10.1080/02619768.2020.1816961

Davin, K. J., Chavoshan, I., & Donato, R. (2018). Images of past teachers: Present when you teach. *System, 72*, 139–150. doi:10.1016/j.system.2017.12.001

Davis, G. B. (1993). *Tools for Teaching*. Jossey-Bass.

Davis, H. A. (2001). The quality and impact of relationships between elementary school students and teachers. *Contemporary Educational Psychology, 26*(4), 431–453. doi:10.1006/ceps.2000.1068 PMID:11681827

De Bot, K., Wander, L., & Verspoor, M. (2007). A Dynamic Systems Theory Approach to Second Language Acquisition. *Bilingualism: Language and Cognition, 10*(1), 7–21. doi:10.1017/S1366728906002732

De Brey, C., Snyder, T. D., Zhang, A., & Dillow, S. A. (2021). Digest of education statistics 2019 (NCES 2021-009). National Center for Education Statistics, Institute of Education Sciences, U.S. Department of Education.

Delahunty, J., Verenikina, I., & Jones, P. (2014). Socio-emotional connections: Identity, belonging and learning in online interactions. A literature review. *Technology, Pedagogy and Education, 23*(2), 243–265. doi:10.1080/1475939X.2013.813405

Denscombe, M. (2007). *The Good Research Guide*. Open University Press.

Department for Education. (2020). *Language Teaching in Schools (England)*. https://researchbriefings.files.parliament.uk/documents/CBP-7388/CBP-7388.pdf

Destianingsih, A., & Satria, A. (2020). Investigating students' needs for effective English online learning during Covid-19 for Polbeng students. *ELT-Lectura: Studies and Perspectives in English Language Teaching, 7*(2), 147–153. doi:10.31849/elt-lectura.v7i2.4657

Dewaele, J.-M. (2012). Affect and Language Teaching. In *The Encyclopedia of Applied Linguistics*. University of London.

Dewaele, J.-M. (2020). If classroom emotions were music, teachers would be conductors and learners would be members of the orchestra. In O. Mentz & K. Papaja (Eds.), *Focus on Language. Challenging language learning and language teaching in peace and global education* (pp. 8–10). Lit Verlag.

Dewey, J. (1938). *Experience and education*. Collier Books.

DeWitt, P. (2019). *12 Critical issues facing education in 2020*. EducationWeek. https://www.edweek.org/leadership/opinion-12-critical-issues-facing-education-in-2020/2019/12?s_kwcid=AL!6416!3!486544088589!b!!g!!&utm_source=goog&utm_medium=cpc&utm_campaign=ew+dynamic+recent%20&ccid=dynamic+ads+recent+articles&ccag=recent+articles+dynamic&cckw=&cccv=dynamic+ad&gclid=CjwKCAjw6qqDBhB-EiwACBs6x3MiJO-4sYfO_KW16kIBEKOkatOVhdUgFsaWMLrrSCDdjy3v-EHPF1BoCnM8QAvD_BwE

Dizdar, D. (1999). Skopostheorie. In M. Snell-Hornby, H. G. Hönig, P. Kußmaul, & P. A. Schmitt (Eds.), *Handbuch Translation* (pp. 104–107). Stauffenburg.

Dizdar, D. (2006). *Translation. Um- und Irrwege*. Frank und Timme Verlag.

Dizdar, D. (2008). Translation zwischen den Disziplinen. *Natur und Geist. Forschungsmagazin der Johannes Gutenberg-Universität, 24*(2), 54–57.

Dockrell, J., Marshall, C., & Wyse, D. (2016). Teachers' reported practices for teaching writing in England. *Reading and Writing*, *29*(3), 409–434. doi:10.100711145-015-9605-9 PMID:26941477

Donalson, J., & Scheffler, A. (2010). *ZOG*. Scholastic Children's Books Euston House.

Donitsa-Schmidt, S., & Ramot, R. (2020). Opportunities and challenges: Teacher education in Israel in the Covid-19 pandemic. *Journal of Education for Teaching*, *46*(4), 586–595. doi:10.1080/02607476.2020.1799708

Dooly, M. (2020). *Virtual Exchange in Teacher Education: Is there an Impact in Teacher Practice?* Academic Press.

Dörnyei, Z. (2007). *Research Methods in Applied Linguistics: Quantitative, Qualitative, and Mixed Methodologies*. Oxford University Press.

Dörnyei, Z., & Ushioda, E. (2011). *Teaching and researching: Motivation*. Routledge.

Dörnyei, Z., & Ushioda, E. (2021). *Teaching and researching motivation* (3rd ed.). Routledge. doi:10.4324/9781351006743

Douglas, P., Cetron, M., & Spiegel, P. (2019). Definitions matter: Migrants, immigrants, asylum seekers and refugees. *Journal of Travel Medicine*, *26*(2). Advance online publication. doi:10.1093/jtm/taz005 PMID:30753575

Dufour, R., Dufour, R., & Eaker, R. (2008). *Revisiting professional learning communities at work: New insights for improving schools*. Solution Tree Press.

Dumford, A. D., & Miller, A. L. (2018). Online learning in higher education: Exploring advantages and disadvantages of engagement. *Journal of Computing in Higher Education*, *30*(3), 452–465. doi:10.100712528-018-9179-z

Dunlop, D., & Xhafer, J. (2016). *Development of synthesizing skills in academic writing. Cambridge English: Research Notes, 64, 52-60.*

Dweck, C. S. (2008). *Mindset: The new psychology of success*. Random House.

Eady, M. J., & Lockyer, L. (2013). Tools for learning: Technology and teaching strategies. Teach in the Primary School, 71-89.

Education Commission of the States. (2020). *State education policy tracking*. https://www.ecs.org/state-education-policy-tracking/

Eickelmann, B., & Drossel, K. (2020). *Schule auf Distanz. Perspektiven und Empfehlungen für den neuen Schulalltag. Eine repräsentative Befragung von Lehrkräften in Deutschland* [Distance education. Perspectives and recommendations for the new everyday school life. A representative survey of teachers in Germany]. Retrieved from https://www.vodafone-stiftung.de/umfrage-co ronakrise-lehrer/

Elliott, J. (1991). *Action Research for Educational Change*. Open University Press.

Ellis, C. (2020). *Revision: Autoethnographic reflections on life and work*. Routledge. ESL at Home. Retrieved February 13, 2021 from, https://eslathome.edublogs.org

Ellis, R. A. (2004). Supporting genre-based literacy pedagogy with technology. In L. Ravelli & R. Ellis (Eds.), *Analysing academic writing: Contextualised frameworks* (pp. 210–232). Continuum.

Ellwood, C., & Nakane, I. (2009). Privileging of speech in EAP and mainstream university classrooms: A critical evaluation of participation. *TESOL Quarterly*, *43*(2), 203–230. doi:10.1002/j.1545-7249.2009.tb00165.x

El-Metoui, L., & Graham-Brown, N. (2021). Emerging from the pandemic: reflections for the ESOL sector. *The ESOL Journal, 32*(1), 7-19. https://www.ingentaconnect.com/content/natecla/esol/2021/00000032/00000001/art00003

Engin, M., & Donanci, S. (2016). Instructional videos as part of a 'flipped' approach in academic writing. *Learning and Teaching in Higher Education: Gulf Perspectives, 13*(1), 73–80. Advance online publication. doi:10.18538/lthe.v13.n1.231

Erdoğan, V. (2019). Integrating 4C skills of 21st century into 4 language skills in EFL classes. *International Journal of Education and Research, 7*(11), 113–124.

Eryansyah, E., Erlina, E., Fiftinova, F., & Nurweni, A. (2019). EFL students' needs of digital literacy to meet the demands of 21st century skills. *Indonesian Research Journal in Education, 3*(2), 442–460.

Eshet, Y. (2004). Digital literacy: A conceptual framework for survival skills in the digital era. *Journal of Educational Multimedia and Hypermedia, 13*(1), 93–106.

European Commission. (2003). *e-Learning: Designing tomorrow's education-A mid-term report*. Retrieved from http://www.elearningeuropa.info/extras/pdf/mid_term_e n.pdf

European Commission. (2019). *Call for digital innovation hubs on artificial intelligence*. Retrieved from https://ec.europa.eu/digital-single-market/en/news/call-digital-innovation-hubs-artificial-intelligence

European Universities Association. (2020). *European higher education in the Covid-19 crisis*. Available online at: https://eua.eu/downloads/publications/briefing_european%20higher%20education%20in%20the%20covid-19%20crisis.pdf

Eurostat. (2019). *Foreign Language Skills Statistics*. https://ec.europa.eu/eurostat/statistics-explained/index.php?title=Foreign_language_skills_statistics

Eurostat. (2020, May 17). *People expanding their knowledge by learning online*. https://ec.europa.eu/eurostat/web/products-eurostat-news/-/edn-20200517-1

Evans, C., Kandiko Howson, C., Forsythe, A., & Edwards, C. (2021). What constitutes high quality higher education pedagogical research? *Assessment & Evaluation in Higher Education, 46*(4), 525–546. doi:10.1080/02602938.2020.1790500

Fagell, P. L. (2020). Career confidential: Distance learning frustrations. *Kappan, 102*(3), 66–67. doi:10.1177/0031721720970708

Fandos-Herrera, C., Jiménez-Martínez, J., Orús, C., & Pina, J. M. (2017). Introducing the discussant role to stimulate debate in the classroom: Effects on interactivity, learning outcomes, satisfaction, and attitudes. *Studies in Higher Education, 44*(2), 380–396. doi:10.1080/03075079.2017.1366437

Farber, B. A. (1984). Stress and burnout in suburban teachers. *The Journal of Educational Research, 77*(6), 325–331. doi:10.1080/00220671.1984.10885550

Fay, R., & Stelma, J. (2016). Criticality, intentionality and intercultural action. In M. Dasli & A. Diaz (Eds.), *The Critical Turn in Language and Intercultural Communication Pedagogy: Theory, Research and Practice* (pp. 126–140). Routledge.

Fedynich, L. V. (2013). Teaching beyond the classroom walls: The pros and cons of cyber learning. *Journal of Instructional Pedagogies, 13*, 1–7.

Feldman, P. (2021). Digital transformation in education: from vision to practice during the pandemic. In A. Plutino & E. Polisca (Eds.), Languages at work, competent multilinguals and the pedagogical challenges of COVID-19 (pp. 39-45). Research-publishing.net. doi:10.14705/rpnet.2021.49.1216

Ferrari, A. (2012). *Digital competence in practice: An analysis of frameworks*. Institute for Prospective Technological Studies, European Commission. Retrieved from http://www.ifap.ru/library/book522. pdf

Flachmann, K., Flachmann, M., Benander, K., & Smith, C. (2003). *The Brief Prose Reader*. Prentice Hall.

Flick, U. (2007). *Qualitative Sozialforschung. Eine Einführung*. Rowohlt.

Flores, M. A., & Gago, M. (2020). Teacher education in times of COVID-19 pandemic in Portugal: National, institutional and pedagogical responses. *Journal of Education for Teaching*, *46*(1), 1–10.

Flower, L., Stein, V., Ackerman, J., Kantz, M. J., McCormick, K., & Peck, W. C. (1990). Reading-to-write: Exploring a Cognitive and Social Process. Oxford University Press. Foundational Principles of Online Writing Instruction.

Fraillon, J., Ainley, J., Schulz, W., Duckworth, D., & Friedman, T. (2019). *IEA international computer and information literacy study 2018 assessment framework*. Springer. doi:10.1007/978-3-030-19389-8

Freedman, S. W., Hull, G. A., Higgs, J. M., & Booten, K. P. (2016). Teaching writing in a digital and global age: Toward access, learning, and development for all. In D. H. Gitomer & C. A. Bell (Eds.), *Handbook of research on teaching* (5th ed., pp. 1389–1450). American Educational Research Association. doi:10.3102/978-0-935302-48-6_23

Freiermuth, M. R., & Huang, H. C. (2012). Bringing Japan and Taiwan closer electronically: A look at an intercultural online synchronic chat task and its effect on motivation. *Language Teaching Research*, *16*(1), 61–88. doi:10.1177/1362168811423341

Freudenberger, H. J. (1974). Staff burnout. *The Journal of Social Issues*, *30*(1), 159–164. doi:10.1111/j.1540-4560.1974.tb00706.x

Friedman, I. A. (1991). High- and low-burnout schools: School culture aspects of teacher burnout. *The Journal of Educational Research*, *84*(6), 325–333. doi:10.1080/00220671.1991.9941813

Friedman, I. A., & Farber, B. A. (1992). Professional self-concept as a predictor of teacher burnout. *The Journal of Educational Research*, *86*(1), 28–35. doi:10.1080/00220671.1992.9941824

Friend, M., & Cook, L. (2002). *Interaction: Collaboration skills for school professionals* (4th ed.). Allyn and Bacon.

Fullan, M. (2001). *The new meaning of educational change*. Teachers College. doi:10.4324/9780203986561

Funamori, M. (2017). The issues Japanese higher education face in the digital age: Are Japanese universities to blame for the slow progress towards an information-based society? *International Journal of Institutional Research and Management*, *1*(1), 37–51. doi:10.52731/ijirm.v1.i1.112

Furlong, C., & Hunt, J. (2009). *ESOL in Wales: Learning from the voluntary sector*. Welsh Assembly and NIACE, Cymru.

Fushino, K. (2010). Causal relationships between communication confidence, beliefs about group work, and willingness to communicate in foreign language group work. *TESOL Quarterly*, *44*(4), 700–724. doi:10.5054/tq.2010.235993

Gallardo del Puerto, F., & Gamboa, E. (2009). The evaluation of computer-mediated technology by second language teachers: Collaboration and interaction in CALL. *Educational Media International*, *46*(2), 137–152. doi:10.1080/09523980902933268

Gall, M., Borg, W., & Gall, J. (2007). *Educational Research: An Introduction* (8th ed.). Allyn & Bacon.

García-Sánchez, S. (2012). English in Class and on the Go: Multimodal U-Learning. *The EuroCALL Review*, *20*(2), 94–102. doi:10.4995/eurocall.2012.11381

García-Sánchez, S. (2016). Online metacognitive tasks for EFL distance learners. *Turkish Online Journal of Distance Education*, *17*(4), 76–90. doi:10.17718/tojde.60563

García-Sánchez, S. (2021). Ubiquitous Digital Literacy and English Language Education: A Systematic Review. Ubiquitous Learning. *International Journal (Toronto, Ont.)*, *15*(1), 37–50. doi:10.18848/1835-9795/CGP/v15i01/37-50

Garrison, D. R. (2007). Online community of inquiry review: Social, cognitive, and teaching presence issues. *Journal of Asynchronous Learning Networks*, *11*(1), 61–72. https://files.eric.ed.gov/fulltext/EJ842688.pdf

Garrison, D. R. (2015). *Thinking collaboratively: Learning in a community of inquiry*. Taylor & Francis Group. doi:10.4324/9781315740751

Garrison, D. R., Anderson, T., & Archer, W. (1999). Critical inquiry in a text-based environment: Computer conferencing in higher education. *The Internet and Higher Education, 2*(2–3), 87–105. doi:10.1016/S1096-7516(00)00016-6

Garrison, D. R., Anderson, T., & Archer, W. (2010). The first decade of the community of inquiry framework: A retrospective. *The Internet and Higher Education, 13*(1-2), 5–9. doi:10.1016/j.iheduc.2009.10.003

Gatcho, A. R. G., & Hajan, B. H. (2019). Check your Face (Book) on page…": Unpacking the pedagogical potentialities of English teachers' wall posts. *Online Submission, 13*(1), 1–9. doi:10.21512/lc.v13i1.5253

Geer, R., & Sweeney, T. A. (2012). Students' voices about learning with technology. *Journal of Social Sciences, 8*(2), 294–303. doi:10.3844/jssp.2012.294.303

Geiger, T., & Pivovarova, M. (2018). The effects of working conditions on teacher retention. *Teachers and Teaching, 24*(6), 604–625. doi:10.1080/13540602.2018.1457524

Genc, Z. S., & Aydin, F. (2017). An Analysis of Learners' Motivation and Attitudes toward Learning English Language at Tertiary Level in Turkish EFL Context. *English Language Teaching, 10*(4), 35–44. doi:10.5539/elt.v10n4p35

Giannikas, C. N. (2019). New Technologies and Language Teacher Education: Are We There Yet? *English Language Teacher Education and Development Journal, 22*, 53–59. http://www.elted.net/uploads/7/3/1/6/7316005/giannikas_vol._22.pdf

Giannikas, C. N. (2020). Prioritizing when Education is in Crisis: The language teacher. *Humanising Language Teaching, 22*(3).

Giannikas, C. N. (2021). Interactive whiteboards in EFL from the Teachers' and students' perspective. *Research Papers in Language Teaching and Learning, 11*(1), 203–219.

Giannikas, C. N. (2021). *Sending our Teachers into the Wild: What we learned about preparedness during COVID-19. Hellenic Association of the Study of English (HASE) Colloquium.*

Gibbons, P. (2015). *Scaffolding language, scaffolding learning: Teaching English language learners in the mainstream classroom* (2nd ed.). Heinemann.

Gibson, J. J. (1979). *The ecological approach to visual perception*. Houghton Mifflin.

Gierdowski, D. C., Brooks, D. C., & Galanek, J. D. (2020). *EDUCAUSE 2020 student technology report: Supporting the whole student*. EDUCAUSE Research.

Gilakjani, A. P. (2017). A review of the literature on the integration of technology into the learning and teaching of English language skills. *International Journal of English Linguistics, 7*(5), 95–106. doi:10.5539/ijel.v7n5p95

Gilster, P. (1997). *Digital Literacy*. John Wiley & Sons, Inc.

Godbey, S. (2018). Testing Future Teachers: A Quantitative Exploration of Factors Impacting the Information Literacy of Teacher Education Students. *College & Research Libraries, 79*(5), 611–623. doi:10.5860/crl.79.5.611

Godwin-Jones, R. (2020). Building the porous classroom: An expanded model for blended language learning. *Language Learning & Technology, 24*(3), 1–18. http://hdl.handle.net/10125/44731

Gold, Y. (1985). Burnout: Causes and solutions. *The Clearing House: A Journal of Educational Strategies, Issues and Ideas, 58*(5), 210–212. doi:10.1080/00098655.1985.9955539

Golombek, P., & Johnson, K. E. (2004). Narrative inquiry as a mediational space: Examining emotional and cognitive dissonance in second-language teachers' development. *Teachers and Teaching, 10*(3), 307–327. doi:10.1080/1354060042000204388

Golonka, E. M., Bowles, A. R., Frank, V. M., Richardson, D. L., & Freynik, S. (2014). Technologies for foreign language learning: A review of technology types and their effectiveness. *Computer Assisted Language Learning, 27*(1), 70–105. doi:10.1080/09588221.2012.700315

Gómez-Trigueros, I. M., Ruiz-Bañuls, M., & Ortega-Sánchez, D. (2019). Digital literacy of teachers in training: Moving from icts (information and communication technologies) to lkts (learning and knowledge technologies). *Education Sciences, 9*(4), 274–284. doi:10.3390/educsci9040274

González-Davies, M. (2012). The Role of Translation in Other Learning Contexts: Towards Acting Interculturally. In S. Hubscher-Davidson & M. Borodo (Eds.), Global Trends in Translator and Interpreter Training: Mediation and Culture (Vol. 161). Academic Press.

González-Davies, M. (2017). The Use of Translation in an Integrated Plurilingual Approach to Language Learning: Teacher Strategies and Best Practices. *Journal of Spanish Language Teaching, 4*(2), 124–135. doi:10.1080/23247797.2017.1407168

González-Lloret, M. (2003). Designing task-based CALL to promote interaction: En busca de esmeraldas. *Language Learning & Technology, 7*(1), 86–104.

Gopalan, C., Butts-Wilmsmeyer, C., & Moran, V. (2021). Virtual flipped teaching during the COVID-19 pandemic. *Advances in Physiology Education, 45*(4), 670–678. doi:10.1152/advan.00061.2021 PMID:34498940

Goria, C. (2021). Reflections on the impact of COVID-19 on teaching and learning in the Faculty of Arts at the University of Nottingham. In A. Plutino & E. Polisca (Eds.), Languages at work, competent multilinguals and the pedagogical challenges of COVID-19 (pp. 47-55). Research-publishing.net. doi:10.14705/rpnet.2021.49.1217

Gov.UK. (2020). *More Afghan interpreters to move to the UK as scheme extends*. https://www.gov.uk/government/news/more-afghan-interpreters-to-move-to-the-uk-as-scheme-extends

Graham, S. (2018). A revised writer(s)-within-community model of writing. *Educational Psychologist, 53*(4), 258–279. doi:10.1080/00461520.2018.1481406

Graham, S., & Hebert, M. A. (2010). *Writing to read: Evidence for how writing can improve reading. A Carnegie corporation time to act report*. Alliance for Excellent Education.

Graham, S., & Rijlaarsdam, G. (2016). Writing education around the globe. *Reading and Writing, 29*(5), 781–792. doi:10.100711145-016-9640-1

Greener, S. (2009). e-Modeling--Helping Learners to Develop Sound e-Learning Behaviours. *Electronic Journal of e-Learning, 7*(3), 265-272.

Greenglass, E. R. (2002). Proactive coping and quality of life management. In E. Frydenberg (Ed.), *Beyond coping: Meeting goals, visions, and challenges*. Oxford University Press., doi:10.1093/med:psych/9780198508144.003.0003

Gregersen, T., MacIntyre, P. D., & Meza, M. D. (2014). The motion of emotion: Idiodynamic case studies of learners' foreign language anxiety. *Modern Language Journal, 98*(2), 574–588. doi:10.1111/modl.12084

Gregersen, T., Mercer, S., & MacIntyre, P. D. (2021). Language Teacher Perspectives on Stress and Coping. *Foreign Language Annals*, 1–19. doi:10.1111/flan.12544

Griffin, J., & Minter, D. (2013). The Rise of the Online Writing Classroom: Reflecting on the Material Conditions of College Composition Teaching. *College Composition and Communication, 65*(1), 140–161. https://www.jstor.org/stable/43490811

Groff, J., & Mouza, C. (2008). A Framework for Addressing Challenges to Classroom Technology Use. *AACE Journal, 16*, 21–46.

Gutiérrez, B. F., & O'Dowd, R. (2021). Virtual Exchange. *Innovative Language Pedagogy Report*, 17.

Guzmán Ibarra, I., & Marín Uribe, R. (2011). La Competencia y las Competencias Docentes: Reflexiones sobre el concepto y la Evaluación. *Revista Electrónica Interuniversitaria de Formación del Profesorado*, 151-172.

Habibi, A., Razak, R. A., Yusop, F. D., Mukminin, A., & Yaqin, L. N. (2020). Factors affecting ICT integration during teaching practices: A multiple case study of three Indonesian universities. *Qualitative Report, 25*(5), 1127–1144. doi:10.46743/2160-3715/2020.4150

Haftador, A. M., Shirazi, F., & Mohebbi, Z. (2021). Online class or flipped-jigsaw learning? Which one promotes academic motivation during the COVID-19 pandemic? *BMC Medical Education, 21*(1), 499. doi:10.118612909-021-02929-9 PMID:34548075

Hajovsky, D. B., Villeneuve, E. F., Reynolds, M. R., Niileksela, Ch. R., Mason, B. A., & Shudak, N. J. (2018). Cognitive ability influences on written expression: Evidence for developmental and sex-based differences in school-age children. *Journal of School Psychology, 67*, 104–118. doi:10.1016/j.jsp.2017.09.001 PMID:29571527

Hall, A. K., Nousiainen, M. T., Campisi, P. J., Dagnone, D., Frank, J. P., Kroeker, K. I., Brzezina, S., Purdy, E., & Oswald, A. (2020). Training disrupted: Practical tips for supporting competency-based medical education during the COVID-19 pandemic. *Medical Teacher, 42*(7), 756–761. doi:10.1080/0142159X.2020.1766669 PMID:32450049

Hall, P., & Simeral, A. (2017). *Creating a culture of reflective practice: Building capacity of schoolwide success*. Association for Supervision & Curriculum Development.

Halupa, C. P., & Bolliger, D. U. (2020). Technology fatigue of faculty in higher education. *Journal of Higher Education and Practice, 11*(18), 16–26. doi:10.7176/JEP/11-18-02

Hampel, R. (2006). Rethinking Task Design for the Digital Age: A Framework for Language Teaching and Learning in a Synchronous Online Environment. *ReCALL, 18*(1), 105–121. doi:10.1017/S0958344006000711

Hamutoğlu, N. B., Savaşçi, M., & Sezen-Gültekin, G. (2019). Digital literacy skills and attitudes towards e-learning. *Journal of Education and Future*, (16), 93–107. doi:10.30786/jef.509293

Haneda, M. (2006). Classrooms as communities of practice: A reevaluation. *TESOL Quarterly, 40*(4), 807–817. doi:10.2307/40264309

Hapsari, C. T. (2021). Distance learning in the time of Covid-19: Exploring students' anxiety. *ELT FORUM, 10*(1), 40–49. doi:10.15294/elt.v10i1.45756

Harasim, L. (2012). *Learning theory and online technologies*. Routledge. doi:10.4324/9780203846933

Hartshorne, R., Baumgartner, E., Kaplan-Rakowski, R., Mouza, C., & Ferdig, R. E. (2020). Special issue editorial: Preservice and inservice professional development during the COVID-19 pandemic. *Journal of Technology and Teacher Education, 28*(2), 137–147.

Hartshorn, K. J., & McMurry, B. L. (2020). The effects of the COVID-19 pandemic on ESL learners and TESOL practitioners in the United States. *International Journal of TESOL Studies, 2*(2), 140–156. doi:10.46451/ijts.2020.09.11

Hashim, H., Md. Yunus, M., Amin Embi, M., & Mohamed Ozir, N. A. (2017). Mobile-assisted Language Learning (MALL) for ESL Learners: A Review of Affordances and Constraints. *Sains Humanika, 9*(1-5). Advance online publication. doi:10.11113h.v9n1-5.1175

Hata, A. (2020, April 22). Japan's students left behind as world embraces online classes: Red tape ensnares schools trying to adapt to new coronavirus restrictions. *Nikkei Asia.* https://asia.nikkei.com/Business/Education/Japan-s-students-left-behind-as-world-embraces-online-classes

Hauck, M., Müller-Hartmann, A., Rienties, B., & Rogaten, J. (2020). Approaches to Researching digital-pedagogical competence development in VE-based teacher education. *Journal of Virtual Exchange, 3*(SI), 5-35.

Heft, H. (2007). Affordances and the body: An intentional analysis of Gibson's ecological approach to visual perception. *Journal for the Theory of Social Behaviour, 19*(1), 1–30. doi:10.1111/j.1468-5914.1989.tb00133.x

Henning, J. E., Gut, D. M., & Beam, P. C. (2019). *Building mentoring capacity in teacher education:A guide to clinically-based practice.* Routledge.

Hewett, B. L. (2015b). The online writing conference: A guide for teachers and tutors (Updated). Boston: Bedford/St. Martin's Press.

Hewett, B. L. (2013). Fully online and hybrid writing instruction. In H. B. Hessler, A. R. Taggart, & K. Schick (Eds.), *A guide to composition pedagogies* (2nd ed., pp. 194–211). Oxford University Press.

Hewett, B. L. (2015a). *Reading to learn and writing to teach: Literacy strategies for online writing instruction.* Bedford/St. Martin's Press.

Hewett, B. L., & DePew, K. E. (2015). *Foundational practices of online writing instruction (Perspective on Writing).* Parlor Press. doi:10.37514/PER-B.2015.0650

Higher Education Policy Institute. (2020). *Action Needed to Avert the Growing Crisis in Language Learning.* https://www.hepi.ac.uk/2020/01/09/action-needed-to-avert-the-growing-crisis-in-language-learning/

Higley, M. (2013). Benefits of Synchronous and Asynchronous e-Learning: Advantages of Using Both Synchronous and Asynchronous Technologies in an Online Learning Environment. *eLearning Industry.* https://elearningindustry.com/benefits-of-synchronous-and-asynchronous-e-learning

Hodges, C., Moore, S., Lockee, B., Trust, T., & Bond, A. (2020). The difference between emergency remote teaching and online learning, *EDUCAUSE Review.* Available at: https://er.educause.edu/articles/2020/3/the-difference-between-emergency-remote-teachingand-online-learning

Hodges, C., Moore, S., Lockee, B., Trust, T., & Bond, A. (2020). *The Difference between Emergency Remote Teaching and Online Learning.* Available online at: https://er.educause.edu/articles/2020/3/the-difference-between-emergency-remote-teaching-andonline-learning

Hodges, C., Moore, S., Lockee, B., Trust, T., & Bond, A. (2020, March 27). The difference between Emergency Remote Teaching and Online Learning. *EDUCAUSE Review.* https://er.educause.edu/articles/2020/3/the-difference-between-emergency-remote-teaching-and-online-learning

Hodges, C., Moore, S., Lockee, B., Trust, T., & Bond, A. (2020). The difference between emergency remote teaching and online learning. *EDUCAUSE Review, 3.* https://er.educause.edu/articles/2020/3/the-difference-between-emergency-remoteteaching-and-online-learning

Holmes, P., Fay, R., & Andrews, J. (Eds.). (2017). Special issue - Education and migration: Languages foregrounded. Language and Intercultural Communication, 17(4).

Holmes, E., O'Connor, R., Perry, V., Tracey, I., Wessly, S., Arseneault, L., & Ballard, C. (2020). Multi-disciplinary research priorities for the COVID-19 pandemic: A call for action for mental health sciences. *The Lancet. Psychiatry*, *7*(6), 547–560. doi:10.1016/S2215-0366(20)30168-1 PMID:32304649

Honarzad, R., & Rassaei, E. (2019). The role of EFL learners' autonomy, motivation and self-efficacy in using technology-based out-of-class language learning activities. *The JALT CALL Journal*, *15*(3), 23–42. doi:10.29140/jaltcall.v15n3.170

Honigsfeld, A., & Dove, M. (2010). *Collaboration and co-teaching: Strategies for English learners*. Corwin.

Howe, D., & Heitner, K. L. (2020, October 1-2). *Faculty satisfaction teaching online in the time of COVID-19* [Paper presentation]. Walden University Research Conference 2020 (online). https://scholarworks.waldenu.edu/researchconference/2020/papers/9/

Huang, F., Teo, T., & Zhou, M. (2019). Factors affecting Chinese English as a foreign language teachers' technology acceptance: A qualitative study. *Journal of Educational Computing Research*, *57*(1), 83–105. doi:10.1177/0735633117746168

Huang, Q. (2018). Examining teachers' roles in online learning. *The EuroCALL Review*, *26*(2), 3. doi:10.4995/eurocall.2018.9139

Huber, E., & Shalavin, C. (2018). Surveying the digital literacy landscape for academic and professional staff in higher education. In M. Campbell, J. Willems, C. Adachi, D. Blake, I. Doherty, S. Krishnan, S. Macfarlane, L. Ngo, M. O'Donnell, S. Palmer, L. Riddell, I. Story, H. Suri & J. Tai (Eds.), *Annual conference of the Australasian society for computers in learning in tertiary education: ASCILITE 2018: Conference Proceedings* (pp. 151-158). ASCILITE.

Hu, G. (2002). Recent important developments in secondary English-language teaching in the People's Republic of China. *Language, Culture and Curriculum*, *15*(1), 30–49. doi:10.1080/07908310208666631

Hu, G. (2003). English language teaching in China: Regional differences and contributing factors. *Journal of Multilingual and Multicultural Development*, *24*(4), 290–318. doi:10.1080/01434630308666503

Hu, G. (2005). English language education in China: Policies, progress, and problems. *Language Policy*, *4*(1), 5–24. doi:10.100710993-004-6561-7

Hussain, Z. (2018). The effects of ICT-based learning on students 'vocabulary mastery in junior high schools in Bandung. *International Journal of Education and Literacy Studies*, *10*(2), 149–156.

Hutchison, A., Beschorner, B., & Schimidt-Crawford, D. (2012). Exploring the use of the ipad for literacy learning. *The Reading Teacher*, *66*(1), 15–23. doi:10.1002/TRTR.01090

Ibrahim, A. I. (2010). ESP at the Tertiary Level: Current Situation, Application and Expectation. *English Language Teaching*, *3*(1), 200–204. doi:10.5539/elt.v3n1p200

Imbernón, F., Silva, P., & Guzmán, C. (2011). Competencias en los procesos de enseñanza-aprendizaje virtual y semipresencial [Teaching skills in virtual and blended learning environments]. *Comunicar*, *36*(36), 107–114. doi:10.3916/C36-2011-03-01

Im, J. H., & Kim, J. (2015). Use of blended learning for effective implementation of English-medium instruction in a non-English higher education context. *International Education Studies*, *8*(11), 1–15. doi:10.5539/ies.v8n11p1

International Association of Universities (2020). *Regional/National Perspectives on the Impact of COVID-19 on Higher Education*. Available online at: iau_covid-19_regional_perspectives_on_the_impact_of_covid-19_on_he_july_2020_.pdf

Irish National Digital Experience (INDEx) Survey: Findings from students and staff who teach in higher education. (2020). National Forum for the Enhancement of Teaching and Learning in Higher Education.

Jagannathan, M. (2021, March 1). *Teachers were already leaving the profession due to stress–then COVID-19 hit.* MarketWatch.com. https://www.marketwatch.com/story/teachers-were-already-leaving-the-profession-due-to-stress-then-covid-19-hit-11614025213

James, L. (2014). The integration of a computer-based early reading program to increase English language learners' literacy skills. *Teaching English with Technology, 14*(1), 9–22.

Jandrić, P., Hayes, D., Truelove, I., Levinson, P., Mayo, P., Ryberg, T., Monzó, L. D., Allen, Q., Stewart, P. A., Carr, P. R., Jackson, L., Bridges, S., Escaño, C., Grauslund, D., Mañero, J., Lukoko, H. O., Bryant, P., Fuentes-Martinez, A., Gibbons, A., ... Hayes, S. (2020). Teaching in The Age of Covid-19. *Postdigital Science and Education, 2*(3), 1069–1230. doi:10.100742438-020-00169-6

Jan, S. (2018). Investigating the Relationship between Students' Digital Literacy and Their Attitude towards Using ICT. *International Journal of Educational Technology, 5*(2), 26–34.

Jeong, J. S., & González-Gómez, D. (2021). A STEM Course Analysis During COVID-19: A Comparison Study in Performance and Affective Domain of PSTs Between F2F and F2S Flipped Classroom. *Frontiers in Psychology, 12*, 669855. doi:10.3389/fpsyg.2021.669855 PMID:34447329

Jewitt, C., Clark, W., & Hadjithoma-Garstka, C. (2011). The use of learning platforms to organise learning in English primary and secondary schools. *Learning, Media and Technology, 36*(4), 335–348. doi:10.1080/17439884.2011.621955

Joe, H. K., Hiver, P., & Al-Hoorie, A. H. (2017). Classroom social climate, self-determined motivation, willingness to communicate, and achievement: A study of structural relationships in instructed second language settings. *Learning and Individual Differences, 53*, 133–144. doi:10.1016/j.lindif.2016.11.005

Johnson Hess, A. (2020, December 14). *27% of teachers are considering quitting because of Covid, survey finds.* CNBC.com. https://www.cnbc.com/2020/12/14/27percent-of-teachers-are-considering-quitting-because-of-covid-survey.html

Johnson, K. E. (2006). The sociocultural turn and its challenges for second language teacher education. *TESOL Quarterly, 40*(1), 235–257. doi:10.2307/40264518

Johnson, K. E. (2007). Tracing teacher and student learning in teacher-authored narratives. *Teacher Development, 11*(2), 175–188. doi:10.1080/13664530701442879

Johnson, K. E. (2009). *Second language teacher education: A sociocultural perspective.* Routledge. doi:10.4324/9780203878033

Johnson, K. E., & Golombek, P. R. (2002). Inquiry into experience. In K. E. Johnson & P. R. Golombek (Eds.), *Teachers' narrative inquiry as professional development* (pp. 1–14). Cambridge University Press.

Johnson, K. E., & Golombek, P. R. (2003). "Seeing" teacher learning. *TESOL Quarterly, 37*(4), 729–737. doi:10.2307/3588221

Johnson, K. E., & Golombek, P. R. (2011). A sociocultural theoretical perspective on teacher professional development. In K. E. Johnson & P. R. Golombek (Eds.), *Research on second language teacher education: A sociocultural perspective on professional development* (pp. 1–12). Routledge. doi:10.4324/9780203844991

Johnson, L., & Kendrick, M. (2017). "Impossible is nothing": Expressing difficult knowledge through digital storytelling. *Journal of Adolescent & Adult Literacy, 60*(6), 667–675. doi:10.1002/jaal.624

Johnson, N., Veletsianos, G., & Seaman, J. (2020). U.S. faculty and administrators' experiences and approaches in the early weeks of the COVID-19 pandemic. *Online Learning Journal, 24*(2), 6–21. doi:10.24059/olj.v24i2.2285

Jonassen, D., Howland, J., Marra, R. M., & Crismond, D. (2008). *How does technology facilitate learning? Meaningful Learning with Technology*. Pearson Allyn Bacon Prentice Hall.

Jukes, I., McCain, T., & Crockett, L. (2010). Understanding the digital generation: Teaching and learning in the new digital landscape. 21st Century Fluency Project.

Jung, Y., Kim, Y., Lee, H., Cathey, R., Carver, J., & Skalicky, S. (2019). Learner perception of multimodal synchronous computer-mediated communication in foreign language classrooms. *Language Teaching Research*, *23*(3), 287–309. doi:10.1177/1362168817731910

Kabilan, M. K., Ahmad, N., & Abidin, M. J. Z. (2010). Facebook: An online environment for learning of English in institutions of higher education? *Internet and Higher Education*, *13*(4), 179–187. doi:10.1016/j.iheduc.2010.07.003

Kahn, J. H., Schneider, K. T., Jenkins-Henkelman, T. M., & Moyle, L. L. (2006). Emotional social support and job burnout among high-school teachers: Is it all due to dispositional affectivity? *Journal of Organizational Behavior*, *27*(6), 793–807. doi:10.1002/job.397

Kamal, M. I., Zubanova, S., Isaeva, A., & Movchun, V. (2021). Distance learning impact on the English language teaching during COVID-19. *Education and Information Technologies*, *26*(6), 7307–7319. Advance online publication. doi:10.100710639-021-10588-y PMID:34075299

Kamarianos, I., Adamopoulou, A., Lambropoulos, H., & Stamelos, G. (2020). Towards an understanding of university students' response in times of pandemic crisis. *European Journal of education. Studies*, *7*, 20–40.

Karabanova, O. A. (2010). Social situation of child's development-the key concept in modern developmental psychology. *Psychology in Russia: State of the Art*, *3*(1), 130–153. doi:10.11621/pir.2010.0005

Karabiyik, C. (2019). The Relationship between Student Engagement and Tertiary Level English Language Learners' Achievement. *International Online Journal of Education & Teaching*, *6*(2), 281–293.

Karalis, Th., & Raikou, N. (2020). Teaching at the Times of COVID-19: Inferences and Implications for Higher Education Pedagogy. *International Journal of Academic Research in Business & Social Sciences*, *10*(5), 479–493. doi:10.6007/IJARBSS/v10-i5/7219

Karalis, Th., & Raikou, N. (2021). Flipping the classroom remotely: Implementation of a flipped classroom course in higher education during the COVID-19 pandemic. *European Journal of Open Education and E-Learning Studies*, *6*(2), 21–38. doi:10.46827/ejoe.v6i2.3809

Katayama, K., & Masutani, F. (2018, May 20). Daigaku kyouin, hansuu ha hijoukin jyoukin mo yonbun no ichi ga "kigentsuki" [Half of university instructors are part-time and one-quarter of full-time instructors are on "fixed-term" contracts]. *Asahi Shimbun*. https://www.asahi.com/articles/ASL5M54SBL5MUTIL00Z.html

Katlianik, I. (2013). *Strategies for increasing the interactivity of children's synchronous learning in virtual environments* (Unpublished doctoral dissertation). University of Oxford.

Kato, S., & Mynard, J. (2015). *Reflective dialogue: Advising in language learning*. Routledge. doi:10.4324/9781315739649

Kaur, M. (2013). Blended Learning- its challenges and future. *Procedia: Social and Behavioral Sciences*, *93*, 612–617. doi:10.1016/j.sbspro.2013.09.248

Kavytska, T., Shovkovyi, V., & Osidak, V. (2021). Source-Based Writing in Secondary School: Challenges and Accomplishments. In C. N. Giannikas (Ed.), *Teaching Practices and Equitable Learning in Children's Language Education* (pp. 63–83). IGI Global. doi:10.4018/978-1-7998-6487-5.ch004

Kemmis, S., & McTaggart, R. (1982). *The Action Research Planner*. Deakin University Press.

Kern, R. (2000). *Literacy and language teaching*. Oxford University Press.

Kim, C. M., Mendenhall, A., & Johnson, T. E. (2010). A design framework for an online English writing course. In Learning and instruction in the digital age (pp. 345-360). New York: Springer. doi:10.1007/978-1-4419-1551-1_21

Kim, J. (2020). Learning and teaching online during Covid-19: Experiences of student teachers in an early childhood education practicum. *International Journal of Early Childhood*, *52*(2), 145–158. doi:10.100713158-020-00272-6 PMID:32836369

King Ramirez, C., & Lafford, B. (2018). Introduction. In Transferable skills for the 21st century: Preparing students for the workplace through world languages for specific purposes (pp.1-20). Sabio Books.

King, J. (2013). *Silence in the second language classroom*. Palgrave Macmillan. doi:10.1057/9781137301482

Kiraly, D. (2000). *A Social Constructivist Approach to Translator Education. Empowerment from Theory to Practice*. St. Jerome.

Klapproth, F., Federkeil, L., Heinschke, F., & Jungmann, T. (2020). Teachers' experiences of stress and their coping strategies during COVID-19 induced distance teaching. *Journal of Pedagogical Research*, *4*(4), 444–452. doi:10.33902/JPR.2020062805

Kleemans, M., & Eggink, G. (2016). Understanding news: The impact of media literacy education on teenagers' news literacy. *Journal of Education*, *5*(1), 75–88.

Klentzin, J. C., Paladino, E. B., Johnston, B., & Devine, C. (2010). Pecha Kucha: Using "Lightning Talk" in University Instruction. *RSR. Reference Services Review*, *38*(1), 158–167. doi:10.1108/00907321011020798

Kniffin, K. M., Narayanan, J., Anseel, F., Antonakis, J., Ashford, S. P., Bakker, A. B., Bamberger, P., Bapuji, H., Bhave, D. P., Choi, V. K., Creary, S. J., Demerouti, E., Flynn, F. J., Gefland, M. J., Greer, L. L., Johns, G., Kesebir, S., Klein, P. G., Lee, S. Y., ... Vugt, M. V. (2021). COVID-19 and the workplace: Implications, issues, and insights for future research and action. *The American Psychologist*, *76*(1), 63–77. doi:10.1037/amp0000716 PMID:32772537

Koehler, M., & Mishra, P. (2009). What is technological pedagogical content knowledge (TPACK)? *Contemporary Issues in Technology & Teacher Education*, *9*(1), 60–70.

Konca, A. S., Ozel, E., & Zelyurt, H. (2016). Attitudes of Preschool Teachers towards Using Information and Communication Technologies (ICT). *International Journal of Research in Education and Science*, *2*(1), 10–15. doi:10.21890/ijres.21816

König, J., Jäger-Biela, D. J., & Glutsch, N. (2020). Adapting to online teaching during COVID-19 school closure: Teacher education and teacher competence effects among early career teachers in Germany. *European Journal of Teacher Education*, *43*(4), 608–622. doi:10.1080/02619768.2020.1809650

Kono, T. (2009). Social affordances and the possibility of ecological linguistics. *Integrative Psychological & Behavioral Science*, *43*(4), 356–373. doi:10.100712124-009-9097-8 PMID:19609627

Ko, S., & Rossen, S. (2010). *Teaching online: A practical guide* (3rd ed.). Routledge. doi:10.4324/9780203855201

Krajka, J., & Marczak, M. (2017). Telecollaboration Projects in Translator Education–Design, Implementation and Evaluation. In E. Smyrnova-Trybulska (Ed.), *Effective Development of Teachers' Skills in the Area of ICT and E-Learning*. University of Silesia - NOA.

Kress, G. R. (2010). *Multimodality: A social semiotic approach to contemporary communication*. Routledge.

Kucer, S. (2014). *Dimensions of Literacy: A Conceptual Base for Teaching, Reading and Writing in School Settings.* Routledge. doi:10.4324/9780203428405

Kuckartz, U. (2014). *Mixed Methods: Methodologie, Forschungsdesigns und Analyseverfahren.* Springer-Verlag.

Kukulska-Hulme, A., & Viberg, O. (2018). Mobile collaborative language learning: State of the art. *British Journal of Educational Technology, 49*(2), 207–218. doi:10.1111/bjet.12580

Kulikowski, K., Przytuła, S., & Sułkowski, Ł. (2021). The motivation of academics in remote teaching during the COVID-19 pandemic in Polish universities: Opening the debate on a new equilibrium in e-learning. *Sustainability, 13*(5), 2752. doi:10.3390u13052752

Kurek, M., & Müller-Hartmann, A. (2017). Task design for telecollaborative exchanges: In search of new criteria. *System, 64*, 7–20. doi:10.1016/j.system.2016.12.004

Laal, M., & Laal, M. (2011). Collaborative Learning: What is it? *Procedia: Social and Behavioral Sciences, 31*, 491–495. doi:10.1016/j.sbspro.2011.12.092

Lacorte, M., & Reyes-Torres, A. (2021). *Didáctica del español como 2/L en el siglo XXI.* Madrid: Arco Libros.

Lam, W. S. E. (2004). Second language socialization in a bilingual chat room: Global and local considerations. *Language Learning & Technology, 8*(3), 44–65.

Lam, W. S. E. (2009). Multiliteracies on Instant Messaging in Negotiating Local, Translocal, and Transnational Affiliations: A Case of an Adolescent Immigrant. *Reading Research Quarterly, 44*(4), 377–397. doi:10.1598/RRQ.44.4.5

Lange, P. G. (2014). *Kids on YouTube: Technical identities and digital literacies.* Left Coast Press.

Lankshear, C., & Knobel, M. (2011). *New literacies.* McGraw-Hill Education.

Lantolf, J. P. (2000). Introducing sociocultural theory. In J. P. Lantolf (Ed.), *Sociocultural theory and second language learning* (pp. 1–26). Oxford University Press.

Lantolf, J. P., & Poehner, M. E. (Eds.). (2008). *Sociocultural theory and the teaching of second languages.* Equinox.

Larsen-Freeman, D., & Long, M. (1994). *Introducción al estudio de la adquisición de segundas lenguas.* Gredos.

Lasfeto, D. (2020). The relationship between self-directed learning and students' social interaction in online learning environment. *Journal of e-Learning and Knowledge Society, 16*(2), 34-41.

Latchem, C., Jung, I., Aoki, K., & Ozkul, A. E. (2008). The tortoise and the hare enigma in e-transformation in Japanese and Korean higher education. *British Journal of Educational Technology, 39*(4), 610–630. doi:10.1111/j.1467-8535.2007.00771.x

Latorre-Cosculluela, C., Suarez, C., Quiroga, S., Sobradiel-Sierra, N., Lozano-Blasco, R., & Rodríguez-Martínez, A. (2020). Flipped Classroom model before and during COVID-19: Using technology to develop 21st century skills. *Interactive Technology and Smart Education, 18*(2), 189–204. doi:10.1108/ITSE-08-2020-0137

Lau, W.W.F., & Yuen, A.H.K. (2014). Developing and Validating of a Perceived ICT Literacy Scale for Junior Secondary School Students: Pedagogical and Educational Contributions. *Computers and Education, 78*, 1–9. doi:10.1016/j.compedu.2014.04.016

Lave, J., & Wenger, E. (1991). *Situated learning: Legitimate peripheral participation.* Cambridge University Press. doi:10.1017/CBO9780511815355

Lazarus, R. S. (2006). Emotions and interpersonal relationships: Toward a person-centered conceptualization of emotions and coping. *Journal of Personality, 74*(1), 9–46. doi:10.1111/j.1467-6494.2005.00368.x PMID:16451225

Lazarus, R. S., & Folkman, S. (1984). *Stress, appraisal and coping.* Springer. https://books.google.com/books?hl=en&lr=&id=i-ySQQuUpr8C&oi=fnd&pg=PR5&dq=Lazarus,+R.+S.,+%26+Folkman,+S.+(1984).+Stress,+appraisal+and+coping.+New+York:+Springer.&ots=DgFRkufgUf&sig=NGhfIg0t2xfz1FpR01rALRqgljM#v=onepage&q=Lazarus%2C%20R.%20S.%2C%20%26%20Folkman%2C%20S.%20(1984).%20Stress%2C%20appraisal%20and%20coping.%20New%20York%3A%20Springer.&f=false

Lee, J. S. (2019). EFL students' views of willingness to communicate in the extramural digital context. *Computer Assisted Language Learning, 32*(7), 692–712. doi:10.1080/09588221.2018.1535509

Lee, J. S. (2019). Informal digital learning of English and second language vocabulary outcomes: Can quantity conquer quality? *British Journal of Educational Technology, 50*(2), 767–778. doi:10.1111/bjet.12599

Lee, J. S. (2020). Informal digital learning of English and strategic competence for cross-cultural communication: Perception of varieties of English as a mediator. *ReCALL, 32*(1), 47–62. doi:10.1017/S0958344019000181

Lee, J. S., & Lee, K. (2019). Informal digital learning of English and English as an international language: The path less traveled. *British Journal of Educational Technology, 50*(3), 1447–1461. doi:10.1111/bjet.12652

Lee, J. S., & Lee, K. (2020). Affective factors, virtual intercultural experiences, and L2 willingness to communicate in in-class, out-of-class, and digital settings. *Language Teaching Research, 24*(6), 813–833. doi:10.1177/1362168819831408

Lee, M., & Lim, K. Y. (2020). Do the technostress creators predict job satisfaction and teacher efficacy of primary school teachers in Korea? *Educational Technology International, 21*(1), 69–95.

Lei, S. I., & So, A. S. I. (2021). Online teaching and learning experiences during the COVID-19 pandemic: A comparison of teacher and student perceptions. *Journal of Hospitality & Tourism Education, 33*(3), 1–15. doi:10.1080/10963758.2021.1907196

Lembani, R., Gunter, A., Breines, M., & Dalu, M. T. B. (2020). The same course, different access: The digital divide between urban and rural distance education students in South Africa. *Journal of Geography in Higher Education, 44*(1), 70–84. doi:10.1080/03098265.2019.1694876

Leoni, F., & Mora, A. (2021). *Caritas Refugee Education End of Year Report (2020-21).* Caritas.

Leu, D., O'Byrne, W., Zawilinski, L., McVerry, J., & Everett-Cacopardo, H. (2009). Expanding the New Literacies Conversation. *Educational Researcher, 38*(4), 264–269. doi:10.3102/0013189X09336676

Liang, M. Y. (2021). Multilingual and multimodal mediation in online intercultural conversations: A translingual perspective. *Language Awareness, 30*(3), 1–21. doi:10.1080/09658416.2021.1941069

Liao, X. (2004). The need for communicative language teaching in China. *ELT Journal, 58*(3), 270–273. doi:10.1093/elt/58.3.270

Li, C. (2020). A positive psychology perspective on Chinese EFL students' trait emotional intelligence, foreign language enjoyment and EFL learning achievement. *Journal of Multilingual and Multicultural Development, 41*(3), 246–263. doi:10.1080/01434632.2019.1614187

Li, J., Shi, Z., & Xue, E. (2020). The problems, needs and strategies of rural teacher development at deep poverty areas in China: Rural schooling stakeholder perspectives. *International Journal of Educational Research, 99*, 1–10. doi:10.1016/j.ijer.2019.101496

Li, L., & Wang, X. (2021). Technostress inhibitors and creators and their impacts on university teachers' work performance in higher education. *Cognition Technology and Work*, *23*(2), 315–330. doi:10.100710111-020-00625-0

Liman-Kaban, A. (2021). The Influence of Online CoI Presences on Learner Satisfaction in Higher Education. *Asian Journal of Distance Education*, *16*(1), 230–246. doi:10.5281/zenodo.5021228

Lin, X., & Gao, L. (2020). Students' sense of community and perspectives of taking synchronous and asynchronous online courses. *Asian Journal of Distance Education*, *15*(1), 169–179. http://www.asianjde.org

Li, Q., & Ma, X. (2010). A Meta-analysis of the Effects of Computer Technology on School Students' Mathematics Learning. *Educational Psychology Review*, *22*(3), 215–243. doi:10.100710648-010-9125-8

Llerena-Izquierdo, J., & Ayala-Carabajo, R. (2021). University teacher training during the COVID-19 emergency: The role of online teaching-learning tools. In *International Conference on Information Technology & Systems* (pp. 90-99). Cham: Springer. 10.1007/978-3-030-68418-1_10

Lockley, T. (2011). Japanese students' experience of ICT and other technology prior to university: A survey. *The JALT CALL Journal*, *7*(1), 93–102. doi:10.29140/jaltcall.v7n1.110

Lomicka, L. (2020). Creating and sustaining virtual language communities. *Foreign Language Annals*, *53*(2), 306–313. doi:10.1111/flan.12456

López-Meneses, E., Sirignano, F. M., Vázquez-Cano, E., & Ramírez-Hurtado, J. M. (2020). University students' digital competence in three areas of the DigCom 2.1 model: A comparative study at three European universities. *Australasian Journal of Educational Technology*, *36*(3), 69–88. doi:10.14742/ajet.5583

López-Sánchez, A. (2009). Re-writing the goals of foreign language teaching: The achievement of multiple literacies and symbolic competence. *International Journal of Learning*, *16*(10), 29–37. doi:10.18848/1447-9494/CGP/v16i10/46632

Lortie, D. (1975). *Schoolteacher: A sociological study*. University of Chicago Press. https://www.jstor.org/stable/2777575

Love, B., Hodge, A., Grandgenett, N., & Swift, A. W. (2014). Student learning and perceptions in a flipped linear algebra course. *International Journal of Mathematical Education in Science and Technology*, *45*(3), 317–324. doi:10.1080/0020739X.2013.822582

Luna, M., Villalon, R., Mateos, M., & Martín, E. (2020). Improving university argumentative writing through an online training. *Journal of Writing Research*, *12*(1), 233–262. doi:10.17239/jowr-2020.12.01.08

Mabuan, R. A. (2017). Developing ESL/EFL Learners' Public Speaking Skills through Pecha Kucha Presentations. *English Review: Journal of English Education*, *6*(1), 1–10. doi:10.25134/erjee.v6i1.765

MacIntyre, P. D., & Charos, C. (1996). Personality, attitudes, and affect as predictors of second language communication. *Journal of Language and Social Psychology*, *15*(1), 3–26. doi:10.1177/0261927X960151001

MacIntyre, P. D., Clément, R., Dörnyei, Z., & Noels, K. A. (1998). Conceptualizing willingness to communicate in a L2: A situational model of L2 confidence and affiliation. *Modern Language Journal*, *82*(4), 545–562. doi:10.1111/j.1540-4781.1998.tb05543.x

MacIntyre, P. D., & Doucette, J. (2010). Willingness to communicate and action control. *System*, *38*(2), 161–171. doi:10.1016/j.system.2009.12.013

MacIntyre, P. D., Gregersen, T., & Mercer, S. (2020). Language teachers' coping strategies during the COVID-19 conversion to online teaching: Correlations with stress, wellbeing and negative emotions. *System*, *94*, 102352. doi:10.1016/j.system.2020.102352

MacIntyre, P. D., & Legatto, J. J. (2011). A dynamic system approach to willingness to communicate: Developing an idiodynamic method to capture rapidly changing affect. *Applied Linguistics*, *32*(2), 149–171. doi:10.1093/applin/amq037

Madalińska-Michalak, J., O'Doherty, T., & Flores, M.A. (2018). Teachers and teacher education in uncertain times. *European Journal of Teacher Education*. . doi:10.1080/02619768.2018.1532024

Mahdy, M. A. A. (2020). The Impact of COVID-19 Pandemic on the Academic Performance of Veterinary Medical Students. *Frontiers in Veterinary Science*, *7*(October), 1–8. doi:10.3389/fvets.2020.594261 PMID:33134368

Maloney, J., Resnick, M., Rusk, N., Silverman, B., & Eastmond, E. (2010). The scratch programming language and environment. *ACM Transactions on Computing Education*, *10*(4), 1–15. doi:10.1145/1868358.1868363

Marczak, M. (2016). *Students' Perspective on Web 2.0-Enhanced Telecollaboration as Added Value in Translator Education*. Research-publishing.net.

Marczak, M. (2017). Concordancer-Enhanced Reflection in Telecollaborative Translation Projects at University Level. *Między oryginałem a przekładem*, (38), 145-168.

Marinoni, G., van't Land, H. & Jensen, T. (2020). *The Impact of COVID-19 on higher education around the world*. IAU Global Survey Report. Available online at: iau_covid19_and_he_survey_report_final_may_2020.pdf

Martínez, J. P., Méndez, I., Ruiz-Esteban, C., Fernández-Sogorb, A., & García-Fernández, J. M. (2020). Profiles of burnout, coping strategies and depressive symptomatology. *Frontiers in Psychology*, *11*(591), 591. Advance online publication. doi:10.3389/fpsyg.2020.00591 PMID:32300323

Maslach, C. (1998). A multidimensional theory of burnout. In C. L. Cooper (Ed.), *Theories of organizational stress*. https://books.google.com/books?hl=en&lr=&id=ahfJ16b-BdUC&oi=fnd&pg=PA68&dq=Maslach,+C.+(1998).+A+multidimensional+theory+of+burnout.+In+C.+L.+Cooper+(Ed.),+Theories+of+organizational+stress,+68%E2%80%9385.&ots=O-cnQIsyAY&sig=rLsoYWYlMgfFmhXi6kptsb0L27c#v=onepage&q&f=false

Maslach, C., & Leiter, M. P. (1997). *The truth about burnout: How organizations cause personal stress and what to do about it*. Jossey-Bass. https://books.google.com/books?hl=en&lr=&id=uzomWhbqcCAC&oi=fnd&pg=PR7&dq=Maslach,+C.,+%26+Leiter,+M.+P.+(1997).+The+truth+about+burnout:+How+organizations+cause+personal+stress+and+what+to+do+about+it.+Jossey-Bass.&ots=9B7rnuPFWz&sig=7ZM2OjzfSWAM-AFGe_pwF_Uy_og#v=onepage&q&f=false

Matz, F., Rogge, M., & Siepmann, P. (Eds.). (2014). *Transkulturelles Lernen im Fremdsprachenunterricht: Theorie und Praxis*. Peter Lang GmbH. doi:10.3726/978-3-653-04068-5

Maxwell, E. E. (2021). *Technostress factors as predictors of job Satisfaction among teachers in K–12 education* [Doctoral dissertation]. Grand Canyon University.

Ma, Y., Hou, X., Huang, J., Wang, W., Li, Y., Zhou, X., & Du, X. (2018). Educational inequality and achievement disparity: An empirical study of migrant children in China. *Children and Youth Services Review*, *87*, 145–153. doi:10.1016/j.childyouth.2018.02.026

McCroskey, J. C., & Baer, J. E. (1985). *Willingness to communicate: The construct and its measurement*. Paper presented at the annual convention of the speech communication association, Denver, CO.

McCroskey, J. C., & Richmond, V. P. (1987). Willingness to communicate. In J. C. McCroskey & J. A. Daly (Eds.), *Personality and interpersonal communication* (pp. 129–155). Sage.

McDougall, J., Readman, M., & Wilkinson, P. (2018). The uses of (digital) literacy. *Learning, Media and Technology*, *43*(3), 263–279. doi:10.1080/17439884.2018.1462206

Mckerlich, R., Riis, M., Anderson, T., & Eastman, B. (2011). Student perceptions of teaching presence, social presence, and cognitive presence in a virtual world. *Journal of Online Learning and Teaching*, *7*(3), 324–336.

McLean, S., Attardi, S. M., Faden, L., & Goldszmidt, M. (2016). Flipped classrooms and student learning: Not just surface gains. *Advances in Physiology Education*, *40*(1), 47–55. doi:10.1152/advan.00098.2015 PMID:26847257

McLelland, N. (2020). Translation and Ideology in the History of Language Learning and Teaching: Changing Purposes, Practices and Prejudices in the Teaching and Learning of Modern Languages. *Zeitschrift für Fremdsprachenforschung*, *31*(1), 23–40.

Means, B., & Neisler, J. (2021). Teaching and Learning in the Time of COVID: The Student Perspective. *Online Learning Journal*, *25*(1), 8–27. doi:10.24059/olj.v25i1.2496

Mehall, S. (2020). Purposeful Interpersonal Interaction in Online Learning: What Is It and How Is It Measured? *Online Learning*, *24*(1), 182–204. doi:10.24059/olj.v24i1.2002

Mellati, M., & Khademi, M. (2015). The impacts of distance interactivity on learners' achievements in online mobile language learning. *International Journal of Web-Based Learning and Teaching Technologies*, *10*(3), 19–35. doi:10.4018/ijwltt.2015070102

Menke, M. R., & Paesani, K. (2019). Analysing Foreign Language Instructional Materials through the Lens of Multiliteracies Framework. *Language, Culture and Curriculum*, *32*(1), 34–49. doi:10.1080/07908318.2018.1461898

Merriam, S. B., Caffarella, R. S., & Baumgartner, L. M. (2007). *Learning in adulthood: A comprehensive guide*. Jossey-Bass.

Meurant, R. C. (2010). The iPad and EFL digital literacy. In *Signal processing and multimedia* (pp. 224–234). Springer. doi:10.1007/978-3-642-17641-8_27

Milheim, W. (2001). Faculty and administrative strategies for the effective implementation of distance education. *British Journal of Educational Technology*, *32*(5), 535–542. doi:10.1111/1467-8535.00223

Miller, E. R., & Gkonou, C. (2018). Language teacher agency, emotion labor and emotional rewards in tertiary-level English language programs. *System*, *79*, 49–59. doi:10.1016/j.system.2018.03.002

Ministry of Education. (2001, November 19). *Jiaoyubu guanyu yinfa yiwujiaoyu kecheng shezhi shiyan fangan de tongzhi* [Announcement on the experimental plan of compulsory education curriculum]. http://www.moe.gov.cn/srcsite/A26/s7054/200111/t20011119_88602.html

Mishra, K. E., Wilder, K., & Mishra, A. K. (2017). Digital literacy in the marketing curriculum: Are female college students prepared for digital jobs? *Industry and Higher Education*, *31*(3), 204–211. doi:10.1177/0950422217697838

MKS – Ministerium für Kultus, Jugend und Sport Baden-Württemberg. (Ed.). (2016). *Gemeinsamer Bildungsplan der Sekundarstufe I, Englisch als Fremdsprache.* www.bildungsplaene-bw.de/,Lde/LS/BP2016BW/ALLG/SEK1/E1

Moore, N. S., & Filling, M. L. (2012). iFeedback: Using video technology for improving student writing. *Journal of College Literacy and Learning*, 3–14.

Moore-Adams, B. L., Monty Jones, W., & Cohen, J. (2016). Learning to Teach Online: A Systematic Review of the Literature on K-12 Teacher Preparation for Teaching Online. *Distance Education*, *37*(3), 333–348. doi:10.1080/01587919.2016.1232158

Moore, J. L., Dickson-Deane, C., & Galyen, K. (2011). e-Learning, online learning, and distance learning environment: Are they the same? *Internet and Higher Education*, *14*(2), 129–135. doi:10.1016/j.iheduc.2010.10.001

Moore, M. G. (1997). Theory of transactional distance. In D. Keegan (Ed.), *Theoretical principles of distance education* (pp. 22–38). Routlege.

Moorhouse, B. L. (2020). Adaptations to a face-to-face initial teacher education course "forced" online due to the COVID-19 pandemic. *Journal of Education for Teaching*, *46*(4), 609–611. Advance online publication. doi:10.1080/02607476.2020.1755205

Mort, P., & Drury, H. (2012). Supporting student academic literacy in the disciplines using genre-based online pedagogy. *Journal of Academic Language and Learning*, *6*(3), A1–A15. https://journal.aall.org.au/

Moser, K. M., Wei, T., & Brenner, D. (2021). Remote teaching during COVID-19: Implications from a national survey of language educators. *System*, *97*, 1–15. doi:10.1016/j.system.2020.102431

Moskowitz, S., & Dewaele, J.-M. (2021). Is teacher happiness contagious? A study of the link between perceptions of language teacher happiness and student attitudes. *Innovation in Language Learning and Teaching*, *15*(2), 117–130. doi:10.1080/17501229.2019.1707205

Motteram, G. (Ed.). (2013). *Innovations in learning technologies for English language teaching*. The British Council.

Motteram, G., Dawson, S., & Al-Masri, N. (2020). WhatsApp supported language teacher development: A case study in the Zataari refugee camp. *Education and Information Technologies*, *25*(6), 5731–5751. Advance online publication. doi:10.100710639-020-10233-0 PMID:32837232

Mudra, H. (2020). Digital literacy among young learners: How do EFL teachers and learners view its benefits and barriers? *Teaching English with Technology*, *20*(3), 3–24.

Müller-Hartmann, A., & Kurek, M. (2016). Virtual group formation and the process of task design in online intercultural exchanges. In R. O'Dowd & T. Lewis (Eds.), Online intercultural exchange (pp. 145-163). Routledge.

Mulyono, H. (2016). Using Quipper as an online platform for teaching and learning English as a foreign language. *Teaching English with Technology*, *16*(1), 59–70.

Mumford, S., & Dikilitaş, K. (2020). Pre-service language teachers reflection development through online interaction in a hybrid learning course. *Computers & Education*, *144*, 103706. doi:10.1016/j.compedu.2019.103706

Munday, D. (2021). Teaching and learning post pandemic. In A. Plutino & E. Polisca (Eds.), Languages at work, competent multilinguals and the pedagogical challenges of COVID-19 (pp. 63-69). Research-publishing.net. doi:10.14705/rpnet.2021.49.1219

Munday, J. (2016). *Introducing translation studies: Theories and applications*. Routledge. doi:10.4324/9781315691862

Murphy, L. (2015). Online Language Teaching: The Learner's Perspective. In R. Hampel & U. Stickler (Eds.), *Developing Online Language Teaching. New Language Learning and Teaching Environments*. Palgrave Macmillan., doi:10.1057/9781137412263_4

Murray, A., & Blyth, A. (2011). A survey of Japanese university students' computer literacy levels. *The JALT CALL Journal*, *7*(3), 307–318. doi:10.29140/jaltcall.v7n3.124

Mynard, J., Burke, M., Hooper, D., Kushida, B., Lyon, P., Sampson, R., & Taw, P. (2020). *Dynamics of a social language learning community: Beliefs, membership and identity*. Multilingual Matters.

Myskow, G., Bennett, P. A., Yoshimura, H., Gruendel, K., Marutani, T., Hano, K., & Li, T. (2018). Fostering collaborative autonomy: The roles of cooperative and collaborative learning. *Relay Journal*, *1*(2), 360–381. doi:10.37237/relay/010212

Nachmias, C., & Nachmias, D. (2007). *Research Methods in the Social Sciences* (7th ed.). Worth Publishers.

Nahar, K., & Chowdhury, R. (2019). Effectiveness of flipped classroom model in distance learning. *Proceedings of the AAEE2019 Conference*.

NALDIC. (2015). *How the EAL needs of bilingual learners in English schools are funded*. Research and information, NALDIC, EAL Funding. https://www.naldic.org.uk/research-and-information/eal-funding/

Nardi, B. A. (2019). *My life as a night elf priest: An anthropological account of world of warcraft*. The University of Michigan Press.

Nash, M., & Churchill, B. (2020). Caring during COVID-19: A gendered analysis of Australian university responses to managing remote working and caring responsibilities. *Gender, Work and Organization*, *27*(5), 833–846. doi:10.1111/gwao.12484 PMID:32837013

National Health Commission of the People's Republic of China. (2020, January 30). *Xinxing guanzhuang bingdu ganran de feiyan gongzhong fanghu zhinan* [Public protection handbook for the pneumonia caused by the novel coronavirus]. http://www.nhc.gov.cn/jkj/s7915/202001/bc661e49b5bc487dba182f5c49ac445b.shtml

National People's Congress. (2019, January 7). *Zhonghua renmin gongheguo yiwujiaoyu fa* [Compulsory education law of the People's Republic of China]. http://www.npc.gov.cn/npc/c30834/201901/21b0be5b97e54c5088bff17903853a0d.shtml

Neumann, M. M., Finger, G., & Neumann, D. L. (2017). A conceptual framework for emergent digital literacy. *Early Childhood Education Journal*, *45*(4), 471–479. doi:10.100710643-016-0792-z

Nevin, A. I., Thousand, J. S., & Villa, R. A. (2009). Collaborative teaching for teacher educators-What does the research say? *Teaching and Teacher Education*, *25*(4), 569–574. doi:10.1016/j.tate.2009.02.009

New London Group. (1996). A pedagogy of multiliteracies: Designing social futures. *Harvard Educational Review*, *66*(1), 60–93. doi:10.17763/haer.66.1.17370n67v22j160u

Nijakowski, N., Lehmann, A., Zdrojewski, J., Nowak, M., & Surdacka, A. (2021). The Effectiveness of the Blended Learning in Conservative Dentistry with Endodontics on the Basis of the Survey among 4th-Year Students during the COVID-19 Pandemic. *International Journal of Environmental Research and Public Health*, *18*, 1–15.

Noels, K. A. (2009). The Internalisation of Language Learning into the Self and Social Identity. In *Motivation, language identity and the L2 self* (pp. 295–313). Multilingual Matters. doi:10.21832/9781847691293-016

Nordquist, R. (2020). *Cause and Effect in Composition*. ThoughtCo. thoughtco.com/cause-and-effect-composition-1689834

Norwegian Directorate of Education and Training. (2020). *English subject curriculum*. Retrieved from https://www.udir.no/lk20/eng01-04?lang=eng

Nuncio, R. V. (2020). Benchmarking ICT for education in Japan: Best practices, trends, challenges and lessons learned for Philippine ICT-based education & development. *Asia–Pacific Social Science Review*, *20*(2), 136–148.

O'Dowd, R., & Dooly, M. (2020). Intercultural communicative competence development through telecollaboration and virtual exchange. In J. Jackson (Ed.), The Routledge Handbook of Language and Intercultural Communication (pp. 361-375). Routledge. doi:10.4324/9781003036210-28

O'Dowd, R. (2018). From Telecollaboration to Virtual Exchange: State of the Art and the Role of UNICollaboration in Moving Forward. *Journal of Virtual Exchange*, *1*, 1–23. doi:10.14705/rpnet.2018.jve.1

O'Dowd, R. (2019). A Transnational Model of Virtual Exchange for Global Citizenship Education. *Language Teaching*, *53*(4), 477–490. doi:10.1017/S0261444819000077

O'Dowd, R. (2021). What do Students Learn in Virtual Exchange? A Qualitative Content Analysis of Learning Outcomes across Multiple Exchanges. *International Journal of Educational Research, 109*, 101804. doi:10.1016/j.ijer.2021.101804

O'Doyd, R., & Dooly, M. (2021). Exploring teachers' professional development through participation in virtual exchange. *ReCALL*, 1–16.

O'Quinn, L., & Corry, M. (2002). Factors that deter faculty from participating in distance education. *Online Journal of Distance Learning Administration, 5*(4). https://www.westga.edu/~distance/ojdla/winter54/Quinn54.htm

OECD Policy Responses to Coronavirus (COVID-19). (2020). *Education responses to COVID-19: Embracing digital learning and online collaboration.* Available online at: https://www.oecd.org/coronavirus/policy-responses/education-responses-to-covid-19-embracing-digital-learning-and-online-collaboration-d75eb0e8/

OECD. (2019). *OECD Skills Outlook 2019: Thriving in a Digital World.* OECD Publishing., doi:10.1787/df80bc12-

OECD. (2020). *Keeping the Internet up and running in times of crisis.* OECD Publishing.

Oliveira, G., Grenha Teixeira, J., Torres, A., & Morais, C. (2021). An exploratory study on the emergency remote education experience of higher education students and teachers during the COVID-19 pandemic. *British Journal of Educational Technology, 52*(4), 1357–1376. doi:10.1111/bjet.13112 PMID:34219758

Olsen, B., & Sexton, D. (2009). Threat rigidity, school reform, and how teachers view their work inside current educational policy contexts. *American Educational Research Journal, 46*(1), 9–44. doi:10.3102/0002831208320573

Online Teaching Japan [David Juteau]. (2021, October 27). *OTJ has members from these countries…* Facebook. https://www.facebook.com/groups/603548090241536/posts/959027178026957

Oppenheim, A. (2001). *Questionnaire design, interviewing and attitude measurement* (4th ed.). Continuum.

Oproiu, G. C. (2015). A Study about Using E-learning Platform (Moodle) in University Teaching Process. *Procedia - Social and Behavioral Sciences, 180*(November), 426–432. doi:10.1016/j.sbspro.2015.02.140

Orsini-Jones, M., & Lee, F. (2018). *Intercultural Communicative Competence for Global Citizenship: Identifying cyber-pragmatic rules of engagement in telecollaboration.* Springer. doi:10.1057/978-1-137-58103-7

Oshima, A., & Hogue, A. (2006). *Writing Academic English* (4th ed.). Pearson Longman.

Owusu-Fordjour, C., Koomson, C. K., & Hanson, D. (2020). The impact of Covid-19 on learning -the perspective of the Ghanaian student. *European Journal of Educational Sciences, 7*(3), 88–101. doi:10.5281/zenodo.3753586

OzimekA. (2020). The future of remote work. https://papers.ssrn.com/sol3/papers.cfm?abstract_id = 3638597

Paesani, K., Allen, H. W., & Dupuy, B. (2016). *Multiliteracies Framework for Collegiate Foreign Language Teaching.* Pearson.

Pandian, A., & Baboo, S. B. (2015). Digital Lifeworlds and Designers of Literacy Practices in Malaysian Schools. In B. Cope & M. Kalantzis (Eds.), *A Pedagogy of Multiliteracies. Learning by Design* (pp. 231–255). Palgrave Macmillan. doi:10.1057/9781137539724_13

Panitsides, E. A., & Karapistola, A. (2020 in press). Enhancing the role of the Hellenic Open University as a Lifelong Learning Organization: Crossing the Rubicon into the e-learning era. In E. Sengupta, P. Blessinger, & M. Makhanya (Eds.), *Humanizing Higher Education: The Role of Technology.* Emerald.

Papadima-Sophocleous, S., Giannikas, C. N., & Kakoulli-Constantinou, E. (2014). ICT in EFL: The global effect of new technologies in the language classroom. In *Proceedings of the 2014 EUROCALL Conference CALL Design: Principles and Practice* (pp. 296-300). Research-publishing. net. 10.14705/rpnet.2014.000234

Papadima-Sophocleous, S., & Loizides, F. (2016). Exploring the benefits and disadvantages of introducing synchronous to asynchronous online technologies to facilitate flexibility in learning. In *CALL communities and culture – short papers from EUROCALL 2016* (Vol. 2016, pp. 363–368). Issue., doi:10.14705/rpnet.2016.eurocall2016.589

Papert, S. (1980). *Mindstorms: Children, Computers, and Powerful Ideas*. Basic Books.

Paquette, P. (2016). Instructing the instructors: Training instructors to use social presence cues in online courses. *The Journal of Educators Online*, *13*(1), 80–108. doi:10.9743/JEO.2016.1.4

Pardo-Ballester, C. (2020). Coronavirus y el futuro de la educación de lenguas extranjeras a nivel universitario. *Puente Atlántico del siglo XXI*, 1-7.

Pardo-Ballester, C. (2021b). Curso de interpretación en línea para acomodar nuevas demandas y desafíos. *Puente Atlántico del siglo XXI*, 1-7.

Pardo-Ballester, C. (2021a). El pasado, presente y futuro de la enseñanza de ELE. *Cuadernos de Aldeuu*, *35*, 335–358.

Parvin, R. H., & Salam, S. F. (2015). The Effectiveness of Using Technology in English Language Classrooms in Government Primary Schools in Bangladesh. *Forum for International Research in Education*, *2*(1), 1–5. doi:10.18275/fire201502011049

Peachey, N. (2017). Synchronous online teaching. In M. Carrier, R. M. Damerow, & K. M. Bailey (Eds.), *Digital language learning and teaching* (pp. 143–155). Routledge. doi:10.4324/9781315523293-12

Peeters, W. (2019). The peer interaction process on Facebook: A social network analysis of learners' online conversations. *Education and Information Technologies*, *24*(5), 1–28. doi:10.100710639-019-09914-2

Peng, J. E., Zhang, L., & Chen, Y. (2017). The mediation of multimodal affordances on willingness to communicate in the English as a foreign language classroom. *TESOL Quarterly*, *51*(2), 302–331. doi:10.1002/tesq.298

Piaget, J. (1968). *Six Psychological Studies*. Vintage Books.

Pianta, R. C. (1999). *Enhancing relationships between children and teachers*. American. Psychological Association. doi:10.1037/10314-000

Pines, A. M. (2002). Teacher burnout: A psychodynamic existential perspective. *Teachers and Teaching*, *8*(2), 121–140. doi:10.1080/13540600220127331

Plota, D., & Karalis, T. (2019). Organization and implementation of a Flipped Classroom course in the Greek University context. *Educational Journal of the University of Patras UNESCO Chair*, *6*, 53–61.

Plutino, A., & Polisca, E. (2021). Introduction. In A. Plutino & E. Polisca (Eds.), Languages at work, competent multilinguals and the pedagogical challenges of COVID-19 (pp. 1-7). Research-publishing.net. doi:10.14705/rpnet.2021.49.1213

Podziewska, J. (2014). The volunteer ethos and the utopian impulse in the ESOL classroom. *Language Issues*, *25*(1), 23–28.

Ponticiello, M., Simmons, M., & Lee, J. S. (2021). The effects of the sudden switch to remote learning due to Covid-19 on HBCU students and faculty. In P. Zaphiris & A. Ioannou (Eds.), Lecture Notes in Computer Science: Vol. 12784. *Learning and Collaboration Technologies: New Challenges and Learning Experiences. HCII 2021*. Springer. doi:10.1007/978-3-030-77889-7_34

Prabjandee, D. (2020). Multilayered motivation of becoming English teachers in Thailand: Beyond intrinsic, extrinsic, and altruistic reasons. *Teacher Learning and Professional Development, 5*(1), 49–61.

Prensky, M. (2001). Digital natives, digital immigrants. *On the Horizon, 9*(5), 1–6. doi:10.1108/10748120110424816

Proietti Ergun, A. L., & Dewaele, J.-D. (2021). Do well-being and resilience predict the foreign language teaching enjoyment of teachers of Italian? *System, 99*, 102506. Advance online publication. doi:10.1016/j.system.2021.102506

Racheva, V. (2018). Social aspects of synchronous virtual learning environments. *AIP Conference Proceedings, 2048*, 020032. doi:10.1063/1.5082050

Raikou, N., Kaltsidis, Ch., Kedraka, K., & Karalis, Th. (2020). Teaching in Times of COVID-19 Pandemic in Two Peripheral Greek Universities: Lessons Learned from Students' Experiences and Opinions. *Research Journal of Education, 6*, 135–143.

Rakitzi, K., Botsoglou, K., & Roussakis, Y. (2020). Applying the Flipped Classroom Model to Higher Education: Students "take the floor". *Open Education, 16*, 132–144.

Raman, K., & Yamat, H. (2014). Barriers teachers face in integrating ICT during English lessons: A case study. *Malaysian Online Journal of Educational Technology, 2*(3), 11–19.

Rasch, G. (1960). *Probabilistic models for some intelligence and attainment tests.* University of Chicago.

Reedy, K., & Parker, J. (2018). *Digital literacy unpacked.* Facet. doi:10.29085/9781783301997

Reich, J., Buttimer, C., Fang, A., Hillaire, G., Hirsch, K., Larke, L., Littenberg-Tobias, J., Moussapour, R. M., Napier, A., Thompson, M., & Slama, R. (2020). *Remote Learning Guidance From State Education Agencies During the COVID-19 Pandemic: A First Look.* doi:10.35542/osf.io/437e2osf.io/437e2

Reinders, H., & Benson, P. (2017). Research agenda: Language learning beyond the classroom. *Language Teaching, 50*(4), 561–578. doi:10.1017/S0261444817000192

Reiss, K., & Vermeer, H. (1984/2013). *Towards a General Theory of Translational Action: Skopos Theory Explained* (C. Nord, Trans.). St Jerome.

Reyes-Torres, A. (2014). Literacy Education: The first step towards Literary Competence. In A. Reyes-Torres, L. Villacañas & B. Soler (Eds.), Thinking Through Children's Literature in the Classroom. (pp. 42-52). Cambridge: Cambridge Scholars Publishing.

Reyes-Torres, A. (2012). Literature in the foreign language syllabus: Engaging the student through active learning. *Tejuelo, 15*, 9–16.

Reyes-Torres, A. (2019). Literatura. In J. Muñoz-Basols, E. Gironzetti, & M. Lacorte (Eds.), *The Routledge Handbook of Spanish Language Teaching* (pp. 628–640). Routledge.

Reyes-Torres, A., & Portalés-Raga, M. (2020). A Multimodal Approach to Foster the Multiliteracies Pedagogy in the Teaching of EFL through Picturebooks: *The Snow Lion. Atlantis (Palma de Mallorca), 42*(1), 1–26. doi:10.28914/Atlantis-2020-42.1.06

Reyes-Torres, A., Portalés-Raga, M., & Bonilla-Tramoyeres, P. (2020). Multimodalidad e innovación metodológica en la enseñanza del inglés: El álbum ilustrado como recurso literario y visual para el desarrollo del conocimiento. *Revista Nebrija de Lingüística Aplicada a la Enseñanza de Lenguas, 14*(28), 54–77.

Rianto, A. (2020). Blended Learning Application in Higher Education: EFL Learners' Perceptions, Problems, and Suggestions. *Indonesian Journal of English Language Teaching and Applied Linguistics*, *5*(1), 55–68. doi:10.21093/ijeltal.v5i1.574

Rias, R. M., & Ismail, F. (2010). Designing interfaces in a mobile environment: An implementation on a programming language. *2010 International Conference on User Science and Engineering (i-USEr)*, 232-237. doi: 10.1109/IUSER.2010.5716758

Rice, K., & Dawley, L. (2009). The Status of Professional Development for K-12 Online Teachers: Insights and Implications. *Journal of Technology and Teacher Education*, *17*(4), 523–545.

Richardson, J. C., & Swan, K. (2003). Examining social presence in online courses in relation to students' perceived learning and satisfaction. *Journal of Asynchronous Learning Networks*, *7*(1), 68–88.

Ridge, E., & Waghid, Y. (2001). Equity and distance education. *Equity & Excellence in Education*, *34*(3), 80–86. doi:10.1080/1066568010340310

Rienties, B., Lewis, T., O'Dowd, R., Rets, I., & Rogaten, J. (2020). The impact of virtual exchange on TPACK and Foreign Language Competence: Reviewing a Large-Scale Implementation Across 23 Virtual Exchanges. *Computer Assisted Language Learning*, 1–27. doi:10.1080/09588221.2020.1737546

Rietdijk, S., van Weijen, D., Jassen, T., van den Bergh, H., & Rijlaarsdam, G. (2018). Teaching writing in primary education: Classroom practice, time, teachers' beliefs and skills. *Journal of Educational Psychology*, *110*(5), 640–663. doi:10.1037/edu0000237

Robinson, H. A., Sheffield, A., Phillips, A. S., & Moore, M. (2017). Introduction to teaching online: Usability evaluation of interactivity in an online social constructivist course. *TechTrends*, *61*(6), 533–540. doi:10.100711528-017-0187-z

Rob, M., & Rob, F. (2018). Dilemma between constructivism and constructionism: Leading to the development of a teaching-learning framework for student engagement and learning. *Journal of International Education in Business*, *11*(2), 273–290. doi:10.1108/JIEB-01-2018-0002

Roche, T. B. (2017). Assessing the role of digital literacy in English for Academic Purposes university pathway programs. *Journal of Academic Language and Learning*, *11*(1), A71–A87.

Rogers, C. R. (1951). *Client-centered Therapy, Its Current Practice, Implications, and Theory*. Houghton Mifflin.

Rogers, M., White, M., Loughbridge, M., & Higgins, I. (2020). *Thinking German Translation. A Course in Translation Method: German to English*. Routledge.

Rony, H. A. Z., & Awal, S. T. (2019). University teachers' training on online teaching-Learning using Online Platform during COVID-19: A case study. *Bangladesh Education Journal*, *18*(2), 57–65.

Rosa, A., & Eschholz, P. (1998). *Models for Writers* (6th ed.). St. Martin's Press.

Rosell-Aguilar, F. (2021). Locked down, but not isolated: Twitter collaboration among teachers in response to COVID-19. In A. Plutino & E. Polisca (Eds.), Languages at work, competent multilinguals and the pedagogical challenges of COVID-19 (pp. 71-77). Research-publishing.net. doi:10.14705/rpnet.2021.49.1220

Rosenblatt, L. M. (1986). The Aesthetic Transaction. *Journal of Aesthetic Education*, *20*(4), 122–128. doi:10.2307/3332615

Rossomondo, A. (2020). Flexibility is the watchword. *Second Language Research & Practice*, *1*(1), 164–167. http://hdl.handle.net/10125/69850

Roy, S., & Covelli, B. (2021). COVID-19 induced transition from classroom to online mid semester: Case study on faculty and students' preferences and opinions. *Higher Learning Research Communications, 11*(0), 10–32. doi:10.18870/hlrc.v11i0.1197

Rozmysłowicz, T. (2019). Translation und Kulturelle Differenz. Kritik und Revision ihrer translationswissenschaftlichen Verhältnisestimmung. In L. Heller & T. Rozmysłowicz (Eds.), *Translation und Interkulturelle Kommunikation/Translation and Intercultural Communication: Beiträge zur Theorie, Empirie und Praxis kultureller Austauschprozesse/Theoretical, Empirical and Practical Perspectives on Cultural Exchanges* (Vol. 106, pp. 51–64). Frank & Timme Verlag.

Russell, V., & Murphy-Judy, K. (2021). *Teaching Language Online: A Guide for Designing, Developing, and Delivering Online, Blended, and Flipped Language Courses.* New York: Routledge.

Russell, V. (2020). Language anxiety and the online learner. *Foreign Language Annals, 53*(2), 338–352. doi:10.1111/flan.12461

Ryan, R. M., & Deci, E. L. (2002). Overview of self-determination theory: An organismic dialectical perspective. In E. L. Deci & R. M. Ryan (Eds.), *Handbook of self-determination research* (pp. 3–33). University of Rochester.

Ryan, R. M., & Deci, E. L. (2017). *Self-determination theory: Basic psychological needs in motivation, development, and wellness.* Guilford. doi:10.1521/978.14625/28806

Ryan, T., & Henderson, M. (2018). Feeling feedback: Students' emotional responses to educator feedback. *Assessment & Evaluation in Higher Education, 43*(6), 880–892. doi:10.1080/02602938.2017.1416456

Saadatmand, M., Uhlin, L., Hedberg, M., Åbjörnsson, L., & Kvarnström, M. (2017). Examining learners' interaction in an open online course through the Community of Inquiry Framework. *European Journal of Open, Distance and E-Learning, 20*(1), 61–79. https://files.eric.ed.gov/fulltext/EJ1187832.pdf

Sadaf, A., & Gezer, T. (2020). Exploring factors that influence teachers' intentions to integrate digital literacy using the decomposed theory of planned behavior. *Journal of Digital Learning in Teacher Education, 36*(2), 124–145. doi:10.1080/21532974.2020.1719244

Sadiku, L. M. (2015). The importance of four skills reading, speaking, writing, listening in a lesson hour. *European Journal of Language and Literature, 1*(1), 29–31. doi:10.26417/ejls.v1i1.p29-31

Sadoux, M. (2021). How to flip it… never again? Towards agile models of work. In A. Plutino & E. Polisca (Eds.), Languages at work, competent multilinguals and the pedagogical challenges of COVID-19 (pp. 89-95). Research- publishing.net. doi:10.14705/rpnet.2021.49.1222

Saldaña, J. (2009). *The coding manual for qualitative researchers.* SAGE.

Sánchez-Caballé, A., Gisbert-Cervera, M., & Esteve-Món, F. (2021). La integración de la competencia digital en educación superior: Un estudio de caso de una universidad catalana. *Educar, 57*(1), 241–258.

Sánchez-Cruzado, C., Santiago Campión, R., & Sánchez-Compaña, M. T. (2021). Teacher Digital Literacy: The Indisputable Challenge after COVID-19. *Sustainability, 13*(4), 1858. doi:10.3390u13041858

Satar, H. M. (2015). Sustaining multimodal language learner interactions online. *CALICO Journal, 32*(3), 480–507. doi:10.1558/cj.v32i3.26508

Satar, H. M. (2016). Meaning-making in online language learner interactions via desktop videoconferencing. *ReCALL, 28*(3), 305–325. doi:10.1017/S0958344016000100

Sato, M., & Ballinger, S. (2016). *Peer interaction and second language learning: Pedagogical potential and research agenda*. John Benjamins. doi:10.1075/lllt.45

Saykili, A. (2018). Distance education: Definitions, generations and key concepts and future directions. *International Journal of Contemporary Educational Research*, *5*(1), 2–17.

Schleicher, A. (2020). *Education disrupted deduction built. Spotlight: Quality education for all during COVID-19 crisis.* Organisation for Economic Co-operation and Development (OECD). https://hundred-cdn.s3.amazonaws.com/uploads/report/file/15/hundred_spotlight_covid-19_digital.pdf

Scholes, R. (1985). *Textual Power: Literary Theory and the Teaching of English*. Yale University Press.

Schreier, M. (2012). *Qualitative Content Analysis in Practice*. Sage Publications.

Scribjab. (2021). Retrieved on February 13, 2021 from, http://www.scribjab.com

Sepulveda-Escobar, P., & Morrison, A. (2020). Online teaching placement during the COVID-19 pandemic in Chile: Challenges and opportunities. *European Journal of Teacher Education*, *43*(4), 587–607. doi:10.1080/02619768.2020.1820981

Serafini, F. (2014). *Reading the visual: An introduction to teaching multimodal literacy*. Teachers College Press.

Shakir Azfar Abdul Halim, M., Hashim, H., & Md Yunus, M. (2020). Pupils' motivation and perceptions on ESL lessons through online quiz-games. *Journal of Education and E-Learning Research*, *7*(3), 229–234. doi:10.20448/journal.509.2020.73.229.234

Shao, Q., & Gao, X. A. (2016). Reticence and willingness to communicate (WTC) of East Asian language learners. *System*, *63*, 115–120. doi:10.1016/j.system.2016.10.001

Shayakhmetova, L., Mukharlyamova, L., Zhussupova, R., & Beisembayeva, Z. (2020). Developing Collaborative Academic Writing Skills in English in CALL Classroom. *International Journal of Higher Education*, *9*(8), 13–18. doi:10.5430/ijhe.v9n8p13

Shima, T. E., & Song, Y. L. (2020). College students' experience of emergency remote teaching due to COVID19. *Children and Youth Services Review*, *119*, 1–7.

Shivastava, A. (2020). Identifying and analyzing occupational stress factors among faculty of autonomous colleges n Madhya Pradesh. *Academic Leadership*, *21*(04).

Shu, D. (2004). *EFL in China: Problems and suggested solutions*. Shanghai Foreign Language Education Press., doi:10.1017/S0305741004000542

Siever, H. (2019). Metaphern für die Figur des Translators. In L. Heller & T. Rozmysłowicz (Eds.), *Translation und Interkulturelle Kommunikation/Translation and Intercultural Communication: Beiträge zur Theorie, Empirie und Praxis kultureller Austauschprozesse/Theoretical, Empirical and Practical Perspectives on Cultural Exchanges* (Vol. 106, pp. 65–88). Frank & Timme Verlag.

Silva, J. S., Usart, M. U., Lázaro-Cantabrana, J. L. L. C., Silva, J., Usart, M., & Lázaro-Cantabrana, J. L. (2019). Teacher's digital competence among final year Pedagogy students in Chile and Uruguay. *Comunicar. Media Education Research Journal*, *27*(2), 33–43.

Simándi, S. (2017). Study circles in Online Learning Environment in the spirit of learning-centered approach. *Acta Technologica Dubnicae*, *7*(2), 96–104. doi:10.1515/atd-2017-0017

Simonson, M., Smaldino, S., Albright, M., & Zvacek, S. (2000). *Teaching and learning at a distance: Foundations of distance education*. Prentice Hall.

Simpson, J. (2019). Policy and adult migrant language education in the UK. In M. Cook & R. Peutrell (Eds.), *Brokering Britain, education citizens* (pp. 25-41). Blue Ridge Summit: Multilingual Matters. doi:10.21832/9781788924634

Simpson, J. (2012). "Bits here and there" — Fragmented ESOL provision in Leeds. *Language Issues, 23*(2), 33–45.

Sims, R. (2003). Promises of interactivity: Aligning learner perceptions and expectations with strategies for flexible and online learning. *Distance Education, 24*(1), 87–103. doi:10.1080/01587910303050

Sindoni, M. G. (2014). *Spoken and written discourse in online interactions: A multimodal approach.* Routledge. doi:10.4324/9780203587935

Singapore Ministry of Education. (2020). *Refreshing our curriculum.* Retrieved from https://www.moe.gov.sg/microsites/cos2020/index.html

Sipe, L. (2008). *Storytime. Young Children's Literary Understanding in the Classroom.* Teachers College Press.

SLGE (The Center for State and Local Government Excellence at ICMA-RC). (2021, February). *Survey findings: K-12 public school employee views on finances, employment outlook, and safety concerns due to COVID-19.* The Center for State and Local Government Excellence at ICMA-RC. https://slge.org/assets/uploads/2021/02/2021-slge-cv19-k12-report.pdf

Sokal, L. J., Eblie Trudel, L. G., & Babb, J. C. (2020b). *How to prevent teacher burnout during the coronavirus pandemic.* The Conversation Canada. Retrieved from https://theconversation.com/how-to-prevent-teacher-burnout-during-the-coronavirus-pandemic-139353

Sokal, L. J., Eblie Trudel, L. G., & Babb, J. C. (2020a). Canadian teachers' attitudes toward change, efficacy, and burnout during the COVID-19 pandemic. *International Journal of Educational Research Open, 1*, 100016. doi:10.1016/j.ijedro.2020.100016

Sokal, L. J., Eblie Trudel, L. G., & Babb, J. C. (2020c). Supporting teachers in times of change: The job demands-resources model and teacher burnout during the COVID-19 pandemic. *International Journal of Contemporary Education, 3*(2), 67–74. doi:10.11114/ijce.v3i2.4931

Soland, J., & Sandilos, L. E. (2021). English language learners, self-efficacy, and the achievement gap: Understanding the relationship between academic and social-emotional growth. *Journal of Education for Students Placed at Risk, 26*(1), 20–44. doi:10.1080/10824669.2020.1787171

Solano, L., Cabrere, P., Ulehlova, E., & Espinoza, V. (2017). Exploring the use of educational technology in EFL teaching: A case study of primary education in the south region of Ecuador. *Teaching English with Technology, 17*(2), 77–86.

Sommers, J. (2013). Response 2.0: Commentary on student writing for the new millennium. *Journal of College Literacy and Learning, 39*, 21–37.

Son, J. B., Park, S. S., & Park, M. (2017). Digital literacy of language learners in two different contexts. *The JALT CALL Journal, 13*(2), 77–96. doi:10.29140/jaltcall.v13n2.213

Sosulski, M. (2020). Responding to COVID-19: A chief academic officer's perspective. *Second Language Research & Practice, 1*(1), 139–143. http://hdl.handle.net/10125/69845

Spante, M., Hashemi, S. S., Lundin, M., & Algers, A. (2018). Digital competence and digital literacy in higher education research: Systematic review of concept use. *Cogent Education, 5*(1), 1519143. doi:10.1080/2331186X.2018.1519143

Spivey, N. N. (2001). *Discourse synthesis: Process and product. In Discourse synthesis: Studies in historical and contemporary social epistemology.* Praeger.

Spivey, N. N., & King, J. R. (1989). Readers as writers composing from sources. *Reading Research Quarterly, 24*(1), 7–26. doi:10.1598/RRQ.24.1.1

Staniscuaski, F., Kmetzsch, L., Soletti, R. C., Reichert, F., Zandonà, E., Ludwig, Z. M., Lima, E. F., Neumann, A., Schwartz, F. P., Mello-Carpes, P. B., Tamajusuku, A. S., Werneck, F. P., Ricachenevsky, F. K., Infanger, C., Seixas, A., Staats, C. C., & de Oliveira, L. (2021). Gender, race and parenthood impact academic productivity during the COVID-19 pandemic: From survey to action. *Frontiers in Psychology, 12*, 663252. Advance online publication. doi:10.3389/fpsyg.2021.663252 PMID:34054667

Stelma, J., & Fay, R. (2014). Intentionality and developing researcher competence on a UK master's course: An ecological perspective on research education. *Studies in Higher Education, 39*(4), 517-533.

Stelma, J., Onat-Stelma, Z., Lee, W., & Kostoulas, A. (2016). Intentional dynamics in TESOL: An ecological perspective. *Working Papers in TESOL and Applied Linguistics, 15*(1), 14-23. https://tesolal.columbia.edu/article/intentional-dynamics-in-tesol/

Stelma, J., & Fay, R. (2019). An ecological perspective on critical action for language education. In A. Kostoulas (Ed.), *Challenging Boundaries in Language Education* (pp. 51–70). Springer.

Stelma, J., Fay, R., & Zhou, X. (2013). Developing intentionality and researching multilingually: An ecological and methodological perspective. *International Journal of Applied Linguistics, 23*(3), 300–315.

Stelma, J., & Kostoulas, A. (2021). *The Intentional Dynamics of TESOL.* De Gruyter Mouton.

Stenhouse, L. (1975). *An Introduction to Curriculum Research and Development.* Heinemann.

Stepp-Greany, J. (2002). Student perceptions on language learning in a technological environment: Implications for the new millennium. *Language Learning & Technology, 6*(1), 165–180.

Stickler, U., Batstone, C., Duensing, A., & Heins, B. (2007). Distant classmates: Speech and silence in online and telephone language tutorials. *European Journal of Open, Distance and E-Learning, 2007*(2).

Stickler, U., & Hampel, R. (2015). Transforming Teaching: New Skills for Online Language Learning Spaces. In R. Hampel & U. Stickler (Eds.), *Developing Online Language Teaching. New Language Learning and Teaching Environments.* Palgrave Macmillan. doi:10.1057/9781137412263_5

Storybooks Canada. (2021). Retrieved on February 13, 2021 from, https://storybookscanada.ca//

Studies in Distance Education. (1997). Theory of transactional distance. In D. Keegan (Ed.), Theoretical principles of distance education (pp. 22-38). Routledge.

Studies in Distance Education. (2013). The effectiveness of online and blended learning: A meta-analysis of the empirical literature. *Teachers College Record, 115*, 1–47.

Su, B., Bonk, C. J., Magjuka, R. J., Liu, X., & Lee, S. (2005). The Importance of Interaction in Web-Based Education: A Program-level Case Study of Online MBA Courses. *Journal of Interactive Online Learning, 4*(1), 1–19. http://www.ncolr.org/jiol/issues/pdf/4.1.1.pdf

Sundqvist, P., & Sylvén, L. K. (2016). *Extramural English in teaching and learning: From theory and research to practice.* Springer. doi:10.1057/978-1-137-46048-6

Sun, P.-C., Tsai, R. J., Finger, G., Chen, Y.-Y., & Yeh, D. (2008). What drives a successful e-Learning? An empirical investigation of the critical factors influencing learner satisfaction. *Computers & Education, 50*(4), 1183–1202. doi:10.1016/j.compedu.2006.11.007

Swan, K., Garrison, D. R., & Richardson, J. C. (2009). A constructivist approach to online learning. *Information Technology and Constructivism in Higher Education*, 43–57.

Swan, K. (2001). Virtual interaction: Design factors affecting student satisfaction and perceived learning in asynchronous online courses. *Distance Education, 22*(2), 306–331. doi:10.1080/0158791010220208

Tabachnick, B. G., & Fidell, L. S. (2001). *Using multivariate statistics* (4th ed.). Allyn & Bacon.

Tang, C. M., & Chaw, L. Y. (2016). Digital literacy: A prerequisite for effective learning in a blended learning environment? *Electronic Journal of E-learning, 14*(1), 54–65.

Tang, T., Abuhmaid, A. M., Olaimat, M., Oudat, D. M., Aldhaeebi, M., & Bamanger, E. (2020). Efficiency of flipped classroom with online-based teaching under COVID-19. *Interactive Learning Environments*, 1–12.

Tanık-Önal, N., & Önal, N. (2020). Teaching science through distance education during the Covid-19COVID pandemic. *International Online Journal of Education & Teaching*, 7(4), 1898–1911. https://iojet.org/index.php/IOJET/article/view/1088

Tarnopolsky, O. (2013). Developing ESP students English speaking, reading, listening, and writing skills in internet-assisted project work. *Journal of Teaching English for Specific and Academic Purposes, 1*(1), 11–20.

Tejedor, S., Cervi, L., Pérez-Escoda, A., & Jumbo, F. T. (2020). Digital literacy and higher education during COVID-19 lockdown: Spain, Italy, and Ecuador. *Publications, 8*(4), 48–65. doi:10.3390/publications8040048

Terenko, O., & Ogienko, O. (2020). How to teach pedagogy courses online at university in COVID-19 pandemic: Search for answers. *Romanian Journal for Multidimensional Education/Revista Romaneasca pentru Educatie Multidimensionala, 12,* 173-179.

The New London Group. (2000). A pedagogy of multiliteracies designing social futures. In B. Cope & M. Kalantzis (Eds.), *Multiliteracies: Literacy learning and the design of social futures* (pp. 9–37). Routledge.

The Times. (2019). *German is more Desirable than French for Employers.* https://www.thetimes.co.uk/article/german-is-more-desirable-than-french-for-employers-z7mbghm5t

Thirumurthy, V., Szecsi, T., Hardin, B. J., & Koo, R. D. (2007). Honoring teachers: A world of perspectives. *Journal of Early Childhood Teacher Education, 28*(2), 181–198. doi:10.1080/10901020701366764

Tompkins, G. (2018). *Literacy for the 21st century: A balanced approach* (7th ed.). Pearson.

Townsend, A. (2013). *Action research: The challenges of changing and researching practice: The challenges of understanding and changing practice.* McGraw-Hill Education.

Tsagari, D., Liontou, J., & Giannikas, C. N. (2020). *Language Educators Working Online during the COVID-19 Pandemic.* International Survey Questionnaire available online at: https://docs.google.com/forms/d/e/1FAIpQLSfAWizub856QxCX_k7bjBKwBKE5UMat5cfYKdxJ2-loaB2CmQ/viewform

Tsai, H. Y. S., Shillair, R., & Cotten, S. R. (2017). Social support and "playing around" an examination of how older adults acquire digital literacy with tablet computers. *Journal of Applied Gerontology, 36*(1), 29–55. doi:10.1177/0733464815609440 PMID:26491029

T-Test Calculator for 2 Dependent Means. (2021, October 12). Retrieved from https://www.socscistatistics.com/tests/ttestdependent/default2.aspx

Turan, Z., & Akdag-Cimen, B. (2020). Flipped classroom in English language teaching: A systematic review. *Computer Assisted Language Learning, 33*(5-6), 590–606. doi:10.1080/09588221.2019.1584117

Turula, A. (2017). Learner autonomy as a social construct in the context of Italki. *Teaching English with Technology*, *17*(2), 3–28.

Ulvik, M., Helleve, I., & Smith, K. (2018). What and how student teachers learn during their practicum as a foundation for further professional development. *Professional Development in Education*, *44*(5), 638–649. doi:10.1080/19415257.2017.1388271

UNESCO COVID-19 Education Response. (2021). *COVID-19: reopening and reimagining universities, survey on higher education through the UNESCO National Commissions*. UNESCO.

Van Dijk, J. A. (2006). Digital divide research, achievements, and shortcomings. *Poetics*, *34*(4-5), 221–235. doi:10.1016/j.poetic.2006.05.004

Vanderslice, R. (2010). Abc's of keeping the best: Attrition, burnout, and climate. *Childhood Education*, *86*(5), 298–301. doi:10.1080/00094056.2010.10521412

Vansteenkiste, M., Sierens, E., Goossens, L., Soenens, B., Dochy, F., Mouratidis, A., Aelterman, N., Haerens, L., & Beyers, W. (2012). Identifying configurations of perceived teacher autonomy support and structure: Associations with self-regulated learning, motivation, and problem behavior. *Learning and Instruction*, *22*(6), 431–439. doi:10.1016/j.learninstruc.2012.04.002

Varga, M. (2017). *The Effects of Teacher-Student Relationships on the Academic Engagement of Students*. Maryland Shared Open Access Repository.

Vasilache, S. (2016). Student perspectives of computer literacy education in an international environment. *Universal Journal of Educational Research*, *4*(6), 1426–1431.

Vázquez-Cano, E., León Urrutia, M., Parra-González, M. E., & López Meneses, E. (2020). Analysis of interpersonal competences in the use of ICT in the Spanish University Context. *Sustainability*, *12*(2), 476–488. doi:10.3390u12020476

Vermeer, H.J. (1996). *Die Welt, in der wir übersetzen. Drei translatologische Überlegungen zu Realität, Vergleich und Prozess*. TextCONText.

Vermeer, H. J. (1978). Ein Rahmen für eine allgemeine Translationstheorie. *Lebende Sprachen*, *3*, 99–102.

Vermote, B., Aelterman, N., Beyers, W., Aper, L., Buysschaert, F., & Vansteenkiste, M. (2020). The role of teachers' motivation and mindsets in predicting a (de)motivating teaching style in higher education: A circumplex approach. *Motivation and Emotion*, *44*(2), 270–294. doi:10.100711031-020-09827-5

Vikneswaran, T., & Krish, P. (2016). Utilising social networking sites to improve writing: A case study with Chinese students in Malaysia. *Technology, Pedagogy and Education*, *25*(3), 287–300. doi:10.1080/1475939X.2015.1030441

Villa, R., Thousand, J., & Nevin, A. (2008). *A guide to co-teaching: Practical tips for facilitating student learning* (2nd ed.). Corwin Press.

Visintini, G. (2021). The "go digital" Bristol experience. In A. Plutino & E. Polisca (Eds.), Languages at work, competent multilinguals and the pedagogical challenges of COVID-19 (pp. 57-62). Research-publishing.net. doi:10.14705/rpnet.2021.49.1218

Vollmer, S. M. (2020) *The Digital Literacy Practices of Newly Arrived Syrian Refugees: a Spatio-Visual Linguistic Ethnography* (PhD thesis). University of Leeds.

Vorobel, O., & Kim, D. (2012). Teaching at a distance: An overview of research. *CALICO Journal*, *29*(3), 548–562. doi:10.11139/cj.29.3.548-562

Vuorikari, R., Punie, Y., Carretero, G. S., & Van Den Brande, G. (2016). *DigComp 2.0: The digital competence framework for citizens. Update Phase 1: The conceptual reference model*. Publication Office of the European Union.

Vygotsky, L. S. (1978). *Mind in society: The development of higher psychological processes*. Harvard University Press.

Vygotsky, L. S. (1978). Mind in Society: The Development of Higher Psychological Processes. In M. Cole, V. John-Steiner, S. Scribner, & E. Souberman (Eds.). Harvard University Press.

Vygotsky, L. S. (1986). *Though and language* (A. Kozulin, Trans.). MIT Press.

Vygotsky, L. S. (1987). *The collected works of LS Vygotsky: The fundamentals of defectology* (Vol. 2). Springer Science & Business Media.

Vygotsky, L. S. (1998). The problem of age (M. J. Hall, Trans.). In RieberR. W. (Ed.), *The collected works of L.S. Vygotsky* (Vol. 5, pp. 187–205). Kluwer Academic/Plenum.

Walker, T. (2020). Helping students and educators recover from COVID-19 trauma. *NEA Today*. https://www. nea. org/advocating-for-change/new-from-nea/helping-students-and-educators-recover-covid-19-trauma

Wang, A. (2015). Facilitating participation: Teacher roles in a multiuser virtual learning environment. *Language Learning & Technology*, *19*(2), 156–176.

Wang, B., Liu, Y., Qian, J., & Parker, S. K. (2021). Achieving effective remote working during the COVID-19 pandemic: A work design perspective. *Applied Psychology*, *70*(1), 16–59. doi:10.1111/apps.12290 PMID:33230359

Wang, C., Hsu, H., & Bonem, E, M., Moss, J, D., Yu S., Nelson D, B., & Levesque-Bristol, C. (2019). Need satisfaction and need dissatisfaction: A comparative study of online and face-to-face learning contexts. *Computers in Human Behavior*, *95*, 114–125.

Warchauer, M., & Mauchniak, T. (2010). New technology and digital worlds: Analyzing evidence of equity in access, use and outcomes. *Review of Research in Education*, *34*(1), 179–225.

Warner, C., & Dupuy, B. (2018). Moving toward Multiliteracies in Foreign Language Teaching: Past and present perspectives ... and beyond. *Foreign Language Annals*, *51*(1), 116–128. doi:10.1111/flan.12316

Warnock, S. (2009). *Teaching writing online: How and why*. National Council of Teachers of English.

Warschauer, M. (1996). *Telecollaboration in foreign language learning*. University of Hawai'i at Manoa: Second Language Teaching and Curriculum Center.

Warschauer, M. (2010). New Tools for Teaching Writing. *Language Learning & Technology*, *14*(1), 3–8.

Warschauer, M., & Kern, R. (Eds.). (2000). *Network-based language teaching: Concepts and practice*. Cambridge University Press. doi:10.1017/CBO9781139524735

Watermeyer, R., Crick, T., Knight, C., & Goodall, J. (2021). COVID-19 and digital disruption in U.K. universities: Afflictions and affordances of emergency online migration. *Higher Education*, *81*(3), 623–641. doi:10.100710734-020-00561-y PMID:32836334

Wattoo, R. M., Latif, M., & Munir, N. (2020). Information Communication Technologies Hauling Out University Students' Effective Learning during COVID-19: A Qualitative Study. *Global Social Sciences Review*, *3*(III), 351–357. doi:10.31703/gssr.2020(V-III).37

Weaver, C. (1994). *Reading Process and Practice from Socio-psycholinguistics to Whole Language*. Heinemann.

Wedenoja, L. (2020). *What to expect when you weren't expecting online classes.* Rockefeller Institute of Government. Retrieved from https://rockinst.org/blog/what-to-expect-when-you-werent-expecting-online-classes/

Wei, Y., & Zhou, S. (2019). Are better teachers more likely to move? Examining teacher mobility in rural China. *The Asia-Pacific Education Researcher, 28*(2), 171–179. doi:10.100740299-018-0423-0

Wells, G. (1986). *The Meaning Makers: Children learning language and using language to learn.* Hodder and Stoughton.

Welsch, W. (1995). Zur veränderten Verfaßtheit heutige Kulturen. *Zeitschrift für Kulturaustausch, 45*(1).

Wessels, F. (2015). The critical role of relationship education. *Hervormde Teologiese Studies, 71*(3), 2702. Advance online publication. doi:10.4102/hts.v71i3.2702

Weston, J.L. (2015). *The Impact of Strategy Instruction on Source-Based Writing* [Doctoral dissertation]. Arizona State University.

Westwood, P. (2008). *What teachers need to know about reading and writing difficulties.* Aust Council for Ed Research.

Wette, R. (2019). Embedded provision to develop source-based writing skills in a Year 1 health sciences course: How can the academic literacy developer contribute? *English for Specific Purposes, 56*, 35–49. doi:10.1016/j.esp.2019.07.002

White, D. S., & Le Cornu, A. (2011). Visitors and Residents: A new typology for online engagement. *First Monday, 16*(9). https://doi.org/10.5210/fm.v16i9.317

White, J. (2015). *Digital literacy skills for FE teachers.* Sage. doi:10.4135/9781473909571

Wiersma, W. (2008). *Research Methods in Education: An Introduction* (9th ed.). Allyn & Bacon.

Williamson, B., Eynon, R., & Potter, J. (2020). Pandemic politics, pedagogies and practices: Digital technologies and distance education during the coronavirus emergency. *Learning, Media and Technology, 45*, 107–114.

Wingate, U., & Dreiss, C. A. (2009). Developing students' academic literacy: An online approach. *Journal of Academic Language and Learning, 3*(1), A14–A25. http://journal.aall.org.au

Witherall, C., & Noddings, N. (Eds.). (1991). *Stories lives tell: Narrative and dialogue in education.* Teachers College Press.

Witte, H. (2000). *Die Kulturkompetenz des Translators. Begriffliche Grundlegung und Didaktisierung.* Stauffenburg.

Wong, M. M. W. (2020). *Mobilizing knowledge processes and lifeworld practices across learning spaces: Exploring grade 6 English language learners' inquiry-based learning experiences in a technology-enhanced classroom* [Unpublished doctoral dissertation]. University of British Columbia. https://open.library.ubc.ca/cIRcle/collections/ubctheses/24/items/1.0395371

Wong, H. L., Shi, Y., Luo, R., Zhang, L., & Rozelle, S. (2014). Improving the health and education of elementary schoolchildren in rural China: Iron supplementation versus nutritional training for parents. *The Journal of Development Studies, 50*(4), 502–519. doi:10.1080/00220388.2013.866223

Wong, M. M. (2014). Smart virtual word walls: Moving away from the traditional into the digital. *English in Texas, 44*(1), 27–29.

Wong, M. M. (2019). "S:ay what you want…:" Rap battles in a technology-enhanced classroom. *Canadian Modern Language Review, 72*(2), 169–182. https://doi.org/10.3138/cmlr.2018-0155

Wong, M. M. (2021). Silly putty: Mobilization of the known across technology-enhanced learning spaces. *Language and Literature, 23*(3), 146–164.

Wong, R. M. H. (2014). An investigation of strategies for student motivation in the Chinese EFL context. *Innovation in Language Learning and Teaching*, *8*(2), 132–154. doi:10.1080/17501229.2013.777449

World Health Organization. (2020). *Coronavirus disease (COVID-19): Schools.* https://www.who.int/news-room/q-a-detail/coronavirus-disease-covid-19-schools

World Health Organization. (2020, April 27). *Archived: WHO timeline – COVID-19.* https://www.who.int/news/item/27-04-2020-who-timeline---covid-19

World Health Organization. (2021, July 1). *Coronavirus disease (COVID-19) advice for the public.* https://www.who.int/emergencies/diseases/novel-coronavirus-2019/advice-for-public

Xia, F., Yang, L. T., Wang, L., & Vinel, A. (2012). Internet of things. *International Journal of Communication Systems*, *25*(9), 1101–1102. doi:10.1002/dac.2417

Xiong, T., & Xiong, X. (2017). The EFL teachers' perceptions of teacher identity: A survey of Zhuangang and Non-zhuangang primary school teachers in China. *English Language Teaching*, *10*(4), 100–110. doi:10.5539/elt.v10n4p100

Yang, C. C. R. (2017). An investigation of the use of the 'flipped classroom' pedagogy in secondary English language classrooms. *Journal of Information Technology Education: Innovations in Practice*, *16*(1).

Yarwood, A., & Lorentzen, A., Wallingford, & A., Wongsarnpigoon, I. (2019b). Exploring Basic Psychological Needs in a Language Learning Center. Part 2: The autonomy-supportive nature and limitations of a SALC. *Relay Journal*, *2*(1), 236–250.

Yarwood, A., Rose-Wainstock, C., & Lees, M. (2019a). Fostering English-use in a SALC through a discussion-based classroom intervention. *Studies in Self-Access Learning Journal*, *10*(4), 256–378.

Yashima, T. (2002). Willingness to communicate in a second language: The Japanese EFL context. *Modern Language Journal*, *86*(1), 54–66.

Yashima, T. (2012). Willingness to communicate: Momentary volition that results in L2 behaviour. In S. Mercer, S. Ryan, & M. Williams (Eds.), *Psychology for language learning: Insights from research, theory and practice* (pp. 119–135). Palgrave Macmillan.

Yashima, T., MacIntyre, P. D., & Ikeda, M. (2018). Situated willingness to communicate in an L2: Interplay of individual characteristics and context. *Language Teaching Research*, *22*(1), 115–137.

Yi Xu, L. J., Deifell, E., & Angus, K. (2021). Emergency Remote Language Teaching and U.S. - Based College-Level World Language Educators' Intention to Adopt Online Teaching in Post-pandemic Times. *Modern Language Journal*, *105*(2), 1–23.

Young, M. F., DePalma, A., & Garrett, S. (2002). Situations, interaction, process and affordances: An ecological psychology perspective. *Instructional Science*, *30*(1), 47–63.

Yu, B., & Zadorozhnyy, A. (2021). Developing students' linguistic and digital literacy skills through the use of multimedia presentations. *ReCALL*, 1–15. doi:10.1017/S0958344021000136

Yunus, M. M., Osman, W. S., & Ishak, N. M. (2011). Teacher-student relationship factor affecting motivation and academic achievement in ESL classroom. *Procedia: Social and Behavioral Sciences*, *15*, 2637–2641. doi:10.1016/j.sbspro.2011.04.161

Záhorec, J., Hašková, A., & Munk, M. (2019). Teachers' professional digital literacy skills and their upgrade. *European Journal of Contemporary Education*, *8*(2), 378–393.

Zainuddin, Z. (2017). First-year college students' experiences in the EFL flipped classroom: A case study in Indonesia. *International Journal of Instruction*, *10*(1), 133–150. doi:10.12973/iji.2017.1019a

Zhang, R. (2020). Exploring blended learning experiences through the community of inquiry framework. *ELT Journal*, *24*(1), 38–53.

Zhang, W., & Zhu, C. (2018). Comparing Learning Outcomes of Blended Learning and Traditional Face-to-Face Learning of University Students in ESL Courses. *International Journal on E-Learning*, *17*(2), 251–273.

Zhao, Y. (2013). Recent developments in technology and language learning: Literature review and meta-analysis. *CALICO Journal*, *21*(1), 7–27. doi:10.1558/cj.v21i1.7-27

Zhao, Y., Llorente, A. M. P., & Gómez, M. C. S. (2021). Digital competence in higher education research: A systematic literature review. *Computers & Education*, *168*, 104212. doi:10.1016/j.compedu.2021.104212

Zioga, C., & Bikos, K. (2020). Collaborative writing using Google Docs in primary education: Development of argumentative discourse. *Turkish Online Journal of Distance Education*, 133–142. doi:10.17718/tojde.690372

About the Contributors

Christina Nicole Giannikas holds a PhD in the field of Applied Linguistics. She is an education and research consultant and has worked with publishers, Ministries of Education and educational institutions worldwide. Christina also works in Higher Education where she lectures courses in Applied Linguistics and is an experienced teacher trainer of pre-service and in-service teacher education programs in Cyprus, Greece and the UK. She specializes in the areas of early language learning, age-appropriate digital pedagogies, digital literacies, assessment, and Teacher Education. Christina has edited and authored a number of books, journal papers, book chapters, and teacher education articles and has been invited to present her work across Europe, Asia, and the United States. For the last four years, Christina has been serving as Chair of the EuroCALL Teacher Education SIG and recently became the EuroCALL National Contact for Greece. She is an invited research collaborator of FLETATIS (Foreign Language Education through Applied Technologies) and EnA research Group at OsloMet. Weblink: https://christinagian.wixsite.com/christinagiannikas.

* * *

Savvi Antoniou is a French language instructor and researcher at the Language Centre of Cyprus University of Technology. She holds a Ph.D. in Language Sciences - Linguistics from Université Bourgogne Franche-Comté an MA in Language Sciences and Teaching French from Université Bourgogne Franche-Comté, an MA in Modern English Language from Huddersfield University, and a BA in French Language and Literature from Aristotle University of Thessaloniki. She has experience in language teaching, both onsite and online. Her research interests include foreign language teaching and learning, Computer-Assisted Language Learning, Psycholinguistics.

Matthew Apple is a Professor in the College of Letters, Ritsumeikan University, Kyoto, Japan. He has taught at various levels of education in Japan since 1999, including junior and senior high school, technical college, undergraduate university, and graduate school. His research interests include CALL, ESP/EAP, and individual differences in SLA. He was lead editor of the edited volumes *Language Learning Motivation in Japan* and *L2 Selves and Motivations in Asian Contexts*.

Petra Bauer is an Assistant Professor (Teaching) of German in the School of Modern Languages and Cultures at Durham University. She wrote her PhD thesis on the translation and reception of ETA Hoffmann's works in 19th century Britain. Her research interests include translation, and in particular literary translation and translation as a means to develop intercultural communicative competence. She is a Fellow of the HEA and a Chartered Linguist (Translation and Education) with the CIoL.

Raphaëlle Beecroft is a teacher educator with a PhD in Foreign Language Pedagogy and a Master's degree in Translation Studies. Her research interests include Translation in Other Learning Contexts (TOLC), the development of ICC through translation and virtual exchange, the implementation of drama methods in task-based foreign language pedagogy to foster oracy as well as English as an International Language in English Language Teacher Education.

Phillip A. Bennett is a learning advisor at Kanda University of International Studies, a member of the Research Institute for Learner Autonomy Education (RILAE), and an editorial team member of Relay Journal. Holding an MA in TESOL from Kanda University of International Studies, he has nearly 20 years of experience in education between Japan and the United States. Over the past 17 years, he has taught all levels and age groups of learners in an array of educational environments in Japan. Currently, his research interests are the learner affect, semiotics, and the development of the symbolic resources of language learners. He hopes to promote advising in language learning and help teachers implement advising in their practice.

Xingtan Cao is a Ph.D. candidate at Faculty of Education, University of Ottawa, Canada. His research interests are citizenship education, second language education, moral education, and international and comparative education. His doctoral research looks at second language education and its roles in the integration of new immigrants to Canada. He served as the Program Chair for the Citizenship Education Research Network (CERN) at the Canadian Society for Studies in Education (CSSE) from 2019 to 2021. He has been teaching for the ESL program at the University of Ottawa since 2019.

Susan Dawson is a Lecturer in Education. Her teaching and research interests include teacher professional development, practitioner research, language education and Aristotle's philosophy.

Melis Dilek graduated from Boğaziçi University, with a bachelor's degree in Foreign Language Education department in 2018. Currently, she is a master's student in Educational Technology Programme at Bahcesehir University. She is also teaching English as a foreign language in a private school in Istanbul, Turkey. Her research interests are online collaborative learning, blended learning, and digital pedagogy.

Richard Fay, Senior Lecturer in Education (TESOL and Intercutural Education), has teaching and research interests including: ecological thinking, epistemic justice, klezmer ensemble performance, narrative research, refugee language education, researching multilingually, and TESOL paradigms.

Ana García-Perera is a graduate of the Universitat de València in Spain with a degree in Primary Education. She currently works as an English Teacher at Pureza de Maria- Cid school. She is interested in foreign language teaching and in the impact of student-teacher relationships on the learning process.

Soraya García-Sánchez (PhD in English Studies) is Associate Professor at the Department of Modern Languages, Translation and Interpreting, Universidad de Las Palmas de Gran Canaria (ULPGC), Spain, where she has been teaching language, culture and literature courses both online and on a face-to-face basis. Her research areas are focused on motivation, e-learning and u-learning (CALL/MALL) environments for EFL/ESP students at university level, and on women's writing and literature in contemporary contexts. She is currently the director of the research group FLETATIS (Foreign Language Education

Through Applied Technologies and Intercultural Sensitivity), and responsible for the research area dealing "Languages, ubiquitous knowledge and international communication". More information is available on her website: https://sorayagarciasanchez.wordpress.com.

Gizem Kara is a master's student in Educational Technology Programme at Bahcesehir University. She is currently teaching young learners at a private school in Istanbul, Turkey.

Kia Karavas is an Associate Professor in the Department of Language and Linguistics of the Faculty of English Language and Literature at the National and Kapodistrian University of Athens, co-coordinator of the Pedagogic and Teaching Competence Programme, and scientific coordinator of the mentor education programme. She is also Deputy Director of the Research Centre for Language Teaching, Testing and Assessment responsible for the develioment of the National KPG exams in English and other nationwide curriculum development and training programmes.

Tamara Kavytska is a PhD holder in Education, Associate Professor at the Department for Teaching Methodology of Ukrainian and Foreign Languages and Literatures, National Taras Shevchenko University of Kyiv, and the author of more than 60 publications in national and international scholarly journals. Her research interests involve Cognitive and Rhetorical Grammar, Teaching Translation, Language Testing and Assessment. With an extensive teaching experience, her career also focuses on translation as a professional activity, particularly – on translation into a second language.

Francesco Leoni is the Deputy Education Coordinator at Caritas Salford. Before completing a teaching qualification in 2018 he worked extensively in the charity sector in the North West of England. He holds an MA in History from the University of Manchester and his areas of interest include the histories of migration and intercultural exchange.

Di Liang is a Ph.D. candidate in Second Language Education at the Pennsylvania State University, USA. He holds an M.Ed. in Foreign Language Education from the University of Pittsburgh. He currently teaches a language teaching method course and supervises World Languages student teachers. Prior to Pennsylvania State University, he taught undergraduate-level Chinese language classes at the University of Pittsburgh. His research interests include second language acquisition and instruction and language teacher education.

Ayşegül Liman Kaban graduated from Marmara University, Department of English Language Teaching in 2009. She completed her master's degree in Interpersonal Communication at Marmara University in 2012. She also completed a course in E-Learning and Digital Culture at The University of Edinburgh in 2013. Between 2013 and 2016, she was the editor of the IATEFL TEASIG Newsletter. She was the editor of IATEFL Learning Technologies Special Interest Group in 2016. In 2020, she completed a doctoral degree in the field of Educational Technologies at Bahcesehir University and she still teaches undergraduate and graduate-level courses. Some of the courses she teaches are online collaborative learning, instructional technologies, distance education, multimedia design, and so on. She has given effective technology integration training to educators in nearly 100 schools and universities in Turkey. She has also given training abroad in England, Germany, the USA, Finland, Italy, and Georgia. She has written two children's books named "Oyun Canavarı" and "Defne'nin Dijital Kimliği" on game addiction and internet security.

Trisevgeni Liontou is an Assistant Professor and English-language Researcher with a Ph.D. in Testing from the Faculty of English Language and Literature, National and Kapodistrian University of Athens. She has worked as an expert item consultant for Second Language Testing, Inc. (Berlitz Corporation), AvantAssessment, USA, a research assistant at the Research Centre for Language Teaching, Testing and Assessment (RCeL) and as a freelance item writer, oral examiner and script rater for various EFL examination boards.

Daniel J. Mills is an associate professor of English as a Foreign Language in the Economics Faculty of Ritsumeikan University (Japan). He holds an M.S.Ed. in TESOL from Shenandoah University and an Ed.D. in Instructional Technology from the University of Wyoming. His research interests include informal learning, autonomy, mobile-assisted language learning, and technology acceptance.

Andres Mora is the Education Coordinator at Caritas Salford. He is a qualified teacher with a Masters in Human Rights Law. His areas of interest include the socio economic rights of asylum seekers and refugees and models of integration that address the holistic wellbeing and aspirations of newly arrived migrants.

Gary Motteram is a Senior Lecturer at the Manchester Institute of Education, where he teaches on MA programmes in TESOL and Digital Technologies. He has published in the fields of technology supported language learning and teacher education. With an interest in online education, more recent research projects have focused on using mobile technologies to work with teachers in challenging circumstances.

Georgios Neokleous completed his PhD in Education at Saint Louis University in 2014, focusing on the use of the mother tongue in EFL classrooms. He holds a post as associate professor of English in the Department of Teacher Education at the Norwegian University of Science and Technology, where he works with pre- and in-service EFL teachers and supervises at BA, MA, and PhD levels.

Cristina Pardo-Ballester is an Associate Professor of Hispanic Linguistics in the Department of World Languages and Cultures at Iowa State University. Her research interests center on Computer Assisted Language Learning (CALL), Second Language Acquisition (SLA), language assessment, and translation studies. She has published and presented scholarly papers dealing with the development of online, hybrid, and blended language courses, the development of online instructional materials, the use of networks for teaching, student attitudes towards the use of CALL, and the integration of technology into the language curriculum.

Caleb Powers, originally from Houston, Texas, earned a Master of Arts in Teaching Foreign Language with a specialization in Language Program Administration from the Middlebury Institute of International Studies at Monterey in 2021. After graduating, Cal was hired as a Curriculum Manager at Voces Digital, an online world language curricula developer. Cal's research interests include teacher burnout, leadership, teacher education/professional development, and mobile-assisted language learning.

Agustín Reyes-Torres is an Associate Professor in the Languages and Literature Education Department at the Universitat de València, Spain. His line of research focuses on foreign language teaching, teachers' education, the Pedagogy of multiliteracies and the use of children's literature in the foreign language class. He has lectured an extensive range of courses and conducted research fellowships at the University of Iowa, University of Virginia, Boston College and Middlebury Language Schools. He is the principal investigator of the research group Lit(T)erart.

Dina Tsagari, PhD, is Professor, Department of Primary and Secondary Teacher Education, Oslo Metropolitan University, Norway. She has also worked for the University of Cyprus, Greek Open University and Polytechnic University of Hong Kong. Her research interests include language testing and assessment, materials design and evaluation, differentiated instruction, multilingualism, distance education and learning difficulties. She is the editor and author of numerous books, journal papers, book chapters, project reports etc. She coordinates research groups, e.g. CBLA SIG – EALTA, EnA OsloMet and is involved in EU-funded and other research projects (e.g. DINGLE, ENRICH, TALE, DysTEFL, PALM, etc.).

Melanie M. Wong, PhD, is an Assistant Professor of Teaching at the University of British Columbia, Canada. She is a former K-12 educator and ELL Strategist at the Calgary Public School District in Canada. Her research interests include K-12 English Language Learners, technology-enhanced learning in K-12 and medical interviews.

Amelia Yarwood is a learning advisor at the Self-Access Learning Center (SALC) and a member of the Research Institute for Learner Autonomy Education (RILAE) at Kanda University of International Studies, Japan. She has worked in education at multiple levels in both Australian and Japanese contexts and while her roles traverse the space between teacher and advisor, she is always developing materials to support her learners' awareness of self, reflective abilities and capacity for self-directed learning. She is currently pursuing a PhD in Foreign Language Education at Kansai University, Japan, and her primary research interests include learners' narrative identity, how emotions mediate learning and autonomous learning behaviours.

Index

A

B

C

D

E

F

G

H

I

K

L

M

N

O

P

R

S

T

U

V

W

Premier Reference Source
Emerging GIS Applications for Emergency and Disaster Management

Premier Reference Source
Managerial Strategies and Green Solutions for Project Sustainability

Premier Reference Source
Comparative Approaches to Using R and Python for Statistical Data Analysis

Premier Reference Source
Solutions for High-Touch Communications in a High-Tech World

CPSIA information can be obtained
at www.ICGtesting.com
Printed in the USA
LVHW060047100222
710699LV00016B/351

9 781799 887188